POLICE OFFICER

Hugh O'Neill

Hy Hammer

E. P. Steinberg

Prentice Hall
New York • London • Toronto • Sydney • Tokyo • Singapore

Eleventh Edition

Prentice Hall General Reference
15 Columbus Circle
New York, NY 10023

An Arco Book

Arco, Prentice Hall and colophons are
registered trademarks of Simon & Schuster, Inc.

Manufactured in the United States of America

1 2 3 4 5 6 7 8 9 10

Library of Congress Cataloging-in-Publication Data

O'Neill, Hugh.
  Police officer / Hugh O'Neill, Hy Hammer, E.P. Steinberg. —11th ed.
  p.   cm.
  "An Arco Book"—T.p. verso.
  ISBN 0-13-678624-3
  1. Police—United States—Examinations, questions, etc.
2. Police—New York (N.Y.)—Examinations, questions, etc.
I. Hammer, Hy.   II. Steinberg, E.P.   III. Title.
HV8143.054   1992   91-45322
363.2'076—dc20   CIP

CONTENTS

What This Book Will Do for You

You want to become a Police Officer. That's great. Every city, every town, every county, every state needs qualified and enthusiastic new recruits to maintain staffing at full level and to cover all posts. You have made a good start toward joining the police force by buying this book.

This book has been carefully researched and has been written to help you through the application and screening process. The information in this book will prepare you for the written exam, forewarn you as to the physical skills on which you must concentrate, and give you valuable tips for your interview and psychological screening.

It is important that you allow the book to help you. Read it carefully. Do not skip over any information. Information about police work itself and the organization of police forces should help psych you for the job. You should get more and more excited about the work as you read about all the possible assignments. The information about the screening process itself should calm you and help to allay your fears. Taken step-by-step the process is not so frightening. Each step has a purpose. There is a way to handle each one. Once you know what to expect, half the battle is won. Thorough preparation for the written exam should win the other half of the battle. If you are prepared, you can feel self-confident. If you feel confident, you can answer questions quickly and decisively, finish the exam, and earn a high score.

So make a study schedule. Assign yourself a period of time each day to devote to preparation for the police screening process. A regular time is best, but the important thing is daily study. Choose a quiet, well-lighted spot with as few distractions as possible. Try to arrange not to be interrupted.

Begin at the beginning of the book. Read. Underline points that you consider significant. Make marginal notes. Flag the pages that you think are especially important with little "post it"™ notes. We have highlighted some pages with colored paper. Read these pages more than once.

The bulk of this book consists of police examinations, real examinations given to candidates by the City of New York within the past several years and practice exams that we have created using questions that have appeared on police exams over the years. Before you attempt these exams, study the three chapters about Police Judgment Questions, Reading-Based Questions, and Observation and Memory. These chapters give you help with the three most common kinds of police exam questions. Many police forces test only in these three areas. Each chapter begins with instructions about the topic and the kind of question. Each gives practical suggestions about how to answer the questions. Read the instructions in each chapter. Try the practice questions in each chapter. Then study the answer explanations. You can learn a great deal from answer explanations. Even when you have answered correctly, the explanation may bring out points that had not occurred to you. This same suggestion—read *all* the explanations— applies throughout this book, to the exams as well as to the instructional chapters.

When you feel that you are well prepared, move on to the exams. If possible, answer an entire exam in one sitting. If you must divide your time, divide into no more than two sessions per exam. You need not do the first exam first. The practice exams are somewhat shorter than the actual New York City exams. It might be wise to save the longest exams for a weekend.

When you do take the exams, treat them with respect. Time yourself accurately and do not peek at the correct answers. Remember, you are taking these for practice; they will not be scored; they do not count. So learn from them. Learn to think; learn to reason like a police officer; learn to pace yourself so that you can answer all the questions. Then learn from the explanations.

IMPORTANT: Do not memorize questions and answers. Any question that has been released will not be used again. You may run into questions that are very similar, but you will not be tested with any of these exact questions. These questions will give you good practice, but they will not give you the answers to any of the questions on your exam.

With all of this emphasis on time, you may be wondering if it is wise to guess. The best policy is, of course, to pace yourself so that you can read and consider each question. Sometimes this does not work. Most civil service exam scores are based only on the number of questions answered correctly. This means that a wild guess is better than a blank space. There is no penalty for a wrong answer, and you just might guess right. If you see that time is about to run out, mark all the remaining spaces with the same answer. By the law of averages, some will be right.

Far better than a wild guess is an educated guess. You make this kind of guess not when you are pressed for time but when you are not sure of the correct answer. Usually, one or two of the choices are obviously wrong. Eliminate the obviously wrong answers and try to reason among those remaining. Then, if necessary, guess from the smaller field. The odds of a right answer increase if you guess from a field of two instead of from a field of four. When you make an educated guess or a wild guess in the course of the exam, you might want to make a note next to the question number in the test booklet. Then, if there is time, you can go back for a second look.

Unless you have applied to a very small police force, your exam will be machine scored. You will mark your answers on a separate answer sheet. Each exam in this book has its own answer sheet so that you can practice marking all your answers in the right way. Tear out the answer sheet before you begin each exam. Do not try to flip pages back and forth. Since your answer sheet will be machine scored, you must fill it out clearly and correctly. You cannot give any explanations to the machine. This means:

1. Blacken your answer space firmly and completely. ● This is the only correct way to mark the answer sheet. ◐, ⊗, ⊘, and ∅ are all unacceptable. The machine might not read them at all.

2. Mark only one answer for each question. If you mark more than one answer you will be considered wrong even if one of the answers is correct.

3. If you change your mind, you must erase your mark. Attempting to cross out an incorrect answer like this ✖ will not work. You must erase any incorrect answer completely. An incomplete erasure might be read as a second answer.

4. All of your answering should be in the form of blackened spaces. The machine cannot read English. Do not write any notes in the margins. If you have done any figuring in the margins of the test booklet itself, be sure to mark the letter of your answer on the answer sheet. Correct answers in the test booklet do not count. Only the answer sheet is scored.

5. Most Important: Answer each question in the right place. Question 1 must be answered in space 1; question 52 in space 52. If you should skip an answer space and mark a series of answers in the wrong places, you must erase all those answers and do the questions over, marking your answers in the proper places. You cannot afford to use the limited time in this way. Therefore, as you answer *each* question, look at its number and check that you are marking your answer in the space with the same number.

6. In general, because of the risk of getting out of line on the answer sheet, we recommend that you answer every question in order, even if you have to guess. Make it an educated guess if you can. If not, make it a wild guess. Just mark the question number in the test booklet so that you can try again if there is time.

On the examination day assigned to you, allow the test itself to be the main event of the day. Do not squeeze it in between other activities. Arrive rested, relaxed, and on time. In fact, plan to arrive early. Leave plenty of time for traffic tie-ups or other complications that might upset you and interfere with your test performance.

In the test room, the examiner will hand out forms for you to fill out. He or she will give you the instructions that you must follow in taking the examination. The examiner will tell you how to fill in the grids on the forms. Time limits and timing signals will be explained. If you do not understand any of the examiner's instructions, Ask Questions. Make sure that you know exactly what to do.

At the examination, you must follow instructions exactly. Fill in the grids on the forms carefully and accurately. Filling in the wrong grid may lead to loss of veterans' credits to which you may be entitled or to an incorrect address for your test results. Do not begin until you are told to begin. Stop as soon as the examiner tells you to stop. Do not turn pages until you are told to. Do not go back to parts you have already completed. Any infraction of the rules is considered cheating. If you cheat, your test paper will not be scored, and you will not be eligible for appointment.

Once the signal has been given and you begin the exam, read every word of every question. Be alert for exclusionary words that might affect your answer: words like "not," "most," "least," "all," "every," and "except."

Read all the choices before you mark your answer. It is statistically true that most errors are made when the last choice is the correct answer. Too many people mark the first answer that seems correct without reading through all the choices to find out which answer is *best*.

If you happen to finish before time is up, return to difficult questions that you marked in the booklet and try them again. There is no bonus for finishing early, so use all your time to perfect your exam paper.

ORGANIZATION OF A MUNICIPAL POLICE FORCE

The entire criminal justice system in the United States starts with the police, and it is the municipal police officer who is most familiar to the average person. Municipal police departments, in both personnel and management practices, are generally organized along semimilitary lines. Police officers wear uniforms, usually blue or brown; they are ranked according to a military system, such as sergeant, lieutenant, captain, colonel; and they are governed by specific, written rules and regulations. Highly trained police officers are found in both large and small cities. Of the more than 17,000 cities in the United States, 55 have populations exceeding a quarter of a million, and these employ about one-third of all police personnel. It is in the cities that American police problems are concentrated, and these problems present the greatest challenges to law enforcement.

All police agencies, large or small, have similar problems and responsibilities. Each engages in common activities that prevent crime and disorder, preserve the peace, and protect individual life and property. Police work is often thought of as a matter of confrontations between police officers and hardened criminals; this frequently is so. In many instances, however, police officers deal with quite different and surprisingly varied situations.

Police activities can be divided into two functions: line and staff. Line functions involve activities that result directly in meeting police service goals; staff activities help administrators organize and manage the police agency. The line functions common to most municipal police departments include patrol, investigation, vice, traffic, juvenile, and crime prevention.

Line Functions

At the center of police law enforcement is patrol. It involves movement of uniformed police personnel, on foot or in vehicles, through designated areas. In most departments, at least half of all police personnel are assigned to patrol. Officers on patrol have a variety of duties that include: interviewing and interrogating suspects and arresting lawbreakers; controlling crowds at public gatherings; enforcing laws regulating public conduct; intervening in personal, family, and public disputes; issuing warnings and citations; and providing miscellaneous services to members of the public. Although patrol officers spend more time carrying out routine police services than in catching criminals, their importance cannot be underestimated. Because their primary duties are performed on the street, patrol officers are the most visible representatives of local government.

Investigation activities come into play when patrol officers are unable to prevent a crime or to arrest a suspect in the act of committing a crime. Investigative specialists, better known as detectives, help to solve crimes by: skillful questioning of victims, witnesses, and suspects; by gathering evidence at crime sites; and by tracing stolen property or vehicles connected with crime. Detectives investigate many types of crimes including murder, manslaughter, robbery, rape, aggravated assault, burglary, auto theft, forgery, embezzlement, and weapons violations. They spend considerable time reviewing physical evidence, clues, interviews, and methods used by the criminal that may provide a break in solving a case. In addition, inves-

1

tigations are coordinated by use of information provided by patrol officers, laboratory personnel, records clerks, and concerned citizens. All of these may lead to the identification of the guilty individual.

Vice operations in the local police agency are aimed at illegal activities that corrupt and destroy the physical, mental, and moral health of the public. Enforcement activities in vice operations are directed principally against illegal gambling, narcotics violations, traffic in liquor, prostitution, pandering, pornography, and obscene conduct. Organized crime is involved in many vice crimes, and vice crimes are directly linked to other types of street crime. For example, gambling is associated with loansharking, and prostitution and drug abuse are linked with robbery. Patrol units have the primary responsibility of enforcing vice laws and can significantly prevent such illegal activities, particularly in high crime areas. In order to be effective, however, there must be a continual exchange of information and coordinated effort between vice units and all other elements of the police department, as well as cooperation with federal law enforcement agencies such as the Drug Enforcement Agency and the Bureau of Alcohol, Tobacco, and Firearms.

Traffic law enforcement seeks the voluntary compliance of citizens with traffic regulations to provide maximum movement of traffic with a minimum of interruption. As no shame is associated with most traffic violations, and the public often breaks traffic regulations without realizing it, breaking these laws is made an unpleasant experience by enforcing penalties such as fines, loss of license, or imprisonment. In addition to vehicular traffic enforcement, uniformed police officers also engage in pedestrian control, traffic direction, investigation of accidents, and traffic education. There is an important relationship between traffic law enforcement and other police services. Stopping a motorist for a routine vehicle check or for a traffic violation often results in an arrest for a nontraffic-related reason, such as weapons or drug possession, stolen vehicle, or flight to avoid prosecution in another jurisdiction. As in the case of other police assignments, traffic officers give court testimony and are often involved in civil cases because of traffic accident investigations.

Most municipal police agencies have specific policy guidelines for dealing with juveniles. However, there may be differences in approach or philosophy among various departments depending on the needs of individual communities. In some cases, police officers are given special training and are assigned to juvenile activities on a full-time basis. In other police departments, the training in this area is minimal, and officers rely on the traditional police methods in dealing with juveniles. A juvenile becomes a delinquent by commiting an act which, if he or she were an adult, would be a crime. The police, however, have greater responsibilities in juvenile matters than merely enforcing laws by taking youthful offenders into custody. Police juvenile efforts are aimed at identifying neglected and dependent children, detecting and preventing predelinquent behavior, finding and investigating delinquency breeding-grounds within the community, and proper disposition of juvenile cases.

The last of the basic line functions of the municipal police agency involves crime prevention. When citizens are hostile to the police agency in their community, it is as real a threat to peace and order as would be police indifference to the needs of the citizens. Police serve all segments of the community, but they cannot preserve law and order and control crime unless the public cooperates and participates in the law enforcement process. Hostility between citizens and police not only creates explosive situations, but, more importantly, can promote crime in the community. Crime is both a police and social problem that will continue to grow unless the public becomes more involved. Community relations programs, for example, help to close the gap between citizens and police by making each aware of the other's problems and providing the impetus to settle their differences. In some municipalities, police agencies have introduced crime prevention techniques such as neighborhood security and watch programs. These encourage citizens to take security measures in their homes and businesses and to report any suspicious persons or activities in the neighborhood.

Staff Functions

Staff functions are activities performed by police officers to help administrators organize and manage the police agency. Personnel recruitment (which includes selection and training), planning, finance, employee services, public relations, and use of civilian personnel are examples of staff work.

Staff is the costliest and most important of all the resources committed to the law enforcement process, and a police agency is only as able and effective as its personnel. To varying degrees, every police department engages in recruitment, selection, and training of personnel. It sets qualifications, recruits candidates, tests and screens applicants, and places them in training facilities. The police department also reviews performance during probation and develops salary schedules and lines of promotion for police officers. In addition, staff units are responsible for providing ongoing training to police officers at all levels in the department as a means of keeping them up-to-date on the latest developments in law enforcement. All of these factors are important because the quality of the personnel and their training determine the character of police performance, and, in the final analysis, the quality of police leadership.

To be effective, police departments must plan and organize numerous activities that characterize around-the-clock operations. The unpredictable nature of police work, however, and the problems that arise from emergency situations sometimes make planning difficult. Work schedules, paydays, patrol assignments, uniforms, and equipment all require planning; this, in turn, involves administrative staff and line operations, extradepartmental plans, and research and development. Good planning by the police agency produces effective police service in the community.

Budgeting is an important part of the staff functions of police personnel. These responsibilities include, but are not limited to, fiscal planning and preparation of cost estimates for personnel, equipment, facilities, and programs necessary to meet the established goals of the police department.

The staff must also provide employee services to members of the police agency. They must explain benefits and help employees and their families to obtain all the services to which they are entitled. For example, in cases of illness, injury, or death, specialists in employee benefits take care of matters with a minimum of inconvenience to the officers and their families.

Police personnel also engage in public relations activities. This entails the development of programs that acquaint the community with police goals and help to gain public support for police activities. Duties include providing information to the press and public, maintaining liaison with community representatives, and working with educational organizations to improve relations with youth in the community.

A number of staff positions and auxiliary staff positions can be filled by handicapped personnel.

A widespread practice is the use of civilian personnel in certain jobs within police agencies. Civilian personnel are assigned to duties that do not require the exercise of police authority or the application of the skills and knowledge of the professional police officer. Work typically performed by civilians includes clerical or secretarial work, maintenance or sanitation work, prisoner booking, and motor vehicle maintenance. Many civilian employees develop an interest in regular police work, and, if they meet the requirements for sworn status, become potential candidates for the police officer position. Some police departments will help pay for the schooling required for their civilian employees to meet the educational standards of the department. Some offer part-time training to their employees.

Besides these primary staff functions, important auxiliary staff services help line and administrative personnel to meet police objectives. These services include crime laboratory, property and detention, transportation, communications, and information systems. In addition, many police departments have intelligence operations and systems of internal discipline. Brief descriptions of these auxiliary services follow.

Auxiliary Staff Services

CRIME LABORATORY

Because solutions to many crimes are found through the application of the physical and biological sciences, the crime laboratory is of great value to law enforcement officers. In an initial critical phase, police officers or specially trained evidence technicians identify, collect, and preserve physical evidence at scenes of crime. Overlooking, contaminating, or accidentally destroying evidence can hinder the progress of an investigation. After the evidence reaches the crime laboratory, qualitative, quantitative, and interpretive analyses are performed by forensic personnel. Crime laboratory personnel are responsible for fingerprint operations, ballistics, polygraph tests, blood and alcohol tests, and examination of questioned documents. Owing to the considerable expense involved with operating crime laboratory facilities, not all police agencies have them. Local and regional laboratories have therefore been established in most states to provide services to law enforcement agencies from different jurisdictions.

PROPERTY AND DETENTION

Regardless of their size, locale, or functions, police agencies are responsible for evidence, personal property, and articles of value confiscated when carrying out police business. In addition, they must take inventory, inspect, replace, and maintain departmental property and facilities. Each police department must ensure the safekeeping of all property and evidence and make provisions for its storage, retrieval, and disposition to authorized police personnel.

Detention activities in a police agency involve temporary confinement of persons arrested and awaiting investigation or trial and permanent imprisonment in city or county facilities for those sentenced by the court. Typical activities include booking, searching, fingerprinting, photographing, and feeding prisoners.

TRANSPORTATION

Police mobility is crucial to crime prevention. Police officers must have the capability of moving safely and swiftly to meet their responsibilities. Police transportation activities center around the acquisition, use, maintenance, cost, and safety of a variety of vehicles. These include automobiles (patrol and unmarked), motorcycles, trucks, buses, motor scooters, aircraft (helicopters and planes), watercraft, and horses. By developing and maintaining an efficient transportation program, the police agency increases its effectiveness and ability to enforce the law.

COMMUNICATIONS

Communications in a police agency are the lifeline of the organization. Most police department communications systems have three parts: the telephone communications system, command and control operations, and radio communications. Though communications systems differ among departments throughout the country because of variation in staffing and funding, they generally operate as follows:

Telephone communications systems aim to reduce crime through rapid and accurate communication with the public. The telephone is the primary link between the police and the community, and, in an emergency, the public must be able to contact the police immediately. This is vitally important because rapid police response to an emergency call can mean the difference between life and death or between the capture and escape of suspects.

Command and control means coordinating operations of radio-equipped field units through exchange of information between field units and communications centers. In its simplest form, it is the receipt, processing, and dispatching of information received in telephone complaints to field units for action. This process becomes more complex as calls increase. In large departments, the use of automated command control equipment is widespread. Regardless of department size, rapid and accurate command and control operations are needed to ensure the safety of the community.

Radio communications, an integral part of police operations, involve use of radio frequencies by command control and police officers both to receive and transmit information. The efficiency of radio communications, however, is often impaired because frequency ranges are limited. In recent years, frequency congestion has been the result of increasing use of communication devices by the public and business. Efforts to solve this problem are receiving constant attention by law enforcement agencies at all levels. Where possible, in addition to radio-equipped vehicles, police departments provide police officers with specialized equipment such as miniature transceivers, mobile and portable radio units, and walkie-talkies. The object is to provide continuous communication among commanders, supervisors, and field personnel.

POLICE INFORMATION SYSTEMS

Another staff service, the information system, can also significantly affect efforts to reduce crime. Such a system consists of three components: reporting, collection and recording of crime data, and information storage and retrieval.

Reporting means thorough and precise reporting of all crimes that come to the department's attention. Included are telephone and field investigation reports and warrant information received from judicial agencies. Such information can assist criminal investigation and is useful in other parts of the criminal justice system.

Collection and recording of crime data helps evaluate crime conditions and the effectiveness of police operations. The data is obtained from the department's reportable incident files, such as precinct and field unit activity logs, accident reports, and criminal investigation reports, as well as summary dossier files consisting of fingerprints, name index to fingerprints, and criminal histories.

Information storage and retrieval, the third part of police information systems, supports police in the field by providing quick and accurate criminal information on request. Field personnel have access, for example, to arrest records, outstanding warrants, stolen vehicles, and serially identified stolen weapons and property. Development of good information systems for police officers contributes significantly to the effectiveness of the police agency.

INTELLIGENCE

Intelligence operations, still another staff service, also contribute to efficient police work. Information is gathered to keep police officials attuned to happenings in their areas of jurisdiction by providing insight into community conditions, potential problem areas, and criminal activities—all essential to law enforcement. This work deals with activities that present a threat to the community. The most common targets of intelligence investigations are organized crime and individuals or groups who cause public disorder. To be effective, intelligence activities must be continuous; the data gathered must be used to plan and carry out crime-fighting programs.

INTERNAL DISCIPLINE

Another auxiliary staff service is internal discipline. Discipline and accountability are vital to any police agency in maintaining its integrity. Internal discipline, also known as internal affairs, involves investigation of complaints related to police department services and personnel. Complaints are lodged by citizens or police personnel themselves. Depending on whether the charges are substantiated, complaints can lead to departmental discipline, dismissal, arrest, prosecution, and imprisonment of those found guilty. By protecting the public from police misconduct and corruption and by taking positive action against employees found guilty of misconduct, the department strengthens morale and gains the support of the community it serves.

When all of the line and staff functions performed in police agencies of any size are considered, it is obvious that effective administration is not easily attained. Large agencies tend to use police officers as specialists in specific types of operations, while smaller departments use officers as generalists performing a wide variety of functions. There are merits to both systems, and their use is generally dictated by the needs and composition of the communities in which they are located.

In addition to the local police agencies in municipalities, other special-purpose public police forces are found in many cities throughout the United States. Their jurisdictions include parks, harbors, airports, sanitation departments, transit systems, housing facilities, and ports. Some of these agencies have full police officer powers within their jurisdictions, while others have more limited authority.

WHAT POLICE OFFICERS DO

The fundamental purpose of the police throughout America is crime prevention through law enforcement, and, to most citizens, the most visible representative of this effort is the uniformed Police Officer. There is no more important police function than day-to-day patrol activities, for the effectiveness of police agencies depends on it. After their basic training, most Police Officers are assigned to patrol duty, and their specific duties and responsibilities are numerous and varied. Unlike the specialist, **Patrol Officers** must perform well in a variety of tasks. Regardless of police department size, these officers have two basic responsibilities: to prevent criminal activities and to furnish day-to-day police service to the community. Patrol Officers protect the public, interpret and enforce the law, control traffic, and perform preliminary investigations. They frequently face situations that require swift yet sound decisions. For example, they must decide whether to take no action in an incident or to offer advice, whether to warn or to arrest persons, perhaps using firearms or substantial force. In some situations they must determine the difference between crime and bizarre behavior or between disturbing the peace and legitimate dissent by citizens. Regardless of the circumstances, their first duty is protection of constitutional guarantees, and their second duty is enforcement of the law.

Police Officers patrol assigned sectors in motor vehicles or on foot, working alone or with a partner, paying close attention to area conditions and inhabitants. During patrol, Police Officers observe suspicious behavior, conditions, or illegal activities in their sector and report incidents by radio to a superior officer prior to taking action. They investigate incidents and question the individuals involved to determine violations of the law. They respond to radio calls sent by police dispatchers or superior officers ordering them to the scene of incidents such as burglaries, bank robberies, homicides, rapes, suicides, assaults, and crimes in progress. They make preliminary investigations, question victims and witnesses, recover stolen property, and take evidence into possession. Where indicated, they arrest suspects at crime scenes or after pursuit and use physical force and firearms to subdue them. When making arrests, they advise suspects of their constitutional rights, as required by law, and transport them in police vehicles to police booking and detention facilities prior to court arraignment. At the time of trial, Police Officers testify in court to provide evidence for prosecuting attorneys.

Traffic control is an essential part of police patrol activities. Police Officers direct and control pedestrian and vehicular traffic in high density areas to ensure safe and rapid movement, observe parked and moving vehicles for evidence of traffic violations, and issue citations for violations of traffic regulations. Other responsibilities include maintaining order and traffic flow during public gatherings, demonstrations, and emergencies such as riots, fires, explosions, auto accidents, and natural disasters, using crowd control and traffic-direction techniques to carry out such assignments. They administer first aid to victims of accidents or crimes and arrange for the dispatch of medical units to the scene. In cases of traffic accidents, they investigate circumstances and causes and record findings for subsequent use by the parties involved and their attorneys.

Assignment to patrol duty requires performance of a number of miscellaneous tasks. Police Officers check entrances and exits of commercial facilities for security during hours of darkness. In some police departments, officers inspect residential buildings for safety and suggest methods of improving security, such as installing special locks, alarms, or improved lighting in entry areas. They inspect premises of public, licensed business establishments to enforce laws, local ordinances, and regulations concerning their operation. Police Officers also provide information and assistance to inquiring citizens, help to settle domestic disputes when called to the scene, and may lend assistance in cases of emergency childbirth. They note conditions that are hazardous to the public such as obstructions, potholes, inoperable street lamps, and defective traffic signals, and report them for appropriate action. At the conclusion of each daily work tour, a Police Officer prepares a written activity report that describes arrests, incidents, and all relevant information gathered and submits it to a superior officer, usually a Police Sergeant.

As noted previously, Police Officers on patrol duty are generalists who perform a number of police functions well. However, many aspects of modern police service are complex and require use of specialized personnel. The degree of specialization within a police agency varies with the size and resources of the department and needs of the community. Small communities usually require less specialization while highly populated areas make specialists a necessity. In small police agencies, specialists are generally used on a part-time basis, while the larger departments usually employ full-time specialists. The following are some examples of the various specialized assignments carried out by Police Officers.

SPECIALIZED ASSIGNMENTS

Bomb Squad Officers are highly trained police personnel who respond to incidents of bomb threats and report to locations where bombs have been detonated. Sophisticated equipment and specially trained dogs may be used to locate and disarm explosive and incendiary devices, many of them real and others cleverly constructed hoaxes.

Community Relations Officers help to develop and maintain contact between the police department and community groups, organizations, and schools in the area. Their objective is to promote understanding of the police role in the community, develop closer working relationships, and keep open the lines of communication between citizens and the police department. These officers meet with members of the community and assist in developing police-sponsored programs to help reduce crime. Other duties include conducting tours of police facilities and addressing student and civic groups on relevant topics such as drug abuse, crime prevention, and traffic safety.

Canine Officers team with specially trained dogs to provide assistance to other police units within the department. For example, they are called to different scenes where their special skills are used to conduct building searches, track suspects in wooded or mountainous terrain, locate lost persons, or help in crowd-control operations. Canine Officers personally train their dogs with the help of professional instructors and are responsible for the animals' general care as well.

Crime Prevention Officers conduct security surveys of multiple dwelling and commercial establishments and suggest methods of improving security, such as the use of burglar alarms, window gates, and better locking devices. Speaking before civic groups to inform citizens of crime prevention and safety methods and presenting slides and movies that demonstrate various crime prevention programs may be other job duties. In some departments, Crime Prevention Officers analyze information contained in police reports for indications of crime patterns or trends. They then alert police units to potential problem areas and methods of operation used by perpetrators. This often effects a reduction in criminal activities.

Emergency Service Officers are highly trained police personnel who are brought into situations that other Police Officers are not equipped to handle. Examples of problems dealt with range from people threatening to jump from bridges or high buildings to persons trapped in automobile wreckage or threatened by a dangerous animal. Such cases require a special expertise, and these officers have the equipment and training needed to do the job.

THE POLICE OFFICER SCREENING PROCESS

Why Do People Become Police Officers?

The police officer on the beat or in the patrol car is a familiar figure on the American scene. Except among certain criminal elements, the officer is highly respected. Law abiding citizens are reassured by the presence of police officers whether those officers are directing traffic, discouraging crime by their visible presence, or helping citizens during actual or potential emergencies.

The respect commanded by the police officer makes him or her a role model to all young children. At some time in his or her childhood, nearly every youngster wants to grow up to be a police officer. Many retain this career goal into their teen years and take active steps to join a police force as they become young adults.

A combination of factors makes police work attractive. The idealistic young person—yes, despite the cynics, there are a great many idealistic young Americans—sees police work as a worthwhile activity. A police officer serves the community. His or her work is absolutely vital to the welfare of the public. Police work gives an opportunity to serve while gaining respect and earning a good living.

The material benefits of police work are very real. Police officers are well-paid public servants; their salary levels are above average, and they receive excellent benefits packages. Police officers can look forward to health and life insurance coverage, to generous time-off and vacation allotments, to opportunities for increased responsibility, advancement, and promotions, and to early, well-paid retirement.

A police department never shuts down. This twenty-four-hour, year-round coverage means that police officers sometimes must work nontraditional hours. While the odd working hours may at times interfere with sleep patterns, they offer benefits as well. Family men, in particular, find it a real asset to have some "prime time" hours at home with their children. Police officers with rotating shifts may have opportunities to share school events or afternoon leisure time with their growing families. Traditional 9-to-5 workers miss these opportunities. Flexible work schedules allow the police officer to attend to personal business without having to borrow precious vacation days. In addition, local police officers do not travel. They are not required to spend long periods on the road away from their homes and families. Police scheduling is one of the appealing features that draws people into this field and which adds to the competitiveness of entry.

One final aspect of police work which draws people into the field is the potential for excitement. A desire for excitement in one's everyday work is not a reason in itself for entering a police force, but it can be an added attraction. Much police work is routine and boring, but the possibility of variety and excitement does exist. Many desk or production jobs are routine and boring with no prospects for interesting relief. Police departments are careful to avoid hiring candidates who seek police work only for the excitement, but they look favorably upon candidates who welcome the challenge of the unexpected.

The popularity of police work makes the field a highly competitive one to enter. There are many more aspiring police officers than there are openings on the force. This situation allows police departments to be very selective in the hiring process. Since they have a large applicant pool, they can afford to hire only those applicants who they feel will succeed in their police training and who they expect to become superior police officers.

The police department is looking for a combination of positive traits in each prospective police officer. The screening process takes each applicant through a series of steps, each designed to measure another trait. The recruit must successfully pass through each of these stages. Failure at any stage eliminates the candidate. Let us discuss the desired traits and the reasons they are so important to the police force.

Traits of a Police Officer

1. **The police officer must be intelligent.** First of all, the recruit must be intelligent enough to make it through the police academy or whatever training program that the particular department offers. The recruit must read well to comprehend written materials, must have good listening skills, and must remember what he or she has been taught. The recruit must be able to synthesize material, that is, be able to learn rules and then to be able to apply them to hypothetical or actual situations. Remembering information is not enough. The candidate must convince the examiners that he or she can understand, interpret, and apply information in the field. The intelligent police officer can separate what is important from what is less important, can make quick judgments, and can express him or herself well in speech and in writing. Most police departments begin the applicant screening process with a written test. Written tests require a minimum of administrative time. They can be administered to a large number of applicants at one sitting. Applicants who do not score well on the written test are dropped from consideration. There is no reason to spend time administering medical exams, physical performance tests, psychological exams, or interviews to candidates who do not demonstrate the intelligence to learn the job and to serve as effective police officers.

2. **The police officer must be healthy and physically strong and agile.** Police work is physically taxing. The officer must be able to spend many hours on his or her feet, to move quickly, to see and hear accurately, and to lift, move, or carry as the emergency requires. Obviously, a police officer who is often ill or who cannot perform all physical activities adequately is not acceptable. Police departments have strict medical standards so that they hire only recruits in excellent health. A great many medical conditions that are not so severe as to interfere with everyday life nor with most occupations are disqualifying for the police officer. Likewise, police departments have carefully devised physical performance tests of strength, speed, and agility. The applicant who cannot qualify on the tests does not show great promise for success as a police officer. Medical and physical screening are important hurdles in the selection process.

3. **The police officer must be emotionally stable.** A police officer carries a gun. Obviously, anyone who is armed must be even tempered, well adjusted, and impartial. When it comes to dealing with firearms, there is no room for error. It is vital that the police officer not become excited nor fire too soon. The police officer must be able to size up a situation without fear or prejudice, then act appropriately. The police officer cannot be ruled by anger; at the same time, the police officer cannot hesitate when prompt action is required. Police brutality, insult, and behavior on the basis of preconceived opinions have no place anywhere in the police force. Choosing the most stable recruits

from among the applicants is one of the more difficult tasks for those in charge of hiring. Applicants who have done well on the written exam and who have passed medical examination and physical fitness tests must often submit to psychological examinations. Psychological examinations are not always satisfactory, but police departments must rely on them to eliminate those candidates who appear to be less than perfectly well adjusted and stable. Because psychological testing tends to be inexact, the test results are often confirmed through interviews. Through a psychological test (often more than one) and interviews, each applicant who has reached this stage of the screening process must prove the stability required for responsible behavior in the police role.

4. **The police officer must be self-confident and tactful.** These personality aspects are the final refinements upon which hiring decisions are based. These judgments are based upon interviews. The police officer must have the self-confidence to make quick decisions and to stick with them. Unwavering decisions and firm actions are vital in maintaining control. Tactful, gentle, but firm: these are the hallmarks of the effective, successful police officer. The interviewer hopes to choose the applicants who best display these qualities in a fine, delicate balance. The judgment cannot be entirely objective, but the interviewer does his or her best. The police officer candidate, in turn, can make a conscious effort to impress the interviewer as a tactful, thoughtful person who can communicate and take over effectively under pressure.

The Written Examination

Step one in the screening process is nearly always the written examination. Police departments want to avoid any possible accusation of favoritism or prejudice in hiring, so they invariably use written examinations to screen out unqualified candidates. The written examination is in almost all cases a multiple-choice examination. Multiple choice assures objectivity. If the questions are well designed, each question has only one right answer. Such exams are easy to score and are generally considered to be fair. The unique feature of entry-level examinations is that they do not presuppose any knowledge. The applicant taking a police officer entry exam is not expected to know police rules, regulations, or procedures. On the other hand, the candidate is expected to reason and even to think like a police officer. Questions that evaluate the candidate's thinking and reasoning processes will include all the necessary information with which to reason. This means that police officer exams tend to include many lists of rules and procedures. They often include long excerpts from manuals and rulebooks. The test taker must read and understand the rules that are the basis for each judgment or reasoning question and then must think through the best answer.

Reading-Based Questions

By now you should have gathered that much of the measure of police intelligence is based upon how well you read and what you do with that which you read. Reading-based questions include questions of fact to be extracted directly from reading passages, questions of inference from reading passages, questions that require a choice of actions based upon rules and a fact situation, and questions of judgment of the behavior of others, again based upon both rules and a fact situation. They may also probe your ability to interpret and judge from what you read by presenting a series of definitions and descriptions of situations and then asking you to classify the situations based on the fact situations.

Since reading-based questions of one form or another constitute the bulk of all police exams, we have devoted a full chapter in the regular text of this book to preparing you for these questions.

Practical Judgment Questions

Closely related to reading-based questions are questions of practical police judgment. These are questions that present you with a fact situation and require you to make a spot decision for appropriate action in that situation. The judgment questions do not presuppose knowledge of the proper police action. Your answer should be based upon good judgment and common sense. However, some familiarity with "police thinking" should stand you in good stead with these questions. The good judgment that you demonstrate in police practical judgment questions should predict the same good judgment in actual police situations. The chapter Police Judgment Quizzer prepares you for police judgment questions and introduces you to "police thinking," which you can then combine with your own common sense in answering the questions. The Judgment Quizzer will give you lots of practice with this important question type, and the answer explanations will all contribute to training you to "think right."

Observation and Memory Questions

The intelligent police officer not only reads well, is able to choose a course of action on the basis of knowledge from reading, and can make good judgments in both emergency and nonemergency situations. He or she must also be a keen observer with a good memory. Observation with instant forgetting is totally useless. Observation and memory questions, which appear on many, though by no means all, police officer exams, serve to identify those recruits who are wide awake and know what to watch for. In a way, they also are a test of judgment, for the test-taker must be able to decide what to focus on. Obviously, no one can notice and remember every detail of a scene or event. The intelligent observer can choose what is most important and commit it to memory. The test situation is not, of course, the same as real life. If your exam does not include this type of question, it is because your police department considers observation and memory questions on a written test to be too artificial to be truly predictive. Since this type of question does appear frequently, we have included a chapter for instruction and practice. The information will prove useful whether or not you must answer observation and memory questions on your exam; you will certainly need to sharpen these skills in order to perform your police duties.

Grammar and Effective Expression Questions

Another important line of questioning on police entrance exams has to do with grammar and effective expression. The reason for these questions is obvious. A police officer must communicate in both speech and in writing; his or her message must come across clearly and accurately. All important information must be included, and it must be stated in logical order. There must be no opportunity for misinterpretation or misunderstanding. Police recruits should present their best language skills along with their other qualifications. Grammar and effective expression are, of course, also related to reading. The person who has done extensive reading should be aware of ways to best express information in clear and orderly fashion. We will not attempt to teach grammar at this late stage. Your logical thinking and your eye for what "looks right" will have to see you through. However, we can forewarn you of various forms that grammar and effective expression questions may take and how to approach them.

Your exam may offer you four sentences and ask you to choose the sentence that is wrong with respect to grammar or English usage. This type of question can prove quite difficult. Often two or even three sentences appear to be wrong. Draw upon your school training. Try the sentences aloud (very softly). You may have to weed out the sentences that you are sure are correct, then guess from among the remaining ones.

Another approach is to offer you four sentences, often all attempting to give the same information, and to ask you which one is best. This is a little easier. Concentrate on literal reading of each sentence. Be sure that the one you choose says what you think it means.

Other exams may ask your advice in rephrasing an awkward sentence or in repositioning a sentence or paragraph for more reasonable presentation.

A common effective expression question gives a series of sentences in random order. You must choose the logical progression of steps—what happened first, next, and so on.

A final form of this question is one that presents a list of facts, then asks you to include all these facts in a statement of one or two sentences. You must take care to include all the facts and to express them in an unambiguous way. Read each choice literally to catch word orders that may make the meaning incorrect or even ridiculous. Check the list of facts often to ensure that all facts are presented clearly and appropriately in the statement.

Related to questions of effective expression are questions of what information is important to include in a statement or report. This type of question relies on judgment as well as on knowing the best way of expressing information. Put yourself in the position of the person receiving and having to act on the information. What would be most useful? What do you need to know? In what order would you find the information most helpful?

Reading Maps

Except in cases of extreme emergency, police officers are required to obey all traffic laws. The police officer who goes to the scene of an accident by entering a one-way street in the wrong direction is likely to create another accident. On the other hand, time may be of the essence. A victim may have injuries that require immediate attention. An officer may have to choose the most efficient legal way to get there. Map questions on police exams involve a combination of reading, logical thinking, and common sense. The police candidate can learn how to use maps effectively while undergoing training; however, the applicant who comes with a well-developed skill will be able to spend more time getting specialized police training. Concentrate on map questions on your exam. Read carefully. Put yourself in the driver's seat, and follow all instructions. Do not hesitate to turn the test booklet as needed to maintain your sense of direction.

Filling Out Forms

Police officers must fill out forms and must read and follow them. A few police exams include questions based upon a form, instructions for filling out the form, and a fact situation. There is no trick to these questions. Read carefully. Be especially alert to instructions which read "fill in blank 3 only if such and such" or "leave number 7 blank unless this and that both apply." Exclusionary and inclusive words present the keys in answering many form questions.

Miscellaneous Questions

There is a variety of miscellaneous questions that appear on isolated police qualification exams. Some or all or none of them may occur on yours. If they are included, they tend not to comprise a significant part of the exam. These questions include arithmetic, synonyms, verbal analogies, spelling, and various types of coding questions. Read directions carefully, then do your best with these.

The Medical Examination

The police officer's beat must be covered at all times. This means that the assigned officer must show up. Otherwise, the scheduling officer must find a substitute and must rearrange the work tours of many other officers. The candidate with a history of frequent illness or one with a chronic ailment that may periodically crop up and interfere with attendance is not an acceptable candidate. Likewise, the applicant with an underlying physical condition that presents no problems in everyday life but which might be aggravated under the stressful activity of a police officer must be rejected.

Every candidate under consideration must undergo a thorough medical examination. This examination always occurs after the applicant has passed the written exam and always before the test of physical fitness or physical performance. The medical examination comes before the physical test so that candidates whose health might be jeopardized by the strenuous activity of the physical test are screened out ahead of time. The police department does not want its applicants collapsing on the floor of the physical testing arena. Only the background check may occur either before or after the medical exam. Since both medical exam and background check require an investment of time by police personnel and yet neither depends upon the other, they may be done in either order. Disqualification on the basis of either background check or medical exam stops the screening process and eliminates the candidate from further consideration.

The medical exam will resemble an army physical more than a visit to your personal physician. You will start by filling out a lengthy questionnaire relating to your medical history. This questionnaire will be used by the physician to single out special health areas for consideration. It may also be used by the personal interviewer when you approach the final step of the screening process.

Do not lie on the medical questionnaire. Your medical history is a matter of record at school, in your service dossier, and in the hospital or clinic files. If you lie you will be found out. If the medical condition does not disqualify you, the fact of your untruthfulness will. On the other hand, there is no need to tell more than is asked. You do not need to expand upon your aches and pains. You needn't make an illness or injury more dramatic than it was. Stick to the facts and do not raise any questions. If you have any current concerns, the police department's examining officer is not the person to ask.

Your medical examination almost certainly will include height and weight measurement, chest x-ray, eye test, hearing test, blood tests, urinalysis, cardiogram, blood pressure, and actual visual and physical examination by the doctor. If you have any doubts as to how you will fare with any of these examinations, you might want to consult your personal physician ahead of time. You may be able to correct a borderline situation before you appear for the exam.

Most police departments provide candidates with height-weight standards and with lists of medical requirements before their scheduled medical examinations. If you receive these, look them over carefully. If they present any problems to you, see your doctor. Your worry may be misplaced, or it may be real. Possibly you will have to change your career goals. Or, likely, you can correct the situation, pass the medical exam, and go on to serve on the police force.

Not all police departments have the same standards for medical conditions. Some will accept conditions that are absolutely disqualifying in others. The height-weight charts and the list of medical requirements on the following pages are illustrative. They are typical of those of many police departments. They should serve you as a general guide at this time. If your own medical position is way out of line, you may need to reconsider or embark on a major health reform campaign right away. Once you get your own department's offical set of guidelines, follow those standards rather than the ones printed here.

Height and Weight for Females

Acceptable Weight in Pounds According to Frame

A		B	C	D
Height (in bare feet)		Small	Medium	Large
Feet	Inches	Frame	Frame	Frame
4	10	102–111	109–121	118–131
4	11	103–113	111–123	120–134
5	0	104–115	113–126	122–137
5	1	106–118	115–129	125–140
5	2	108–121	118–132	128–143
5	3	111–124	121–135	131–147
5	4	114–127	124–138	134–151
5	5	117–130	127–141	137–155
5	6	120–133	130–144	140–159
5	7	123–136	133–147	143–163
5	8	126–139	136–150	146–167
5	9	129–142	139–153	149–170
5	10	132–145	142–156	152–173
5	11	135–148	145–159	155–176
6	0	138–151	148–162	158–179

NOTE: Although the above table commences at a specified height, no minimum height requirement has been prescribed. This table of height and weight will be adhered to in all instances except where the Civil Service examining physician certifies that weight in excess of that shown in the table (up to a maximum of twenty pounds) is lead body mass and not fat. Decision as to frame size of a candidate shall be made by the examining physician.

The following tests will be part of the physical examination:

- Vision
- Hearing
- Serology
- Urinalysis
- Chest X-Ray
- Blood Pressure
- Electrocardiogram

Height and Weight for Males

Acceptable Weight in Pounds According to Frame

A		B	C	D
Height (in bare feet)		**Small**	**Medium**	**Large**
Feet	**Inches**	**Frame**	**Frame**	**Frame**
5	2	128–134	131–141	138–150
5	3	130–136	133–143	140–153
5	4	132–138	135–145	142–156
5	5	134–140	137–148	144–160
5	6	136–142	139–151	146–164
5	7	138–145	142–154	149–168
5	8	140–148	145–157	152–172
5	9	142–151	148–160	155–176
5	10	144–154	151–163	158–180
5	11	146–157	154–166	161–184
6	0	149–160	157–170	164–188
6	1	152–164	160–174	168–192
6	2	155–168	164–178	172–197
6	3	158–172	167–182	176–202
6	4	162–176	171–187	181–207

NOTE: Although the above table commences at a specified height, no minimum height requirement has been prescribed. This table of height and weight will be adhered to in all instances except where the Civil Service examining physician certifies that weight in excess of that shown in the table (up to a maximum of twenty pounds) is lead body mass and not fat. Decision as to frame size of a candidate shall be made by the examining physician.

The following tests will be part of the physical examination:

- Vision
- Hearing
- Serology
- Urinalysis
- Chest X-Ray
- Blood Pressure
- Electrocardiogram

Candidates are required to meet the physical and medical requirements stated below and in the announcement at the time of the medical examination, at the time of appointment, and at appropriate intervals thereafter.

1. **Weight.** Candidates should have weight commensurate to frame. Weight should not interfere with candidate's ability to perform the duties of the position of Police Officer.

2. **Vision.** Candidates must have binocular visual acuity not less than 20/20 with or without correction; if correction is required, binocular visual

acuity not less than 20/40 without correction. Binocular peripheral vision should not be less than 150 degrees.

3. **Color Vision.** Be able to distinguish individual basic colors against a favorable background.

4. **Hearing.** Candidates must be able to pass an audiometric test of hearing acuity in each ear. A binaural hearing loss of greater than 15% in the frequency ranges of 500, 1000, 2000 Hz would be considered disqualifying. Hearing appliances should correct the deficiency so the binaural hearing loss in the combined frequency level of 500, 1000, 2000 Hz is no greater than 15%.

5. **Heart.** Candidates must be free of functionally limiting heart disease. Must have a functional cardiac classification of no greater than Class I. This determination to be made clinically or by cardiac stress test.

6. **Lungs.** The respiratory system must be free of chronic disabling conditions that would interfere with the candidate's performance of required duties.

7. **Diabetes.** Candidates who are diabetic must not require insulin injections or oral hypoglycemic agents for control.

8. **Neurological Health.** Candidates must be free of neurological disorders that may affect job performance. Candidates with epilepsy or seizure disorders must provide evidence of one-year seizure free history without drug control.

9. **Musculoskeletal Health.** Candidates must be free of musculoskeletal defects, deformities, or disorders which may affect job performance. Functional use of the arms, hands, legs, feet and back must be demonstrable at the examination. Candidates will be asked to demonstrate physical fitness through tests of strength, agility, flexibility and endurance.

10. **Hernia.** Candidates must be free of abdominal and inguinal herniae which would interfere with job performance.

11. **Blood Vascular Health.** Candidates must be free of blood or vascular disorders that interfere with the performance of duties. Candidates with uncontrolled high blood pressure will be disqualified remediable.

12. **Mental Health.** Candidates must be free of mental illness, serious emotional disturbances or nervous disorders, alcoholism, drug dependence or abuse.

13. **General Medical Statement.** Candidates must be free of any medical and/or nervous condition that would jeopardize safety and health of others. Candidates with communicable diseases will be disqualifed remediable.

Formulation of Medical Requirements from Another Police Department

The duties of these positions involve physical exertion under rigorous environmental conditions, irregular and protracted hours of work, patrol duties on foot, motor vehicle, and aircraft; and participation in physical training. Applicants must be in sound physical condition and of good muscular development.

Vision

- Binocular vision is required and must test 20/40 (Snellen) without corrective lenses,
- Uncorrected vision must test at least 20/70 in each eye,
- Vision in each eye must be corrected to 20/20,
- Near vision, corrected or uncorrected, must be sufficient to read Jaeger Type 2 at 14 inches, and
- Ability to distinguish basic colors by pseudoisochromatic plate test (missing no more than four plates) is required, as is normal peripheral vision.

Hearing

- Without using a hearing aid, the applicant must be able to hear the whispered voice at 15 feet with each ear; or
- Using an audiometer for measurement, there should be no loss of 30 or more decibels in each ear at the 500, 1,000, and 2,000 levels.

Speech

- Diseases or conditions resulting in indistinct speech are disqualifying.

Respiratory System

- Any chronic disease or condition affecting the respiratory system which would impair the full performance of duties of the position is disqualifying; e.g., conditions that result in reduced pulmonary function, shortness of breath, or painful respiration.

Cardiovascular System

The following conditions are disqualifying:

- Organic heart disease (compensated or not),
- Hypertension with repeated readings which exceed 150 systolic and 90 diastolic without medication, and
- Symptomatic peripheral vascular disease and severe varicose veins.

Gastrointestinal System

- Chronic symptomatic diseases or conditions of the gastrointestinal tract are disqualifying.
- Conditions requiring special diets or medications are disqualifying.

Endocrine System

- Any history of a systemic metabolic disease, such as diabetes or gout, is disqualifying.

Genito-Urinary Disorders

- Chronic, symptomatic diseases or conditions of the genito-urinary tract are disqualifying.

Extremities and Spine

- Any deformity or disease that would interfere with range of motion, or dexterity, or that is severe enough to affect adversely the full performance of the duties of the position is disqualifying.

Hernias

- Inguinal and femoral hernias with or without the use of a truss are disqualifying. Other hernias are disqualifying if they interfere with performance of the duties of the position.

Nervous System

- Applicants must possess emotional and mental stability with no history of a basic personality disorder.
- Applicants with a history of epilepsy or convulsive disorder must have been seizure free for the past two years without medication.
- Any neurological disorder with resulting decreased neurological or muscular function is disqualifying.

Miscellaneous

Though not mentioned specifically above, any other disease or condition that interferes with the full performance of duties is also grounds for medical rejection.

Before entrance on duty, all applicants must undergo a pre-employment medical examination and be medically suitable to perform the full duties of the position efficiently and without hazard to themselves and others. Failure to meet any one of the required medical qualifications will be disqualifying for appointment. These standards are considered minimum standards and will not be waived in any case. Applicants found to have a correctable condition may be restored to any existing list of eligibles for further consideration for appointment when the disqualifying condition has been satisfactorily corrected or eliminated.

Physical Performance Tests

The physical performance requirements for all police officers are very similar. All police officers must be able to jump into action in an instant, must be able to move very quickly, must be strong, must have the stamina to maintain speed and strength for a long time, and must be able to continue physically stressful activity at a high level while withstanding discomfort and pain. The ideal police officer is "Superman." The actual police officer does well to approach those qualities.

While police departments have similar physical performance requirements, they tend to measure fitness in many different ways. Three different police officer physical fitness tests follow. Read them through and note the variations. Try each out to the extent that you can without the actual testing course. See how you do. You may need to get yourself into a regular body-building routine some time before you are called for examination. Strength and fitness cannot be developed overnight. You will need to work yourself up to par over a long period. Set up a program and get started right away. You will not be called for a physical fitness test until after you have passed the written examination and the medical examination. The background check may also be conducted before your physical fitness test. You have time, but not that much time. Start now.

A Typical Qualifying Physical Fitness Test for Police Officer

Instructions for Candidates

These subtests are electronically timed by your stepping on the Start Mat and the Finish Mat.

STAIR CLIMB/RESTRAIN: (One Trial) (Maximum Time Allowed: Two Minutes)

In this subtest, you will be expected to run up 3 flights of stairs, down 1 flight, push and pull a box 5 times, and run 5 feet to the finish line.

- On the signal GO, step on the Start Mat, run up the stairs on your right, and continue up to the landing on the third floor.
- Both feet must be placed on the landing.
- Run quickly down one flight of stairs and into the lobby.

- Grab the box and pull it towards you until the front of the box reaches the tape on the floor.
- Now push it back to its starting position.
- Repeat 4 more times as the examiner announces the count.
- After the last trip, turn RIGHT and step on the Finish Mat.

DUMMY DRAG: (Two Trials)
(Maximum Time Allowed: One Minute)

In this subtest, you will be expected to drag a dummy 30 feet.

- Step on the Start Mat.
- Grab the dummy under the shoulders.
- Holding the dummy in this position, move backwards around the traffic cone set 15 feet away and return.
- Place the dummy EXACTLY as you found it in the starting position.
- Step on the Finish Mat.

WALL CLIMB/OBSTACLE RUN: (Two Trials)
(Maximum Time Allowed: One Minute)

In this subtest, you will be expected to go over the 5-foot wall and continue through the obstacle run.

- Step on the Start Mat.
- Run to the wall and go over. You are NOT allowed to use the support bars.
- Follow the tape on the floor around the cones.
- If you miss a cone or go around it the wrong way, you must go back and go around the cone CORRECTLY.
- If you knock a cone over, you must STOP and set it up before you continue.
- Step on the Finish Mat.

Another
Physical Fitness Test

Medical evidence to allow participation in the physical fitness test may be required, and the Department of Personnel reserves the right to exclude from the physical test any eligibles who, upon examination of such evidence, are apparently medically unfit. Eligibles will take the physical fitness test at their own risk of injury, although efforts will be made to safeguard them.

Candidates must complete the *entire* course consisting of seven events in not more than *65 seconds*.

Candidates who do not successfully complete events 3, 5, and 6 will fail the test.

Description of Events

1. Run up approximately 40 steps.

2. Run approximately 40 yards following a designated path including at least four 90° turns, to a sandbag.

3. Push the sandbag, weighing approximately 100 pounds, forward a distance of approximately five yards and then back to its original position. (Failure to meet all of the conditions for this event will result in failure in the test as a whole.)

4. Run approximately 10 yards to a dummy, weighing approximately 110 pounds, which is hanging with its lowest point approximately 3 feet above the floor.

5. Raise the dummy so as to lift the attached ring off the metal pipe. Allow the dummy to slide onto the floor or place it on the floor. *You must not drop it or throw it down*. (Failure to meet all of the conditions for this event will result in failure in the test as a whole.)

6. Step up approximately 18 inches and walk across a 12 foot beam by placing one foot in front of the other until you reach the other end. (You must be in control at all times, and falling off the beam will result in failure of the test as a whole.)

7. Run approximately 10 yards to the finish line.

Candidates who fail the test on their first trial will be allowed a second trial on the same date after a rest period.

Candidates who do not successfully complete all the events in their proper sequence will fail the test.

One More Physical Fitness Test, Very Different in Style

The candidates who qualify on the medical examination will be required to pass the qualifying physical fitness test. A total score of twenty is required for passing this test; the scores attained on the five individual tests are added together to obtain your final score.

Test I: Trunk Flexion Test (Three Chances)

Candidates will assume a sitting position on the floor with the legs extended at right angles to a line drawn on the floor. The heels should touch the near edge of the line and be five inches apart. The candidate should slowly reach with both hands as far forward as possible on a yardstick that is placed between the legs with the fifteen-inch mark resting on the near edge of the heel line. The score is the most distant point (in inches) reached on the yardstick with fingertips.

Rating	Trunk Flexion (Inches)	Points
Excellent	22 and over	6
Good	20–21	5
Average	14–19	4
Fair	12–13	3
Poor	10–11	2
Very Poor	9 and under	1

Test II: Hand Grip Strength Test (Three Chances)

The candidate places the dynamometer (hand grip tester) at the side and, without touching the body with any part of the arm, hand or the dynamometer, should grip the dynamometer as hard as possible in one quick movement. The best of the three tries will be recorded.

Rating	Hand Grip in Kg.	Points
Excellent	65 and above	6
Good	57–64	5
Average	45–56	4
Fair	37–44	3
Poor	30–36	2
Very Poor	29 and under	1

Test III: Standing Broad Jump (Three Chances)

Candidates will be permitted three chances in consecutive order, and the longest distance will be credited. Candidates will be required to jump from a standing position, both feet together. Distance of jump will be recorded from starting point to back of heels. It is each candidate's responsibility to have a non-skid surface on the soles of his or her sneakers.

Rating	Distance	Points
Excellent	7'10" or better	6
Good	7' to 7'9"	5
Average	6'1" to 6'11"	4
Fair	5'6" to 6'0"	3
Poor	5'0" to 5'5"	2
Very Poor	Less than 5'	1

Test IV: One Minute Sit-Up Test

The candidate will start by lying on the back with the knees bent so that the heels are about eighteen inches away from the buttocks. An examiner will hold the ankles to give support. The candidate will then perform as many correct sit-ups (elbows alternately touching the opposite knee) as possible within a one-minute period. The candidate should return to the starting position (back to floor) between sit-ups.

Rating	Sit-Ups in 1 Minute	Points
Excellent	35	6
Good	30–34	5
Average	20–29	4
Fair	15–19	3
Poor	10–14	2
Very Poor	9 and under	1

Test V: Three Minute Step Test

The candidate will step for three minutes on a one-inch bench at a rate of twenty-four steps per minute. The time will be maintained by a metronome. Immediately after the three minutes of stepping, the subject will sit down and relax without talking. A sixty-second heart rate count is taken starting five seconds after the completion of stepping.

Rating	Pulse	Points
Excellent	75–84	6
Good	85–94	5
Average	95–119	4
Fair	120–129	3
Poor	130–139	2
Very Poor	Over 140	1

The Background Check

The police officer is in a position of public trust. He or she must be deserving of that trust. The police department must feel very certain that the police officer will not use his or her position for personal gain, will not use it to harass individuals or groups that he or she dislikes, will not be easily corrupted, and will not take advantage of privileged knowledge.

The standard predictor of future behavior is past behavior. The police department must find out how you have behaved in the past. It will do this by first having you fill out a questionnaire. As with the medical questionnaire, there is no point in lying or cheating. You will be found out and will be disqualified. State the facts clearly. Explain fully and factually.

If you have a totally clean record and face no problems in your personal or family life, then you need have no concern about the background check. Fill in the blanks. List references, and inform those people whose names you have given, so that they are not upset when they are contacted by the police.

Most people have something in their backgrounds that can spark more inquiry. The problem may be financial: If you are strapped for money, the police department may fear that you might be corruptible. The problem may be marital: The police department may worry that you will be distracted. The problem may be one of frequent job changes: The police department questions your stability and the value of investing in your training. The problem may be one of poor credit: Are you responsible and reliable? Or the problem may be one of a brush with the law, minor or major. Most minor infractions can be explained at an interview; reassure the interviewer that these were youthful indiscretions unlikely to recur. Arrests for felonies, and, worse still, convictions present greater obstacles. It may be wise to consult an attorney who specializes in expunging criminal records to see what can be done to clear your name. Some offenses are absolutely disqualifying. You may as well know ahead of time and take all possible steps to make yourself employable by the police department.

A felony record needs the services of an attorney. So might multiple misdemeanor convictions. You can help yourself in many other situations. If you have a poor credit rating, pay up and have your rating upgraded. If you are behind on alimony payments, catch up. If you have an unanswered summons, go to court and answer it. Pay your parking tickets. Even if these past problems turn up in the background check, your positive attitude in clearing them up will be in your favor.

Be sure that you are able to document any claims you make with reference to diplomas, degrees, and honors. You may have to produce these at an interview. Likewise, be certain that you understand the nature and gravity of the problems in your background. Be prepared to admit that you misbehaved and to reassure the examiners that you have matured into a responsible citizen.

The Psychological Evaluation

The Purpose of the Psychological Evaluation

Some jurisdictions subject all police officer candidates to a psychological evaluation before appointment; others, because of the expense involved, limit psychological evaluations to those cases where there are signs that one might be necessary. However, in all cases the sole purpose of a psychological evaluation is to determine the candidate's mental fitness for performing the specific duties of a police officer. The evaluation is *not* concerned with other aspects of mental well-being. In fact, because of this exclusive focus on police work, a candidate might be judged psychologically unfit to be a police officer even if he or she is perfectly suited for other types of employment.

What makes police work so different from other occupations? Soon after orientation and the usual training at the police academy, the police officer begins functioning more or less independently. Although the officer functions under supervison, that supervision is present only periodically; and although the officer should be guided by the department's rules of procedure, many times the officer will be thrust into situations where immediate action is required to save lives or protect property. For example, the officer who encounters a pregnant woman about to give birth must take decisive action at once. In such situations, there is no time to consult the rules of procedure. The officer must do whatever is necessary right away.

Another crucial difference is that the police officer carries a gun as part of the job. Prudent use of this weapon requires not only conformance to the rules of procedure but also a good sense of police judgment. The officer who must decide in an emergency whether to use that gun must have a very high degree of psychological stability.

Psychological evaluations of police officer candidates are usually conducted by a psychologist or psychiatrist who is trained to detect signs of deficiencies that could interfere with the proper performance of police work. The job is twofold: to look for signs of potential trouble and to evaluate the sincerity of the candidate. For example, consider the possible responses when the psychologist asks, "Why do you want to become a police officer?" A proper response would be "I want a career in the public service, and I feel that effective law enforcement will make for a better society for my children and eventually for my grandchildren." There is nothing wrong with this response. The only thing to be judged is the sincerity of the candidate. Now look at the following response to the same question: "I have always liked uniforms. They bring respect and admiration, and they permit you to perform your duties without interference." Something is wrong here. Or consider this response: "I hate criminals. They take advantage of the weak and elderly. They are cowards, and I want to do everything I can to eliminate them." This intense hatred may indicate the need for further investigation of this candidate's psychological stability.

Typical Evaluation Questions

The questions that you will be asked will, for the most part, be quite predictable. The majority of them will be based on your responses to application forms and other papers that you have been required to file. The psychologist will ask you to amplify or to explain the personal data that you listed on those papers. Sometimes you will be asked to describe your feelings about events that happened to you. Also, as a way of encouraging you to talk, you may be asked more open-ended questions about your personal likes, dislikes, or emotions.

You may also be asked your opinion about what you might do in a hypothetical police work situation, but such questions are unlikely to form the bulk of the evaluation. In this case, the psychologist is not testing your knowledge of police procedures, but only your ability to make reasoned judgments and to avoid rash behavior. Because most of the questions you will be asked are predictable, it is relatively easy to prepare answers for them. Begin your preparation by looking over the application forms that you filled out and any other papers that you were required to file. You should be able to pick out the points that a psychologist will want you to clarify or explain.

Typical questions you might encounter include the following:

- Why did you choose your area of concentration in school?
- What particularly interests you about that subject?
- Why did you transfer from school x to school y?
- How did you get the job with _____?
- Which of the duties described in your second job did you like best? Which least? Why?
- What did you do during the nine months between your second and third jobs?
- Explain the circumstances of your leaving a particular job.
- Please clarify: armed forces service, arrest record, hospitalization record, etc., as applicable.

Other questions are much like those asked at a routine job interview. They can be anticipated and prepared for as well.

- Why do you want to leave the kind of work you are doing now?
- Why do you want to be a police officer?
- How does your family feel about your becoming a police officer?
- What do you do in your leisure time?
- Do you have any hobbies? What are they? What do you particularly like about _____?
- What is your favorite sport? Would you rather play or watch?
- How do you react to criticism? If you think the criticism is reasonable? If you consider the criticism unwarranted?
- What is your pet peeve?
- What are your greatest strengths? Weaknesses?
- What could make you lose your temper?
- Of what accomplishment in your life are you most proud?
- What act do you most regret?
- If you could start over, what would you do differently?
- What traits do you value most in a co-worker? In a friend?
- What makes you think you would make a good police officer?

Still other questions may be more specific to police work. You should have prepared answers to:

- How much sleep do you need?
- Are you afraid of heights?
- What is your attitude toward irregular hours?
- Do you prefer working alone or on a team?
- Are you afraid of dying?
- What would you do with the rest of your life if your legs were crippled in an injury?
- How do you deal with panic? Your own? That of others?
- What is your attitude toward smoking? Drinking? Drugs? *Playboy* magazine? Gambling?
- What is your favorite TV program? How do you feel about watching news? Sports? Classical drama? Rock music? Opera? Game shows?

Now make a list of your own. The variety of evaluation questions is endless, but most can be answered with ease. Preparation makes the whole process much more pleasant and less frightening.

There is one question that strikes terror into the heart of nearly every candidate for police officer or any other job. This question is likely to be the first and, unless you are prepared for it, may well throw you off your guard. The question is, "Tell me about yourself." For this question you should have a prepared script (in your head, not in your hand). Think well ahead of time about what you want to tell. What could the psychologist be interested in? This question is not seeking information about your birthweight nor about your food preferences. The psychologist wants you to tell about yourself with relation to your interest in and qualifications for police work. Think of how to describe yourself with this goal in mind. What information puts you into a good light with reference to the work for which you are applying? Organize your presentation. Then analyze what you plan to say. What is a psychologist likely to pick up on? To what questions will your speech lead? You must prepare to answer these questions to which you have opened yourself.

Towards the end of the evaluation, the psychologist will most likely ask if you have any questions. You undoubtedly will have had some beforehand and should have come prepared to ask them. If all of your questions have been answered in the course of the evaluation, you may tell this to the psychologist. If not, or if the evaluation has raised new questions in your mind, by all means ask them. The evaluation should serve for your benefit; it is not just to serve the purposes of the Police Department.

The invitation of your questions tends to be the signal that the evaluation is nearly over. The psychologist is satisfied that he or she has gathered enough information. The time allotted to you is up. Be alert to the cues. Do not spoil the good impression you have made by trying to prolong the evaluation.

Should You Reveal Personal Opinions and Feelings?

The psychologist does not expect candidates to be devoid of personal feelings. After all, everyone has likes and dislikes. However, the mature, psychologically stable person is able to keep those feelings from interfering with the performance of job duties. The police officer will encounter a very wide variety of people on the job. Some the officer may find personally likeable; others may be unlikeable, even downright unpleasant. However, whatever the officer's true feelings about the persons encountered, he or she must service those individuals in an effective manner or serious repercussions—even loss of life—may result. This type of behavior takes mental maturity and stability, qualities every officer must possess. It is these qualities that the psychologist is looking for at the evaluation, not an absence of personal feelings. The successful candidate does not have to like everyone he or she meets. What is important is the ability to control personal feelings in order to function effectively.

Sometimes during an evaluation a candidate will express "extreme" views on certain subjects. Unlike more typical opinions or feelings, these may indeed be cause for disqualification. An obvious example is a display of unreasoning dislike for people from a particular ethnic or religious background. To the psychologist, this is a sure sign of trouble. The candidate who says, "People from ethnic group X are always the ones who commit the violent crimes" will never be appointed a police officer.

Should You Volunteer Information?

One very important point to remember at the evaluation is to limit your responses to what is asked. An evaluation session of this type is one of the very few opportunities most people have to reveal their true inner selves to others. The psychologist knows this and will often encourage the person being evaluated to talk freely and openly about personal matters and opinions. An unthinking candidate may use this opportunity to bring up matters that ordinarily he or she would never discuss. The talkative candidate might even know that he or she is getting in too deep but may be unable to refrain from continuing. The psychologist will encourage this type of individual to talk at length in order to reveal personal matters that will indicate the level of the candidate's psychological stability.

One device that psychologists use to make candidates keep talking is to assume a facial expression that indicates that further explanation is expected. It is very important not to respond to this suggestion! If you do, you are likely to say things that can only be harmful to you. Try to be satisfied with your original response, and have the maturity to stand by it no matter what expression you see on the psychologist's face. Display a sense of self-assurance that convinces the psychologist that you are satisfied with your answers.

How to Explain Problem Incidents in Your Past

One concern of many police officer candidates is how to handle questions about problem incidents in their past. More than a few candidates have at some time—usually in their youth—gotten into trouble in some incident involving property damage or even personal injury to others. Such incidents almost always come to light during the candidate's background check, often through school, court, or military records. If you have such an incident in your past and are questioned about it by the psychologist, the wisest course is to accept full responsibility for it and to attribute it to your youthful immaturity at the time. Claiming that the record is false or giving excuses for your bad behavior is not likely to be regarded favorably. The psychologist is much more apt to respond positively if you accept responsibility and—just as important—you attribute any such incident to an immature outlook that you have now outgrown. One mistake of this type will not necessarily disqualify you if you can convince the psychologist that you have become a fully responsible adult and will never do anything of the kind again.

"Pencil-and-Paper" Evaluations

As part of the psychological evaluation, some jurisdictions use standardized personality tests that you answer by marking a sheet of paper. These tests may contain a hundred or more questions. Your responses help the psychologist determine your specific personality traits. Your answer to any one question by itself usually means very little, but your answers to a group of questions, taken together, will have significance to the psychologist. Your wisest course when taking one of these written personality tests is to give honest, truthful answers. Any attempt to make yourself appear different from the way you really are is not likely to be successful.

Keep A Positive Attitude

One final word of advice: it is important to approach all psychological evaluations with a positive attitude. Think of the evaluation not as an ordeal that you must endure, but rather as an opportunity to prove that you are qualified to become a police officer. In truth, the psychologist will be looking for traits that qualify you, not ones that disqualify you. And if disqualifying evidence exists, it is the psychologist's responsibility to consider every factor before making a negative recommendation. So go into the evaluation with confidence and be prepared to "sell" yourself to the psychologist. You will be given every chance to prove your worth.

Evaluation Checklist

Here are some valuable points to remember as you prepare for the psychological evaluation.

1. Get a good night's sleep the night before the evaluation.

2. Do not take any medication beforehand to calm yourself. You may be tested for drugs before the evaluation.

3. Dress neatly and conservatively.

4. Be polite to the psychologist or psychiatrist.

5. Respond to all questions honestly and forthrightly.

6. Use as few words as possible to communicate your thoughts. When you have finished answering a question, do not let the psychologist's behavior lead you to think that you have not said enough.

7. Admit responsibility for any youthful indiscretions and attribute them to your immaturity at the time of the incident.

8. Do not permit any deep-seated prejudices to assert themselves. If you can control them during the evaluation, you will be able to control them while performing the duties of a police officer.

9. Most important, be yourself. You're bound to do better than if you pretend to be someone you're not.

Appeals

A police officer candidate who is marked "not qualified" on the psychological evaluation will be afforded an opportunity to appeal. In most jurisdictions, a notice of disqualification will include information on appeal procedures and on any time limitations.

Because the official disqualification is made by a psychologist or psychiatrist, the best way for the candidate to appeal is to engage another psychologist or psychiatrist to testify on the candidate's behalf. To start preparing the appeal, the candidate should obtain the official notice of the examination, the medical standards on which the evaluation was based, and a document telling the precise reason for the disqualification. If these items are not furnished by the examining agency, the candidate should petition for them at once. If necessary, the candidate should be prepared to resort to the procedures specified in the Freedom of Information Act in order to find out the exact reasons for rejection. This information is crucial to preparing a proper appeal. Any psychological testimony on the candidate's behalf must respond to the reasons given for disqualification. It is not enough for a psychologist to simply assert that the candidate is generally mentally stable. The psychologist must show that the candidate is in fact psychologically competent to perform the specific duties of a police officer.

If you are disqualified as a result of the psychological evaluation, you should certainly consider filing an appeal. Often this kind of show of determination has influenced a hiring jurisdiction to take a chance on a "borderline" candidate. You will find many psychologists and psychiatrists who specialize in helping rejected police officer candidates.

Police Officer Organizations

Many city police departments have a wide variety of religious, fraternal, and ethnic organizations. These groups do not appear on any official roster, yet they are as much a part of the average police officer's life as his or her gun or shield.

Formed to represent the diverse cultural and religious heritage of their respective members, it might be said that they are the heart of the department. Collectively, they represent almost all members of the service of every rank and assignment.

Most organizations serve as a vital resource to their members, providing counseling, both spiritual and practical. They fill a social void through pride in belonging.

All of the organizations provide either tangible personal benefits to members and their families or perform charitable acts within the community. Most do both. The groups provide many police officers with their closest friends and with the opportuity for socialization.

Occasionally, one hears the criticism that fraternal and ethnic organizations, instead of providing an enjoyable means of helping individuals find and respect their own identity and heritage, actually highlight the differences between groups of people. This is a false assumption. Members of these organizations often meet and exchange ideas and concerns. Differences are discussed and possible solutions are offered. Dialogue is, after all, the key to understanding.

We encourage Police Officers of all backgrounds to join one or more of these organizations. For the names of the organizations in your town, check with your police department. The following pages list organizations recognized by the New York City Police Department.

AMERICAN LEGION POLICE POST

The New York City American Legion Post 460 was founded August 31, 1920. Its membership consists of both active and retired police officers who served in the United States Military during time of war.

The purpose of the Police Post 460 is to foster friendship, promote comraderie, and preserve the rights of all veterans in police civil service.

The American Legion's accomplishments to date include: the G.I. Bill, V.A. Home Loan Program, preference in civil service job examinations, and real estate tax exemptions.

Dates of service eligibility:

World War II—	12/7/41 to 12/31/46
Korea—	6/25/50 to 1/31/55
Vietnam—	12/22/61 to 5/7/75

ANCHOR CLUB

The Anchor Club was founded in September 1922 by men of the New York City Police Department who were members of the Knights of Columbus. This Club Branch #1 was the first Anchor Club in America.

The Anchor Club has made it its goal to provide annual programs for all widows and children of deceased police officers.

1. Outing to Coney Island's Astroland and New York Aquarium with all rides, lunch, and parking provided.

2. A day at Yankee Stadium with lunch and parking provided.

3. Annual Christmas party with gifts, food, and entertainment for the children.

4. Annual memorial mass for all deceased members of the Department with a luncheon served after.

5. A boat ride or other outing for a day during the summer.

We have established the Joseph L Melody Fund which helps seminarians to complete their studies.

We raise funds for outings and Christmas parties to provide pleasure for children of any deceased member of the Police Department regardless of race, creed, or religion.

ASIAN—JADE SOCIETY

The Asian Jade Society was founded in 1980 by its ten charter members. The society is open to members of the Police Department (active and retired) of Asian-Pacific Islander heritage including Chinese, Japanese, Korean, Phillipino, Indian, etc.

The goals of the society are:

* To establish lasting friendships among members and their families.
* To assist and support each other in times of need.
* To provide mutual advancement in the best interest of our members.
* To foster good relations in the Asian Pacific communities.

Events—Annual Chinese New Year Dinner Dance; Summer picnic for members and their families

COLUMBIA ASSOCIATION

Columbia Association held its first meeting in 1929.

Membership: 4,500 members from the New York City Police Department of Italian ancestry (active and retired uniformed members in all ranks).

Objectives:

1. To promote, practice and cherish the spirit of brotherhood among people irrespective of race or religion.
2. To develop an understanding and appreciation of the contributions made by Italians and Italian-Americans toward the development of our great nation.
3. To increase our knowledge and understanding of the cultural heritage that unites us all.

Events: Installation of officers (bi-annual), Concord weekend, dinner-dance, golf outing, Mount Airey Lodge weekend, high school and college scholarship exams, annual Columbus Day parade and post parade party, and scholarship awards night.

Benefits:

1. Provide counsel and legal aid.
2. A minimum amount of $4,000.00 in high school and college scholarship awards provided for children of members who successfully compete in a scholarship examination.
3. Death benefit to beneficiary of member.
4. Promotion classes for members preparing for the Sergeant's Examination.

5. Wristwatches awarded to members in good standing promoted to the rank of Sergeant.
6. Thirty-five year members will be awarded dues-free Life Membership Cards.
7. Dinners served at general meetings.
8. Organization prizes for recreational activities.
9. When a death occurs in the immediate family of a member, the deceased will be remembered at perpetual masses.
10. To keep members abreast of the Association's activities, a newspaper is mailed to their homes.
11. Columbia Medal for Valor.

Affiliations: National Council of Columbia Associations in Civil Service; Coalition of Italo-American Associations, Inc.

EMERALD SOCIETY

The Emerald Society of the Police Department of the City of New York takes this opportunity to extend to all new Police Officers a hearty and sincere *Ceade Mile Failte*—A Hundred Thousand Welcomes.

The Emerald Society was founded in 1953 and now boasts of the highest membership ever. The purpose of the Emerald Society is to maintain a close relationship with the culture, tradition, and well-being of the country of our heritage. Our programs are religious, benevolent, charitable, patriotic, social, musical and athletic.

Our objectives are to develop a spirit of brotherhood, good will, and fellowship and to encourage a fuller participation in the activities of the many organizations within the Police Department.

Through the support of the Board of Officers, the general membership, active and retired, and our many friends in the Irish-American community, we offer a wide range of programs annually:

Annual Winter Weekend
High School Scholarships—Test and Awards
Annual Dinner Dance
Irishman of the Year Award
Saint Patrick's Day Parade and Celebration
Retired Members' Night
Flights to Ireland
Moonlight Cruise
Patrick J. O'Connor Medal of Valor
College Scholarship Lottery
Affiliated with the Grand Council of United Emerald Societies, Inc.
Associated with the Irish American Immigration Committee
Committee of Police Services
Cruises and Flights
Golf Tournaments

GUARDIANS ASSOCIATION

The Guardians Association, a fraternal organization, was recognized by the New York Police Department in 1949. Our membership is open to all law enforcement officers and civilians in the New York Police Department. Our services are voluntary. Our hope is to help with the progress and peace in our city.

Our off-hours "beat" is unlimited. The Guardians Association has consistently and persistently pursued a policy of on-going police and community efforts over the years. Christmas never saw Harlem Hospital without our toys for confined children. We played a leadership role in A. Philip Randolph's two school marches on Washington in 1957 and 1958, as well as the historical August 28, 1963, March on Washington for Jobs and Freedom. We have served as the "Dutch Uncles" for minority group police aspirants. The membership is engaged in on-the-street off-duty police recruitment programs.

We believe in fair, impartial enforcement of law for all people. As police officers this is our sworn duty, and we will vigorously protest infractions by fellow officers or by any other agencies of the law.

We believe that a mutual understanding between police and the people they serve would result in far more effective law enforcement in black communities. We therefore stand for intensive recruitment of more qualified blacks with the New York City Police Department.

We stand for involvement; for deeds, not words, and for educational efforts that promote respect for the law.

HISPANIC SOCIETY

The Hispanic Society of the City Of New York Police Department was founded in January, 1957, by a handful of energetic Hispanic officers set on the premise that in order to serve the people of the City of New York and in order to create a more harmonious relationship with other police officers there should exist a fraternal organization, an organization capable of understanding and able to address the needs of Hispanic officers.

The Society is dedicated to strengthening the fraternal atmosphere among all members of Hispanic origin. Also, inspired by a collective desire for recognition, we came together to gain strength through unity, brotherhood through participation, and mutual respect through hard work.

The society now enjoys the reputation of being among the foremost of organizations dedicated to promoting good will and fostering support in our community. This example has stimulated other Hispanic groups in public service to organize along these same lines.

Presently, we are pursuing an aggressive program to encourage growth, secure recognition, and stimulate the prosperity of Hispanics in the Police Department and in this City.

HOLY NAME SOCIETY
Manhattan, Bronx, Staten Island

Founded: In January 1914, we are the largest and oldest religious organization in the New York City Police Department.

Membership: 11,000 active and retired members of the New York City Police Department who work or worked in Manhattan, Bronx, and Staten Island.

Objective: Promoting the spiritual welfare of Catholic Police Officers employed within or retired from the Police Department of the City of New York in the Boroughs of Manhattan, Bronx, and Staten Island by encouraging and assisting them to observe the practices of the confraternity of The Most Holy Name of Jesus, namely the frequent reception of the sacraments, the honoring of The Most Holy Name by an active religious life, and the working against all things which offend The Most Holy Name.

Annual Events: Communion mass and breakfast awarding ten Catholic High School Scholarships annually; annual memorial mass for deceased members of the New York Police Department (first Saturday in Nov.); Project Hands for the Handicapped; Special Olympics for the handicapped; president night (in June); presents Medal For Valor On Medal Day for Police Department; March in St. Patrick's Day Parade; Holy Name Society weekend away, plus our Holy Name Retreat.

Benefits: Eligibility for life insurance program, personal guidance and counseling, masses for sickness and death, scholarship program for children, annual police retreat.

Affiliate: National Holy Name Society, Archdiocese of New York. We are Branch number 175.

HOLY NAME SOCIETY
Brooklyn & Queens

The Brooklyn and Queens Holy Name Society of the New York City Police Department was founded in 1919. Our first Spiritual Director, Monsignor Lawrence H. Bracken, was sworn in on January 20, 1919. Monsignor Bracken served the Police Department and our Society for 45 years.

The Diocese of Brooklyn consists of the two counties of Brooklyn and Queens. Our Society consists of 1,600 Catholic officers, of all ranks, who work for the Police Department within the Diocese of Brooklyn.

The Society holds an Annual Communion Breakfast, preceded by the Bishop's celebration of Holy Mass. At the Breakfast the Society presents scholarship awards to the children of our members to assist them with their future education.

Throughout the year the Society has several meetings at which our members meet socially to continue their long friendships and to establish new associations with other members.

The Society wishes to extend a cordial welcome to all the new Police Officers who have entered our Department in recent years.

THE HONOR LEGION

The Honor Legion, founded in 1912, is the oldest fraternal organization in the New York City Police Department.

The Honor Legion is composed of members of the Police Force of the City of New York, comprising all ranks, who during the history of the Honor Legion, have received department recognition and have been awarded medals or honorable mention for deeds of valor performed at imminent risk of life or who have been commended for meritorious acts at personal risk, and who are entitled to wear the insignia of their department.

It holds in one great bond of comradeship the Honor Members of the Department, the Finest of the Finest. It recognizes no rank. It is a force, a tower of strength to combat evil, an inspiration from within, a beacon of hope for the weak, a leaven for good. Its tenets: self-respect, courage, loyalty and devotion to duty.

The underlying purpose of the organization is to render aid and comfort to the survivors of the members of the service who have made the supreme sacrifice in the performance of their duty: (*Fidelis Ad Mortem.*)

This purpose is carried out by the members of the Honor Legion with the thoughtfulness of mind that "there but for the grace of God go I."

The Honor Legion is a fraternal organization which through social functions fosters comradeship and brotherhood recognizing no ethnicity or religious differences.

The Board of Officers of the Honor Legion of the Police Department of the City of New York is proud and honored to announce that our membership rolls are open to all law enforcement personnel throughout our nation, providing they meet the Honor Legion's high standards for membership.

POLICEWOMEN'S ENDOWMENT ASSOCIATION

Founded: 1921 by Rose Taylor, Ada Bearry, Mary McGuire, Minnie Ernest and Mary Sullivan

Objective: To unite and promote the interest and welfare of the female uniformed members of the Police Department of the City of New York; to promote equal opportunities of appointment, assignment and promotion; and to provide benefits as determined by the constitution and bylaws.

Membership: Open to all females who are uniformed members of the service of the Police Department of the City of New York. (Active and retired) Membership is open on a yearly basis.

Events: Conferences, dinner dances, various sports, installation of officers, disco, and trips.

Programs: Self-Help Group, Big Sister/Little Sister program, Child Care

Newsletter: "On Target" bi-monthly publication.

History: 1964 First Sgts. Exam for females
1965 First Female Sgts. Sworn in
1967 First Female Lts. Sworn in
1971 First Female Capt. Sworn in
1972 First Policewomen assigned to patrol
1973 Policewomen became Police Officers

Note: As of 1987 the New York City Police Department has the largest number of female officers due to the efforts of the Policewomen's Endowment Association.

POLICE SELF SUPPORT GROUP

The Police Self Support Group was formed by Det. Richard Pastorella of the Bomb Squad who on December 31, 1982, was severely injured at Police Headquarters while trying to disarm an F.A.L.N. terrorist device. After convalescing at Bellevue Hospital, and later at home, he became painfully aware of the secondary trauma associated with his injuries—that of being "forgotten."

He resolved that no other police officer sustaining line-of-duty injuries would ever stand alone again and soon formed what has now come to be known as the Police Support Group.

The police department formally recognized our group in May 1985.

On June 25th of this year, we were formally accepted into the Committee of Police Societies (C.O.P.S.)

THE PULASKI ASSOCIATION

In September of 1956 a small group of 31 police officers of Polish heritage met at Prospect Hall, Brooklyn, New York. Sergeant Michael Labowski was elected to lead this group to petition the New York City Police Department for permission to establish a Polish fraternal organization.

Sergeant Labowski and the other founders, in searching for a name for the organization, decided on Pulaski in honor of the great Polish freedom fighter, General Casimir Pulaski. The founders saw in General Pulaski an unselfish bravery and dedication to freedom that was consistent with the goals of the organization they had established.

The Pulaski Association has grown to a membership of over 1,500 police officers of Polish and Slavic heritage. To qualify for membership a member or his/her spouse must be of Polish or Slavic heritage. The Association is at the forefront of fraternal organizations within the New York City Police Department. It is known for its support of brotherhood and its scholarship program as well as for sponsoring the best social functions, vacations and fraternal meetings within the Police Department.

THE SHOMRIM SOCIETY

The name Shomrim comes from the Hebrew word meaning watcher or protector.

Founded: October 16, 1924 (incorporated February 28, 1925).

Membership: 2,600 members of the Jewish faith from the New York City Police Department (active and retired) including police officers and civilian members of the Department.

Objective: To foster the ideals of charity, benevolence and brotherhood.

Events: Installation of officers dinner dance, Oneg Shabbat, Passover charity distribution, trips, Israeli Day parade, Solidarity Day parade, picnic, mid-year weekend, Memorial Service, spiritual breakfast, Chanukah festival, and winter weekend outing.

Benefits: Membership in a Jewish religious and fraternal organization comprised of uniformed and civilian members of the Police Department of all ranks. Participation in charitable activities fostering the ideals of Judaism, benevolence and brotherhood. Visit the sick, pay shiva calls. Establish long lasting friendship of members and their families and participation in many social activities. Death benefits and burial grounds provided in the New York area for all members, spouse, and any unmarried children. (Perpetual care in Shomrim Field—no fee.) Scholarship program for children and grandchildren of members.

Affiliations: National Conference of Shomrim Societies; Council of Jewish Organizations in Civil Service.

The Shomrim Society maintains the concept of having all members of the Police Department of the Jewish faith join for the welfare of all.

STEUBEN ASSOCIATION

Functions

1. Monthly meetings—Meetings with old friends and the making of new ones.
2. Installation dinner-dance.
3. May wine festival and October beer festival.
4. Father and son/daughter meeting.
5. Ladies'-Night meeting.

6. Old-Timers' night.
7. Picnic in summer.
8. Steuben parade in September and a reception afterwards for members who march and their families.
9. Christmas party for members' and deceased members' children and grandchildren and for all children of members of the Police Department who have died in the performance of duty.
10. Flight to Germany, winter week-end in the Catskills, bus tours, etc.
11. Liaison between the Police Department and the German-American community.

Benefits

1. Fraternalism.
2. Death benefit for survivors of members in good standing.
3. Dental plan for members and their families.
4. High school and college scholarship awards.
5. Christmas gifts to widows of deceased members who were in good standing before their demise.
6. Forming of study group for members interested in promotion.

The Steuben Association is also concerned with charitable endeavors and with the making of donations to various charitable and religious organizations each year.

As the Steuben Association grows, so will all the activities, benefits, and charitable endeavors grow. It is our desire to maintain a vibrant and progressive organization whereby the Steuben Association will maintain its high integrity and loyalty and whereby each person will say that he or she is proud to be a member of the Steuben Association—P.D.N.Y.

ST. GEORGE ASSOCIATION

All Protestant Members of the Department
Lutheran, Methodist, Baptist, Episcopalian, Congregational, etc.

For many years Chaplain A. Hamilton Nesbitt had a dream of uniting the Protestant members of the New York City Police Department into an organization that would minister to and serve them and their families spiritually, socially and, if needed, economically. After consultation with the Police Commissioner and encouragement from other official leaders in the department, his dream became a reality. The St. George Association was organized and officers elected at Police Headquarters in 1937.

Since 1937 the St. George Association has grown into a healthy organization of more than 5,000 members from various Protestant denominations. The Executive Board meets every second Thursday of each month. In addition there are spiritual and social functions throughout the year such as the Communion breakfast and German, Chinese and Christmas dinner meetings, which all members are invited to attend. Every other year we have an Installation Dinner and Dance. All meetings and activities are made known through the St. George Association's monthly bulletin and precinct delegates.

The St. George Association presents scholarships to the sons and daughters of active paid-up members, retired members and the children of deceased members of the organization.

The name St. George Association of the United States of America was selected because of the unique correlation between the aims of this Association and those of St. George, the great Christian crusader, famed in legend and myth for his perfect Christian knighthood. St. George was the hero of many colorful and varied legends, the most famous of which is known as the "Golden Legend" wherein "St. George, on a fiery white steed, rescued from a monstrous dragon a virgin who was standing on a rock at the brink of a large body of water." Authentic history reveals, however, that St. George was born in Athens, Greece and became a captain in the Roman Army during the reign of the Roman Emperor Diocletian, which lasted from 284 to 305 A.D. This marked the highest point in cruel persecution of the Christians. He steadfastly refused to capitulate, and, against all odds, fought desperately for the cause of Christianity. He was the standard bearer for right, brotherly love, and the protection of womanhood. He gave his life for this great cause and became a patron saint of Christian crusaders. St. George is the emblem of Christian progressiveness.

ST. PAUL'S SOCIETY

Founded: January 1958 (incorporated January 1967)

Membership: 350 members of Eastern Orthodox Faith from the New York City Police Department. Included are members from the Housing Police and Port Authority Police Department. Members are active, retired, life members and civilians.

Objective: To promote a fraternal spirit, strengthen friendship and promote each other's welfare among all members of the Police Department. To increase our knowledge and understanding of the Eastern Orthodox faith.

Annual Event: Annual Holy Communion service and breakfast held each year. Installation of officers at our annual Christmas party. Greek-American Day parade up 5th Ave.

Benefits: Provide spiritual counseling for those in need. To sponsor a scholarship award program for children of members in good standing (including deceased members). To keep members abreast of the society and the society's activities in a monthly news letter.

Affiliations: Olympia Association,
New York City,
Transit Police Department.

Greek (Orthodox Archdiocese of North and South America.)

The St. Paul's Society was formed for the understanding of the cultural heritage that unites us all.

TRAFFIC SQUAD

The Traffic Squad Benevolent Association is the oldest fraternal organization within the New York City Police Department. Founded in 1906 and incorporated in 1909, the Traffic Squad has strived to actively represent the best interests of its members.

This organization has many goals which provide for the mutual advancement and fraternalism of its members in a professional manner.

The Traffic Squad Benevolent Association is proud to be an active member association in the New York City Police Department as well as in the Committee of Police Societies, Inc. (C.O.P.S.)

In addition to its police functions, the T.S.B.A. shows an active concern to community affairs and problems. We know that without the continued cooperation and support of the public that we serve our tasks would be insurmountable.

VIKING ASSOCIATION

The name Viking was selected because of identification with the ancestors of those hailing from the nations of Scandinavia.

Founded: May 17, 1985

Membership: The Viking Association bylaws provide that membership is open to those currently engaged in, or retired from, police work contracted for by the City of New York or its subsidiary authorities. Such employment may include sworn or civilian service, but is limited to only those who trace an ancestral or marital bond to Sweden, Norway, Denmark, Finland, or Iceland.

Objectives: To foster the ideals of charity, benevolence and fraternity through the collective efforts of Scandinavian Americans.

Events: Installation of officers, 17th of May parade and party, scholarship program, nursing home visits, orphaned children's Christmas party, baseball game outing and members' Christmas.

Benefits: Viking membership provides the heretofore missing element of ethnic identification to those eligible to join. The performance of such acts as visits to orphaned children and the elderly in nursing homes serves as the common ground necessary to form deep and long lasting relationships.

Civilian Support Group

THE NEW YORK'S FINEST FOUNDATION

The New York's Finest Foundation organization is not an organization of police officers. It is an organization of private citizens from all walks of life and of all political persuasions who have only one thing in common—a love for the City of New York and a deep concern for the safety of its citizens. These business executives, salesmen, and professional people have joined for the common purpose of helping our city by helping our police.

Membership in the New York's Finest Foundation is open to men and women who feel that an efficient police force is essential to the welfare of all the people of New York City and who are willing to give of their time and talents in this cause.

No member, board member or officer of the New York's Finest Foundation receives any financial remuneration. All he receives is the gratification which comes with knowing that he is doing his part to repay the police officers who serve this city with such distinction.

The New York's Finest Foundation raises money for the police since—by law—the police are not permitted to raise money for themselves. This money is used to help the police officer and his family in many ways. Here are just a few examples:

We assist the widows of police officers killed in the line of duty.

We select the Police Officers for the "Cop of the Month" Program awarded by the Police Commissioner and fund this program.

We provide scholarships to the children of police officers of all ethnic and religious groups.

We were a major contributor to the Bullet Proof Vest Program.

We help encourage policemen to continue their education through college and beyond. We participate in Medal Day ceremonies, donating a Police Valor Medal.

We do everything we can to help raise the morale of police officers by letting them know that there are civilians who care about them and appreciate their efforts.

In some police agencies, Police Officers are assigned to **Fugitive Search Units** where they are responsible for conducting investigations to locate and return fugitives for prosecution by criminal justice agencies. Data received from national, regional, and state crime information centers is examined and employers and other law enforcement agencies are contacted to develop leads. Once a fugitive is located, these officers obtain the legal documents necessary for custody and may be required to travel to other criminal justice agencies throughout the country to return prisoners wanted for unlawful flight.

Harbor Patrol is a specialized unit in which Police Officers are responsible for patrolling municipal harbors to detect and apprehend criminals and to aid persons in distress. Patrol is usually in power launches and may involve rescuing drowning victims, recovering bodies, or assisting ships in distress. These officers also cooperate with other law enforcement agencies in an effort to apprehend criminals and prevent smuggling or entry of illegal aliens.

Hostage Negotiation Teams are another area in which some Police Officers may specialize. Members of these units are specially trained officers who have the difficult task of rescuing hostages from their captors without bloodshed or violence. This is hardly easy because persons holding hostages are often nervous and desperate. Such situations require cool, calm, and logical actions on the part of each officer.

Police Officers in certain police departments are members of **Intelligence Units**. These units gather and compile information about community conditions, potential problems, organized crime, and lawlessness in the form of civil disorder. To obtain this data, officers often work undercover to infiltrate organized crime and terrorist groups or seemingly legitimate businesses used as fronts for criminal activities. They coordinate their activities with other law enforcement agencies, and furnish current information about the location and activities of members of organized crime and subversive groups to local, state, and federal agents.

Police Officers assigned to **Juvenile Units** have the responsibility of conducting juvenile investigations, providing assistance to field officers in matters involving juvenile problems, and of coordinating efforts with other agencies such as courts, schools, and social service and counseling agencies. Juvenile Officers investigate not only juvenile offenses but also cases of lost or runaway children to discover their whereabouts and to locate their parents. They take into custody delinquent or neglected children and refer cases involving serious offenses to the juvenile court system. They also patrol neighborhoods where youths gather, investigate reports of large gatherings that might indicate trouble, and enlist the help of the community in preventing potential juvenile problems.

Mounted Police Officers are specially trained officers who patrol their assigned areas on horseback or motorcycle. Officers on horseback perform the basic duties of the Patrol Officer but their skills are particularly effective in crowd-control activities. Through skillful handling of their mounts, these officers preserve order where large crowds congregate, such as at parades and sporting events, and, in cases of riot or civil unrest, disperse unruly crowds. Officers patrolling on motorcycles perform important traffic-control duties in congested areas by helping to facilitate the flow of traffic. In many cases, patrol cars are unable to reach the scene of disturbances or accidents, and motorcycle officers, first on the scene, provide assistance to sick or injured persons, direct traffic around fires or explosions, and perform general police work by keeping order and apprehending criminals.

Another specialized assignment that may be available to Police Officers is the **Property Unit**. Property Officers are responsible for property confiscated as evidence, removed from suspects, lost or stolen, or purchased by police department officials. Work also involves keeping detailed records of all properties under their control and, when authorized, releasing property to arresting officers for use as evidence in legal proceedings. They return personal property to suspects being released from custody and contact owners of lost or stolen property to claim articles upon proof of ownership. Property Officers keep extensive records of articles confiscated during arrests, such as narcotics and firearms, and arrange for their transfer to official disposal sites when required by law. Responsibility may also include receiving and examining property purchased by the department to verify the completeness and satisfactory condition of these purchases against invoices or other records.

Aviation programs in which Police Officers are trained as **Police Pilots** provide another area of police specialization. Because aircraft are not restricted by roads or traffic congestion, larger areas can be patrolled, and aircraft can be used for aerial surveillance missions, high-speed transportation, and police rescue missions. Police pilots may fly helicopters, conventional fixed-wing aircraft, or Short Takeoff and Landing (STOL) aircraft in carrying out their assignments. Helicopters are very effective in urban patrol as part of helicopter-automobile patrol teams. They can shorten response time to crime scenes, hover, or patrol at slow speeds to observe ground activities or illuminate an area at night. Conventional fixed-wing aircraft are very effective in highway speed enforcement as part of air-ground teams and in search and surveillance operations. Unlike the helicopter, however, they cannot hover or cruise at reduced speeds needed in urban areas. STOL aircraft combine some of the characteristics of the helicopter with those of conventional, fixed-wing aircraft. These aircraft can take off and land in shorter distances than those required for other fixed-wing aircraft. Faster than most helicopters, they can cruise at slower speeds than other fixed-wing craft and can stay airborne without refueling twice as long as rotary-wing aircraft. Regardless of the type of aircraft they fly, Police Pilots play a crucial role in law enforcement activities.

In some departments, cases of rape and sexual assault are the responsibility of Police Officers assigned to **Sex Crimes Units**. These crimes create special problems for both victims and the criminal justice system. Fear of harassment or humiliation during police investigations and medical examinations makes victims reluctant to report such crimes and to go through the ordeal of a trial. Sex Crimes Units are staffed with both male and female officers who are specially trained and sensitive to the plight of victims and can provide needed support during medical examinations, interviews with police and public prosecutors, and subsequent investigations. In some departments, rape victims, if they so desire, can deal exclusively with other women who act both as interviewers and as criminal investigators. These officers can also provide referral to community agencies that give special help to victims of sex crimes.

Anti-Crime or Street-Crime Units are a successful innovation being used by many departments throughout the country. Police Officers assigned to these units work in high-crime areas, out of uniform, and pose as unsuspecting citizens from various walks of life. Their objective is to present themselves as targets for assaults and robberies and to apprehend suspects who attempt to commit such crimes. These decoys team with backup units in the area so that a response is made when suspects attempt to carry out crimes against the decoy officers. Members of these units also conduct surveillance activities on stakeouts.

Many police agencies have developed **Tactical Forces**—highly mobile units that can be deployed rapidly against special crime problems. Normally made up of Police Officers from within the police agency, and varying in size from a few officers on small forces to several hundred on larger forces, these units are motorized and assigned to areas where patterns of serious crimes are occurring. The work can be varied and officers may find themselves working in plainclothes on a robbery detail and then be abruptly assigned to work in uniform on a different type of assignment. When no specific crime problems occur in a particular area, these officers are deployed over a wider area and then, if needed, can be called back quickly to work as a unit on a particular case. In some police agencies, these officers are members of specially trained units, such as sniper-suppression teams and special weapons attack teams (SWAT), which are used during specified emergency situations. The overall purpose of Tactical Forces is to strengthen the regular patrol force and help the line units to meet their goals.

Police Instructors are another example of the varied specializations into which Police Officers may move. These training officers instruct police recruits in basic phases of police work and in the duties and responsibilities of the Police Officer. They conduct lectures, discussions, and demonstrations and use audio-visual materials to teach basic core skills to new personnel. Subject matter of the training sessions includes criminal law, traffic regulations, human relations, criminal investigation, patrol techniques, report writing, firearms, and physical training. In addition to training police recruits, Police Instructors train veteran officers through inservice courses and refresher sessions. Some instructors specialize in one area of training, and the educational and background qualifications for this position vary among departments.

Traffic Officers are members of specialized police units whose aim is to produce voluntary obedience to traffic regulations and provide maximum mobility of traffic with a minimum of interruption. These enforcement units operate in preselected locations where high rates of vehicular and pedestrian accidents, auto thefts, and traffic-law violations occur. Traffic enforcement is closely related to other police activities because, in many instances, persons stopped for traffic violations are found to be involved in criminal activities or are fugitives wanted in another jurisdiction.

In addition to the Police Officers who work in local and county police agencies, there are others who are employed by special purpose public police forces in many cities throughout the United States. Some typical examples include park, harbor, airport, sanitation, transit, housing, and port police forces. Some of these agencies have full peace-officer powers within their limited jurisdictions, while others have limited authority. In New York City, for example, there are three major public police forces besides the New York City Police Department. They are the forces of the New York City Housing Authority, the New York City Transit Authority, and the New York Port Authority. The following are brief descriptions of the work of Police Officers in these departments.

Housing Authority Officers patrol grounds, cellars, roofs, stairwells, and elevators of public housing projects. Officers are assigned to housing projects around the clock based on the incidence of crime in various locations. They conduct investigations of all crimes and disturbances on properties within their jurisdiction, and apprehend and arrest suspects, using physical force or firearms if necessary. If the situation justifies it, these officers can request assistance from the New York City Police Department (N.Y.P.D.). Both agencies cooperate closely, the N.Y.P.D. providing records, booking, laboratory, and detention services for both forces.

Transit Authority Officers enforce the law and provide security services for the New York City Transit System, which contains nearly 500 subway stations. These officers patrol subway stations and trains, particularly during high-crime hours, usually 8 P.M. to 4 A.M. They apprehend and arrest suspects and use physical force and firearms if necessary to carry out their duties. The jurisdiction of Transit Authority Officers is not limited to Transit Authority property, as they have full police powers to enforce all local and state laws anywhere in New York City. The New York City Police Department and the Transit Police cooperate closely. In cases of emergency, the N.Y.P.D. will respond to crime or emergency scenes. Conversely, Transit Authority Officers take action if they witness a crime occurring off Transit Authority property.

Port of New York Authority Police are responsible for policing and providing security in bus, rail, and air terminals; tunnels and bridges; and any properties or facilities operated by the Port Authority. Port Authority Officers enforce the law and apprehend and arrest suspects, using physical force or firearms if necessary. Other responsibilities include controlling traffic and crowds and handling emergency situations occurring within their jurisdiction.

WORKING CONDITIONS

Police Officers work in many locations, which range from boroughs, townships, and counties to urban areas of varying sizes. Working conditions vary considerably according to location, size, organization, and jurisdiction of the police agency. Those who work in small towns and rural communities most certainly face problems different from those met by their counterparts in the inner cities of larger urban areas. There are definite differences in pace, types of criminal activities encountered, and availability of manpower and services needed to provide adequate police protection to the public. But all Police Officers, regardless of where they work, share certain problems. They constantly deal with human suffering, yet must always maintain self-control and act in a calm, efficient manner. They face danger, difficulty, and frustration, perhaps daily, but can do little to prevent it from happening. They also share the problems of long, irregular hours and, in some communities, a lack of public support for police officers.

As a rule, most Police Officers, while conducting patrols or carrying out other assignments, work outdoors in all types of weather. Some officers on special duty may perform their duties indoors at police facilities. Depending on the size of the department, Police Officers work alone or may have a partner. Because police agencies operate 24 hours a day, officers are usually required to work five-day rotating shifts, including holidays and weekends. Police Officers are on call at all times and, during periods of emergency or manpower shortages, are required to work additional tours of duty. All Police Officers, regardless of where they work or the size of the employing police agency, *must live with the very real threat of physical injury or death*. The apprehension of suspects who may be armed and dangerous, situations involving high-speed chases, or the rescue of individuals attempting suicide are some of the possibilities that make this work *hazardous*. Such hazards should be fully considered by individuals thinking about a police career. In most police agencies, Police Officers have fringe benefits that include some or all of the following: paid vacation, sick leave, and holidays; overtime pay; life, medical, and disability insurance; uniform allowances; tuition assistance or refund programs for college studies; and retirement pension. In some departments, officers may retire after 20 years of service if they are from 50 to 55 years of age. In departments with different standards, Police Officers may retire after 20 years of service regardless of age.

TRAINING AND PROMOTION OPPORTUNITIES

Following the completion of training, new officers are assigned to work under the supervision of a veteran officer. The experienced officer evaluates their work performance from time to time during the probationary period, which may last one year to 18 months. New officers may also team with experienced officers who provide them with practical instruction and field experience. After successfully completing the probationary period, these officers become permanent licensed or certified law enforcement officers; then they are sworn in and awarded a badge.

Once entry into this work is made, promotional prospects are generally good and are usually governed by merit or civil service system regulations. Police Officers as a rule become eligible for promotion after a specified number of years (three to five in most police agencies). Promotions are made according to the officer's position on a promotion list, determined by scores on a written, competitive examination as well as ratings of on-the-job performance. The first promotional level for uniformed Police Officers is the position of Sergeant. Thereafter they are eligible to compete for other positions such as Lieutenant Captain, or higher command positions the titles of which vary among police agencies throughout the country. A Police Officer might instead opt for lateral promotion into the Detective division. The officer would then begin as a Police Detective, moving up the ranks to Detective Sergeant, Detective Lieutenant, Detective Captain, and even beyond as merited by education, performance, and scores on competitive examinations.

Police Detective

DUTIES OF THE JOB

Police Detectives, key members of the police law enforcement team, conduct investigations to prevent crime, protect life and property, and solve criminal cases, which can range from misdemeanors to homicide. As a rule, crimes are initially investigated by uniformed Police Officers who are dispatched to crime scenes to apprehend suspects, question witnesses, and preserve evidence. If arrests are not made or the crime remains unsolved, Detectives take over the criminal investigation. Working in plainclothes, Detectives assigned to a case report to the scene, where possible, and determine the nature of the incident, exact location and time of the occurrence, and probable reason for the crime. They obtain reports from uniformed Police Officers; question witnesses, victims and suspects if they have been apprehended; and arrange for official statements to be given at a police station or headquarters. In addition, they search the area carefully to detect clues and gather evidence for use in the investigation. Detectives then direct Evidence Technicians to examine the scene to locate and lift latent fingerprints and to photograph the scene and any evidence obtained for eventual use in preparing the case for court. In some police departments, Detectives trained in fingerprinting and photography perform these duties themselves.

In seeking solutions to crimes, Detectives use all the resources of the police agency, such as ballistics experts, police chemists, laboratory technicians, computers, and speedy communication systems. Once all of the available information has been compiled, they analyze the results to determine the direction the investigation will take. Detectives study the files and records of suspects, if any, evaluate police laboratory findings, and prepare detailed reports including descriptions of evidence, names and statements of witnesses and victims, circumstances of the crime, and statements made by suspects. In attempts to develop leads, copies of fingerprints found at the crime scene may be transmitted to the State Crime Information Center (S.C.I.C.) and National Crime Information Center (N.C.I.C.) for comparison with those found at scenes in other localities. Information may also be given to police artists in their own departments or state and local law enforcement agencies for use in preparing composite sketches of suspects. Members of police patrol units are advised about crimes occurring in various areas and about the methods of operation used by perpetrators. In many instances, Police Detectives question informants on their knowledge of a crime or on their information about the personal habits, associates, characteristics, and aliases of crime suspects.

As evidence begins to develop, court-approved wire tapping or electronic surveillance methods may be used to gather data pertinent to the investigation. Detectives conduct surveillance of suspects on foot or in vehicles to uncover illegal activities; they participate in stakeouts at specific locations to gather evidence or prevent commission of crimes. When all investigative efforts have been made, each Detective prepares a written progress report of the case assigned and submits it to the Detective Sergeant or other superior officer for criticism and suggestions. At this point, the Detective usually plans what action is to be taken to resolve the case based on the evidence gathered and the recommendations of Supervisory Officers. Police Detectives arrest, or participate in the arrest of, suspects based on this evidence and as authorized by appropriate legal warrants.

During the process of arrest, they are authorized to use firearms and/or physical force where necessary to subdue suspects. At the time of arrest, they advise suspects of their constitutional rights and escort them to the police station or headquarters for booking, interrogation, and detention. Suspects are turned over to designated police personnel for fingerprinting, photographing, recording of personal effects, and checking of their records by the records section of the department against outstanding warrants in other jurisdictions.

An important responsibility of Police Detectives involves the preparation of criminal cases scheduled for trial. This entails preparing a written summary of facts gathered during the investigation, including evidence obtained and official statements made by witnesses, victims, Police Officers, and defendants. Prior to trial, Detectives usually review the case summary with the prosecutor to detect legal flaws; they may have to supply supplemental data to strengthen the case for the prosecution. Detectives spend many hours in court testifying as arresting officers and appearing as witnesses for the prosecution. In instances of unsolved cases, Detectives usually forward copies of the fingerprints gathered during the investigation to the Federal Bureau of Investigation (FBI) for comparison with prints which will be recorded during future arrests made nationwide by other law enforcement agencies.

The duties just described are common to Police Detectives in most local, county, and state investigative units. The increasing complexities of police work, however, have caused many agencies to use Detectives as specialists in various types of investigations. The size and resources of the department plus the needs of the community determine the extent of such specialization. Detectives in small police agencies tend to specialize less and are usually generalists who investigate a wide range of crimes. Detectives in large departments in heavily populated urban or suburban areas are more likely to specialize. The following are examples of some of the specialized assignments carried out by Police Detectives.

SPECIALIZED ASSIGNMENTS

Bombing/arson cases are those in which Detectives investigate incidents of suspected arson or the use or presence of explosive devices. Arson is the intentional or attempted destruction, by fire or explosion, of the property of another, or of one's own property, with the intent to defraud. Bombing incidents involve detonation or attempted detonation of an explosive or incendiary device for a criminal purpose or with disregard for the safety and property of others. In some departments, Detectives supervise or actually remove suspected explosive devices to the safe areas, using special skills and equipment to reduce the risk to police personnel and public safety.

Detectives assigned to **Burglary/Robbery Units** specialize in the investigation of such incidents to solve current criminal cases and to prevent future crimes of this sort. Burglary is the actual or attempted entry of a structure, with or without force, with the intent to steal or commit a felony (serious crime). Robbery is the unlawful taking or attempted taking of property in the immediate possession of another person by force or threat of force, with or without a deadly weapon.

Detectives, Fraud and Embezzlement, specialize in crimes involving embezzlement, fraud, forgery, and counterfeiting. Embezzlement is the illegal appropriation of entrusted property with the intention of defrauding the legal owner or beneficiary. Fraud involves deceit or intentional misrepresentation with the aim of illegally depriving a person of his/her property or legal rights. Forgery is the creation or alteration of a written or printed document with the intention to defraud by claiming it is the act of an unknown second party. In a check forgery, for example, the forged signature is accepted as being legitimate and the transaction is completed. Counterfeiting involves manufacture of a copy or imitation of a negotiable instrument with value set by law. Examples include currency, coins, postage, food stamps, and bearer bonds. The investigations into these "white-collar crimes" bring Detectives into close association with representatives of banks, brokerage firms, hotels, and retail establishments, as well as law enforcement agencies.

Homicide Detectives investigate criminal homicide cases in which one person is killed by another or other cases where death appears imminent as the result of aggravated assault. Criminal homicides are those that involve the death of another person without justification or excuse and include acts such as murder and voluntary, involuntary, and vehicular manslaughter.

Detectives assigned to a **Juvenile Section or Division** specialize in investigating cases involving juveniles (youths under 18 years of age who are subject to the jurisdiction of a juvenile court). These Detectives investigate all cases of juvenile crimes. They maintain surveillance in areas where youths gather to keep abreast of happenings and to develop case leads and arrest juveniles suspected of violating the law. Cases involving serious offenses are referred to the Juvenile Court, and parents or guardians are notified to advise them of circumstances in the case. Meetings may also be held with parents or guardians of juveniles in detainment, but not arrested or charged, to stress the need for increased supervision to prevent development of delinquent behavior.

Narcotics Detectives conduct specialized investigations to identify and apprehend persons suspected of illegal use or sale of narcotics and dangerous drugs. Narcotics Detectives examine physicians' and pharmacists' records to determine the legality of sales and to monitor the distribution of narcotics and the quantity of drugs in stock. They must often perform undercover work to investigate known or suspected drug suppliers and handlers who have been identified through surveillance or informants. Detectives purchase narcotics from suspects for use as evidence and arrest individuals identified as distributors, suppliers, and pushers. Narcotics Detectives also work on a cooperative basis with other police agencies involved in narcotics investigations and with federal agencies such as the Drug Enforcement Administration (DEA).

Detectives in some police agencies are part of **Organized Crime Activities Units** and specialize in investigating such activities. They gather data about members of organized criminal groups through the use of informers, surveillance, and infiltration by undercover officers. Not only are cases involving members of organized crime solved by such efforts, but numerous criminal acts are prevented from occurring at all. Often, participation in the Federal Organized Strike Force Programs and work with members of law enforcement agencies from all levels of government is part of these Detectives' assignments.

Motor Vehicle Theft and Truck Hijacking is another type of investigative specialization. Detectives question salvage and junkyard operators, motor vehicle and motor parts dealers, owners of retail stores, and pawnbrokers to uncover possible leads. They check inventories and records to make certain that stocks are legitimate. They maintain surveillance of known thieves and fences who illegally dispose of stolen property, use informers, and take suspects into custody when sufficient evidence has been gathered. Other duties include identification of stolen property and making arrangements for its return to owners.

Investigation of establishments and persons suspected of violating morality and antivice laws pertaining to liquor, gambling, and prostitution is the concern of **Vice Squad Detectives**. They monitor places where liquor is sold to check on hours of operation, underage patrons, and general adherence to the law. Establishing surveillance of suspects and locations to gather evidence of gambling and/or prostitution activities and working undercover to gain access are also part of the job. When sufficient evidence is gathered, necessary legal warrants are obtained, raids on suspects' establishments are conducted, and accused persons are taken into custody. In addition to those just mentioned, Detectives may, in some police agencies, specialize in the investigation of sex offenses, kidnappings, bank robberies, and missing person cases.

WORKING CONDITIONS

Local, county, and state police agencies employ Detectives. Working conditions differ widely according to the size, location, organization, and jurisdiction of the police agency. During investigations, considerable time is spent in office work, reviewing files, gathering data, evaluating and preparing reports, meeting with other Police Officers, and making telephone inquiries. A good deal of time is also spent away from police officers working in a variety of locations, in all kinds of weather, reporting to crime scenes, questioning suspects and witnesses, conducting surveillance and stakeouts, and making arrests. Detectives drive unmarked police vehicles. They may work alone or with partners. Their basic work schedule is rotating shifts of five days a week, eight hours a day, including weekends and holidays. At times they work long, irregular hours; a considerable amount of overtime may be necessary during the investigation of certain cases. As with other Police Officers, Detectives are on call at all times and may be recalled to duty during periods of emergency. *Although detective work is a challenging career, there are times when it is tedious, routine, and frustrating.* Furthermore, *Detectives are often exposed to the risks of bodily injury and death* during the course of criminal investigations.

In most police agencies, Detectives receive fringe benefits including some or all of the following: paid vacation, sick leave, and holidays; overtime pay; life, medical, and disability insurance; tuition assistance or refund programs for college studies; and retirement pension. In some departments, Detectives can retire after 20 years of service if they are in the 50- to 55-year age bracket. Other departments have different standards, and Detectives may retire after 20 years of service regardless of age.

TRAINING AND PROMOTION OPPORTUNITIES

After successfully completing their training, new Detectives remain on probation. They are assigned to work with experienced investigative personnel who provide practical guidance and assistance under actual field conditions. After demonstrating the ability to perform this job on an independent basis, newly hired Detectives are permanently assigned.

Advancement prospects for Detectives are governed by work performance, as well as the personnel practices and size of the agency. Promotional opportunities are usually good and are made according to merit system or civil service regulations. Detectives are, as a rule, eligible for promotion after satisfactory service for a specified period of time, say two to four years. When skills are developed through training, experience, and further education, it is possible to compete for the position of Sergeant, the first step in the promotion ladder. Subsequently, qualified candidates can compete for such positions as Lieutenant, Captain, and other high-level jobs known in different parts of the country by various titles such as Inspector, Major, Lieutenant Colonel, and Colonel.

POLICE RECRUIT QUALIFICATIONS

Entry requirements for Police Officers vary to a certain degree among police agencies throughout the country. As a rule, however, applicants must be U.S. citizens between the ages of 20 and 35 at the time of appointment to service. Time served in the military is usually deducted from a candidate's chronological age in meeting the upper age requirement. Most police agencies require completion of high school or its equivalent as the educational minimum, although some insist on completion of a specified number of college credits and, in some instances, a college degree. Secondary and postsecondary courses helpful in preparing for police work include government, English, psychology, sociology, American history, physics, and foreign languages. In addition, over 1000 junior colleges, colleges, and universities offer programs in police science or criminal justice. The vast majority of police agencies in the United States operate under civil service systems and select candidates accordingly. Candidates must pass a competitive examination and obtain a qualifying rating on an interview conducted by senior police officers. Each applicant must pass a comprehensive medical examination, which in some agencies includes psychological and psychiatric evaluations to determine emotional stability and acceptability for police work. Performance tests designed to gauge strength, agility, and stamina must be passed, and departmental standards with regard to height, weight, and eyesight must also be met. Because good judgment and a sense of responsibility are essential in police work, a thorough background investigation is conducted to assess general character, past history, honesty, and general suitability for this work. As a rule, possession of a valid driver's license is also required prior to employment by the police agency. Meeting the preceding requirements is the typical way of beginning a police career. In some localities, however, young high school graduates or law enforcement students in college can enter this field as police cadets or interns. These individuals, hired as paid civilian employees of the police agency, perform nonenforcement duties and attend classes to learn basic police skills. Those who successfully complete this type of program and meet the basic entry requirements for Police Officer may be appointed to the regular force at age 21.

Newly hired Police Officers enter training on a probationary basis prior to being assigned to duty. Programs vary widely with regard to length and content. In small departments, there is less formal instruction and a greater degree of on-the-job training as a means of developing skills. In large police agencies, formalized programs of instruction are the rule and may last from several weeks to six months, depending on department policy and availability of training facilities. Newly hired officers receive instruction in a variety of subjects including criminal law; motor vehicle codes; arrest, search, and seizure procedures; constitutional law; civil rights; methods of patrol, surveillance, and communications; traffic control; accident investigation; laws of evidence; crime prevention and criminal investigation procedures; pursuit driving; armed and unarmed defense tactics; use of various types of firearms; physical conditioning; crowd control; first aid; community relations; preparation of reports; court procedures; use of legal warrants; police ethics; and departmental regulations. Some departments combine this formal training with field experience to reinforce concepts learned in the classroom.

Following the completion of training, new officers are assigned to work under the supervision of an experienced officer. The experienced officers with whom probationary officers are teamed provide them with practical instruction and field experience and evaluate their work performance from time to time during the probationary period. Probation may last from a year to 18 months, after which the new officer becomes a permanent member of the force.

Police officers usually become eligible for promotion after a specified length of service. In a large department, promotion may allow an officer to specialize in one type of police work such as laboratory work, traffic control, communications, or work with juveniles. Promotions to the rank of sergeant, lieutenant, and captain are usually made according to a candidate's position on a promotion list, as determined by scores on a written examination and on-the-job performance.

Many types of training help police officers improve their performance on the job and prepare for advancement. Through training given at police department academies and colleges, officers keep abreast of crowd-control techniques, civil defense, legal developments that affect their work, and advances in law enforcement equipment. Many police departments encourage officers to work toward college degrees, and some pay all or part of the tuition.

IMPORTANT NOTE: If you are a veteran of the United States Armed Forces, be sure to make this fact known. Veterans receive some form of employment preference when they apply for any government position—local, state, or federal. The veteran's preference sometimes takes the form of points added to the examination score. For some positions, the maximum age of entry is raised by the number of years served. Service-connected disability, if it is not disqualifying for the job, can add still more weight to the application. Even if your experience in the Armed Forces was such that it cannot be counted towards the experience requirements of the position, be sure that you get credit for the very fact of that service.

A TYPICAL NOTICE OF EXAMINATION

Police Officer Series

N.Y.C. POLICE DEPARTMENT
N.Y.C. TRANSIT POLICE DEPARTMENT
N.Y.C. HOUSING AUTHORITY POLICE DEPARTMENT

The general provisions of the notice of examination and the general examination regulations of the New York City Department of Personnel are part of this notice of examination.

The eligible list resulting from this examination will be established expressly for positions in the N.Y.C. Police Department. At the time of list establishment or earlier, the City Personnel Director will determine whether to establish the list expressly for the positions in the N.Y.C. Transit Police Department and the N.Y.C. Housing Authority Police Department as well. If the list is expressly established for all three positions, then a candidate who declines any one of these positions will not be considered for positions in the other two agencies. That is in accordance with the Rules and Regulations of the City Personnel Director, Section VIII of Rule IV, which also provide that a candidate may apply to the City Personnel Director to possibly be restored to the list either at the bottom of the list or at the candidate's original position, as determined by the City Personnel Director. In addition, appointment to any one of these positions shall result in ineligibility for further certification from the list.

Requirements

Minimum requirements: High school graduation or evidence of having passed an examination for the high school equivalency diploma, the GED.

Applicants must be United States citizens.

The education and citizenship requirements must be met by the date of appointment.

License Requirements: At the date of appointment as a Police Officer, possession of a valid New York State driver's license is required.

Age Requirements: *N.Y.C. Police Department and N.Y.C. Transit Police Department:* The N.Y.C. Administrative Code and the N.Y. Public Authorities Law provide that only persons who shall be less than 35 years of age on the date of the filing of the application for the examination may be appointed as a Police Officer in these two agencies. Thus, candidates must not have reached their 35th birthday by the first date of filing. *N.Y.C. Housing Authority Police Department:* The N.Y. Civil Service Law provides that only persons who have not passed their 35th birthday on the date of appointment may be appointed to this agency.

Exception to the age requirement: All persons who were engaged in military duty, as defined in Section 243 of the Military Law, may deduct from their actual age the length of time spent in such military duty provided that the total deduction for military duty does not exceed six years, of which not more than four years may be for voluntary service after May 7, 1975.

A candidate must have attained age 20 to be appointed as a Police Officer.

All applicants must have reached their 17th birthday by the last date for filing. However, in accordance with Section 54 of the N.Y. Civil Service Law, this requirement shall in no case prohibit an applicant who is within six months of this requirement from taking the examination.

Character and Background: Proof of good character and satisfactory background will be an absolute prerequisite to appointment. In accordance with the provisions of law, persons convicted of a felony or receiving a dishonorable discharge from the armed forces are not eligible for appointment to this position. Persons convicted of petit larceny may be declared ineligible for appointment.

Probationary Period: The probationary period for Police Officer is 18 months. Each appointee will be required to pass the Police Academy firearms, academic, physical performance, and driving tests, among other things.

Residence: Any person entering N.Y.C. employment as a Police Officer must be a resident of the City of New York, or of Nassau, Westchester, Suffolk, Orange, Rockland, or Putnam Counties.

Investigation: At the time of appointment and at the time of investigation, candidates must present all the official documents and proof required to qualify. At the time of investigation, candidates will be required to present proof of date of birth by transcript of records of the Bureau of Vital Statistics or other satisfactory evidence. Proof of military service and similar documents may be required. Failure to present required documents, including proof of educational or license requirements, will result in disqualification for appointment or a direction to terminate services.

Any willful misstatement or omission will be cause for disqualification.

Job Description

Duties and responsibilities: To perform general police duties in the following police agencies: N.Y.C. Transit Police Department and N.Y.C. Housing Authority Police Department.

Medical and physical standards: Eligibles must meet the medical standards required and pass a physical performance test. Candidates must pass a qualifying physical fitness test and a qualifying medical test. Eligibles will be rejected for any medical, psychiatric, or physical impairment that restricts their ability to perform the duties of Police Officer. Periodic reexaminations of employees in these titles will be required in accordance with Executive Order No. 31, dated October 10, 1966.

There are no height requirements for this position.

Career Opportunities: Employees in the title of Police Officer are accorded promotional opportunities to the title of Sergeant and are also accorded an opportunity for Detective designation.

Currently educational requirements for the satisfactory completion of probation at successive ranks are: (1) Sergeant - satisfactory completion of two years (64 credits) of coursework at an accredited college or university; (2) Lieutenant - satisfactory completion of three years (96 credits) of coursework at an accredited college or university; (3) Captain - attainment of a Baccalaureate degree from an accredited college or university. College credits which are earned as a result of satisfactorily completing the Police Academy curriculum can be used towards meeting the educational requirements.

A candidate who is prevented from participating in the examination on the test date because of religious beliefs may request a special examination in accordance with the provisions of Personnel Director Rule 4.4.6. Requests for special examinations can only be made in accordance with the provisions of Rules 4.4.5 and 4.4.6.

Appointment Information

The eligible list resulting from this examination may be selectively certified to fill vacancies for Police Officer that require a working knowledge of both English and another language. Those who pass the written test and are placed on the eligible list will be permitted to take a qualifying oral test to determine ability to speak and understand other languages as needed. Candidates wishing to take such a qualifying test must indicate at the time of the test the language for which they wish to be tested. Only those candidates who pass this qualifying oral test will be eligible for such selective certification.

POLICE JUDGMENT QUIZZER

About the Police Judgment Quizzer

Early Police Officer examinations were a strange mixture of questions covering municipal government, municipal geography, spelling, grammar, first aid, everything, in fact, that every person should know something about, but very little that was specific to measuring the ability of future police officers to do their job well. As testing methods matured and examiners gained experience in mass testing, they determined that the best measure of a good police officer is a measure of his or her judgment in actual police situations. So the emphasis shifted from factual to actual exams. "Let the questions supply the facts," the examiners reasoned, "and let the aspiring police officers display their judgment in choosing the correct answers."

What Would You Do If . . .

This is the essential form of the practical question on police officer exams. Assume you are a police officer. Here is a given situation. How would you respond to it? This is a very subtle and efficient method of testing. Questions are often based on actual patrol situations. What would you do if you saw a woman walking down the street dressed only in a sheet and leading a doe on a leash? Arrest her? On what charge? Take the doe to an animal shelter? Take the woman to a doctor? Ask her for her phone number? It actually happened. What would you do?

TEST-TAKING STRATEGY FOR PRACTICAL JUDGMENT QUESTIONS

Police applicants are placed in a peculiar position by practical judgment questions in that the correct answers for these questions are influenced by actual police department procedures. As an applicant taking the exam, you are not expected to know the police department's policies or procedures. Yet test-makers often assume that police departmental policies or procedures are just common sense. To do really well on practical judgment questions, you need something more than common sense. You need a good understanding of ordinary police department policies and procedures as they apply to routine patrol situations. This is the reason why close relatives of police officers tend to earn high scores on the police officer exam. Their familiarity with "police language" and "police thinking" stands them in good stead when they must choose the correct answers to police practical judgment questions.

This chapter will familiarize you with many of the "common sense" ideas that underlie police practical judgment questions. The chapter will serve as "your brother the police officer," teaching you to think like a patrol officer. By the time you have finished studying this material, you will be thinking like a patrol officer. You will then be prepared to score high on your police officer exam.

THE POLICE ROLE

To start with, you must understand the role of a police officer. This role varies according to size, location, and philosophy of the police department. State police find that their role encompasses major problems like traffic pileups and serious accidents, as well as the more routine problems of stranded motorists. Small-town police find that they have a broad role in maintaining public safety and assuring law and order. Big-city police tend to have a more narrow role because in big cities other agencies take on primary responsibility for certain tasks: medics handle health situations beyond emergency first-aid; traffic department personnel deal with many traffic situations; social workers handle many crises concerning the elderly, children, and the mentally ill. Part of your preparation for your own exam should be acquiring some familiarity with the ordinary role of police officers in the department to which you are applying.

With this information in mind, you must follow one basic rule when answering police practical judgment questions—fulfill the police role and only the police role. This means:

1. Be professional. Avoid emotional responses, show of bias, or incurring any kind of indebtedness to persons on your beat.

2. Avoid all roles other than the police role, e.g., parent, physician, tradesman, private security, etc. Sometimes you may find it hard to draw the line, such as that between emergency first-aid and the role of the medic. In an emergency where time is pressing, the police officer must provide assistance to people to the full extent of his or her competence. Where more time is available, leave doubtful roles to others.

3. Fulfill the police role of assisting endangered people twenty-four hours a day. Be prepared to assist in keeping the peace at any time and to take the initiative in urgent situations. Fulfilling the police role does not necessarily mean making arrests when there is no great need to do so. In practical judgment questions, think of the police role as one of keeping the peace rather than one of making arrests, especially in the off-duty situation.

4. Avoid even the slightest appearance of corruption. Maintain police integrity. Avoid all partiality. Do not accept any gifts or favors. Do not refer business to any particular businessman, company, or professional person.

POLICE PRIORITIES

A *hierarchy* is an arrangement of things according to their importance. Something near the top of a hierarchy is more important than something near the bottom of the hierarchy. Basically it is an arrangement of things or activities according to their priorities.

There are five basic functions in police work. These have a definite hierarchical order. If an officer finds him- or herself in a situation in which several of these functions must be done, the officer should consider the hierarchical order, or order of priorities, and act in accordance with the position of each function in that order.

1. *Assist endangered people.* Essentially this means assisting:
   a. seriously injured persons.
   b. physically endangered persons (e.g., victims of a crime in progress, drowning persons, etc.).

2. *Keep the peace.* Calm any major disorder. Prevent tumult, aggression, or destruction of property.

3. *Enforce the law.* Where no actual harm to persons or property is threatened, peace-keeping and maintaining order may be adequate. Where there is unlawful injury or loss, arrest may be necessary in addition to the restoring of order.

4. *Assist people who are not immediately endangered but who need help*. This means assisting:
   a. physically or mentally needy persons: children, the elderly, the handicapped, the homeless, and persons who appear to be sick, mentally ill, or intoxicated.
   b. crime victims, lost persons, and stranded persons.

5. *Maintain order on the beat*. This involves:
   a. Investigating suspicious persons or circumstances. Something is suspicious if it is *unusual* for the time or the place or the persons involved.
   b. Regulating the use of streets and sidewalks for safety and for the efficient flow of traffic.
   c. Knowing the beat. You must be familiar with the physical features of the beat, you must be aware of routine events, and you must develop positive contacts with the people on the beat.
   d. Making recommendations that will improve safety or flow of traffic in the area. Remember to stay "professional" by recommending only activities, not particular products or businesses.

THE PRINCIPLE OF USE OF MINIMUM NECESSARY FORCE

Many police practical judgment questions concern the possible use of force. Police officers are empowered to use force, even deadly force, under certain circumstances. In general, common sense should rule judgments about the use of force. There are some basic principles that are part of "common sense."

Police officers should always handle problems with the *minimum amount of force necessary* to resolve the problem. Never use more force than the problem deserves. Obviously, a police officer should not shoot somebody for failing to show identification, even if the person were being unreasonably stubborn. A police officer's action should not cause greater harm than the problem the officer is trying to resolve. In other words, a problem should not be handled in such a way as to create an even bigger problem.

When a police officer is evaluating the gravity of a situation to determine how much force is necessary (or when a candidate is making this choice in an examination), the officer must consider the physical setting, the actual actions and the apparent intentions of the people involved, and the intent of the law. Differences in physical settings require differences in policies and regulations. Big-city police departments, for example, practically never permit police officers to fire warning shots, to shoot at moving vehicles, or to shoot at people on public streets. It is assumed that such shooting would endanger innocent bystanders. On the other hand, state police departments often do allow warning shots, shooting at moving vehicles, and even shooting at people on the road because they assume a highway setting without any innocent bystanders in the line of fire.

THE VALUE HIERARCHY

Occasionally a police officer has to make a quick decision in a situation that involves value conflicts. For example, it may be necessary to choose between risking serious injury to a hostage or letting a dangerous criminal escape. Such a decision involves a value judgment. An officer makes the decision based on the order of priorities.

If a police department's hierarchy of values is spelled out clearly, officers are assisted in making rapid and proper judgments. Police exam candidates can rely on the same list of priorities. The list below is the value hierarchy that has been the basis for practical judgment questions on police officer exams for many years. In order of priority:

1. Protection of life and limb.
2. Obeying orders in an emergency situation.
3. Protection of property.
4. Obeying orders in a non-emergency situation.
5. Maintaining the assigned role.
6. Efficiency in getting the job done.
7. Avoiding blame or earning praise or respect.

Use the hierarchy of values in making decisions. If a situation presents a conflict of values, always choose the value that is highest on the list. Here are two examples:

Example 1. You are assigned to stay in a particular spot during an emergency situation, but by leaving that spot you will save a life. You are justified in choosing to save a life (1) rather than obeying orders (2). The understanding is, of course, that leaving your spot will not result in other lives being lost. "Protecting life and limb" is your number one priority, the highest value in the police hierarchy of values.

Example 2. You are assigned to watch a prisoner, and a fellow officer is assigned to write up the arrest report. Stay in your own role even if you are more skilled than the other officer at writing up arrest reports. The conflict is between carrying out an assigned duty (5) and getting a job done efficiently (6). Choose the higher priority.

One more: You are patrolling alone at night, and you come across a business that has been burglarized with the front door smashed in. At this hour you are expected to be making a routine check of illegal parking on a certain street. The police department might be criticized by residents if the illegal parking is not acted on, but the store is likely to be further burglarized if you leave this spot. Stay where you are and protect the property (3) rather than carrying out your assigned illegal parking patrol (5) or concerning yourself with criticism of the department (7). Always choose the highest value.

Please note that no value is given to the officer's personal gains or benefits or reputation. Personal consideration is *never* a good reason for doing anything so far as a civil service exam question is concerned.

As the hierarchy of values suggests, the best reason for any action is the protection of life and limb. If safety is a real issue in the fact pattern of the question, then safety is the number one priority in choosing the answer. Sometimes there is no real issue of safety. In such a case, the next value assumes the greatest importance. If there is an emergency situation and you have been given specific orders, your priority is to carry out those orders. If not, the next priority is the protection of property. Property includes public property and police department property as well as private property. If there are no threats to property, you are expected to carry out routine, non-emergency orders and to fulfill your assigned duties. Doing what you were told to do and carrying out your routine assignments as a police officer take priority over efficiency. A police force is a highly organized bureaucracy. The organization will function best as a whole if each person does just his or her own assigned job.

Read each question carefully. Is there really something in the question situation to indicate that there is an issue of life and limb at stake? Would a proposed answer based on efficiency really be possible and efficient? Be realistic. Unless told otherwise, assume that the officer is an ordinary police officer and not a sharpshooter or a trained firefighter.

When all other reasoning fails you, answer to the Chief. In other words, the Chief of Police is testing you for your job. If you are faced with a difficult choice in making a decision, imagine that the question is being asked you personally by the Chief of Police. Give the answer the Chief would want you to give.

Answering The Questions

This quizzer contains questions that have actually appeared on examinations for entry-level law enforcement positions conducted over a considerable number of years. The questions have been carefully screened for current relevancy.

Answering these questions will accomplish much in preparing you to do your best on the examination. Ideally, you can consider yourself well prepared if on the day of the examination you are thinking like a police officer. This quizzer will help you get in that frame of mind. Most of the questions found here concern incidents that a police officer may encounter on a daily basis.

The position of police officer is unique in that, although it is an entry-level position, it involves a great deal of responsibility and requires the ability to make reliable on-the-spot decisions. Therefore, accurate judgment is perhaps the most important qualification of the police officer. In order to make accurate police decisions, the officer must thoroughly understand the duties of the position and the police officer's role in society.

By the time you finish the Police Judgment Quizzer, you no doubt will be thinking like a police officer, and you thus will be well on your way towards earning that high examination score.

Choose from among the four suggested answers the *best* answer to each question. Write the letter of your answer choice beside the corresponding question number. The correct answers appear on page 50. Following the answer key is a full explanation of the police reasoning behind each correct answer choice.

1. An off-duty police officer was seated in a restaurant when two men entered, drew guns, and robbed the cashier. The officer made no attempt to prevent the robbery or apprehend the criminals. Later he justified his conduct by stating that an officer, when off duty, is a private citizen with the same duties and rights of all private citizens. The officer's conduct was

   (A) wrong; a police officer must act to prevent crimes and apprehend criminals at all times
   (B) right; the police officer was out of uniform at the time of the robbery
   (C) wrong; he should have obtained the necessary information and descriptions after the robbers left
   (D) right; it would have been foolhardy for him to intervene when outnumbered by armed robbers

2. While you are on traffic duty, a middle-aged man crossing the street cries out with pain, presses his hand to his chest, and stands perfectly still. You suspect that he may have suffered a heart attack. You should

   (A) help him to cross the street quickly in order to prevent his being hit by moving traffic

   (B) permit him to lie down flat in the street while you divert traffic
   (C) ask him for the name of his doctor so that you can summon him
   (D) request a cab to take him to the nearest hospital for immediate treatment

3. Assume that you have been assigned to a traffic post at a busy intersection. A car bearing out-of-state license plates is about to turn into a one-way street going in the opposite direction. You should blow your whistle and stop the car. You should then

   (A) hand out a summons to the driver in order to make an example of him, since out-of-town drivers notoriously disregard our traffic regulations
   (B) pay no attention to him and let him continue in the proper direction
   (C) ask him to pull over to the curb and advise him to get a copy of the latest New York City traffic regulations
   (D) call his attention to the fact that he was violating a traffic regulation and permit him to continue in the proper direction

4. Assume that you are a police officer. A woman has complained to you about a man's indecent exposure in front of her house. As you approach the house, the man begins to run. You should

   (A) shoot to kill as the man may be a dangerous maniac
   (B) fire a warning shot to try to halt the man
   (C) summon other police officers in order to apprehend him
   (D) pursue and try to seize the man

5. You have been assigned to a patrol post in the park during the winter months. You hear the cries of a boy who has fallen through the ice. The first thing you should do is to

   (A) rush to the nearest telephone and call an ambulance
   (B) call upon a passerby to summon additional police officers
   (C) rush to the spot from which the cries came and try to save the boy
   (D) rush to the spot from which the cries came and question the boy concerning his identity so that you can summon his parents

6. While you are patrolling your post, you find a flashlight and a screwdriver lying near a closed bar and grill. You also notice some jimmy marks on the door. You should

   (A) continue patrolling your post after noting in your memorandum book what you have seen
   (B) arrest any persons standing in the vicinity
   (C) determine whether the bar has been robbed
   (D) telephone the owner of the bar and grill to relate what you have seen outside the door

7. You are on your way to report for an assignment when you see two men fighting on the street. For you to attempt to stop the fight would be

   (A) unjustified; it is none of your business
   (B) justified; a fight between individuals may turn into a riot
   (C) unjustified; you may get hurt with the result that you will not be able to report for duty
   (D) justified; as a police officer, it is your duty to see that the public peace is kept

8. Suppose a police officer's tour of duty extends from 12:00 midnight to 8:00 A.M. While on the first round of her tour, she notices that the night light in the front of a small candy store is out. In the past, the proprietor has always left the light on. The door to the store is locked. Of the following, the most appropriate action for the officer to take *first* is to

   (A) use her flashlight to light the store interior so that she may inspect it for unusual conditions
   (B) continue on her beat, since the light probably burned out
   (C) break open the door lock to conduct a thorough search of the store
   (D) call the storekeeper to say that the night light is out

9. While on patrol at 2 A.M., you notice a man and a woman walking down the street and arguing in loud tones. They do not see you as you are standing in the shadows. The pair stops in front of a large apartment house. The man takes a bunch of keys from his pocket and finds the one that will open the door. While he is doing this, the woman taps her foot impatiently. At this point, as the two are entering the apartment house, you should

   (A) notify headquarters of the incident
   (B) permit them to enter but follow closely behind them to see what they do
   (C) ignore the incident and continue on your patrol
   (D) force them to show identification

10. While patrolling a post late Saturday night, a police officer notices a well-dressed man break a car window with a rock, open the front door, and enter the car. He is followed into the car by a female companion. Of the following, the most essential action for the officer to take is to

    (A) point a gun at the car, enter the car, and order the man to drive to the station house to explain his actions
    (B) approach the car and ask the man why it was necessary to break the car window
    (C) take down the license number of the car and note the description of both the man and the woman in the event that the car is later reported as stolen
    (D) request proof of ownership of the car from the man

11. Assume that a police officer is assigned to duty in a radio patrol car. The situation in which it would be *least* advisable for the officer to use the siren to help clear traffic when answering a call is when a report has come in that

    (A) a man is involved in an argument with a cleaning store proprietor
    (B) a man is holding up a liquor store
    (C) two cars have crashed, resulting in loss of life
    (D) two gangs of juveniles are engaged in a street fight

12. You notice that a man is limping hurriedly, leaving a trail of blood behind him. You question him and his explanation is that he was hurt accidentally while he was watching a man clean a gun. You should

    (A) let him go as you have no proof that his story is not true
    (B) have him sent to the nearest city hospital under police escort so that he may be questioned further after treatment
    (C) ask him whether the man has a license for his gun
    (D) ask him to lead you to the man who cleaned his gun so that you may question him further about the accident

13. At 10 A.M. on a regular school day, a police officer notices a boy about 11 years old wandering in the street. When asked why he is not in school, the boy replies that he attends school in the neighborhood, but that he felt sick that morning. The officer then takes the boy to the principal of the school. This method of handling the situation was

    (A) bad; the officer should have obtained verification of the boy's illness
    (B) good; the school authorities are best equipped to deal with the problem
    (C) bad; the officer should have obtained the boy's name and address and reported the incident to the attendance officer
    (D) good; seeing the truant boy escorted by a police officer will deter other children from truancy

14. "A police officer should know the occupations and habits of the people on his or her beat. In heavily populated districts, however, it is too much to ask that the officer know all the people on the beat." If this statement is correct, which of the following would be the most practical course for a police officer to follow?

    (A) Concentrate on becoming acquainted with the oldest residents on his or her beat.
    (B) Limit his or her attention to people who work as well as live in the district.
    (C) Limit his or her attention to people with criminal records.
    (D) Concentrate on becoming acquainted with key people such as janitors and local merchants.

15. Police officers are instructed to pay particular attention to anyone apparently making repairs to an auto parked in the street. The most important reason for this rule is that

    (A) the person making the repairs may be stealing the auto
    (B) the person making the repairs may be obstructing traffic
    (C) working on autos is prohibited on certain streets
    (D) many people injure themselves while working on autos

16. A police officer, walking his beat at 3 A.M., notices heavy smoke coming out of a top floor window of a large apartment house. Of the following, the action the officer should take *first* is to:

    (A) make certain that there really is a fire
    (B) enter the building and warn all the occupants of the apartment house
    (C) attempt to extinguish the fire before it gets out of control
    (D) call the fire department

17. Inspections of critical points on a post are purposely made at irregular intervals to

    (A) permit leaving the post when arrests are necessary
    (B) make it difficult for wrongdoers to anticipate the inspections
    (C) allow for delays due to unusual occurrences at other points
    (D) simplify the scheduling of lunch reliefs and rest periods

18. A police officer making her rounds notices that one storekeeper has not cleared the snow from the sidewalk in front of his store. After reminding the storekeeper that he is breaking the law if the sidewalk is not cleared, the officer also points out that a dangerous situation may arise if ice forms. This method of handling the situation is usually

    (A) bad; the storekeeper broke the law and should be punished
    (B) good; the storekeeper will clear the sidewalk and no one will be hurt
    (C) bad; the police officer should have forced the storekeeper to clear the sidewalk of snow immediately
    (D) good; threatening severe punishment is the most desirable method to achieve compliance with the law

19. "Because the woman had been acting suspiciously, the police officer halted her for questioning. Immediately a man joined the two. Though the police officer directed his questioning at the woman, it was the man who responded." On the basis of these data, it is *most* reasonable to infer that

    (A) the woman is incapable of speech or is intellectually incompetent
    (B) an effort is being made to conceal information
    (C) the police officer's suspicions are badly grounded
    (D) what appears to be suspicious is often proved to be law abiding

20. "The woman approached the police officer with the tearful request that he call her at home in order to put the fear of the law into her 11-year-old son. The boy, she said, was associating with a group of wild, older youths who were leading the boy astray." The officer should have

    (A) complied with the the woman's request
    (B) obtained further information before committing himself to any cooperative relations with the woman
    (C) cooperated with the woman in whatever manner seemed appropriate, provided that the boy's history has been reported accurately by his mother
    (D) denied the woman's request

21. Suppose that, at 11 A.M., while you are patrolling your post, a young girl runs up to you, saying that a man has just dropped dead on the street a block away. Of the following, your *first* action under the circumstances should be to

    (A) request the young girl to describe the man who is said to be dead
    (B) approach furtively the scene of the alleged death in order to investigate all the circumstances fully
    (C) proceed immediately to the place where the man is alleged to have dropped dead
    (D) request the young girl to identify herself

22. A group of boys about 17 years of age is standing on a street corner, talking loudly, shouting, and, in general, making a good deal of noise in a residential district in the early hours of the morning. A police officer who comes upon this scene should attempt to

    (A) arrest the boy who appears to be the leader
    (B) arrest the entire group
    (C) disperse the group
    (D) summon assistance

23. Suppose that, in the course of your duties, you are called to the scene of a disturbance in which some seven or eight people are involved. Of the following, the action most likely to end the disturbance quickly and effectively is for you to

    (A) divide the disorderly group immediately into three approximately equal sections
    (B) take the nearest person promptly into custody and remove that person from the scene
    (C) announce your authority and call for order in a firm and decisive manner
    (D) question a bystander in detail about the reasons for the disorder

24. A newly appointed officer of a uniformed force may *least* reasonably expect an immediate supervising officer to

    (A) help him or her avoid errors
    (B) give him or her specific instructions
    (C) check on the progress he or she is making
    (D) make all necessary decisions for him or her

25. In lecturing on the law of arrest, an instructor remarked: "To go beyond is as bad as to fall short." The one of the following that most nearly expresses the same thing is

    (A) never undertake the impossible
    (B) extremes are not desirable
    (C) look before you leap
    (D) too much success is dangerous

26. In addressing a class, an instructor remarked: "Carelessness and failure are twins." The one of the following that most nearly expresses the same thing is
    (A) negligence seldom accompanies success
    (B) incomplete work is careless work
    (C) conscientious work is never attended by failure
    (D) a conscientious person never makes mistakes

27. The primary function of a police department is
    (A) the prevention of crime
    (B) the efficiency and discipline of its members
    (C) to preserve property values
    (D) to minimize conflicts

28. Law enforcement officials receive badges with numbers on them so that
    (A) their personalities may be submerged
    (B) they may be more easily identified
    (C) they may be spied upon
    (D) their movements may be kept under constant control

29. The best attitude for an officer to take is to
    (A) be constantly on the alert
    (B) be hostile
    (C) vary watchfulness with the apparent necessity for it
    (D) regard tact as the most effective weapon for handling any degree of disorder

30. Ten percent of the inmates released from a certain prison are arrested as parole violators. It follows that
    (A) 90 percent have reformed
    (B) 10 percent have reformed
    (C) none has reformed
    (D) none of the foregoing is necessarily true

31. A certain committee found that over 90 percent of the murders in the United States are committed by use of pistols. It follows that
    (A) almost all murders are caused by the possession of pistols
    (B) 90 percent of all murders can be eliminated by eliminating the sale and use of pistols
    (C) the pistol is a mechanical aid to crime
    (D) no information is available with regard to the way murders happen

32. A criminal is typically one who
    (A) has a peculiarly shaped head
    (B) exhibits a most degenerate kind of behavior
    (C) is an intelligent, well-educated person
    (D) looks like other people

33. There would be no crime if there were no
    (A) weapons
    (B) criminals
    (C) stupid laws
    (D) private property

34. An officer receives instructions from his supervisor that he does not fully understand. For the officer to ask for a further explanation would be
    (A) good; chiefly because his supervisor will be impressed with his interest in his work
    (B) poor; chiefly because the supervisor's time will be needlessly wasted
    (C) good; chiefly because proper performance depends on full understanding of the work to be done
    (D) poor; chiefly because officers should be able to think for themselves

35. Which of the following statements concerning the behavior of law enforcement officers is most accurate?
    (A) A show of confident assurance on the part of a law enforcement officer will make it possible to cover a shortage of knowledge in any given duty.
    (B) In ordinary cases, when a newly appointed officer does not know what to do, it is always better to do too much than to do too little.
    (C) It is not advisable that officers recommend the employment of certain attorneys for individuals taken into custody.
    (D) A prisoner who is morose and refuses to talk will need less watching by an officer than one who is suicidal.

36. In dealing with children, a law enforcement officer should always
    (A) treat them the same as adults
    (B) instill in them a fear of the law
    (C) secure their confidence
    (D) impress them with the right of the law to punish them for their wrongdoings

37. The one of the following which is the most probable reason for the considerably increasing proportion of serious crimes committed by women is
    (A) that the proportion of women in the population is increasing
    (B) the increasing number of crime gangs in operation
    (C) the success of women in achieving social equality with men
    (D) the increasing number of crime stories in the movies and on television

38. Increased police vigilance would probably be *least* successful in preventing
    (A) murder
    (B) burglary
    (C) prostitution
    (D) auto theft

39. It frequently happens that a major crime of an unusual nature is followed almost immediately by an epidemic of several crimes, in widely scattered locations, with elements similar to the first crime. Of the following, the most likely explanation for this situation is that
    (A) the same criminal is likely to commit the same type of crime
    (B) a gang of criminals will operate in several areas simultaneously
    (C) newspaper publicity on a major crime is apt to influence other would-be criminals
    (D) the same causes which are responsible for the first crime are also responsible for the others

40. "A member of the department shall not indulge in intoxicants while in uniform. A member of the department, not required to wear a uniform, and a uniformed member, while out of uniform, shall not indulge in intoxicants to an extent unfitting him or her for duty." It follows that a
    (A) member off duty, not in uniform, may drink intoxicants to any degree desired
    (B) member on duty, not in uniform, may drink intoxicants

(C) member on duty, in uniform, may drink intoxicants
(D) uniformed member, in civilian clothes, may not drink intoxicants

41. The reason police officers have greater authority than private citizens in making arrests is
    (A) to protect citizens against needless arrest
    (B) to ensure a fair trial
    (C) that they have greater knowledge of the law
    (D) that they are in better physical shape

42. "The treatment given to the offender cannot alter the fact of the offense, but we can take measures to reduce the chances of similar acts occurring in the future. We should banish the criminal, not in order to exact revenge nor directly to encourage reform, but to deter him or her and others from further illegal attacks on society." According to this quotation, the principal reason for punishing criminals is to
    (A) prevent the commission of future crimes
    (B) remove them safely from society
    (C) avenge society
    (D) teach them that crime does not pay

43. When arrested, boys under 16 years of age are not brought to the same place of detention as older men. The reason for this separation is most likely to
    (A) keep them with others of their own age
    (B) protect them from rough police methods
    (C) help them get sound legal aid
    (D) keep them from contact with hardened criminals

44. Many criminals dress well and look intelligent but have no regard for a human life if it stands in their way. A reasonable conclusion from this statement is that
    (A) it is almost certain death to combat a criminal
    (B) criminals are frequently intelligent
    (C) even some intelligent people have no regard for human life
    (D) a well-dressed person may be a criminal

45. A police officer stationed along the route of a parade has been ordered not to allow cars to cross the route while the parade is in progress. An ambulance driver on an emergency run attempts to drive an ambulance across the route while the parade is passing. Under these circumstances, the officer should

(A) ask the driver to wait while the officer calls headquarters and obtains a decision

(B) stop the parade long enough to permit the ambulance to cross the street

(C) direct the ambulance driver to the shortest detour available, which will add at least ten minutes to the run

(D) hold up the ambulance in accordance with the order

46. An off-duty police officer in civilian clothes riding in the rear of a bus notices two teenage boys tampering with the rear emergency door. The most appropriate action for the officer to take is to

(A) tell the boys to discontinue their tampering, pointing out the dangers to life that their actions create

(B) report the boys' actions to the bus operator and let the bus operator take whatever action is deemed best

(C) signal the bus operator to stop, show the boys the police badge, and then order them off the bus

(D) show the boys the police badge, order them to stop their actions, and take down their names and addresses

47. Assume that you are on your way home late at night. You notice smoke pouring out of one of the windows of a house in which several families reside. Your first consideration under these circumstances should be to

(A) determine the cause of the smoke

(B) arouse all the residents in the house

(C) carry out to safety any persons overcome by smoke

(D) call the fire department to the scene

48. While present at a performance in a theater, you are notified that there is a fire under the stage. Under these circumstances, you would *least* expect to

(A) transmit the alarm from the nearest box

(B) remove fire appliances from their places

(C) ascertain whether there is a fire

(D) announce to the audience that there is a fire in the theater and everyone should leave quietly

49. You notice something unusual on your post. You should immediately

(A) report the matter in writing to your superior

(B) look up the rules on the matter

(C) investigate the matter

(D) wait for a time to see whether anything will happen

50. A police officer is summoned into a subway station where a man has collapsed and is lying unconscious on the floor. His breath smells strongly of alcohol. For the officer to summon medical aid immediately is

(A) undesirable; the man is merely intoxicated and can be handled by the police officer alone

(B) desirable; the man's unconsciousness may have a medical cause

(C) undesirable; the commotion caused by the incident will be aggravated by the appearance of an ambulance

(D) desirable; medical aid is necessary to help him regain consciousness in any event

51. A police officer notices a two-year-old child standing by himself in front of a supermarket and crying. Which of the following actions should the officer take *first*?

(A) Call the precinct to find out if the child has been reported missing.

(B) Look for possible identification on the child's clothing.

(C) Take the child to the police precinct until he is claimed.

(D) Inquire in the supermarket in an attempt to find his parent.

52. At a crowded bus stop, a police officer notices that a child about seven years old has been pushed out of the bus involuntarily. The crowd piling into the bus is so thick that the child is unable to get back into it. After the bus has gone, the officer learns from the child that her mother was on the bus but was probably unable to get out because of the crowd pushing in. The child knows her own address, a considerable distance away, and in an opposite direction from the one in which she was traveling. Of the following, the best action for the officer to take *first* is to

    (A) take the child home
    (B) explain to the child how to go home and let her go alone
    (C) leave the child with instructions to wait until her mother returns
    (D) wait at the stop with the child long enough to give the mother a chance to return from the next stop

53. Which of the following is the most accurate statement concerning the proper attitude of a police officer towards persons in his or her custody?

    (A) Ignore any serious problems of those in custody, if they have no bearing on the charges preferred.
    (B) Do not inform the person who has been arrested of the reason for the arrest.
    (C) Do not permit a person in custody to give vent to feelings at any time.
    (D) Watch a brooding or silent person more carefully than one who loudly threatens suicide.

54. Two rival youth gangs have been involved in several minor clashes. The officer working in the area believes that a serious clash will occur if steps are not taken to prevent it. Of the following, the *least* desirable action for the officer to take in the effort to head off trouble is to

    (A) arrest the leaders of both gangs as a warning
    (B) warn the parents of the dangerous situation
    (C) obtain the cooperation of religious and civic leaders in the community
    (D) report the situation to a superior

55. If, while you are on traffic duty at a busy intersection, a pedestrian asks you for directions to a particular place, the best course of conduct is for you to

    (A) ignore the question and continue directing traffic

    (B) tell the pedestrian to ask an officer on foot patrol
    (C) answer the question in a brief, courteous manner
    (D) leave your traffic post only long enough to give clear and adequate directions

56. Suppose that, while you are patrolling your post, a middle-aged woman informs you that three men are holding up a nearby bank. You rush immediately to the scene of the holdup. While you are still about 75 feet away, you see the three men, revolvers in their hands, emerge from the bank and run towards what is apparently their getaway car, which is pointed in the opposite direction. Of the following, your *first* consideration in this situation should be to

    (A) enter the bank in order to find out what the men have taken
    (B) maneuver quickly so as to get the getaway car between you and the bank
    (C) make a mental note of the descriptions of the escaping men for immediate alarm
    (D) draw your gun and shout for the men to surrender

57. A storekeeper has complained to you that every day at noon several peddlers congregate outside his store in order to sell their merchandise. You should

    (A) inform him that such complaints must be made directly to the Police Commissioner
    (B) inform him that peddlers have a right to earn their living too
    (C) make it your business to patrol that part of your post around noon
    (D) pay no attention to him as this storekeeper is probably a crank inasmuch as nobody else has complained

58. A police officer is approached by an obviously upset woman who reports that her husband is missing. The *first* thing the officer should do is to

    (A) check with the hospitals and the police station
    (B) tell the woman to wait a few hours and call the police station if her husband has not returned
    (C) obtain a description of the missing man so that an alarm can be broadcast
    (D) ask the woman why she thinks her husband is missing

59. When approaching a suspect to make an arrest, it is *least* important for the police officer to guard against the possibility that the suspect may

    (A) be diseased
    (B) have a gun
    (C) use physical force
    (D) run away

60. An acceptable proof of the present address of the person to whom a police officer is issuing a summons would logically be

    (A) a recent photograph
    (B) society membership cards
    (C) recently postmarked letters addressed to that person
    (D) the deed to a house

61. "In any uniformed service, strict discipline is essential." Of the following, the best justification for requiring that subordinates follow the orders of superior officers without delay is that

    (A) not all orders can be carried out quickly
    (B) it is more important that an order be obeyed accurately than promptly
    (C) prompt obedience makes for efficient action in emergencies
    (D) some superior officers are too strict

62. Suppose that you receive directions from your supervisor that you do not altogether understand. Of the following, the best action for you to take is to

    (A) request a more experienced employee to assist you in your work
    (B) go ahead and do the best you can
    (C) follow only those directions that you understand perfectly
    (D) ask your supervisor to repeat those instructions that are not clear

63. As a police officer, if you think of an idea for improving the police protection in certain areas, your best procedure would be to

    (A) get the opinions of all the people working in those areas
    (B) suggest it to your superiors immediately
    (C) forget it because the department has experts thinking about such problems all the time
    (D) consider the idea carefully before suggesting it.

64. A person is making a complaint to an officer which seems unreasonable and of little importance. Of the following, the best action for the officer to take is to

    (A) criticize the person making the complaint for taking up valuable time
    (B) laugh over the matter to show that the complaint is minor and silly
    (C) tell the person that anyone responsible for the grievance will be arrested
    (D) listen to the person making the complaint and tell him or her that the matter will be investigated

65. When reporting a robbery to headquarters over the police telephone system, a police officer should make the report as brief as possible so as to avoid

    (A) long entries in the record book
    (B) confusing the listener
    (C) errors in fact
    (D) tying up the line

66. Police officers are instructed to confer with the assistant district attorney before preparing a formal written complaint. The most probable reason is to

    (A) keep it brief
    (B) agree on the facts of the case
    (C) avoid legal errors
    (D) assure a conviction

67. In submitting a report of an unusual arrest or other unusual occurrence, the first paragraph of the report should contain

    (A) a brief outline of what occurred
    (B) your conclusions and recommendations
    (C) the authority and reason for the investigation of the arrest or occurrence
    (D) complete and accurate answers to the questions who?, what?, where?, when?, why?, and how?

68. "If an officer is not relieved at the expiration of a tour of duty, he or she shall not abandon the post, but shall communicate with the desk officer or control sergeant and comply with the instructions received." Of the following, the best reason for this rule is that

    (A) it gives the officer definite control over all earned overtime
    (B) the service given to an officer's relief may be repaid at another time when he or she is late
    (C) it gives the officer a chance to make up time which he or she may owe due to previous lateness
    (D) it is necessary for the safety of the public that a post be manned at all times

69. A factory manager asks a police officer to escort the payroll clerk to and from the local bank when payroll money is withdrawn. The police officer knows that it is against departmental policy to provide payroll escort service. The officer should

    (A) refuse and explain why he or she cannot do what is requested
    (B) refer the manager to the precinct commander
    (C) tell the manager that police officers have more important tasks to perform
    (D) advise the manager that he or she will provide this service if other duties do not interfere

70. A police officer in civilian clothes appearing as a witness in a court must wear his or her shield over the left breast. This procedure

    (A) helps the officer in reporting for duty promptly if called
    (B) impresses the judge
    (C) identifies the witness as a police officer
    (D preserves order

71. The printed departmental rules may logically be expected to include information on

    (A) which posts are the most dangerous
    (B) where to purchase uniforms and equipment cheaply

    (C) how many days a week overtime work will be required
    (D) what must be included in an accident report

72. Orders issued to police officers remain in effect until cancelled. An example of an order that will be be fulfilled at a definite time known in advance is one which

    (A) warns police officers to be on the lookout for certain known hoodlums
    (B) informs police officers of a new reporting procedure
    (C) assigns additional police officers to the entertainment district area on New Year's Eve
    (D) reminds police officers of a rule that is sometimes overlooked

73. Certain orders and instructions are transmitted by means of bulletins posted on the precinct bulletin boards. Such a bulletin order would most likely be rescinded if it

    (A) conflicted with another order that was issued later
    (B) was not readily understood by the entire force
    (C) had been in force for a long time
    (D) was frequently violated

74. A thorough knowledge of printed departmental regulations will help a police officer to know

    (A) how to recognize a forgery
    (B) when it is proper to make an arrest
    (C) how to take care of the police uniform
    (D) when to expecct vandalism

75. According to the police manual, when circumstances permit, not more than one prisoner shall be confined in a cell. Of the following, the most important reason for this regulation is to

    (A) ensure reasonable privacy for the prisoners
    (B) minimize the development of troublesome situations
    (C) protect the civil rights of the prisoners
    (D) separate the hardened from the less hardened criminals

76. "Parking is prohibited here," the police officer said. "You'll have to move further down." The driver then informed the police officer that he was a good friend of an important local political figure and indicated that the officer should attend to other more significant matters. Of the following courses of action, the one that the officer ought to select is to

    (A) permit the driver to park there for a brief time
    (B) request the name of the alleged important political figure
    (C) insist that the car be parked elsewhere
    (D) attract the attention of bystanders to the incident in order to demonstrate police impartiality

77. Suppose that while you are directing traffic at Columbus Circle, a young man approaches and asks "How can I get to Columbus Circle?" You should say

    (A) "On your way, young man."
    (B) "This seems paradoxical. You seek what you have."
    (C) "Columbus Circle is at 59th Street and Broadway."
    (D) "This is Columbus Circle. Where do you want to go?"

78. A motorist who has been stopped by an officer for speeding acts rudely. He hints about his personal connections with high officials in the city government and demands the officer's name and shield number. The officer should

    (A) ask the motorist why he wants the information and give it only if the answer is satisfactory
    (B) give both name and shield number without comment
    (C) ignore the request since both name and shield number will appear on the summons the officer will issue
    (D) give name and shield number but increase the charges against the motorist

79. At 3:00 A.M. while on his tour of duty, a police officer notices a traffic light at an intersection is not operating. There is little traffic at night at this intersection. Under these circumstances, the most appropriate action for the police officer to take is to

    (A) report this matter to a superior at the end of his tour of duty

    (B) station himself at the intersection to direct traffic until the appearance of daylight reduces the hazard of a collision
    (C) report this matter immediately to the precinct
    (D) post a sign at the intersection stating that the traffic light is not operating

80. "While Police Officer Y was patrolling his post, he noticed that a traffic light at an important intersection was not operating. Traffic was beginning to become snarled. He immediately stepped out into the intersection and directed traffic until the traffic load eased up, whereupon he resumed his patrol." Of the following, the chief criticism of Officer Y's action in this situation is that he should

    (A) have remained at the intersection directing traffic until the end of his tour of duty
    (B) not have attempted to direct traffic at all, since that is not his duty
    (C) have called his superior so that his regular post could have been covered
    (D) not have waited until traffic eased up before taking the responsibility of leaving his post

81. "Driver 1 claimed that the collision occurred because, as he approached the intersection, Driver 2 started to make a left turn suddenly and at a high speed, even though the light had been red for 15 to 20 seconds." Suppose that you have been assigned to make a report on this accident. The position of the vehicles after the accident is indicated in the diagram below. The point in each case indicates the front of the vehicle. On the basis of this diagram, the best reason for concluding that Driver 1's statement is false is that

    (A) Driver 2's car is beyond the center of the intersection
    (B) Driver 2's car is making the turn on the proper side of the road
    (C) Driver 1's car is beyond the sidewalk line
    (D) Driver 1's car is on the right-hand side of the road

82. While patrolling a bridge approach road alone in a radio car, you are signaled to stop by a private car traveling in the opposite direction. The driver tells you that be was robbed by two men in a sedan ahead of him. Your car cannot cross the concrete safety-strip to get into the other lane. Of the following, the best course of action for you to take is to

    (A) tell the driver you cannot cross to his lane and ask him to report the matter
    (B) leave your car where it is, cross over to the private car, and use it to pursue the suspects
    (C) notify headquarters over your radio
    (D) make a U-turn in your car and chase the suspect vehicle on the wrong side of the parkway

83. "A courteous warning by an officer to a vehicle operator who has committed a minor traffic violation is usually more effective than a summons." Of the following statements, the one that best supports this point of view is:

    (A) An officer should issue a summons whenever one is called for and never show favoritism.
    (B) A warning should always be issued for a first offense.
    (C) The inconvenience and expense of a summons will keep most motorists from repeating the offense.
    (D) The operator who receives a warning for a minor violation will try to avoid repeating the offense.

84. A police officer using hand signals is directing traffic at a congested intersection. It is *least* important that

    (A) the officer be visible
    (B) the officer be accessible
    (C) the signs used by the officer be uniform
    (D) the signs used by the officer be simple

85. It is suggested that an officer should keep all persons away from the area of an accident until an investigation has been completed. This suggested procedure is

    (A) good; witnesses will be more likely to agree on a single story
    (B) bad; such action blocks traffic flow and causes congestion
    (C) good; objects of possible use as evidence will be protected from damage or loss

    (D) bad; the flow of normal pedestrian traffic provides an opportunity for an investigator to determine the cause of the accident

86. Before permitting automobiles involved in an accident to depart, a police officer should take certain measures. Of the following, it is *least* important that the officer make certain that

    (A) both drivers are properly licensed
    (B) the automobiles are in safe operating condition
    (C) the drivers have exchanged names and license numbers
    (D) he or she obtains the names and addresses of drivers and witnesses

87. A radio motor patrol team arrives on the scene a few minutes after a pedestrian has been killed by a hit-and-run driver. After obtaining a description of the car, the first action the officer should take is to

    (A) radio a description of the fleeing car to precinct headquarters
    (B) try to overtake the fleeing car
    (C) obtain complete statements from everyone at the scene
    (D) inspect the site of the accident for clues

88. The most effective method of crime prevention is, in general,

    (A) severe punishment of malefactors
    (B) probation
    (C) parole
    (D) eradication of causal factors

89. A businessman requests advice concerning good practice in the use of a safe in his office. Of the following points, which should be stressed in the use of safes?

    (A) A safe should not be placed where it can be seen from the street.
    (B) The combination should be written down and carefully hidden in the office.
    (C) A safe located in a dark place is more tempting to a burglar than one that is located in a well-lighted place.
    (D) Factors of size and weight alone determine the protection offered by a safe.

90. It has been claimed that a person who commits a crime sometimes has an unconscious wish to be punished, which is caused by strong unconscious feelings of guilt. Of the following actions by a criminal, the one which may be partly due to an unconscious desire for punishment is

(A) claiming that he or she doesn't know anything about the crime when questioned by the police

(B) running away from the state where the crime was committed

(C) revisiting the place where the crime was committed

(D) taking care not to leave any clues at the scene of the crime

91. Which of the following statements about fingerprints is *least* accurate?

(A) The value of fingerprints left at the scene of the crime does not vary with the distinctness of the fingerprint impressions.

(B) It is of value to fingerprint a person with an abnormal number of fingers.

(C) Fingerprints of different persons have never been found to be alike.

(D) The prime value of fingerprints lies in their effectiveness in identifying people.

92. According to a police manual, the delivery for laboratory examination of any article required as evidence must be made by the member of the force finding or coming into the possession of such evidence. Of the following, the most likely reason for this procedure is that it

(A) assists in the establishment of the authenticity of the evidence

(B) encourages a more careful search of the crime scene for all physical evidence that may be related to the crime

(C) ensures that the evidence will be properly marked or tagged for future identification

(D) prevents the undue delay that might result from a delivery through official channels

93. You are getting the description of a lost diamond bracelet. Of the following, the most important piece of information, in addition to knowing that the missing item is a diamond bracelet, is

(A) value—$10,000

(B) design—two intertwining snakes

(C) diamonds—many small and several large diamonds

(D) owner—Mrs. H. Jones

94. You are watching a great number of people leave a ball game. Of the persons who are described below, the one whom it would be easiest to spot would be

(A) female; age 15; height 5'6"; weight 130 lbs.; long straight black hair

(B) male; age 50; height 5'8"; weight 150 lbs.; missing toe on right foot

(C) male; age 60; height 5'7"; weight 170 lbs.; all false teeth

(D) male; age 25; height 6'3"; weight 220 lbs.; pockmarked

95. You are preparing a description of a woman to be broadcast. Of the following characteristics, the one which would be of most value to an officer driving a squad car is

(A) wanted for murder

(B) age 45 years

(C) height 6'1"

(D) smokes very heavily

96. Assume that on a hot summer day, you are stationed on the grass at the south bank of a busy parkway looking at southbound traffic for a light blue 1974 Ford two door sedan. If traffic is very heavy, which of the following additional pieces of information would be most helpful to you in identifying the car?

(A) All chrome is missing from the left side of the car.

(B) There is a bullet hole in the left front window.

(C) The paint on the right side of the car is somewhat faded.

(D) The front bumper is missing.

97. You are watching a great number of people leave a sports arena after a boxing match. Of the characteristics listed below, the one which would be of greatest value to you in spotting a man wanted by the department is

(A) height: 5′3″; weight: 200 lbs.
(B) eyes: brown; hair: black, wavy; complexion: sallow
(C) that he frequents bars and grills and customarily associates with females
(D) scars: thin ½″ scar on left upper lip; tattoos: on right forearm—"Pinto"

98. "Social Security cards are not acceptable proof of identification for police purposes." Of the following, the most important reason for this rule is that the Social Security card

(A) is easily obtained
(B) states on its face "for Social Security purposes—not for identification"
(C) is frequently lost
(D) does not contain a photograph, description, or fingerprints of the person

99. "Photographs of suspected persons should not be shown to the witness if the suspect himself can be arrested and placed on view for identification." This recommendation is

(A) inadvisable; this procedure might subject the witness to future retribution by the suspect
(B) advisable; a photograph cannot be used for identification purposes with the same degree of certainty as the suspect in person
(C) inadvisable; the appearance of the suspect may have changed since the commission of the crime
(D) advisable; photography as an art has not achieved an acceptable degree of perfection

100. Stationed at a busy intersection, you are given the description of a vehicle that has been stolen. Of the following characteristics, the one which will permit you to eliminate most easily a large number of vehicles is

(A) no spare tire
(B) make—Buick, two-door sedan, 1976
(C) color—black
(D) tires—750 × 16, white-walled

101. If a sick or injured woman, to whom a male police officer is rendering aid, is unknown and the officer has reason to believe that her clothing contains means of identification, he should

(A) immediately search the clothing for such identification and remove any identification found therein
(B) send for a female officer to search the clothing before the woman is sent to a hospital
(C) ask any female present to search the clothing for such identification
(D) accompany her to the hospital and there seek the necessary information from the hospital authorities.

102. Which of the following means of avoiding identification would be most likely to meet with success?

(A) growing a beard
(B) shaving off the beard if there was one originally
(C) burning the fingers so as to remove the fingerprints
(D) changing the features by facial surgery

103. In asking a witness of a crime to identify a suspect, it is a common practice to place the suspect with a group of persons and ask the witness to pick out the person in question. Of the following, the best reason for this practice is that it will

(A) make the identification more reliable than if the witness were shown the suspect alone
(B) protect the witness against reprisals
(C) make sure that the witness is telling the truth
(D) help select other participants in the crime at the same time

104. Suppose that a police officer observes an individual acting suspiciously while in a department store. Of the following, the most desirable procedure for her to follow is to

(A) arrest the person
(B) warn the salespeople that this person may be a thief
(C) continue to observe this person until sufficient data is present for the formulation of a final decision
(D) telephone headquarters for assistance as there may soon be a disturbance

105. A police officer who is off duty observes a woman busily engaged in examining fabrics at a counter in a large store. The woman's handbag is open. A number of other persons are at this counter also engaged in examining fabrics. Of the following, the best procedure for the officer to follow *first* is to

(A) tell the woman that her handbag is open

(B) keep the woman under close observation

(C) direct a clerk to inform the woman that her handbag is open

(D) approach the woman and engage her in conversation, by asking a question like, "Do you have the time? My watch seems to have stopped."

106. "The four witnesses to the bank robbery, including the bank president and the cashier, were left together for one hour in the president's office at the bank before they were questioned." This kind of procedure is

(A) desirable and considerate as there is no point in treating respectable citizens as criminals

(B) unwise as it permits undue pressure to be brought upon some of the witnesses

(C) unwise as it permits an exchange of actual and imagined details that may result in invalid testimony

(D) wise as it keeps the witnesses all in one place

107. Assume that you are questioning a victim in order to obtain a description of a mugger. Of the following, the best example of the type of question to be avoided is:

(A) Did you notice any scars or unusual features?

(B) Did he wear a brown or black coat?

(C) What color were his shoes?

(D) Approximately how tall was he?

108. Suppose that you are questioning witnesses to a hit-and-run accident. Of the following, the information that will probably be *least* valuable for the purpose of sending out an alarm for the hit-and-run automobile is the

(A) direction which the automobile took after the accident

(B) number of occupants in the automobile at the time of the accident

(C) speed at which the automobile was moving when it struck the victim

(D) part of the automobile that struck the victim of the accident

109. The marks left on a bullet by a gun barrel are different from those left by any other gun barrel. This fact is most useful in directly identifying the

(A) direction from which a shot was fired

(B) person who fired a particular gun

(C) gun from which a bullet was fired

(D) bullet that caused a fatal wound

110. Uniformed officers are constantly urged to consider every revolver loaded until proven otherwise. Of the following, the best justification for this recommendation is that

(A) no time is lost when use of the revolver is required

(B) there are many accidents involving apparently empty revolvers

(C) less danger is involved when facing armed criminals

(D) ammunition deteriorates unless replaced periodically.

111. Of the following, the best method to use in shooting a revolver is to keep

(A) both eyes closed

(B) both eyes open

(C) the right eye open

(D) the left eye open

112. A police officer should fire a pistol

(A) only as a last resort

(B) at no time

(C) primarily to inspire fear

(D) to impress upon citizens the need for respect

113. The police officer must inform the person arrested of his or her authority and of the cause of arrest except when the

(A) crime charged is a felony

(B) person arrested is a habitual offender

(C) officer is in uniform so that authority is apparent

(D) person is arrested in the actual commission of the crime

114. "A woman about thirty years of age accosted a police officer with the complaint that her husband had just attacked her with a pair of scissors. 'My husband nearly gouged my eyes out,' the woman said. 'He poked me in the face not once but four or five times. He cut my face into ribbons. He's a dangerous man and I want him arrested. I have five or six witnesses to the attack.' The officer saw no marks on the woman's face." On the basis of these data, the officer may most reasonably take the position that

(A) the husband ought to be taken into custody immediately
(B) the woman's story is at least partially inaccurate
(C) no scissors were involved in the accident
(D) the incident occurred some time ago

115. Generally, before making an arrest for a serious crime, the police officer must have facts to provide a reasonable basis for believing the person to be guilty." The best reason for this rule is to

(A) reduce the number of arrests
(B) protect himself or herself against being charged with false arrest
(C) safeguard the rights of citizens against improper arrest
(D) place the burden of disproving the charges upon accused

116. Suppose that a police officer arrests a man accused of molesting a young girl. In an instance of this type, the officer should

(A) behave toward the accused in the same manner as toward any other individual accused of a crime
(B) be a little rough in handling the man
(C) inform the man in no uncertain terms that the act of which he is accused is most contemptible
(D) assume that the man is psychopathic and rightfully a case for institutionalization

117. Suppose that a police officer is summoned by a Mr. Smith who accuses a Mr. Jones of having aided a Mr. Brown to do an injury to Mr. Smith. The nature of the claimed injury is not such as to give the officer the right to make an arrest. The officer should *first*

(A) prove to Mr. Smith that there is insufficient merit in his case

(B) refer Mr. Smith to the captain of the precinct
(C) explain to Mr. Smith the reason why an arrest cannot be made
(D) refer Mr. Smith to the nearest court

118. When sent to make an arrest, a police officer should be sure he or she is arresting the correct person in order to avoid

(A) publicity
(B) detaining an innocent person
(C) having to use force
(D) having to appear in court

119. If a police officer is called upon to eject a disorderly person from a bus station, the most important consideration must necessarily be to

(A) avoid damaging transit system property
(B) earn good public opinion
(C) avoid endangering other passengers
(D) get the person off the property

120. "When making arrests, the police officer should treat all suspects in the same manner." This suggested rule is

(A) undesirable; the specific problems presented should govern the officer's actions
(B) desirable; this is the only democratic solution to the problem
(C) undesirable; persons who are only suspected are not criminals and should not be treated as such
(D) desirable; only by setting up fixed and rigid rules can officers know what is expected of them

121. A police officer observes a young man who is obviously very excited, walking unusually fast, and repeatedly halting to look behind him. Upon stopping the young man, the officer finds that he is carrying a gun and has just held up a liquor store a few blocks away. This incident illustrates that

(A) circumstances that are not suspicious in themselves frequently provide clues for the solution of crimes
(B) an experienced officer can pick the criminal type out of a crowd by alert observation
(C) action is always to be preferred to thought
(D) a police officer should investigate suspicious circumstances

122. A police officer positively recognizes a woman on a busy street as one wanted for passing bad checks. Of the following, the most appropriate action for the officer to take is to

(A) approach and then arrest the woman
(B) follow the women until a place is reached where there are few people, then take out a gun, and arrest the woman
(C) immediately take out a gun, stop the woman, and search her
(D) follow the woman as she may lead the way to associates.

123. A woman has her husband arrested for severely beating their five-year-old son. A crowd of angry neighbors has gathered around the husband. In making the arrest, the arresting officer should

(A) treat the husband like any other person accused of breaking the law
(B) deal with the husband sympathetically since the man may be mentally ill
(C) handle the husband harshly since his crime is a despicable one
(D) treat the husband roughly only if he shows no remorse for his actions

124. The purpose of a raid is to

(A) apprehend criminals
(B) disclose the members of a certain criminal group
(C) secure the probable cause required for the issuance of a search warrant
(D) know the fields of observation from a suspected place

125. There has been a series of burglaries in a residential area consisting of one-family houses. You have been assigned to select a house in this area in which detectives can wait secretly for an attempted burglary of that house so that the burglars can be apprehended in the act. Which of the following would be the best house to select for this purpose?

(A) The house that was recently burglarized and from which several thousand dollars worth of clothing and personal property were taken.

(B) The house whose owner reports that several times the telephone has rung, but the person making the call hung up as soon as the telephone was answered.
(C) The house that is smaller and looks much less pretentious than other houses in the same area.
(D) The house that is occupied by a widower who works long hours but who lives with an invalid mother requiring constant nursing service.

126. Suppose that a police officer observes a young girl picking up small articles of merchandise as she passes from one counter to another of a large department store. The girl does not stop to pay for any of the articles. For the officer to wait until the girl is about to leave the store before apprehending her is

(A) inadvisable; she may escape
(B) advisable; evidence is thereby more firmly established
(C) inadvisable if she has an accomplice waiting outside
(D) advisable if the police officer has a witness to confirm the observations

127. Jones is accused of having assaulted Smith at a particular time and place. Police investigation disclosed that Jones was present at the time and place where the alleged assault took place. This information makes admissible the conclusion that

(A) Jones assaulted Smith
(B) Smith assaulted Jones
(C) Jones may have assaulted Smith
(D) Smith may have assaulted Jones

128. Suppose that a lawyer is attacked in a washroom by a man who delivered several blows from behind with a carpenter's mallet. From this information only, it is safe to infer

(A) that the attacker is young and strong
(B) that the mallet was either recently purchased or stolen
(C) that the washroom is located in an office building
(D) none of the foregoing

129. Suppose that a police officer is seeking information designed to locate the perpetrator of a known assault. Of the following, the question that would be most useful in assisting the officer to ascertain the identity of the guilty person is
    (A) Where did the assault occur?
    (B) At what time did the assault occur?
    (C) Who was the victim of the assault?
    (D) Who was the assailant?

130. During a quarrel on a crowded city street, one man stabs another and flees. A police officer arriving at the scene a short time later finds the victim unconscious, calls for an ambulance, and orders the crowd to leave. The officer's action is
    (A) bad; there may have been witnesses to the assault among the crowd
    (B) good; it is proper first aid procedure to give an injured person room and air
    (C) bad; the assailant is probably among the crowd
    (D) good; a crowd may destroy needed evidence

131. Green is accused on apparently good evidence of having stolen a radio from Brown at 8:30 P.M., January 18. If Green is able to prove that at 10:00 P.M. of the same day he was not in possession of any radio, Green has
    (A) proved his innocence
    (B) yet to establish his innocence
    (C) implied his guilt since evidence for the period 8:30 P.M. to 10:00 P.M. is absent
    (D) proved that Brown is mistaken or lying

132. Clothes valued at $800 as well as $1000 in cash were stolen from the home of one of the residents of a police officer's post. The officer learns that Albert Jones, a man 27 years old and not known ever to possess more than a few dollars at one time, has, shortly after the occasion of the robbery, displayed what seemed to be a large roll of bills. The officer may most profitably take, as the basis for first action, the position that
    (A) a large roll of bills is sometimes obtained as the result of a burglary
    (B) despite the fact that the clothing is valued at $800, a considerably smaller

sum is likely to be realized when the clothing is sold to a secondhand dealer
    (C) Albert Jones may recently have gotten a job
    (D) reputation must be distinguished from character

133. A resident on your post informs you that a valuable diamond ring has been stolen from her apartment. About two weeks later, a boy gives you what appears to be a diamond ring that he says be found on the street. Of the following, the question that would be *least* significant in this situation is:
    (A) Did the boy actually find the ring on the street?
    (B) Is this the same ring the resident mentioned?
    (C) Was the ring really stolen?
    (D) Did the resident wait for more or less than two hours before reporting the theft of the ring?

134. "Goods valued at $75,000 were reported burglarized from a loft. Investigation proved conclusively that it was impossible for burglars either to have entered or left the loft building without having been detected." On the basis of these data, the police officer may most reasonably deduce that
    (A) more than $75,000 worth of goods were stolen
    (B) the burglary was committed by a person unfamiliar with the habits of the people in the loft where the crime occurred
    (C) what was reported to be a burglary is actually an assault
    (D) the alleged crime did not occur

135. Suppose that a police officer observes that a certain company on his post pays out a large sum in cash weekly in payroll. If the officer were asked to suggest the best method for eliminating the possibility of a successful payroll robbery in this company, he would suggest
    (A) the hiring of several armed guards
    (B) that payday occur at irregular intervals
    (C) that payment be made at a place other than at the offices of the company
    (D) payment by check

136. "Many thieves conceal themselves in a building during business hours, and, when they have accomplished their purpose, escape through a rear door or window." The reason for such concealment in the building is most probably that after business hours

(A) without a key, locked doors are sometimes difficult to open
(B) poor lighting is conducive to undetected criminal activity
(C) to accomplish a purpose, one must have a goal
(D) rear doors ordinarily serve as exits

137. "When investigating a burglary, a police officer should obtain as complete descriptions as possible of articles of value that were stolen, but should list, without describing, stolen articles that are relatively valueless." This suggested procedure is

(A) poor; what is valueless to one person may be of great value to another
(B) good; it enables the police to concentrate on recovering the most valuable articles
(C) poor; articles of little value frequently provide the only evidence connecting the suspect to the crime
(D) good; the listing of the inexpensive items is probably incomplete

138. Looking through the window of a jewelry store, a police officer sees a man take a watch from the counter and drop it into his pocket while the jeweler is busy talking to someone else. The man looks around the store and then walks out. The officer should

(A) stop the man and bring him back into the store so that both he and the jeweler can be questioned
(B) ignore the incident; if the man were performing an illegal act, the jeweler would have called for help
(C) arrest the man, take him to the station house, and then return to obtain the jeweler's statement
(D) ignore the incident; if the man were a thief, the jeweler would not have left the watches unattended

139. A radio police officer who responded at 2 A.M. to a radio call that a burglary had been committed in an apartment heard the sound of clashing tools coming from the adjoining apartment. For the officer to investigate the noise would be

(A) undesirable; the officer may not search without a warrant
(B) desirable; the thief may be found
(C) undesirable; unusual noises in apartments are common
(D) desirable; the victim would tend to be impressed by the concern shown

140. Assume that you are driving a police car, equipped with a two-way radio, along an isolated section of the parkway at 3 A.M. You note that the headlights of a car pulled to the side of the road are blinking rapidly. When you stop to investigate, the driver of the car informs you that he was just forced to the side of the road by two men in a green station wagon, who robbed him of a large amount of cash and jewelry at gunpoint and then sped away. Your *first* consideration in this situation should be to

(A) drive rapidly along the parkway in the direction taken by the criminals in an effort to apprehend them before they escape
(B) question the driver carefully, looking for inconsistencies indicating that he made up the whole story
(C) obtain a complete listing and identification of all materials lost
(D) notify your superior to have the parkway exits watched for a car answering the description of the getaway car

141. A police officer finds a man dying in one of the city parks. There are several stab wounds in the man's chest and his skull is fractured. Just before dying, the man manages to say that he was the victim of an assault and robbery. Upon investigation by the officer, a bloodstained shoemaker's awl is found nearby. Of the following, the most useful assumption to make *first* in attempting to solve the crime is that

(A) for some reason the man lied, so tentatively, his statement ought to be disregarded
(B) there were no witnesses to the possible crime
(C) the awl was deliberately placed near the scene of the crime to mislead the police
(D) the murderer had access to shoemaker's tools

142. "At 2 A.M., while patrolling your post, you find the body of a man lying on the street. A knife is protruding from the man's back." On the basis of these data only, it is *least* likely that the man was lying

    (A) on his left side
    (B) face downward
    (C) on his back
    (D) on his right side

143. In a recent case of suicide, the body was found slumped in a chair and no revolver, knife, or razor was found in the room. Of the following, the most reasonable hypothesis from the data given is that

    (A) the person had taken some poison
    (B) the person had hanged himself
    (C) the person had died as a result of a heart attack
    (D) the murderer had taken the weapon

144. Suppose that while patrolling your post in an unfrequented area at 1:00 A.M., you find a man sprawled on the ground in an alley. The man's throat has been cut and he is dead. There is considerable blood on the ground, but the man does not appear to be bleeding. Of the following, the *first* step you should take is to

    (A) straighten the man out so he is resting comfortably
    (B) telephone your precinct
    (C) investigate to determine whether the blood on the ground is the blood of the dead man
    (D) carry the man out to the street

145. Suppose that A, the proprietor of a fur business, is found dead at his place of business at 8:00 A.M. His death appears to have occurred as a result of the fact that he is hanging from a rope tied to a water pipe. In the pockets of A's trousers are a number of pawn tickets for furs and a lapsed insurance policy for $10,000. On the basis of this information only, the best inference is that

    (A) A committed suicide because of business difficulties
    (B) A had been working late and was murdered by thieves
    (C) A's death is the consequence of an accident

    (D) it is safe only to declare that A probably did not commit suicide. The fact that so few articles were found in his pockets is a substantial basis for extended additional investigation

146. When the bodies of two women were found stabbed in an inner room of an apartment, it was first believed that it was a case of mutual homicide. Of the following clues found at the scene, the one that indicates that it was more likely a case of murder by a third party is the fact that

    (A) the door to the apartment was found locked
    (B) there were bloodstains on the outer door of the apartment
    (C) there was a switchblade knife in each body
    (D) no money could be found in the room where the bodies were

147. "The questioning of witnesses is often much less truth-revealing than are physical clues found at the scene of the crime." Of the following, the chief justification for this statement is that

    (A) most witnesses rarely tell the truth
    (B) physical clues are always present if examination is thorough
    (C) questioning of witnesses must be supported by other evidence
    (D) the memory of witnesses is often unreliable

148. Jones, who is suspected of having committed a crime of homicide at 8:30 P.M. in the building where he lives, claims that he could not have committed the act because he worked overtime until 8:00 P.M. In order to prove that Jones actually could not have committed the act in question, it is most important to know

    (A) how long it takes to get from Jones' building to Jones' place of work
    (B) if there are any witnesses to the fact that Jones worked overtime
    (C) Jones' reputation in the community
    (D) what kind of work Jones does

149. A police officer on a post hears a cry for help from a woman in a car with two men. He approaches the car and is told by the woman that the men are kidnapping her. The men claim to be the woman's husband and doctor, and they state that they are taking her to a private mental hospital in Westchester County. Of the following, the officer should

(A) take all of them to the station house for further questioning
(B) permit the car to depart on the basis of the explanation
(C) call for an ambulance to take the woman to the nearest city mental hospital
(D) accompany the car to the private mental hospital

150. Suppose that a seven-year-old boy has been kidnapped as he was returning home from a playground at dusk. The following day, his parents received an anonymous letter that told them the child was well and designated a close friend of the family, who was known to be very fond of the boy, as an intermediary to arrange payment of a ransom. On the basis of these data only, we may most reasonably assume that

(A) the friend kidnapped the boy
(B) the friend was probably an accessory in the kidnapping
(C) further investigation is necessary to determine the identity of the kidnapper
(D) the boy is dead

151. The most frequent cause among the following for making a person a criminal is

(A) mental retardation
(B) good education
(C) bad environmental conditions
(D) superior ability in a trade

152. A view widely held among criminologists is that the severity of laws dealing with criminals is not so effective a deterrent to crime as is

(A) the enactment of less severe laws, coupled with lenient administration
(B) a well-organized parole system for even the most hardened criminals
(C) psychiatric treatment, as most crimes are committed by persons with emotional and mental difficulties

(D) certainty that the criminal will be apprehended and sentenced properly

153. A representative group of young criminals in a certain state were found to be normal in intelligence, but 86 percent were behind from one to six grades in school. The best inference from these data is that

(A) lack of intelligence is highly correlated with delinquency
(B) criminals should be removed from the school system
(C) educational maladjustments are closely associated with delinquency
(D) the usual rate at which criminals progress educationally represents the limit of their learning powers

154. "One study shows that boys' clubs and similar programs aimed at the prevention of crime and the rehabilitation of the juvenile delinquent tend to attract the good boys, while the bad boys stay away." This quotation implies most directly that the number of instances in which juvenile delinquents are rehabilitated through such programs as boys' clubs is

(A) relatively large
(B) relatively small
(C) a quantity the size of which cannot be estimated even loosely and approximately
(D) greater for good boys than for bad boys

155. Two police officers patrolling the downtown business streets at 1 A.M. observe a young girl dressed in a manner to attract attention, walking slowly down the street. The girl approaches a young man, who disregards her. After a short time, she approaches another man, who also disregards her. The officers should

(A) follow the girl until they are in a position to make a double arrest
(B) ignore the situation, since the girl is obviously not a professional prostitute
(C) approach and question the men as well as the girl since they may give evidence to prove solicitation
(D) separate, one continuing to observe the girl, the other calling the Missing Persons Bureau to check up on descriptions of missing girls

156. "Where a satisfactory adjustment can be made without arresting the delinquent minor, it is done. Court action is only taken where it seems best for the minor or the community." Of the following, the best justification for this procedure is that

(A) court cases are costly to the community
(B) rehabilitation of the delinquent minor is of primary importance
(C) arresting minors may become a source of inconvenience if not discouraged
(D) juvenile delinquency can increase if juvenile delinquents are not arrested

157. Suppose that, while on patrol late at night, you find a woman lying in the street, apparently a victim of a hit-and-run accident. She seems to be injured seriously, but you wish to ask her one or two questions in order to help apprehend the driver of the hit-and-run car. Of the following, the first question to ask is:

(A) Which direction did the car go?
(B) What time did it happen?
(C) What kind of car was it?
(D) How many persons were in the car?

158. Of the following, the information that would be *least* helpful to the police officer assigned to the case of a 14-year-old girl who has been reported by her mother as a runaway is

(A) the possible cause for her running away
(B) a detailed description of her clothing
(C) a detailed description of her scholastic abilities
(D) a detailed description of her features

159. A plainclothes police officer in a market comes upon a woman who is complaining that a fruit dealer has fraudulent scales. Upon questioning, she offers as evidence a bag of grapes she has just purchased. Of the following, the most appropriate action for the officer to take would be to

(A) buy some fruit from the dealer and later check the weight on scales known to be true
(B) return with the woman to the dealer and ask him to weigh the grapes again
(C) take the woman's bag of grapes and weigh it on true scales to verify her claim
(D) weigh the bag of grapes on a nearby dealer's scale as a check

160. A violin is reported as missing from the home of Mrs. Brown. It would be *least* important to the police, before making a routine check of pawn shops, to know that this violin

(A) is of a certain unusual shade of red
(B) has one tuning key with a chip mark on it in the shape of a triangle
(C) has a well-known manufacturer's label stamped inside the violin
(D) has a hidden number given to the police by the owner

161. Merely looking at a criminal is enough to tell an intelligent officer

(A) how educated the person is
(B) whether the person will be a troublemaker
(C) whether the person is truly a criminal
(D) little or nothing

162. Assume that you are investigating a case of reported suicide. You find the deceased sitting in a chair, sprawled over his desk, a revolver still clutched in his right hand. In your examination of the room, you find that the window is partly open. Only one bullet has been fired from the revolver. The bullet has lodged in the wall. Assume that the diagram above is a scale drawing of the scene. D indicates the desk, C indicates the chair, W indicates the window, and B indicates the bullet. Of the following, which indicates most strongly the deceased did not commit suicide?

(A) the distance between the desk and the bullet hole
(B) the relative position of the bullet hole and the chair
(C) the fact that the window was partly open
(D) the relative position of the desk and the window.

163. As the police officer approaches a lighted delicatessen late at night, two men emerge and walk rapidly in the opposite direction. Suspicious of the behavior of these men, the officer looks through the window into the store. Of the following, the circumstances tending most strongly to confirm his suspicions are

(A) several persons are waiting to be served inside the store
(B) the clerk is standing at the counter with his back to the officer
(C) the clerk and a customer are engaged in a conversation
(D) no one at all is visible inside the store

164. About 9:00 P.M., a police officer observed two men loitering near a neighborhood movie theater. He had not seen either man in the neighborhood before. The agent for the theater usually deposited the night receipts in the local bank's night deposit vault between 9:00 and 9:15 P.M. The most appropriate action for the officer to take was to

(A) station himself so that he could observe their actions until the theater's money had been deposited
(B) demand that they tell him their place of residence and the reason for their presence near the theater
(C) pay no further attention since they were obviously waiting for someone in the theater
(D) enter the theater by the side entrance and warn the manager to be prepared for a possible robbery attempt

165. The proprietor of a tavern summons a police officer and turns over a loaded revolver that was found in one of the tavern's booths. The *least* appropriate action for the officer to take is to

(A) unload the gun and place it in an inside pocket
(B) determine exactly when the revolver was found
(C) obtain the names or descriptions of the persons who occupied the booth before the revolver was found
(D) question the proprietor very closely concerning the matter

166. Assume that you have stopped a 1978 Dodge four-door sedan, which you suspect is a car reported as stolen the day before. The items of information that would be most useful in determining whether or not this is the stolen car is that

(A) the stolen car's license number was QA2356; this car's license number is U21375
(B) the stolen car's engine number was AB6231; this car's engine number is CS2315
(C) the windshield of the stolen car was not cracked; this car's windshield is cracked
(D) the stolen car had whitewall tires; this car does not have whitewall tires

167. Crime statistics indicate that property crimes such as larceny, burglary, and robbery are more numerous during winter months than in summer. The explanation that most adequately accounts for this situation is that

(A) human needs, such as clothing, food, heat, and shelter, are greater in summer
(B) criminal tendencies are generally aggravated by climatic changes
(C) there are more hours of darkness in winter and such crimes are usually committed under cover of darkness
(D) urban areas are more densely populated during winter months, affording greater opportunity for such crimes

168. Blackmail is an especially troublesome problem for the police. The best justification for this statement is that the

(A) victim of a blackmail plot usually hesitates to cooperate with the police for fear of publicity
(B) blackmailer is usually a hardened criminal who will not hesitate to murder the victim
(C) facts constituting the subject matter of a blackmail are seldom known to the victim
(D) victim of a blackmail plot is usually anxious to expose all details to the police

169. In some states, statutes forbid the payment of ransom to kidnappers. Such statutes are

(A) actually in violation of the due process of law clause of the federal constitution
(B) necessary to encourage kidnappers to return the kidnapped person unharmed
(C) harmful because kidnapping is encouraged by such legislation
(D) examples of laws that protect society although sometimes working hardships on individuals

170. Any change in insurance coverage immediately prior to a fire should be investigated. Strange as it may seem, most such changes made by convicted arsonists are made to a smaller amount. The most probable reason for such changes is that the arsonist

(A) was trying to divert suspicion
(B) decided to set the fire after the change was made
(C) did not have enough money to pay for the full amount
(D) reduced the insurance to the amount he or she expected to be lost in the fire

ANSWER KEY

We are providing this key to the correct answers so that you can check your answers quickly and easily. Be sure to continue and study all the answer explanations that follow. The explanations point out the police reasoning and judgment involved in the correct answer choices.

1. A	18. B	35. C	52. D	69. A	86. C	103. A	120. A	137. C	154. B
2. A	19. B	36. C	53. D	70. C	87. A	104. C	121. D	138. A	155. C
3. D	20. D	37. C	54. A	71. D	88. D	105. A	122. A	139. B	156. B
4. D	21. C	38. A	55. C	72. C	89. C	106. C	123. A	140. D	157. C
5. C	22. C	39. C	56. C	73. A	90. C	107. B	124. A	141. D	158. C
6. C	23. C	40. B	57. C	74. B	91. A	108. C	125. B	142. C	159. A
7. D	24. D	41. C	58. D	75. B	92. A	109. C	126. B	143. A	160. C
8. A	25. B	42. A	59. A	76. C	93. B	110. B	127. C	144. B	161. D
9. C	26. A	43. D	60. C	77. D	94. D	111. B	128. D	145. A	162. B
10. D	27. A	44. D	61. C	78. B	95. C	112. A	129. D	146. B	163. D
11. A	28. B	45. B	62. D	79. C	96. D	113. D	130. A	147. D	164. A
12. B	29. A	46. A	63. D	80. C	97. A	114. B	131. B	148. A	165. A
13. B	30. D	47. D	64. D	81. A	98. D	115. C	132. A	149. A	166. B
14. D	31. C	48. D	65. D	82. C	99. B	116. A	133. D	150. C	167. C
15. A	32. D	49. C	66. C	83. D	100. B	117. C	134. D	151. C	168. A
16. D	33. B	50. B	67. A	84. B	101. D	118. B	135. D	152. D	169. D
17. B	34. C	51. D	68. D	85. C	102. D	119. C	136. A	153. C	170. A

Answer Explanations

1. **(A)** A police officer is always a police officer, even when not officially on duty. Off-duty status does not relieve a police officer from fulfilling the police role.

2. **(A)** The first thing to do is to protect the man's life by escorting him out of danger. Securing medical assistance should follow.

3. **(D)** Obviously, going the wrong way on a one-way street creates a dangerous situation for many people. By stopping the driver, you have averted the danger. The out-of-towner has not actually committed a violation, he was just about to. It would be wise to point out to him exactly how one-way streets are marked in your town.

4. **(D)** If the man is that close, you may be able to catch him yourself. Summoning other officers might lose valuable time and allow the man to escape. The offense is not such as to warrant shooting the man nor endangering bystanders by discharging your gun.

5. **(C)** Drowning occurs very quickly. Try to rescue the boy.

6. **(C)** Anything unusual should be investigated as soon as possible. The first thing to do is to determine whether or not a burglary has occurred. Then the premises should be secured and the owner notified. If the premises were not entered, they should be kept under surveillance in case the burglar returns.

7. **(D)** Stopping fights is part of keeping the peace and of maintaining order on your beat.

8. **(A)** A burglar may be inside and have turned off the light to escape detection. If there is no evidence of intruders, the storekeeper should be called to turn on the light or to replace the burned-out bulb. This question illustrates the need for a police officer to be observant and to remember how things usually appear on the beat.

9. **(C)** No one has broken the law, and there is nothing suspicious in anyone's behavior. People are entitled to argue. There is no reason to suspect that the keys on the man's key ring were not his own.

10. **(D)** You can assume that these people are up to no good. The quickest way to find this out is to ask for registration papers, for proof of ownership. If the keys were simply locked inside the car, the owner should readily clear up your suspicion. If ownership cannot be proved, arrest is indicated.

11. **(A)** An argument in a cleaning store is not an emergency situation. There is no need to disrupt traffic nor to create alarm. On the other hand, the situation could lead to blows so the officer should stop in to try to calm the tempers.

12. **(B)** Your first consideration must be protection of life and limb. Get the man to the hospital for medical attention but have him escorted for futher questioning. Gunshot wounds always should be investigated.

13. **(B)** Absolutely. Schools are prepared to deal with unauthorized absences and with children's illness.

14. **(D)** Janitors and local merchants tend to be out on the street often and are very aware of what is happening in the neighborhood. These people also would prefer to avoid having any trouble in the area and, if on friendly terms with a trusted police officer, are likely to alert the officer to situations they feel the officer should know about.

15. **(A)** The owner may indeed be caring for his or her car, in which case the owner can prove ownership. An open hood can also be a sign of car theft by means of jump start or of battery theft in progress.

16. **(D)** A police officer is a police officer, not a firefighter. It is the job of firefighters to ascertain whether or not there really is a fire and to put it out. Fires spread rapidly. The practical move is to call the fire department rather than trying to run through the building alone trying to rouse all occupants.

17. **(B)** A pattern of regular inspections gives fair notice to prospective wrongdoers as to when no one will be looking.

18. **(B)** No storekeeper wants the liability of a pedestrian's being injured because of his fail-

ure to do what was required. Pointing out the danger to the storekeeper should be sufficient.

19. **(B)** It may well be that the man is simply a "take charge" type. However, you must answer by choosing one of the four statements. Of these, it is most likely that the man feels better equipped to answer so as to conceal some information.

20. **(D)** The police officer must maintain the role of police officer. He may not assume the role of parent. Rather than simply turning the woman down, he might suggest that she contact the proper social agency.

21. **(C)** Rush to the scene. The girl may have misjudged the situation and the man may be in need of emergency medical assistance. If the man is indeed dead, his body should not lie in the street unattended.

22. **(C)** Dispersing a noisy group of teenagers is generally sufficient to quiet things down.

23. **(C)** Seven or eight people do not constitute an unruly crowd. The appearance of a person of authority demanding order should end the disturbance.

24. **(D)** A newly appointed officer assumes some responsibility immediately. The supervising officer will give guidance but will not make all decisions.

25. **(B)** Common sense. Extremes are not desirable. You must respect the rights of the innocent even as you make sure to arrest the guilty.

26. **(A)** The careless person is not likely to succeed; the negligent person will probably fail.

27. **(A)** You have four choices. Of these, crime prevention is the primary function of a police department.

28. **(B)** Police badges serve as identification of the police officers.

29. **(A)** The police officer must be alert at all times.

30. **(D)** If 10 percent of the inmates released from a prison are arrested as parole violators, the one conclusion that may be drawn is that 10 percent have violated parole and have been caught. The statement gives no basis for any other conclusions.

31. **(C)** Murders are not caused by pistols; pistols are often used in the commission of murders. Clearly the pistol is a mechanical aid to crime, and some crimes might be avoided if pistols were unavailable, but there is no one-to-one correspondence between pistols and murders.

32. **(D)** A police officer cannot allow his or her professional judgment to be influenced in any way by misinformation or personal prejudice.

33. **(B)** This is a truism. Common sense should give you the answer.

34. **(C)** The officer must understand what he or she is to do in order to do it. Watch out for distracting answers like that offered by choice (A). Self-interest is never the reason for doing anything when taking a civil service exam.

35. **(C)** Remember not to step out of the police officer's role. The police officer must never recommend individuals, not even a choice of individuals. The most the police officer may do is recommend that the individual contact the local bar association or consult directories in a library.

36. **(C)** In police exams, older children are generally referred to as juveniles. "Children" means young children. In dealing with children, whether protecting them or arresting them, the police officer must secure their confidence to get maximum cooperation.

37. **(C)** Criminal behavior is not exempt from the struggle for equality.

38. **(A)** Since murder is often a crime of passion, the police may have little means to foresee or prevent it. Burglary, prostitution, and auto theft are premeditated and, to some extent, visible. Police vigilance can help prevent opportunities for such crimes to occur.

39. **(C)** This phenomenon is called "copycat crime." It is an unfortunate but unavoidable consequence of a free press.

40. **(B)** This question requires careful reading and interpreting rather than judgment. A member on duty but not in uniform may drink intoxicants but not to an extent to make him- or herself unfit for duty. Judgment enters into the situation in that the officer must judge for him- or herself at what point to stop drinking.

41. **(C)** Police officers are trained in the law and in the law of arrest. They are better able to judge when arrest is called for.

42. **(A)** Imprisonment serves to prevent that offender's commission of future crimes, at least so long as the offender remains in prison. It is hoped that the imprisonment of offenders serves to deter others from crime and thus further prevents the commission of future crimes.

43. **(D)** Boys under sixteen are very impressionable and learn readily. Society's interests are best served by not allowing them contact with hardened criminals.

44. **(D)** According to the statement, it is certainly true that a well-dressed person may be a criminal. Statement (C) is on its face also true, but the statement speaks only of criminals who *look* intelligent, not of criminals who *are* intelligent.

45. **(B)** The police officer's first priority is to save lives. An ambulance on an emergency run is on a mission to save a life. Lifesaving supersedes all other orders.

46. **(A)** Even though in civilian clothes and off duty, the police officer has the duty to save lives. By educating the youngsters in the dangers of their actions, the police officer may be saving their lives and possibly the lives of other passengers on very crowded buses. One must hope that this instruction will also restrain them from tampering with emergency doors in future bus rides.

47. **(D)** Even when the fire is in a house rather than an apartment building, your first duty is to summon firefighters. They most likely can save more lives than you can alone by attempting to rouse residents.

48. **(D)** Common sense. No responsible person would start a stampede in a crowded theater by shouting "Fire!" In addition, as a police officer you must never contribute to disorder.

49. **(C)** Your job is to investigate anything unusual along your beat and to deal with threats to persons or property.

50. **(B)** Remain in the police role. A police officer is a police officer, not a paramedic.

Send for professional assistance and leave medical decisions to medical personnel.

51. **(D)** This is a true common-sense question. An inquiry over the supermarket's public address system is most likely to produce a parent who had not yet missed the child. If not, proceed with other actions.

52. **(D)** Again common sense. The mother is most likely to return to the spot at which she became separated from the youngster.

53. **(D)** If you do not really know the answer to this question, you can reach it by a process of elimination. (A) is incorrect because a medical problem cannot be ignored; (B) is incorrect because the person must be informed of the reason for arrest; (C) is incorrect because the person is certainly allowed to speak and to express feelings. (D) is your best choice. While all suicide threats must be taken seriously, the person newly taken into custody may well be blustering. Suicide in custody is a serious problem. The silent, brooding, distressed prisoner must be carefully watched.

54. **(A)** Note the word *least*. Arresting the leaders who have not been involved in criminal activity would be illegal and foolhardy. Gang members are very loyal to their own, and you could start a riot. All the other choices represent potentially positive steps.

55. **(C)** The police officer is the department's representative to the public. The officer should be as helpful as possible without neglecting assigned duties.

56. **(C)** Your first consideration is public safety. You are outnumbered by armed men who are desperate to escape. If you shout, they are likely to shoot, thereby endangering bystanders in the intervening 75 feet. Do your best to identify the men so that officers better positioned to apprehend them can be alerted by alarm.

57. **(C)** Police presence is often sufficient to discourage prohibited activity. The police officer should always attempt to accomplish his or her purpose with the least aggressive action.

58. **(D)** The woman is upset, but you must not act too hastily. Ascertain that the husband is really missing before you spend time getting a description and searching for the man.

59. **(A)** Even in this age of AIDS, the officer must be *least* concerned with diseases the suspect may carry. The officer must be more concerned with the possibility that the suspect will use a gun or physical force to resist arrest or that he or she will try to flee.

60. **(C)** Of course, a person may be having mail directed to an address from which he or she has recently moved or even where he or she has never lived; however, it is most likely that mail delivered to an address is meant for persons who reside there. Of the choices, this is clearly the best.

61. **(C)** Your superiors have the advantage of years of training and experience. Their judgment is quicker, and they must be obeyed without question at the site of an emergency.

62. **(D)** You are likely to see this type of question more than once. You *must* know what you are to do. If you do not understand, ask.

63. **(D)** Of course there are experts trying to improve the police system, so you should not rush to present every idea. On the other hand, as an active police officer you are in daily contact with the special demands of your work. If you have a good idea, consider it carefully, then present it to your superiors.

64. **(D)** Public relations is important, and a little tact can work wonders. You can be polite and noncommital and satisfy the complainant.

65. **(D)** Obviously, the police emergency telephone lines must be kept open to receive emergency calls. Further, the less time spent talking, the sooner there will be action.

66. **(C)** The police role is to perform police work. The police officer is not a lawyer and is not expected to understand the fine points of preparation of legal documents. An assistant district attorney is equipped to give proper legal advice.

67. **(A)** An introductory statement describing the occurrence establishes the framework on which to hang details and conclusions.

68. **(D)** Both common sense and proper police practice require that a police officer's post be covered at all times. In answering questions on a civil service exam, personal gain is *never* the correct answer.

69. **(A)** A police officer must adhere to rules and regulations and so cannot provide a prohibited service. On the other hand, it is easy to be polite and caring. Explain to the manager the reason for your refusal.

70. **(C)** The police badge is an identifying emblem. The police officer who serves as a witness must be identified as such.

71. **(D)** To answer this question, read through the choices and find which one constitutes a rule. Obviously that is the one which will appear in printed departmental rules.

72. **(C)** Obviously, an order which concerns police activity on New Year's Eve will be fulfilled on New Year's Eve.

73. **(A)** Two conflicting orders cannot remain in effect at the same time. If a new order is issued and conflicts with a previously issued order, the previous order is thereby rescinded.

74. **(B)** Read carefully. The question asks about printed department rules and regulations. You can eliminate choices (A) and (D). Regulations may include standards for condition of the uniform but not instructions for its care. Rules for arrest procedure belong in the printed regulations.

75. **(B)** Pure common sense. Overcrowding leads to friction. Furthermore, convicts in constant close proximity have more opportunity to plan trouble together.

76. **(C)** A police officer must never bow to political pressure nor give the appearance of doing so. The officer must politely but firmly insist upon obedience to the law.

77. **(D)** A police officer must be polite and helpful.

78. **(B)** It is true that the officer's name and shield number will appear on the summons,

but there is no harm in giving these to the motorist. Professional behavior requires that the summons be given without further discussion.

79. **(C)** Since there is not much danger of traffic accidents caused by the malfunctioning light at this hour, report the matter immediately to allow maximum opportunity for the light's repair before morning traffic. Then post a temporary sign to alert traffic until the light is repaired. If the light cannot be repaired in time, your prompt report to the precinct allows time for a special officer to be assigned to direct traffic in the morning.

80. **(C)** A police officer must make quick judgments on the job. The assigned post must be covered; yet emeregencies must be dealt with. Snarled traffic could have waited the brief time it would have taken for Officer Y to contact his precinct.

81. **(A)** You do not need to have had training in investigation of traffic accidents to recognize from the diagram that car 2 is too far beyond the center of the intersection to have been attempting a left turn. Driver 1 is trying to cover himself with a false statement about driver 2.

82. **(C)** You have a radio. Use it. The alleged robbers should be pursued promptly and safely.

83. **(D)** The vast majority of people wish to be law-abiding citizens. A summons must be issued for a major offense, even if it is a first offense, but a courteous warning may be sufficient for a minor offense that the operator may not even have recognized as an offense.

84. **(B)** The police officer directing traffic at a congested intersection must be visible, must use simply understood signals, and must consistently use the same signals. It is *least* important that the officer be physically accessible to motorists or to pedestrians.

85. **(C)** Access to the area of an accident should be limited to those who are attending to the injured. Beyond lifesaving, the first priority is to preserve evidence. Inconvenience to the public is a later consideration.

86. **(C)** The police role at the scene of a property-damage accident is to be certain that both drivers are licensed drivers and are authorized to drive the vehicles, that the automobiles are safe to operate on the public roadway, and that information has been obtained for police files as to those involved in the accident and witnesses. It is not the role of the police officer to be concerned with the parties' arrangements to collect damages from one another.

87. **(A)** A hit-and-run driver must be pursued and apprehended as quickly as possible. The efficient way to intercept the hit-and-run car is to radio a description of the car to precinct headquarters for instant broadcast to patrol cars in the vicinity.

88. **(D)** The accepted answer is that eradication of the cause of crime should be the most effective means of crime prevention.

89. **(C)** There is no question that fewer crimes are committed in locations with high visibility. A safe in a well-lighted place is more secure from tampering than one in a dark place. It is permissible and advisable to give this type of general safety advice to businesspeople. On the other hand, were a businessperson to ask for advice about the best kind of safe, the police officer would have to decline. A police officer cannot recommend products or merchants.

90. **(C)** The person with an unconscious wish to be punished, also known as a "death wish," will draw attention to him- or herself with respect to the crime. Revisiting the crime scene is a common means of doing this. The other choices represent efforts to avoid detection and punishment.

91. **(A)** Read carefully. *The least accurate* format of the question makes it tricky to answer. Choices (B), (C), and (D) make correct, positive statements. Choice (A) makes a wrong statement. The value of fingerprints left at the scene of the crime *does* vary with the distinctness of the fingerprint impressions. Clearer fingerprints are more valuable.

92. **(A)** In general, the fewer people who handle a piece of evidence, the fewer things can go wrong. Personal delivery of the evidence

makes for less hearsay. Choice (C) is incorrect because of the strong word "ensures." Evidence can still be mismarked even with personal delivery and initially correct information.

93. **(B)** The description that focuses on the unique character of a missing item is most useful for search and recovery.

94. **(D)** Descriptions (B) and (C) are of no use whatsoever. Watching people leave a ball game, you have no way of knowing who is missing a toe nor who has false teeth. Choice (A) describes a very typical young girl. Choice (D) is a big man who stands out in a crowd, and his pockmarked face is further visible identification

95. **(C)** Common sense. How many 6'1" women do you see roaming the streets?

96. **(D)** As the car is coming towards you, the most useful information is that the front bumper is missing. A bullet hole would be too small to see in a moving car on a busy highway.

97. **(A)** A 5'3" man weighing 200 lbs. is obese. He should be relatively easy to spot if you are alerted to watch for him. All these identification judgment questions are meant to test your judgment as to what you would report if other officers were to search on the basis of your descriptions.

98. **(D)** A Social Security card is not acceptable proof of identification for any purpose because it does not identify. The Social Security card contains no picture nor descriptive text of any sort.

99. **(B)** One picture may be worth a thousand words, but a good look at the person in the flesh leads to greater ease and accuracy of identification than studying photographs.

100. **(B)** Common sense. There are a great number of black cars. Spare tire or lack thereof and tire size are ridiculous characteristics by which to attempt to identify a vehicle in a busy intersection. Make, body style, and year give you something definite to go by.

101. **(D)** The key is that the woman is sick or injured and needs medical attention. The first step is to get her to the hospital. Identification is secondary.

102. **(D)** Surgery would be most successful. Few criminals resort to surgery to avoid identification because of the time and pain involved and the need to find a competent person to perform the operation confidentially.

103. **(A)** Identification from a lineup is more reliable. The witness cannot simply say "yes" or "no."

104. **(C)** Citizens have rights that may not be abridged unless they commit some infraction. Suspicious actions are no grounds for arrest, alarm, or embarrassment of the person. The police officer who considers behavior suspicious is, in effect, facing an unusual situation on the post. Continued observation is called for.

105. **(A)** An open handbag is a danger to the woman's property. By all means, bring the open handbag to the woman's attention.

106. **(C)** You want the personal recollection of each individual witness, not the consensus of a committee.

107. **(B)** Questions should be of the open sort, such as "Was the mugger wearing an outer garment?" Giving an either-or choice limits the answer and may miss important descriptive information.

108. **(C)** The speed at which an automobile was traveling when it hit a victim may affect the extent of damage to the vehicle, but it is the *least* valuable information from among the choices. The direction in which the automobile fled can direct the chase; the number of occupants helps with identification; the part of the automobile that struck the victim may be distinctively damaged.

109. **(C)** Markings on a bullet left by a gun barrel serve the same purpose as fingerprints. Since they are unique, they effectively identify the gun from which the bullet was fired.

110. **(B)** Common sense. Read the newspapers for confirmation.

111. **(B)** You need proper depth vision to shoot accurately. Depth vision is achieved with both eyes open.

112. **(A)** Of course, there are police regulations concerning the firing of guns. Common

sense dictates that the officer has a pistol to use if necessary, but that there must be a very good reason to use that gun.

113. **(D)** A person who is in the physical process of committing a crime is fully aware of that fact. When arresting such person, it is unnecessary to tell the person that he or she is being arrested because he or she is in the process of committing a crime.

114. **(B)** The woman's intact, scarless face must certainly lead the police officer to question her story. The correct answer choice is generous in giving the benefit of some credence to the woman. The situation bears investigation for the sake of the woman who might likely require psychiatric attention.

115. **(C)** Our Constitution protects the rights of the individual. A police officer must learn to recognize reasonable basis for arrest so as to protect the rights of the innocent while taking into custody those who, on the basis of evidence, appear to be guilty.

116. **(A)** Professionalism requires that a police officer not allow personal prejudices nor emotions to interfere with the manner in which he or she performs duties. In giving the reason for arrest, the officer must state the facts without commentary.

117. **(C)** Much of the work of a police officer falls into the realm of public relations. The officer must be patient and tactful in explaining action or inaction on the specific complaint.

118. **(B)** The civil rights of the innocent citizen must be protected. The possibility of personal embarrassment or embarrassment of the police force are not the paramount considerations.

119. **(C)** The number one priority is the safety of the general public.

120. **(A)** This is not an attitude question; it is an action question. Situations vary greatly. Procedures differ on the basis of circumstances such as: Is the suspect armed? Is the suspect injured and in need of immediate medical attention? Is the suspect in the midst of a crowd? Does the suspect hold hostages? Is the suspect at home in bed?

121. **(D)** Do not read extra meaning into a straightforward question. The young man was acting suspiciously, and the officer correctly investigated his suspicious behavior. The fact that the man had indeed committed a crime confirms that investigation of suspicious incidents is worthwhile and may produce results.

122. **(A)** Where a police officer is positive of his or her identification and where immediate arrest threatens no danger, he or she should inform the suspect of the reason for the arrest and should take the suspect into custody.

123. **(A)** Once again, professionalism is the key to the answer. The police officer must not let any personal feelings intrude upon performance of duties.

124. **(A)** The ultimate purpose of a raid upon a premises, with legal search warrant already in hand, is to secure evidence that leads to the apprehension of criminals or to apprehend the criminals themselves.

125. **(B)** Eliminate choice (A). The burglars know there is nothing more to steal in that house. Eliminate choice (C). Burglars tend to hit houses that look as if the takings would be more worthwhile. Eliminate choice (D). This house is never unoccupied so would be difficult to burglarize. Chances are that the party that calls the house in choice (B) and hangs up when the phone is answered is waiting for a time when the phone is not answered and the house is presumably unattended as an opportunity to burglarize.

126. **(B)** The police officer must continue to observe the young girl but cannot apprehend her until she signals intent to steal the merchandise by leaving the store without paying. Merely carrying merchandise around in the store is not a prohibited activity.

127. **(C)** You must not jump to conclusions. The fact that Jones was present at the time and place of the assault does not mean that he actually committed the assault. On the other hand, the possibility cannot be ruled out, since he was there. If it had been proven that Jones had been elsewhere at the time of the assault, then it could have been

positively stated that Jones did not assault Smith.

128. **(D)** From this fact statement, we know only that the lawyer was attacked from behind in a washroom by a male who had access to the washroom and to a carpenter's mallet. No conclusions can be drawn.

129. **(D)** The only way to ascertain identity is to know who the person is.

130. **(A)** The officer's immediate sending for an ambulance is correct. However, once the injured is medically cared for, the officer's next responsibility is to learn what happened. Among the bystanders, a witness or several witnesses may be able to describe the circumstances of the stabbing and possibly to identify or at least to describe the assailant.

131. **(B)** Green must prove that he did not steal the radio. One-and-one-half hours is ample time to fence a radio, so nonpossession is not automatic proof of innocence.

132. **(A)** Note that the question merely suggests the given facts as a basis for first action, not that Jones should be assumed guilty. Much police investigative work is based upon reasonable assumptions.

133. **(D)** The length of time that the resident waited before reporting the theft of the ring is totally irrelevant. All the other questions are valid ones.

134. **(D)** If burglary was physically impossible at this site and time, then, from among the choices, we must assume that the crime of burglary did not occur and that the report is a false one. Beyond the scope of the question, an investigator might reasonably suspect an internal theft with the claim of burglary as coverup.

135. **(D)** Since the question has to do with protection of property, the police officer is within the scope of the police role to make a suggestion. The suggestion, without reference to a specific bank or payroll service, is entirely proper.

136. **(A)** The thief who is already inside the premises to be burglarized avoids the risk of attracting attention by the act of forcing entrance.

137. **(C)** Thieves are likely to be careful with items of value but to pay less attention to articles they consider worthless. This carelessness combined with care taken by police officers can lead to apprehension of the thieves.

138. **(A)** Immediate confrontation will ascertain that the watch was indeed taken from the given jewelry store. If, by chance, the man was authorized to take the watch (if, for example it had been repaired for him), then the matter will be readily clarified. If the police officer has indeed observed the man in the process of stealing the watch, this prompt action will make for a neat case.

139. **(B)** A police officer must investigate unusual occurrences. The sound of clashing tools at 2 A.M. is certainly worth investigating, especially in an apartment next door to one in which there had just been a burglary.

140. **(D)** You can't catch the robbers yourself; they have already gone too far. On the other hand, you must not allow them to exit the parkway while you are questioning the victim. Radio to have the exits monitored. A limited access parkway offers possibilities for interception of thieves that are absent on city streets.

141. **(D)** The only immediate assumption is that the murderer had access to shoemaker's tools. This is a useful piece of knowledge. If no shoe repair shop has reported a theft, the field of suspects can be reasonably narrowed.

142. **(C)** Common sense. For the knife to be protruding from his back, the man is unlikely to be lying on his back.

143. **(A)** Read carefully. The question describes a suicide, thereby eliminating choices (C) and (D). A body slumped in a chair is not consistent with hanging.

144. **(B)** The man is dead; there is nothing you can do for him now. On the other hand, there is a body on the ground. Phone your precinct at once. Investigation of circumstances of death will follow.

145. **(A)** The pawn tickets serve as a very good clue. A man in the fur business should sell furs, not pawn them. Obviously, this man

was in deep financial trouble. The lapsed insurance policy is further indication of desperation. No businessman willingly allows insurance of property or self (the question does not specify which) to lapse.

146. **(B)** The blood on the door bears investigation. It was likely left by the murderer at exit.

147. **(D)** Unfortunately, observation is often incomplete and memory may fill in the gaps or even distort the facts.

148. **(A)** The first question to be raised is the amount of time taken to travel from Jones' place of work to his home. If it is determined that it does indeed take longer than one half hour, then Jones must supply proof that he really was working at 8 P.M. If the distance can be covered in less than a half hour, whether or not Jones was really working at 8 P.M. is irrelevant.

149. **(A)** This is an unusual situation that bears investigation. Admission to a private mental hospital is not an emergency situation, especially since the alleged patient will be under observation at the station house, so by all means bring the whole party in for questioning.

150. **(C)** With these facts, the only certainty is that further investigation is warranted on an urgent basis.

151. **(C)** Bad environmental conditions—poverty, poor housing, lack of opportunity, immoral companions—combine to create criminals.

152. **(D)** It is generally assumed that the best deterrent to crime is the expectation that one will be caught and swiftly punished.

153. **(C)** A person who is normal in intelligence but is below grade level in school is educationally maladjusted. The fact that 86 percent of delinquents appear to be normally intelligent but below grade level points to a close association of educational maladjustment with delinquency. With this information, we can describe a correlation but not a causal relationship. The data do not indicate that educational maladjustment causes delinquency nor that delinquency leads to educational maladjustment, only that they are related.

154. **(B)** Unfortunately, the boys who might be most helped by boys' clubs do not join.

155. **(C)** A man who has responded to a prostitute is unlikely to cooperate with the police, but a man who has spurned her advances will probably answer your questions. Both the girl and one or two men should be questioned, for the girl will undoubtedly deny that she is soliciting. Indeed, it may be that she is not, and, if police officers approach her, she may ask for needed instructions or assistance. You must not assume guilt without first investigating.

156. **(B)** The expectation and hope is that minors are not incorrigible; that is, their behavior can be corrected and improved. If this can be accomplished without arrest, so much the better.

157. **(C)** The most important information when seeking a hit-and-run vehicle is the appearance of the car. Of the choices, "What kind of car was it?" is by far the most useful.

158. **(C)** One of the last things a runaway is likely to do is to enroll in a school. Therefore, knowledge of her scholastic abilities would not be very helpful in the search for the girl. Detailed description of her features would be most helpful.

159. **(A)** The officer cannot be certain that the woman has not eaten some grapes; therefore, no determination can be made on the basis of the bag she presents. The officer must buy his own fruit to check the weights.

160. **(C)** The label of the well-known manufacturer is found in many violins. It does not distinguish this violin from many other violins. All the other choices would help in making a positive identification.

161. **(D)** This is a probe of your prejudices. Looks tell nothing about intelligence, personality, or character.

162. **(B)** For the deceased to have committed suicide with the bullet lodged as indicated, the shot would have had to come from a revolver in his left hand. The revolver is in his right hand.

163. **(D)** It is most unlikely that a lighted delicatessen is left unattended late at night. The officer should confirm suspicions further by

entering the delicatessen to search for foul play with reference to the proprietor or employees.

164. **(A)** Loitering just before theater deposits are about to be made could be either a coincidence or a plan for robbery. People do loiter around theaters waiting for others or just passing the time away. You must be prepared, but you can take no action unless some crime is committed. The best action is to keep the men under observation until the money has been safely deposited.

165. **(A)** This is unintelligent handling of evidence. Fingerprints and ballistics evidence may be destroyed. It would be wise to close off the booth to the public so as to safeguard possible clues such as match covers, bits of paper with notes on them, and fingerprints on drinking glasses.

166. **(B)** Comparison of engine numbers is usually the determining factor in establishing whether or not a car is indeed the stolen one in question. Engine numbers are changed only with great difficulty; it is most unlikely that this would be accomplished in one day. This 1978 Dodge is probably not the car that was reported stolen. License plates and tires are easily changed and cannot serve as positive identification of stolen cars. A stolen car can easily acquire a cracked windshield.

167. **(C)** Statistical studies show that crimes against property reach a maximum in winter months when human needs are greatest. During winter months, crimes such as larceny, burglary, and robbery show a decided increase for the further reason that longer periods of darkness reduce probability of

detection. Crimes against persons and morals (assaults, rapes, homicides, etc.) show an increase during the warm months when the contacts between persons are more frequent.

168. **(A)** The very subject matter of the blackmail is precisely the reason the victim is unlikely to cooperate with the police. The victim of a blackmail plot usually has some secret that he or she does not wish to reveal to the public by way of the police. It may concern some event, scandalous or otherwise, which occurred in the past and which if revealed may hold him or her up to public ridicule. Because of this, victims are reluctant to cooperate with the police in the prosecution of blackmailers.

169. **(D)** This is a situation in which individual interests must be subverted for the common good. The individual family wants its kidnapped member back at any price. However, allowing kidnappers to profit from kidnapping encourages other kidnappers. The principle is the same as the principle of not negotiating with terrorists. Wrongdoers must not achieve their goals through their wrongdoing. Hopefully, prospective kidnappers who know that they will fail in their attempt to collect ransom will be discouraged from kidnapping.

170. **(A)** As strange as it may seem, intent to defraud the insurer may not always be manifested by increasing insurance just before have the commission of the crime. There have been many instances in which the insurance was deliberately reduced in order to divert suspicion.

READING-BASED QUESTIONS

A recent survey of police officer examinations given nationwide indicates that there is wide variation in the subject matter of these exams. The single topic that is common to all exams is reading. Some exams include classic reading comprehension questions that present a passage and then ask questions on the details of the passage and, perhaps, on its meaning. Other exams require candidates to indicate proper behavior based on their reading of printed procedures and regulations. Still another type of reading-based question requires candidates to reason and choose next steps on the basis of information presented in a reading passage. There are, of course, nearly as many variations of the reading-based question as there are testmakers. In fact, reading skill enters into form-completion questions, arithmetic problems based on fact situations, and police judgment questions as well.

Before you begin to devote attention to strategies for dealing with reading-based questions, give some thought to your reading habits and skills. Of course, you already know how to read. But how well do you read? Do you concentrate? Do you get the point on your first reading? Do you notice details?

Between now and the test day, you must work to improve your reading concentration and comprehension. Your daily newspaper provides excellent material to improve your reading. Make a point of reading all the way through any article that you begin. Do not be satisfied with the first paragraph or two. Read with a pencil in hand. Underscore details and ideas that seem to be crucial to the meaning of the article. Notice points of view, arguments, and supporting information. When you have finished the article, summarize it for yourself. Do you know the purpose of the article? The main idea presented? The attitude of the writer? The points over which there is controversy? Did you find certain information lacking? As you answer these questions, skim back over your underlinings. Did you focus on important words and ideas? Did you read with comprehension? As you repeat this process day after day, you will find that your reading will become more efficient. You will read with greater understanding, and will get more from your newspaper.

One aspect of your daily reading that deserves special attention is vocabulary building. The effective reader has a rich, extensive vocabulary. As you read, make a list of unfamiliar words. Include in your list words that you understand within the context of the article, but that you cannot really define. In addition, mark words that you do not understand at all. When you put aside your newspaper, go to the dictionary and look up *every* new and unfamiliar word. Write the word and its definition in a special notebook. Writing the words and their definitions helps seal them in your memory far better than just reading them, and the notebook serves as a handy reference for your own use. A sensitivity to the meanings of words and an understanding of more words will make reading easier and more enjoyable even if none of the words you learn in this way crops up on your exam. In fact, the habit of vocabulary building is a good lifetime habit to develop.

Success with reading questions depends on more than reading comprehension. You must also know how to draw the answers from the reading selection, and be able to distinguish the *best* answer from a number of answers that all seem to be good ones, or from a number of answers that all seem to be wrong.

Strange as it may seem, it's a good idea to approach reading comprehension questions by reading the questions—not the answer choices, just the questions themselves—before you read the selection. The questions will alert you to look for certain details, ideas, and points of view. Use your pencil. Underscore key words in the questions. These will help direct your attention as you read.

Next skim the selection very rapidly to get an idea of its subject matter and its organization. If key words or ideas pop out at you, underline them, but do not consciously search out details in the preliminary skimming.

Now read the selection carefully with comprehension as your main goal. Underscore the important words as you have been doing in your newspaper reading.

Finally, return to the questions. Read each question carefully. Be sure you know what it asks. Misreading of questions is a major cause of error on reading comprehension tests. Read *all* the answer choices. Eliminate the obviously incorrect answers. You may be left with only one possible answer. If you find yourself with more than one possible answer, reread the question. Then skim the passage once more, focusing on the underlined segments. By now you should be able to conclude which answer is *best*.

Reading-based questions may take a number of different forms. In general, some of the most common forms are as follows:

1. **Question of fact or detail**. You may have to mentally rephrase or rearrange, but you should find the answer stated in the body of the selection.

2. **Best title or main idea**. The answer may be obvious, but the incorrect choices to the "main idea" question are often half-truths that are easily confused with the main idea. They may misstate the idea, omit part of the idea, or even offer a supporting idea quoted directly from the text. The correct answer is the one that covers the largest part of the selection.

3. **Interpretation**. This type of question asks you what the selection means, not just what it says. On police exams, the questions based upon definitions of crimes, for example, fall into this category.

4. **Inference.** This is the most difficult type of reading comprehension question. It asks you to go beyond what the selection says, and to predict what might happen next. You might have to choose the best course of action to take, based upon given procedures and a fact situation, or you may have to judge the actions of others. Your answer must be based upon the information in the selection and your own common sense, but not upon any other information you may have about the subject. A variation of the interference question might be stated as, "The author would expect that...." To answer this question, you must understand the author's point of view, and then make an inference from that viewpoint based upon the information in the selection.

5. **Vocabulary**. Some police reading sections, directly or indirectly, ask the meanings of certain words as used in the selection.

Let's now work together on some typical reading comprehension selections and questions.

Selection for Questions 1 to 4

The recipient gains an impression of a typewritten letter before beginning to read the message. Factors that give a good first impression include margins and spacing that are visually pleasing, formal parts of the letter that are correctly placed according to the style of the letter, copy that is free of obvious erasures and overstrikes, and transcript that is even and clear. The problem for the typist is how to produce that first, positive impression of her work.

There are several general rules that a typist can follow when she wishes to prepare a properly spaced letter on a sheet of letterhead. The width of a letter should ordinarily not be less than four inches, nor more than six inches. The side margins should also have a proportionate relation to the bottom margin, as well as the space between the letterhead and the body of the letter. Usually the most appealing arrangement is when the side margins are even, and the bottom margin is slightly wider than the side margins. In some offices, however, a standard line length is used for all business letters, and the secretary then varies the spacing between the date line and the inside address according to the length of the letter.

1. The best title for the preceding paragraph is   **1.** Ⓐ Ⓑ Ⓒ Ⓓ
- (A) Writing Office Letters
- (B) Making Good First Impressions
- (C) Judging Well-Typed Letters
- (D) Good Placing and Spacing for Office Letters

2. According to the preceding paragraphs, which of the following might   **2.** Ⓐ Ⓑ Ⓒ Ⓓ
be considered the way that people quickly judge the quality of work
that has been typed?
- (A) by measuring the margins to see if they are correct
- (B) by looking at the spacing and cleanliness of the typescript
- (C) by scanning the body of the letter for meaning
- (D) by reading the date line and address for errors

3. According to the preceding paragraphs, what would be definitely   **3.** Ⓐ Ⓑ Ⓒ Ⓓ
undesirable as the average line length of a typed letter?
- (A) 4″
- (B) 5″
- (C) 6″
- (D) 7″

4. According to the preceding paragraphs, when the line length is kept   **4.** Ⓐ Ⓑ Ⓒ Ⓓ
standard, the secretary
- (A) does not have to vary the spacing at all because this also is standard
- (B) adjusts the spacing between the date line and inside address for different lengths of letters
- (C) uses the longest line as a guideline for spacing between the date line and inside address
- (D) varies the number of spaces between the lines

Begin by skimming the questions and underscoring key words. Your underscored questions should look more or less like this:

1. What is the best title for the preceding paragraphs?
2. According to the preceding paragraphs, which of the following might be considered the way that people quickly judge the quality of work that has been typed?
3. According to the preceding paragraphs, what would be definitely undesirable as the average line length of a typed letter?
4. According to the preceding paragraphs, when the line length is kept standard, the secretary does what?

Now skim the selection. This quick reading should give you an idea of the structure of the selection and of its overall meaning.

Next read the selection carefully and underscore words that seem important or that you think hold keys to the question answers. Your underscored selection should look something like this:

The recipient gains an impression of a typewritten letter before he begins to read the message. Factors that give a good first impression include margins and spacing that are visually pleasing, formal parts of the letter that are correctly placed according to the style of the letter, copy that is free of obvious erasures and overstrikes, and transcript that is even and clear. The problem for the typist is how to produce that first, positive impression of her work.

There are several general rules that a typist can follow when she wishes to prepare a properly spaced letter on a sheet of letterhead. The width of a letter should ordinarily not be less than four inches, nor more than six inches. The side margins should also have a proportionate relation to the bottom margin as well as the space between the letterhead and the body of the letter. Usually the most appealing arrangement is when the side margins are even, and the bottom margin is slightly wider than the side margins. In some offices, however, a standard line length is used for all business letters, and the secretary then varies the spacing between the date line and the inside address according to the length of the letter.

Finally, read the questions and answer choices, and try to choose the correct answer for each question.

The correct answers are: 1. (**D**), 2. (**B**), 3. (**D**), 4. (**B**). Did you get them all right? Whether you made any errors or not, read these explanations.

1. (**D**) The best title for any selection is the one that takes in all of the ideas presented without being too broad or too narrow. Choice (D) provides the most inclusive title for this passage. A look at the other choices shows you why. Choice (A) can be eliminated because the passage discusses typing a letter, not writing one. Although the first paragraph states that a letter should make a good first impression, the passage is clearly devoted to the letter, not the first impression, so choice (B) can be eliminated. Choice (C) puts the emphasis on the wrong aspect of the typewritten letter. The passage concerns how to type a properly spaced letter not how to judge one.

2. (**B**) Both spacing and cleanliness are mentioned in paragraph 1 as ways to judge the quality of a typed letter. The first paragraph states that the margins should be "visually pleasing" in relation to the body of the letter, but that does not imply margins of a particular measure, so choice (A) is incorrect. Meaning is not discussed in the passage, only the look of the finished letter, so choice (C) is incorrect. The passage makes no mention of errors, only the avoidance of erasures and overstrikes, so choice (D) is incorrect.

3. (**D**) This answer comes from the information provided in paragraph 2, that the width of a letter "should not be less than four inches nor more than six inches." According to this rule, seven inches is an undesirable line length.

4. (**B**) The answer to this question is stated in the last sentence of the reading passage. When a standard line length is used, the secretary "varies the spacing between the date line and the inside address according to the length of the letter." The passage offers no support for any other choice.

Let us try another together.

Selection for Questions 5 to 9

Cotton fabrics treated with the XYZ Process have features that make them far superior to any previously known flame-retardant-treated cotton fabrics. XYZ

Process treated fabrics endure repeated laundering and dry cleaning; are glow resistant as well as flame resistant; when exposed to flames or intense heat form tough, pliable, and protective chars; are inert physiologically to persons handling or exposed to the fabric; are only slightly heavier than untreated fabrics; and are susceptible to further wet and dry finishing treatments. In addition, the treated fabrics exhibit little or no adverse change in feel, texture, and appearance, and are shrink-, rot-, and mildew-resistant. The treatment reduces strength only slightly. Finished fabrics have "easy care" properties in that they are wrinkle resistant and dry rapidly.

5. It is most accurate to state that the author in the preceding selection presents   5. Ⓐ Ⓑ Ⓒ Ⓓ

   (A) facts but reaches no conclusion concerning the value of the process
   (B) a conclusion concerning the value of the process and facts to support that conclusion
   (C) a conclusion concerning the value of the process unsupported by facts
   (D) neither facts nor conclusions, but merely describes the process

6. Of the following articles, for which is the XYZ process most suitable?   6. Ⓐ Ⓑ Ⓒ Ⓓ

   (A) nylon stockings
   (B) woolen shirt
   (C) silk tie
   (D) cotton bedsheet

7. Of the following aspects of the XYZ process, which is *not* discussed in the preceding selection?   7. Ⓐ Ⓑ Ⓒ Ⓓ

   (A) costs
   (B) washability
   (C) wearability
   (D) the human body

8. The main reason for treating a fabric with the XYZ Process is to   8. Ⓐ Ⓑ Ⓒ Ⓓ

   (A) prepare the fabric for other wet and dry finishing treatment
   (B) render it shrink-, rot-, and mildew-resistant
   (C) increase its weight and strength
   (D) reduce the chance that it will catch fire

9. Which of the following would be considered a minor drawback of the XYZ process?   9. Ⓐ Ⓑ Ⓒ Ⓓ

   (A) it forms chars when exposed to flame
   (B) it makes fabrics mildew-resistant
   (C) it adds to the weight of fabrics
   (D) it is compatible with other finishing treatments

Skim the questions and underscore the words which you consider to be key. The questions should look something like this:

   5. It is most accurate to state that the author, in the preceding selection, <u>presents</u>
   6. Of the following articles, for which is the <u>XYZ process</u> <u>most suitable</u>?
   7. Of the following <u>aspects</u> of the XYZ process, which is *not* <u>discussed</u> in the preceding selection?
   8. The <u>main reason for treating</u> a fabric with the XYZ process is to
   9. Which of the following would be considered a <u>minor drawback</u> of the XYZ process?

Skim the reading selection. Get an idea of the subject matter of the selection and of how it is organized.

Now read the selection carefully and underscore the words which you think are especially important. This fact-filled selection might be underlined like this:

Cotton fabrics treated with the XYZ Process have features that make them far superior to any previously known flame-retardant-treated cotton fabrics. XYZ Process treated fabrics endure repeated laundering and dry cleaning; are glow resistant as well as flame resistant; when exposed to flames or intense heat form tough, pliable, and protective chars; are inert physiologically to persons handling or exposed to the fabric; are only slightly heavier than untreated fabrics; and are susceptible to further wet and dry finishing treatments. In addition, the treated fabrics exhibit little or no adverse change in feel, texture, and appearance, and are shrink-, rot-, and mildew-resistant. The treatment reduces strength only slightly. Finished fabrics have "easy care" properties in that they are wrinkle resistant and dry rapidly

Now read each question and all its answer choices, and try to choose the correct answer for each question.

The correct answers are: 5. (**B**), 6. (**D**), 7. (**A**), 8. (**D**), 9. (**C**). How did you do on these? Read the explanations.

5. (**B**) This is a combination main idea and interpretation question. If you cannot answer this question readily, reread the selection. The author clearly thinks that the XYZ process is terrific and says so in the first sentence. The rest of the selection presents a wealth of facts to support the initial claim.

6. (**D**) At first glance you might think that this is an inference question requiring you to make a judgement based upon the few drawbacks of the process. Closer reading, however, shows you that there is no contest for correct answer here. This is a simple question of fact. The XYZ Process is a treatment for cotton fabrics.

7. (**A**) Your underlinings should help you with this question of fact. Cost is not mentioned; all other aspects of the XYZ Process are. If you are having trouble finding mention of the effect of the XYZ Process on the human body, add to your vocabulary list "inert" and "physiologically."

8. (**D**) This is a main idea question. You must distinguish between the main idea and the supporting and incidental facts.

9. (**C**) Obviously a drawback is a negative feature. The selection mentions only two negative features. The treatment reduces strength slightly, and it makes fabrics slightly heavier than untreated fabrics. Only one of these negative features is offered among the answer choices.

You should be getting better at reading and at answering questions. Try this next selection on your own. Read and underline the questions. Skim the selection. Read and underline the selection. Read questions and answer choices and mark your answers. Then check your answers against the answers and explanations that follow the selection.

Selection for Questions 10 to 12

Language performs an essentially social function: It helps us get along together, communicate, and achieve a great measure of concerted action. Words are signs that have significance by convention, and those people who do not adopt the conventions simply fail to communicate. They do not "get along," and a social force arises that encourages them to achieve the correct associations. By "correct" we mean as used by other members of the social group. Some of the vital points about language are brought home to an English visitor to America, and vice versa, because our vocabularies are nearly the same—but not quite.

10. As defined in the preceding selection, usage of a word is "correct" when it is

    10. Ⓐ Ⓑ Ⓒ Ⓓ

    (A) defined in standard dictionaries
    (B) used by the majority of persons throughout the world who speak the same language
    (C) used by the majority of educated persons who speak the same language
    (D) used by other persons with whom we are associating

11. In the preceding selection, the author is concerned primarily with the

    11. Ⓐ Ⓑ Ⓒ Ⓓ

    (A) meaning of words
    (B) pronunciation of words
    (C) structure of sentences
    (D) origin and development of language

12. According to the preceding selection, the main language problem of an English visitor to America stems from the fact that an English person

    12. Ⓐ Ⓑ Ⓒ Ⓓ

    (A) uses some words that have different meanings for Americans
    (B) has different social values than the Americans
    (C) has had more exposure to non-English speaking persons than Americans have had
    (D) pronounces words differently than Americans do

The correct answers are: 10. (D), 11. (A), 12. (A).

10. (D) The answer to this question is stated in the next-to-last sentence of the selection.

11. (A) This main idea question is an easy one to answer. You should have readily eliminated all of the wrong choices.

12. (A) This is a question of fact. The phrasing of the question is quite different from the phrasing of the last sentence, but the meaning is the same. You may have found this reading selection more difficult to absorb than some of the others, but you should have had no difficulty answering this question by eliminating the wrong answers.

Now try this reading selection and its questions. Once more, explanations follow the correct answers. Follow the procedure you have learned, and be sure to read the explanations even if you have a perfect score.

Selection for Questions 13 to 18

Since almost every office has some contact with data-processed records, a Senior Stenographer should have some understanding of the basic operations of data processing. Data processing systems now handle about one third of all office paper work. On punched cards, magnetic tape, or on other mediums, data are recorded before being fed into the computer for processing. A machine such as the key punch is used to convert the data written on the source document into the coded symbols on punched cards or tapes. After data has been converted, it must be verified to guarantee absolute accuracy of conversion. In this manner data becomes a permanent record that can be read by electronic computers that compare, store, compute, and otherwise process data at high speeds.

One key person in a computer installation is a programmer, the man or woman who puts business and scientific problems into special symbolic languages that can be read by the computer. Jobs done by the computer range all the way from payroll operations to chemical process control, but most computer applications are directed toward management data. About half of the programmers employed by business come to their positions with college degrees; the remaining half are promoted to their positions, without regard to education, from within the organization on the basis of demonstrated ability.

13. Of the following, the best title for the preceding selection is   13. Ⓐ Ⓑ Ⓒ Ⓓ
   - (A) The Stenographer as Data Processer
   - (B) The Relation of Key Punching to Stenography
   - (C) Understanding Data Processing
   - (D) Permanent Office Records

14. According to the preceding selection, a Senior Stenographer should   14. Ⓐ Ⓑ Ⓒ Ⓓ
   understand the basic operations of data processing because
   - (A) almost every office today has contact with data processed records by computer
   - (B) any office worker may be asked to verify the accuracy of data
   - (C) most offices are involved in the production of permanent records
   - (D) data may be converted into computer language by typing on a key punch

15. According to the preceding selection, the data that the computer   15. Ⓐ Ⓑ Ⓒ Ⓓ
   understands is most often expressed
   - (A) as a scientific programming language
   - (B) as records or symbols punched on tape, cards, or other mediums
   - (C) as records on cards
   - (D) as records on tape

16. According to the preceding selection, computers are used most   16. Ⓐ Ⓑ Ⓒ Ⓓ
   often to handle
   - (A) management data
   - (B) problems of higher education
   - (C) the control of chemical processes
   - (D) payroll operations

17. Computer programming is taught in many colleges and business   17. Ⓐ Ⓑ Ⓒ Ⓓ
   schools. The preceding selection implies that programmers in
   industry
   - (A) must have professional training
   - (B) need professional training to advance
   - (C) must have at least a college education to do adequate programming tasks
   - (D) do not need college education to do programming work

18. According to the preceding selection, data to be processed by com-   18. Ⓐ Ⓑ Ⓒ Ⓓ
   puter should be
   - (A) recent
   - (B) complete
   - (C) basic
   - (D) verified

The correct answers are: 13. (**C**), 14. (**A**), 15. (**B**), 16. (**A**), 17. (**D**), 18. (**D**).

13. (**C**) Choosing the best title for this selection is not easy. Although the Senior Stenographer is mentioned in the first sentence, the selection is really not concerned with stenographers or with their relationship to key punching. Eliminate choices (A) and (B). Permanent office records are mentioned in the selection, but only along with other equally important uses for data processing. Eliminate choice (D). When in doubt, the most general title is usually correct.

14. (**A**) This is a question of fact. Any one of the answer choices could be correct, but the answer is given almost verbatim in the first sentence. Take advantage of answers that are handed to you in this way.

15. (**B**) This is a question of fact, but it is a tricky one. The program language is a symbolic language, not a scientific one. Reread carefully and eliminate choice (A). (B) includes more of the information in the selection than either (C) or (D), and so is the best answer.

16. (**A**) This is a question of fact. The answer is stated in the next to the last sentence.

17. (**D**) Remember that you are answering the questions on the basis of the information given in the selection. In spite of any information you may have to the contrary, the last sentence of the selection states that half the programmers employed in business achieved their positions by moving up from the ranks without regard to education.

18. (**D**) Judicious underlining proves very helpful to you in finding the correct answer to this question buried in the middle of the selection. Since any one of the answers might be correct, the way to deal with this question is to skim the underlined words in the selection, eliminate those that are not mentioned, and choose the appropriate answer.

On police exams, many reading passages will relate to legal definitions, laws, and police procedures. When reading these passages, you must pay special attention to details relating to exceptions, special preconditions, combinations of activities, choices of actions, and prescribed time sequences. Sometimes the printed procedure specifies that certain actions are to be taken only when there is a combination of factors such as that a person actually breaks a window *and* has a gun. At other times, the procedures give choices of action under certain circumstances. You must read carefully to determine if the passage requires a combination of factors or gives a choice, then make the appropriate judgment. And when a time sequence is specified, be certain to follow that sequence in the prescribed order.

The remaining selections in this chapter are based on police-type questions. Beyond requiring reading comprehension skills, they require the special police exam emphasis we have just discussed.

Selection for Questions 19 to 23

If we are to study crime in its widest social setting, we will find a variety of conduct that, although criminal in the legal sense, is not offensive to the moral conscience of a considerable number of persons. Traffic violations, for example, do not brand the offender as guilty of moral offense. In fact, the recipient of a traffic ticket is usually simply the subject of some good-natured joking by friends. Although there may be indignation among certain groups of citizens against gambling and liquor law violations, these activities are often tolerated, if not openly supported, by the more numerous residents of the community. Indeed, certain social and service clubs regularly conduct gambling games and lotteries for the purpose of raising funds. Some communities regard violations involving the sale of liquor with little concern in order to profit from increased license fees and taxes paid by dealers. The thousand and one forms of political graft and corruption which infest our urban centers only occasionally arouse public condemnation and official action.

19. According to the passage, all types of illegal conduct are   19. Ⓐ Ⓑ Ⓒ Ⓓ

   (A) condemned by all elements of the community
   (B) considered a moral offense, although some are tolerated by a few citizens
   (C) violations of the law, but some are acceptable to certain elements of the community
   (D) found in a social setting and therefore not punishable by law

20. According to the passage, traffic violations are generally considered by society to be   20. Ⓐ Ⓑ Ⓒ Ⓓ

   (A) crimes requiring the maximum penalty set by the law
   (B) more serious than violations of the liquor laws
   (C) offenses against the morals of the community
   (D) relatively minor offenses requiring minimum punishment

21. According to the passage, a lottery conducted for the purpose of raising funds for a church   21. Ⓐ Ⓑ Ⓒ Ⓓ

   (A) is considered a serious violation of the law
   (B) may be tolerated by a community that has laws against gambling
   (C) may be conducted under special laws demanded by the more numerous residents of a community
   (D) arouses indignation in most communities

22. On the basis of the passage, the most likely reaction in the community to a police raid on a gambling casino would be   22. Ⓐ Ⓑ Ⓒ Ⓓ

   (A) more an attitude of indifference than interest in the raid
   (B) general approval of the raid
   (C) condemnation of the raid by most people
   (D) demand for further action, since this raid is not sufficient to end gambling activities

23. Of the following, which best describes the central thought of this passage and would be most suitable as a title?   23. Ⓐ Ⓑ Ⓒ Ⓓ

   (A) Crime and the Police
   (B) Public Condemnation of Graft and Corruption
   (C) Gambling Is Not Always a Vicious Business
   (D) Public Attitude Toward Law Violations

The correct answers are: 19. (C), 20. (D), 21. (B), 22. (A), 23. (D).

19. (C) The words "although" and "occasionally," which pop up in this passage, are the clues to the answer. Although illegal conduct is, by definition, violation of law, much illegal conduct is not repulsive to many elements of the community. Choice (A) is a direct contradiction of the meaning of the passage as is choice (B). (D) is unsupported by the passage.

20. (D) The third sentence supports this answer. The fourth sentence directly contradicts choice (B) in its statement that gambling and liquor law violations may raise some indignation.

21. **(B)** The clear implication is that law-abiding citizens readily engage in gambling and lotteries for fund-raising purposes. Nothing is said about special laws enabling this activity, so (C) is not a correct choice.

22. **(A)** Since gambling is not considered a serious criminal activity by the bulk of the populace, a raid on a gambling establishment would meet with indifference rather than with either approval or disapproval.

23. **(D)** Choice (A) is too broad; the passage deals specifically with certain kinds of crime. (B) is opposite in thought to the content of the passage. (C) is too narrow since other crimes are discussed in addition to gambling.

Selection for Questions 24 to 26

The law enforcement agency is one of the most important agencies in the field of juvenile delinquency prevention. This is so, however, not because of the social work connected with this problem, for this is not a police matter, but because the officers are usually the first to come in contact with the delinquent. The manner of arrest and detention makes a deep impression on the delinquent and affects his or her lifelong attitude toward society and toward the law. The juvenile court is perhaps the most important agency in this work. Contrary to general opinion, however, it is not primarily concerned with putting children into correctional schools. The main purpose of the juvenile court is to save the child and to develop his or her emotional makeup so that he or she can grow up to be a decent and well-balanced citizen. The system of probation is the means by which the court seeks to accomplish these goals.

24. According to the passage, police work is an important part of a program to prevent juvenile delinquency because

    24. Ⓐ Ⓑ Ⓒ Ⓓ

    (A) social work is no longer considered important in juvenile delinquency prevention
    (B) police officers are the first to have contact with the delinquent
    (C) police officers jail the offender in order to be able to change his or her attitude toward society and the law
    (D) it is the first step in placing the delinquent in jail

25. According to the passage, the chief purpose of the juvenile court is to

    25. Ⓐ Ⓑ Ⓒ Ⓓ

    (A) punish the child for the offense
    (B) select a suitable correctional school for the delinquent
    (C) use available means to help the delinquent become a better person
    (D) provide psychiatric care for the delinquent

26. According to the passage, the juvenile court directs the development of a delinquent under its care chiefly by:

    26. Ⓐ Ⓑ Ⓒ Ⓓ

    (A) placing the child under probation
    (B) sending the child to a correctional school
    (C) keeping the delinquent in prison
    (D) returning the child to his or her home

The correct answers are: 24. **(B)**, 25. **(C)**, 26. **(A)**.

24. **(B)** The correct answer is stated in the second sentence: "...officers are usually the first to come in contact with the delinquent." The point with reference to social work

is not that social work is unimportant but that it is not a police matter. Choices (C) and (D) are in direct contradiction to the passage.

25. **(C)** The purpose of the juvenile court is to choose the best possible method to "save the child." The passage implies that punishment and reform school are not the methods of choice, that probation is preferred. While psychiatric care may be the correct method in some cases, it is not mentioned in the passage and is certainly not the best answer choice.

26. **(A)** Some questions are easier than others. Careful reading makes this answer obvious.

Selection for Question 27

When a person commits a traffic infraction, a Police Officer should:

1. Inform the violator of the offense committed.
2. Request the violator to show his or her driver's license, vehicle registration, and insurance identification card. Failure to produce this required material may result in additional tickets. (Taxis, buses, and other rented vehicles do not require insurance identification cards.)
3. Enter only one infraction on each ticket.
4. Use a separate ticket for each additional infraction.

27. Police Officer Herrmann has been assigned to curb traffic violations at the intersection of Main Street and Central Avenue. Officer Herrmann observes a taxi cab going through a red light at this intersection and signals the driver to pull over. The officer informs the cab driver of his violation and asks for the required material. The driver surrenders his license and registration to the officer. Police Officer Herrmann should

    27. Ⓐ Ⓑ Ⓒ Ⓓ

(A) issue the cab driver a ticket for the red light violation and issue him a separate ticket for not surrendering his insurance card
(B) issue the cab driver one ticket including both the red light violation and the absence of the insurance card
(C) issue the cab driver a ticket only for the red light violation
(D) issue the cab driver a ticket only for not having an insurance card

The correct answer is **(C)**.

27. **(C)** The taxi driver violated the law by going through a red light. Officer Herrmann correctly informed the driver of this infraction and must issue a ticket. If the violator had been driving a private automobile, Officer Herrmann would have had to issue a separate ticket for his not producing an insurance card (see rules 3 and 4). However, in this case, the exception applies. The exception is that taxis, along with buses and rented vehicles, do not need to have insurance identification cards. You have to read carefully to determine exactly which rule applies in this case.

Selection for Questions 28 to 29

Police Officers while on patrol may observe a recently vacated building that can create a safety hazard. In such situations, Police Officers should follow these procedures, in the order given:

1. Walk through the vacated building to determine if a safety hazard exists.
2. If a safety hazard exists, notify the supervisor on patrol.
3. Write an entry in the Activity Log.
4. Report the facts concerning the safety hazard in the vacant building to the Telephone Switchboard Operator.
5. Place barriers in front of the vacated building if directed by the Patrol Supervisor.

28. Police Officer Wolff notes that a building on his patrol route has recently been vacated. What action should Officer Wolff take next?

28. Ⓐ Ⓑ Ⓒ Ⓓ

(A) Report the safety hazard in the vacant building to the Telephone Switchboard Operator.
(B) Radio the supervisor on patrol.
(C) Make an entry in his Activity Log.
(D) Determine if there is a safety hazard.

29. Police Officer Furumoto has noticed a safety hazard in a vacant building. He first notified the supervisor on patrol and then made an entry in the Activity Log. He is about to place barriers in front of the building to safeguard the public. Officer Furumoto is acting

29. Ⓐ Ⓑ Ⓒ Ⓓ

(A) correctly. Public safety is the police officer's first duty.
(B) incorrectly. The Patrol Supervisor has not directed him to place barriers.
(C) incorrectly. He must first report the safety hazard to the Telephone Switchboard Operator.
(D) incorrectly. He should radio for additional police officers to assist him in protecting the public from this hazard.

The correct answers are: 28. **(D)**, 29. **(C)**.

28. **(D)** The introductory sentence says that a recently vacated building can create a safety hazard, not that it necessarily does so. Officer Wolff must enter the building and look around to determine whether or not there is indeed a safety hazard. Only if he decides that there is a hazard, should he proceed with notification and other actions.

29. **(C)** The procedure lists steps to be taken in the order given. While Officer Furumoto is justly concerned with public safety, the hazard in the vacant building hardly constitutes a pressing emergency. Having made the entry in the Log, his next act must be to notify the Telephone Switchboard Operator. Then he must await instructions from the Patrol Supervisor. The Supervisor may feel that the hazard does not warrant barricades.

Selection for Questions 30 to 31

Police Officer DiSisto has observed that there is a pattern to criminal activity in her sector. She has noticed that burglaries tend to occur on High Street while auto thefts occur on York Street. Most rapes take place on Chapel Street and most assaults on Whitney. The rapes occur between 10 P.M. and 4 A.M., auto thefts between midnight and 6 A.M., burglaries between 10 A.M. and 4 P.M., and assaults between 6 P.M. and 10 P.M. Auto thefts seem most common on Monday, Tuesday, and Thursday. Assaults occur most often on Friday, Saturday, and Sunday. Most rapes happen over the weekend and most burglaries on Monday, Wednesday, and Saturday.

30. Police Officer DiSisto would most likely be able to reduce the incidence of rape by concentrating her patrol on

30. Ⓐ Ⓑ Ⓒ Ⓓ

(A) York Street between midnight and 8 A.M.
(B) Chapel Street between 7 P.M. and 3 A.M.
(C) High Street between 2 A.M. and 10 P.M.
(D) Chapel Street between 4 P.M. and midnight

31. Auto theft has been a special problem in the precinct, and Police Officer DiSisto's supervisor has requested that she make a special effort to eliminate auto theft on her patrol. Officer DiSisto should request assignment to patrol on

31. Ⓐ Ⓑ Ⓒ Ⓓ

(A) Sunday through Thursday from 10 P.M. to 6 A.M.
(B) Friday through Wednesday from 3 A.M. to 11 A.M.
(C) Monday through Friday from 8 A.M. to 4 P.M.
(D) Wednesday through Sunday from 2 P.M. to 10 P.M.

The correct answers are: 30. **(B)**, 31. **(A)**.

30. **(B)** You must read for details and then use these details to reason. This type of question highlights the value of reading the questions before you read the paragraph. Question 30 deals with rape; question 31 with auto theft. In your initial reading of the paragraph, you will underscore details concerning rape and auto theft, ignoring information relating to burglary and assault. With your information thus narrowed, note that the rape area is Chapel Street. Eliminate choices (A) and (C). The rapes occur in the six-hour span from 10 P.M. to 4 A.M. Choice (B) covers five hours of this six-hour span while (D) covers only the two hours from 10 P.M. to midnight.

31. **(A)** Approach this question in the same way. Auto theft appears to be a mid-week event. Only choices (A) and (C) include the three target days of Monday, Tuesday, and Thursday. Auto thefts occur under cover of darkness making (C) a poor choice.

Selection to Question 32

Harassment occurs when a person annoys or alarms another person, but does not intend or cause physical injury.

Menacing occurs when a person threatens to cause serious physical injury to another person, but does not cause a serious physical injury.

Assault occurs when a person causes physical injury to another person.

32. On a foggy Friday night after work, a group of men met at the Jolly-O Tavern for a few beers. The conversation centered on the merits of the two local hockey teams, and Warren Wu stoutly defended his favorite team against that of Tomas Ramos. Ramos could stand just so much taunting. As he became more angry, Ramos told Wu that he had better "shut up" before he, Tomas Ramos, knocked Wu's block off. Wu continued to praise his team, whereupon Ramos gave him such a punch to the jaw that Wu's lip was split and a tooth was knocked out. Based on the definitions above, Ramos should be charged with

32. Ⓐ Ⓑ Ⓒ Ⓓ

(A) harassment, menacing, and assault
(B) menacing and assault
(C) assault
(D) no crime

The correct answer is (**C**).

32. (**C**) The fact of assault seems clear. Ramos caused physical injury to Wu. According to the definitions, assault is the only charge. Harassment requires that no injury be intended, but Ramos stated intent to harm Wu. Menacing requires that no injury be caused. These definitions are mutually exclusive. Only one can apply. Definitions of other crimes may allow for one definition to be included within another. Careful reading is the number one requirement.

Use the skills and techniques you have just developed to practice with the traditional-style reading comprehension questions in the following chapter. Then apply your new expertise to the exams in this book and to your Police Officer exam.

Before you begin the exercises, review this list of hints for scoring high on reading comprehension questions.

1. Read the questions and underline key words.

2. Skim the selection to get a general idea of the subject matter, the point that is being made, and the organization of the material.

3. Reread the selection giving attention to details and point of view. Underscore key words and phrases.

4. If the author has quoted material from another source, be sure that you understand the purpose of the quote. Does the author agree or disagree?

5. Carefully read each question or incomplete statement. Determine exactly what is being asked. Watch for negatives or all-inclusive words such as *always, never, all, only, every, absolutely, completely, none, entirely, no.*

6. Read all the answer choices. Eliminate those choices that are obviously incorrect. Reread the remaining choices and refer to the selection, if necessary, to determine the *best* answer.

7. Avoid inserting your own judgments into your answers. Even if you disagree with the author or even if you spot a factual error in the selection, you must answer on the basis of what is stated or implied in the selection.

8. Do not allow yourself to spend too much time on any one question. If looking back at the selection does not help you to find or figure out the answer, choose from among the answers remaining after you eliminate the obviously wrong answers, mark the question in the test booklet, and go on. If you have time at the end of the exam or exam portion, reread the selection and the question. Often a fresh look provides new insights.

PRACTICE WITH READING COMPREHENSION QUESTIONS

1. "The force reconciling and coordinating all human conflicts and directing people in the harmonious accomplishment of their work is the supervisor. To deal with people successfully, the first one a supervisor must learn to work with is him- or herself." According to the quotation, the most accurate of the following conclusions is:

   (A) Human conflicts are the result of harmonious accomplishment.
   (B) A supervisor should attempt to reconcile all the different views subordinates may have.
   (C) A supervisor who understands him- or herself is in a good position to deal with others successfully.
   (D) The reconciling force in human conflicts is the ability to deal with people successfully.

2. "Law must be stable and yet it cannot stand still," means most nearly that

   (A) law is a fixed body of subject matter
   (B) law must adapt itself to changing conditions
   (C) law is a poor substitute for justice
   (D) the true administration of justice is the firmest pillar of good government.

3. "The treatment to be given the offender cannot alter the fact of the offense; but we can take measures to reduce the chance of similar acts occurring in the future. We should banish the criminal, not in order to exact revenge nor directly to encourage reform, but to deter that person and others from further illegal attacks on society." According to the quotation, prisoners should be punished in order to

   (A) alter the nature of their offenses
   (B) banish them from society
   (C) deter them and others from similar illegal attacks on society
   (D) directly encourage reform.

4. "On the other hand, the treatment of prisoners on a basis of direct reform is foredoomed to failure. Neither honest persons nor criminals will tolerate a bald proposition from anyone to alter their characters or habits, least of all if we attempt to gain such a change by a system of coercion." According to this quotation, criminals

   (A) are incorrigible
   (B) are incapable of being coerced
   (C) are not likely to turn into law-abiding citizens
   (D) possess very firm characters.

5. "While much thought has been devoted to the question of how to build walls high enough to keep persons temporarily in prison, we have devoted very little attention to the treatment necessary to enable them to come out permanently cured, inclined to be friends rather than enemies of their law-abiding fellow citizens." According to this quotation, much thought has been devoted to the problem of prisons as

   (A) vengeful agencies
   (B) efficient custodial agencies
   (C) efficient sanatoria
   (D) places from which society's friends might issue.

6. "Community organization most often includes persons whose behavior is unconventional in relation to generally accepted social definition, if such persons wield substantial influence with the residents." The inference one can most validly draw from this statement is that

   (A) influential persons are often likely to be unconventional
   (B) the success of a community organization depends largely on the democratic processes employed by it
   (C) a gang leader may sometimes be an acceptable recruit for a community organization
   (D) the unconventional behavior of a local barkeeper may often become acceptable to the community.

7. "The safeguard of democracy is education. The education of youth during a limited period of more or less compulsory attendance at school does not suffice. The educative process is a lifelong one." The statement most consistent with this quotation is:

(A) The school is not the only institution that can contribute to the education of the population.

(B) All democratic peoples are educated.

(C) The entire population should be required to go to school throughout life.

(D) If compulsory education were not required, the educative process would be more effective.

8. "The police officer's art consists in applying and enforcing a multitude of laws and ordinances in such degree or proportion and in such manner that the greatest degree of social protection will be secured. The degree of enforcement and the method of application will vary with each neighborhood and community." According to this statement,

(A) each neighborhood or community must judge for itself to what extent the law is to be enforced

(B) a police officer should only enforce those laws that are designed to give the greatest degree of social protection

(C) the manner and intensity of law enforcement is not necessarily the same in all communities

(D) all laws and ordinances must be enforced in a community with the same degree of intensity.

9. "As a rule, police officers, through service and experience, are familiar with the duties and the methods and means required to perform them. Yet, left to themselves, their aggregate effort would disintegrate and the vital work of preserving the peace would never be accomplished." According to this statement, the most accurate of the following conclusions is:

(A) Police officers are sufficiently familiar with their duties as to need no supervision.

(B) Working together for a common purpose is not efficient without supervision.

(C) Police officers are familiar with the methods of performing their duties because of rules.

(D) Preserving the peace is so vital that it can never be said to be completed.

Answer questions 10 through 12 on the basis of the information given in the following passage.

Criminal science is largely the science of identification. Progress in this field has been marked and sometimes very spectacular because new techniques, instruments, and facts flow continuously from the scientists. But the crime laboratories are understaffed; trade secrets still prevail; and inaccurate conclusions are often the result. However, modern gadgets cannot substitute for the skilled intelligent investigator; he or she must be their master.

10. According to this passage, criminal science

(A) excludes the field of investigation

(B) is primarily interested in establishing identity

(C) is based on the equipment used in crime laboratories

(D) uses techniques different from those used in other sciences.

11. Advances in criminal science have been, according to the passage,

(A) extremely limited

(B) slow but steady

(C) unusually reliable

(D) outstanding.

12. A problem that has not been overcome completely in crime work is, according to the passage,

(A) unskilled investigators

(B) the expense of new equipment and techniques

(C) an insufficient number of personnel in crime laboratories

(D) inaccurate equipment used in laboratories.

13. "While the safe burglar can ply his or her trade the year round, the loft burglar has more seasonal activities, since only at certain periods of the year is a substantial amount of valuable merchandise stored in lofts." The generalization, which this statement best illustrates, is that

(A) nothing is ever completely safe from a thief
(B) there are safe burglars and loft burglars
(C) some types of burglarly are seasonal
(D) the safe burglar considers safecracking a trade.

Answer questions 14 through 17 on the basis of the information given in the following passage.

When a vehicle has been disabled in a tunnel, the officer on patrol in this zone shall press the emergency truck light button. In the fast lane, red lights will go on throughout the tunnel; in the slow lane, amber lights will go on throughout the tunnel. The yellow zone light will go on at each signal control station throughout the tunnel and will flash the number of the zone in which the stoppage has occurred. A red flashing pilot light will appear only at the signal control station at which the emergency truck button was pressed. The emergency garage will receive an audible and visual signal indicating the signal control station at which the emergency truck button was pressed. The garage officer shall acknowledge receipt of the signal by pressing the acknowledgement button. This will cause the pilot light at the operated signal control station in the tunnel to cease flashing and to remain steady. It is an answer to the officer at the operated signal control station that the emergency truck is responding to the call.

14. According to this passage, when the emergency truck light button is pressed,
(A) amber lights will go on in every lane throughout the tunnel
(B) emergency signal lights will go on only in the lane in which the disabled vehicle is located
(C) red lights will go on in the fast lane throughout the tunnel
(D) pilot lights at all signal control stations will turn amber.

15. According to this passage, the number of the zone in which the stoppage has occurred is flashed
(A) immediately after all the lights in the tunnel turn red
(B) by the yellow zone light at each signal control station
(C) by the emergency truck at the point of stoppage
(D) by the emergency garage

16. According to the passage, an officer near the disabled vehicle will know that the emergency tow truck is coming when
(A) the pilot light at the operated signal control station appears and flashes red
(B) an audible signal is heard in the tunnel
(C) the zone light at the operated signal control station turns red
(D) the pilot light at the operated signal control station becomes steady.

17. Under the system described in the passage, it would be correct to come to the conclusion that
(A) officers at all signal control stations are expected to acknowledge that they have received the stoppage signal
(B) officers at all signal control stations will know where the stoppage has occurred
(C) all traffic in both lanes of that side of the tunnel in which the stoppage has occurred must stop until the emergency truck has arrived
(D) there are two emergency garages, each able to respond to stoppages in traffic going in one particular direction.

Answer questions 18 through 20 on the basis of the information given in the following passage.

The use of a roadblock is simply an adaptation of the military practice of encirclement by the police. Successful operation of a roadblock plan depends almost entirely on the amount of advance study and planning given to such operations. A thorough and detailed examination of the roads and terrain under the jurisdiction of a given police agency should be made with the locations of the roadblocks pinpointed in advance. The first principle to be borne in mind in the location of each roadblock is the time element. Its location must be at a point beyond which the fugitive could not have possibly traveled in the time elapsed from the commission of the crime to the arrival of the officers at the roadblock.

18. According to the passage,
    (A) military operations have made extensive use of roadblocks
    (B) the military practice of encirclement is an adaptation of police use of roadblocks
    (C) the technique of encirclement has been widely used by military forces
    (D) a roadblock is generally more effective than encirclement.

19. According to the passage,
    (A) advance study and planning are of minor importance in the success of roadblock operations
    (B) a thorough and detailed examination of all roads within a radius of fifty miles should precede the determination of a roadblock location

    (C) consideration of terrain features is important in planning the location of roadblocks
    (D) a roadblock operation can seldom be successfully undertaken by a single police agency.

20. According to the passage,
    (A) the factor of time is the sole consideration in the location of a roadblock
    (B) the maximum speed possible in the method of escape is of major importance in roadblock location
    (C) the time the officers arrive at the site of a proposed roadblock is of little importance
    (D) a roadblock should be sited as close to the scene of the crime as the terrain will permit.

Answer questions 21 through 22 on the basis of the information given in the following passage.

A number of crimes, such as robbery, assault, rape, certain forms of theft, and burglary, are high visibility crimes in that it is apparent to all concerned that they are criminal acts prior to or at the time they are committed. In contrast to these, check forgeries, especially those committed by first offenders, have low visibility. There is little in the criminal act or in the interaction between the check passer and the person cashing the check to identify it as a crime. Closely related to this special quality of the forgery crime is the fact that, while it is formally defined and treated as a felonious or "infamous" crime, it is informally held by the legally untrained public to be a relatively harmless form of crime.

21. According to the passage, crimes of "high visibility"
    (A) are immediately recognized as crime by the victims
    (B) take place in public view
    (C) always involve violence or the threat of violence
    (D) are usually committed after dark.

22. According to the passage
    (A) the public regards check forgery as a minor crime
    (B) the law regards check forgery as a minor crime
    (C) the law distinguishes between check forgery and other forgery
    (D) it is easier to spot inexperienced check forgers than other criminals.

Answer questions 23 and 24 on the basis of the information given in the following passage.

The racketeer is primarily concerned with business affairs, legitimate or otherwise, and preferably those that are close to the margin of legitimacy. The racketeer gets the best opportunities from business organizations that meet the need of large sections of the public for goods or services that are defined as illegitimate by the same public, such as prostitution, gambling, illicit drugs, or liquor. In contrast to the thief, the racketeer and the establishments controlled deliver goods and services for money received.

23. It can be deduced from the passage that suppression of racketeers is difficult because

 (A) victims of racketeers are not guilty of violating the law
 (B) racketeers are generally engaged in fully legitimate enterprises
 (C) many people want services that are not obtainable through legitimate sources
 (D) laws prohibiting gambling and prostitution are unenforceable.

24. According to the passage, racketeering, unlike theft, involves

 (A) objects of value
 (B) payment for goods received
 (C) organized gangs
 (D) unlawful activities.

25. "In examining the scene of a homicide, one should not only look for the usual, standard traces—fingerprints, footprints, etc.—but should also have eyes open for details that at first glance may not seem to have any connection with the crime." The most logical inference to be drawn from this statement is that

 (A) in general, standard traces are not important
 (B) sometimes one should not look for footprints
 (C) usually only the standard traces are important
 (D) one cannot tell in advance what will be important.

Answer questions 26 and 27 on the basis of the information given in the following passage.

If a motor vehicle fails to pass inspection, the owner will be given a rejection notice by the inspection station. Repairs must be made within ten days after this notice is issued. It is not necessary to have the required adjustment or repairs made at the station where the inspection occurred. The vehicle may be taken to any other garage. Reinspection after repairs may be made at any official inspection station, not necessarily the same station that made the initial inspection. The registration of any motor vehicle for which an inspection sticker has not been obtained as required, or which is not repaired and inspected within ten days after inspection indicates defects, is subject to suspension. A vehicle cannot be used on public highways while its registration is under suspension.

26. According to the passage, the owner of a car that does not pass inspection must

 (A) have repairs made at the same station that rejected the car
 (B) take the car to another station and have it reinspected
 (C) have repairs made anywhere and then have the car reinspected
 (D) not use the car on a public highway until the necessary repairs have been made.

27. According to the passage, the one of the following which may be cause for suspension of the registration of a vehicle is that

 (A) an inspection sticker was issued before the rejection notice had been in force for ten days
 (B) it was not reinspected by the station that rejected it originally
 (C) it was not reinspected either by the station that rejected it originally or by the garage that made the repairs
 (D) it has not had defective parts repaired within ten days after inspection.

28. A statute states: "A person who steals an article worth less than $100 where no aggravating circumstances accompany the act is guilty of petit larceny. If the article is worth $100 or more, it may be larceny second degree." If all you know is that Edward Smith stole an article worth $100, it may reasonably be said that

(A) Smith is guilty of petit larceny
(B) Smith is guilty of larceny second degree
(C) Smith is guilty of neither petit larceny nor larceny second degree
(D) precisely what charge will be placed against Smith is uncertain.

Answer questions 29 through 30 on the basis of the information given in the following passage.

The City Police Department will accept for investigation no report of a person missing from his residence if such residence is located outside of the city. The person reporting same will be advised to report such fact to the police department of the locality where the missing person lives, which will, if necessary, communicate officially with the City Police Department. However, a report will be accepted of a person who is missing from a temporary residence in the city, but the person making the report will be instructed to make a report also to the police department of the locality where the missing person lives.

29. According to the passage, a report to the City Police Department of a missing person whose permanent residence is outside of the city will

(A) always be investigated provided that a report is also made to local police authorities
(B) never be investigated unless requested officially by local police authorities
(C) be investigated in cases of temporary residence in the city, but a report should always be made to local police authorities
(D) always be investigated and a report will be made to the local police authorities by the City Police Department.

30. Mr. Smith of Oldtown and Mr. Jones of Newtown have an appointment in the city, but Mr. Jones doesn't appear. Mr. Smith, after trying repeatedly to phone Mr. Jones the next day, believes that something has happened to him. According to the passage, Mr. Smith should apply to the police of

(A) Oldtown
(B) Newtown
(C) Newtown and the city
(D) Oldtown and the city.

31. A police department rule reads as follows: "A Deputy Commissioner acting as Police Commissioner shall carry out the orders of the Police Commissioner, previously given, and such orders shall not, except in cases of extreme emergency, be countermanded." This means most nearly that, except in cases of extreme emergency,

(A) the orders given by a Deputy Commissioner acting as Police Commissioner may not be revoked
(B) a Deputy Commissioner acting as Police Commissioner should not revoke orders previously given by the Police Commissioner
(C) a Deputy Commissioner acting as Police Commissioner is vested with the same authority to issue orders as the Police Commissioner
(D) only a Deputy Commissioner acting as Police Commissioner may issue orders in the absence of the Police Commissioner.

32. "A 'crime' is an act committed or omitted in violation of a public law either forbidding or commanding it." This statement implies most nearly that

    (A) crimes can be omitted
    (B) a forbidding act, if omitted, is a crime
    (C) an act of omission may be criminal
    (D) to commit an act not commanded is criminal.

33. "He who by command, counsel, or assistance procures another to commit a crime is, in morals and in law, as culpable as the visible actor himself, for the reason that the criminal act, whichever it may be, is imputable to the person who conceived it and set the forces in motion for its actual accomplishment." Of the following, the most accurate inference from this statement is that

    (A) a criminal act does not have to be committed for a crime to be committed

    (B) acting as counselor for a criminal is a crime
    (C) the mere counseling of a criminal act can never be a crime if no criminal act is committed
    (D) a person acting only as an adviser may be guilty of committing a criminal act.

34. "A 'felony' is a crime punishable by death or imprisonment in a state prison, and any other crime is a 'misdemeanor.'" According to this quotation, the decisive distinction between "felony" and "misdemeanor" is the

    (A) degree of criminality
    (B) type of crime
    (C) place of incarceration
    (D) judicial jurisdiction.

Question 35 is to be answered on the basis of the information given in the following passage.

If the second or third felony is such that, upon a first conviction, the offender would be punishable by imprisonment for any term less than his or her natural life, then such person must be sentenced to imprisonment for an indeterminate term, the minimum of which shall be not less than one-half of the longest term prescribed upon a first conviction, and the maximum of which shall be not longer than twice such longest term; provided, however, that the minimum sentence imposed hereunder upon such second or third felony offender shall in no case be less than five years; except that where the maximum punishment for a second or third felony offender hereunder is five years or less, the minimum sentence must be not less than two years.

35. According to this passage, a person who has a second felony conviction shall receive as a sentence for that second felony an indeterminate term

    (A) not less than twice the minimum term prescribed upon a first conviction as a maximum
    (B) not less than one-half the maximum term of the first conviction as a minimum
    (C) not more than twice the minimum term prescribed upon a first conviction as a minimum
    (D) with a maximum of not more than twice the longest term prescribed for a first conviction for this crime.

ANSWER KEY

1.	C	8.	C	15.	B	22.	A	29.	C
2.	B	9.	B	16.	D	23.	C	30.	B
3.	C	10.	B	17.	B	24.	B	31.	B
4.	C	11.	D	18.	C	25.	D	32.	C
5.	B	12.	C	19.	C	26.	C	33.	D
6.	C	13.	C	20.	B	27.	D	34.	C
7.	A	14.	C	21.	A	28.	D	35.	D

ANSWER EXPLANATIONS

1. **(C)** Before understanding and working with others, one must first understand one's own motivation and working habits. The supervisor with good self-understanding is an effective supervisor.

2. **(B)** Adaptation is changing in response to changing conditions without a total change of substance.

3. **(C)** This quotation expresses the philosophy that the purpose of punishment is neither to make the offender "pay for his/her crime" nor to reform the offender, but rather to protect society from the specific criminal and to serve, by example, as a deterrent to others.

4. **(C)** The philosophy expressed here is "Once a criminal, always a criminal." Attempts at reform and rehabilitation are futile. (Remember: Answer questions based on reading passages on the information in the passages. You may disagree; you may even know that the information is incorrect. However, your answer must be based on the passage, not upon your opinions or your knowledge.)

5. **(B)** This question deals with a philosophy contrary to those expressed in the previous two questions. It states that we have devoted attention to means of making prisons secure places in which to keep offenders but have not given much thought to rehabilitation.

6. **(C)** You may find this principle difficult to accept, but it does represent accepted practice in many quarters. The concept is that if the person with leadership qualities—even if with antisocial behaviors—is drawn into the mainstream, that person can learn to accept certain norms of the majority and transmit these more acceptable attitudes and behaviors to the group that respects him or her. The term used to describe the drawing into the inner circle of the unconventional leader is "co-opting."

7. **(A)** Since education continues throughout life, yet schooling is of limited duration, obviously education occurs in places other than schools.

8. **(C)** The needs and desires of communities vary, therefore degree and manner of enforce-ment of different laws in different communities will also vary.

9. **(B)** The meaning of this quotation is that good intentions and thorough knowledge of duties are not sufficient. Organization and supervision are vital to efficient operation of the police function.

10. **(B)** The science of identification is primarily interested in establishing identity.

11. **(D)** Marked and spectacular progress is outstanding.

12. **(C)** Understaffed laboratories have insufficient personnel.

13. **(C)** The concept may be novel to you, but the question itself is an easy one. The answer is stated directly in the paragraph.

14. **(C)** See the second sentence. When a reading passage is crammed with details, most of the questions will be strictly factual.

15. **(B)** See the third sentence.

16. **(D)** See the last two sentences.

17. **(B)** The yellow zone light goes on at each signal control station and flashes the number of the zone in which the stoppage has occurred, so all officers receive this information.

18. **(C)** If the military practice of encirclement was adapted for use by the police, we may assume that it was widely and successfully used. Choice (B) reverses the order of the adaptation.

19. **(C)** This is the clear implication of the third sentence.

20. **(B)** The roadblock must be placed beyond the point that the fugitive could have possibly reached, so maximum speed of escape is vitally important in the establishment of a roadblock.

21. **(A)** See the first sentence.

22. **(A)** See the last sentence.

23. **(C)** The racketeer provides goods and services that are officially illegal but that are desired by otherwise respectable members of

the general public. Since the public wants these services, active effort to suppress the providers is unlikely.

24. **(B)** See the last sentence.

25. **(D)** The police officer must always be observant and alert to both abnormalities and routine details in the environment. This useful quality in a police officer is the reason many police officer exams include a section testing powers of observation and memory.

26. **(C)** The state is not concerned with who makes repairs nor with who does the inspection, only that these be accomplished.

27. **(D)** See the next-to-last sentence.

28. **(D)** Beware of qualifying words and definite statements. If the article is worth $100 or more, it *may* be larceny second degree, but not necessarily.

29. **(C)** See the last sentence.

30. **(B)** Mr. Jones is a resident of Newtown, so the missing person report must be filed with the Newtown police. The meeting of Smith and Jones was to have taken place in the city, but Jones was not a temporary resident of the city, so the city police are not involved in this case.

31. **(B)** The word "countermand" means "revoke." The Deputy Commissioner carries out the orders of the Police Commissioner and revokes them only in cases of extreme emergency.

32. **(C)** An act of omission, if it is in violation of a public law commanding said act, is a crime. The act of omission is not a crime if it is not in violation of a public law.

33. **(D)** The person who conceives and sets in motion the forces for the accomplishment of a crime—in other words, the advisor who convinced another to commit a criminal act, may well be deemed guilty of committing the criminal act.

34. **(C)** Imprisonment in a state prison is incarceration in the state prison. Imprisonment or incarceration in any other institution is the punishment for a misdemeanor. Crimes are defined by the place of incarceration or imprisonment.

35. **(D)** You may have to do some very careful reading and rereading to find the answer to this question. You will find it in the last clause before the first semicolon.

OBSERVATION AND MEMORY

To function effectively, a police officer must possess a keen memory for details. He or she must be on the constant alert for physical characteristics that will help to identify key people, places, or things, thereby leading to the apprehension of a criminal or the solution of a criminal investigation.

Most people have distinguishing features that are difficult to disguise: the contour of the face; the size, shape, and position of the ears; the shape of the mouth. Any of these may be sufficient for an officer to detect an individual wanted for criminal activities. On the other hand, the color or style of an individual's hair or the first impression of his or her face may change drastically with the addition of a wig, mustache, or beard. In addition, eye color can be altered with tinted contact lenses. Therefore, the police officer must focus attention on those physical features that cannot be changed easily and might serve as the basis of a positive identification of that person at some time in the future.

Observation is not limited to the act of seeing. In addition, the officer must learn to recognize and recall distinctive features of people, places, and things. An official record in the memorandum book may serve as a refresher for the facts stored in the officer's mental record. The officer should be aware of the people who frequent his or her post, and of the surrounding buildings and stores on that post, so that important details may be brought to bear in a case when necessary. An officer without a keen sense of recall cannot perform his or her duties effectively.

Because police departments all over the country recognize the importance of a good memory for details and a good sense of recall in the officer's job, examinations for the position frequently contain sections that evaluate these skills. To best sharpen your memory and sense of recall, you must practice using these skills. You need only walk around your neighborhood and observe. Keep your eyes open to everything you see. Later try to recall details of buildings or people that you saw. Remember, your environment is your study aid: Virtually any place you go, you can practice observing and recalling details.

Police Observation of Persons, Places, and Things

The police officer must be thoroughly observant at all times. The nonobservant officer is soon found out by the criminal element who will take advantage of this deficiency to commit crimes on the officer's post. Good observation is a matter of training and knowledge. A police officer may have perfect eyesight yet be blind when it comes to observing matters calling for police action.

Many dangerous criminals have been arrested by virtue of a police officer's keen observation. An officer should observe the customary activities on his or her post as well as the people who live in or frequent it, so that the officer can quickly spot a stranger or an unusual activity. Some places will call for more observation than others: banks, jewelry stores, taverns, service stations, and any place where crime is likely to occur or where the criminal element may gather.

An essential element in observation is the ability to remember details. Officers should practice observation by giving themselves such tests as describing a man or a woman encountered casually or trying to remember details on a billboard. The identification of persons, places, and things depends on accurate observation. Many witnesses testify inaccurately in court because they failed to observe properly at the time of the incident's occurrence. A failure of this kind is *inexcusable* on the part of an officer.

Memory is a very individualized skill. Some people remember details of what they see and hear, others remember only the most obvious facts. Some people memorize easily, others find memorizing very difficult. Some people remember forever, others forget in a short time. Some people can memorize in a systematic manner, others are haphazard in their methods or have no method at all. Systematic observation tends to lead to more efficient memorization. Some sort of meaningful grouping of people and activities helps to secure the descriptions, the activities, and the interactions in your mind. Whether the material is pictorial or narrative, try to organize it in some meaningful way.

We really cannot tell you how to memorize. We can, however, teach you how to look at pictures and point out the details on which you should concentrate.

Photograph for Exercise 1

(Photograph courtesy of General Motors)

Exercise 1

Let us begin by looking together at the photograph on page 88.

Start with the people:

1. How many people are in the photograph?

2. How many men? How many women?

3. What do the people appear to be doing?

4. Are the people all working together? If not, how many are working alone? How many together? Is the man on the right working?

5. Note the clothing. Dark pants, dark socks, light shirts crossed across the chest and tied in back. The two men in the foreground have on the same type of shoes, but the other visible pair of shoes is a different type.

6. Note glasses. Which men wear them?

7. Note hair. Which men have dark hair? Which light? Can you describe the hairstyles of the light-haired men?

8. One man is sitting on a stool. Which man? How many legs does the stool have? Of what does the stool appear to be made? Does it move on casters?

9. Which of the men have beards? Mustaches?

10. Is anyone wearing a watch? Who?

Observe the action:

11. What does the man in the right foreground have in his hand? What is he probably doing?

12. What does the man who is standing appear to be doing? What about the man kneeling beside him?

13. What might be the relationship of the older man to the younger ones?

Note the background:

14. There are pictures of cars on the walls. Parts of how many cars are visible? How many tires are shown?

15. What else can be seen on the walls? Telephone? Calendar? Bookcase?

16. Is the car on which the men are working up on a lift?

17. How many levels of floor are visible? Is the floor clean?

18. There is a number on one piece of equipment. Did you notice the number? Remember it!

A good question writer could easily develop ten questions based upon these observations. Would you have noticed everything and made note as well about what was not there at all?

In looking at a photograph, focus first on the people. Notice their clothing, physical features, and activities. Count, but also make note of which person or persons are wearing what, doing what, interacting with whom, and so on. Then notice the prominent objects. Next, turn your attention to the background, floors, walls, etc. Finally, start at the left side of the photograph and move your eyes very slowly to the right, noticing special details such as numbers, calibrations, dirt spots, unidentified objects, etc. If you work very hard at noticing, you are likely to remember what you noticed, at least for the duration of the exam.

Photograph for Exercise 2

(Photograph courtesy of The Coleman Company, Inc.)

Exercise 2

Let us look at another photograph on page 90.

1. The people in the picture are...number, sex, age.

2. The people are wearing...notice the boy's belt, label on jeans (even if you cannot read it, you should notice that it is there), long-sleeved plaid shirts.

3. Notice hair color, type (curly or straight), and length.

4. Note that no shoes are visible; neither person wears glasses nor a watch nor hat.

5. What is the boy doing? What is the girl doing?

6. Who is standing? Who sitting? On What?

7. On what is the soda can resting? On what is the cooler resting?

8. What else is on the table? Notice lantern, covered pot, box, and coffeepot.

9. How many slats make up the table? The bench?

10. What is on the ground? Snow? Sand? Gravel? Lawn? Rocks? Flowers? Wild grasses?

11. The day is...cold? warm? rainy? cloudy? sunny? Where is the sun in the picture?

12. In the background are (is)...mountains? trees? water? boats? tents? more grass? other people? animals?

13. What can you see in the sky? What is on or in the water? What else is there on the land?

14. Does the cooler have a handle on top? Where? Is it all one color? How many colors? Describe the design of the cooler.

15. Where is the fill valve on the lantern?

16. Does the coffeepot have a handle?

17. Does the tent have a visible window?

18. Describe the end of the bench? Squared off? Rounded? Other?

How did you do with this photograph? Are you developing skill at noticing everything?

Photograph for Exercise 3

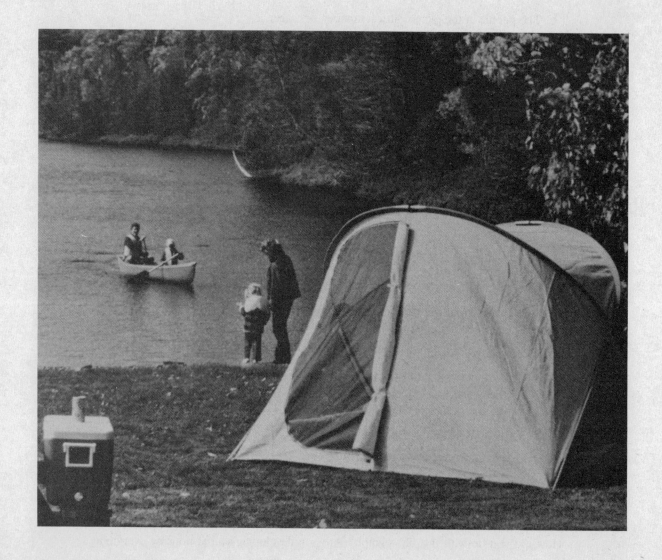

(Photograph courtesy of The Coleman Company, Inc.)

Exercise 3

Study the photograph on page 92. On a plain piece of paper make as comprehensive a list as you can. Try to notice every detail on which you could possibly be quizzed. When you have completed your list, compare it with ours, which follows. If you noticed everything that we did, you are becoming very observant. Perhaps you found details that we missed. If so, congratulate yourself and keep up the good work.

Here is our list:

1. There are four people in the photograph, two adults and two children.

2. Two people are in a canoe, a man and a child.

3. The man in the canoe is sitting in the stern (rear) and is paddling on his left side.

4. The child in the canoe is in the bow (front) and is paddling on his right side.

5. The child in the canoe is blond, the man is dark-haired. Both are wearing shirts with long sleeves.

6. A woman and a little girl are standing on the shore.

7. The little girl is blonde; the woman's hair is darker.

8. Both the woman and the girl are wearing jackets. The little girl's jacket is a winter jacket with a fleece-lined hood.

9. In the foreground is a cooler with white top, white handle and drainage valve.

10. On top of the cooler is a soda can.

11. Also in the foreground is a light colored tent of modified quonset shape.

12. A door flap of the tent is rolled back.

13. The opening of the tent is screened.

14. The water is calm.

15. The bank is grassy.

16. The body of water is lined with trees and shrubs.

17. Not visible: sky, end of body of water, background beyond the tree line, other people, and animals.

By now your powers of observation should be considerably keener.

Photograph for Exercise 4

Exercise 4

Make this exercise an observation and memory exercise rather than just an observation exercise. Study the photograph on page 94 for five minutes. Make mental notes of as many details as you possibly can, but do not do any writing while you look at the photo. Then close the book and write as many details as you can remember. When you have written all that you can remember, draw a line on your paper and reopen the book. Add to the list details that you forgot and details that you previously overlooked. Then compare your list with ours.

1. The scene is a classroom. The students are women; the instructor is a man.

2. The students are all seated; the teacher is standing.

3. The teacher has dark, curly hair. He wears white pants and a white knit, collared sport shirt with some dark strips.

4. The teacher wears a watch on his left wrist and a bracelet on his right. He has something in each hand.

5. The teacher has some slender object in each breast pocket.

6. The teacher is not wearing glasses. He is clean shaven. His mouth is closed.

7. Parts of thirteen students are visible.

8. The class is racially mixed.

9. The students are wearing a uniform that consists of a white short-sleeved blouse with cuffs on the sleeves and wide pointed collar, dark slacks, and dark overblouse vest.

10. Footwear is not part of the uniform though low white shoes seem to be favored.

11. One student is wearing a long-sleeved print shirt under her uniform blouse. That student is black and wears glasses.

12. Most students are seated on folding chairs with writing arms. One student is sitting in a chair without an arm. That student is closest to the camera. She has her notebook open on her lap, wears her hair in a bun, has side combs in her hair and loop earrings, is wearing white shoes, and has a watch on her left wrist and a ring on one finger of her left hand.

13. The students all appear to be very attentive.

14. While some students are holding pen or pencil, none appears to be writing, and some even have notebooks closed.

15. There is a cane leaning on the wall right next to the door.

16. The room lighting is not visible.

17. The floor is made of square tiles.

18. On the floor in the foreground can be seen parts of three suitcases or large briefcases and two large plastic bags with something dark inside each.

19. Beside the teacher is a low table. On that table is a model of a woman's head and a spray bottle.

20. Behind the low table is a white cabinet with two doors. On top of the cabinet is a book and two small unidentifiable objects.

21. Part of a second white cabinet is visible beside the first.

22. In the left background is a sink with a depression in its front rim.

23. On a shelf behind the sink is a stack of unidentifiable objects.

24. Pasted on the wall over and around the door are sixteen separate pictures. Some of these feature only one woman; some have a number of smaller snapshots on a standard size background.

25. The largest number of separate heads one can count in any one of these pictures is seven. (Top picture of far left group.)

26. The part of the room to the right is deeper than that on the left.

27. There is a dark colored, molded shape chair behind the instructor.

28. Two students are supporting their chins with one hand. One student is using her left hand, the other her right.

29. Of all the students, only one is obviously wearing glasses.

30. One student is wearing high-heeled open shoes.

Exercise 5
Observation and Recognition of Faces

This exercise measures your ability to recognize the basic differences and similarities in the faces of people. Many alleged criminals being sought by the police disguise their facial features to make it difficult for the police to apprehend them. Aside from surgery, there are many things that the wanted person can do to make recognition difficult. The addition and removal of beards and mustaches, or even change in hair color or hair style, are relatively easy to accomplish. As noted previously, tinted contact lenses, now very common, can alter the color of eyes. However, there are some features that an individual cannot change easily. These are the features a police officer should concentrate on when attempting to identify wanted persons: the size, shape, and position of the ears; the shape of the jaw. The shape of the nose and the jaw are difficult to change without surgery. The police officer should also recognize that the wanted male with a distinctive jaw would likely try to disguise that feature by growing a beard.

DIRECTIONS: Answer the following ten questions by selecting the face, labeled (A), (B), (C), or (D), which is most likely to be the same as that of the suspect on the left. You are to assume that no surgery has taken place since the sketch of the suspect was made. Only observation and recognition are factors in this exercise. Do not try to memorize features of these faces. Circle the letter of the face you choose. Explanations follow the last question.

Answer Key

1. D   3. C   5. C   7. B   9. B
2. B   4. D   6. D   8. A   10. A

Answer Explanations

1. **(D)** Choice (A) has a different nose; (B) and (C) have different chins.

2. **(B)** Choice (A) has a longer face; (C) has a fuller face with different chin; (D) has a different nose.

3. **(C)** Choice (A) has a longer face; (B) has dark eyes; (D) has much fuller lips.

4. **(D)** Choice (A) has thinner lips; (B) has a different nose; (C) has different ears.

5. **(C)** Choice (A) has a different mouth; (B) has a different nose; (D) has different eyes.

6. **(D)** Choice (A) has a different chin; (B) has a different mouth; (C) has different eyes.

7. **(B)** Choice A has different eyes; (C) has a different nose; (D) has a different mouth.

8. **(A)** Choice (B) has different eyes and nose; (C) has a wider face at the jaw line; (D) has different nose and chin. It would appear that the original face has larger eyes than any of the choices. Be aware that makeup can create illusions in the original face as well as in the choices.

9. **(B)** Choice (A) has different ears; (C) has a different mouth; (D) has less prominent nostrils. The difference in hairline may also be significant. The original could be wearing a wig, but judging from his hairstyle that is unlikely.

10. **(A)** Choice (B) has a different nose; (C) has different ears; (D) has different eyes and, again, the original's hairline suggests that it is natural, not a wig.

ANSWER SHEET

NEW YORK CITY EXAM—OCTOBER 29, 1988

1. Ⓐ Ⓑ Ⓒ Ⓓ	29. Ⓐ Ⓑ Ⓒ Ⓓ	57. Ⓐ Ⓑ Ⓒ Ⓓ	85. Ⓐ Ⓑ Ⓒ Ⓓ	113. Ⓐ Ⓑ Ⓒ Ⓓ
2. Ⓐ Ⓑ Ⓒ Ⓓ	30. Ⓐ Ⓑ Ⓒ Ⓓ	58. Ⓐ Ⓑ Ⓒ Ⓓ	86. Ⓐ Ⓑ Ⓒ Ⓓ	114. Ⓐ Ⓑ Ⓒ Ⓓ
3. Ⓐ Ⓑ Ⓒ Ⓓ	31. Ⓐ Ⓑ Ⓒ Ⓓ	59. Ⓐ Ⓑ Ⓒ Ⓓ	87. Ⓐ Ⓑ Ⓒ Ⓓ	115. Ⓐ Ⓑ Ⓒ Ⓓ
4. Ⓐ Ⓑ Ⓒ Ⓓ	32. Ⓐ Ⓑ Ⓒ Ⓓ	60. Ⓐ Ⓑ Ⓒ Ⓓ	88. Ⓐ Ⓑ Ⓒ Ⓓ	116. Ⓐ Ⓑ Ⓒ Ⓓ
5. Ⓐ Ⓑ Ⓒ Ⓓ	33. Ⓐ Ⓑ Ⓒ Ⓓ	61. Ⓐ Ⓑ Ⓒ Ⓓ	89. Ⓐ Ⓑ Ⓒ Ⓓ	117. Ⓐ Ⓑ Ⓒ Ⓓ
6. Ⓐ Ⓑ Ⓒ Ⓓ	34. Ⓐ Ⓑ Ⓒ Ⓓ	62. Ⓐ Ⓑ Ⓒ Ⓓ	90. Ⓐ Ⓑ Ⓒ Ⓓ	118. Ⓐ Ⓑ Ⓒ Ⓓ
7. Ⓐ Ⓑ Ⓒ Ⓓ	35. Ⓐ Ⓑ Ⓒ Ⓓ	63. Ⓐ Ⓑ Ⓒ Ⓓ	91. Ⓐ Ⓑ Ⓒ Ⓓ	119. Ⓐ Ⓑ Ⓒ Ⓓ
8. Ⓐ Ⓑ Ⓒ Ⓓ	36. Ⓐ Ⓑ Ⓒ Ⓓ	64. Ⓐ Ⓑ Ⓒ Ⓓ	92. Ⓐ Ⓑ Ⓒ Ⓓ	120. Ⓐ Ⓑ Ⓒ Ⓓ
9. Ⓐ Ⓑ Ⓒ Ⓓ	37. Ⓐ Ⓑ Ⓒ Ⓓ	65. Ⓐ Ⓑ Ⓒ Ⓓ	93. Ⓐ Ⓑ Ⓒ Ⓓ	121. Ⓐ Ⓑ Ⓒ Ⓓ
10. Ⓐ Ⓑ Ⓒ Ⓓ	38. Ⓐ Ⓑ Ⓒ Ⓓ	66. Ⓐ Ⓑ Ⓒ Ⓓ	94. Ⓐ Ⓑ Ⓒ Ⓓ	122. Ⓐ Ⓑ Ⓒ Ⓓ
11. Ⓐ Ⓑ Ⓒ Ⓓ	39. Ⓐ Ⓑ Ⓒ Ⓓ	67. Ⓐ Ⓑ Ⓒ Ⓓ	95. Ⓐ Ⓑ Ⓒ Ⓓ	123. Ⓐ Ⓑ Ⓒ Ⓓ
12. Ⓐ Ⓑ Ⓒ Ⓓ	40. Ⓐ Ⓑ Ⓒ Ⓓ	68. Ⓐ Ⓑ Ⓒ Ⓓ	96. Ⓐ Ⓑ Ⓒ Ⓓ	124. Ⓐ Ⓑ Ⓒ Ⓓ
13. Ⓐ Ⓑ Ⓒ Ⓓ	41. Ⓐ Ⓑ Ⓒ Ⓓ	69. Ⓐ Ⓑ Ⓒ Ⓓ	97. Ⓐ Ⓑ Ⓒ Ⓓ	125. Ⓐ Ⓑ Ⓒ Ⓓ
14. Ⓐ Ⓑ Ⓒ Ⓓ	42. Ⓐ Ⓑ Ⓒ Ⓓ	70. Ⓐ Ⓑ Ⓒ Ⓓ	98. Ⓐ Ⓑ Ⓒ Ⓓ	126. Ⓐ Ⓑ Ⓒ Ⓓ
15. Ⓐ Ⓑ Ⓒ Ⓓ	43. Ⓐ Ⓑ Ⓒ Ⓓ	71. Ⓐ Ⓑ Ⓒ Ⓓ	99. Ⓐ Ⓑ Ⓒ Ⓓ	127. Ⓐ Ⓑ Ⓒ Ⓓ
16. Ⓐ Ⓑ Ⓒ Ⓓ	44. Ⓐ Ⓑ Ⓒ Ⓓ	72. Ⓐ Ⓑ Ⓒ Ⓓ	100. Ⓐ Ⓑ Ⓒ Ⓓ	128. Ⓐ Ⓑ Ⓒ Ⓓ
17. Ⓐ Ⓑ Ⓒ Ⓓ	45. Ⓐ Ⓑ Ⓒ Ⓓ	73. Ⓐ Ⓑ Ⓒ Ⓓ	101. Ⓐ Ⓑ Ⓒ Ⓓ	129. Ⓐ Ⓑ Ⓒ Ⓓ
18. Ⓐ Ⓑ Ⓒ Ⓓ	46. Ⓐ Ⓑ Ⓒ Ⓓ	74. Ⓐ Ⓑ Ⓒ Ⓓ	102. Ⓐ Ⓑ Ⓒ Ⓓ	130. Ⓐ Ⓑ Ⓒ Ⓓ
19. Ⓐ Ⓑ Ⓒ Ⓓ	47. Ⓐ Ⓑ Ⓒ Ⓓ	75. Ⓐ Ⓑ Ⓒ Ⓓ	103. Ⓐ Ⓑ Ⓒ Ⓓ	131. Ⓐ Ⓑ Ⓒ Ⓓ
20. Ⓐ Ⓑ Ⓒ Ⓓ	48. Ⓐ Ⓑ Ⓒ Ⓓ	76. Ⓐ Ⓑ Ⓒ Ⓓ	104. Ⓐ Ⓑ Ⓒ Ⓓ	132. Ⓐ Ⓑ Ⓒ Ⓓ
21. Ⓐ Ⓑ Ⓒ Ⓓ	49. Ⓐ Ⓑ Ⓒ Ⓓ	77. Ⓐ Ⓑ Ⓒ Ⓓ	105. Ⓐ Ⓑ Ⓒ Ⓓ	133. Ⓐ Ⓑ Ⓒ Ⓓ
22. Ⓐ Ⓑ Ⓒ Ⓓ	50. Ⓐ Ⓑ Ⓒ Ⓓ	78. Ⓐ Ⓑ Ⓒ Ⓓ	106. Ⓐ Ⓑ Ⓒ Ⓓ	134. Ⓐ Ⓑ Ⓒ Ⓓ
23. Ⓐ Ⓑ Ⓒ Ⓓ	51. Ⓐ Ⓑ Ⓒ Ⓓ	79. Ⓐ Ⓑ Ⓒ Ⓓ	107. Ⓐ Ⓑ Ⓒ Ⓓ	135. Ⓐ Ⓑ Ⓒ Ⓓ
24. Ⓐ Ⓑ Ⓒ Ⓓ	52. Ⓐ Ⓑ Ⓒ Ⓓ	80. Ⓐ Ⓑ Ⓒ Ⓓ	108. Ⓐ Ⓑ Ⓒ Ⓓ	136. Ⓐ Ⓑ Ⓒ Ⓓ
25. Ⓐ Ⓑ Ⓒ Ⓓ	53. Ⓐ Ⓑ Ⓒ Ⓓ	81. Ⓐ Ⓑ Ⓒ Ⓓ	109. Ⓐ Ⓑ Ⓒ Ⓓ	137. Ⓐ Ⓑ Ⓒ Ⓓ
26. Ⓐ Ⓑ Ⓒ Ⓓ	54. Ⓐ Ⓑ Ⓒ Ⓓ	82. Ⓐ Ⓑ Ⓒ Ⓓ	110. Ⓐ Ⓑ Ⓒ Ⓓ	138. Ⓐ Ⓑ Ⓒ Ⓓ
27. Ⓐ Ⓑ Ⓒ Ⓓ	55. Ⓐ Ⓑ Ⓒ Ⓓ	83. Ⓐ Ⓑ Ⓒ Ⓓ	111. Ⓐ Ⓑ Ⓒ Ⓓ	139. Ⓐ Ⓑ Ⓒ Ⓓ
28. Ⓐ Ⓑ Ⓒ Ⓓ	56. Ⓐ Ⓑ Ⓒ Ⓓ	84. Ⓐ Ⓑ Ⓒ Ⓓ	112. Ⓐ Ⓑ Ⓒ Ⓓ	140. Ⓐ Ⓑ Ⓒ Ⓓ

TEAR HERE

PRACTICE EXAMINATION 1

DEPARTMENT OF PERSONNEL

Social Security No. _____

Room No. _____

Seat No. _____

School _____

POLICE OFFICER SERIES
EXAMINATION NO. 7197

First Memory Booklet
October 29, 1988

DO NOT OPEN THIS BOOKLET UNTIL THE SECOND SIGNAL IS GIVEN!

Write your Social Security Number, Room Number, Seat Number, and School in the appropriate spaces at the top of this page.

You *must* follow the instructions found on the TEST INSTRUCTION SHEET.

ANYONE DISOBEYING ANY OF THE INSTRUCTIONS FOUND ON THE TEST INSTRUCTION SHEET MAY BE DISQUALIFIED— RECEIVE A ZERO ON THE ENTIRE TEST.

This booklet contains one scene. Try to remember as many details in the scene as you can. You should pay equal attention both to objects and to people shown in the scene.

DO *NOT* WRITE OR MAKE *ANY* NOTES WHILE STUDYING THE SCENE.

DO NOT OPEN THIS BOOKLET UNTIL THE
SECOND SIGNAL IS GIVEN!

[NOTE: You will have five (5) minutes to study the scene shown.]

The New York City Department of Personnel makes no commitment, and no inference is to be drawn, regarding the content, style, or format of any future examination for the position of Police Officer.

Department of Personnel

Social Security No. _____
Room No. _____
Seat No. _____
School _____

Police Officer Series
Examination No. 7197

Second Memory Booklet
October 29, 1988

DO NOT OPEN THIS BOOKLET UNTIL THE FOURTH SIGNAL IS GIVEN!

Write your Social Security Number, Room Number, Seat Number, and School in the appropriate spaces at the top of this page.

You *must* follow the instructions found on the TEST INSTRUCTION SHEET.

ANYONE DISOBEYING ANY OF THE INSTRUCTIONS FOUND ON THE TEST INSTRUCTION SHEET MAY BE DISQUALIFIED— RECEIVE A ZERO ON THE ENTIRE TEST.

This booklet contains Questions 1 through 6, which are based on Scene 1 as shown in the First Memory Booklet. Answer Questions 1 through 6 after the fourth signal. At the *FIFTH SIGNAL*, you should turn to Scene 2. Try to remember as many details in the scene as you can. You should pay equal attention both to objects and to people shown in the scene.

DO NOT OPEN THIS BOOKLET UNTIL THE FOURTH SIGNAL IS GIVEN!

[Note: You will have five (5) minutes to study the scene shown.]

The New York City Department of Personnel makes no commitment, and no inference is to be drawn, regarding the content, style, or format of any future examination for the position of Police Officer.

Answer questions 1 through 6 solely on the basis of sketch number 1.

1. Which one of the following vehicles is parked on Elm Road?

   (A) A police car
   (B) An ambulance
   (C) A tow truck
   (D) A fire truck.

2. What are the words printed on the side of the bus?

   (A) Northside Bus
   (B) Southside Bus
   (C) Eastside Bus
   (D) Westside Bus.

3. The man with the gun is wearing a

   (A) white shirt with black stripes
   (B) tee shirt with the words SPOT NEWS
   (C) sweat shirt with the word ACE
   (D) white shirt with black dots.

4. The taxi which is being repaired is parked in a

   (A) No Standing Zone
   (B) No Parking Zone
   (C) Towaway Zone
   (D) Authorized Vehicles Only Zone.

5. The license plate number of the vehicle which is closest to the person lying on the street is

   (A) G498
   (B) 8K46
   (C) 302L
   (D) 31S4.

6. The person in the second floor window is directly above

   (A) Uncle Dan's Lunch
   (B) Mandley Discount Clothing Outlet
   (C) Cafeteria Europa
   (D) M & P Music World.

DEPARTMENT OF PERSONNEL

Social Security No. _____

Room No. _____

Seat No. _____

School _____

POLICE OFFICER SERIES
EXAMINATION NO. 7197

Question Booklet
October 29, 1988

Written Test: Weight 100
Time Allowed: 4½ Hours

DO NOT OPEN THIS BOOKLET UNTIL THE SEVENTH SIGNAL IS GIVEN!

Record your answers on the Official Answer Sheet before the last signal. If you wish, you may also record your answers in the Question Booklet before the last signal is given. This will be your only official record of answers.

This Question Booklet contains procedures and definitions which are to be used to answer certain questions. These procedures and definitions are not necessarily those of the New York City Police Department. However, you are to answer these questions solely on the basis of the material given.

After the seventh signal is given, open this Question Booklet and begin to work. You will have 4½ hours to complete this test. Answer questions 7 through 11 before answering any other questions.

You may make notes in this booklet and use the scrap paper on your desk. If you need additional scrap paper, ask the monitor.

Remember, only your Official Answer Sheet will be rated, so be sure to mark *all* your answers on the Official Answer Sheet before the eighth signal. *No additional time* will be given for marking your answers after the test has ended.

DO NOT OPEN THIS BOOKLET UNTIL THE SEVENTH SIGNAL IS GIVEN!

The New York City Department of Personnel makes no commitment, and no inference is to be drawn, regarding the content, style, or format of any future examination for the position of Police Officer.

Answer questions 7 through 11 solely on the basis of sketch 2.

7. The robbery at knifepoint is occurring on

    (A) The corner of Brady Avenue and E. 7th Street
    (B) Brady Avenue in front of Mario's Pizza Hole
    (C) The corner of Brady Avenue and W. 7th Street
    (D) Brady Avenue in front of Sparta Senior Center.

8. The street musician is standing closest to

    (A) Crane Hotel
    (B) The subway entrance
    (C) Mario's Pizza Hole
    (D) Blair Savings Bank.

9. The youth holding the knife is wearing a

    (A) black ski cap, plaid shirt, and white pants
    (B) white ski cap, plaid shirt, and black pants
    (C) black baseball cap, white shirt, and plaid pants
    (D) white baseball cap, white shirt, and black pants.

10. Which one of the following best describes the person holding the gun?

    (A) White male, white pants, and a plaid shirt.
    (B) Asian male, black pants, and a heart print shirt.
    (C) White male, plaid pants, and a black jacket.
    (D) Black male, black pants, and a white jacket.

11. What is the number on the shirt of the man running towards the subway?

    (A) 49
    (B) 54
    (C) 45
    (D) 94.

Please check your Answer Sheet to make sure that you have written in and blackened your Social Security number correctly. If you have not yet written in and blackened your Social Security number, please do so immediately. If you have incorrectly written in or blackened your Social Security number, please correct the mistake immediately. Failure to correctly blacken your Social Security number may result in your Answer Sheet NOT being rated.

Answer questions 12 through 14 solely on the basis of the following passage.

At 11:30 P.M., while parked in front of 945 Howard Street, Police Officers Abbott and Johnson received a radio call of a family dispute at 779 Seward Street, Apartment 1928. The radio dispatcher informed the Officers that the call came from Mrs. Debra Lacoste who lives in Apartment 1930. The officers arrived at the location and heard yelling and screaming. When the Officers knocked on the door a woman crying hysterically opened the door. The woman, Gloria Ross, informed the Officers that her husband, Sam Ross, was in her apartment. She said he was drunk, had yelled at her, and had made threats to hurt her if she did not let him see his children. Mrs. Ross then presented a letter to Officer Abbott, which he recognized as being an Order of Protection issued by Family Court. The Order of Protection stated that Mr. Ross was not to be seen anywhere near his wife, including her residence and place of employment. Furthermore, the Order stated that he had no right to see the children or to yell at his wife or use obscene language in his wife's presence. Mrs. Ross told the Officer that she wanted her husband arrested for violating the Order of Protection. Officer Johnson quickly read the Order of Protection and informed Officer Abbott that the Order was valid. Officer Abbott ordered Sam Ross to turn around with his hands behind his back and Officer Abbott handcuffed him and placed him under arrest.

12. Which of the following persons first made the authorities aware of the family dispute?
    (A) A neighbor
    (B) The victim
    (C) A Police Officer
    (D) The suspect.

13. The Police Officers responded to a report of a disturbance at

    (A) 945 Howard Street, Apartment 1928
    (B) 779 Seward Street, Apartment 1930
    (C) 779 Seward Street, Apartment 1928
    (D) 945 Howard Street, Apartment 1930.

14. Which of the following actions caused Mr. Ross to be arrested?

    (A) He called his children on the telephone.
    (B) He tried to visit his children.
    (C) He waited for his wife in front of her job.
    (D) He yelled at his children.

Answer question 15 solely on the basis of the following information.

Sexual Abuse 3rd Degree—occurs when a person intentionally subjects an individual to sexual contact without the individual's consent.

15. Which one of the following situations is the best example of Sexual Abuse in the Third Degree?

(A) Joe is riding a crowded train and bumps into JoAnn when the train comes to a sudden stop.
(B) When Jean carelessly steps on Bob's toe, Bob curses at her and uses sexually explicit language.
(C) John is standing on a crowded train and starts rubbing himself against a woman's buttocks.
(D) Bill accidentally brushes his newspaper against a woman's chest while he is reading on a crowded train.

Answer question 16 solely on the basis of the following information.

Police Officers are required to provide assistance to sick or injured persons. Upon arrival at the scene of a sick or injured person a Police Officer should do the following in the order given:

1. Give reasonable aid to the sick or injured person.
2. Request an ambulance or doctor, if necessary.
3. Wait outside to direct the ambulance, or have some responsible person do so.
4. Make a second call in 20 minutes if ambulance does not arrive.

16. Police Officer Jones, while on patrol, is approached by John Rutherford who informs the Officer that his business partner, Silvio Monteleone, tripped on the 5th floor stairs outside his apartment located at 1276 Stork Lane. When Officer Jones and Rutherford arrive at the scene, the Officer finds that Silvio may have broken his right arm. At 12:20 P.M. Officer Jones radios for an ambulance to take Silvio to the hospital. While waiting, Officer Jones attempts to locate a blanket to place over Silvio who is lying on a cold tile floor. After knocking at three apartments, Officer Jones receives a blanket from Mrs. Flores. It is now 12:35 P.M. and the ambulance has not arrived. The next step Officer Jones should take is to

(A) call his patrol supervisor
(B) send Silvio's friend John down to the street to direct the medical personnel
(C) call the ambulance a second time to request assistance
(D) radio for a patrol car to transport Silvio to the hospital

17. Sergeant Burroughs assigns Police Officer Holland to patrol the area between Webster and St. Paul Avenues. She informs Officer Holland that over the past month there has been a sharp increase in the number of burglaries. She instructs Officer Holland to pay close attention to any suspicious activities. To which one of the following situations should Officer Holland give the most attention?

(A) Two young children who knock on doors and run away.
(B) Two teenagers who live around the corner, sitting on the stairs of a building listening to the radio.
(C) A group of elderly men sitting on a bench in front of a row of buildings.
(D) Two men going from door to door asking if Mr. Jones is home.

18. While on patrol, Police Officer Fuentes is approached by a woman who states that she has just been robbed. Officer Fuentes obtains the following information relating to the robbery:

Place of Occurrence:	168 Delancey Street
Time of Occurrence:	5 minutes earlier
Description of Suspect:	Male, white, 6 feet tall, wearing a black jacket, grey pants, and white sneakers
Direction of Flight:	Northbound on Delancey Street

Officer Fuentes radios this information to the other Officers. Which one of the following expresses the above information *most clearly* and *accurately*?

(A) I have a robbery. The suspect is six feet tall wearing a black jacket, grey pants, and white sneakers. The robbery occurred five minutes ago at 168 Delancey Street. A white male fled northbound on Delancey Street.
(B) A robbery occurred five minutes ago at 168 Delancey Street. The suspect fled northbound on Delancey Street. He is a white male, approximately 6 feet tall, wearing a black jacket, grey pants, and white sneakers.
(C) I have a robbery. The suspect fled northbound on Delancey Street and is a male, approximately 6 feet tall five minutes ago. Suspect is white and is wearing a black jacket, grey pants, and white sneakers. The robbery occurred at 168 Delancey Street.
(D) A robbery has occurred at 168 Delancey Street. The suspect is wearing white sneakers. He fled northbound wearing a black jacket on Delancey Street and he is approximately 6 feet tall, wearing grey pants. The robbery took place five minutes ago with a white male.

19. Police Officer Waters was the first person at the scene of a fire which may have been the result of arson. He obtained the following information:

Place of Occurrence:	35 John Street, Apartment 27
Time of Occurrence:	4:00 P.M.
Witness:	Daisy Logan
Incident:	Fire (possible Arson)
Suspect:	Male, white, approximately 18 years old, wearing blue jeans and a plaid shirt, running away from incident.

Officer Waters is completing a report on the incident. Which one of the following expresses the above information *most clearly* and *accurately*?

(A) At 4:00 P.M., Daisy Logan saw a white male, approximately 18 years old who was wearing blue jeans and a plaid shirt, running from the scene of a fire at 35 John Street, Apartment 27.

(B) Seeing a fire at 35 John Street, a white male approximately 18 years old, wearing blue jeans and a plaid shirt was seen running from Apartment 27 at 4:00 P.M. reported Daisy Logan.

(C) Approximately 18 years old and wearing blue jeans and a plaid shirt, Daisy Logan saw a fire and a white male running from 35 John Street, Apartment 27 at 4:00 P.M.

(D) Running from 35 John Street, Apartment 27, the scene of the fire, reported Daisy Logan at 4:00 P.M., was a white male approximately 18 years old and wearing blue jeans and a plaid shirt.

20. Police Officer Sullivan obtained the following information at the scene of a two-car accident:

Place of Occurrence:	2971 William Street
Drivers and Vehicles Involved:	Mrs. Wilson, driver of blue 1984 Toyota Camry; Mr. Bailey, driver of white 1981 Dodge Omni
Injuries Sustained:	Mr. Bailey had a swollen right eye; Mrs. Wilson had a broken left hand

Which one of the following expresses the above information *most clearly* and *accurately*?

(A) Mr. Bailey, owner of a white, 1981 Dodge Omni, at 2971 William Street, had a swollen right eye. Mrs. Wilson, with a broken left hand, is the owner of the blue 1984 Toyota Camry. They were in a car accident.

(B) Mrs. Wilson got a broken left hand and Mr. Bailey a swollen right eye at 2971 William Street. The vehicles involved in the car accident were a 1981 Dodge Omni, white, owned by Mr. Bailey, and Mrs. Wilson's blue 1984 Toyota Camry.

(C) Mrs. Wilson, the driver of the blue 1984 Toyota Camry, and Mr. Bailey, the driver of the white 1981 Dodge Omni, were involved in a car accident at 2971 William Street. Mr. Bailey sustained a swollen right eye, and Mrs. Wilson broke her left hand.

(D) Mr. Bailey sustained a swollen right eye and Mrs. Wilson broke her left hand in a car accident at 2971 William Street. They owned a 1981 white Dodge Omni and a 1984 blue Toyota Camry.

Answer question 21 solely on the basis of the following information.

When a Police Officer observes a person who is in possession of a firearm, the Officer is required to:

1. Ask the person to produce identification and the pistol license.
2. Verify the pistol license, if it is questionable, by telephoning the New York City Police Department License Division during business hours between 9:00 A.M. and 5:00 P.M., Monday to Friday.
3. Make an Activity Log entry including the person's name, address, date of birth, and the pistol license number and expiration date.
4. Remove person to station house if license has expired.
5. If license is valid, return all identification and notify Desk Officer.

21. At 3:00 P.M. on September 10, 1988, Police Officer Rogers sees a man walking towards him with a gun in his waistband. The Officer stops the man and asks him for identification and his pistol license. The man gives the Officer his pistol license and driver's license. The information on the pistol license identifies the man as John Wilson, residing at 4 Auburn Street, Apt. #1B. Mr. Wilson is 34 years old, and was born on May 15, 1954. His pistol license number is 71554, and the expiration date is September 9, 1988. His driver's license indicates the same name, address, and date of birth. The Officer makes an Activity Log entry listing all of the required information obtained from Mr. Wilson, returns both licenses to him, and then notifies the Desk Officer. In this situation, the actions taken by Officer Rogers were

    (A) proper, primarily because Mr. Wilson was not a New York City resident
    (B) improper, primarily because the Officer did not verify the pistol license with the License Division
    (C) proper, primarily because he returned the pistol license to Mr. Wilson and notified the Desk Officer that the license was valid
    (D) improper, primarily because Mr. Wilson should have been brought to the station house.

Answer question 22 solely on the basis of the following information.

Police Officers must sometimes rely on eyewitness accounts of incidents, even though eyewitnesses may make mistakes with regard to some details.

22. Police Officer Colon responded to a report of a purse snatch on 110th Street. Upon arrival at the scene she interviewed the complainant, Mrs. Smith, and three other witnesses who had been standing at a bus stop. The witnesses saw two men fleeing from the scene in a black car. The following are license plate numbers provided by the complainant and witnesses. Which one of these numbers should Officer Colon consider most likely to be correct?

    (A) P-51856
    (B) T-58166
    (C) P-51886
    (D) T-41685

Answer question 23 solely on the basis of the following information.

When Police Officers receive a report of a missing person they should do the following in the order given:

1. Report to the location of the complainant who reported the missing person.
2. Interview the complainant.
3. Obtain a physical description of the missing person and a description of the clothes worn by the missing person.
4. Determine where the missing person was last seen.
5. Start a search at the location where the missing person was last seen.
6. Request a Patrol Supervisor to respond to the scene.

23. Police Officer Jane Anderson responds to a report of a missing 15-year-old at 187 Rockwell Avenue, Apt. 6F. The teenager's mother, the complainant, informs Officer Anderson that her son is 5'5", 140 lbs., and was wearing a red striped shirt and black shorts. Police Officer Anderson should next

(A) search the apartment building for the teenager
(B) begin searching the neighborhood
(C) ask the mother where her son was last seen
(D) request a Patrol Supervisor to respond to the scene.

Answer question 24 solely on the basis of the following information.

Grand Larceny 4th Degree—occurs when a person steals property and:

1. the value of the property is more than one thousand dollars; or
2. the property, regardless of its nature and value, is taken from the victim; or
3. the property consists of one or more firearms.

24. Which one of the following is the best example of Grand Larceny in the Fourth Degree?

(A) Samuel, a security guard working at Beacon's Warehouse, enters an unauthorized area and steals a clock radio.
(B) Jonathan enters Lacy's Department Store, loads $500 worth of merchandise into a large shopping bag, and leaves the store.
(C) Harry is walking down the street at night when a shabbily dressed woman pulls out a gun and tells him to put his hands up.
(D) Mildred discovers that the man, who just bumped into her, has stolen her wallet containing $20 in cash from her pants pocket.

25. Officer Johnson has issued a summons to a driver and has obtained the following information:

Place of Occurrence:	Corner of Foster Road and Woodrow Avenue
Time of Occurrence:	7:10 P.M.
Driver:	William Grant
Offense:	Driving through a red light
Age of Driver:	42
Address of Driver:	23 Richmond Avenue

Officer Johnson is making an entry in his memo book regarding the incident. Which one of the following expresses the above information *most clearly* and *accurately*?

(A) William Grant, lives at 23 Richmond Avenue at 7:10 P.M., went through a red light. He was issued a summons at the corner of Foster Road and Woodrow Avenue. The driver is 42 years old.
(B) William Grant, age 42, who lives at 23 Richmond Avenue, was issued a summons for going through a red light at 7:10 P.M. at the corner of Foster Road and Woodrow Avenue.
(C) William Grant, age 42, was issued a summons on the corner of Foster Road and Woodrow Avenue for going through a red light. He lives at 23 Richmond Avenue at 7:10 P.M.
(D) A 42-year-old man who lives at 23 Richmond Avenue was issued a summons at 7:10 P.M. William Grant went through a red light at the corner of Foster Road and Woodrow Avenue.

26. Police Officer Frome has completed investigating a report of a stolen auto and obtained the following information:

Date of Occurrence:	October 26, 1988
Place of Occurrence:	51st Street and 8th Avenue
Time of Occurrence:	3:30 P.M.
Crime:	Auto Theft
Suspect:	Michael Wadsworth
Action Taken:	Suspect arrested

Officer Frome is preparing a report on the incident. Which one of the following expresses the above information *most clearly* and *accurately*?

(A) Arrested on October 26, 1988 was a stolen auto at 51st Street and 8th Avenue at 3:30 P.M. driven by Michael Wadsworth.
(B) For driving a stolen auto at 3:30 P.M., Michael Wadsworth was arrested at 51st Street and 8th Avenue on October 26, 1988.
(C) On October 26, 1988 at 3:30 P.M. Michael Wadsworth was arrested at 51st Street and 8th Avenue for driving a stolen auto.
(D) Michael Wadsworth was arrested on October 26, 1988 at 3:30 P.M. for driving at 51st Street and 8th Avenue. The auto was stolen.

Answer questions 27 and 28 solely on the basis of the following information.

As a result of numerous interviews of complainants and witnesses of violent crimes, Officer Wells has noticed a serious rise in the number of certain crimes in his patrol area over the past three months. He has observed that most of the rapes take place on E. 98th Street between Lott Avenue and Herk Place; assaults happen on Lott Avenue between Chester Avenue and E. 98th Street; and the majority of the robberies occur on Lott Avenue between E. 98th Street and Hughes Place. The assaults take place between 1:00 A.M. and 3:00 A.M. All of the robberies happen between 1:00 A.M. and 6:00 A.M. and most of the rapes happen between 8:00 A.M. and 11:00 A.M. The rapes usually occur on Mondays and Wednesdays, the robberies on Fridays and Saturdays, and the assaults on Saturdays and Sundays.

27. Officer Wells would most effectively reduce the number of robberies by patrolling

(A) Lott Avenue between E. 98th Street and Hughes Place on Fridays and Saturdays between 1:00 A.M. and 8:00 A.M.
(B) Lott Avenue between E. 98th Street and Chester Avenue on Saturdays and Sundays between 1:00 A.M. and 6:00 A.M.
(C) E. 98th Street between Lott Avenue and Herk Place on Saturdays and Sundays between 1:00 A.M. and 3:00 A.M.
(D) E. 98th Street between Herk Place and Chester Avenue on Mondays and Wednesdays between 8:00 A.M. and 11:00 A.M.

28. Officer Wells has been informed by his supervisor that he will be assigned to a patrol each week that would allow him to concentrate on reducing the number of rapes. What would be the most appropriate patrol for Officer Wells to work?

(A) Tuesday through Saturday, 8:00 P.M. to 4:00 P.M.
(B) Monday through Friday, 7:30 A.M. to 3:30 P.M.
(C) Wednesday through Sunday, noon to 8:00 P.M.
(D) Monday through Friday, 3:00 P.M. to 11:00 P.M.

29. Police Officers are required to remove potentially dangerous property from a prisoner prior to placing him in a jail cell. Which of the following items should be removed from a prisoner?

(A) An empty wallet.
(B) A gold wedding ring.
(C) A box of cough drops.
(D) A pair of shoe laces.

Answer question 30 solely on the basis of the following information.

When a Police Officer makes an arrest, the Officer should do the following in the order given:

1. Inform the prisoner of the reason for the arrest.
2. Handcuff the prisoner's hands behind his back.
3. Search the prisoner and the nearby area for weapons and evidence.
4. Advise the prisoner of his legal rights before questioning.

30. Police Officer Golden arrests Roy Owen and informs Mr. Owen that he is being arrested for the robbery of a jewelry store. While properly handcuffing the prisoner, the Officer notices a small handgun in Mr. Owen's back pants pocket. The Officer finishes handcuffing the prisoner and then removes the handgun from his pants pocket. The Officer should next

(A) inform the prisoner of his rights
(B) question the prisoner
(C) return, with the prisoner, to the jewelry store
(D) search the prisoner and the immediate area for weapons and evidence.

31. Police Officer Wright has finished investigating a report of Grand Larceny and has obtained the following information:

Time of Occurrence:	Between 1:00 P.M. and 2:00 P.M.
Place of Occurrence:	In front of victim's home, 85 Montgomery Avenue
Victim:	Mr. Williams, owner of the vehicle
Crime:	Automobile broken into
Property Taken:	Stereo valued at $1,200

Officer Wright is preparing a report on the incident. Which one of the following expresses the above information *most clearly* and *accurately*?

(A) While parked in front of his home Mr. Williams states that between 1:00 P.M. and 2:00 P.M. an unknown person broke into his vehicle. Mr. Williams, who lives at 85 Montgomery Avenue, lost his $1,200 stereo.
(B) Mr. Williams, who lives at 85 Montgomery Avenue, states that between 1:00 P.M. and 2:00 P.M. his vehicle was parked in front of his home when an unknown person broke into his car and took his stereo worth $1,200.
(C) Mr. Williams was parked in front of 85 Montgomery Avenue, which is his home, when it was robbed of a $1,200 stereo. When he came out he observed between 1:00 P.M. and 2:00 P.M. that his car had been broken into by an unknown person.
(D) Mr. Williams states between 1:00 P.M. and 2:00 P.M. that an unknown person broke into his car in front of his home. Mr. Williams further states that he was robbed of a $1,200 stereo at 85 Montgomery Avenue.

Answer questions 32 through 35 solely on the basis of the following passage.

Police Officers Grice and Sexton were working a 4:00 P.M. to midnight tour of duty on Friday, December 5, when they were assigned to investigate a burglary. They were told to respond to 355 Grand Street, the 14th floor, Apartment 1402, and to speak to the complainant, Ms. Starr. Upon arrival, Officer Sexton interviewed Ms. Starr, who stated that when she returned home from work at approximately 6:10 P.M. she was unable to unlock her door because the keyhole had been stuffed with toothpicks. After the door was opened by building maintenance, she entered her apartment and saw that her jewelry box had been emptied and was laying on the floor.

Officer Grice, who is qualified in the recovery of fingerprints, dusted the jewelry box and the front door in an attempt to recover any fingerprints that the burglar may have left. The Officers also interviewed Mrs. Caputo, who lives in Apartment 1404 and Mr. Babbit who lives in Apartment 1407. Both individuals stated that they neither saw nor heard anything unusual.

The next night, Saturday, December 6, Officers Grice and Sexton responded to Apartment 1514 in the same building on a call of a burglary. The complainant, Ms. Chung, stated that when she returned home from shopping she discovered that her lock had been stuffed with chewing gum and that her apartment had been burglarized. Officer Grice dusted the front door and a dresser, which had been opened, for prints.

Ten days after the last burglary, Detective Carrano, who had been assigned to investigate the burglaries, was informed by Mr. Hunt of the fingerprint identification unit that the prints recovered from both apartments belonged to Peter Remo of 355 Gravel Street, Apartment 1705. Later that evening after obtaining an arrest warrant, Detective Carrano arrested Peter Remo for the burglaries.

32. Who lived on the same floor as Ms. Starr?
    (A) Ms. Chung
    (B) Peter Remo
    (C) Mr. Babbit
    (D) Mr. Hunt.

33. Who was responsible for recovering the fingerprints that were used to identify Peter Remo?
    (A) Officer Grice
    (B) Mr. Hunt
    (C) Detective Carrano
    (D) Officer Sexton.

34. When was Peter Remo arrested?
    (A) December 5
    (B) December 6
    (C) December 15
    (D) December 16.

35. Why was Ms. Starr unable to unlock her door?

    (A) She lost her keys.
    (B) Chewing gum had been stuffed into the lock.
    (C) Her keys had been taken from her jewelry box.
    (D) The lock was stuffed with toothpicks.

Answer question 36 solely on the basis of the following information.

Upon arriving at the scene of any offense committed between members of the same family or household, a Police Officer should do the following in the order given:

1. Ascertain all the facts.
2. Obtain medical assistance, if needed.
3. Determine whether:
   a. a family offense has been committed; or
   b. an Order of Protection has been obtained by the complainant in order to keep the offender from entering the complainant's home or workplace.
4. Begin a search of the immediate area for the offender, if the offender has fled the scene.
5. If the search produces no results advise the complainant/victim to call the police when the offender returns.
6. Prepare a Complaint Report.

36. Police Officer Laura Molina responds to 285 Oak Street, Apartment 3A, in regard to a possible violent family offense. Upon arrival, Police Officer Molina is met at the apartment door by Ms. Martin. Officer Molina notices that Ms. Martin had been bleeding from a cut over her right eye. Ms. Martin tells Police Officer Molina that she and her husband had been having serious marital problems for the past six months. She said that just last week she had gotten an Order of Protection against her husband. However, her husband had returned to their home drunk and hit her on the head with a glass bottle. Police Officer Molina noticed broken glass on the floor in the living room. Police Officer Molina asked Ms. Martin if she needed an ambulance, but Ms. Martin told the Officer that she did not. Ms. Martin further explained that after her husband hit her, he ran out of the apartment. Ms. Martin added that he was wearing white sneakers, green army fatigue pants, and a light blue shirt. The next step P.O. Molina should take is to

(A) call an ambulance
(B) search the area for Mr. Martin
(C) prepare a Complaint Report
(D) advise Ms. Martin to call the police when her husband returns.

Answer question 37 solely on the basis of the following information.

When handcuffing a prisoner, a Police Officer should:

1. Handcuff person with hands behind his back.
2. Search person for weapons, evidence, or contraband.
3. Escort person to station house and inform the supervisor of the charges.
4. Remove handcuffs and place the person in a cell.

37. While on patrol, Police Officer Lewis arrests Robert Hendricks for assaulting his wife, Mrs. Hendricks. Police Officer Davis, who is also on patrol, arrives to assist Officer Lewis and observes her handcuffing the prisoner with his hands in front of his body. When Officer Lewis begins to search the prisoner for weapons, the prisoner swings his arms around and hits Officer Lewis on the side of the head. Officer Davis then steps in to subdue the prisoner. A patrol car arrives to transport the prisoner to the station house. There, Officer Lewis informs the Supervisor of the charges against the prisoner, removes the handcuffs, and places him in a cell. In this situation, Officer Lewis' actions were

(A) improper, primarily because she should not have removed the handcuffs from the prisoner until he was safely in his cell
(B) proper, primarily because she did not place the handcuffs on the legs or ankles of the prisoner
(C) improper, primarily because the prisoner's hands were not handcuffed behind his back
(D) proper, primarily because she placed the handcuffs on the prisoner in the presence of another Police Officer.

Answer question 38 solely on the basis of the following information.

Police Officers must sometimes rely on eyewitness accounts of incidents, even though eyewitnesses may make mistakes with regard to some details.

38. While crossing the street, Robert Green was struck by a delivery truck. Police Officer Luther was called to the scene and spoke with four witnesses who saw the truck that struck Mr. Green. The following are descriptions of the truck given by the witnesses. Which one of the descriptions should Officer Luther consider most likely to be correct?

(A) A brown GMC truck, Plate G-1843
(B) A black Ford truck, Plate G-1854
(C) A brown Ford truck, Plate G-1845
(D) A brown Ford truck, Plate C-1845.

Answer question 39 solely on the basis of the following information.

Police Officers may be required to safeguard the property of a deceased person who lived alone. When safeguarding the property, a Police Officer should do the following in the order given:

1. Request a Patrol Supervisor to respond to the scene.
2. In the presence of the Patrol Supervisor, search the body for valuables and documents concerning identity.
3. Remove all property except clothing.
4. Enter in Memo Book a complete list of property removed from deceased.
5. Complete the Property Clerk's Invoice Work Sheet indicating what property was removed.
6. Deliver all property and the Property Clerk's Invoice Work Sheet to the Desk Officer at the precinct.

39. Police Officer Frey responds to 220 E. 5th Street, Apt. 8M. He finds Mr. Johnson lying dead on the living room floor. The building superintendant, who had let Officer Frey into the apartment, informs Officer Frey that Mr. Johnson lived alone. The Officer radios the dispatcher and requests the Patrol Supervisor to respond to the scene. When Sergeant O'Malley, the Patrol Supervisor arrives, he and Officer Frey search the body. They find a wallet with various personal papers and $3,200 in cash. Officer Frey removes the property. The next step Officer Frey should take is to

(A) continue searching the area around the body for any additional property
(B) deliver the property to the precinct and give it to the Desk Officer
(C) prepare the Property Clerk's Invoice Work Sheet
(D) make a Memo Book entry listing the wallet and its contents.

40. On August 31st at 2:30 P.M., Police Officer Jones is assigned to a post at the West Side Shopping Mall. Captain Franks tells Officer Jones that there has been a sharp increase in shoplifting at the mall over the past three weeks. He instructs the Officer to watch closely any persons whose behavior appears to be suspicious. Officer Jones observes the following four situations. Which person should Officer Jones watch more closely?

(A) A woman who is dressed in jeans and a winter overcoat is looking at a display counter in a dress shop.
(B) A woman with a large shopping bag who appears to be counting money while leaving a store.
(C) An old man who is pushing a stroller with a two-year-old child in the toy department of a large store.
(D) Two teenaged boys who are looking in the display window of an electronics store.

Answer questions 41 through 42 solely on the basis of the following map. The flow of traffic is indicated by the arrows. If there is only one arrow shown, then traffic flows only in the direction indicated by the arrow. If there are two arrows shown, then traffic flows in both directions. You must follow the flow of traffic.

41. Police Officers Gold and Warren are at the intersection of Maple Road and Hampton Drive. The radio dispatcher has assigned them to investigate an attempted auto theft in the parking lot on Dusty Road. Which one of the following is the shortest route for the Officers to take in their patrol car to get to the entrance of the parking lot on Dusty Road, making sure to obey all traffic regulations?

(A) Travel north on Hampton Drive, then west on Dusty Road to the parking lot entrance.

(B) Travel west on Maple Road, then north on Beck Drive, then west on Dusty Road to the parking lot entrance.

(C) Travel north on Hampton Drive, then west on Anderson Street, then north on Merrick Street, then west on Dusty Road to the parking lot entrance.

(D) Travel west on Maple Road, then north on Merrick Street, then west on Dusty Road to the parking lot entrance.

42. Police Officer Gladden is in a patrol car at the intersection of Beach Drive and Anderson Street when he spots a suspicious car. P.O. Gladden calls the radio dispatcher to determine if the vehicle was stolen. P.O. Gladden then follows the vehicle north on Beach Drive for three blocks, then turns right and proceeds for one block and makes another right. He then follows the vehicle for two blocks and then they both make a left turn and continue driving. P.O. Gladden now receives a call from the dispatcher stating the car was reported stolen and signals for the vehicle to pull to the side of the road. In what direction was P.O. Gladden heading at the time he signaled for the other car to pull over?

(A) North   (C) South
(B) East   (D) West.

Answer question 43 solely on the basis of the following information.

Criminal Possession of Stolen Property 3rd Degree—occurs when a person knowingly possesses stolen property in order to benefit himself or another person who does not own the property.

43. Which one of the following situations is the best example of Criminal Possession of Stolen Property in the Third Degree?

(A) Police Officers enter Mr. Hanson's home and discover a stolen television. Hanson shows the Officers a receipt for the television from what he thought was an honest dealer.

(B) While walking to work, Anne finds a diamond ring in the street and keeps it.

(C) John purchases what he believes is an expensive stolen stereo, which is actually a low-priced stereo that the dealer obtained properly.

(D) Tim warns his customers that the stereos he has for sale are stolen and shouldn't be brought to authorized dealers for repairs.

44. Police Officer Fontaine obtained the following details relating to a suspicious package:

Place of Occurrence:	Case Bank, 2 Wall Street
Time of Occurrence:	10:30 A.M.
Date of Occurrence	October 10, 1988
Complaint:	Suspicious package in doorway
Found by:	Emergency Service Unit

Officer Fontaine is preparing a report for department records. Which one of the following expresses the above information *most clearly* and *accurately*?

(A) At 10:30 A.M. the Emergency Service Unit reported they found a package on October 10, 1988 which appeared suspicious. This occurred in a doorway at 2 Wall Street, Case Bank.

(B) A package which appeared suspicious was in the doorway of Case Bank. The Emergency Service Unit reported this at 2 Wall Street at 10:30 A.M. on October 10, 1988 when found.

(C) On October 10, 1988 at 10:30 A.M. a suspicious package was found by the Emergency Service Unit in the doorway of Case Bank at 2 Wall Street.

(D) The Emergency Service Unit found a package at the Case Bank. It appeared suspicious at 10:30 A.M. in the doorway of 2 Wall Street on October 10, 1988.

45. Police Officer Reardon receives the following information regarding a case of child abuse:

Victim:	Joseph Mays
Victim's Age:	10 years old
Victim's Address:	Resides with his family at 42 Columbia Street, Apartment 1B
Complainant:	Victim's uncle, Kevin Mays
Suspects:	Victim's parents

Police Officer Reardon is preparing a report to send to the Department of Social Services. Which one of the following expresses the above information *most clearly* and *accurately*?

(A) Kevin Mays reported a case of child abuse to his ten-year-old nephew, Joseph Mays, by his parents. He resides with his family at 42 Columbia Street, Apartment 1B.

(B) Kevin Mays reported that his ten-year-old nephew, Joseph Mays, has been abused by the child's parents. Joseph Mays resides with his family at 42 Columbia Street, Apartment 1B.

(C) Joseph Mays has been abused by his parents. Kevin Mays reported that his nephew resides with his family at 42 Columbia Street, Apartment 1B. He is ten years old.

(D) Kevin Mays reported that his nephew is ten years old. Joseph Mays has been abused by his parents. He resides with his family at 42 Columbia Street, Apartment 1B.

46. While on patrol Police Officer Hawkins was approached by Harry Roland, a store owner, who found a leather bag, valued at $200.00, outside his store. Officer Hawkins took the property into custody and removed the following

- 2 Solex watches, each valued at $500.00
- 4 14-kt. gold necklaces, each valued at $315.00
- Cash $519.00
- 1 diamond ring valued at $400.00

Officer Hawkins is preparing a report on the found property. Which one of the following is the total value of the property and cash found?

(A) $1,734.00   (C) $3,179.00

(B) $3,171.00   (D) $3,379.00.

Answer question 47 solely on the basis of the following information.

During the month of September, three rapes were committed near Pier 21 on Westerly Avenue. The description of each of the suspects given by the victims, is as follows:

Rape No. 1—Male, white, mid thirties, 5'8", 190 lbs., long wavy hair, wearing dark sunglasses, black jacket, green pants, black boots, moustache.

Rape No. 2—Male, white, late 20's, 5'8", slim build, moustache, closely cropped hair, brown eyes, black jacket, blue jeans, black boots.

Rape No. 3—Male, white, 35, 5'7", 180 lbs., long hair, moustache, dark glasses, blue denim jacket, blue jeans, black boots.

On October 3, 1988, a fourth rape was committed. The suspect was arrested by Police Officer Jackson. The description of the suspect is as follows:

Rape No. 4—Male, white, 30–35, 5'7", 185 lbs., long curly hair, moustache, grey jacket, blue jeans, baseball cap, white boots.

47. Based on the above descriptions of the suspects in the first three rapes, Officer Jackson should consider the suspect in the fourth rape as a suspect in

(A) Rape No.1, but not Rape No. 2 or Rape No.3
(B) Rape No.1 and Rape No. 3, but not Rape No. 2
(C) Rape No. 2 and Rape No. 3, but not Rape No. 1
(D) Rape No. 1, Rape No. 2, and Rape No. 3.

Answer question 48 solely on the basis of the following information.

When a warrant has been issued for the arrest of a parent who has physically abused or neglected a child, Police Officers should do the following in the order given:

1. Respond to the location and arrest the parent(s) named in the warrant if the parent is present.
2. Remove the child from the home, even if parent named in warrant is not present and an arrest is not made.
3. Deliver the child to Family Court between the hours of 9 A.M. and 5 P.M.
4. If Family Court is not in session, bring the child to the precinct station house and locate temporary housing.
5. If either the child or parent is not home, attempt to locate child or parent.

48. Officers Batts and Peters are informed by the Desk Officer that a warrant has been issued for the arrest of Mr. Hughes. It has been reported that Mr. Hughes has physically abused his five-year-old son, Michael. The Officers arrive at the Hughes home at 1:00 A.M. They find Michael at home alone. When asked where his parents are, he informs the Officers that his father went away yesterday and that his mother doesn't live with them. Michael tells the Officers that his uncle has been visiting but hasn't been home all day. The Officers return to the station house with Michael and locate temporary housing for him. What should the Officers do next?

(A) Attempt to locate Michael's uncle.
(B) Take Michael to Family Court.
(C) Try to locate Michael's parents.
(D) Hold Michael in the station house until his mother is located.

Answer question 49 solely on the basis of the following information.

Police Department policy requires that a vehicle pursuit should be ended whenever the pursuit causes a greater risk to Police Officers and the public than the danger to the community if the suspect is not caught. If the chase is ended, the Officers should attempt to obtain enough information to apprehend the suspect at a later time.

49. Officer Jordan is in her patrol car when she sees a blue Ford, license plate #7744-AEK, hit an unoccupied red Chevrolet, and speed away from the scene of the accident. Officer Jordan pursues the blue Ford at 80 M.P.H. on a busy street. While in pursuit, Officer Jordan weaves in and out of traffic, causing some cars to skid and swerve. After a few blocks the blue Ford skids and Officer Jordan's car crashes into it. Officer Jordan immediately arrests the driver of the Ford. In this situation Officer Jordan's actions were

(A) proper, primarily because it is her duty to arrest criminal suspects
(B) improper, primarily because Officer Jordan should not have pursued the blue Ford without knowing how badly the red Chevrolet was damaged
(C) proper, primarily because Officer Jordan arrested the driver without causing serious injury to another person
(D) improper, primarily because Officer Jordan should have discontinued the pursuit and tried to arrest the suspect at another time.

50. While on patrol, Police Officer Blake observes a man running from a burning abandoned building. Officer Blake radios the following information:

Place of Occurrence:	310 Hall Avenue
Time of Occurrence:	8:30 P.M.
Type of Building:	Abandoned
Suspect:	Male, white, about 35 years old
Crime:	Arson

Officer Blake is completing a report on the incident. Which one of the following expresses the above information *most clearly* and *accurately*?

(A) An abandoned building located at 310 Hall Avenue was set on fire at 8:30 P.M. A white male, approximately 35 years old, was observed fleeing the scene.
(B) A white male, approximately 35 years old, at 8:30 P.M. was observed fleeing 310 Hall Avenue. The fire was set at an abandoned building.
(C) An abandoned building was set on fire. A white male, approximately 35 years old, was observed fleeing the scene at 8:30 P.M. at 310 Hall Avenue.
(D) Observed fleeing a building at 8:30 P.M. was a white male, approximately 35 years old. An abandoned building, located at 310 Hall Avenue, was set on fire.

Answer question 51 solely on the basis of the following information.

Police Officers must sometimes rely on eyewitness accounts of incidents, even though eyewitnesses may make mistakes with regard to some details.

51. While on patrol, Police Officer Hanson was approached by a woman who was screaming that her pocketbook had just been stolen. Officer Hanson questions four witnesses who saw the robbery. The following are descriptions of the suspect given by the witnesses. Which one of the descriptions should Officer Hanson consider most likely to be correct?

(A) Male, white, 40 years old, wearing a black hat and red sneakers.
(B) Male, black, 25 years old, wearing a black hat and red sneakers.
(C) Male, white, 25 years old, wearing a black hat and red sneakers.
(D) Male, white, 20 years old, wearing a grey hat and maroon sneakers.

52. Police Officers may be required to transport to a hospital persons who are in need of immediate treatment when an ambulance is not immediately available. It would be most appropriate for a Police Officer to transport which one of the following individuals?

(A) An elderly woman who twists her ankle while walking to the grocery store.
(B) A 4-year-old boy who trips and breaks his arm while walking to school with his mother.
(C) A man who has a heart attack and is lying unconscious in the street.
(D) A man who bangs his forehead in a car accident and claims he might have a broken nose.

53. Police Officer Winters responds to a call regarding a report of a missing person. The following information was obtained by the Officer:

Time of Occurrence:	3:30 P.M.
Place of Occurrence:	Harrison Park
Reported by:	Louise Dee—daughter
Description of Missing Person:	Sharon Dee, 70 years old, 5'5", brown eyes, black hair—mother

Officer Winters is completing a report on the incident. Which one of the following expresses the above information *most clearly* and *accurately*?

(A) Mrs. Sharon Dee, reported missing by her daughter Louise, was seen in Harrison Park. The last time she saw her was at 3:30 P.M. She is 70 years old with black hair, brown eyes, and 5'5"
(B) Louise Dee reported that her mother, Sharon Dee, is missing. Sharon Dee is 70 years old, has black hair, brown eyes, and is 5'5". She was last seen at 3:30 P.M. in Harrison Park.
(C) Louise Dee reported Sharon, her 70-year-old mother at 3:30 P.M., to be missing after being seen last at Harrison Park. Described as being 5'5", she has black hair and brown eyes.
(D) At 3:30 P.M. Louise Dee's mother was last seen by her daughter in Harrison Park. She has black hair and brown eyes. Louise reported Sharon is 5'5" and 70 years old.

Answer questions 54 through 57 solely on the basis of the following passage.

While working an 8:00 A.M. to 4:00 P.M. shift on January 14, 1988, Police Officers Jones and Smith received a radio call at 1:45 P.M. to investigate a report of a man with a gun in front of 103 Lexington Avenue. Mary Holmes had called 911 from her home at 1:43 P.M. and explained that two days ago while on her way home from work, she had been threatened by a man with a gun in front of her home at 113 Lowell Street. She told the police operator that the same man was now standing in front of Harry's Lounge at 103 Lexington Avenue, drinking a beer. She described him as being between 30 and 40 years old, 5'6", 160 lbs., wearing a gray coat, gray brim hat, and gold wire rim glasses. The Officers responded to the location and observed a male fitting the description given by Miss Holmes. The Officers approached the suspect and, while searching his right front waist band, Officer Jones found a chromeplated .38 caliber revolver licensed and registered under the name of Joseph Fitz. Miss Holmes was brought to the scene and identified the suspect as the person who had threatened her earlier. Officer Smith then placed the man, identified as Joseph Fitz, under arrest.

54. On what day did the suspect threaten Miss Holmes?

(A) January 10
(B) January 12

(C) January 14
(D) January 16.

55. Officer Jones recovered the gun from the suspect's

(A) left front waist band
(B) right rear waist band

(C) left rear waist band
(D) right front waist band.

56. Miss Holmes stated that the suspect had threatened her in front of

(A) Harry's Lounge
(B) her home

(C) a bar
(D) her office.

57. Joseph Fitz was arrested because he

(A) illegally possessed a weapon
(B) was drinking in a public place
(C) committed a robbery two days earlier
(D) was identified as the suspect in a previous incident.

58. While on patrol, Police Officers Mertz and Gallo receive a call from the dispatcher regarding a crime in progress. When the Officers arrive they obtain the following information:

Time of Occurrence:	2:00 P.M.
Place of Occurrence:	In front of 2124 Bristol Avenue
Crime:	Purse Snatch
Victim:	Maria Nieves
Suspect:	Carlos Ortiz
Witness:	Jose Perez, who apprehended the suspect

The Officers are completing a report on the incident. Which one of the following expresses the above information *most clearly* and *accurately*?

(A) At 2:00 P.M., Jose Perez witnessed Maria Nieves. Her purse was snatched. The suspect, Carlos Ortiz was apprehended in front of 2124 Bristol Avenue.

(B) In front of 2124 Bristol Avenue, Carlos Ortiz snatched the purse belonging to Maria Nieves. Carlos Ortiz was apprehended by a witness to the crime after Jose Perez saw the purse snatch at 2:00 P.M.

(C) At 2:00 P.M., Carlos Ortiz snatched a purse from Maria Nieves in front of 2124 Bristol Avenue. Carlos Ortiz was apprehended by Jose Perez, a witness to the crime.

(D) At 2:00 P.M., Carlos Ortiz was seen snatching the purse of Maria Nieves as seen and apprehended by Jose Perez in front of 2124 Bristol Avenue.

59. Police Officers Willis and James respond to a crime in progress and obtain the following information:

Time of Occurence:	8:30 A.M.
Place of Occurrence:	Corner of Hopkin Avenue and Amboy Place
Crime:	Chain snatch
Victim:	Mrs. Paula Evans
Witness:	Mr. Robert Peters
Suspect:	white male

Officers Willis and James are completing a report on the incident. Which one of the following expresses the above information *most clearly* and *accurately*?

(A) Mrs. Paula Evans was standing on the corner of Hopkin Avenue and Amboy Place at 8:30 A.M. when a white male snatched her chain. Mr. Robert Peters witnessed the crime.

(B) At 8:30 A.M., Mr. Robert Peters witnessed Mrs. Paula Evans and a white male standing on the corner of Hopkin Avenue and Amboy Place. Her chain was snatched.

(C) At 8:30 A.M., a white male was standing on the corner of Hopkin Avenue and Amboy Place. Mrs. Paula Evans' chain was snatched and Mr. Robert Peters witnessed the crime.

(D) At 8:30 A.M., Mr. Robert Peters reported he witnessed a white male snatching Mrs. Paula Evans' chain while standing on the corner of Hopkin Avenue and Amboy Place.

Answer question 60 solely on the basis of the following information.

When a Police Officer reasonably suspects that a person has committed, is committing, or is about to commit a crime, the Officer, in order to protect himself from being injured, should do the following in the order given:

1. Stop the person and request identification and an explanation of the person's conduct.
2. Frisk the person by running hands over the person's clothing if the Officer thinks his life may be in danger.
3. Search the person by placing hands inside pockets and interior parts of the person's clothing if a frisk reveals an object that appears to be a weapon.
4. Prepare a Stop and Frisk Report for each person stopped if:
   a. person was stopped by use of force; or
   b. person was stopped and frisked or searched; or
   c. person was stopped and arrested.

60. Police Officers Darcey and Sanchez are investigating a report of a man with a gun on the corner of Boston Road and Montana Avenue. The Officers stop a man fitting the description they were given. Officer Darcey asks the man why he is in the area. Officer Darcey then asks the man for some proper identification. He then frisks the man and feels an object which seems to be an address book in the man's shirt pocket. Officer Darcey should next

(A) complete a Stop and Frisk Report
(B) search the man's clothing
(C) request the man's identification and an explanation of his conduct
(D) place the man under arrest for possession of a weapon.

Answer question 61 solely on the basis of the following information.

Robbery 3rd Degree—occurs when a person forcibly steals property.

61. Which one of the following situations is the best example of Robbery in the Third Degree?

(A) Stephanie was riding the train to Coney Island. When the train reached her stop, she realized her briefcase was missing.
(B) June was walking north on 119 Avenue to the bus stop when Sam approached her and snatched her bag. As she struggled with the attacker, he knocked her to the ground and fled south on 119 Avenue.
(C) Clifton was riding the train to Chambers Street during rush hour when Joe brushed past him, picked his pocket, and got off at the next stop.
(D) Denise's purse was hanging on the back of her chair while she ate at a local coffee shop, when Bill slit the purse strap with a razor and fled with the purse.

Answer question 62 solely on the basis of the following information.

Police Officer Gray has been instructed by his supervisor to help search for a suspected murderer who was seen running into an abandoned building after committing the crime. The description of the suspect is as follows:

Male, white, about 38 years old, 6'5", 225 lbs., short hair, gray pants, brown sweat shirt, brown construction boots, moustache, 2" scar above right eye.

Officer Gray has also been informed that there were three other murders committed on the same block since the beginning of the year and has been given the following descriptions of the suspects:

Murder No. 1—Male, white, 40 years old, 6'4", 220 lbs., short black hair, black pants, brown shirt, black jacket, construction boots, moustache, scar on face.

Murder No. 2—Male, white, 25 years old, 6'3", 170 lbs., short afro, gray pants, brown sweat shirt, brown boots, moustache, beard.

Murder No. 3—Male, white, 35 years old, 6'0", 225 lbs., black hair, gray pants, brown sweat shirt, brown shoes, moustache, long sideburns.

62. Based on the above descriptions of the suspects in the three previous murders, Officer Gray should tell his supervisor that the suspect in the last murder should also be considered a suspect in

    (A) Murder No. 1, but not Murder No. 2 or Murder No. 3
    (B) Murder No. 3, but not Murder No. 1 or Murder No. 2
    (C) Murder No. 1 and Murder No. 2, but not Murder No. 3
    (D) Murder No. 2 and Murder No. 3, but not Murder No. 1.

Answer question 63 solely on the basis of the following information.

When a Police Officer responds to the scene of an incident, the Officer may find it necessary to request the immediate assistance of another Department such as Fire, Sanitation, etc.

63. In which of the following incidents would an Officer most likely request the assistance of another Department?

    (A) A man reports that he was robbed at gunpoint.
    (B) Two teenage boys are caught spray-painting their names on a factory wall.
    (C) A truck carrying a poisonous liquid overturns and spills the liquid onto a crowded street.
    (D) A box of jewelry is found in the basement of an apartment house.

Answer question 64 solely on the basis of the following information.

When a juvenile, who is less than 16 years old, is arrested by a Police Officer and charged with a felony, the Officer must take the following steps in the order given:

1. Transport juvenile to Central Booking.
2. Place juvenile in a cell separate from adult prisoners.
3. Notify juvenile's parents of arrest.
4. Deliver arrest report to Central Booking Supervisor.
5. Have juvenile fingerprinted and photographed.
6. Deliver juvenile to Spofford Juvenile Center for detention.

64. Police Officer Wilson arrested 15-year-old Johnny Leon after Leon was seen threatening and eventually hitting Mr. Perez over the head with an ax handle. Leon was charged with Assault 1st Degree. Officer Wilson placed Leon in the patrol wagon. When they arrive at Central Booking, Officer Wilson should next

(A) ensure that Leon is not put in a cell with adult prisoners
(B) telephone Leon's parents
(C) have Leon fingerprinted and photographed
(D) submit arrest report to Supervisor at Central Booking.

Answer question 65 solely on the basis of the following information.

When evidence is required for presentation in court, a Police Officer must:

1. Request evidence from the Officer assigned to the Property Clerk facility where it is stored.
2. Give the Officer the Property Clerk's Index Number.
3. Present shield and identification card.
4. Sign a receipt for evidence.

65. Police Officer Dana is informed that she is scheduled to testify in court about a narcotics arrest she made four months ago. The case involves evidence stored at the Property Clerk's Office. Since Officer Dana was scheduled to work on patrol that day, she appears at the Property Clerk's Office in full police uniform. She requests the evidence from Officer Baskin, who is assigned to the Property Clerk's Office, and gives the clerk the correct Property Clerk's Index Number. Officer Dana presents her shield to Officer Baskin and signs a receipt for the evidence. She then proceeds to court. Officer Dana's actions in this situation were

(A) proper, primarily because she was scheduled to work patrol that day
(B) improper, primarily because a patrol supervisor should have been present to witness the transfer of property
(C) proper, primarily because the evidence was critical to the case
(D) improper, primarily because she did not show proper identification to Officer Baskin.

66. Police Officers Cleveland and Logan responded to an assault that had recently occurred. The following information was obtained at the scene:

Place of Occurrence:	Broadway and Roosevelt Avenue
Time of Occurrence:	1:00 A.M.
Crime:	Attempted robbery, assault
Victim:	Chuck Brown, suffered a broken tooth
Suspect:	Lewis Brown, victim's brother

Officer Logan is completing a report on the incident. Which one of the following expresses the above information *most clearly* and *accurately*?

(A) Lewis Brown assaulted his brother Chuck on the corner of Broadway and Roosevelt Avenue. Chuck Brown reported his broken tooth during the attempted robbery at 1:00 A.M.

(B) Chuck Brown had his tooth broken when he was assaulted at 1:00 A.M. on the corner of Broadway and Roosevelt Avenue by his brother, Lewis Brown, while Lewis was attempting to rob him.

(C) An attempt at 1:00 A.M. to rob Chuck Brown turned into an assault at the corner of Broadway and Roosevelt Avenue when his brother Lewis broke his tooth.

(D) At 1:00 A.M., Chuck Brown reported that he was assaulted during his brother's attempt to rob him. Lewis Brown broke his tooth. The incident occurred on the corner of Broadway and Roosevelt Avenue.

67. Police Officer Mannix has just completed an investigation regarding a hit-and-run accident which resulted in a pedestrian being injured. Officer Mannix has obtained the following information:

Make and Model of Car:	Pontiac, Trans Am
Year and Color of Car:	1986, white
Driver of Car:	Male, black
Place of Occurrence:	Corner of W. 15th Street and 8th Avenue
Time of Occurrence:	1:00 P.M.

Officer Mannix is completing a report on the accident. Which one of the following expresses the above information *most clearly* and *accurately*?

(A) At 1:00 P.M., at the corner of W. 15th Street and 8th Avenue, a black male driving a white 1986 Pontiac Trans Am was observed leaving the scene of the accident after injuring a pedestrian with the vehicle.

(B) On the corner of W. 15th Street and 8th Avenue, a white Pontiac, driven by a black male, a 1986 Trans Am injured a pedestrian and left the scene of the accident at 1:00 P.M.

(C) A black male driving a white 1986 Pontiac Trans Am, injured a pedestrian and left with the car while driving on the corner of W. 15th Street and 8th Avenue at 1:00 P.M.

(D) At the corner of W. 15th Street and 8th Avenue, a pedestrian was injured by a black male. He fled in his white 1986 Pontiac Trans Am at 1:00 P.M.

Answer questions 68 and 69 solely on the basis of the following information.

Police Officer Jones has been made aware by merchants on her post that an increase in crimes has been occurring in her area. All of the assaults seem to take place on Pitt Avenue between Van Syck Street and Stone Street. Most of the robberies take place on Pitt Avenue between Amboy Place and Herzl Street. All of the larcenies take place on Amboy Place between Pitt Avenue and East Avenue. The robberies usually occur on Fridays and Saturdays; the larcenies occur on Sundays and Mondays; and the assaults occur on Wednesdays and Thursdays. Most of the larcenies occur between 4:00 P.M. and 8:00 P.M, all of the robberies occur between 1:00 P.M. and 3:00 P.M., and the assaults occur between 1:00 A.M. and 4:00 A.M.

68. In order to reduce the number of larcenies, Officer Jones should inform the merchants that she will increase patrol on

   (A) Pitt Avenue between Amboy Place and Herzl Street on Sundays and Mondays between 4:00 P.M. and 8:00 P.M.
   (B) Amboy Place between Pitt Avenue and East Avenue on Mondays and Tuesdays between 3:00 A.M. and 8:00 A.M.
   (C) Amboy Place between East Avenue and Pitt Avenue on Sundays and Mondays between 3:00 P.M. and 10:00 P.M.
   (D) Herzl Street between Amboy Place and Pitt Avenue on Wednesdays and Thursdays between 1:00 A.M. and 9:00 A.M.

69. Officer Jones would be most effective in reducing the number of robberies if she patrolled from

   (A) 10:00 A.M. to 6:00 P.M., Monday through Friday
   (B) 1:00 P.M. to 9:00 P.M., Saturday through Wednesday
   (C) 1:00 A.M. to 9:00 A.M., Wednesday through Sunday
   (D) 8:00 A.M. to 4:00 P.M., Tuesday through Saturday.

70. Under certain circumstances, Police Officers are required to request the assistance and advice of a supervisor. Which one of the following situations would most likely require a supervisor?

   (A) Two men are verbally arguing over a parking space.
   (B) Several teenagers are listening and dancing to loud music in the schoolyard.
   (C) A woman threatens to jump from the twelfth floor of a building.
   (D) A man complains that his next door neighbor smokes marijuana in the building hallways.

Answer question 71 solely on the basis of the following information.

Reckless Endangerment 1st Degree—occurs when, under circumstances that clearly show a total disregard for human life, a person acts in a manner that creates a grave risk of death to another person.

71. Which one of the following is the best example of Reckless Endangerment in the First Degree?

(A) James, while attending a football game where his favorite team is losing, fires a rifle into the stands to get the crowd to stop cheering for the opposing team.
(B) A woman threatens to kill herself if her husband is not immediately released from prison.
(C) A motorist whose gas pedal is stuck hits a woman who is pushing a baby carriage down the block, causing her death.
(D) A person continues to throw garbage out of his second floor window into an empty lot, even after he is warned he could injure someone.

Answer question 72 solely on the basis of the following information.

When a Police Officer recovers a stolen vehicle, the following should be done in the order given:

1. Make a Memo Book entry describing the vehicle and where the vehicle was found.
2. Notify the Desk Officer.
3. Prepare a Property Clerk's Invoice.
4. Notify the owner, if known.

72. While on patrol, Police Officer Vasquez notices an unoccupied vehicle with lit head-lights on the corner of 101st and Kane Avenue. She recalls seeing that same vehicle parked in the same place with its engine running one hour earlier. Officer Vasquez requests the radio dispatcher to run a check on the vehicle's Florida license plate ZBF293. She is informed that the vehicle is registered to Ms. Patti Tucci of Miami Beach. Officer Vasquez notices that the steering column of the vehicle has been broken. Officer Vasquez suspects that the vehicle has been stolen. Officer Vasquez should next

(A) notify the owner of the vehicle
(B) record all details related to the vehicle in her Memo Book
(C) prepare a Property Clerk's Invoice
(D) call the Desk Officer.

Answer question 73 through 76 solely on the basis of the following passage.

On April 6, at 5:25 A.M., while patrolling the #8 train southbound to Brooklyn, Transit Police Officer O'Rourke noticed a young woman at the end of the car who appeared to be ill. Officer O'Rourke approached the woman and asked her if she was feeling all right. The woman was crying and began speaking incoherently. Officer O'Rourke escorted the woman off the train at the next southbound #8 platform in order to obtain information from her. After speaking with her for fifteen minutes, Officer O'Rourke learned that her name was Carol Rivers and that she had been assaulted and sexually molested while waiting for the southbound #8 train about a half hour before meeting the Officer. Miss Rivers described the suspect as a white male, in his forties, with gray hair, glasses, a red shirt, black pants, and a brown hat. The suspect fled on a northbound #8 train with the victim's pocketbook. Officer O'Rourke then radioed for an ambulance to respond to the location to assist Miss Rivers.

The next day at approximately 5:30 A.M., while Officer O'Rourke was standing on the subway platform waiting to board the uptown #7 train to Queens, he noticed an individual coming down the steps from the southbound platform. The man was in his forties, with gray hair, dark glasses, and the same clothing described by Miss Rivers the day before, except for his shirt, which was white. Office O'Rourke, believing the man to be the same perpetrator, decided to follow him in order to observe the suspect's actions. The man was walking alongside a woman on the northbound platform and attempted to snatch her pocketbook. The woman held onto her purse and started to yell for the police. The man immediately released his hold on the pocketbook and ran down the platform onto an awaiting #7 train to Manhattan. Officer O'Rourke pursued the man onto the train and subsequently placed him under arrest two stations later.

73. Officer O'Rourke requested that the ambulance respond to the subway platform of the

(A) northbound #8 train   (C) downtown #7 train
(B) uptown #7 train   (D) southbound #8 train.

74. At approximately what time was Miss Rivers assaulted?

(A) 4:55 A.M.   (C) 5:25 A.M.
(B) 5:10 A.M.   (D) 5:40 A.M.

75. The suspect arrested by Officer O'Rourke was wearing a

(A) red shirt and blue pants   (C) red shirt and black pants
(B) white shirt and black pants   (D) white shirt and red pants.

76. On April 7, Officer O'Rourke boarded a train to

(A) Manhattan   (C) the Bronx
(B) Queens   (D) Brooklyn.

77. Police Officer Brown has responded to a domestic dispute and has obtained the following information:

Time of Complaint:	3:20 P.M.
Complainant:	Mrs. Jenny Shawn
Address of Complainant:	39 Waring Place
Complaint:	Husband and wife screaming, and threatening each other with knives
People involved:	Mr. and Mrs. George Roberts

Officer Brown is completing a report on the incident. Which one of the following expresses the above information *most clearly* and *accurately?*

(A) At 39 Waring Place Mrs. Jenny Shawn called the police because Mr. and Mrs. George Roberts were screaming and threatening each other with knives at 3:20 P.M.

(B) At 3:20 P.M., Mrs. Jenny Shawn reported Mr. and Mrs. George Roberts to the police. At 39 Waring Place they were screaming and threatening each other with knives.

(C) Mrs. Jenny Shawn reported to the police of 39 Waring Place at 3:20 P.M., that Mr. and Mrs. George Roberts were screaming and threatening each other with knives.

(D) At 3:20 P.M., Mrs. Jenny Shawn, of 39 Waring Place, called the police because Mr. and Mrs. George Roberts were screaming and threatening each other with knives.

78. While on patrol, Police Officer Beckman witnesses the following incident:

Incident:	Person hit by brick that was thrown from 12th floor of a building
Place of Incident:	In front of 227 20th Street
Time of Incident:	11:21 A.M.
Victim:	Mr. George Manson, Injured
Suspect:	Mr. Brian Mor

Officer Beckman is completing a report regarding this incident. Which one of the following expresses the above information *most clearly* and *accurately?*

(A) At 11:21 A.M., in front of 227 20th Street a brick was thrown. Mr. George Manson was walking and injured by Mr. Brian Mor on the 12th floor of a building.

(B) A brick was thrown from the 12th floor window of a building in front of 227 20th Street. Mr. George Manson was walking at 11:21 A.M. and was injured by Mr. Brian Mor.

(C) Mr. Brian Mor threw a brick in front of 227 20th Street. At 11:21 A.M. Mr. George Manson was injured when walking from the 12th floor of a building.

(D) At 11:21 A.M., Mr. George Manson was walking in front of 227 20th Street. He was injured by a brick that Mr. Brian Mor threw from the 12th floor of a building.

Answer question 79 solely on the basis of the following information.

When a Police Officer investigates a complaint of a rape or an attempted rape, the Officer should do the following in the order given:

1. Interview the complainant and witnesses and attempt to obtain the facts.
2. Search for and remove any evidence from the location of the complaint.
3. Notify the Sex Crime Squad if the victim was raped.
4. Prepare a Complaint Report Worksheet.
5. Notify supervisor upon completion of investigation.

79. Police Officers King and Ross respond to 110-30 11th Avenue. Upon arriving at the location they find Mary Jones and Sam Dean sitting on the front steps of the building. Mr. Dean informs the Officers that as he was walking home he heard screams, ran into an alley, and discovered a man threatening Mary Jones with a knife. Mr. Dean ran towards the man who dropped his knife and ran away. Mary Jones confirms what Mr. Dean told the Officers and added that when the man had threatened her with a knife he said he was going to rape her. She said that if Mr. Dean hadn't chased the man away she would have been raped. The next step that Officers King and Ross should take is to

(A) prepare a Complaint Report Worksheet
(B) interview Mr. Dean
(C) search for the knife
(D) call the Sex Crime Squad.

Answer question 80 solely on the basis of the following information.

Police Officer Selma is assigned to patrol Blum and Tan Streets in order to reduce the sale of drugs. Officer Selma is informed that drugs are being sold at 416 Blum Street in Apt. 1A and at 428 Tan Street in Apt. 1B. Most of the drug sales in Apt. 1A occur between 10:30 A.M. and 4:00 P.M. Most of the drug sales in Apt. 1B take place from 5:00 P.M. to 8:00 P.M. Officer Selma is also informed that most of the drug sales are taking place on Thursdays and Sundays on Tan Street and Wednesdays and Fridays on Blum Street.

80. Officer Selma would most likely reduce the number of drug sales taking place in Apt. 1A by patrolling in the area of

(A) 428 Tan Street from 9:00 A.M. to 5:00 P.M.
(B) 416 Blum Street from 9:00 A.M. to 5:00 P.M.
(C) 428 Tan Street from 3:00 P.M. to 11:00 P.M.
(D) 416 Blum Street from 3:00 P.M. to 11:00 P.M.

Answer question 81 solely on the basis of the following information.

When a Police Officer stops a vehicle and discovers that the operator is driving with a suspended license, the Officer should

1. Take away the driver's license.
2. Give the operator of the vehicle a receipt for the license.
3. If the operator has two or more unrelated suspensions, or if the driver's license has been revoked for any reason, arrest the motorist.
4. Do not mark or mutilate the license in any manner.
5. Have the violator's vehicle parked in a legal parking area until removed by a licensed operator.

81. Police Officers Wells and Cortese, while on patrol, observed the driver of a blue Firebird make an illegal U-turn at an intersection. Officer Wells directed the driver to pull over to the curb. The Officer approached the driver and requested his driver's license and car registration. While inspecting the license, Officer Wells noticed that the license had been revoked. Officer Wells took the license, issued a receipt, and placed the driver under arrest. Officer Cortese legally parked the car under a tree. In this situation the actions taken by Officers Wells and Cortese were

(A) proper, primarily because the driver had a revoked license
(B) improper, primarily because he should have taken the license and registration
(C) proper, primarily because the driver almost caused an accident
(D) improper, primarily because the vehicle should have been removed by a licensed driver.

Answer question 82 solely on the basis of the following information.

Under certain circumstances Police Officers may be required to use their hand guns.

82. In which one of the following situations would it be most appropriate for an Officer to remove his gun from his holster?

(A) A man enters a subway station without paying a fare and as he runs towards a train he knocks a woman to the ground.
(B) A person grabs a woman's handbag and runs down a crowded street.
(C) A woman hits a young boy with her car and begins to drive away without stopping.
(D) A person is swinging an axe in a crowded area and threatens to kill anyone who comes near him.

83. Police Officer Spencer received the following information from a Grand Larceny victim:

Time of Occurrence:	3:45 P.M.
Place of Occurrence:	Uptown #4 train, 14th Street station
Victim:	Louis Smith
Witness:	Cindy Lewis (Smith's girlfriend)
Description of Suspect:	Unknown
Crime:	Grand Larceny, chain snatch

Officer Spencer is completing a report on the Grand Larceny. Which one of the following expresses the above information *most clearly* and *accurately*?

(A) Cindy Lewis stated that at 3:45 P.M., while aboard the uptown #4 train, an unknown man reached into the train while it was stopped at the 14th Street station and snatched the chain of her boyfriend, Louis Smith.

(B) A male, unidentified by Louis Smith, reached in and stole his chain from an uptown #4 train at the 14th Street station. Cindy Lewis said she was his girlfriend and unable to identify the suspect, who did the snatch at 3:45 P.M.

(C) On the #4 train going uptown, Louis Smith had his chain snatched at the 14th Street station when a man reached in the train. He was traveling with his girlfriend, Cindy Lewis, and they were both unable to identify him when it occurred at 3:45 P.M.

(D) At 3:45 P.M., Cindy Lewis was unable to identify the man who snatched her boyfriend's chain at the 14th Street station. They were traveling uptown on the #4 train when someone reached in and took Smith's chain.

84. While on patrol, Officer Casio responds to a Grand Larceny. The following details were obtained at the scene:

Time of Crime:	Between 9:30 P.M. and midnight
Place of Crime:	In front of 119-30 Long Street
Crime:	Car theft
Vehicle stolen:	1983 Renault
Victim:	Sam Andrews
Suspect:	Unidentified

Officer Casio is completing a report on the incident. Which one of the following expresses the above information *most clearly* and *accurately*?

(A) Between 9:30 P.M. and midnight, Sam Andrews was in front of 119-30 Long Street. A 1983 Renault was stolen by an unidentified person.

(B) An unidentified person stole Sam Andrews' 1983 Renault from in front of 119-30 Long Street between 9:30 P.M., and midnight.

(C) An unidentified person in front of 119-30 Long Street stole a car between 9:30 P.M. and midnight. Sam Andrews has a 1983 Renault.

(D) A 1983 Renault was stolen in front of Sam Andrews at 119-30 Long Street between 9:30 P.M. and midnight by an unidentified person.

Answer questions 85 through 87 solely on the basis of the following map. The flow of traffic is indicated by arrows. If there is only one arrow shown, then traffic flows only in the direction indicated by the arrow. If there are two arrows shown, then traffic flows in both directions. You must follow the flow of traffic.

85. Police Officers Gannon and Vine are located at the intersection of Terrace Street and Surf Avenue when they receive a call from the radio dispatcher stating that they need to respond to an attempted murder at Spruce Street and Fine Avenue. Which one of the following is the shortest route for them to take in their patrol car, making sure to obey all traffic regulations?

   (A) Travel west on Surf Avenue, then north on Prospect Street, then east on Noble Avenue, then south on Poplar Street, then east on Fine Avenue to Spruce Street.
   (B) Travel east on Surf Avenue, then south on Poplar Street, then east on Fine Avenue to Spruce Street.
   (C) Travel west on Surf Avenue, then south on Prospect Street, then east on Fine Avenue to Spruce Street.
   (D) Travel south on Terrace Street, then east on Fine Avenue to Spruce Street.

86. Police Officers Sears and Ronald are at Nostrand Boulevard and Prospect Street. They receive a call assigning them to investigate a disruptive group of youths at Temple Boulevard and Surf Avenue. Which one of the following is the shortest route for them to take in their patrol car, making sure to obey all traffic regulations?

   (A) Travel north on Prospect Street, then east on Surf Avenue to Temple Boulevard.
   (B) Travel north on Prospect Street, then east on Noble Avenue, then south on Temple Boulevard to Surf Avenue.
   (C) Travel north on Prospect Street, then east on Fine Avenue, then north on Temple Boulevard to Surf Avenue.
   (D) Travel south on Prospect Street, then east on New York Avenue, then north on Temple Boulevard to Surf Avenue.

87. While on patrol at Prospect Street and New York Avenue, Police Officers Ross and Rock are called to a burglary in progress near the entrance to the Apple-Terrace Co-ops on Poplar Street midway between Fine Avenue and Nostrand Boulevard. Which one of the following is the shortest route for them to take in their patrol car, making sure to obey all traffic regulations?

   (A) Travel east on New York Avenue, then north on Poplar Street.
   (B) Travel north on Prospect Street, then east on Fine Avenue, then south on Poplar Street.
   (C) Travel north on Prospect Street, then east on Surf Avenue, then south on Poplar Street.
   (D) Travel east on New York Avenue, then north on Temple Boulevard, then west on Surf Avenue, then south on Poplar Street.

88. While on patrol, Officer Smith responded to the scene of a robbery. Upon his arrival, Mrs. Mary Taylor told Officer Smith that the following items were taken from her at gun point:

● Cash	$150.00
● 3 bracelets, each valued at	95.00
● 2 rings, each valued at	70.00
● 1 leather handbag, valued at	100.00

Later that day, Mary Taylor telephoned Officer Smith and informed him that she found a receipt for the leather bag that was taken, and it is actually valued at $159.00.

Officer Smith is preparing a Complaint Report on the robbery. Which one of the following is the total value of the property and cash taken from Mrs. Taylor

(A) $415.00 (C) $675.00
(B) $474.00 (D) $734.00

Answer question 89 solely on the basis of the following information.

Three rapes occurred in the 141st Precinct during the month of April. The reported description of each of the suspects is as follows:

Rape No. 1—Male, white, about 25 years old, short brown hair, gray pants, white tank top shirt, black shoes, scar above right eye and across right cheek, earring in left ear.

Rape No. 2—Male, white, early 40's black hair, gray pants, white shirt, black shoes, black suit jacket, wearing sun glasses.

Rape No. 3—Male, white, 21 years old, black hair, blue dungarees, white sneakers, black leather vest, white T-shirt, tattoo on left arm, earring in right ear.

On April 21, Police Officer Johnson arrested a suspect during an attempted rape. The description of the suspect is as follows:

Rape No. 4—Male, white, 20 years old, short black hair, blue jeans, white sneakers, white T-shirt, tattoo of a ghost on left arm, earring in left ear.

89. Based on the descriptions of the suspects in the first three rapes, Officer Johnson should consider the suspect in the fourth rape as a suspect in

(A) Rape No. 1, but not Rape No. 2 or Rape No. 3
(B) Rape No. 3, but not rape No. 1 or No. 2
(C) Rape No. 1 and Rape No.3, but not Rape No. 2
(D) Rape No. 1 and Rape No. 2, but not Rape No. 3

90. While on patrol, Police Officer Rucco witnesses a robbery and apprehends the suspect. The following information relates to this incident:

Place of Robbery:	In front of 311 Sutter Avenue
Victim:	Veronica Stables, not injured
Suspect:	Male, white, wearing blue jeans, white sneakers, leather jacket
Action Taken:	Suspect apprehended and arrested on the corner of Canal and Vestry Streets.

Officer Rucco is completing a report on the incident. Which one of the following expresses the above information *most clearly* and *accurately*?

(A) Wearing blue jeans, white sneakers, and a leather jacket in front of 311 Sutter Avenue, Veronica Stables was robbed by the suspect and not injured. The white male was apprehended and arrested on the corner of Canal and Vestry Streets.
(B) On the corner of Canal and Vestry Streets was apprehended and arrested a white male. Veronica Stables was robbed and not injured by the suspect wearing blue jeans, white sneakers, and a leather jacket in front of 311 Sutter Avenue.
(C) A white male wearing blue jeans, white sneakers, and a leather jacket in front of 311 Sutter Avenue was apprehended and arrested on the corner of Canal and Vestry streets. Veronica Stables was not injured and robbed by the suspect.
(D) A white male wearing blue jeans, white sneakers, and a leather jacket robbed Veronica Stables in front of 311 Sutter Avenue. The suspect was apprehended and arrested on the corner of Canal and Vestry Streets.

Answer question 91 solely on the basis of the following information.

Police Officers may arrest a person for driving while under the influence of alcohol and then test the person for alcohol use at a police facility. Upon making such an arrest, a Police Officer should do the following in the order given:

1. Remove the prisoner to the precinct station house.
2. Inform the Desk Officer of the arrest.
3. Request the Communications Division to dispatch Highway Police Officers to the testing location where the alcohol test will be conducted.
4. Remove the prisoner to the testing location in order to have the Highway Police Officers conduct a chemical test of the prisoner.
5. Record the results of the test on an Intoxicated Driver Examination Report.
6. Return the prisoner to the precinct station house.

91. While on patrol, Police Officers Riglioni and Cardaci observe the driver of a red Chevrolet driving erratically. The Officers stop the vehicle and ask the driver to get out. The driver gets out of the vehicle and is obviously drunk. The Officers arrest the driver for operating a vehicle while under the influence of alcohol. The Officers take the prisoner to the precinct station house and report the arrest to the Desk Officer. The next step the Officers should take is to

(A) request the Communications Division to send the Highway Police
(B) bring the prisoner to the testing location
(C) conduct a test to determine if the prisoner is drunk
(D) complete the Intoxicated Driver Examination Report.

Answer question 92 solely on the basis of the following information.

Police Officers must sometimes rely on eyewitness accounts of incidents, even though eyewitnesses may make mistakes with regard to some details.

92. Mrs. Levy was the victim of a hit-and-run accident. When Police Officer Murphy arrived at the scene, he interviewed four witnesses who saw a black car strike the victim and leave the scene. The following are license plate numbers provided by the four witnesses. Which one of these numbers should Officer Murphy consider most likely to be correct?

(A) P-82324
(B) P-82342

(C) F-83424
(D) F-62323.

Answer question 93 solely on the basis of the following information.

When Police Officers respond to investigate a complaint of unnecessary loud noise, they should do the following in the order given:

1. Respond to the location of the unnecessary noise.
2. Interview the complainant, if possible.
3. Interview the violator.
4. Correct the condition by advising and warning the violator.
5. Give the violator a summons if the warning is ignored.
6. Make a Memo Book entry concerning the incident.
7. Report all actions taken to the Desk Officer.

93. While on patrol, Police Officer Ryan receives a call at 3 A.M. to respond to 225 Kent Street, Apt. 4J, concerning a complaint of loud music. Upon his arrival, the Officer is met by Mr. Templer who states that his neighbor has been continuously playing his stereo very loudly. As the Officer is speaking to Mr. Templer, he hears a loud stereo playing from the next-door apartment. Officer Ryan goes to the apartment and informs the violator, Mr. Nelson, that Mr. Templer has complained about the noise. Mr. Nelson immediately apologizes for playing his stereo loudly and then lowers the stereo saying he will be more thoughtful in the future. Police Officer Ryan should next

(A) interview Mr. Templer
(B) give Mr. Nelson a summons
(C) make a Memo Book entry
(D) give Mr. Templer a summons.

94. When a motorist commits a traffic violation, a Police Officer may give the motorist either a warning or a traffic ticket. In which one of the following situations should a Police Officer issue a traffic ticket instead of a warning?

(A) A woman is adjusting her child's seat belt while driving.
(B) A man who is driving on a busy street turns his head away from the road to watch a young woman pass by.
(C) A woman who is applying lipstick while driving goes through a stop sign.
(D) A man who is talking to his friend comes to a sudden halt at a red traffic light.

Answer question 95 solely on the basis of the following information.

Grand Larceny 2nd Degree—occurs when a person steals property and when the value of the property is greater than $1500.

Unauthorized Use of a Vehicle—occurs when a person knowingly takes, operates, rides in or otherwise uses a vehicle without the consent of the owner.

95. Will Walker, a car mechanic at a gas station, repairs Mr. Smith's car. Knowing that Mr. Smith is away, Walker decides to borrow the car for the weekend. He drives the car home, parks it on the street, and accidentally leaves the keys in the ignition. Several hours later, Ben Barnes walks past the car and notices the keys in the ignition. Knowing that the car is worth at least $7,000, Barnes breaks into the car and drives it away. Barnes later sells the car to a used car salesman for $8,000. In this situation

(A) both Barnes and Walker should be charged only with Grand Larceny 2nd Degree

(B) Barnes should be charged with Grand Larceny 2nd Degree and Unauthorized Use of a Vehicle, and Walker should be charged with Unauthorized Use of a Vehicle

(C) both Barnes and Walker should be charged only with Unauthorized Use of a Vehicle

(D) Barnes should be charged with Unauthorized Use of a Vehicle and Walker should be charged with Grand Larceny 2nd Degree and Unauthorized Use of a Vehicle.

96. Police Officer Clay obtained the following information at the scene of burglary:

Time of Occurrence:	3:00 P.M.
Place of Occurrence:	350 Lenox Avenue
Suspect:	Male
Crime:	Burglary; TV and VCR stolen
Witness:	Ed Simms
Victim:	Mrs. Lester

Police Officer Clay is preparing a report on the burglary. Which one of the following expresses the above information *most clearly* and *accurately*?

(A) At 3:00 P.M., Mrs. Lester's house at 350 Lenox Avenue was burglarized. Ed Simms reported seeing a man leaving Mrs. Lester's house with a TV and VCR.

(B) Mrs. Lester's house was burglarized at 3:00 P.M. A man took a TV and a VCR. Mr. Ed Simms saw a man. She lives at 350 Lenox Ave.

(C) At 350 Lenox Ave., Mrs. Lester's house was burglarized. Mr. Ed Simms saw a man leaving her house at 3:00 P.M. He was carrying a TV and a VCR.

(D) Ed Simms stated that he witnessed a burglary. It happened at 350 Lenox Ave., at 3:00 P.M. A man took a TV set and a VCR from Mrs. Lester's house.

Answer question 97 solely on the basis of the following information.

While on patrol in September 1988, Police Officer Harris received several reports from people who were robbed as they exited the Georgia Street subway station. The description of each suspect is as follows:

Robbery No. 1—Male, black, early 20's, 5'10", 180 lbs., dark hair, moustache, blue jeans, black jacket, running shoes.

Robbery No. 2—Male, black, 25 to 30 years old, 5'9", 165 lbs., dark hair, dark moustache, glasses, black jeans, green sweat shirt, running shoes.

Robbery No. 3—Male, black, 40 to 45 years old, 5'8", 150 lbs., dark hair, clean shaven, blue jeans, black jacket, running shoes.

On October 6, 1988, a woman was robbed by a male who was loitering near the Georgia Street subway station. Police Officer Harris witnessed the robbery and apprehended the suspect four blocks away. The description of the suspect is as follows:

Robbery No. 4—Male, black, 20-25 years old, 5'10", 175 lbs., dark hair, moustache, blue jeans, black jacket, black cap, sneakers.

97. Based on the above description of the suspects in the first three robberies, Officer Brown should consider the suspect in the fourth robbery as a suspect in

(A) Robbery No. 1, but not Robbery No. 2 or Robbery No. 3
(B) Robbery No. 1 and Robbery No. 2, but not Robbery No. 3
(C) Robbery No. 2 and Robbery No. 3, but not Robbery No. 1
(D) Robbery No. 1, Robbery No. 2, and Robbery No. 3

98. Officer Stanley obtained the following information regarding a call for help:

Time of Occurrence:	6:40 A.M.
Place of Occurrence:	452 Hull Street, Apt. 4A
Crime:	Rape
Victim:	Jane Allen
Suspect:	Male, white

Officer Stanley is completing a report on the incident. Which one of the following expresses the above information *most clearly* and *accurately*?

(A) Raped at 452 Hull Street, at 6:40 A.M., was Jane Allen in Apt. 4A by a white male.
(B) At 6:40 A.M., Jane Allen was raped by a white male living at 452 Hull Street, Apt. 4A.
(C) A white male at 452 Hull Street, Apt. 4A raped Jane Allen at 6:40 A.M.
(D) At 6:40 A.M., Jane Allen was raped at 452 Hull Street, Apt. 4A, by a white male.

Answer question 99 solely on the basis of the following information.

Complaint—is a report of an unlawful or improper act, or any condition that requires investigation by the Police to determine if an unlawful act has occurred.

Complaints should be recorded in a particular precinct when:

1. There is an arrest for an unlawful act in that precinct; or
2. A resident of that precinct is reported missing; or
3. A dead human body is found on the piers or in the waters bordering that precinct; or
4. Property is lost and the loss is first discovered in that precinct.

99. Police Officer Menke of the 126th Precinct is assigned to prepare the Precinct's Complaint Reports. Which one of the following situations should be recorded as a Complaint by Officer Menke?

(A) While having lunch in the 44th Precinct, Ray Shaw, a businessman who lives in the 126th Precinct, discovers that his briefcase has been stolen.
(B) David Spooner, who lives in the 126th Precinct, is arrested for possession of cocaine in the 56th Precinct.
(C) A dead human body is found floating in the West River approximately fifteen feet from the riverbank bordering the 126th Precinct.
(D) Richard Warman, of the 126th Precinct, reports that his 23-year-old daughter, who lives in the 130th Precinct, has been missing for 48 hours.

Answer question 100 solely on the basis of the following information.

Police Officers Smith and Jones are on patrol when, at approximately 10:00 A.M., James Banks runs up to the patrol car and informs the Officers that he has just been robbed. Mr. Banks is told to get into the patrol car and the Officers proceed to drive around the immediate area in search of the suspect. Mr. Banks gives the following description of the suspect:

Male, black, about 18 years old, 6'1", 190 lbs., wearing blue dungarees, red button-down shirt, red and white sneakers, blue cap, long sideburns, and has a gold front tooth.

Officer Smith is aware that this is the fourth robbery in this area during the past month. The reported descriptions of the suspects involved in the previous three robberies are as follows:

Robbery No.1—Male, black, 21 years old, 6'0", 180 lbs., wearing blue pants, red shirt, red sneakers, blue ski cap, wearing a slight beard.

Robbery No.2—Male, black, 19 years old, 6'0", 185 lbs., wearing blue jeans, red shirt, white sneakers, blue baseball cap, wearing long sideburns.

Robbery No.3—Male, black, 18 years old, 5'7", 150 lbs., wearing blue dungarees, red sweat shirt, red and white sneakers, blue hat, wearing long sideburns.

100. Based on the descriptions that were given of the suspects for the first three robberies, Officer Smith should consider the suspect in the Banks robbery as a suspect in

(A) Robbery No. 2, but not Robbery No. 1 or Robbery No. 3
(B) Robbery No. 1 and Robbery No. 2, but not Robbery No. 3
(C) Robbery No. 2 and Robbery No. 3, but not Robbery No. 1
(D) Robbery No. 1, Robbery No. 2, and Robbery No. 3.

101. Police Officer Roland responded to 233 Main Street to investigate a past burglary. Officer Roland arrived at the scene and interviewed Mrs. Joan Bates. Mrs. Bates stated that her apartment was broken into and the following items were missing:

- 1 Ring valued at $415.00
- Cash $220.00
- Coin Collection valued at $410.00
- 3 Cameras, each valued at $175.00

Officer Roland is preparing a report on the burglary. Which one of the following is the total value of the missing property and cash?

(A) $1,220.00
(B) $1,395.00
(C) $1,570.00
(D) $1,615.00

Answer questions 102 through 104 solely on the basis of the following passage.

Police Officers Ryder and Brown respond to a call concerning a past burglary in a private house located at 1296 Brentwood Road. When the Officers arrive, they are met by William Parker, who owns the house. Mr. Parker tells the Officers that he had been out of town for the entire weekend and, upon his return twenty minutes ago, discovered that the lock on his back door was broken. He also discovered that several items were missing from around his house. At this point, Officer Ryder asks Mr. Parker to show her where the burglars entered. Meanwhile Officer Brown makes a search of the immediate area. Officer Ryder's investigation reveals that the burglars cut a wire located by the front basement window in order to disable the alarm system. The burglars then forced open the lock with a metal bar of some kind. Officer Brown's search of the area uncovers no evidence. Office Ryder then asks Mr. Parker to describe the items which are missing. Mr. Parker says that his 19″ color television and clock radio are gone, along with several items that were borrowed from various friends. Among the missing items are a compact disc player owned by David Mills, a videotape recorder owned by Samantha Burns, and a portable tape player with headphones owned by Roger Denning. Officer Ryder lists the missing items and the owners' names in her report and tells Mr. Parker to call the station house in the morning to obtain a report number which he can use if he files an insurance claim.

102. The thieves broke the lock of which entrance?

(A) Side
(B) Front
(C) Basement
(D) Back.

103. Which of the missing items were owned by William Parker?

(A) Color television and clock radio
(B) Compact disc player and tape player
(C) Videotape recorder and compact disc player
(D) Portable tape player and headphones.

104. What crime is this passage primarily concerned with?

(A) Arson
(B) Assault
(C) Burglary
(D) Fraud.

Answer question 105 solely on the basis of the following information.

When a person commits an offense for which a summons may be served, a Police Officer should:

1. Inform the violator of each offense committed.
2. Request that the violator show proof of identity and residence.
3. Take the violator to the station house for investigation if doubt exists concerning his identity.
4. Enter only one offense on a summons.
5. Use a separate summons for any additional offense.

105. Police Officer Hayes stops a motorist for driving through a red light and asks him for his driver's license, registration, and insurance card. The motorist apologizes to Officer Hayes and explains that he left his house in a hurry and forgot his wallet, which contains all of his identification. Officer Hayes asks the driver to state his name and address and advises him that, in addition to receiving a summons for going through the red light, he will receive three summonses for driving without his license, registration, and insurance card. The actions taken by Officer Hayes in this situation were

(A) proper, primarily because the driver may have been lying when he said that he forgot his wallet.
(B) improper, primarily because he did not take the driver to the station house.
(C) proper, primarily because there was no need to investigate further since the driver willingly gave his name and address.
(D) improper, primarily because he should have followed the driver home to check his identification.

106. Police Officer Greg responds to the apartment of a complainant who just reported a child missing. He obtains the following information.

Complainant:	Francis Fallon
Missing Child:	Johnny Red
Age of Child:	5 years old
Description of child:	Male, white, wearing a red T-shirt and blue jeans
Time and place last seen:	Thomas Park, 4:20 P.M.

Officer Greg is about to radio this information to the dispatcher. Which one of the following expresses the above information *most clearly* and *accurately*?

(A) Francis Fallon reported that Johnny Red, a 5-year-old white male, was last seen at 4:20 P.M. in Thomas Park. He was wearing a red T-shirt and blue jeans.

(B) Wearing a red T-shirt and blue jeans, Francis Fallon reported that Johnny Red was last seen at 4:20 P.M. in Thomas Park. He is a white 5-year-old male.

(C) In Thomas Park, Francis Fallon reported that 5-year-old, Johnny Red, a white male, was last seen wearing a red T-shirt and blue jeans at 4:20 P.M.

(D) At 4:20 P.M., Francis Fallon reported in Thomas Park that 5-year-old Johnny Red, a white male, was last seen wearing a red T-shirt and blue jeans.

107. Police Officer Zacks responds to 57th Avenue and Broadway and obtains the following information regarding a vandalism complaint:

Time of Occurrence:	12:00 P.M.
Place of Occurrence:	In front of 5716 Broadway
Damage:	Shattered front windshield of car
Complainant:	Daniel Molley, owner of car
Suspect:	Unidentified teenager

Officer Zacks is completing a report on the incident. Which one of the following expresses the above information *most clearly* and *accurately*?

(A) At 12:00 P.M., an unidentified teenager shattered his car's front windshield in front of 5716 Broadway reported Daniel Molley.

(B) At 12:00 P.M., in front of 5716 Broadway, an unidentified teenager shattered the front windshield of Daniel Molley's car.

(C) At 12:00 P.M., Daniel Molley reported an unidentified teenager in front of 5716 Broadway. His front car windshield was shattered.

(D) A teenager, unidentified, was in front of 5716 Broadway. At 12:00 P.M. Daniel Molley's front windshield was shattered on his car.

Answer question 108 solely on the basis of the following information.

When a juvenile, less than 16 years old, is arrested and charged as a juvenile offender, the arresting Police Officer should do the following in the order given:

1. Bring the juvenile to the station house
2. Notify parents that the juvenile is in custody and of the location of the juvenile.
3. If parents are unavailable to come to the station house, then:
   a. advise juvenile of constitutional rights; and
   b. begin questioning the juvenile.
4. If parents are coming to the station house, then:
   a. advise juvenile of constitutional rights in the parents' presence;
   b. begin questioning the juvenile in the parents' presence.
5. Prepare an Arrest Report.

108. While patrolling, Police Officer Martin observes a male juvenile carrying a gun and robbing an elderly woman. Officer Martin confiscates the gun and arrests 15-year-old Tom Hill. The Officer takes Hill to the station house. The Desk Officer advises Officer Martin to take Hill to the room selected for the questioning of juveniles. Officer Martin then contacts Hill's parents. They inform her that they will be there as soon as possible. Officer Martin should next

(A) begin questioning the juvenile about the offense
(B) prepare an Arrest Report detailing the events of the crime
(C) inform the juvenile of his constitutional rights once his parents arrive and are in the room
(D) request the parents to wait in another room during questioning.

109. While on patrol, Officer Woods responds to a robbery that occurred earlier. Officer Woods obtains the following information at the scene:

Crime: Robbery
Time of Crime: 7:30 P.M.
Place of Crime: 1177 103rd Avenue
Victim: Erica Russell
Suspect: Floyd Benett
Witness: Ben Jamin

Officer Woods is completing a report on the incident. Which one of the following expresses the above information *most clearly* and *accurately*?

(A) At 1177 103rd Avenue, Ben Jamin stated that Floyd Benett was seen robbing Erica Russell at 7:30 P.M.
(B) At 7:30 P.M., Ben Jamin witnessed Floyd Benett rob Erica Russell at 1177 103rd Avenue.
(C) At 7:30 P.M., Ben Jamin stated that he saw Floyd Benett rob Erica Russell at 1177 103rd Avenue.
(D) Ben Jamin witnessed Floyd Benett at 1177 103rd Avenue. At 7:30 P.M., Erica Russell was robbed.

110. Police Officer Joplin has finished investigating a report of Grand Larceny and has obtained the following information:

Place of Occurrence:	Orchard Street Furs, 121 Orchard Street
Time of Occurrence:	4:00 P.M.
Victim:	Sam Houston, owner of store
Crime:	$3000 stolen
Suspect:	Unknown black male

Officer Joplin is preparing a report on the incident. Which one of the following expresses the above information *most clearly* and *accurately*?

(A) Sam Houston, owner of Orchard Street Furs, located at 121 Orchard Street, reported that at 4:00 P.M. an unknown black male stole $3000 from his store.
(B) Orchard Street Furs is located at 121 Orchard Street. Sam Houston reported at 4:00 P.M. an unknown black male stole $3000 from his store.
(C) At 4:00 P.M., $3000 was stolen from the owner of Orchard Street Furs. Sam Houston was robbed by a black male at 121 Orchard Street.
(D) At 4:00 P.M., an unknown black male stole $3000. Sam Houston's store, Orchard Street Furs, is located at 121 Orchard Street.

111. Officers Reed and Shaw respond to the scene of robbery and obtain the following information from a witness:

Crime:	Bank Robbery, $20,000 stolen
Bank:	Federal Conserve Bank
Time of Crime:	2:30 P.M.
Suspect:	Female, white, armed with a shotgun
Witness:	Frank Count, bank teller

Officer Reed is recording the details of the crime in her memo book. Which one of the following expresses the above information *most clearly* and *accurately*?

(A) At 2:30 P.M., Frank Count, a bank teller at Federal Conserve Bank reported a robbery. The bank was robbed of $20,000 by a shotgun and a white female.
(B) Frank Count, a bank teller, reported that the Federal Conserve Bank was robbed of $20,000 at 2:30 P.M. by a white female armed with a shotgun.
(C) A bank teller, reported Frank Count, robbed the Federal Conserve bank of $20,000. She was white and armed with a shotgun.
(D) At 2:30 P.M., the Federal Conserve Bank was robbed of $20,000. Frank Count, a bank teller, reported a white female armed with a shotgun.

Answer question 112 solely on the basis of the following information.

When a Police Officer receives property found by someone other than a Police Officer he should:

1. Issue a receipt including a description of the property to the person delivering the property.
2. Enter the facts in the Activity Log.
3. Prepare a Property Clerk's Invoice.
4. Deliver the property and invoice to the Desk Officer.
5. Resume patrol.

112. Arlene Harris found a brown leather wallet containing twenty dollars and two credit cards. She approached Police Officer Taylor, who was patrolling on the corner of Concorde and Broadway. Officer Taylor took the wallet and handed Ms. Harris a signed note which stated: "Received property from Ms. Arlene Harris." He thanked Ms. Harris for her honesty and then entered the events including Ms. Harris' address and telephone number in his Activity Log. He then went directly to the precinct where he prepared a Property Clerk's Invoice which he gave, along with the wallet, to Sgt. Mead, the Desk Officer. Officer Taylor then returned to patrol. In this situation Officer Taylor's actions were

(A) proper, primarily because he thanked Ms. Harris for her honesty
(B) improper, primarily because he should have asked Ms. Harris to take the wallet to the precinct
(C) proper, primarily because he did not leave his post to return the wallet
(D) improper, primarily because he did not give Ms. Harris a proper receipt for the wallet.

113. Police Officer Hoff responds to the scene of a hit-and-run accident and obtains the following information:

Occurrence:	Woman hit by a speeding car
Time of Occurrence:	1:30 P.M.
Location of Occurrence:	35th Avenue between 4th and 5th Streets
Description of Car:	Green Ford
Victim:	Lois Nettle
Injuries:	Broken right leg

Officer Hoff is radioing for an ambulance. Which one of the following expresses the above information *most clearly* and *accurately*?

(A) Lois Nettle broke her right leg between 4th and 5th Streets on 35th Avenue. At 1:30 P.M., a woman was hit by a speeding green Ford.
(B) A car hit Lois Nettle and broke her right let at 1:30 P.M. A green Ford was speeding on 35th Avenue between 4th and 5th Streets.
(C) Lois Nettle broke her right leg when a speeding green Ford hit her at 1:30 P.M. on 35th Avenue between 4th and 5th Streets.
(D) At 1:30 P.M., a green Ford was speeding. On 35th Avenue, between 4th and 5th Streets Lois Nettle broke her right leg when she was hit.

Answer questions 114 through 116 solely on the basis of the following passage.

Police Officers Wilson and Mills receive a radio call to investigate an auto accident involving injuries. Upon their arrival, Officer Mills approaches a Mustang convertible which had been driven into the side of an Oldsmobile sedan. There is also a small Dodge truck several feet away which had crashed into a fire hydrant. Officer Mills immediately determines that no one is injured and radios the dispatcher to cancel the ambulance. Meanwhile, Officer Wilson interviews Sam Thomas, who is the owner and driver of the Mustang. Mr. Thomas states that he was driving south on Bedford Avenue when a large Oldsmobile pulled out of a parking lot in front of him. Mr. Thomas goes on to say that he immediately hit his brakes but slid into the side of the Oldsmobile. Officer Mills interviews Thomas Parker, who is the driver of the Oldsmobile. Mr. Parker admits that he drove out of the parking lot without looking for oncoming traffic. He tells Officer Mills that he is not used to driving and borrowed the Oldsmobile from his brother, Harold Parker, who is the owner of the car. Finally, Officer Wilson interviews Rutger Schmidt, who is the driver of the Dodge truck. Mr. Schmidt indicates that, in an attempt to avoid the accident, he swerved out of the way, lost control of the truck, and ran into a fire hydrant. Mr. Schmidt tells Officer Wilson that he works for the Acme Exterminating Company, which owns the truck. Following the interviews, the two Officers write their accident report and indicate the damage to each vehicle. The Mustang had a damaged front bumper and grill, and broken headlights; the Oldsmobile had a dented driver's side quarter panel; the Dodge truck had a crumpled bumper and blown right front tire.

114. Who was the owner of the Oldsmobile sedan?

(A) Sam Thomas   (C) Harold Parker

(B) Thomas Parker   (D) Rutger Schmidt

115. What was damaged on the Dodge truck?

(A) Driver's side quarter panel.   (C) Tailgate and tail lights.

(B) Bumper and right front tire.   (D) Front bumper, grill, and headlights.

116. The driver of which vehicle was the primary cause of the accident?

(A) The Mustang convertible   (C) The Dodge truck

(B) The Patrol Car   (D) The Oldsmobile sedan.

Answer question 117 solely on the basis of the following information.

Upon observing a vehicle accident, a Police Officer should do the following in the order given:

1. Park the patrol car so that it will not block traffic.
2. Determine if there are any injuries and request an ambulance if needed.
3. Divert traffic if necessary.
4. Obtain drivers' licenses, vehicle registrations, and insurance identification cards of the drivers involved.
5. Have vehicles removed from the roadway.
6. Determine the cause of the accident.

117. Officer Jackson responds to the scene of an accident. Upon arrival, Officer Jackson parks his patrol car in a spot where it is not blocking traffic. As he approaches the intersection on foot, he sees that a taxicab and a white Toyota have been involved in a head-on collision. He also notices that a large crowd has gathered around the damaged vehicles. Traffic is backed up in all directions leading into the intersection, and a man who is bleeding from the head is lying on the roadway. The next step Officer Jackson should take is to

(A) request an ambulance
(B) direct traffic away from the accident
(C) have the vehicles removed from the roadway
(D) determine the cause of the accident

118. Police Officer Boyle was driving his patrol car in the snow when he was involved in a car accident. The following information was obtained at the scene of the accident:

Place of Occurrence:	Intersection of Canal and Church Streets
Time of Occurrence:	10:15 A.M.
Vehicle Number:	5729
Damage to Vehicle:	Hood, right fender, and windshield
Injuries Sustained by Officer:	Two broken arms.

Police Officer Nevins is completing a report on the accident. Which one of the following expresses the above information *most clearly* and *accurately*?

(A) Police Officer Boyle had two broken arms at 10:15 A.M. Vehicle 5729 was in a car accident at the intersection of Canal and Church Streets. It has a damaged hood, right fender, and windshield.
(B) At 10:15 A.M., vehicle 5729 and Police Officer Boyle were in a car accident. At the intersection of Canal and Church Streets they suffered two broken arms, a damaged hood, right fender, and windshield.
(C) Vehicle 5729 had a damaged hood, right fender, and windshield at 10:15 A.M. At the intersection of Canal and Church Streets Police Officer Boyle had two broken arms in a car accident.
(D) At 10:15 A.M., Police Officer Boyle was in a car accident at the intersection of Canal and Church Streets. Officer Boyle suffered two broken arms, and vehicle 5729 sustained damage to the hood, right fender, and windshield.

Answer question 119 solely on the basis of the following information.

Juvenile—a child who is at least seven years of age but less than sixteen years of age.

A juvenile report should be prepared for the following:

1. All violations and offenses except felonies, unlawful assembly, and photographable offenses.
2. Petty violations.
3. A juvenile in need of supervision.
4. An intoxicated juvenile.
5. A stranded juvenile.
6. A runaway juvenile (New York City resident).

119. Police Officer Fillmore apprehends Walter Gardiner, who is fifteen years old. Walter was participating in a political demonstration in front of his 5th Avenue apartment in Manhattan. The protesters did not have a valid permit allowing them to demonstrate at that location. A witness states that she saw Walter drinking alcohol, but P.O. Fillmore sees no indication that the youth is intoxicated. The Officer believes that the youth's parents were also participants in the demonstration. Walter has no previous arrest record. Officer Fillmore decides to prepare a Juvenile Report for unlawful assembly for Walter. The action taken by Police Officer Fillmore is

(A) improper, primarily because a Juvenile Report should not be prepared for unlawful assembly
(B) proper, primarily because Walter is a New York City resident who has not reached his sixteenth birthday
(C) improper, primarily because Walter has the right to express his political beliefs
(D) proper, primarily because a Juvenile Report should be prepared for a juvenile who has been drinking.

120. Police Officer Frankle responds to the scene of an abused child. Officer Frankle obtains the following information:

Complaint:	Gladys Jones
Date of Complaint:	October 12, 1988
Time of Complaint:	2:00 P.M.
Name of Child:	Henry Worth
Child's Injuries:	Bruises to face and arms

Police Officer Frankle is notifying the Bureau of Child Welfare about this incident. Which of the following expresses the above information *most clearly* and *accurately*?

(A) On October 12, 1988, Henry Worth had bruises on his face and arms, reported Gladys Jones at 2:00 P.M.
(B) With bruises to the face and arms, Gladys Jones reported Henry Worth on October 12, 1988, at 2:00 P.M.
(C) On October 12, 1988, at 2:00 P.M., Gladys Jones reported that Henry Worth had bruises on his face and arms.
(D) Henry Worth, with bruises to his face and arms, reported Gladys Jones on October 12, 1988 at 2:00 P.M.

Answer question 121 solely on the basis of the following information.

Burglary 1st Degree—occurs when a person knowingly enters or remains unlawfully in a dwelling with intent to commit a crime therein, and when, in entering or while in the dwelling or in immediate flight from it, he or another participant in the crime:

1. Is armed with explosives or a deadly weapon; or
2. Causes physical injury to any person who is not a participant in the crime; or
3. Displays what appears to be a pistol, revolver, rifle, shotgun, machine gun, or other firearm.

Dwelling—a building which is usually occupied by a person living there at night.

121. Which one of the following situations is the best example of Burglary in the First Degree?

(A) Carrying only a flashlight, Thomas Jackson climbs through the dining room window of the Bentley estate and steals $20,000 worth of jewelry.

(B) Bill Watson breaks into a house to steal a VCR. While in the house he sees Mrs. Campbell. Watson then pulls out a gun and tells her to give him her VCR or he will kill her.

(C) Joe Smith and Mark Star, each carrying revolvers, unlawfully break into an office building to commit a robbery. While inside the building they hear a noise and try to run out. On their way out, Star pushes Smith to the ground, causing him physical injury.

(D) Tommy Taylor breaks into a department store at 2:00 A.M. to steal a television set. When a security guard confronts him, Taylor pulls out a gun and pushes the guard to the ground, causing him physical injury.

Answer question 122 solely on the basis of the following information.

To ensure fair and proper proceedings when investigations are conducted, a Police Officer must do the following in the order given:

1. Inform the suspect that he must appear in a lineup for identification in connection with the crime.
2. Arrest the suspect if he does not agree to voluntarily appear in the lineup.
3. Notify the detective supervisor who will personally supervise the lineup.
4. Give the suspect Miranda Warnings if he is to be questioned before or after the lineup.

122. Police Officers Shore and Thompson are looking for a male who was involved in a robbery and stabbing. A witness to the crime gives the Officers a description that matches the description of a person named Rodney Pitts. The Officers find Mr. Pitts at his home and tell him that he must appear in a lineup because he fits the description of a man who committed a robbery and stabbing. Mr. Pitts angrily denies his involvement with the crimes, but agrees to take part in the lineup. The next step the Officers should take is to

(A) tell Mr. Pitts that he must appear in a lineup
(B) contact the detective supervisor
(C) place the suspect under arrest
(D) advise Mr. Pitts of Miranda Warnings.

123. Police Officer Pepper responds to a shooting and obtains the following information:

Victim:	John Rice
Suspect:	Rudy Johnson
Witness:	Mary Rice, wife of victim
Location:	Rudy's Bar, 1492 York Avenue
Weapon:	.38 caliber revolver
Injury:	Wound to left leg

Officer Pepper is preparing a report on the incident. Which one of the following expresses the above information *most clearly* and *accurately*?

(A) Rudy Johnson, witnessed by his wife Mary Rice shot John Rice with a .38 caliber revolver in Rudy's Bar, 1492 York Avenue. Mr. Rice had a wound to his left leg.
(B) With a wound to the left leg, Mary Rice witnessed Rudy Johnson shoot John Rice in Rudy's Bar at 1492 York Avenue. Mr. Johnson had a .38 caliber revolver.
(C) Mary Rice witnessed Rudy Johnson shoot her husband, John Rice, with a .38 caliber revolver in Ruby's Bar at 1492 York Avenue. Mr. Rice was wounded in the left leg.
(D) Rudy Johnson was in Rudy's Bar at 1492 York Avenue. Mary Rice witnessed her husband shot by a .38 caliber revolver in the left leg.

124. Police Officers Simon and Peters receive a call to respond to a possible child abuse case. The following information was obtained by the Officers:

Occurrence:	Child found alone in apartment
Time of Occurrence:	11:00 P.M.
Place of Occurrence:	463 Lott Street, Apt. 3A
Child Found By:	Deborah Fields, neighbor
Child:	Angela Bolds, three years old
Parent of Child:	Mary Bolds, mother

Officers Simon and Peters are completing a report for the Bureau of Child Welfare. Which one of the following expresses the above information *most clearly* and *accurately*?

(A) Angela Bolds, three years old, was found in Apt. 3A of 463 Lott Street, by herself without her mother, Mary Bolds, by a neighbor who is named Deborah Fields at 11:00 P.M.

(B) At 463 Lott Street, Apt. 3A, Deborah Fields, a neighbor, found Angela Bolds, who is three years old, by herself in her apartment. Her mother, Mary Bolds, was not home at 11:00 P.M.

(C) Deborah Fields, a neighbor, found Angela Bolds, three years old, by herself in Apt. 3A at 11:10 P.M. The child's mother, Mary Bolds, who resides at 463 Lott Street, was not home.

(D) At 11:00 P.M., Deborah Fields, a neighbor, found three-year-old Angela Bolds alone in Apt. 3A of 463 Lott Street. Mrs. Fields stated that the child's mother, Mary Bolds, was not at home.

125. Police Officer Johnson responds to the scene of an assault and obtains the following information:

Time of Occurrence:	8:30 P.M.
Place of Occurrence:	120-18 119th Avenue, Apt. 2A
Suspects:	John Andrews, victim's ex-husband and unknown white male
Victim:	Susan Andrews
Injury:	Broken right arm

Officer Johnson is preparing a complaint report on the incident. Which one of the following expresses the above information *most clearly* and *accurately*?

(A) Susan Andrews was assaulted at 120-18 119th Avenue, Apt. 2A. At 8:30 P.M. her ex-husband, John Andrews, and an unknown white male broke her arm.

(B) At 8:30 P.M., Susan Andrews was assaulted at 120-18 119th Avenue, Apt, 2A by her ex-husband, John Andrews, and an unknown white male. Her right arm was broken.

(C) John Andrews, an unknown white male, and Susan Andrews's ex-husband, assaulted and broke her right arm at 8:30 P.M., at 120-18 119th Avenue, Apt. 2A.

(D) John Andrews, ex-husband of Susan Andrews, broke her right arm with an unknown white male at 120-18 119th Avenue, at 8:30 P.M. in Apt. 2A.

Answer questions 126 through 128 solely on the basis of the following passage.

Police Officer Lombardo was dispatched to the scene of an apparently dead human body. His supervisor and another Officer were at the scene, as were two paramedics. The paramedics, Pete Lizzo and Erick Clark, had just pronounced the body dead at 6:55 p.m. There were no relatives present and a neighbor, Eddie Torres, told Officer Lombardo that the dead person lived alone and had no family. Mr. Torres agreed to be a witness to the search of the premises. Officer Lombardo knew that the police were required to voucher or hold all valuables and important papers for safekeeping if a close relative did not live with the dead person. The apartment was filled with a large number of possessions including two gold rings, a gold watch, $200 in cash, and kitchen and living room furniture. They also found an old black and white television set, old clothing, and numerous kitchen utensils. In a tin box, the Officer found a birth certificate, social security card, and the dead person's diary. After the search was completed, the jewelry, cash, birth certificate, and social security card were vouchered. Eddie Torres signed Officer Lombardo's memo book.

126. Of the following, which items were vouchered by Officer Lombardo?

    (A) Two gold rings, a gold watch, a social security card, birth certificate, and $200 in cash
    (B) A gold watch, two gold rings, $200 cash, a diary, and a social security card
    (C) A birth certificate, social security card, diary, jewelry, and $200 cash
    (D) A social security card, two gold watches, a gold ring, a birth certificate, and $200 cash.

127. The search was witnessed by

    (A) a neighbor
    (B) a relative
    (C) a police officer
    (D) a paramedic.

128. Officer Lombardo vouchered the dead person's property because

    (A) the paramedics were present
    (B) a supervisor was not available
    (C) there was only one witness
    (D) there was no relative living with the dead person.

Answer question 129 solely on the basis of the following information.

When Police Officers arrive at the scene of a fire, they should do the following in the order given:

1. Send an alarm or make sure one has been sent.
2. Direct a responsible person to remain at the alarm box in order to direct fire vehicles.
3. Park the patrol car in a location that will not interfere with fire-fighting operations.
4. Warn and assist occupants in evacuation of building.
5. Upon arrival of fire vehicles, establish police lines beyond the fire apparatus and hydrants in use.

129. While on patrol, Police Officers Gannett and James see flames and smoke coming from the top floor of an apartment building and notice that the Fire Department is not on the scene. Officer Gannett double-parks his vehicle in front of the building. Officer James immediately walks to the alarm box on the corner, pulls the alarm, and awaits the arrival of the Fire Department. The next step Officer Gannett should take is to

(A) ask the building landlord to find an alarm box and direct Fire Department vehicles
(B) enter the building in order to warn and evacuate occupants
(C) establish police lines so that fire vehicles will be able to get to the building
(D) park his patrol car in a spot where it will not block fire vehicles.

130. While on patrol, Officers Banks and Thompson see a man lying on the ground bleeding. Officer Banks records the following details about the incident:

Time of Incident:	3:15 P.M.
Place of Incident:	Sidewalk in front of 517 Rock Avenue
Incident:	Tripped and fell
Name of Injured:	John Blake
Injury:	Head wound
Action Taken:	Transported to Merry Hospital

Officer Banks is completing a report on the incident. Which one of the following expresses the above information *most clearly* and *accurately*?

(A) At 3:15 P.M., Mr. John Blake was transported to Merry Hospital. He tripped and fell injuring his head on the sidewalk in front of 517 Rock Avenue.
(B) Mr. John Blake tripped and fell on the sidewalk at 3:15 P.M. in front of 517 Rock Avenue. He was transported to Merry Hospital while he sustained a head wound.
(C) Mr. John Blake injured his head when he tripped and fell on the sidewalk in front of 517 Rock Avenue at 3:15 P.M. He was transported to Merry Hospital.
(D) A head was wounded on the sidewalk in front of 517 Rock Avenue at 3:15 P.M. Mr. John Blake tripped and fell and was transported to Merry Hospital.

172 / Police Officer

Answer question 131 solely on the basis on the following information.

When assigned to investigate a complaint, a Police Officer should

1. Interview witnesses and obtain facts.
2. Conduct a thorough investigation of circumstances concerning the complaint.
3. Prepare a Complaint Report.
4. Determine if the Complaint Report should be closed or referred for further investigation.
5. Enter Complaint Report on the Complaint Report Index and obtain a Complaint Report Number at the station house.

131. While on patrol, Police Officer John is instructed by his supervisor to investigate a complaint by Mr. Stanley Burns, who was assaulted by his brother-in-law, Henry Traub. After interviewing Mr. Burns, Officer John learns that Mr. Traub has been living with Mr. Burns for the past two years. Officer John accompanies Mr. Burns to his apartment but Mr. Traub is not there. Officer John fills out the Complaint Report and takes the report back to the station house where it is entered on the Complaint Report Index and assigned a Complaint Report Number. Officer John's actions were

   (A) improper, primarily because he should have stayed at Mr. Burns' apartment and waited for Mr. Traub to return in order to arrest him
   (B) proper, primarily because after obtaining all the facts, he took the report back to the station house and was assigned a Complaint Report Number
   (C) improper, primarily because he should have decided whether to close the report or refer it for further investigation
   (D) proper, primarily because he was instructed by his supervisor to take the report from Mr. Burns even though it involved his brother-in-law.

132. Police Officers are sometimes required to respond to family disputes and, when appropriate, refer a person to Family Court for counseling or other appropriate services. In which one of the following situations would it be most appropriate for an Officer to refer the person involved to Family Court?

   (A) A husband who is threatening to harm his wife because she spends too much money.
   (B) Two sisters arguing over the use of the telephone.
   (C) Three roommates arguing about their recent rent increase.
   (D) A mother yelling at her 16-year-old son for failing his history test.

Answer questions 133 through 140 on the basis of the following sketches. The first face on top is a sketch of an alleged criminal based on witnesses' descriptions at the crime scene. One of the four sketches below that face is the way the suspect looked after changing appearance. Assume that NO surgery has been done on the suspect.

133.

(A)   (B)

(C)   (D)

134.

(A)

(B)

(C)

(D)

135.

(A)   (B)

(C)   (D)

136.

(A) (B)

(C) (D)

137.

138.

139.

(A)

(B)

(C)

(D)

140.

(A) (B)

(C) (D)

Please check your Answer Sheet to make sure that you have written in and blackened your Social Security number correctly. If you have not yet written in and blackened your Social Security number, please do so immediately. If you have incorrectly written in or blackened your Social Security number, please correct the mistake immediately. Failure to correctly blacken your Social Security number may result in your Answer Sheet not being rated.

PROTEST PROCEDURE

Any candidate wishing to file a protest to one or more key answers on this examination must submit an original and four copies of the protest, together with supporting evidence, to PROTEST—Police Officer, Department of Personnel, 220 Church Street, NY, NY 10013. Protests will be accepted for a period of thirty (30) days beginning October 31, 1988. Protests must be *received* by the last day of the protest period (November 30, 1988).

Protests must be submitted in the following form. For each proposed key answer you protest, you must start a new page and each page must be headed by the following: Examination title, examination number, question number, test date, your Social Security Number. The protest must include a statement explaining why the answer you selected is as good as or better than the proposed key answer, and must include any additional supporting evidence you wish to submit. You may not modify or add to your protest once it is submitted. However, you may submit separate protests to additional questions within the thirty (30) day protest period.

After you have prepared the four copies, print your name and address on the original pages only and sign the last page of the original protest. Do not include your name or address on any other copies. You must print *only* your Social Security Number on each page of the four copies. *PROTESTS SENT WITHOUT THE FOUR COPIES WILL NOT BE CONSIDERED!*

In order to be informed of the availability of the Validation Board Report for this test, please include a postage-paid, self-addressed, business-size envelope with your protests.

RECORD YOUR ANSWERS IN THIS TEST BOOKLET BEFORE THE LAST SIGNAL

ANSWER SHEET COLLECTION—When you finish the test, remain seated and signal the monitor to collect your answer sheet. Leave the building quickly and quietly.

DO NOT telephone this Department to request information on the progress of the rating of this test. Such information will *NOT* be given. You will be notified individually by mail of your rating after all papers have been rated. Notify this Department promptly in writing of any change of your address. You should indicate your Social Security Number and the title and number of the examination in any correspondence to the Department of Personnel with respect to this examination.

TAKE THIS QUESTION BOOKLET WITH YOU

Proposed Answer Key for Written Test
Held on October 29, 1988

1. B	29. D	57. D	85. D	113. C
2. A	30. D	58. C	86. C	114. C
3. D	31. B	59. A	87. B	115. B
4. C	32. C	60. A	88. D	116. D
5. B	33. A	61. B	89. B	117. A
6. D	34. D	62. A	90. D	118. D
7. A	35. D	63. C	91. A	119. A
8. D	36. B	64. A	92. A	120. C
9. C	37. C	65. D	93. C	121. B
10. A	38. C	66. B	94. C	122. B
11. D	39. D	67. A	95. B	123. C
12. A	40. A	68. C	96. A	124. D
13. C	41. C	69. D	97. B	125. B
14. B	42. B	70. C	98. D	126. A
15. C	43. D	71. A	99. C	127. A
16. B	44. C	72. B	100. B	128. D
17. D	45. B	73. D	101. C	129. D
18. B	46. D	74. A	102. B	130. C
19. A	47. B	75. B	103. A	131. C
20. C	48. C	76. B	104. C	132. A
21. D	49. D	77. D	105. B	133. B
22. C	50. A	78. D	106. A	134. C
23. C	51. C	79. C	107. B	135. D
24. D	52. C	80. B	108. C	136. A
25. B	53. B	81. A	109. B	137. A
26. C	54. B	82. D	110. A	138. D
27. A	55. D	83. A	111. B	139. B
28. B	56. B	84. B	112. D	140. C

ANSWER EXPLANATIONS

1. **(B)** You may not have considered the ambulance to be parked; you may not have remembered that the ambulance was on Elm Street. However, you must choose from among four choices. Of the choices offered, only an ambulance appears anywhere in the picture.

2. **(A)** The only bus is a Northside Bus.

3. **(D)** The man with a gun, dark glasses, and a necklace in his hand is wearing a white shirt with black dots.

4. **(C)** The cab that is undergoing a tire change has been pulled up in a towaway zone.

5. **(B)** The car that is angled across Elm Street near the man lying in the roadway bears the license plate 8K46. This is the only license plate visible in the picture.

6. **(D)** There is a man standing at the open second-floor window of M & P Music World.

7. **(A)** You probably noticed that the robbery at knifepoint was occurring at the corner and that the streets were Brady and 7th. You do have to focus on tiny details like East and West, or in this case simply E.

8. **(D)** There is a violinist standing mid-block, just in front of the Blair Savings Bank.

9. **(C)** The young man with the knife is wearing a black baseball cap, a short-sleeved white shirt, and plaid trousers.

10. **(A)** The person in the lower right-hand corner who is holding a gun is a bearded white male wearing light-colored pants and a plaid shirt with sleeves rolled up.

11. **(D)** The purse-snatcher running towards the subway has the number 94 on his shirt. From these last three questions, you should recognize that you must direct your attention especially to pictures of people who appear to be involved in some sort of wrongdoing. Focus in on both appearance and location.

12. **(A)** The family dispute was in Apartment 1928. The call came from Mrs. Debra Lacoste in Apartment 1930, obviously a neighbor.

13. **(C)** The officers were parked in front of 945 Howard Street, but the disturbance was at 779 Seward Street in Apartment 1928.

14. **(B)** The Order of Protection stated that Mr. Ross was not to see his children, yet he had come to his wife's apartment (also against the order) to visit the children. This was the direct cause for the arrest. Ross yelled at his wife, not at his children. Paragraphs that are full of details like this one tend to ask very specific questions, which are answered by careful reading and attention to the details. Since this is not a memory series, you may look back to check the facts. Careful initial reading with underlining of facts should save you time.

15. **(C)** Again, careful reading is the key. The word that governs the correct answer is "intentionally."

16. **(B)** Pay special attention to questions that offer you a set procedure to follow in numbered steps. Officer Jones has given reasonable aid with the blanket and has radioed for an ambulance. The call was made only 15 minutes ago; it is not yet time to call again. The correct procedure is to post a responsible person (John Rutherford, the business partner, is a good choice) outside to direct the medics.

17. **(D)** This is a relatively easy judgment question. Obviously, the activity that must arouse greatest suspicion in an area plagued by burglaries is a door-to-door check, presumably to learn which premises are unattended.

18. **(B)** All four choices include all the necessary information; therefore, your task is to choose the best organized statement. Remember that other officers must rely on the information to pursue the suspect. They must know: time, place, full description and clothing of suspect, and direction of flight. If information is given in haphazard order, as in (C) "approximately 6 feet tall five minutes ago," valuable time will be lost while the message is interpreted.

19. **(A)** Some "clearly and accurately" questions are more obvious than others. Here the statement in choice (A) is so far superior in organization to any of the others that you have no doubt. This type of question gives you a chance to prove the logic and orderliness of your thinking.

20. **(C)** You should be catching on to this type of question. All information that logically belongs together must be presented together. Thus, we must know who belongs to which car and who sustained which injury. There might be an even better way to express the information, but you must choose the best way offered.

21. **(D)** The pistol license expired on September 9, 1988, and the date of this incident is September 10, 1988. Directive #4 states that the person must be taken to the station house if the license has expired.

22. **(C)** Approach this question by counting the elements that are common to the greatest number of accounts. Choices (A) and (C) both begin with P-518 whereas the other two witnesses have given quite different versions, so chances are that either (A) or (C) is correct. As a fourth digit, "8" appears twice while "5" is only reported once, so consider (C) to be the most likely answer. Go on to the final digit. "6" is reported three times, and (C) is one of the times it is reported. While you have no guarantee of accuracy, (C) is the best choice based upon common elements.

23. **(C)** Officer Anderson has reported to the location of the complainant and has obtained a description of the missing person. Before she can begin the search, she must find out where the missing person was last seen.

24. **(D)** In choice (C) nothing is taken. In the other three choices, no property is valued at more than one thousand dollars nor are firearms taken. In choice (D) the value of the property is only $20, but the property is taken directly from the person of the victim, so the action is classified as Grand Larceny in the Fourth Degree.

25. **(B)** The organization: who is involved, description of the person, what happened, when, and where.

26. **(C)** Choices (A) and (D) are ridiculous. The stolen auto was not arrested nor was Michael Wadsworth arrested for driving at 51st Street and 8th Avenue. (B) is not incorrect, but (C) reads much more smoothly and sensibly.

27. **(A)** Take this step by step. The robberies take place on Lott Avenue between E. 98th Street and Hughes Place. Only choice (A) offers you

this location, so you need search no farther for the correct answer. If more than one choice had named the same blocks, you would have had to make your choice on the basis of days of the week and possibly time of day as well.

28. **(B)** The rapes seem to occur on Mondays and Wednesdays, so Officer Wells should not be working a weekend patrol. Since the rapes take place in the morning, choice (B), weekdays from 7:30 A.M. to 3:30 P.M., would seem the most effective period for rape control.

29. **(D)** Prisoners have been known to hang themselves with shoelaces. The other three choices offer no conceivable danger.

30. **(D)** The officer has found and removed a weapon, but this find was only incidental to the process of handcuffing. Regulations state that the officer must actually search the prisoner and the nearby area for weapons and evidence before advising the prisoner of his legal rights.

31. **(B)** This choice identifies the victim, tells where he lives, when and where the crime took place, what happened, and the nature and value of the stolen property.

32. **(C)** Ms. Starr lives in Apartment 1402, on the 14th floor. Mr. Babbit lives in Apartment 1407, obviously the same floor. Recognize this as the beginning of a series of detail questions. Refer to the passage as needed.

33. **(A)** Officer Grice is qualified in the recovery of fingerprints.

34. **(D)** The first burglary occurred on December 5. The last burglary occurred on December 6. Peter Remo was arrested ten days after the last burglary, December 16.

35. **(D)** Ms. Starr's lock had been stuffed with toothpicks. It was Ms. Chung's lock that was stuffed with chewing gum.

36. **(B)** Officer Molina has ascertained the facts, has been assured that Ms. Martin does not need medical attention, and has learned that Mr. Martin has left the apartment. She is up to step 4 and must now begin searching the area for Mr. Martin.

37. **(C)** Regulation 1 states that the person should be handcuffed with hands behind back. The

activity was improper because it was against regulations. The narrative illustrates the reason for this regulation by telling of the blow to the side of Officer Lewis's head. You do not need to know the reasons for regulations; you must simply follow them.

38. **(C)** This is a "greatest number of common elements" question. The descriptions of witnesses (C) and (D) are almost identical. You should certainly consider that the vehicle was a brown Ford truck with the license number 1845. Since three witnesses saw the letter on the plate as "G" and only one as "C," go with "G."

39. **(D)** Officer Frey has properly followed procedure to this point. Reading the description along with the regulations, you know that Officer Frey has completed step 3, has removed the wallet and papers, and must now go to step 4, entering in the Memo Book a list of the property removed.

40. **(A)** The date is August 31. Why is the woman wearing a winter overcoat? Could she be planning to hide objects under that coat? Watch her.

41. **(C)** Try the routes to see which one works. Dusty Road is not a through street from Hampton Drive, so eliminate (A). Maple Road is one-way eastbound, so neither (B) nor (D) can be correct. Choice (C) works.

42. **(B)** To choose the answer, do exactly what Officer Gladden did. Locate the intersection of Beach Drive and Anderson Street. With pencil or finger follow the route, turning the map as needed to be sure you are keeping right and left straight. You should end up headed East on Main Street.

43. **(D)** Only this choice satisfies the requirement of both the goods' being stolen and knowing possession.

44. **(C)** Where date and time are indicated in a report, the most coherent summary usually begins with this information. Focus first on the choice that begins with date and time, but do not take it for granted. Be sure to read it through to be certain that it includes all other pertinent information in logical arrangement.

45. **(B)** The report must make it clear just who was abused, who is accused of the abusing, who has made the report, and where the abused and abusers may be found. You can be certain only from choice (B).

46. **(D)** The arithmetic is simple. Don't forget the value of the leather bag itself.

2 watches at $500 each	=	$1000
4 necklaces at $315 each	=	1260
cash of $519	=	519
1 ring at $400	=	400
leather bag at $200	=	+ 200
total	=	$3379

47. **(B)** The rapist might easily wear different clothing on different days so you must concentrate on the physical description. The rapist in #2 seems to be younger and thinner than the others and has short hair. The other descriptions are quite similar.

48. **(C)** It is the middle of the night, and the police have removed a child from his home and placed him in temporary housing. The next step, according to printed procedure, is to try to locate a parent.

49. **(D)** The officer has enough information—make and color of offending car and its license plate number—to make an arrest at a later time. The driver of the Ford is a reckless driver who has left the scene of an accident, but no victim was abandoned bleeding in the street and no heinous crime was committed. Considering the danger to self and public caused by Officer Jordan's 80-M.P.H. weaving through traffic, we must conclude that Officer Jordan used bad judgment in continuing the pursuit.

50. **(A)** This question does not ask for your judgment but only for which of four choices expresses the information most clearly and accurately. Choice (A) is best.

51. **(C)** Clearly the suspect is male, white, and in his 20s. Three witnesses agree that he was wearing a black hat and red sneakers. Choice (C) contains the greatest number of common elements.

52. **(C)** In this question, you must make a judgment as to which is the greatest medical emergency. A heart attack requires the most immediate medical attention.

53. **(B)** This is a well-written report. It states the nature of the problem: a missing person;

describes the missing person; and tells when and where that person was last seen.

54. **(B)** Miss Holmes called the police on January 14. She told them that the man had threatened her two days earlier, January 12.

55. **(D)** Officer Jones found the revolver while searching the suspect's right front waistband.

56. **(B)** Miss Holmes said that the threat had occurred in front of her home at 113 Lowell Street.

57. **(D)** The gun appeared to be legally registered. Fitz was arrested because Miss Holmes identified him as the person who had threatened her earlier.

58. **(C)** All other versions are hopelessly garbled.

59. **(A)** This is the best statement of what happened to whom, when, and where. It makes clear the identity of the witness.

60. **(A)** In this case, the officers may reasonably omit step 3 and follow the instruction at 4b. An address book is not a lethal weapon. There is no basis for the officers to believe that their lives are in danger, so they have no right to search the man's clothing. They did, however, stop and frisk him, so they must prepare a Stop and Frisk Report.

61. **(B)** Clearly, the event described in choice (B) represents the use of force in stealing June's bag.

62. **(A)** The suspect in murder #2 is too young. The suspect in murder #3, while a tall man, is estimated at a full 5" shorter than the suspect in the most recent murder. The suspect in murder #1 fits the current description very closely.

63. **(C)** Police officers are trained and equipped to deal with robbery, vandalism, and recovered property. While the police might well deal with crowd control at the site of a spill of poisonous liquid, the main problem is the concern of other departments.

64. **(A)** The steps must be followed in order. Upon arrival at Central Booking, Leon must be put into a cell that does not contain adult prisoners.

65. **(D)** Sometimes you may have to read over a description a number of times to pick up

a single word on which the answer depends. Step 3 states that the officer must present shield *and* identification card. The description says only that Officer Dana presented her shield to Officer Baskin before signing the receipt.

66. **(B)** The information could be stated even more clearly, but choice (B) is the best of the four offered.

67. **(A)** The sentence is a bit awkward, but it is accurate and does get its message across clearly.

68. **(C)** Narrow your choices as quickly as possible. The larcenies occur on Amboy Place between Pitt Avenue and East Avenue. Of course, this means that they occur equally on Amboy Place between East Avenue and Pitt Avenue. Narrow to (B) and (C). Larcenies occur on Sundays and Mondays, so choose (C). You would need to consider the time of day only if two answer choices led you to both the correct blocks and days of the week.

69. **(D)** The robberies occur on Fridays and Saturdays, so eliminate (A) and (B) as choices that do not span those days. The robberies occur from 1 to 3 P.M., so Officer Jones would not be very effective in reducing robberies in the choice (C) night shift.

70. **(C)** Look over the choices and decide which represents an emergency life-and-death situation that might be disastrous if not handled correctly. You would want the benefit of your supervisor's experience.

71. **(A)** The firing of a rifle into the stands is so obvious a case of total disregard for human life and creating grave risk of death to others that the other choices would have to be very convincing. (C) is pure accident; (B) is a threat to one's own life, not the life of another; (D) is recklessness with risk of injury rather than death.

72. **(B)** Officer Vasquez has been busy and has properly investigated the automobile. Up to this point, she has not fulfilled any of the duties required upon recovery of a stolen vehicle. Therefore, she must now enter the details in her Memo Book.

73. **(D)** Officer O'Rourke met the victim on a southbound #8 train.

74. **(A)** The officer met the victim at 5:25 A.M. She reported that she had been assaulted about a half hour before, at about 4:55 A.M.

75. **(B)** The arrested suspect was wearing a white shirt and the same color pants as the day before, black.

76. **(A)** On April 7, Officer O'Rourke entered the subway station intending to take a #7 train to Queens. However, when he recognized the suspect and observed him attempting to snatch a purse, he pursued the man and instead boarded a train to Manhattan.

77. **(D)** This is a clear and accurate statement.

78. **(D)** This report is clear, accurate, and complete.

79. **(C)** The police officers have conducted their interview, during which they learned of the presence of the knife that was dropped. The knife constitutes evidence. They must now search for the knife.

80. **(B)** Apartment 1A is at 416 Blum Street. Narrow to (B) or (D). The 1A sales are midday sales, so 9:00 A.M. to 5:00 P.M. is the best time to patrol.

81. **(A)** The officers did all the right things. The driver's license had been revoked, not merely suspended, so arrest was mandated.

82. **(D)** A police officer must always hesitate to use his gun in a crowd because of the danger to innocent bystanders. In this case, however, the man with the axe is already presenting a clear and present danger to the people who surround him. A well-aimed shot to the man with the axe may preserve the safety of a far greater number. The officer must take this calculated risk.

83. **(A)** This is a difficult incident to describe in only a few words. Choice (A) does it most clearly.

84. **(B)** This is the only statement that makes sense.

85. **(D)** Choice (A) would get them there, but it is the long way around; Surf Avenue is one-way west, eliminate (B); Prospect Street is one-way north, eliminate (C). (D) is quick and legal.

86. **(C)** Eliminate (A) because Surf is one-way westbound; eliminate (B) because it is an unnecessarily long route; eliminate (D) because Prospect is one-way northbound. (C) is direct and permissible.

87. **(B)** Choice (D) entails too long a route; (A) and (C) are prohibited by one-way streets. (B) works well. Follow the routes yourself to answer map questions.

88. **(D)** This is a simple arithmetic problem. Be careful not to count the handbag twice.

Cash of $150	=	$150
3 bracelets at $95 each	=	285
2 rings at $70 each	=	140
1 handbag at $159	=	+ 159
total	=	$734

89. **(B)** The suspect in Rape 1 has the wrong color hair and what is described as a highly visible scar. Since this scar was not reported in any of the other rapes, the man is probably only a suspect in Rape 1. The rapist in Rape 2 is too old. The descriptions of the rapists in Rape 3 and Rape 4 contain one major discrepancy, namely the location of the earring. Victims do make mistakes. The correspondence of the descriptions in all other details, including the left arm tattoo, makes the identity likely. Even if you were to disagree about the possibility of a victim's mistaking which ear, you would have to choose (B). You are not offered a choice that discounts all three previous rapists.

90. **(D)** This is the only clear and accurate statement.

91. **(A)** According to the printed procedure, Highway Police Officers conduct the alcohol test at the precinct station house. The next step in this case is to send for these officers.

92. **(A)** Reconstruct the number as best you can based on the principle of frequently occurring elements. The digits 8-2-3-2 all appear in three of the four eyewitness accounts in these respective positions. Of the final digits, only "4" appears more than once. Your choice must be far from certain, but in balance (A) is the best bet.

93. **(C)** Officer Ryan has interviewed both complainant and violator. The violator, Mr. Nelson, is very cooperative and agrees at once to correct the violation. There is no need for

a summons. Skip step 5 and enter a report in the Memo Book.

94. **(C)** The woman has gone through a stop sign, a serious moving violation. The fact that she missed the stop sign because she was putting on lipstick does not constitute extenuating circumstances. On the contrary, she was truly negligent.

95. **(B)** Walker did not steal the property. He fully intended to return the car to Mr. Smith after the weekend. Barnes consciously stole the valuable car, drove it without authorization, and resold it. His actions constituted both Grand Larceny Second Degree and Unauthorized Use of the Vehicle.

96. **(A)** Choice (B) is hopelessly garbled. Choice (C) leaves doubt as to who was carrying a TV and a VCR. Choice (D) is accurate but is awkwardly stated; (A) is better.

97. **(B)** The suspect in Robbery 3 is too old. Descriptions of the robbers in No. 1 and No. 2 coincide quite closely with Officer Harris's suspect in terms of age, height, weight, and moustache.

98. **(D)** The statement clearly states when, who, what, where, and by whom.

99. **(C)** The dead body found in the waters off the precinct must be reported as a Complaint in the precinct. In (A) the loss is discovered outside the precinct; in (B) the unlawful act is committed outside the precinct; in (D) the missing person resides outside the precinct.

100. **(B)** Although he fits in most respects, the suspect in Robbery 3 is too small. Victims' estimates of height and weight may vary, but not to so great a degree. The other two suspects closely resemble the current suspect.

101. **(C)** This problem presents no pitfalls.

1 ring at	=	$415
cash at	=	220
coin collection at	=	410
3 cameras at $175 each	=	+ 525
total	=	$1570

102. **(D)** The thieves broke the lock of the back door. They cut a wire at the basement window.

103. **(A)** The 19″ color television and clock radio belonged to Parker himself. The other items were borrowed from his friends.

104. **(C)** You, as an applicant, are not expected to know the classification of crimes, but this answer is given in the first sentence. Officers Ryder and Brown responded to a call concerning a burglary.

105. **(B)** Since the driver was unable to produce proof of identity and residence, doubt existed concerning his identity. The regulations state that if there is doubt concerning the identity of the violator, the violator must be taken to the station house.

106. **(A)** Only this statement correctly sorts out who made the report, who is missing, description of missing person, and time and place of last sighting.

107. **(B)** This is a clear, simple statement.

108. **(C)** Since Hill's parents are on their way, Officer Martin must be patient and wait for them to arrive. Only after the parents are in the room, should Officer Martin advise Tom Hill of his rights and begin questioning him about the offense.

109. **(B)** This statement is clear and accurate. Choice (C) confuses time of the crime with time of the report.

110. **(A)** Clear and accurate.

111. **(B)** If choice (B) were not offered, (D) would be acceptable. (B) is clearer. (A) mistakenly states that the bank was robbed by a shotgun; (C) states that a bank teller robbed the bank.

112. **(D)** The receipt should include a description of the property.

113. **(C)** You might think it more accurate to state that Lois Nettle's right leg was broken when the car hit her, as in choice (B). However, (C) gets the total message across much more clearly. For purposes of the ambulance crew, it is sufficient to know that the leg is broken.

114. **(C)** Thomas Parker was the driver of the Oldsmobile, but his brother, Harold Parker, was its owner. This begins a series of ques-

tions of fact, which may be answered by careful reading of the passage.

115. **(B)** The Dodge truck had a crumpled bumper and blown right front tire.

116. **(D)** The driver of the Oldsmobile sedan caused the accident by pulling out of a parking lot without looking for oncoming traffic.

117. **(A)** By now you should be aware that personal injuries always must receive the first attention. This is confirmed by the printed regulations as the first priority after the officer gets out of the car.

118. **(D)** Only this last statement tells what happened and to whom and to what.

119. **(A)** The regulation clearly states that unlawful assembly is a violation or offense for which a juvenile report should *not* be prepared.

120. **(C)** Date, time, who made the report, what was reported. Clearly and accurately stated.

121. **(B)** Only choice (B) fulfills all the requirements for Burglary in the First Degree: Watson is armed, he breaks into a dwelling, and in addition he threatens the owner with his gun. In (A) there is no weapon and no injury; in (C) the building is not a dwelling and the injured is party to the crime; in (D) though the suspect is armed and the guard is injured, the building is not a dwelling.

122. **(B)** Mr. Pitts has, however reluctantly, agreed to appear in the lineup. Since he has agreed to appear, he should not be arrested. The detective supervisor should be notified to expect him.

123. **(C)** This is the only statement that is clear, complete, and accurate.

124. **(D)** All the statements give all the information, but (D) is the clearest statement.

125. **(B)** This statement is by far the clearest and most accurate.

126. **(A)** Read carefully. The facts are there.

127. **(A)** Eddie Torres, a neighbor, served as witness to the search and signed the Memo Book.

128. **(D)** Regulations require that the police voucher the property of any deceased who has no relative living with him or her.

129. **(D)** Officer Gannett double-parked in front of the building so Officer James could jump out and send the alarm. The police car now represents an obstacle to the firefighters. Gannett must move the police car before entering the building to assist in evacuation of tenants.

130. **(C)** Only one statement is clear and accurate.

131. **(C)** Officer John neglected to make a decision as to whether the report should be closed or referred for further investigation.

132. **(A)** A threat of bodily harm might best be dealt with by professional counseling arranged through Family Court. The other disputes are routine household occurrences that pose no threat to anyone's safety.

133. **(B)** Focus on distinctive features. (A) has the wrong chin; (C) has a scar or cleft between nose and lips; (D) has the wrong lips.

134. **(C)** Choice (A) has the wrong nose; (B) has the wrong lips; (D) has the wrong chin.

135. **(D)** Choice (A) has the wrong nose; (B) has the wrong eyes (glasses may make the eyes appear larger, but B's are more deeply set); (C) has the wrong lips.

136. **(A)** Choice (B) has the wrong ears; (C) has the wrong mouth; (D) has the wrong nose.

137. **(A)** Choice (B) has the wrong ears; (C) has a more narrow lower face; (D) has the wrong nose.

138. **(D)** Choice (A) has the wrong lips; (B) has a cleft chin; (C) has the wrong eyes. A dramatic change of hairstyle on head or face often makes an effective change of appearance. If you are having difficulty choosing the disguised face, give special attention to the hair.

139. **(B)** Choice (A) has the wrong eyes; (C) has the wrong chin; (D) has the wrong lips.

140. **(C)** Choice (A) has the wrong lips; (B) has the wrong chin; (D) has the wrong nose.

ANSWER SHEET

New York City Exam—October 24, 1987

1. Ⓐ Ⓑ Ⓒ Ⓓ	31. Ⓐ Ⓑ Ⓒ Ⓓ	61. Ⓐ Ⓑ Ⓒ Ⓓ	91. Ⓐ Ⓑ Ⓒ Ⓓ	121. Ⓐ Ⓑ Ⓒ Ⓓ
2. Ⓐ Ⓑ Ⓒ Ⓓ	32. Ⓐ Ⓑ Ⓒ Ⓓ	62. Ⓐ Ⓑ Ⓒ Ⓓ	92. Ⓐ Ⓑ Ⓒ Ⓓ	122. Ⓐ Ⓑ Ⓒ Ⓓ
3. Ⓐ Ⓑ Ⓒ Ⓓ	33. Ⓐ Ⓑ Ⓒ Ⓓ	63. Ⓐ Ⓑ Ⓒ Ⓓ	93. Ⓐ Ⓑ Ⓒ Ⓓ	123. Ⓐ Ⓑ Ⓒ Ⓓ
4. Ⓐ Ⓑ Ⓒ Ⓓ	34. Ⓐ Ⓑ Ⓒ Ⓓ	64. Ⓐ Ⓑ Ⓒ Ⓓ	94. Ⓐ Ⓑ Ⓒ Ⓓ	124. Ⓐ Ⓑ Ⓒ Ⓓ
5. Ⓐ Ⓑ Ⓒ Ⓓ	35. Ⓐ Ⓑ Ⓒ Ⓓ	65. Ⓐ Ⓑ Ⓒ Ⓓ	95. Ⓐ Ⓑ Ⓒ Ⓓ	125. Ⓐ Ⓑ Ⓒ Ⓓ
6. Ⓐ Ⓑ Ⓒ Ⓓ	36. Ⓐ Ⓑ Ⓒ Ⓓ	66. Ⓐ Ⓑ Ⓒ Ⓓ	96. Ⓐ Ⓑ Ⓒ Ⓓ	126. Ⓐ Ⓑ Ⓒ Ⓓ
7. Ⓐ Ⓑ Ⓒ Ⓓ	37. Ⓐ Ⓑ Ⓒ Ⓓ	67. Ⓐ Ⓑ Ⓒ Ⓓ	97. Ⓐ Ⓑ Ⓒ Ⓓ	127. Ⓐ Ⓑ Ⓒ Ⓓ
8. Ⓐ Ⓑ Ⓒ Ⓓ	38. Ⓐ Ⓑ Ⓒ Ⓓ	68. Ⓐ Ⓑ Ⓒ Ⓓ	98. Ⓐ Ⓑ Ⓒ Ⓓ	128. Ⓐ Ⓑ Ⓒ Ⓓ
9. Ⓐ Ⓑ Ⓒ Ⓓ	39. Ⓐ Ⓑ Ⓒ Ⓓ	69. Ⓐ Ⓑ Ⓒ Ⓓ	99. Ⓐ Ⓑ Ⓒ Ⓓ	129. Ⓐ Ⓑ Ⓒ Ⓓ
10. Ⓐ Ⓑ Ⓒ Ⓓ	40. Ⓐ Ⓑ Ⓒ Ⓓ	70. Ⓐ Ⓑ Ⓒ Ⓓ	100. Ⓐ Ⓑ Ⓒ Ⓓ	130. Ⓐ Ⓑ Ⓒ Ⓓ
11. Ⓐ Ⓑ Ⓒ Ⓓ	41. Ⓐ Ⓑ Ⓒ Ⓓ	71. Ⓐ Ⓑ Ⓒ Ⓓ	101. Ⓐ Ⓑ Ⓒ Ⓓ	131. Ⓐ Ⓑ Ⓒ Ⓓ
12. Ⓐ Ⓑ Ⓒ Ⓓ	42. Ⓐ Ⓑ Ⓒ Ⓓ	72. Ⓐ Ⓑ Ⓒ Ⓓ	102. Ⓐ Ⓑ Ⓒ Ⓓ	132. Ⓐ Ⓑ Ⓒ Ⓓ
13. Ⓐ Ⓑ Ⓒ Ⓓ	43. Ⓐ Ⓑ Ⓒ Ⓓ	73. Ⓐ Ⓑ Ⓒ Ⓓ	103. Ⓐ Ⓑ Ⓒ Ⓓ	133. Ⓐ Ⓑ Ⓒ Ⓓ
14. Ⓐ Ⓑ Ⓒ Ⓓ	44. Ⓐ Ⓑ Ⓒ Ⓓ	74. Ⓐ Ⓑ Ⓒ Ⓓ	104. Ⓐ Ⓑ Ⓒ Ⓓ	134. Ⓐ Ⓑ Ⓒ Ⓓ
15. Ⓐ Ⓑ Ⓒ Ⓓ	45. Ⓐ Ⓑ Ⓒ Ⓓ	75. Ⓐ Ⓑ Ⓒ Ⓓ	105. Ⓐ Ⓑ Ⓒ Ⓓ	135. Ⓐ Ⓑ Ⓒ Ⓓ
16. Ⓐ Ⓑ Ⓒ Ⓓ	46. Ⓐ Ⓑ Ⓒ Ⓓ	76. Ⓐ Ⓑ Ⓒ Ⓓ	106. Ⓐ Ⓑ Ⓒ Ⓓ	136. Ⓐ Ⓑ Ⓒ Ⓓ
17. Ⓐ Ⓑ Ⓒ Ⓓ	47. Ⓐ Ⓑ Ⓒ Ⓓ	77. Ⓐ Ⓑ Ⓒ Ⓓ	107. Ⓐ Ⓑ Ⓒ Ⓓ	137. Ⓐ Ⓑ Ⓒ Ⓓ
18. Ⓐ Ⓑ Ⓒ Ⓓ	48. Ⓐ Ⓑ Ⓒ Ⓓ	78. Ⓐ Ⓑ Ⓒ Ⓓ	108. Ⓐ Ⓑ Ⓒ Ⓓ	138. Ⓐ Ⓑ Ⓒ Ⓓ
19. Ⓐ Ⓑ Ⓒ Ⓓ	49. Ⓐ Ⓑ Ⓒ Ⓓ	79. Ⓐ Ⓑ Ⓒ Ⓓ	109. Ⓐ Ⓑ Ⓒ Ⓓ	139. Ⓐ Ⓑ Ⓒ Ⓓ
20. Ⓐ Ⓑ Ⓒ Ⓓ	50. Ⓐ Ⓑ Ⓒ Ⓓ	80. Ⓐ Ⓑ Ⓒ Ⓓ	110. Ⓐ Ⓑ Ⓒ Ⓓ	140. Ⓐ Ⓑ Ⓒ Ⓓ
21. Ⓐ Ⓑ Ⓒ Ⓓ	51. Ⓐ Ⓑ Ⓒ Ⓓ	81. Ⓐ Ⓑ Ⓒ Ⓓ	111. Ⓐ Ⓑ Ⓒ Ⓓ	141. Ⓐ Ⓑ Ⓒ Ⓓ
22. Ⓐ Ⓑ Ⓒ Ⓓ	52. Ⓐ Ⓑ Ⓒ Ⓓ	82. Ⓐ Ⓑ Ⓒ Ⓓ	112. Ⓐ Ⓑ Ⓒ Ⓓ	142. Ⓐ Ⓑ Ⓒ Ⓓ
23. Ⓐ Ⓑ Ⓒ Ⓓ	53. Ⓐ Ⓑ Ⓒ Ⓓ	83. Ⓐ Ⓑ Ⓒ Ⓓ	113. Ⓐ Ⓑ Ⓒ Ⓓ	143. Ⓐ Ⓑ Ⓒ Ⓓ
24. Ⓐ Ⓑ Ⓒ Ⓓ	54. Ⓐ Ⓑ Ⓒ Ⓓ	84. Ⓐ Ⓑ Ⓒ Ⓓ	114. Ⓐ Ⓑ Ⓒ Ⓓ	144. Ⓐ Ⓑ Ⓒ Ⓓ
25. Ⓐ Ⓑ Ⓒ Ⓓ	55. Ⓐ Ⓑ Ⓒ Ⓓ	85. Ⓐ Ⓑ Ⓒ Ⓓ	115. Ⓐ Ⓑ Ⓒ Ⓓ	145. Ⓐ Ⓑ Ⓒ Ⓓ
26. Ⓐ Ⓑ Ⓒ Ⓓ	56. Ⓐ Ⓑ Ⓒ Ⓓ	86. Ⓐ Ⓑ Ⓒ Ⓓ	116. Ⓐ Ⓑ Ⓒ Ⓓ	146. Ⓐ Ⓑ Ⓒ Ⓓ
27. Ⓐ Ⓑ Ⓒ Ⓓ	57. Ⓐ Ⓑ Ⓒ Ⓓ	87. Ⓐ Ⓑ Ⓒ Ⓓ	117. Ⓐ Ⓑ Ⓒ Ⓓ	147. Ⓐ Ⓑ Ⓒ Ⓓ
28. Ⓐ Ⓑ Ⓒ Ⓓ	58. Ⓐ Ⓑ Ⓒ Ⓓ	88. Ⓐ Ⓑ Ⓒ Ⓓ	118. Ⓐ Ⓑ Ⓒ Ⓓ	148. Ⓐ Ⓑ Ⓒ Ⓓ
29. Ⓐ Ⓑ Ⓒ Ⓓ	59. Ⓐ Ⓑ Ⓒ Ⓓ	89. Ⓐ Ⓑ Ⓒ Ⓓ	119. Ⓐ Ⓑ Ⓒ Ⓓ	149. Ⓐ Ⓑ Ⓒ Ⓓ
30. Ⓐ Ⓑ Ⓒ Ⓓ	60. Ⓐ Ⓑ Ⓒ Ⓓ	90. Ⓐ Ⓑ Ⓒ Ⓓ	120. Ⓐ Ⓑ Ⓒ Ⓓ	150. Ⓐ Ⓑ Ⓒ Ⓓ

TEAR HERE

PRACTICE EXAMINATION 2

DEPARTMENT OF PERSONNEL

Social Security No. _____

Room No. _____

Seat No. _____

School _____

POLICE OFFICER SERIES
EXAMINATION NO. 7009

First Memory Booklet
October 24, 1987

DO NOT OPEN THIS BOOKLET UNTIL THE SECOND SIGNAL IS GIVEN!

Write your Social Security Number, Room Number, Seat Number, and School in the appropriate spaces at the top of this page.

You *must* follow the instructions found on the TEST INSTRUCTION SHEET.

ANYONE DISOBEYING ANY OF THE INSTRUCTIONS FOUND ON THE TEST INSTRUCTION SHEET MAY BE DISQUALIFIED— RECEIVE A ZERO ON THE ENTIRE TEST.

This booklet contains one scene. Try to remember as many details in the scene as you can. You should pay equal attention both to objects and to people shown in the scene

DO *NOT* WRITE OR MAKE *ANY* NOTES WHILE STUDYING THE SCENE.

DO NOT OPEN THIS BOOKLET UNTIL THE SECOND SIGNAL IS GIVEN!

[NOTE: You will have five (5) minutes to study the scene shown.]

The New York City Department of Personnel makes no commitment, and no inference is to be drawn, regarding the content, style, or format of any future examination for the position of Police Officer.

DEPARTMENT OF PERSONNEL

Social Security No. _____

Room No. _____

Seat No. _____

School _____

POLICE OFFICER SERIES
EXAMINATION No. 7009

Second Memory Booklet
October 24, 1987

DO NOT OPEN THIS BOOKLET UNTIL THE FOURTH SIGNAL IS GIVEN!

Write your Social Security Number, Room Number, Seat Number, and School in the appropriate spaces at the top of this page.

You *must* follow the instructions found on the TEST INSTRUCTION SHEET.

ANYONE DISOBEYING ANY OF THE INSTRUCTIONS FOUND ON THE TEST INSTRUCTION SHEET MAY BE DISQUALIFIED— RECEIVE A ZERO ON THE ENTIRE TEST.

This booklet contains Questions 1 through 6, which are based on Scene 1 as shown in the First Memory Booklet. Answer Questions 1 through 6 after the fourth signal. At the *FIFTH SIGNAL*, you should turn to Scene 2. Try to remember as many details in the scene as you can. You should pay equal attention both to objects and to people shown in the scene.

DO NOT OPEN THIS BOOKLET UNTIL THE FOURTH SIGNAL IS GIVEN!

[NOTE: You will have five (5) minutes to study the scene shown.]

The New York City Department of Personnel makes no commitment, and no inference is to be drawn, regarding the content, style, or format of any future examination for the position of Police Officer.

Answer questions 1 through 6 solely on the basis of sketch number 1.

1. Which one of the following is printed on the side of the black vehicle with the open hood?
   - (A) Richard Printing
   - (B) Archie's Business School
   - (C) Bob's Painters
   - (D) Nature's Food.

2. When is parking prohibited on East Avenue?

   - (A) Monday–Friday, 7:00 A.M. to 11:00 P.M.
   - (B) Friday–Saturday, 7:00 P.M. to 11:00 A.M.
   - (C) Monday–Saturday, 7:00 A.M. to 11:00 A.M.
   - (D) Friday–Saturday, 7:00 P.M. to 11:00 P.M.

3. Which one of the following is printed on the side of the white vehicle on Bay Street?
   - (A) Bob's Painters
   - (B) Uptown Express
   - (C) Guido's
   - (D) Fast Movers.

4. The man standing on the sidewalk with the woman is wearing

   - (A) black pants and is holding a white jacket
   - (B) a white jacket and black pants
   - (C) white pants and is holding a black jacket
   - (D) a black jacket and white pants.

5. Which one of the following is shown as a one-way street?
   - (A) East Avenue
   - (B) Bay Street
   - (C) Jewel Street
   - (D) West Avenue.

6. How many men are standing next to the station wagon with the hood up?
   - (A) one
   - (B) two
   - (C) three
   - (D) four.

DEPARTMENT OF PERSONNEL

Social Security No. _____
Room No. _____
Seat No. _____
School _____

POLICE OFFICER SERIES
EXAMINATION NO. 7009

Question Booklet
October 24, 1987

Written Test: Weight 100
Time Allowed: 5 Hours

DO NOT OPEN THIS BOOKLET UNTIL THE SEVENTH SIGNAL IS GIVEN!

Record your answers on the official Answer Sheet before the last signal. If you wish, you may also record your answers in the Question Booklet before the last signal is given. This will be your only official record of answers.

This Question Booklet contains procedures and definitions which are to be used to answer certain questions. These procedures and definitions are not necessarily those of the New York City Police Department. However, you are to answer these questions solely on the basis of the material given.

After the seventh signal is given, open this Question Booklet and begin to work. You will have 5 hours to complete this test.

You may make notes in this booklet and use the scrap paper on your desk. If you need additional scrap paper, ask the monitor.

Remember, only your official Answer Sheet will be rated, so be sure to mark *all* your answers on the official Answer Sheet before the eighth signal. *No* additional time will be given for marking your answers after the test has ended.

DO NOT OPEN THIS BOOKLET UNTIL THE SEVENTH SIGNAL IS GIVEN!

The New York City Department of Personnel makes no commitment, and no inference is to be drawn, regarding the content, style, or format of any future examination for the position of Police Officer.

Answer questions 7 through 12 solely on the basis of sketch number 2.

7. What words are written on the shirt of the man carrying a knife?

(A) Beach Bum
(B) Grateful Dead
(C) He-Man
(D) Big Blue.

8. Which one of the following best describes the victim of the crime?

(A) white female, striped pants, and blonde hair
(B) white female, dark hair, and black and white blazer
(C) Asian female, black pants, wearing glasses
(D) black female, striped pants, and white blazer.

9. A man is shown taking something from a woman's purse. The man is using his

(A) right hand, and the purse is on the woman's right shoulder
(B) left hand, and the purse is on the woman's right shoulder
(C) right hand, and the purse is on the woman's left shoulder
(D) left hand, and the purse is on the woman's left shoulder.

10. The youth who is holding a knife is wearing

(A) jeans and a jacket
(B) shorts and a short-sleeve shirt
(C) jeans and a short-sleeve shirt
(D) shorts and a T-shirt.

11. Which store has a "closed" sign in its window?

(A) Ave. R. Discount
(B) Gourmet Supermarket
(C) Book Store
(D) Rubber Stamps.

12. The Electronics store is located

(A) on Ave. R
(B) at the corner of Ave. R and E. 3rd St.
(C) on E. 3rd St.
(D) at the corner of Ave. R and W. 3rd St.

Please check your Answer Sheet to make sure that you have written in and blackened your Social Security number correctly. If you have not yet written in and blackened your Social Security number, please do so immediately. If you have incorrectly written in or blackened your Social Security number, please correct the mistake immediately. Failure to correctly blacken your Social Security number may result in your Answer Sheet NOT being rated.

Answer questions 13 and 14 solely on the basis of the following information.

Police Officer Thomas is aware that within his assigned sector all rapes occur on Clark Street, all robberies occur on Gaston Street, and all assaults occur on Pine Grove Avenue. Most robberies occur on Wednesdays and Fridays, most rapes occur on Tuesdays and Thursdays, and most assaults occur on Mondays and Tuesdays. Most rapes occur between 7:00 A.M. and 11:30 A.M., most assaults occur between 2:30 P.M. and 5:00 P.M., and most robberies occur between 3:30 P.M. and 9:30 P.M.

13. Officer Thomas would most likely be able to reduce the number of robberies if he patrolled

    (A) Pine Grove Avenue on Wednesdays from 8:00 A.M. to 4:00 P.M.
    (B) Gaston Street on Wednesdays from midnight to 8:00 A.M.
    (C) Gaston Street on Fridays from 4:00 P.M. to midnight
    (D) Clark Street on Mondays from 2:00 P.M. to 10:00 P.M.

14. To reduce the number of rapes, Officer Thomas is assigned to work a steady tour. For this purpose it would be most appropriate for Officer Thomas to work

    (A) Saturday through Wednesday, 8:00 A.M. to 4:00 P.M.
    (B) Thursday through Monday, 2:00 P.M. to 10:00 P.M.
    (C) Monday through Friday, 5:00 P.M. to 1:00 A.M.
    (D) Sunday through Thursday, 6:00 A.M. to 2:00 P.M.

15. Police Officer Salley has been selected to serve on a special task force designed to identify possible locations of drug sales in the precinct. He is assigned a post at the intersection of Rochester Avenue and Bergen Street between the hours of 9:00 A.M. and 5:00 P.M., Mondays through Fridays.

Which one of the following observations made by Officer Salley most likely indicates possible drug activity?

    (A) A continuous flow of people frequent Benny's Grocery Store and leave without packages.
    (B) A hot dog vendor arrives at the Bergen Street construction site each day at 11:30 A.M. and leaves at 2:00 P.M.
    (C) Many of the students from Rochester Avenue Elementary School go into Harry's Candy Store after school.
    (D) Many students from Bergen Street High School gather in the video arcade on Rochester Avenue during lunch periods and after school.

16. Police Officer Gattuso responded to a report of a robbery and obtained the following information regarding the incident:

Place of Occurrence:	Princess Grocery, 6 Sutton Place
Time of Occurrence:	6:00 P.M.
Crime:	Robbery of $200
Victim:	Sara Davidson, owner of Princess Grocery
Description of Suspect:	White, female, red hair, blue jeans, and white T-shirt
Weapon:	Knife

Officer Gattuso is preparing a report on the incident. Which one of the following expresses the above information *most clearly* and *accurately*?

(A) Sara Davidson reported at 6:00 P.M. her store Princess Grocery was robbed at knifepoint at 6 Sutton Place. A white woman with red hair took $200 from her wearing blue jeans and a white T-shirt.

(B) At 6:00 P.M. a red-haired woman took $200 from 6 Sutton Place at Princess Grocery owned by Sara Davidson, who was robbed by the white woman. She was wearing blue jeans and a white T-shirt and used a knife.

(C) In a robbery that occurred at knifepoint, a red-haired white woman robbed the owner of Princess Grocery. Sara Davidson, the owner of the 6 Sutton Place store which was robbed of $200, said she was wearing blue jeans and a white T-shirt at 6:00 P.M.

(D) At 6:00 P.M., Sara Davidson, owner of Princess Grocery, located at 6 Sutton Place, was robbed of $200 at knifepoint. The suspect is a white female with red hair wearing blue jeans and a white T-shirt.

Answer question 17 solely on the basis of the following information.

Murder 1st Degree—occurs when a person intentionally causes the death of another person.

17. Which one of the following situations is the best example of Murder in the First Degree?

(A) Sam is riding the train with Brenda who suddenly passes out, stops breathing, and dies even though Sam attempts to revive her.

(B) Jennifer shoots and kills her husband after a friend tells her that her husband is seeing another woman.

(C) A taxi driver goes through a red light because he is in a hurry and runs over Albert, breaking his arm and leg.

(D) Joe is standing on a very crowded subway platform when he accidentally pushes an elderly woman who falls onto the tracks and is killed by an oncoming train.

18. Police Officer Martinez responds to a report of an assault and obtains the following information regarding the incident:

Place of Occurrence:	Corner of Frank and Lincoln Avenues
Time of Occurrence:	9:40 A.M.
Crime:	Assault
Victim:	Mr. John Adams of 31-20th Street
Suspect:	Male, white, 5'11", 170 lbs., dressed in gray
Injury:	Victim suffered a split lip
Action Taken:	Victim transported to St. Mary's Hospital

Officer Martinez is completing a report on the incident. Which one of the following expresses the above information *most clearly* and *accurately*?

(A) At 9:40 A.M., John Adams was assaulted on the corner of Frank and Lincoln Avenues by a white male, 5'11", 170 lbs., dressed in gray, suffering a split lip. Mr. Adams lives at 31-20th Street and was transported to St. Mary's Hospital.

(B) At 9:40 A.M., John Adams was assaulted on the corner of Frank and Lincoln Avenues by a white male, 5'11", 170 lbs., dressed in gray, and lives at 31-20th Street. Mr. Adams suffered a split lip and was transported to St. Mary's Hospital.

(C) John Adams, who lives at 31-20th street, was assaulted at 9:40 A.M. on the corner of Frank and Lincoln Avenues by a white male, 5'11", 170 lbs., dressed in gray. Mr. Adams suffered a split lip and was transported to St. Mary's Hospital.

(D) Living at 31-20th Street, Mr. Adams suffered a split lip and was transported to St. Mary's Hospital. At 9:40 A.M., Mr. Adams was assaulted by a white male, 5'11", 170 lbs., dressed in gray.

Answer question 19 solely on the basis of the following information.

Police Officer Hooks has been instructed by his Precinct Commander to identify the locations in his patrol area where particular patterns of complaints have been reported. In reviewing recent complaint reports, Officer Hooks finds that most noise complaints occur on Beeker Street between Bay Boulevard and 79th Avenue. Larceny complaints are reported along Sutton Place between Church Street and Jerome Avenue. The majority of complaints concerning double-parked cars occur on Main Street between Flushing Street and Ocean Boulevard. Most of the larcenies occur between 7:00 A.M. and 10:00 A.M., the noise complaints between 11:00 P.M. and 2:00 A.M., and the complaints regarding double-parked cars between 1:00 P.M. and 4:00 P.M.

19. Officer Hooks is working a 1:00 P.M. to 9:00 P.M. shift. From which area should he receive the most complaints?

(A) Sutton Place between Jerome Avenue and Church Street.
(B) Beeker Street between Bay Boulevard and 79th Avenue.
(C) Main Street between Flushing Street and Ocean Boulevard.
(D) Main Street between Jerome Avenue and Church Street.

Answer questions 20 through 23 solely on the basis of the following passage.

Police Officer Richards, performing an 8:00 A.M. to 4:00 P.M. tour of duty, is designated as the station house cell block attendant. During Officer Richards' patrol, he hears moaning sounds coming from cell block number six, which is occupied by Sam Galvez. Mr. Galvez is complaining of abdominal pain and requests to go to the hospital. Officer Richards follows the procedure for a prisoner requiring medical attention by requesting that an ambulance respond to the precinct and also notifying the Desk Officer, Lt. Schwinn, who is talking with Captain Small. When the Emergency Medical Service attendants arrive, Officer Richards escorts them toward the cell block. John Ross, a medical attendant, determines after a brief examination of Mr. Galvez that his pain is probably due to his appendix.

John Ross and Jack Ryan, the other medical attendant, recommend that the prisoner be removed to the hospital. Lieutenant Schwinn assigns Police Officer Ellen Gray to rear handcuff Mr. Galvez and escort him to the hospital in the ambulance. At the hospital, Mr. Galvez is seen by Dr. Keegan, the attending physician, who requests that Officer Gray remove the handcuffs so he may conduct a complete physical examination. Officer Gray complies with Dr. Keegan's request. After Dr. Keegan examines the patient, he recommends that Mr. Galvez be admitted for an appendectomy. Police Officer Gray notifies the Hospitalized Prisoner Unit at the Court Division, completes the entries on the Medical Treatment of Prisoners form, and remains with Mr. Galvez until the arrival of a uniformed Police Officer who relieves her.

20. Who assigned Officer Gray to accompany the prisoner?
    (A) Police Officer Richards
    (B) Captain Small
    (C) Police Officer Ryan
    (D) Lieutenant Schwinn.

21. The Medical Treatment of Prisoner form was completed by the
    (A) escorting officer
    (B) cell block attendant
    (C) desk officer
    (D) medical attendant.

22. Prior to examining Mr. Galvez, Dr. Keegan requested that Officer Gray
    (A) handcuff Mr. Galvez
    (B) leave the examination room
    (C) remove the handcuffs from Mr. Galvez
    (D) submit a copy of the Medical Treatment form.

23. Officer Gray obtained the medical diagnosis from Dr. Keegan and then notified the
    (A) Hospitalized Prisoner Unit at the Court Division
    (B) Emergency Medical Service attendant, John Ross
    (C) Desk Officer, Lieutenant Schwinn
    (D) Cell Block Attendant, Police Officer Richards.

24. The Commanding Officer of each precinct often assigns Police Officers to special conditions patrols which are designed to handle problems unique to that precinct. Officers Martin and Spector are assigned to a special narcotics vehicle. Which one of the following should they give the most attention to as a possible drug dealing location?

   (A) A schoolyard where a group of fifteen youths are playing basketball and listening to the radio at 4:30 P.M.
   (B) A street corner where a group of people are standing next to an out-of-order telephone at 3:30 A.M.
   (C) Outside a YMCA center where a group of kids are getting on bicycles at 10:30 P.M.
   (D) Near an outdoor pool where twenty teenagers are waiting for an approaching bus at 4:00 P.M.

Answer question 25 solely on the basis of the following information.

While reviewing crime statistics for his patrol area, Police Officer Jones, of the 25th Precinct, notices that most of the homicides occur between 1:00 A.M. and 3:00 A.M., chain snatches between 10:00 A.M. and 2:00 P.M., and assaults between 5:00 A.M. and 6:00 A.M. Most of the homicides seem to occur on Thursdays, most of the chain snatches on Fridays, and most of the assaults on Fridays and Saturdays.

25. Police Officer Jones is instructed to work a steady tour that would allow him to concentrate on homicides and assaults within his patrol area. In order to do this it would be most appropriate for Officer Jones to work

   (A) 1:00 A.M. to 9:00 A.M., Monday through Friday
   (B) 5:00 A.M. to 1:00 P.M., Tuesday through Saturday
   (C) Midnight to 8:00 A.M., Wednesday through Sunday
   (D) 10:00 A.M. to 6:00 P.M., Monday through Friday.

Answer question 26 solely on the basis of the following information.

Assault 3rd Degree—occurs when a person intentionally causes physical injury to another person.

26. Which one of the following situations is the best example of Assault in the Third Degree?

   (A) Jennifer and Joe were talking on a street corner when Sam approached Jennifer, snatched her pocketbook, and fled.
   (B) Arthur and Jennifer were standing on a street corner arguing over Jennifer's daughter when Arthur punched Jennifer in the face, causing her mouth to bleed.
   (C) Sam and Arthur were arguing on a street corner when Sam's head was struck and bruised by a brick falling from a nearby building.
   (D) In order to avoid paying a debt, Sam ran away from Joe, who was chasing after him on foot. Joe was then hit by a passing car.

27. The following information was obtained by Police Officer Adams at the scene of an auto accident:

Date of Occurrence:	August 7, 1987
Place of Occurrence:	541 W. Broadway
Time of Occurrence:	12:45 P.M.
Drivers:	Mrs. Liz Smith and Mr. John Sharp
Action Taken:	Summons served to Mrs. Liz Smith

Officer Adams is completing a report on the accident. Which one of the following expresses the above information *most clearly* and *accurately*?

(A) At 541 W. Broadway Mr. John Sharp and Mrs. Liz Smith had an auto accident at 12:45 P.M. Mrs. Smith received a summons on August 7, 1987.

(B) Mrs. Liz Smith received a summons at 12:45 P.M. on August 7, 1987 for an auto accident with Mr. John Sharp at 541 W. Broadway.

(C) Mr. John Sharp and Mrs. Liz Smith were in an auto accident. At 541 W. Broadway on August 7, 1987 at 12:45 P.M. Mrs. Smith received a summons.

(D) On August 7, 1987 at 12:45 P.M. at 541 W. Broadway, Mrs. Liz Smith and Mr. John Sharp were involved in an auto accident. Mrs. Smith received a summons.

28. Police Officer Gold and his partner were directed by the radio dispatcher to investigate a report of a past burglary. They obtained the following information at the scene:

Date of Occurrence:	April 2, 1987
Time of Occurrence:	Between 7:30 A.M. and 6:15 P.M.
Place of Occurrence:	124 Haring Street, residence of victim
Victim:	Mr. Gerald Palmer
Suspect:	Unknown
Crime:	Burglary
Items stolen:	Assorted jewelry, $150 cash, T.V., VCR

Officer Gold must complete a report on the incident. Which one of the following expresses the above information *most clearly* and *accurately*?

(A) Mr. Gerald Palmer stated that on April 2, 1987, between 7:30 A.M. and 6:15 P.M., while he was at work, someone broke into his house at 124 Haring Street and removed assorted jewelry, a VCR, $150 cash, and a T.V.

(B) Mr. Gerald Palmer stated while he was at work that somebody broke into his house on April 2, 1987 and between 7:30 A.M. and 6:15 P.M. took his VCR, T.V., assorted jewelry, and $150 cash. His address is 124 Haring Street.

(C) Between 7:30 A.M. and 6:15 P.M. on April 2, 1987 Mr. Gerald Palmer reported an unknown person at 124 Haring Street took his T.V., VCR, $150 cash, and assorted jewelry from his house. Mr. Palmer said he was at work at the time.

(D) An unknown person broke into the house at 124 Haring Street and stole a T.V., VCR, assorted jewelry, and $150 cash from Mr. Gerald Palmer. The suspect broke in on April 2, 1987 while he was at work, reported Mr. Palmer between 7:30 A.M. and 6:15 P.M.

Answer question 29 solely on the basis of the following information.

When a Police Officer observes a person in custody or possession of a rifle or shotgun in public, the Officer should do the following in the order given:

1. Determine if person possesses a valid permit or certificate of registration.
2. Inform person not possessing permit or certificate of registration that:
   a. he may accompany the Officer to the precinct and surrender the firearm; or
   b. he may surrender the firearm at the scene, after which a receipt will be given.
3. Serve a summons returnable to appropriate criminal court.
4. Make a prompt arrest if violator refuses to surrender weapon.
5. Prepare a Property Clerk's Invoice and voucher weapons as evidence.

29. Police Officers Stromm and Rivers receive a call from the radio dispatcher that a male black, wearing sunglasses, is creating a disturbance in front of Joe's Grocery Store, located at 592 Pit Avenue. When they arrive, the Officers observe a male fitting the description showing the rifle to a small crowd that has gathered. The man, identified as Jerry Perkins, informs the Officers that he does not have a permit for the rifle and has no intention of accompanying them to the precinct to surrender his gun. The next thing that the Officers should do is

    (A) promptly place Perkins under arrest at the scene
    (B) inform Perkins that a receipt will be given him if he surrenders the weapon on the spot
    (C) issue Perkins a summons returnable to the appropriate criminal court
    (D) inform Perkins that he must have a valid permit or certificate of registration.

Answer question 30 solely on the basis of the following information.

Police Officers must sometimes rely on eyewitness accounts of incidents, even though eyewitnesses may make mistakes with regard to some details.

30. While on patrol, Police Officers Black and Beck receive a call from the radio dispatcher regarding a bank robbery in progress. When they arrive on the scene, they see that one of the bank employees has been wounded. While Officer Beck attends to the wounded employee, Officer Black interviews four witnesses who saw a man carrying a gun get into a blue late-model Cadillac and flee from the scene. The following are license plate numbers that were observed by the witnesses. Which one of these plates should Officer Black consider most likely to be the correct one?

    (A) N.J. Plate ACE-1780
    (B) N.Y. Plate ADE-1780
    (C) N.Y. Plate BDE-1780
    (D) N.J. Plate ADE-1680.

31. While on patrol, Police Officers Morris and Devine receive a call to respond to a reported burglary. The following information relating to the crime was obtained by the Officers:

Time of Occurrence:	2:00 A.M.
Place of Occurrence:	2100 First Avenue
Witness:	David Santiago
Victim:	John Rivera
Suspect:	Joe Ryan
Crime:	Burglary, video tape recorder stolen

The Officers are completing a report on the incident. Which one of the following expresses the above information *most clearly* and *accurately*?

(A) David Santiago, the witness reported at 2:00 A.M. he saw Joe Ryan leave 2100 First Avenue, home of John Rivera, with a video tape recorder.

(B) At 2:00 A.M., David Santiago reported that he had seen Joe Ryan go into 2100 First Avenue and steal a video tape recorder. John Rivera lives at 2100 First Avenue.

(C) David Santiago stated that Joe Ryan burglarized John Rivera's house at 2100 First Avenue. He saw Joe Ryan leaving his house at 2:00 A.M. with a video tape recorder.

(D) David Santiago reported that at 2:00 A.M. he saw Joe Ryan leave John Rivera's house, located at 2100 First Avenue, with Mr. Rivera's video tape recorder.

Answer question 32 solely on the basis of the following information.

When a Police Officer responds to an incident involving the victim of an animal bite, the Officer should do the following in the order given:

1. Determine the owner of the animal.
2. Obtain a description of the animal and attempt to locate it for an examination if the owner is unknown.
3. If the animal is located and the owner is unknown, comply with the Care and Disposition of Animal procedure.
4. Prepare a Department of Health form 480BAA and deliver it to the Desk Officer with a written report.
5. Notify the Department of Health by telephone if the person has been bitten by an animal other than a dog or cat.

32. Police Officer Rosario responds to 1225 South Boulevard where someone has been bitten by a dog. He is met by John Miller who informs Officer Rosario that he was bitten by a large German Shepard. Mr. Miller also states that he believes the dog belongs to someone in the neighborhood but does not know who owns it. Officer Rosario searches the area for the dog but is unable to find it. What should Officer Rosario do next?

(A) Locate the owner of the animal.
(B) Notify the Department of Health by telephone.
(C) Prepare a Department of Health form 480BAA.
(D) Comply with the Care and Disposition of Animal procedure.

33. The following details were obtained by Police Officer Howard at the scene of a hit and run accident:

Place of Occurrence:	Intersection of Brown Street and Front Street.
Time of Occurrence:	11:15 A.M.
Victim:	John Lawrence
Vehicle:	Red Chevrolet, License Plate 727PQA
Crime:	Leaving the scene of an accident

Officer Howard is completing a report on the incident. Which one of the following expresses the above information *most clearly* and *accurately*?

(A) A red Chevrolet license plate 727PQA hit John Lawrence. It left the scene of the accident at 11:15 A.M. at the intersection of Brown and Front Streets.

(B) At 11:15 A.M., John Lawrence was walking at the intersection of Brown Street and Front Street when he was struck by a red Chevrolet, license plate 727PQA, which left the scene.

(C) It was reported at 11:15 A.M. that John Lawrence was struck at the intersection of Brown Street and Front Street. The red Chevrolet, license plate 727PQA, left the scene.

(D) At the intersection of Brown Street and Front Street, John Lawrence was the victim of a car at 11:15 A.M. which struck him and left the scene. It was a red Chevrolet license plate 727PQA.

34. Police Officer Donnelly has transported an elderly male to Mt. Hope Hospital after finding him lying on the street. At the hospital, Nurse Baker provided Officer Donnelly with the following information:

Name:	Robert Jones
Address:	1485 E. 97th St.
Date of Birth:	May 13, 1917
Age:	70 years old
Type of Ailment:	Heart condition

Officer Donnelly is completing an Aided Report. Which one of the following expresses the above information *most clearly* and *accurately*?

(A) Mr. Robert Jones, who is 70 years old, born on May 13, 1917, collapsed on the street. Mr. Jones, who resides at 1485 E. 97th Street, suffers from a heart condition.

(B) Mr. Robert Jones had a heart condition and collapsed today on the street, and resides at 1485 E. 97th Street. He was 70 years old and born on May 13, 1917.

(C) Mr. Robert Jones, who resides at 1485 E. 97th Street, was born on May 13, 1917, and is 70 years old, was found lying on the street from a heart condition.

(D) Mr. Robert Jones, born on May 13, 1917, suffers from a heart condition at age 70 and was found lying on the street residing at 1485 E. 97th Street.

214 / *Police Officer*

35. Police Officers on patrol are often called to a scene where a response from the Fire Department might be necessary. In which one of the following situations would a request to the Fire Department to respond be most critical?

(A) A film crew has started a small fire in order to shoot a scene on an October evening.
(B) Two man-hole covers blow off on a September afternoon.
(C) Homeless persons are gathered around a trash can fire on a February morning.
(D) A fire hydrant has been opened by people in the neighborhood on a July afternoon.

Answer question 36 solely on the basis of the following information.

Upon coming into possession of found property, a Police Officer should do the following in the order given:

1. Issue a receipt to person delivering property if other than a Police Officer.
   a. If property is turned in at station house, Station House Clerk will prepare a Property Clerk's Invoice and give finder a copy as a receipt.
   b. If property is delivered to a Police Officer on patrol, prepare a receipt including a description of the property and signature of receiving Officer.
2. Enter facts in memo book.
3. Prepare worksheet of Property Clerk's Invoice.
4. Deliver property and worksheet to Station House Officer.
5. Verify accuracy of Property Clerk's Invoice by signing name in the appropriate box.

36. Police Officer Bestwell, while on patrol, finds a black leather purse near a subway entrance. The bag contains a wallet with personal papers and other miscellaneous items. After logging the items that were contained in the bag into his memo book, Officer Bestwell asks Mrs. Robinson, a witness, to sign the book to verify that he found the property and that he was going to deliver it to the station house. Officer Bestwell's next step should be to

(A) give Mrs. Robinson a receipt describing the property
(B) have the Station House Clerk prepare a Property Clerk's Invoice and give a copy to Mrs. Robinson
(C) prepare a worksheet of the Property Clerk's Invoice
(D) deliver property and Property Clerk's Invoice to the Station House Officer.

37. Police Officer Rogers was dispatched to investigate a report of drugs being sold. The Officer obtained the following information:

Place of Occurrence:	In front of 109-30 Hollis Avenue
Time of Occurrence:	Between 3:00 P.M. and 6:00 P.M.
Reporter:	Mrs. Williams, who resides at 109-30 Hollis Avenue
Crime:	Drug sales
Suspects:	Male students from PS 182

Officer Rogers is preparing a report on the investigation. Which one of the following expresses the above information *most clearly* and *accurately*?

(A) Mrs. Williams reports between the hours of 3:00 P.M. and 6:00 P.M. drugs are sold. She lives at 109-30 Hollis Avenue where a group of boys from PS 182 sell drugs outside of her home.
(B) Male students selling drugs from PS 182 are creating a problem for Mrs. Williams. She reports this takes place in front of her home. She resides at 109-30 Hollis Avenue. The sales take place from 3:00 P.M. to 6:00 P.M.
(C) Drugs are being sold in front of 109-30 Hollis Avenue. Mrs. Williams reported a group of boys from PS 182 are responsible in front of her home at 109-30 Hollis Avenue. The drugs sell from 3:00 P.M. to 6:00 P.M.
(D) Mrs. Williams reports that a group of boys from PS 182 are selling drugs in front of her home at 109-30 Hollis Avenue. She further reports that the drug sales occur between 3:00 P.M. to 6:00 P.M.

Answer question 38 solely on the basis of the following information.

Rape 1st Degree—occurs when a male engages in sexual intercourse with a female:

1. by forcible compulsion; or
2. who is incapable of consent by reason of being physically helpless; or
3. who is less than eleven years old.

38. Liz and Marie while returning home from school walked by a wooded area near their home. The girls, both 10 years old, were spotted by their neighbor, Mr. Walls, who invited them to his house for ice cream. The girls followed Mr. Walls home where Joe, Mr. Walls' friend, joined them. After finishing their ice cream, the girls decided to go home but were unable to leave because Joe had locked the door. The girls were pushed into a room by Joe and Mr. Walls. The men then tore the girls' clothes off and tied them to a bed. Mr. Walls engaged in sexual intercourse with the girls while Joe watched. Who should be charged with Rape 1st Degree?

(A) Mr. Walls should be charged with Rape 1st Degree but Joe should not.
(B) Joe should be charged with Rape 1st Degree but Mr. Walls should not.
(C) Joe and Mr. Walls should both be charged with Rape 1st Degree.
(D) Neither Joe nor Mr. Walls should be charged with Rape 1st Degree.

Answer questions 39 through 40 solely on the basis of the following map. The flow of traffic is indicated by the arrows. If there is only one arrow shown, then traffic flows only in the direction indicated by the arrow. If there are two arrows shown, then traffic flows in both directions. You must follow the flow of traffic.

39. Police Officers Glenn and Albertson are on 111th Street at Henry Street when they are dispatched to a past robbery at Beach Boulevard and 115th Street. Which one of the following is the shortest route for the Officers to follow in their patrol car, making sure to obey all traffic regulations?

(A) Travel north on 111th Street, then east on Edelman Avenue, then north on 112th Street, then east on Beach Boulevard, then north on 114th Street, then east on Nassau Boulevard, then one block south on 116th Street.

(B) Travel north on 111th Street, then east on Beach Boulevard, then north on 114th Street, then east on Nassau Boulevard, then one block south on 115th Street.

(C) Travel north on 111th Street, then east on Merrick Boulevard, then two blocks south on 115th Street.

(D) Travel north on 111th Street, then east on Nassau Boulevard, then south on 112th Street, then east on Beach Boulevard, then north on 114th Street, then east on Nassau Boulevard, then one block south on 115th Street.

40. Later in their tour, Officers Glenn and Albertson are driving on 114th Street. If they make a left turn to enter the parking lot at Andersen Avenue, and then make a U-turn, in what direction would they now be headed?

(A) North   (C) East
(B) South   (D) West

41. On Monday, October 12, Police Officers Reynolds and Cornan responded to a past burglary at the Electronic Center. The manager of the store stated that the following merchandise was taken:

- 2 Portable tape players, each valued at $99.00
- 3 Compact Disc players, each valued at $290.00
- 5 Telephone sets, each valued at $50.00
- 1 VCR valued at $470.00
- 1 TV set valued at $600.00
- 1 Stereo rack system valued at $975.00
- 1 Walkman stereo valued at $70.00

In addition to the above items, the manager told the Officers that his calculator, worth $50, was also taken from behind the counter.

Officer Reynolds is preparing a Complaint Report on the burglary. Which one of the following is the total value of the property stolen?

(A) $2,554.00   (C) $3,433.00
(B) $2,604.00   (D) $3,483.00.

Answer Question 42 through 46 solely on the basis of the following passage.

At 10:30 P.M., while parked in front of a clothing store at 1925 First Avenue, Police Officers Cole and Reese received a radio call to investigate a possible burglary at 1423 Second Avenue. The Officers were to meet the complainant in front of the location given by the dispatcher.

Upon arriving at the scene, the Officers were met by Mr. Rivers, the owner of the Melody Grocery Store located at 1425 Second Avenue. He explained that he had called the police because he noticed the bicycle shop next door had been left open. Mr. Rivers further stated that the shop owner, Mr. Rose, usually closes at 9:00 P.M. Mr. Reyes, who lives at 1923 First Avenue and works with Mr. Rivers, noticed that the store gate had been partially closed and upon checking saw that the lights were off and the door was not locked.

At 10:40 P.M., Police Officer Reese radioed for a Supervisor before entering the premises. Sgt. Parker arrived ten minutes later and supervised a search to find out if the owner was sick, injured, or incapacitated somewhere in the store. The results proved negative. Apparently nothing had been taken or disturbed and there were no visible signs of a forced entry. The Sergeant instructed Officer Reese to guard the premises while his partner contacted Police Officer Craig, the Precinct Telephone Switchboard Operator, who would check the precinct merchant index file and then notify Mr. Rose of the situation.

42. The Sergeant supervised a search to determine if

    (A) the store was being burglarized
    (B) the owner was sick or injured
    (C) the store had been ransacked
    (D) the owner was working late.

43. The Police dispatcher received a call regarding a possible burglary at

    (A) 1423 Second Avenue
    (B) 1923 First Avenue
    (C) 1425 Second Avenue
    (D) 1925 First Avenue.

44. What type of business was left unsecured?

    (A) Florist Shop
    (B) Bicycle Shop
    (C) Grocery Store
    (D) Clothes Store.

45. At what time did the Sergeant arrive?

    (A) 10:30 P.M.   (C) 10:45 P.M.
    (B) 10:40 P.M.   (D) 10:50 P.M.

46. Which Police Officer would attempt to contact the store owner?

    (A) Reese   (C) Craig
    (B) Parker   (D) Cole.

47. While on patrol, Police Officer Willis responds to a report of unusual odors at an apartment complex. The following information was obtained by the Officer:

Place of Occurrence:	173 Concord Avenue, Apartment 17
Time of Occurrence:	1:10 A.M.
Caller:	Mrs. Denise Mathis
Odors:	Gas and ammonia
Source of Odors:	Janitor's supply room
Action Taken:	Fire Department called

Officer Willis is completing a report on the incident. Which one of the following expresses the above information *most clearly* and *accurately*?

(A) At 173 Concord Avenue, Apartment 17, the smell of gas and ammonia prompted Mrs. Denise Mathis to call 911. The Fire Department responded to the scene of the janitor's supply room. It was 1:10 A.M.

(B) Mrs. Denise Mathis smelled gas and ammonia from her home at 173 Concord Avenue, Apartment 17. She called 911. The source was found in the janitor's supply room after being noticed at 1:10 A.M. and the Fire Department was called.

(C) At 1:10 A.M., Mrs. Denise Mathis of 173 Concord Avenue, Apartment 17, smelled gas and ammonia, and called 911. The odors were found to be coming from the janitor's supply room. The Fire Department was called to the scene.

(D) Unusual odors of gas and ammonia were noticed by Mrs. Denise Mathis at 173 Concord Avenue, Apartment 17 at 1:10 A.M. The janitor's supply room was responsible. She called 911. The Fire Department was called.

Answer question 48 solely on the basis of the following information.

Police Officers must sometimes rely on eyewitness accounts of incidents, even though eyewitnesses may make mistakes with regard to some details.

48. While crossing the street, ten-year-old Nerissa King is struck by a car at the corner of James Street and Paul Avenue. Police Officer Lou responds to the scene and questions four witnesses who saw the vehicle that struck Nerissa. The following are descriptions of the vehicle given by the witnesses. Which one of these descriptions should Officer Lou consider most likely to be correct?

(A) Red Ford Mustang, NY Plate 2198 CAT
(B) Red Ford Mustang, NY Plate 2998 KAT
(C) Burgundy Ford Pinto, NY Plate 2198 CAT
(D) Red Ford Mustang, NY Plate 2198 COT

49. Police Officer Kelly responds to a call from the radio dispatcher regarding a small boy who has fallen down while running in a school yard. Officer Kelly has obtained the following information:

Time of Incident:	8:00 A.M.
Place of Incident:	PS 27 school yard at 1313 Thorn Lane
Victim:	Henry Ruiz
Injury:	Broken right index finger

Officer Kelly is writing a report on the incident. Which one of the following expresses the above information *most cleary* and *accurately*?

(A) While running in the PS 27 school yard, Henry Ruiz broke his right index finger. At 8:00 A.M. an accident occurred at 1313 Thorn Lane.

(B) At 8:00 A.M., a little boy broke his finger in the school yard at 1313 Thorn Lane. Henry Ruiz was running and it was his right index finger he broke at PS 27.

(C) Henry Ruiz fell down while running at 8:00 A.M. at 1313 Thorn Lane. The small boy broke his right index finger in the school yard of PS 27.

(D) At 8:00 A.M. in the school yard of PS 27, 1313 Thorn Lane, Henry Ruiz fell down while running and broke his right index finger.

50. Police Officer Covatti was on patrol when he received the following information relating to a person in need of assistance:

Place of Occurrence:	Canal Street and Ludlow Place
Date of Occurrence:	May 25
Person Aided:	Unidentified woman, unconscious and bleeding from the head
Reporter:	Laura Gallo
Disposition:	Victim transported by ambulance to Beth Israel Hospital

Officer Covatti is about to enter the details regarding this incident in his memo book. Which one of the following expresses the above information *most clearly* and *accurately*?

(A) An unconscious woman was transported to Beth Israel Hospital by ambulance. Laura Gallo reported that she was bleeding from the head at the corner of Canal Street and Ludlow Place on May 25th. She was unidentified.

(B) On May 25th, Laura Gallo reported that there was an unconscious woman bleeding from the head on the corner of Canal Street and Ludlow Place. An ambulance responded and transported the woman, who was unidentified, to Beth Israel Hospital.

(C) Laura Gallo reported that there was an unconscious unidentified woman bleeding from the head on the corner of Canal Street and Ludlow Place. On May 25th, an ambulance transported the woman to Beth Israel Hospital.

(D) An ambulance transported an unconscious woman, bleeding from the head, to Beth Israel Hospital. On May 25th, Laura Gallo reported that an unidentified woman was on the corner of Canal Street and Ludlow Place.

Answer question 51 solely on the basis of the following information.

When transporting emotionally disturbed people, a Police Officer should:

1. Have person removed to the hospital in an ambulance.
   a. Restraining equipment including handcuffs may be used if patient is violent or resists.
   b. When possible, a female patient being transported should be accompanied by another female or by an adult member of her immediate family.
2. Ride in body of ambulance with patient.
   a. Two police officers are needed if more than one patient is being transported.
   b. If an ambulance is not available and the situation warrants, transport the patient to the hospital by patrol car, if able to do so with reasonable restraint.

51. On Monday, while working an 8:00 P.M. to 4:00 A.M. shift, Police Officer Crown is assigned to patrol the Broadway-Lafayette subway station. At 2:15 A.M. he observes a middle-aged man wearing only red shorts pacing up and down the platform yelling, "Aliens are coming. Aliens are coming." Officer Crown approaches the man, later identified as Robert Grover, and asks, "What's the matter?" Mr. Grover begins swinging his arms at the Officer and shouts, "Don't touch me. When the next train comes, I'm jumping in front of it." Officer Crown immediately handcuffs him and calls for an ambulance. When it arrives, Officer Crown places Mr. Grover into the back of the ambulance. Just as the ambulance is about to leave for the hospital, Police Officer Cook arrives with two emotionally disturbed females, both in handcuffs. The women are placed into the ambulance along with Mr. Grover. Officer Cook stays behind to console Mrs. Susan Helms, the mother of one of the two females. Officer Crown accompanies Mr. Grover and the females to the hospital, telling Officer Cook, "I'll see you later at the hospital." In this situation, the actions taken by the Officer were

(A) proper, primarily because Officer Cook attempted to console Mrs. Helms, the mother of one of the women
(B) improper, primarily because Officer Crown handcuffed Mr. Grover without good cause
(C) proper, primarily because Officer Cook accompanied the females to the hospital in an ambulance
(D) improper, primarily because Officer Crown accompanied more than one patient to the hospital.

Answer questions 52 and 53 solely on the basis of the following information.

Police Officer Malone is instructed by his supervisor to analyze the crime statistics in his patrol sector in order to reduce the number of burglaries, auto thefts, and robberies. Through his analysis, Officer Malone finds that a large percentage of the burglaries take place on East 99th Street, the majority of auto thefts along East 100th Street, and most of the robberies on Park Avenue. The burglaries occur after most people go to bed, the auto thefts during the afternoon rush hours, and the robberies during the evening hours. For the most part, burglaries take place on Thursdays and Fridays, auto thefts on Mondays and Wednesdays, and robberies on Fridays and Saturdays.

52. Officer Malone would be most effective in reducing the number or burglaries and robberies if he patrolled from

(A) 9:00 P.M. to 5:00 A.M., Wednesday through Sunday, on E. 99th Street and Park Avenue
(B) 8:00 A.M. to 4:00 P.M., Monday through Friday, on E. 99th and E. 100th Streets
(C) noon to 8:00 P.M., Wednesday through Sunday, on E. 99th Street and Park Avenue
(D) 1:00 A.M. to 9:00 A.M., Friday through Tuesday, on Park Avenue and E. 100th Street.

53. In order to most effectively reduce the number of auto thefts in his sector, Officer Malone's Supervisor asked him to work a steady tour that would allow him to concentrate on that crime. For this purpose it would be most appropriate for Officer Malone to work

(A) Tuesday through Saturday, 3:00 A.M. to 11:00 A.M.
(B) Saturday through Wednesday, 8:00 A.M. to 4:00 P.M.
(C) Monday through Friday, 4:00 P.M. to midnight
(D) Monday through Friday, midnight to 8:00 A.M.

54. It is sometimes necessary for a Police Officer to call for back-up assistance in certain situations. In which one of the following situations would it be most appropriate for Police Officers to call for back-up?

(A) A group of people playing a radio loudly in the park.
(B) Two children fighting in front of a school.
(C) A shop owner who wants a drunk removed from his doorway.
(D) Two men shaking sticks at each other while arguing in front of a bar.

Answer question 55 solely on the basis of the following information.

Police Officers coming into possession of a recovered weapon are required to voucher it by taking the following steps in the order given:

1. Unload ammunition from the chamber or magazine.
2. Scratch an identifying mark on the side of each cartridge case removed from the weapon.
3. Place the ammunition in an envelope.
4. Write "Ammunition Removed from Firearm" and the weapon's serial number (if available) across the face of the envelope.
5. Place additional ammunition, other than that removed from firearm, in a separate envelope.
6. Deliver the firearm and ammunition to the Desk Officer of the precinct of occurrence.

55. Police Officer Black is acting as vouchering officer for recovered weapons at the Midtown South Precinct. He is given a loaded .357 magnum revolver and 20 additional rounds of ammunition to be vouchered. Officer Black removes the bullets from the revolver's chamber and, with a nail, engraves "P.O.B." on the side of each cartridge case. He then places the bullets into a large brown envelope and writes "Ammunition Removed from Firearm" and the revolver's serial number across the envelope's face. The next step Officer Black should take is to

(A) scratch an identifying mark on each of the additional 20 rounds of ammunition
(B) put the additional 20 rounds of ammunition in another envelope
(C) give the revolver and bullets to the Desk Officer of the precinct where the revolver was recovered
(D) scratch an identifying mark on the barrel of the revolver.

Answer question 56 solely on the basis of the following information.

Police Officers Davis and Lewis are assigned to cover Sector A. They have been working this area for six months now and have noticed that a lot of the rapes take place on Saturdays, most of the drug sales take place on Fridays and Saturdays, and the majority of the robberies occur on Mondays and Fridays. The primary hours when the rapes occur are between 3:00 P.M. and 10:00 P.M., the drug sales take place between 9:00 A.M. and 6:00 P.M., and the robberies happen between 1:00 P.M. and midnight.

56. The Officers are instructed to work a steady tour that would allow them to concentrate on robberies and rapes within their patrol area. For this purpose it would be most appropriate for the Officers to work

(A) 3:00 P.M. to 11:00 P.M., Thursday through Monday
(B) 10:00 A.M. to 6:00 P.M., Tuesday through Saturday
(C) 8:00 A.M. to 4:00 P.M., Monday through Friday
(D) 4:00 P.M. to midnight, Wednesday through Sunday.

Answer questions 57 through 59 solely on the basis of the following passage.

Police Officers Wilson and Jost are assigned to a patrol car and receive a call from the dispatcher to respond to a shooting at 236 Bever Street between Hoyt and Clinton Avenues. The two Officers arrive at the scene at 5:20 P.M. and see a man, later identified as David Smith of 242 Bever Street, lying on the sidewalk and bleeding from the chest. An ambulance arrives at 5:35 P.M. and the attendant, Peter Johnson, pronounces Mr. Smith dead from a gunshot wound on the left side of the chest. Officer Jost begins to walk along Bever Street looking for witnesses. Suddenly, William Jones comes out of his store, located at 239 Bever Street, and tells Officer Jost that he heard a gunshot at 5:15 P.M. and saw two white males going through the victim's pockets. Meanwhile, Walter Garvey, of 247 Bever Street, approaches Officer Wilson and tells him that he saw the victim fall to the ground and then observed two white males search the victim before they ran west on Bever Street toward Clinton Avenue. Mr. Garvey describes one suspect as having blond hair and wearing a blue jacket and black jeans, and the other suspect as having brown hair and wearing a white jacket and blue jeans.

After interviewing Mr. Jones, Officer Jost is approached by Doris Finkle, owner of the Sweet Shop located at 238 Bever Street. She tells him that the victim was walking along Bever Street when two white males came from behind and pushed Mr. Smith against the wall. She also says that a man with blond hair started talking to the victim when suddenly a man wearing a white jacket fired a gun and Mr. Smith fell to the ground. Mrs. Finkle tells the Officer that the two suspects searched the victim and then ran away.

57. Who pronounced David Smith dead?

   (A) William Jones
   (B) Doris Finkle
   (C) Peter Johnson
   (D) Walter Garvey.

58. Which of the following persons was the first to report hearing a gunshot?

   (A) Police Officer Jost
   (B) Walter Garvey
   (C) Peter Johnson
   (D) William Jones.

59. Who was the first witness to give a description of the suspects' clothing?

   (A) Mrs. Finkle
   (B) Mr. Garvey
   (C) Mr. Jones
   (D) Mr. Johnson.

60. Police Officers Carrano and Lee have responded to the scene of a burglary and obtained the following information:

Place of Occurrence:	289 Orchard Street
Time of Occurrence:	1:35 A.M.
Witness:	Ms. Perez
Suspect:	A Female Hispanic, 5'10", 140 lbs., wearing a black jacket and blue jeans
Crime:	Burglary of a clothing store, three coats taken

Officers Lee and Carrano are filing the initial report on the incident. Which one of the following expresses the above information *most clearly* and *accurately*?

(A) At 1:35 A.M., Ms. Perez reported a woman stole three coats while wearing a black jacket and blue jeans in the store at 289 Orchard Street. The Hispanic is 5'10" and 140 lbs.

(B) A female Hispanic witnessed by Ms. Perez was wearing blue jeans and a black jacket. A store at 289 Orchard Street was robbed of three coats by a suspect weighing 140 lbs. at 5'10" at 1:35 A.M.

(C) Ms. Perez witnessed a burglary when she saw a woman steal three coats. She was wearing blue jeans and a black jacket. At 1:35 A.M., she burglarized a store at 289 Orchard Street. The Hispanic suspect was 5'10" and 140 lbs.

(D) At 1:35 A.M., Ms. Perez reportedly saw a female Hispanic steal three coats from a store at 289 Orchard Street. The suspect was described as being 5'10", 140 lbs., wearing blue jeans and a black jacket.

61. Police Officer Sanchez has just finished investigating a report of a rape and has obtained the following information:

Time of Occurrence:	9:10 A.M.
Place of Occurrence:	Tony's Bodega, 109 Victory Boulevard
Victim:	Joyce Rivera, employee
Crime:	Rape
Suspect:	Male, white, carrying a gun

Officer Sanchez is completing a report on the incident. Which one of the following expresses the above information *most clearly* and *accurately*?

(A) Joyce Rivera is an employee at Tony's Bodega located at 109 Victory Boulevard. She reported that at 9:10 A.M. a white male went into the Bodega and raped her at gun point.

(B) While working in Tony's Bodega, located at 109 Victory Boulevard, Joyce Rivera reported at 9:10 A.M., she was raped at gun point by a male white.

(C) The time was 9:10 A.M., when a white male went into Tony's Bodega and pointed a gun at an employee. He then raped Joyce Rivera. The Bodega is located at 109 Victory Boulevard.

(D) At 9:10 A.M., Joyce Rivera reported that she was in Tony's Bodega, located at 109 Victory Boulevard. A white male went in and raped her while she was working at gun point.

Answer question 62 solely on the basis of the following information.

When evidence is required for presentation in court a Police Officer must do the following:

1. Request evidence from Officer assigned to Property Clerk facility where it is stored.
2. Give the Officer the Property Clerk's Invoice Number.
3. Present shield and identification card.
4. If the evidence is held by the court, obtain a receipt and notify the Property Clerk's Office.
5. If the evidence is not held, return all evidence to the Property Clerk's Office.

62. Police Officer Johnson of the 105th Precinct was notified to appear in Queens Supreme Court to testify in a case involving an arrest he made the previous month. Officer Johnson needed the evidence, which consisted of two 9mm pistols and one hunting knife, before he could testify. Officer Johnson went to the 112th Precinct, where the Property Clerk's Office is located, gave the invoice number for the evidence and presented his shield and I.D. card. Officer Johnson obtained the evidence and proceeded to the court house. After four hours of testimony by various witnesses, the trial was adjourned for the day and the weapons were taken into custody by the court officer. After obtaining a receipt, Officer Johnson returned to the 105th where he completed his tour. In this situation the actions taken by Officer Johnson were

(A) proper, primarily because he obtained a receipt for the evidence before going to court
(B) improper, primarily because he did not notify the Property Clerk's Office
(C) proper, primarily because he presented his shield and I.D. card to obtain the evidence from the court officer
(D) improper, primarily because he did not return the evidence before ending his tour.

63. Captain Rutherford assigns Police Officer Haskel to a post in the Washington Avenue subway station. Officer Haskel is informed that there has been an increase in chain snatchings at the location, and he is instructed to observe anyone who looks suspicious. Which one of the following situations should Officer Haskel monitor more closely?

(A) A teenage boy who is standing on the platform and constantly checking the time on his watch.
(B) A man wearing a white robe selling incense and jewelry on the platform.
(C) A woman who has been standing against a post for the past hour watching passengers as they exit trains.
(D) Two teenagers walking down the stairs and onto an awaiting train.

64. Police Officer Mercardo has been assigned to inspect patrol car #785 for its equipment and general condition. The following information has been obtained by the Officer:

1. Total mileage of car: 76,561
2. Exterior of car: poor
   a. Broken right headlight
   b. Dents on right fender and right door
   c. Front tires flat
3. Interior of car: poor
   a. Seats ripped
   b. Dashboard lights broken
   c. Glove compartment door missing

Officer Mercardo is completing a report on his inspection of the car. Which one of the following expresses the above information *most clearly* and *accurately*?

(A) Patrol car #785 has a total mileage of 76,561 miles and is in poor condition in that the exterior of the car has a broken right headlight. It also has flats on both front tires and dents are on right fender and door. The interior of the car shows ripped seats and no glove compartment door with the dashboard lights broken.

(B) Patrol car #785, which is in poor condition, has a total mileage of 76,561 miles. The exterior of the car has a broken right headlight and dents on the right fender and right door. Both front tires are flat. The interior of the car reveals that the seats are ripped, the dashboard lights don't work, and the door to the glove compartment is missing.

(C) Patrol car #785 has on the exterior a broken right headlight, dents to the fender and door which can be found on the right side, and two flat tires in the front. For the interior, the seats are ripped, the dashboard lights are broken, and the glove compartment needs to be fixed. The general condition of the car is poor, which has a total mileage of 76,561.

(D) Patrol car #785 has in the interior ripped seats and a missing glove compartment door. Also the dashboard lights don't come on. The condition of the car is poor, it has a total mileage of 76,561 miles on it. The exterior of the car has two front tires that are flat, a broken right headlight and dents to the right fender. The door is also dented.

Answer question 65 solely on the basis of the following information.

Police Officers may become involved in cases regarding children who are lost. When a lost child is brought to a Police Officer, the Officer should do the following in the order given:

1. Notify Desk Officer and radio dispatcher.
2. Conduct a brief investigation in vicinity of place where child was found.
3. Bring child to the Precinct station house if parents or relatives are not found.
4. Prepare an Aided Report.
5. Telephone Missing Persons Squad and give a description.
6. Complete captions on Aided Report and process in normal manner.

65. Police Officer Davis, while assigned to patrol on White Street, was approached by Mr. Franklin, the custodian at 274 Lafayette Street, and a small child. Mr. Franklin explained that he found the child walking alone on the fifth floor of his building. Officer Davis radioed the dispatcher, telephoned his Desk Officer, and then escorted the child to the station house. When Officer Davis arrived at the precinct, the Desk Officer reminded him that, prior to bringing the child in, Officer Davis should have

(A) prepared an Aided Report
(B) called the radio dispatcher
(C) notified the Missing Persons Squad
(D) made inquiries in the building about the child.

66. Police Officer Cohen is on patrol and receives a call to respond to a disturbance at a local grocery store. The following information is given to the Officer at the scene:

Place of Occurrence:	Joe's Mini-Mart
Complainant:	Tom Callas
Crime:	Loitering and using abusive language
Suspect:	Male, Hispanic
Action Taken:	The suspect was removed from premises

Officer Cohen is completing a report on the incident. Which one of the following expresses the above information *most clearly* and *accurately*?

(A) Tom Callas called the Police because a male Hispanic was loitering and using abusive language in Joe's Mini-Mart. The male Hispanic was removed from the premises by Police.
(B) A male Hispanic was removed from Joe's mini-Mart. Tom Callas called the Police. He was loitering and using abusive language when he was removed from the premises.
(C) At Joe's Mini-Mart, a male Hispanic was loitering and using abusive language. Tom Callas called the Police. They removed him from the premises.
(D) The Police removed a male Hispanic from Joe's Mini-Mart. Tom Callas called them because he was loitering and using abusive language.

Answer questions 67 and 68 solely on the basis of the following information.

Upon notification or observation of a vehicle accident, a Police Officer should do the following in the order given:

1. Park radio motor patrol car behind vehicles involved so that traffic will not be blocked.
2. Determine if there are any injuries and request an ambulance if needed.
3. Divert traffic if necessary.
4. Obtain the drivers license, vehicle registration, and insurance identification card of driver(s) so that required information can be recorded.
5. Determine the cause of the accident by inquiry and observation.
6. Prepare one copy of Police Accident Report.

67. While on Highway Patrol, Police Officer Quinn witnesses a serious three vehicle accident and immediately stops to assist. While exiting his patrol car, he notices that one of the drivers involved in the accident is bleeding heavily from the mouth and that a serious traffic condition is developing on both sides of the intersection. The next step Officer Quinn should take is to

(A) reduce congestion by diverting the traffic
(B) request drivers licenses, vehicle registrations, and insurance cards from the drivers
(C) obtain medical assistance for the injured
(D) radio for a tow truck to remove accident vehicles.

68. Police Officers Velazquez and Degas are on vehicle patrol and passing through an intersection when a pedestrian flags them down to report a traffic accident. Officer Velazquez stops behind the vehicles involved in the accident, gets out of the car, and asks the two drivers if anyone is injured. They both say that they are all right. Officer Velazquez then asks them for their licenses, registrations, and insurance cards. Officer Degas notices that traffic is beginning to back up at the intersection, so she starts to direct traffic around the accident. The next step that Officers Velazquez and Degas should take is to

(A) request that an ambulance respond to the scene
(B) divert traffic if necessary
(C) prepare one copy of a Police Accident Report
(D) determine the cause of the accident.

69. During his last tour of duty, Police Officer Meehan observed a robbery in progress and arrested the suspect. The following details are related to the robbery:

Place of Occurrence:	Corner of Ludlow and Rivington Streets
Date of Occurrence:	June 10
Weapon:	.357 Magnum
Crime:	Robbery

Officer Meehan is completing a request for departmental recognition for this arrest. Which one of the following expresses the above information *most clearly* and *accurately*?

(A) On June 10th, I apprehended a perpetrator without assistance on the corner of Ludlow and Rivington Streets. I observed a robbery in progress and recovered a .357 Magnum.
(B) On June 10th, I observed a robbery in progress on the corner of Ludlow and Rivington Streets. I apprehended the perpetrator without assistance and recovered a .357 Magnum.
(C) I observed a robbery in progress and without assistance I apprehended the perpetrator with a .357 Magnum. This took place on the corner of Ludlow and Rivington Streets. The incident occurred on June 10.
(D) On June 10th, I recovered a .357 Magnum when I observed a robbery in progress. I apprehended the perpetrator on Ludlow and Rivington Streets without assistance.

Answer question 70 solely on the basis of the following information.

After a suspicious person has been stopped, questioned, and frisked, the Police Officer should do the following in the order given:

1. Request the person's name and address.
2. Prepare a Stop and Frisk report.
3. Enter the details in the Activity Log.
4. Inform the supervisor of the facts.
5. Submit a Stop and Frisk report to the Desk Officer.
6. Get the Precinct Log number.

70. Police Officer O'Boyle is dispatched to investigate a suspicious male with a knife in Van Cortland Park. When the Officer arrives on the scene, he notices a male fitting the description he has been given. Officer O'Boyle stops, questions, and frisks the male but finds nothing on him. What should the Officer do next?

(A) Inform his supervisor of the facts.
(B) Prepare a Stop and Frisk report.
(C) Request the person's name and address.
(D) Enter the details in the Activity Log.

Answer question 71 solely on the basis of the following information.

During the winter, when the temperature drops below 32° and the Department of Health declares a Cold Weather Emergency, Police Officers are required to:

1. Require all homeless people to go to a shelter.
2. Give transportation to homeless people looking for shelter.
3. If a homeless person refuses to go to a shelter and has no home, use force if necessary to get the person to a hospital for psychiatric evaluation.

71. It is 3:00 A.M. on a Tuesday and the temperature has dropped from 34° to 28°. A Cold Weather Emergency has just been declared. During his patrol, Police Officer Georgia notices a middle-aged woman lying near a metal grate on the sidewalk near the corner of Main Street and Craig Avenue. The woman is surrounded by shopping bags and appears to be disoriented. The Officer asks her where she lives and she says "many places." He asks if she has any friends or relatives and she says that she does not know anyone. The Officer asks her if she would like to go to a shelter and she refuses. When asked for identification, she hands the Officer a wallet containing a few meaningless scraps of paper. The Officer then calls for a supervisor and an ambulance to transport her to a hospital for psychiatric evaluation. In this situation, the actions taken by Officer Georgia were

    (A) improper, primarily because the woman had not committed a crime or bothered anyone
    (B) proper, primarily because she was obviously in need of psychiatric evaluation
    (C) improper, primarily because the woman was more in need of shelter than of a psychiatric evaluation
    (D) proper, primarily because the woman had refused shelter despite the Cold Weather Emergency.

Answer question 72 solely on the basis of the following information.

Criminal Sale of a Controlled Substance 5th Degree—occurs when a person knowingly and unlawfully sells a controlled substance, such as cocaine, marihuana, heroin.

Sell means to sell, give or dispose of to another, or to offer or agree to do the same.

72. Which one of the following situations is the best example of Criminal Sale of a Controlled Substance in the Fifth Degree?

    (A) James and Cathy dispose of six vials of cocaine by burying them in their back yard.
    (B) Harry and Jack sit in a stairwell and pass a lit pipe filled with marihuana between them.
    (C) Thomas opens his dresser drawer and exchanges a bag full of cocaine for a bag of marihuana.
    (D) John laces his neighbor's dog food with heroin.

Answer question 73 solely on the basis of the following information.

After arresting a suspect, Police Officers are required to take fingerprints in order to establish positive identification. When taking fingerprints, Police Officers must do the following in the order given:

1. Police Officers should be extremely careful when fingerprinting to have no weapons on their person.
2. Inform person to relax hands and fingers and let the Officer do the rolling.
3. Prepare fingerprint charts as follows:
   a. Two copies of Criminal Fingerprint Record
   b. One copy of FBI Fingerprint Chart
   c. One copy of N.Y. State Fingerprint Chart
4. In the case of a juvenile, prepare one copy of N.Y. State Juvenile Fingerprint Chart.
5. Whenever arrested persons are fingerprinted, palm prints and photographs may also be taken.

73. Police Officer Lane has arrested a juvenile and is about to process his arrest. Before taking the fingerprints, Officer Lane hands his revolver to Lt. Cronin, who secures it in the weapons locker. The youth is told to relax his hands and fingers and to let Officer Lane do the rolling. The Officer begins to prepare two Criminal Fingerprint Records, and FBI Fingerprint Chart and a N.Y. State Fingerprint Chart. After completing this, the next step Officer Lane should take is to

   (A) take palm prints and photographs of the juvenile
   (B) prepare an additional Criminal Fingerprint Record
   (C) deliver the fingerprint reports to the appropriate agency
   (D) prepare a N.Y. State Juvenile Fingerprint Chart.

74. Police Officer Roach responded to the home of Audrey Seager regarding a past burglary. Ms. Seager reported that, while she was at work, someone broke into her home and stole the property listed below. She further stated that a piece of her luggage worth approximately $150.00 was also taken and was probably used by the robber to carry the following property out of her apartment:

• 2 35mm Cameras, each valued at	$289.00
• 2 Video Cassette Recorders, each valued at	$329.00
• Miscellaneous jewelry valued at	$455.00
• Cash	$350.00
• Stock certificates valued at	$1,500.00

Officer Roach is completing a Complaint Report. Which one of the following is the total value of the property and cash stolen from Ms. Seager?

   (A) $2,923.00
   (B) $3,073.00
   (C) $3,691.00
   (D) $3,991.00.

Answer question 75 solely on the basis of the following information.

Serious Physical Injury—injury that creates a substantial risk of death, or serious and prolonged disfigurement, prolonged impairment of health, or loss or impairment of function of any bodily organ.

Assault 2nd Degree—occurs when, with intent to cause physical injury to another, a person causes such injury to such person or to a third person by means of a deadly weapon or dangerous instrument.

Manslaughter 1st Degree—occurs when, with intent to cause serious physical injury to another, a person causes death to that person or to a third person.

Murder 2nd Degree—occurs when, with intent to cause the death of another, a person causes the death of such person or a third person.

75. Police Officers Harris and Linden were dispatched to Clare's Bar. Upon their arrival they observed two dead bodies lying on the floor. After interviewing witnesses at the bar, they learned that an elderly man known as "Whiskey Bill" had given the victims home-made liquor. Whiskey Bill was placed under arrest. During the interrogation, Bill admitted that he knew that the liquor would be fatal if someone drank it, but he wanted to get even with Joe, who was one of the victims. It would be most appropriate for the Officers to charge Bill with

(A) Murder 2nd Degree
(B) Serious Physical Injury
(C) Assault 2nd Degree
(D) Manslaughter 1st Degree.

Answer question 76 solely on the basis of the following information.

Police Officer Miller is assigned to the 72nd Precinct and observes that most of the rapes in his sector are committed on Bay Street between President Street and Alabama Street. All the assaults are committed on Nelson Street between Carroll Street and Lewis Street, and all the homicides are committed on Third Avenue between Tinton Street and Union Street. Most of the rapes happen on Thursdays and Fridays between 10:00 P.M. and 2:00 A.M.; the assaults on Saturdays between 10:00 A.M. and 1:00 P.M.; and most of the homicides on Saturdays and Sundays between 1:00 A.M. and 4:00 A.M.

76. Officer Miller would most likely be able to reduce the number of homicides by patrolling

(A) Bay Street on Thursdays and Fridays between 10:00 P.M. and 2:00 A.M.
(B) Alabama Street on Saturdays between 10:00 A.M. and 1:00 P.M.
(C) Carroll Street on Wednesdays between 11:00 A.M. and 3:00 P.M.
(D) Third Avenue on Saturdays and Sundays between 1:00 A.M. and 4:00 A.M.

Answer questions 77 through 79 solely on the basis of the following map. The flow of traffic is indicated by the arrows. If there is only one arrow shown, then traffic flows only in the direction indicated by the arrow. If there are two arrows shown, then traffic flows in both directions. You must follow the flow of traffic.

77. Police Officers Simms and O'Brien are located at Roundsman Avenue and Washington Street. The radio dispatcher has assigned them to investigate a motor vehicle accident at the corner of Pierson Street and Rose Place. Which one of the following is the shortest route for them to take in their patrol car, making sure to obey all traffic regulations?

    (A) Travel west on Roundsman Avenue, then north on Temple Street, then east on Thames Street, then north on Pierson Street to Rose Place.
    (B) Travel east on Roundsman Avenue, then north on Oak Avenue, then west on Rose Place to Pierson Street.
    (C) Travel west on Roundsman Avenue, then north on Temple Street, then east on Rose Place to Pierson Street.
    (D) Travel east on Roundsman Avenue, then north on Oak Avenue, then west on Thames Street, then north on Temple Street, then east on Rose place to Pierson Street.

78. Police Officers Sears and Castro are located at Cedar Street and Roundsman Avenue. They are called to respond to the scene of a burglary at Rose Place and Charles Street. Which one of the following is the shortest route for them to take in their patrol car, making sure to obey all traffic regulations?

    (A) Travel east on Roundsman Avenue, then north on Oak Avenue, then west on Rose Place to Charles Street.
    (B) Travel east on Roundsman Avenue, then north on Washington Street, then east on Rose Place to Charles Street.
    (C) Travel west on Roundsman Avenue, then north on Wolowski Street, then east on Trinity Place, then south on Charles Street to Rose Place.
    (D) Travel east on Roundsman Avenue, then north on Charles Street to Rose Place.

79. Police Officer Glasser is in an unmarked car at the intersection of Rose Place and Temple Street when he begins to follow two robbery suspects. The suspects go south for two blocks, then turn left for two blocks, then make another left turn for one more block. The suspects realize they are being followed and make a left turn and travel two more blocks and then make a right turn. In what direction are the suspects now headed?

    (A) North   (C) East
    (B) South   (D) West

80. Police Officer Ross has been assigned to investigate a recent increase in the number of token booth hold-ups committed by pairs of youths in the Chambers Street Station. He has been instructed to pay special attention to any activity that appears to be suspicious. Which one of following situations should Officer Ross monitor more closely?

(A) A male youth talking to the token clerk while the clerk is counting money.
(B) A youth looking at a subway map near the booth while holding a black canvas bag.
(C) One youth standing by the token booth while his friend waits on the stairs.
(D) Two female youths engaged in fistfight near the turnstile.

Answer question 81 solely on the basis of the following information.

When a prisoner in custody is admitted to a hospital, the arresting Police Officer should do the following in the order given:

1. Notify Desk Officer in the precinct of arrest.
2. Search male prisoner at hospital in presence of witnesses if prisoner was removed from scene of arrest directly to hospital.
3. Have hospital personnel search female prisoners.
4. Search prisoner's personal clothing, after removal by hospital personnel, for weapons, evidence, or contraband.
5. Give hospital authorities receipt for property received.
6. Enter in Activity Log list of property removed and any information necessary to process arrest.
7. Report to precinct of arrest to continue arrest processing when relieved by guarding Officer.

81. While Police Officer Smith was arresting Michelle Hart for the robbery of a jewelry store, Ms. Hart suffered an asthma attack and had to be hospitalized immediately. Officer Smith requested that an ambulance respond to the scene and informed Lt. Brandon, the Desk Officer in the precinct, of details regarding the arrest. He then rode to the hospital in the ambulance with his prisoner. After informing hospital personnel of the circumstances concerning the arrest, the next thing Officer Smith should do is

(A) report to the precinct of arrest and continue arrest processing
(B) search the prisoner in presence of hospital personnel
(C) enter in his Activity Log the time of arrest and identity of prisoner
(D) direct hospital personnel to search the prisoner.

Answer question 82 solely on the basis of the following information.

When a person is arrested for possession of a firearm, the arresting Officer should:

1. Seize the weapon.
2. Base the charge on the violation of Penal Law or Administrative Code.
3. Prepare the Request for Laboratory Examination form.
4. Bring weapon and Request form to the Ballistics Unit.
5. After examination by Ballistics Unit, deliver weapon to Property Clerk with Property Clerk's Invoice.

82. Police Officer Livingston has received a call from the dispatcher regarding shots fired. Upon arriving at the scene, Officer Livingston finds a loaded 9mm automatic pistol in the possession of John Blake. Officer Livingston secures the firearm and arrests John Blake, charging him with Criminal Use of a Firearm in the 1st Degree, a violation of the Penal Law. Once at the station house, Officer Livingston is instructed to prepare a form requesting a Laboratory Examination of the firearm. After this has been completed, Officer Livingston leaves the form with his supervisor and takes the firearm to the Ballistics Unit, where it is examined. It is learned that the gun was used in a number of crimes, including the shooting of a Police Officer. Officer Livingston delivers the gun to the Property Clerk's Office with a Property Clerk's Invoice. Officer Livingston's actions were

    (A) improper, primarily because the laboratory request was not brought to the Ballistics Unit
    (B) proper, primarily because the gun was brought to the Ballistics Unit where it was learned that the gun was used in other crimes
    (C) improper, primarily because the Property Clerk's Invoice should have been given to his supervisor after it was completed
    (D) proper, primarily because Mr. Blake was charged with Criminal Use of a Firearm in the First Degree, a violation of the Penal Law.

83. Police Officers are sometimes required to request emergency transportation for seriously injured people. For which one of the following people would it be most appropriate for a Police Officer to request emergency transportation?

    (A) A pregnant woman who complains of feeling faint.
    (B) An elderly man who has been drinking complains about his vision.
    (C) A young boy who is roller-skating falls down and is knocked unconscious.
    (D) A teenage girl slips while ice-skating and limps off the ice.

Answer questions 84 through 87 solely on the basis of the following passage.

On May 10, at 5:30 P.M., Police Officers Swift and Monroe were on routine patrol when they were dispatched to 1180 Albany Avenue, Apartment 3C on an assault in progress. They arrived at the apartment at 5:40 P.M. and were met by Mr. Raymond Ambrose. Mr. Ambrose said he called the police because he heard yelling and screaming coming from Apartment 3A, but it had since stopped. Mr. Ambrose told the Officers that the tenant in 3A, Helen Gray, lived alone ever since her divorce.

Officer Monroe knocked on the door of Apartment 3A and noticed that the door was partially opened. The Officers cautiously entered the apartment, which appeared to have been ransacked. Officer Swift checked the fire escape while his partner searched the bedroom where he found Mrs. Gray, unconscious, lying on the floor and bleeding heavily from the head. A blood-covered baseball bat was found next to her. The Officer called for an ambulance to respond while Officer Swift tried to gather information from neighbors.

Mary Grable, age 68, of Apartment 3B; Ben Grim, age 16, of Apartment 1A; and Angela Arnold, age 27, of 1162 Albany Avenue were standing in the hallway. Ms. Arnold stated that she and Mrs. Gray are close friends and she became concerned when she saw Stuart Gray in the neighborhood around 5:10 P.M. Ms. Arnold told Officer Swift, "Since they've been divorced, Stuart visits Helen to get money to support a 'crack' habit, and it always leads to an argument." Grable said she had heard a commotion, but didn't know who was involved. Grim told Officer Swift that he saw Stuart Gray running from the building at about 5:35 P.M. with blood on his hands and shirt.

Paramedics arrived at 5:50 P.M. and transported Mrs. Gray to the hospital where she died at 6:30 P.M. without regaining consciousness. Stuart Gray was arrested at 7:15 the next morning at the home of his mother, Valerie Gray, and was charged with the homicide.

84. From the information given, it is most likely that the crime was committed between

(A) 5:10 A.M.–5:35 A.M.
(B) 5:10 P.M.–5:35 P.M.
(C) 5:30 P.M.–5:35 P.M.
(D) 5:30 P.M.–5:50 P.M.

85. Who was the first person to find Mrs. Gray?

(A) Officer Monroe
(B) Mr. Ambrose
(C) Officer Swift
(D) Ms. Arnold.

86. Whose information tied Stuart to the crime?

(A) Ms. Arnold and Ben Grim
(B) Mr. Ambrose and Ms. Arnold
(C) Ben Grim and Valerie Gray
(D) Ms. Arnold and Ms. Grable.

87. Stuart Gray was arrested on

(A) May 10 at 6:30 P.M.
(B) May 11 at 7:15 P.M.
(C) May 10 at 7:15 A.M.
(D) May 11 at 7:15 A.M.

88. The following details were obtained by Police Officer Dwight at the scene of a family dispute:

Place of Occurrence:	77 Baruch Drive
Victim:	Andrea Valdez, wife of Walker
Violator:	Edward Walker
Witness:	George Valdez, victim's brother
Crime:	Violation of Order of Protection
Action Taken:	Violator arrested

Police Officer Dwight is preparing a report on the incident. Which one of the following expresses the above information *most clearly* and *accurately*?

(A) George Valdez saw Edward Walker violate his sister's Order of Protection at 77 Baruch Drive. Andrea Valdez's husband was arrested for this violation.

(B) Andrea Valdez's Order of Protection was violated at 77 Baruch Drive. George Valdez saw his brother-in-law violate his sister's Order. Edward Walker was arrested.

(C) Edward Walker was arrested for violating an Order of Protection held by his wife, Andrea Valdez. Andrea's brother, George Valdez, witnessed the violation at 77 Baruch Drive.

(D) An arrest was made at 77 Baruch Drive when an Order of Protection held by Andrea Valdez was violated by her husband. George Valdez, her brother, witnessed Edward Walker.

Answer question 89 solely on the basis of the following information.

Endangering the Welfare of a Child—occurs when a person knowingly acts in a manner likely to be injurious to the physical, mental, or moral welfare of a male child less than 16 years old or a female child less than 17 years old.

89. Which one of the following situations is the best example of Endangering the Welfare of a Child?

(A) John spanks his seven-year-old son because he has been misbehaving in school.

(B) Linda slaps her sixteen-year-old brother for punishing her child.

(C) Beverly leaves her four-year-old son unattended to go to a party in the next building.

(D) Gary sends his twelve-year-old daughter to her room with no dinner for bringing home a bad report card.

90. Police Officer Clay responds to the scene of a found child where he obtains the following information:

Child's Name:	Craig Gildae
Age:	4 years
Location Found:	Wandering around in front of 501 E. 204th Street
Description:	Male, white, blond hair, blue eyes, wearing red overalls, white T-shirt, and blue high-top sneakers.

Officer Clay is about to transmit this information to the radio dispatcher. Which one of the following expresses the above information *most clearly* and *accurately*?

(A) In front of 501 E. 204th Street a male white, Craig Gildae, was found wandering around with blond hair, blue eyes, wearing a white T-shirt, red overalls, and blue high-top sneakers. The child is four years old.

(B) Four-year-old Craig Gildae was found wandering around in front of 501 E. 204th Street. He is a male, white, blond hair, blue eyes, wearing red overalls, a white T-shirt, and blue high-top sneakers.

(C) A blond hair, blue-eyed male was found wandering around wearing red overalls, white T-shirt, and blue high-top sneakers. Four-year-old Craig Gildae was found in front of 501 E. 204th Street.

(D) Found wandering around in front of 501 E. 204th Street male, white, with blond hair, blue eyes, wearing red overalls, white T-shirt, and blue high-top sneakers identified as four-year-old Craig Gildae.

91. The following details were obtained by Police Officer Jackson at the scene of a robbery:

Place of Occurrence:	Chambers Street, northbound A platform
Victim:	Mr. John Wells
Suspect:	Joseph Miller
Crime:	Robbery, armed with knife, wallet taken
Action Taken:	Suspect arrested

Officer Jackson is completing a report on the incident. Which one of the following expresses the above information *most clearly* and *accurately*?

(A) At Chambers Street northbound A platform Joseph Miller used a knife to remove the wallet of John Wells while waiting for the train. Police arrested him.

(B) Mr. John Wells, while waiting for the northbound A train at Chambers Street, had his wallet forcibly removed at knifepoint by Joseph Miller. Joseph Miller was later arrested.

(C) Joseph Miller was arrested for robbery. At Chambers Street John Wells stated that his wallet was taken. The incident occurred at knifepoint while waiting on northbound A platform.

(D) At the northbound Chambers Street platform, John Wells was waiting for the A train. Joseph Miller produced a knife and removed his wallet. He was arrested.

Answer question 92 solely on the basis of the following information.

When a Police Officer stops a vehicle and discovers that the operator is driving with a suspended or revoked drivers license, the Officer should do the following in the order given:

1. Confiscate the driver's license.
2. Prepare a Seized Drivers License Report.
3. Give operator of vehicle a receipt for license.
   a. If operator has two or more unrelated suspensions, or his license has been revoked for any reason, remove the motorist to the precinct of arrest and process a Desk Appearance Ticket.
   b. If operator has one or more suspensions regarding the same violation, a Universal Summons should be issued.
4. Do not mark or mutilate license in any manner.
5. Have the violator's vehicle parked in a legal parking area until the registered owner can arrange to have the vehicle removed from the scene by a licensed operator.

92. Police Officers Harris and Lowe are on patrol in their radio car when they stop a vehicle driven by Dennis Clarke. Clarke, whose license had been suspended once before for speeding, was driving over the speed limit. Officer Harris confiscates Clarke's license, prepares the required report, and issues him a receipt for his license. The next thing Officer Harris should do is

(A) have Clarke park his vehicle in a legal parking area until he can arrange to have a licensed operator remove it
(B) issue Clarke a Universal Summons and have him drive his vehicle to his home
(C) remove Clarke to the precinct and process him for a Desk Appearance Ticket
(D) issue Clarke a Universal Summons and have his car parked in a legal parking area.

93. Police Officer Hayes is informed by Sergeant Holt that drugs are being sold from autos on Officer Hayes' post. He is directed to observe stopped vehicles if he believes the occupants' actions are suspicious. Which one of the following should Officer Hayes consider most suspicious?

(A) Two men sit in a parked auto in front of a school yard during recess and after school.
(B) An auto drops off a man and then quickly speeds away.
(C) A car service driver reads a newspaper and is parked in the same spot for 45 minutes.
(D) Four teenagers sit in a parked convertible by a busy recreation area while listening to a radio.

Answer question 94 solely on the basis of the following information.

Upon uncovering illegal drugs during an investigation, Police Officers should do the following in the order given:

1. Bring the drugs to the station house of the precinct where the discovery was made.
2. Notify the Station House Officer.
3. Prepare a Property Clerk's Invoice.
4. Request a laboratory analysis of the drugs.
5. Mark the drugs for future identification.
6. Request specially secured envelopes from the Station House Officer.
7. Deliver the drugs to the laboratory.

94. In the course of a drug investigation in the 2nd Precinct, Police Officer Wells has come into possession of 100 vials of refined cocaine. He brought his find to the Station House Officer in the 2nd Precinct, filled out a Property Clerk's Invoice, and called for a laboratory analysis of the narcotics, He then labelled each individual vial so that the vials could be identified by other Officers if necessary. The next step Officer Wells should take is to

(A) deliver the drugs to the laboratory
(B) consecutively number all the vials of cocaine with the Officer's initials
(C) ask the Station House Officer for specially secured envelopes
(D) prepare a request for a laboratory examination of the drugs.

Answer question 95 solely on the basis of the following information.

Theft of Services—occurs when a person intentionally fails to pay or avoids the payment of lawful charges for any public transportation service.

95. Which one of the following is the best example of Theft of Services?

(A) A shabbily dressed elderly man crawls under a turnstile in a subway station to retrieve a quarter he accidentally dropped. When a train pulls into the station, he retrieves the quarter and quickly gets on.
(B) In the middle of dinner at a restaurant, Tom and Janet complain about the quality of service. They refuse to pay their bill and immediately leave the restaurant and hail a taxi.
(C) Harry is driving home and pulls up to a toll booth to pay a quarter toll. Harry misses the coin box with the quarter and drives away.
(D) John hails a cab to take him to his office. When he arrives he realizes that he has no cash with him and asks the cab driver to wait while he gets some from his office safe.

96. Police Officer Bellows responds to a report of drugs being sold in the lobby of an apartment building. He obtains the following information at the scene:

Time of Occurrence:	11:30 P.M.
Place of Occurrence:	1010 Bath Avenue
Witnesses:	Mary Markham, John Silver
Suspect:	Harry Stoner
Crime:	Drug Sales
Action Taken:	Suspect was gone when Police arrived

Officer Bellows is completing a report of the incident. Which one of the following expresses the above information *most clearly* and *accurately*?

(A) Mary Markham and John Silver witnessed drugs being sold and the suspect flee at 1010 Bath Avenue. Harry Stoner was conducting his business at 11:30 P.M. before Police arrival in the lobby.

(B) In the lobby, Mary Markham reported at 11:30 P.M. she saw Harry Stoner, along with John Silver, selling drugs. He ran from the lobby at 1010 Bath Avenue before Police arrived.

(C) John Silver and Mary Markham reported that they observed Harry Stoner selling drugs in the lobby of 1010 Bath Avenue at 11:30 P.M. The witnesses stated that Stoner fled beford Police arrived.

(D) Before Police arrived, witnesses stated that Harry Stoner was selling drugs. At 1010 Bath Avenue, in the lobby, John Silver and Mary Markham said they observed his actions at 11:30 P.M.

97. While on patrol, Police Officer Fox receives a call to respond to a robbery. Upon arriving at the scene, he obtains the following information:

Time of Occurrence:	6:00 P.M.
Place of Occurrence:	Sal's Liquor Store at 30 Fordham Road
Victim:	Sal Jones
Suspect:	White male wearing a beige parka
Description of Crime:	Victim was robbed in his store at gunpoint

Officer Fox is completing a report on the incident. Which one of the following expresses the above information *most clearly* and *accurately*?

(A) I was informed at 6:00 P.M. by Sal Jones that an unidentified white male robbed him at gunpoint at 30 Fordham Road while wearing a beige parka at Sal's Liquor Store.

(B) At 6:00 P.M., Sal Jones was robbed at gunpoint in his store. An unidentified white male wearing a beige parka came into Sal's Liquor Store at 30 Fordham Road, he told me.

(C) I was informed at 6:00 P.M. while wearing a beige parka an unidentified white male robbed Sal Jones at gunpoint at Sal's Liquor Store at 30 Fordham Road.

(D) Sal Jones informed me that at 6:00 P.M. he was robbed at gunpoint in his store, Sal's Liquor Store, located at 30 Fordham Road, by an unidentified white male wearing a beige parka.

Answer question 98 solely on the basis of the following information.

Police Officer Daily has been informed by Sergeant Newman that there have been three purse snatches on his post during the past two weeks. The description of each of the suspects is as follows:

Incident No. 1—Male, black, 24 years old, 5′9″, 185 lbs., scar on left side of face, blue dungarees, white sneakers, long brown hair, earring in right ear.

Incident No. 2—Male, black, about 25 years old, 170 lbs., 5′9″, long black hair, black dungarees, white sneakers, white tank top, scar on right side of face.

Incident No. 3—Male, black, 27 to 30 years old, 5′8″, 190 lbs., long curly hair, blue T-shirt, earring in left ear, black sneakers, black dungarees, tattoo on right arm.

On April 20, Police Officer Daily arrested a suspect during an attempted purse snatch. The description of the suspect is as follows:

Incident No. 4—Male, black, 5′9″, 180 lbs., 23 years old, white tank top, white sneakers, long, straight brown hair, black dungarees, gold earring in right ear, scar on left side of face.

98. Based on the above descriptions of the suspects in the first three incidents, Officer Daily should consider the suspect in the fourth purse snatching as a suspect in

   (A) Incident No. 1, but not Incident No. 2 or Incident No. 3
   (B) Incident No. 3, but not Incident No. 1 or Incident No. 2
   (C) Incident No. 1 and Incident No. 2, but not Incident No. 3
   (D) Incident No. 2 and Incident No. 3, but not Incident No. 1.

Answer question 99 solely on the basis of the following information.

Robbery—occurs when a person steals property by using or threatening the immediate use of physical force upon another person.

99. Which one of the following is the best example of Robbery?

   (A) Bill casually bumps into Raymond, removes Raymond's wallet from his back pocket, and runs away.
   (B) Carol and John are approached by Marty, who takes their money after saying he would slash Carol's face with a knife.
   (C) Karen approaches Grace, who is sleeping on the train, slices her purse strap with a razor, grabs the purse and walks away.
   (D) Fred threatens to find Peter's daughter and hurt her if Peter does not hand over his gold watch.

100. The following details were obtained by Police Officer Connors at the scene of a bank robbery:

Time of Occurrence:	10:21 A.M.
Place of Occurrence:	Westbury Savings and Loan
Crime:	Bank Robbery
Suspect:	Male, dressed in black, wearing a black woolen face mask
Witness:	Mary Henderson of 217 Westbury Avenue
Amount Stolen:	$6141 U.S. currency

Officer Connors is completing a report on the incident. Which one of the following expresses the above information *most clearly* and *accurately*?

(A) At 10:21 A.M. the Westbury Savings and Loan was witnessed being robbed by Mary Henderson of 217 Westbury Avenue. The suspect fled dressed in black with a black woolen face mask. He left the bank with $6141 in U.S. currency.

(B) Dressed in black wearing a black woolen face mask, Mary Henderson of 217 Westbury Avenue saw a suspect flee with $6141 in U.S. currency after robbing the Westbury Savings and Loan. The robber was seen at 10:21 A.M.

(C) At 10:21 A.M., Mary Henderson, of 217 Westbury Avenue, witness to the robbery of the Westbury Savings and Loan, reports that a male, dressed in black, wearing a black face mask, did rob said bank and fled with $6141 in U.S. currency.

(D) Mary Henderson, of 217 Westbury Avenue, witnessed the robbery of the Westbury Savings and Loan at 10:21 A.M. The suspect, a male, was dressed in black and was wearing a black woolen face mask. He fled with $6141 in U.S. currency.

Answer question 101 solely on the basis of the following information.

Police Officers sometimes have to make notifications to the Bureau of Child Welfare when they determine that a child may have been abused, maltreated, or neglected.

101. In which one of the following cases would it be most appropriate for a Police Officer to notify the Bureau of Child Welfare?

(A) A woman is pulling a screaming child across the street while the traffic light is about to turn red against them.

(B) A man is spanking his son with his bare hand because his son refused to get out of the swimming pool when he was told to.

(C) A mother is cooking with hot oil while her children are running around in the kitchen. One bangs into the stove and burns his hand slightly.

(D) A father is playing softball in the park while his infant takes a nap alone in their apartment.

102. At the scene of a dispute, Police Officer Johnson made an arrest after obtaining the following information:

Place of Occurrence:	940 Baxter Avenue
Time of Occurrence:	3:40 P.M.
Victim:	John Mitchell
Suspect:	Robert Holden, arrested at scene
Crime:	Menacing
Weapon:	Knife
Time of arrest:	4:00 P.M.

Officer Johnson is completing a report of the incident. Which one of the following expresses the above information *most clearly* and *accurately*?

(A) John Mitchell was menaced by a knife at 940 Baxter Avenue. Robert Holden, owner of the weapon, was arrested at 4:00 P.M., twenty minutes later, at the scene.

(B) John Mitchell reports at 3:40 P.M. he was menaced at 940 Baxter Avenue by Robert Holden. He threatened him with his knife and was arrested at 4:00 P.M. at the scene.

(C) John Mitchell stated that at 3:40 P.M. at 940 Baxter Avenue he was menaced by Robert Holden, who was carrying a knife. Mr. Holden was arrested at the scene at 4:00 P.M. .

(D) With a knife Robert Holden menaced John Mitchell at 3:40 P.M. The knife belonged to him and he was arrested at the scene of 940 Baxter Avenue at 4:00 P.M.

103. Officer Nieves obtained the following information after he was called to the scene of a large gathering:

Time of Occurrence:	2:45 A.M.
Place of Occurrence:	Mulberry Park
Complaint:	Loud music
Complainant:	Mrs. Simpkins, 42 Mulberry Street, Apartment 25
Action Taken:	Police Officer dispersed the crowd

Officer Nieves is completing a report on the incident. Which one of the following expresses the above information *most clearly* and *accurately*?

(A) Mrs. Simpkins, who lives at 42 Mulberry Street, Apartment 25, called the Police to make a complaint. A large crowd of people were playing loud music in Mulberry Park at 2:45 A.M. Officer Nieves responded and dispersed the crowd.

(B) Officer Nieves responded to Mulberry Park because Mrs. Simpkins, the complainant, lives at 42 Mulberry Street, Apartment 25. Due to a large crowd of people who were playing loud music at 2:45 A.M., he immediately dispersed the crowd.

(C) Due to a large crowd of people who were playing loud music in Mulberry Park at 2:45 A.M., Officer Nieves responded and dispersed the crowd. Mrs. Simpkins called the Police and complained. She lives at 42 Mulberry Street, Apartment 25.

(D) Responding to a complaint by Mrs. Simpkins, who resides at 42 Mulberry Street, Apartment 25, Officer Nieves dispersed a large crowd in Mulberry Park. They were playing loud music. It was 2:45 A.M.

104. While patrolling the subway, Police Officer Clark responds to the scene of a past robbery where he obtains the following information:

Place of Occurrence:	Northbound E train
Time of Occurrence:	6:30 P.M.
Victim:	Robert Brey
Crime:	Wallet and jewelry taken
Suspects:	2 male whites armed with knives

Officer Clark is completing a report on the incident. Which one of the following expresses the above information *most clearly* and *accurately*?

(A) At 6:30 P.M., Robert Brey reported he was robbed of his wallet and jewelry. On the northbound E train, two white males approached Mr. Brey. They threatened him before taking his property with knives.

(B) While riding the E train northbound, two white men approached Robert Brey at 6:30 P.M. They threatened him with knives and took his wallet and jewelry.

(C) Robert Brey was riding the E train at 6:30 P.M. when he was threatened by knives by two whites. The men took his wallet and jewelry as he was traveling northbound.

(D) Robert Brey reports at 6:30 P.M. he lost his wallet to two white men as well as his jewelry. They were carrying knives and threatened him aboard the northbound E train.

Answer question 105 solely on the basis of the following information.

Whenever a Police Officer responds to the scene of a family offense, the Officer should do the following in the order given:

1. Determine all the facts.
2. Obtain medical assistance if requested or need is apparent.
3. Determine if:
   a. a crime has been committed; or
   b. an Order of Protection has been obtained by complainant.
4. Arrest offender if a crime has been committed.

105. Police Officers Harley and Morris are dispatched to the scene of a family dispute at 734 E. 108th Street, Apartment 2E. As the Officers enter the apartment, they see a man and a woman struggling on the floor while cursing at each other. The Officers immediately separate the two, who are identified as Herbert and Mary Jones. Officer Harley attempts to question the two individuals to determine what happened, while Officer Morris keeps them separated. Both parties blame each other for starting the fight. Although neither spouse seems to be physically hurt, Mrs. Jones insists she be examined by a doctor. What should the Officers do next?

(A) Call for medical assistance.
(B) Arrest Mr. Jones for committing the offense.
(C) Find out if Mrs. Jones has obtained an Order of Protection.
(D) Determine whether a family offense has been committed by either spouse.

Answer questions 106 through 109 solely on the basis of the following passage.

While returning to the 15th Precinct from court, Police Officer Moody encountered an armed robbery in progress outside of 238 Madison Street. When the perpetrator saw the Officer, he fled into the building and attempted to enter the second floor apartment of Maria Vasquez. Ms. Vasquez had previously opened the door when she heard the noise downstairs. When Ms. Vasquez saw the perpetrator approaching her with a gun in his hand, she immediately closed and locked the door. Since the perpetrator was not able to gain entrance to the apartment, he jumped out of the hallway window and hid in the courtyard. When Officer Moody arrived at the bottom of the second floor stairway he heard Ms. Vasquez crying hysterically from inside the apartment. He banged on the door and called to her to see if she was all right. Ms. Vasquez did not speak English and, thinking it was the perpetrator, she refused to open the door. As a result, Officer Moody assumed that the woman was being held hostage by the perpetrator. Officer Moody immediately stepped away from the door, advised the radio dispatcher of the circumstances, and requested back-up assistance.

Every sector car in the precinct responded to assist Officer Moody and each, with the exception of sectors Adam and Charlie, took up a strategic location outside of the building. Officers O'Connor and Torres, of sector Adam, went up to the second floor to guard the apartment door with Officer Moody. Officer Perez, of sector Charlie, went up to the roof. Officer Donadio, also of sector Charlie, started to enter the courtyard when he observed the perpetrator hiding in the bushes. Officer Donadio quickly took cover behind the cement wall entrance of the courtyard and ordered the perpetrator at gun point to surrender. The perpetrator surrendered his weapon and allowed himself to be easily apprehended. Officer Donadio then advised the other Officers by radio that the perpetrator was in custody and that Ms. Vasquez was not being held hostage.

106. Which Officer went up to the roof?

(A) Officer O'Connor
(B) Officer Perez
(C) Officer Donadio
(D) Officer Moody.

107. Officer Moody chased the perpetrator because

(A) he was trying to get into the apartment of Maria Vasquez
(B) he was holding Maria Vasquez hostage
(C) he was attempting to commit an armed robbery
(D) he jumped out the second floor hallway window.

108. Which Officer was *not* on the second floor?

(A) Officer Moody
(B) Officer Torres
(C) Officer O'Connor
(D) Officer Donadio.

109. While Officer Moody was standing at the bottom of the stairs, the suspect was

(A) in Ms. Vasquez's apartment
(B) in the courtyard
(C) on the roof
(D) on the second floor fire escape.

Answer question 110 solely on the basis of the following information.

Police Officers must sometimes rely on eyewitness accounts of incidents, even though eyewitnesses may make mistakes with regard to some details.

110. While coming from the bank, Sal Shure was mugged and killed at the corner of W. 238th Street and Oxford Avenue. Police Officer Farris responds to the scene and questions four witnesses who saw the person that killed Shure. The following are descriptions of the suspect given by the witnesses. Which one of these descriptions should Officer Farris consider most likely to be correct?

   (A) Male, white, 5'9", 185 lbs., brown hair, black eyes.
   (B) Male, Hispanic, 5'11", 175 lbs., brown hair, brown eyes.
   (C) Male, white, 5'10", 190 lbs., black hair, hazel eyes.
   (D) Male, white, 5'11", 190 lbs., brown hair, brown eyes

111. Police Officer Johnson has just finished investigating a report of a burglary and has obtained the following information:

Place of Occurrence:	Victim's residence
Time of Occurrence:	Between 8:13 P.M. and 4:15 A.M.
Victim:	Paul Mason of 1264 Twentieth Street, Apartment 3D
Crime:	Burglary
Damage:	Filed front door lock

   Officer Johnson is preparing a report of the incident. Which one of the following expresses the above information *most clearly* and *accurately*?

   (A) Paul Mason's residence was burglarized at 1264 Twentieth Street, Apartment 3D, between 8:13 P.M. and 4:15 A.M. by filing the front door lock.
   (B) Paul Mason was burglarized by filing the front door lock and he lives at 1264 Twentieth Street, Apartment 3D, between 8:13 P.M. and 4:15 A.M.
   (C) Between 8:13 P.M. and 4:15 A.M. the residence of Paul Mason, located at 1264 Twentieth Street, Apartment 3D, was burglarized after the front door lock was filed.
   (D) Between 8:13 P.M. and 4:15 A.M., at 1264 Twentieth Street, Apartment 3D, after the front door lock was filed, the residence of Paul Mason was burglarized.

Answer question 112 solely on the basis of the following information.

Grand Larceny 4th Degree—occurs when a person steals property and when:

1. The value of the property is greater than one thousand dollars; or
2. The property consists of secret scientific material; or
3. The property consists of a credit card; or
4. The property, regardless of its nature and value, is taken from the body or clothing of another person; or
5. The property, regardless of its nature and value, is obtained through fear.

112. Which one of the following is the best example of Grand Larceny in the Fourth Degree?

 (A) Jim finds a briefcase on the downtown 'E' train. Inside the briefcase he notices an envelope which contains $900.00. He removes the money from the envelope and exits the train, leaving the briefcase behind.
 (B) Jane finds on the street a wallet, which contains several papers and an American Express card, which she sends back to the company.
 (C) Bruce, a gang member, goes into an all-night produce market and orders the owner, Mr. Wong, to pay him $50.00 for protection or his store will be destroyed. Mr. Wong refuses and dials 911 as Bruce flees from the store.
 (D) Without Elaine's knowledge, Grace removes a costume jewelry bracelet valued at about $15.00 from Elaine's wrist.

113. Police Officer Lowell has just finished investigating a burglary and has received the following information:

Place of Occurrence:	117-12 Sutphin Boulevard
Time of Occurrence:	Between 9:00 A.M. and 5:00 P.M.
Victim:	Mandee Cotton
Suspects:	Unknown

Officer Lowell is completing a report on this incident. Which one of the following expresses the above information *most clearly* and *accurately*?

 (A) Mandee Cotton reported that her home was burglarized between 9:00 A.M. and 5:00 P.M. Ms. Cotton resides at 117-12 Sutphin Boulevard. Suspects are unknown.
 (B) A burglary was committed at 117-12 Sutphin Boulevard reported Mandee Cotton between 9:00 A.M. and 5:00 P.M. Ms. Cotton said unknown suspects burglarized her home.
 (C) Unknown suspects burglarized a home at 117-12 Sutphin Boulevard between 9:00 A.M. and 5:00 P.M. Mandee Cotton, homeowner, reported.
 (D) Between the hours of 9:00 A.M. and 5:00 P.M. it was reported that 117-12 Sutphin Boulevard was burglarized. Mandee Cotton reported that unknown suspects are responsible.

Answer question 114 solely on the basis of the following information.

When a prisoner in custody requires medical or psychiatric treatment, a Police Officer should do the following in the order given:

1. Request an ambulance and remove prisoner to hospital directly from place of arrest, if necessary.
   a. Accompany prisoner to hospital.
   b. Notify Desk Officer.
2. Handcuff prisoner, hands in rear, before transporting.
3. Remain with prisoner at all times in hospital.
4. Request room change if security is inadequate.
5. Do not remove handcuffs, unless requested by attending physician.
6. Remain immediately outside room and attempt to maintain visual contact, even if requested to leave examination room after informing physician of circumstances of arrest.

114. Police Officer Schultz calls for an ambulance to remove a prisoner from the precinct to Grant Hospital's Emergency Room due to chest pains which the prisoner is experiencing. The Desk Officer, Lt. Collins, orders Officer Schultz to ride in the ambulance with the prisoner and reminds him to rearcuff the prisoner before removing him from the holding cell. Officer Schultz does so and escorts the prisoner into the ambulance. When they arrive at the hospital, Officer Schultz questions Dr. Carson about the security status of the Emergency Room. Dr. Carson informs Officer Schultz that they haven't had any problems since the hospital opened ten years ago. Officer Schultz's next step should be to

(A) remove the prisoner's handcuffs to allow Dr. Carson to examine him
(B) describe the details of the prisoner's arrest to Dr. Carson
(C) keep an eye on the prisoner if requested to leave the examining room by Dr. Carson
(D) ask Dr. Carson to examine the prisoner in a more secure location in the hospital.

Answer question 115 solely on the basis of the following information.

Under certain circumstances, Police Officers are authorized to search a person suspected of having committed a crime.

115. Which of the following people would a Police Officer most likely search?

(A) A person who is suspected by a store owner of selling watches on the street without a license.
(B) A motorist who is stopped by a Traffic Enforcement Agent for going through a red light.
(C) A poorly dressed man who is obviously intoxicated staggering down the street.
(D) A man who is recognized by a woman as being recently involved in an armed robbery.

Answer question 116 solely on the basis of the following information.

Larceny—occurs when a person, without the use of threat of force, wrongfully takes, obtains, or withholds property from the owner.

Robbery—occurs when a person uses, or threatens the immediate use of, force on the victim or an another person in the course of stealing property.

Burglary—occurs when a person knowingly and unlawfully enters or remains in a building with intent to commit a crime therein.

116. Kevin Watts follows Jane Robinson, his ex-girlfriend, to her home one night after work and decides that he wants to make her pay for breaking off their engagement. While Jane is in the kitchen preparing her dinner, Kevin climbs up the fire escape and enters her bedroom through the window. He then threatens to beat Jane "to a pulp" if she tries to stop him from taking her cash, jewelry, and television set. Kevin takes her property and leaves. In this situation, Watts should be charged with

(A) Burglary and Larceny
(B) Burglary and Robbery
(C) Robbery and Larceny
(D) Robbery, Burglary, and Larceny.

117. Police Officer Dale has just finished investigating a report of attempted theft and has obtained the following information:

Place of Occurrence:	In front of 103 W. 105th Street
Time of Occurrence:	11:30 A.M.
Victim:	Mary Davis
Crime:	Attempted theft
Suspect:	Male, black, scar on right side of face
Action Taken:	Drove victim around area to locate suspect

Officer Dale is preparing a report on the incident. Which one of the following expresses the above information *most clearly* and *accurately*?

(A) Mary Davis was standing in front of 103 W. 105th Street when Officer Dale arrived after an attempt to steal her pocketbook failed at 11:30 A.M. Officer Dale canvassed the area looking for a black male with a scar on the right side of his face with Ms. Davis in the patrol car.
(B) Mary Davis stated that, at 11:30 A.M., she was standing in front of 103 W. 105th Street when a black male with a scar on the right side of his face attempted to steal her pocketbook. Officer Dale canvassed the area with Ms. Davis in the patrol car.
(C) Officer Dale canvassed the area by putting Mary Davis in a patrol car looking for a black male with a scar on the right side of his face. At 11:30 A.M. in front of 103 W. 105th Street she said he attempted to steal her pocketbook.
(D) At 11:30 A.M., in front of 103 W. 105th Street, Officer Dale canvassed the area with Mary Davis in a patrol car who said that a black male with a scar on the right side of his face attempted to steal her pocketbook.

118. While on patrol, Police Officer Santoro received a call to respond to the scene of a shooting. The following details were obtained at the scene:

Time of Occurrence:	4:00 A.M.
Place of Occurrence:	232 Senator Street
Victim:	Mike Nisman
Suspect:	Howard Conran
Crime:	Shooting
Witness:	Sheila Norris

Officer Santoro is completing a report on the incident. Which one of the following expresses the above information *most clearly* and *accurately*?

(A) Sheila Norris stated at 4:00 A.M. she witnessed a shooting of her neighbor in front of her building. Howard Conran shot Mike Nisman and ran from 232 Senator Street.

(B) Mike Nisman was the victim of a shooting incident seen by his neighbor. At 4:00 A.M. Sheila Norris saw Howard Conran shoot him and run in front of their building. Norris and Nisman reside at 232 Senator Street.

(C) Sheila Norris states that at 4:00 A.M. she witnessed Howard Conran shoot Mike Nisman, her neighbor, in front of their building at 232 Senator Street. She further states she saw the suspect running from the scene.

(D) Mike Nisman was shot by Howard Conran at 4:00 A.M. His neighbor, Sheila Norris, witnessed him run from the scene in front of their building at 232 Senator Street.

Answer question 119 solely on the basis of the following information.

When a Police Officer arrives at a scene where there is a dead human body, the Officer should do the following in the order given:

1. Request an ambulance and a patrol supervisor.
2. Exclude unauthorized persons from the scene.
3. Obtain the names of witnesses and keep them at the scene if the death is suspicious.
4. Screen the area from public view, if possible.
5. Cover the body with waterproof covering if publicly exposed.

119. Police Officer Wong is dispatched to 365 E. 52nd Street. Upon arriving, he sees a man who is apparently dead and lying face down in an alley behind the building. Officer Wong immediately calls for an ambulance and his patrol supervisor. While waiting, the Officer notices that a large crowd is beginning to gather around the uncovered body. The next step Officer Wong should take is to

(A) cover the body with a waterproof covering
(B) keep unauthorized people away from the scene
(C) screen the area from public view
(D) obtain the names of witnesses.

120. Police Officer Taylor responds to the scene of a serious traffic accident in which a car struck a telephone pole, and obtains the following information:

Place of Occurrence:	Intersection of Rock Street and Amboy Place
Time of Occurrence:	3:27 A.M.
Name of Injured:	Carlos Black
Driver of Car:	Carlos Black
Action Taken:	Injured taken to Beth-El Hospital

Officer Taylor is preparing a report on the accident. Which one of the following expresses the above information *most clearly* and *accurately*?

(A) At approximately 3:27 A.M. Carlos Black drove his car into a telephone pole located at the intersection of Rock Street and Amboy Place. Mr. Black, who was the only person injured, was taken to Beth-El Hospital.

(B) Carlos Black, injured at the intersection of Rock Street and Amboy Place, hit a telephone pole. He was taken to Beth-El Hospital after the car accident that occurred at 3:27 A.M.

(C) At the intersection of Rock Street and Amboy Place, Carlos Black injured himself and was taken to Beth-El Hospital. His car hit a telephone pole at 3:27 A.M.

(D) At the intersection of Rock Street and Amboy Place at 3:27 A.M., Carlos Black was taken to Beth-El Hospital after injuring himself by driving into a telephone pole.

121. While on patrol in the Jefferson Housing Projects, Police Officer Johnson responds to the scene of a Grand Larceny. The following information was obtained by officer Johnson:

Time of Occurrence:	6:00 P.M.
Place of Occurrence:	Rear of Building 12A
Victim:	Maria Lopez
Crime:	Purse snatched
Suspect:	Unknown

Officer Johnson is preparing a report on the incident. Which one of the following expresses the above information *most clearly* and *accurately*?

(A) At the rear of Building 12A, at 6:00 P.M., by an unknown suspect, Maria Lopez reported her purse snatched in the Jefferson Housing Projects.

(B) Maria Lopez reported that at 6:00 P.M. her purse was snatched by an unknown suspect at the rear of the Building 12A in the Jefferson Housing Projects.

(C) At the rear of Building 12A, Maria Lopez reported at 6:00 P.M. that her purse had been snatched by an unknown suspect in the Jefferson Housing Projects.

(D) In the Jefferson Housing Projects, Maria Lopez reported at the rear of Building 12A that her purse had been snatched by an unknown suspect at 6:00 P.M.

Answer question 122 solely on the basis of the following information.

Criminal Possession of Stolen Property 2nd Degree—occurs when a person knowingly possesses stolen property with intent to benefit himself or a person other than the owner, or to prevent its recovery by the owner, and when:

1. The value of the property exceeds two hundred fifty dollars; or
2. The property consists of a credit card; or
3. The person is a pawnbroker or is in the business of buying, selling, or otherwise dealing in property; or
4. The property consists of one or more firearms, rifles, or shotguns.

122. Which one of the following is the best example of Criminal Possession of Stolen Property in the Second Degree?

(A) Mary knowingly buys a stolen camera valued at $225.00 for her mother's birthday.
(B) John finds a wallet containing $100.00 and various credit cards. John keeps the money and turns the credit cards in at his local precinct.
(C) Mr. Varrone, a pawnbroker, refuses to buy Mr. Cutter's stolen VCR valued at $230.00.
(D) Mr. Aquista, the owner of a toy store, knowingly buys a crate of stolen water pistols valued at $260.00.

123. Police Officer Dale has just finished investigating a report of menacing and obtained the following information:

Time of Occurrence:	10:30 P.M.
Place of Occurrence:	(Hallway) 77 Hill Street
Victim:	Grace Jackson
Suspect:	Susan, white female, 30 years of age
Crime:	Menacing with a knife

Officer Dale is preparing a report on the incident. Which one of the following expresses the above information *most clearly* and *accurately*?

(A) At 10:30 P.M., Grace Jackson was stopped in the hallway of 77 Hill Street by a 30-year-old white female known to Grace as Susan. Susan put a knife to Grace's throat and demanded that Grace stay out of the building or Susan would hurt her.
(B) Grace Jackson was stopped in the hallway at knife point and threatened to stay away from the building located at 77 Hill Street. The female who is 30 years of age known as Susan by Jackson stopped her at 10:30 P.M.
(C) At 10:30 P.M. in the hallway of 77 Hill Street Grace Jackson reported a white female 30 years of age put a knife to her throat. She knew her as Susan and demanded she stay away from the building or she would get hurt.
(D) A white female 30 years of age known to Grace Jackson as Susan stopped her in the hallway of 77 Hill Street. She put a knife to her throat and at 10:30 P.M. demanded she stay away from the building or she would get hurt.

Answer questions 124 through 126 solely on the basis of the following passage.

Police Officer Berman has been assigned to a steady post from Hartman Boulevard to Bement Street on Forest Avenue for the past two years. Officer Berman's duties involve walking along Forest Avenue and in and out of stores talking with the people on his post to ensure that everything is all right. While on duty at 11:30 on Saturday morning, Officer Berman walks into Pete Arturo's Boutique, which is normally filled with female customers because of the type of merchandise sold there. Today the Officer sees only three young men in the store. Officer Berman looks around and notices that Pete is not in sight. Officer Berman notices a thin man whom he has never seen behind the register. Officer Berman decides to ask for Mrs. Arturo, knowing that Pete is not married, because he suspects that something is wrong. The thin man replies with a smile, "She will be in a little later." Officer Berman then walks out of the boutique and calls for back-up assistance on a possible robbery in progress. At 11:40, Police Officers Fernandez and Heck arrive at the side of Arturo's Boutique. Five minutes later Police Officer Jones arrives in his scooter. The Officers are now waiting for a Supervisor to arrive so they can proceed with the plan of action which they have already discussed. Two minutes after Officer Jones arrives, Sgt. Demond pulls up with his driver, Police Officer Ricco, and gathers all of the information. Sgt. Demond then calls the boutique by phone, identifies himself, and advises the man who answers to give himself up so that nobody will get hurt. Sgt. Demond also tells the man on the phone that he has the store surrounded and will give them five minutes to surrender. The three men walk out of the boutique with Mr. Arturo, who is unharmed. Officer Berman recovers three loaded .38 caliber revolvers from the suspects.

124. How many police personnel responded to Officer Berman's call for assistance?

(A) Four
(B) Five
(C) Six
(D) Seven.

125. At what time did Sgt. Demond arrive at the boutique?

(A) 11:40 A.M.
(B) 11:42 A.M.
(C) 11:45 A.M.
(D) 11:47 A.M.

126. Which of the following Officers arrived in the scooter?

(A) Berman
(B) Fernandez
(C) Jones
(D) Heck.

Answer questions 127 through 129 solely on the basis of the following information.

Police Officer Keenan has been ordered to improved the traffic flow on his post by issuing summonses on West 231st Street from Maple Lane to Kingsway Avenue. Officer Keenan has noticed that, between 8:00 A.M. and 10:00 A.M. at W. 231st and Maple Lane, cars park in the bus stop on the north side of the street. This has forced the buses to stop in the middle of the street, blocking traffic for several minutes at a time. In addition, from 10:00 A.M. to 3:00 P.M., cars double park on both sides of W. 231st Street from Maple Lane to Kingsway Avenue, which slows the traffic throughout the day. Officer Keenan has also noticed that from 4:00 P.M. to 6:00 P.M. cars park in the bus stop on the south side of W. 231st Street and Kingsway Avenue, again forcing the buses to stop in the middle of the street.

127. Officer Keenan would be most effective at improving the traffic condition between 8:00 A.M. and 9:00 A.M. by issuing summonses

(A) between Kingsway Avenue and Maple Lane
(B) on the north side of W. 231st Street and Maple Lane
(C) on the south side of W. 231st Street and Maple Lane
(D) between Kingsway Avenue and W. 231st Street.

128. In order to keep traffic flowing between noon and 1:00 P.M., Officer Keenan should issue summonses on

(A) the north side of Kingsway Avenue
(B) both sides of Maple Lane
(C) both sides of W. 231st Street
(D) the south side of Kingsway Avenue.

129. To keep traffic flowing between 5:00 P.M., and 6:00 P.M., Officer Keenan should issue summonses on the

(A) south side of W. 231st Street and Kingsway Avenue
(B) south side of W. 231 Street and Maple Lane
(C) north side of W. 231st Street and Kingsway Avenue
(D) north side of W. 231st Street and Maple Lane.

130. Police Officer Bennett responds to the scene of a car accident and obtains the following information from the witness:

Time of Occurrence: 3:00 A.M.
Victim: Joe Morris, removed to Methodist Hospital
Crime: Struck pedestrian and left the scene of accident
Description of Auto: Blue 1984 Thunderbird, license plate BOT-3745

Officer Bennett is preparing an Accident Report. Which one of the following expresses the above information *most clearly* and *accurately*?

(A) Joe Morris, a pedestrian, was hit at 3:00 A.M. and removed to Methodist Hospital. Also a blue Thunderbird, 1984 model left the scene, license plate BOT-3745.

(B) A pedestrian was taken to Methodist Hospital after being struck at 3:00 A.M. A blue automobile was seen leaving the scene with license plate BOT-3745. Joe Morris was knocked down by a 1984 Thunderbird.

(C) At 3:00 A.M. Joe Morris, a pedestrian, was struck by a blue 1984 Thunderbird. The automobile, license plate BOT-3745, left the scene. Mr. Morris was taken to Methodist Hospital.

(D) Joe Morris, a pedestrian at 3:00 A.M. was struck by a Thunderbird. A 1984 model, license plate BOT-3745, blue in color left the scene and the victim was taken to Methodist Hospital.

Answer question 131 solely on the basis of the following information.

Burglary—occurs when a person knowingly enters or remains unlawfully in a building with the intent to commit a crime therein.

131. Which one of the following situations is the best example of Burglary?

(A) John Moss, an employee at the Forever Toys Warehouse, enters the locked warehouse at 10:30 P.M. through an open window in order to get his wallet, which he had forgotton in his desk when he left work at 5:30 P.M.

(B) Mary Hargrove, not wanting to walk around the block to get to the train station, decides to take a short-cut by slipping through a hole in the fence and walking across a field. There are signs posted that state the field is a restricted area and unauthorized persons would be prosecuted. Although Hargrove is not authorized to be on the property, she continues anyway.

(C) Wayne Moore, after being locked out of his home by his wife, goes to a neighbor's house in the hope that he would be able to spend the night. Although the neighbors are not home, Moore notices that a window leading to the basement is unlocked. He climbs through the window and falls asleep on a basement sofa.

(D) Harold Weeks decides to steal from an antique store valuable items, which he will later sell. Weeks enters the premises by picking the lock on the back door and is confronted by the owner before he is able to take anything.

Answer questions 132 through 134 solely on the basis of the following passage.

Police Officer Smith was reassigned to the Parkhill Housing Complex, which consists of nine 8-story buildings. He was told that nine rapes had occurred in the last eight days in the complex and all had taken place between 9:00 A.M. and 6:00 P.M. On May 2, Officer Smith was working the 10:00 A.M. to 6:00 P.M. shift. At the beginning of Officer Smith's shift his supervisor, Sergeant Larry, gave him the suspected rapist's description, which had been obtained on April 27 from Nancy Lewis, one of the rape victims. The suspect was described as a male, black, 6'2", aproximately 210 lbs., having a light complexion and the word "Budda" tattooed on his left forearm.

While on patrol several blocks from the Parkhill Complex at noon of the same day, Officer Smith was called by the dispatcher and told to respond to a complaint at 110 Park Avenue, Apartment 3C, located in the complex. Upon his arrival at the apartment, he was met by Mary Wilson, who told him that her 16-year-old daughter Tammy had just been raped in the building elevator. Tammy stated that when she entered her building, a black male, approximately 26 years old, about 6'1", wearing a suit, had been waiting for the elevator. She also told Officer Smith that when she entered the elevator with this man, he forced her to the floor, raped her and pushed her out of the elevator on the 7th floor.

On May 3, at 8:00 A.M., an individual fitting the description given by Ms. Lewis was apprehended in front of 55 Hill Street, another building in the Parkhill Complex. The suspect's name was John Jones. At 12:30 P.M. of the same day, Ms. Wilson and Ms. Lewis went to the Precinct Station House and identified John Jones as the person who raped them.

132. Who was the first person to give Officer Smith a description of the rapist?

(A) Sergeant Larry
(B) Tammy Wilson
(C) Mary Wilson
(D) Nancy Lewis.

133. Where was Tammy Wilson raped?

(A) In the elevator at 55 Hill Street
(B) On the 5th floor at 110 Park Avenue
(C) In the elevator at 110 Park Avenue
(D) On the 7th floor at 55 Hill Street.

134. John Jones was apprehended

(A) the same day as the rape of Nancy Lewis
(B) the day after the rape of Nancy Lewis
(C) the same day as the rape of Tammy Wilson
(D) the day after the rape of Tammy Wilson.

135. At 11:30 A.M., Police Officers Newman and Johnson receive a radio call to respond to a reported robbery. The Officers obtained the following information:

Time of Occurrence:	11:20 A.M.
Place of Occurrence:	Twenty-four hour newsstand at 2024 86th Street
Victim:	Sam Norris, owner
Amount Stolen:	$450.00
Suspects:	Two male whites

Officer Newman is completing a complaint report on the incident. Which one of the following expresses the above information *most clearly* and *accurately*?

(A) At 11:20 A.M. it was reported by the newsstand owner that two male whites robbed $450.00 from Sam Norris. The twenty-four hour newsstand is located at 2024 86th Street.
(B) At 11:20 A.M., Sam Norris, the newsstand owner, reported that the twenty-four hour newsstand located at 2024 86th Street was robbed by two male whites who took $450.00.
(C) Sam Norris, the owner of the twenty-four hour newsstand located at 2024 86th Street, reported that at 11:20 A.M. two white males robbed his newsstand of $450.00.
(D) Sam Norris reported at 11:20 A.M. that $450.00 had been taken from the owner of the twenty-four hour newsstand located at 2024 86th Street by two male whites.

Answer question 136 solely on the basis of the following information.

Police Officers are often required to handle cases where the occupant of a residence has died. Upon arrival at the scene of a dead human body, Police Officers should do the following in the order given:

1. Request an ambulance and patrol supervisor to respond.
2. Determine if the death is suspicious or of natural causes.
3. Determine facts and notify the Desk Officer as soon as possible.
4. Notify station house and get aided and complaint report numbers.
5. Notify medical examiner and get log number
6. Notify precinct Detective Unit.
7. If apparent homicide or suicide notify Crime Scene Unit.

136. Police Officer Casin and his supervisor, Sgt. Velez, are in Apartment 1-H at 3333 Hudson Parkway. The occupant of the apartment, Tom Acheson, age 65, is lying face up on the kitchen floor, dead. The ambulance attendant is present and informs the Sergeant that the occupant died of natural causes and has probably been dead for about four days. Officer Berberich arrives on the scene and Sgt. Velez gives Officer Berberich the above information instructing him to make the proper notifications. Which one cf the following should Officer Berberich notify first?

(A) The Desk Officer
(B) The precinct Detective Unit
(C) The occupant's immediate family
(D) The medical examiner.

137. While on patrol, Police Officer Adams is dispatched to investigate a reported burglary. When he arrives, Officer Adams is informed by Ms. Bond, an artist, that when she returned home from an appointment, she found that her front door had been forced open and the following pieces of her artwork were missing:

• 3 Sculptures, each valued at	$2000.00
• 2 Oil paintings, each valued at	$500.00
• 1 Ceramic vase valued at	$375.00
• 1 Portrait valued at	$2500.00
• 2 Small watercolors, each valued at	$75.00

In addition to the artwork, Ms. Bond told Officer Adams that a brooch and bracelet, each valued at $250.00, and $50.00 in cash were also missing. Officer Adams is preparing a Complaint Report on the burglary. Which one of the following is the total value of the property and cash stolen?

(A) $5,450.00
(B) $5,750.00
(C) $10,325.00
(D) $10,575.00.

Answer question 138 solely on the basis of the following information.

Police Officers are often required to respond to the scene of a serious crime, such as robbery, rape, or burglary. When a Police Officer responds to a crime scene, he should do the following in the order given:

1. Interview the complainant and witnesses, obtain the facts, and gather evidence.
2. Conduct a thorough field investigation.
3. Prepare a Complaint Report.
4. Determine if the complaint should be closed or referred for further investigation.

138. Police Officers Pastorino and Longo are driving down Longwood Avenue near Snyder Street while on patrol. They notice that a woman, later identified as Grace Thomas, is lying on the sidewalk in front of 1237 Snyder Street. Officer Pastorino approaches her, notices that she has sustained a minor stab wound on her left arm, and radios for an ambulance. Officer Longo then asks the victim to explain what happened. She tells him that she has just been robbed and assaulted and gives a description of the suspect. Meanwhile, Officer Pastorino searches the area thoroughly and finds a knife but no witnesses. The next step that the Officers should take is to

(A) prepare a Complaint Report
(B) determine if the complaint should be closed or referred for further investigation
(C) conduct a thorough field investigation
(D) interview the complainant and witnesses.

Answer question 139 solely on the basis of the following information.

Dwelling—a building that is usually occupied by a person lodging there at night.

Burglary 1st Degree—occurs when a person knowingly enters or remains unlawfully in a dwelling at night with the intent to commit a crime therein, and when, while entering or while in the dwelling, or in immediate flight therefrom, he or another participant in the crime:

1. Is armed with explosives or a deadly weapon; or
2. Causes physical injury to any person who is not a participant in the crime; or
3. Uses or threatens the immediate use of a dangerous instrument; or
4. Displays what appears to be a pistol, revolver, rifle, shotgun, machine gun, or other firearm.

139. Which one of the following situations is the best example of Burglary in the First Degree?

(A) Sam enters Joanne's apartment by breaking the lock on her door in order to get warm during the cold weather.
(B) Ernest remains in Doreen's Department Store after store hours and removes five diamond rings from the showcase. On his way out, he injures a security guard who tries to apprehend him.
(C) Roger enters the courtyard of a large apartment building and breaks a bedroom window with the butt of his pistol in order to gain entry. The tenant awakens moments later and sees Roger leaving through the window with her VCR.
(D) At 2:00 A.M. on a Sunday, Kevin enters Tom's 24-Hour Deli, removes two cases of beer without paying for them, and runs to an awaiting vehicle.

140. While on patrol, Police Officers Carter and Popps receive a call to respond to an assault in progress. Upon arrival they receive the following information:

Place of Occurrence:	27 Park Avenue
Victim:	John Dee
Suspect:	Michael Jones
Crime:	Stabbing during a fight
Action Taken:	Suspect arrested

The Officers are completing a report on the incident. Which one of the following expresses the above information *most clearly* and *accurately*?

(A) In front of 27 Park Avenue, Michael Jones was arrested for stabbing John Dee during a fight.
(B) Michael Jones was arrested for stabbing John Dee during a fight in front of 27 Park Avenue.
(C) During a fight, Michael Jones was arrested for stabbing John Dee in front of 27 Park Avenue.
(D) John Dee was stabbed by Michael Jones, who was arrested for fighting in front of 27 Park Avenue.

Answer question 141 solely on the basis of the following information.

When a child under ten years of age is reported to be missing, a Police Officer should:

1. Respond to the scene and interview the complainant in order to obtain details, including an accurate description of the child and the location where last seen.
2. Notify Desk Officer of details.
3. Start an immediate search for the child.
4. Request Patrol Supervisor to respond.

141. Police Officers Cippillone and Carey are dispatched to 2501 Richmond Road to investigate a report of a missing child. When the Officers arrive at the location, they are told by Mr. and Mrs. William that their eight-year-old daughter Jill was due back from her friend's house three hours ago and she has still not returned. The Williams describe Jill as 4'3" tall, having brown hair, green eyes and weighing 60 lbs. She was wearing a yellow dress and a white sweater when she left home. The Officers ask the Williams for the name and address of Jill's friends, particularly the last one she had visited. After obtaining this information, the Officers notify their Desk Officer and begin a thorough search for Jill. After a half hour, Officer Carey finds Jill inside a nearby candy store and returns her to her parents' home. Officer Cippillone informs the Desk Officer of the situation and both Officers go back out on patrol. In this situation the actions taken by the Officers were

(A) proper, primarily because they conducted a thorough search and located Jill
(B) improper, primarily because they should have broadcasted Jill's description to other Officers over the radio
(C) proper, primarily because they were able to locate the child without the help of their supervisor
(D) improper, primarily because the Patrol Supervisor should have been requested.

Answer questions *142* through *150* on the basis of the following sketches. The first face on top is a sketch of an alleged criminal based on witnesses' descriptions at the crime scene. One of the four sketches below that face is the way the suspect looked after changing appearance. *Assume that NO surgery has been done on the suspect.* Select the face that is most likely that of the suspect.

142.

(A)

(B)

(C)

(D)

143.

(A)
(B)
(C)
(D)

144.

(A)   (B)

(C)   (D)

145.

146.

(A)   (B)

(C)   (D)

147.

(A)　　　　　(B)

(C)　　　　　(D)

148.

(A) (B)

(C) (D)

149.

(A)

(B)

(C)

(D)

150.

(A)

(B)

(C)

(D)

Please check your Answer Sheet to make sure that you have written in and blackened your Social Security number correctly. If you have not yet written in and blackened your Social Security number, please do so immediately. If you have incorrectly written in or blackened your Social Security number, please correct the mistake immediately. Failure to correctly blacken your Social Security number may result in your Answer Sheet *not* being rated.

PROTEST PROCEDURE

Any candidate wishing to file a protest to one or more key answers on this examination must submit an original and four copies of the protest, together with supporting evidence, to PROTEST-Police Officer, Department of Personnel, 220 Church Street, NY, NY 10013. Protests will be accepted for a period of thirty (30) days beginning October 26, 1987. Protests must be *received* by the last day of the protest period (November 25, 1987).

Protests must be submitted in the following form. For each proposed key answer you protest, you must start a new page and each page must be headed by the following: Examination title, examination number, question number, test date, your Social Security Number. The protest must include a statement explaining why the answer you selected is as good as or better than the proposed key answer, and must include any additional supporting evidence you wish to submit. You may not modify or add to your protest once it is submitted. However, you may submit separate protests to additional questions within the thirty (30) day protest period.

After you have prepared the four copies, print your name and address on the original pages only and sign the last page of the original protest. Do not include your name or address on any other copies. You must print *only* your Social Security Number on each page of the four copies. PROTESTS SENT WITHOUT THE FOUR COPIES WILL NOT BE CONSIDERED!

In order to be informed of the availability of the Validation Board Report for this test, please include a postage-paid, self-addressed business-size envelope with your protests.

RECORD YOUR ANSWERS IN THIS TEST BOOKLET BEFORE THE LAST SIGNAL.

ANSWER SHEET COLLECTION—When you finish the test, remain seated and signal the monitor to collect your answer sheet. Leave the building quickly and quietly.

DO NOT telephone this Department to request information on the progress of the rating of this test. Such information will *NOT* be given. You will be notified individually by mail of your rating after all papers have been rated. Notify this Department promptly in writing of any change of your address. You should indicate your Social Security Number and the title and number of the examination in any correspondence to the Department of Personnel with respect to this examination.

TAKE THIS QUESTION BOOKLET WITH YOU

FINAL ANSWER KEY FOR WRITTEN TEST
HELD ON OCTOBER 24, 1987

1. C	31. D	61. A	91. B	121. B
2. C	32. C	62. B	92. D	122. D
3. D	33. B	63. C	93. A	123. A
4. A	34. A	64. B	94. C	124. B
5. B	35. B	65. D	95. A	125. D
6. B	36. C	66. A	96. C	126. C
7. A	37. D	67. C	97. D	127. B
8. B	38. A	68. D	98. A	128. C
9. D	39. B	69. B	99. B	129. A
10. C	40. C	70. C	100. D	130. C
11. D	41. D	71. D	101. D	131. D
12. A	42. B	72. B	102. C	132. A
13. C	43. A	73. D	103. A	133. C
14. D	44. B	74. C	104. B	134. D
15. A	45. D	75. A	105. A	135. C
16. D	46. C	76. D	106. B	136. A
17. B	47. C	77. C	107. C	137. D
18. C	48. A	78. A	108. D	138. A
19. C	49. D	79. A	109. B	139. C
20. D	50. B	80. C	110. D	140. B
21. A	51. D	81. D	111. C	141. D
22. C	52. A	82. A	112. D	142. A
23. A	53. C	83. C	113. A	143. C
24. B	54. D	84. B and/or C	114. B	144. B
25. C	55. B	85. A	115. D	145. D
26. B	56. A	86. A	116. B	146. A
27. D	57. C	87. D	117. B	147. B
28. A	58. D	88. C	118. C	148. D
29. B	59. B	89. C	119. B	149. B
30. B	60. D	90. B	120. A	150. C

ANSWER EXPLANATIONS

1. **(C)** The black car in the lower left portion of the picture with its hood open is the station wagon of Bob's Painters. The other choices are all business establishments in the picture.

2. **(C)** The only "No Parking" sign in the picture, and it is indeed on East Avenue, reads NO PARKING MON.—SAT. 7A.M.—11A.M.

3. **(D)** A white panel truck belonging to Fast Movers is parked on Bay Street.

4. **(A)** The man standing on the sidewalk talking to the woman in the dotted dress is wearing dark pants and a long-sleeved white shirt. He is holding a white jacket.

5. **(B)** The ONE WAY sign is on the signpost pointing in the direction of Bay Street. This is a certain answer. The sign that prohibits left turns into West Avenue does not necessarily indicate that West Avenue is a one-way street. The left turn may be prohibited only in the interest of traffic flow.

6. **(B)** There are two men attempting to determine the problem with the Bob's Painters station wagon. A woman is sitting in the car waiting.

7. **(A)** When studying pictures for memory questions, be sure to pay special attention to the people who may be involved in any sort of criminal activities. The shirt of the man with a knife says "Beach Bum."

8. **(B)** The crime in the question has nothing to do with the knife. The crime is the pickpocketing in progress. The victim is a white woman (note the legs) with dark hair and a black and white jacket.

9. **(D)** The woman's bag is hanging on her left shoulder. The pickpocket is reaching across his body with his left arm and is lifting the wallet with his left hand.

10. **(C)** The young man with the knife is wearing jeans and a short-sleeved shirt.

11. **(D)** 1802 Avenue R, a Rubber Stamps store, has a "closed" sign in its window. This question is a reminder that a police officer must be aware of all circumstances on the post. A store that is closed or out of business should not show much activity. Movement or lights should be cause for investigation.

12. **(A)** The Electronics store is located mid-block on Avenue R at number 1806. The store could not be at a corner because there is no space between it and either number 1804 or number 1808.

13. **(C)** All robberies occur on Gaston Street, so immediately narrow your choices to (B) and (C). The robberies generally occur in late afternoon and early evening so a 4:00 P.M. to midnight patrol would be most effective in reducing robberies.

14. **(D)** Since most rapes occur on Tuesdays and Thursdays, rape patrol must be conducted on those days. Eliminate choices (A) and (B). Since rapes occur between 7:00 A.M. and 11:30 A.M., Officer Thomas should be on the post from 6:00 A.M. to 2:00 P.M.

15. **(A)** The legitimate reason for people to go to a grocery store is to buy groceries. One or two people might come out empty-handed because they did not find what they wanted, but a steady stream of empty-handed patrons is cause for suspicion. The other choices describe very normal activities.

16. **(D)** Who was robbed and by whom? Who was wearing what? When and where did it happen? Choice (D) tells it best.

17. **(B)** Jennifer has a motive and intentionally kills her husband. In (D) the death is accidentally caused; in (A) the death is from natural causes; in (C) there is no death.

18. **(C)** Only this statement clearly expresses where the victim lives, where the assault occurred, the clothing of the suspect, and the nature of the injury. Organization is the key to this type of question.

19. **(C)** The 1:00 P.M. to 9:00 P.M. shift entirely encompasses the 1:00 P.M. to 4:00 P.M. period during which the major complaint concerns double-parked cars. The majority of double-parked car complaints come from the area of Main Street between Flushing Street and Ocean Boulevard.

20. **(D)** A fairly long reading passage, which is filled with names and details, is usually followed by a series of questions about those details. Read this type of passage with pencil in hand, and mark details that you think may

be important. The questions are meant only to test the accuracy of your reading, not your memory for the details, so you may keep referring to the passage while finding the answers. In the second sentence of the second paragraph, Lieutenant Schwinn assigns Officer Ellen Gray to handcuff and escort the prisoner.

21. **(A)** In the last sentence, Officer Gray, the escorting officer, completes the Medical Treatment of Prisoners form.

22. **(C)** The doctor requested that the handcuffs be removed so that he could conduct a complete physical examination.

23. **(A)** This information is given in the last sentence.

24. **(B)** This is a police judgment question. The drug dealing is most likely where people are congregated for no visible purpose. The youngsters playing basketball after school are busy; the children leaving the YMCA by bicycle at 10:30 P.M. may be running a risk of accident, but they do not give rise to suspicion for drug dealing. The bus stop is a normal place for people to congregate. But, what are those people doing at 3:30 A.M. next to the phone booth?

25. **(C)** This is not a difficult question, but you do have to pay close attention. The crimes, on which Officer Jones is to concentrate, appear to occur during the early morning hours (between 1:00 A.M. and 6 A.M.), so narrow to choices (A) and (C). Thursday, Friday, and Saturday appear to be the heaviest crime days in the area, so Wednesday through Sunday are the better days for Jones to work.

26. **(B)** Arthur committed Assault Third Degree when he intentionally punched Jennifer in the face and caused her mouth to bleed.

27. **(D)** Most often if the list of facts includes data and time of occurrence, the best organization of the information begins with date and time. You may save time by looking first at answer choices beginning with date and time if offered. In this question, the date, time, and place organization is the clearest.

28. **(A)** The best organization in this instance begins with a brief introductory statement and then continues with date, time, and description of the incident.

29. **(B)** Perkins has said that he has no intention of accompanying the officers to the precinct, but not that he will not surrender the rifle. He should be arrested only if he refuses to surrender the weapon. First, he must be informed that he may surrender the rifle on the spot and receive a receipt.

30. **(B)** Since two witnesses agree that the plate began with ADE, consider that they are probably correct. Three witnesses agree that the numbers were 1780, so they are likely to be right. The disagreement as to state is somewhat surprising, but you must base your conclusion on the elements recalled in common by the greatest number of witnesses and choose plate ADE-1780.

31. **(D)** This is a well-organized sentence that gives all the necessary information clearly and accurately.

32. **(C)** In questions based upon stated regulations and fact situations, you must limit your answer to the information on the test paper, even if you have other information or knowledge. In this question, do not allow yourself to be distracted by your concern for the dog-bite victim. According to these regulations, since Officer Rosario is unable to find the dog, he must next prepare the Department of Health Form 480BAA.

33. **(B)** This is a well-organized statement that gives all the facts.

34. **(A)** All the statements are accurate and give the information unambiguously. Choose the one that gives the information in the most reasonable order and that reads most smoothly.

35. **(B)** Man-hole covers do not simply blow off. There must be something unusual going on under the streets. The Fire Department is best equipped to investigate the causes of explosions. The contained fires in (A) and (C) should be watched but do not represent a present emergency. The Fire Department should be made aware of the open hydrant, but they need not be called to the scene.

36. **(C)** Officer Bestwell has entered a description of the items into his memo book and must now prepare a worksheet of the Property Clerk's Invoice. Mrs. Robinson does not need a receipt since she is not the person who found or turned in the property.

37. **(D)** All of the choices get the message across, but choice (D) is clearest and simplest to understand.

38. **(A)** Mr. Walls had sexual intercourse with girls under the age of eleven by forcible compulsion. He is guilty of Rape First Degree. Joe may be guilty of a number of illegal acts, but he did not have intercourse with the girls so is not guilty of Rape First Degree.

39. **(B)** Choice (D) would be possible, but it is a much longer route. (A) is incorrect because Edelman Avenue is one way westbound; (C) is incorrect because Merrick Boulevard does not go through to 115th Street.

40. **(C)** Follow the route. The officers are driving north, they turn left, which is west. A U-turn will head them in the opposite direction, which is east.

41. **(D)** This is an arithmetic problem. When adding up the list, do not forget to include the calculator.

2 tape players at $99 each	=	$198
3 compact disc players at $290 each	=	870
5 telephone sets at $50 each	=	250
1 VCR at $470	=	470
1 TV set at $600	=	600
1 stereo rack system at $975	=	975
1 Walkman stereo at $70	=	70
1 calculator at $50	=	+ 50
total		$3,483

42. **(B)** This is a reading-for-details series of questions. The Sergeant supervised a search to determine if the owner was sick, injured, or otherwise incapacitated.

43. **(A)** The first sentence tells of a possible burglary at 1423 Second Avenue.

44. **(B)** 1423 Second Avenue was a bicycle shop.

45. **(D)** At 10:40 P.M. Officer Reese radioed for a Supervisor who arrived ten minutes later, at 10:50 P.M.

46. **(C)** Police Officer Craig, the Precinct Telephone Switchboard Operator, would attempt to contact the store owner.

47. **(C)** This statement gives all the information in the most logical order.

48. **(A)** Three witnesses agree that the car was a red Ford Mustang; three witnesses agree that the plate number was 2198; two witnesses agree that the plate ended with CAT. Choice (A) includes the greatest number of common elements.

49. **(D)** The details are uncomplicated. The report should be equally straightforward.

50. **(B)** There are few details. Choice (B) expresses them well, leaving no doubt as to what happened and to whom.

51. **(D)** The regulation states: "Two police officers are needed if more than one patient is being transported." Here there are three patients.

52. **(A)** This question is not as time-consuming as it first appears. Burglaries and robberies seem to occur at night. Only choice (A) suggests a nighttime patrol, so you needn't concern yourself with days of the week or location of patrol.

53. **(C)** The auto thefts occur on Mondays and Wednesdays during evening rush hours, roughly 3:30 P.M. to 7:00 P.M., so a Monday through Friday, 4:00 P.M. to midnight tour should be most effective.

54. **(D)** In stepping in to stop a flight between armed persons, a police officer runs some risk of personal injury. Back-up assistance should help break up the fight more efficiently and with less danger.

55. **(B)** Read the steps and the narrative description carefully. The next step, in order, is to place the additional ammunition into another envelope.

56. **(A)** Robberies and rapes occur in the afternoon and night, so eliminate (B) and (C). The days of the week that are most important to cover are Monday, Friday, and Saturday. Choice (D) would leave Monday uncovered, so (A) is the answer.

57. **(C)** The ambulance attendant, Peter Johnson, pronounced Smith dead.

58. **(D)** William Jones came out of his store and reported hearing a gunshot at 5:15 P.M.

59. **(B)** Walter Garvey described the hair color and clothing of the two suspects.

60. **(D)** Only this statement makes clear descriptions of witness, suspect, and action.

61. **(A)** This is the only clear and accurate statement.

62. **(B)** Regulation item 4 requires that the police officer notify the Property Clerk's Office if evidence is held by the court.

63. **(C)** The teenage boy who keeps looking at his watch could be putting on a guise of waiting for a train in order to avoid special attention; but the woman, who has stood for a full hour without showing any impatience that the person she is awaiting has not arrived, must arouse greater suspicion and should be monitored more closely.

64. **(B)** There is no question that this is a well-organized report, which presents all the information clearly and accurately.

65. **(D)** Item 2 says that the officer should conduct a brief investigation in the vicinity of the place where the child was found. This means that the officer should have inquired within the building to learn if anyone was missing a child or if anyone had any information about this particular youngster.

66. **(A)** This is the simplest statement and clearly includes all the facts.

67. **(C)** The officer's first act at the scene of the accident must be to request medical assistance for the injured.

68. **(D)** No one was injured, so an ambulance is unnecessary; Officer Degas is already diverting the traffic. Now the officers must attempt to determine the cause of the accident so that they will have complete information to enter on the Police Accident Report.

69. **(B)** This is a short statement that includes all of the facts clearly and accurately.

70. **(C)** The activity described has all occurred before the list of procedures even begins. Therefore, the officer is now at the top of the list. The first official act must be to request the person's name and address.

71. **(D)** Officer Georgia has followed regulations. The homeless woman refused shelter during the Cold Weather Emergency, so Officer Georgia was required to have her hospitalized.

72. **(B)** Since, by the definition, "sell" means "give to another," and since Harry and Jack have been giving the marihuana pipe to each other, Harry and Jack have been involved in Criminal Sale of a Controlled Substance Fifth Degree. No one else sold or gave to another.

73. **(D)** The suspect is a juvenile so, following the printed procedure, the next step is to prepare a N.Y. State Juvenile Fingerprint Chart.

74. **(C)** Multiply and add as indicated. Do not forget about the suitcase.

2 35mm Cameras at $289 each	=	$578
2 Video Cassette Recorders at $329 each	=	658
Miscellaneous jewelry	=	455
Cash	=	350
Stock Certificates totalling	=	1500
Luggage	=	+ 150
total	=	$3,691

75. **(A)** Whiskey Bill knew that the liquor would be fatal and deliberately gave some to Joe to drink. Bill's action constitutes Murder Second Degree.

76. **(D)** The homicides are all on Third Avenue, and only one choice suggests that Officer Miller should patrol Third Avenue. Spend no extra time on a question that can be answered so easily.

77. **(C)** Choice (D) is also possible but is by no means the shortest route. (A) is impossible because Thames Street is one way westbound; (B) is impossible because Rose Place is not a through street.

78. **(A)** Choice (C) is not really a bad one, but it is somewhat longer than (A). (B) cannot be taken because Rose Place at Washington Street is one way westbound; (D) cannot be taken because Charles Street is one way southbound.

79. **(A)** Put yourself in the driver's seat and follow the route, turning the map as needed to

be certain of right and left from the driver's point of view. Starting at Rose Place and Temple Street, go south two blocks to Roundsman Avenue. Turn left and go east for two blocks to Washington Street. Turn left and travel one block north to Thames Street. Turn left and go two more blocks west to Temple Street. The final right turn will leave you headed north.

80. **(C)** The youth looking at a subway map while holding a black canvas bag might very well raise suspicion; however, this question speaks of pairs of youths who have been conducting the hold-ups. Since you are looking for two youths, and in (C) one boy appears to be acting as a lookout, choice (C) represents the pair that should be monitored closely.

81. **(D)** The prisoner was removed from the scene of the arrest directly to the hospital and so must be searched at the hospital. Since the prisoner, Michelle Hart, is female, Officer Smith must direct hospital personnel to conduct the search.

82. **(A)** Directive 4 requires that both weapon and Request for Laboratory Examination form be brought to the Ballistics Unit.

83. **(C)** A fall that renders a person unconscious is a serious injury. It requires emergency transportation for medical assistance.

84. **(B)** or **(C)** Eliminate choice (A) at once; the crime was committed in the afternoon, not in the morning. Stuart Gray was seen running from the building at 5:35 P.M., so the crime had to have been committed before that time. Stuart Gray was seen nearby at about 5:10 P.M., so the crime could not have been committed before that time. The question asks for the "most likely" time. The best answer is choice (B). The time span 5:10 to 5:35 allows for Gray to have entered the apartment, argued, hit Mrs. Gray over the head, rummaged through drawers to find money for his crack habit, and run off. (C) is acceptable as an answer because it is also possible that Gray went through drawers as Valerie Gray argued with him and that he hit her over the head as his last act before exiting the apartment. Since the

crime had to have been committed no later than 5:35 and the time span 5:30 to 5:35 is offered, there is no reason to accept choice (D) as an answer, even though it might technically be correct.

85. **(A)** Officer Swift checked the fire escape while his partner, Officer Monroe, searched the bedroom where he found Mrs. Gray.

86. **(A)** Ben Grim saw Stuart Gray run from the building with blood on his hands. Ms. Arnold's statement, of having seen Gray in the neighborhood before the crime, ties him only very circumstantially. However, Ben Grim must be part of the answer, and Valerie Gray having never regained consciousness cannot be part of the answer, so (A) is the only choice.

87. **(D)** The homicide took place on May 10. Gray was arrested at 7:15 the next morning, that is, on May 11 at 7:15 A.M.

88. **(C)** This is a clear and accurate statement of the facts.

89. **(C)** A parent is permitted to reasonably discipline a child. A mother's leaving a four-year-old at home alone for purposes of her partying can offer no benefit to the child. Quite to the contrary, a child is not equipped to deal with emergencies and might even cause them. This is a good example of Endangering the Welfare of a Child.

90. **(B)** This information is presented in logical, useful order.

91. **(B)** This statement keeps the parties straight and tells what happened.

92. **(D)** Clarke has one previous suspension for the same violation so should be issued a Universal Summons. No person may operate a motor vehicle with a suspended license, so Clarke must park his car in a legal area and arrange for a licensed operator to fetch it.

93. **(A)** The most suspicious car is that in which two men sit near the schoolyard during recess and after school. It is difficult to think of a legitimate reason for their being there, and they must be closely observed. The car

service driver could be selling drugs and using his legitimate role as a cover, and the teenagers could be selling drugs from their car, but the question asks which is *most suspicious.*

94. **(C)** Officer Wells has proceeded through step 5 and has marked the separate vials of drugs. He must now move to step 6 and request specially secured envelopes from the Station House Officer.

95. **(A)** The man crawled under the turnstile and then rode the subway train. Had he not intended to avoid payment, he could have dropped a token into the turnstile, gone through and then retrieved the quarter. The diners in (B) refused to pay for food, not for transportation services. In (C), Harry paid even though his payment may not have registered.

96. **(C)** All other choices are very unclear.

97. **(D)** Only this choice makes clear when and where the crime was committed and leaves no doubt as to who was wearing a beige parka.

98. **(A)** All suspects are within the same age, height, and weight range. The suspects in incidents 1 and 4 have three features in common that are not reported in suspects 2 and 3. These are long brown hair, not common in blacks and therefore highly significant, a scar on the left side of the face, and an earring in the right ear.

99. **(B)** Choices (A) and (C) involve stealing without physical force. In choice (D) there is threat of physical force, but not threat of *immediate* force and nothing is stolen. In (B), on the other hand, the threat is real and immediate and the money is stolen.

100. **(D)** All of the other choices present the information inaccurately and with much room for doubt as to real meaning.

101. **(D)** Instances (A) and (B) represent normal disciplinary action by parents. (C) is a household accident. It is the duty of parents to care for their defenseless and helpless infants. Leaving a baby at home alone, to go out to play softball out of sight and earshot may well constitute neglect.

102. **(C)** When two people of the same sex are involved in an interaction, you must take special care to use their names more often to avoid confusion of "he," "him," and "his." Choice (C) keeps both people and time sequence straight.

103. **(A)** This is the best organized and simplest statement.

104. **(B)** All four statements present the information accurately, but choice (B) is clearest.

105. **(A)** The officers do not perceive a need for medical attention, but Mrs. Jones has requested it. According to step 2, the officers must obtain medical assistance if it is requested.

106. **(B)** Officer Perez of sector Charlie went up to the roof.

107. **(C)** Go back to the first sentence. Officer Moody encountered an armed robbery in progress and chased the perpetrator.

108. **(D)** Officer Donadio was in the courtyard.

109. **(B)** Read carefully. By the time Officer Moody arrived at the bottom of the second floor stairway, the suspect had jumped out the hall window and was in the courtyard.

110. **(D)** Three witnesses agree that the suspect is a white, non-Hispanic male, so immediately eliminate (B). The array of estimates of height leads to infer that the man is on the taller side, so narrow to (C) and (D). Three witnesses recall that the man had brown hair and dark eyes; so (D), as the description with the greatest number of common elements, is the best choice.

111. **(C)** This statement is clear, logical and accurate.

112. **(D)** This constitutes Grand Larceny Fourth Degree because the bracelet, even though inexpensive, was removed from the victim's body. (A) is not the answer because the value of the stolen property is less than one thousand dollars and the property was not taken from the person of another nor obtained through fear. In (B) the credit card is not stolen. In (C) a threat is made but nothing is stolen.

113. **(A)** The information is sketchy and simple. There is no need to complicate it with a confusing report.

114. **(B)** The doctor has not requested that Officer Schultz remove the handcuffs, so he should not do so at this time. Officer Schultz must now inform Dr. Carson of the details of the prisoner's arrest.

115. **(D)** A man who is recognized as being recently involved in an armed robbery is most certainly a person suspected of having committed a crime. The Police Officer is authorized to search him.

116. **(B)** Larceny and robbery cannot occur at the same time, since one entails the use or threat of force, while the other occurs only without force. Kevin Watts threatened to beat Jane up, then stole her property. He committed robbery. Watts also unlawfully entered the apartment by way of the fire escape for purposes of robbery, thereby committing burglary as well.

117. **(B)** This is by far the most clear and accurate statement.

118. **(C)** This statement includes all of the facts and expresses them clearly.

119. **(B)** According to the prescribed order of actions to be taken, Officer Wong must now keep unauthorized people away from the scene. In answering questions, remember to be bound by the printed instructions that accompany the question.

120. **(A)** This is a well-organized, useful statement.

121. **(B)** All the other statements are garbled.

122. **(D)** The stolen water pistols that Mr. Aquista buys are only toys, not firearms, but their value is in excess of $250 so his purchase with knowledge of their stolen status constitutes Criminal Possession of Stolen Property Second Degree. (A) does not qualify because the value of the camera is under $250.

123. **(A)** This statement gets all the facts straight and expresses them clearly.

124. **(B)** The officers who responded to Officer Berman's call for back-up assistance are: Officers Fernandez and Heck; Officer Jones (on a scooter); and Sergeant Desmond with his driver, Officer Ricco.

125. **(D)** Officers Fernandez and Heck arrived at 11:40. Officer Jones arrived five minutes later, at 11:45. Sergeant Demond arrived two minutes after Jones, at 11:47.

126. **(C)** We know that Officer Berman was walking. There is no information as to how Officers Fernandez and Heck arrived. The passage tells us that Jones arrived by scooter.

127. **(B)** Between 8:00 A.M. and 10:00 A.M., the traffic problem is caused by cars parked in the bus stop on the north side of West 231st Street and Maple Lane.

128. **(C)** Midday traffic congestion is created by the cars that double-park on both sides of West 231st Street.

129. **(A)** During the evening rush hour, cars park in the bus stop on the south side of West 231st Street and Kingsway Avenue.

130. **(C)** This statement is clear, accurate, and well organized.

131. **(D)** Although Weeks did not actually steal anything, he broke into the store with intent to steal, and his action therefore constitutes burglary. No other choice involves criminal intent.

132. **(A)** Sergeant Larry gave Officer Jones the description of the rapist as reported by Nancy Lewis.

133. **(C)** Tammy Wilson was raped in the elevator at 110 Park Avenue, then was pushed out of the elevator at the 7th floor.

134. **(D)** Tammy Wilson was raped on the same day that Officer Smith was given the description of the rapist, May 2. John Jones was apprehended on May 3, the day after the rape of Tammy Wilson.

135. **(C)** Only this choice accurately states that the robbery occurred at 11:20 A.M. All other choices give 11:20 A.M. as the time of the report of the robbery.

136. **(A)** Whether the death is suspicious or of apparently natural causes, the first person to be notified is the Desk Officer.

137. **(D)** Read carefully so as to be sure to include all items in your total. Don't miss the brooch and the bracelet *each* valued at $250.

3 sculptures at $2000 each	=	$6,000
2 oil paintings at $500 each	=	1,000
1 ceramic vase at $375	=	375
1 portrait at $2500	=	2,500
2 small watercolors at $75 each	=	150
1 brooch at $250	=	250
1 bracelet at $250	=	250
cash of $50	=	+ 50
total		$10,575

138. **(A)** The officers have interviewed the complainant and have thoroughly searched the area for evidence. Since there are no witnesses, their next act must be to prepare a Complaint Report.

139. **(C)** There is no question that entry of a bedroom at night, pistol in hand, and stealing a VCR constitutes Burglary First Degree. Choice (B) fits all the requirements for Burglary First Degree except that a department store is not a dwelling.

140. **(B)** All the statements do make clear who was stabbed, who was arrested, and where it happened. Choice (B) makes the statement most clearly.

141. **(D)** The officers did not follow through on all required procedures. They should have requested a Patrol Supervisor.

142. **(A)** Choice (B) has a different chin; (C) has different nostrils and a pierced right ear rather than left; (D) has a totally different shape head and face.

143. **(C)** Choice (A) has a different shape chin; (B) has different ears; (D) has a different chin. The beauty marks and heavy glossed lips are cosmetic changes only and cannot be used as a basis of comparison.

144. **(B)** Choice (A) has a different nose and ears; (C) has different eyes; (D) has different ears and lips. The hole from a pierced ear is difficult to remove so is significant if the comparison face has one. It is easy to pierce an ear, so the addition of a hole in an ear of one of the choices is meaningless.

145. **(D)** Choice (A) has a different mouth; (B) has different face shape and different eyes; (C) has different eyes.

146. **(A)** The beard effectively disguises the distinctive chin, but choice (A) must be your man because (B) and (D) have wrong chins and (C) has different eyes and ears.

147. **(B)** Choice (A) has a different chin (look carefully through the stubble on the comparison face); choice (C) has an entirely different nose; (D) has different ears.

148. **(D)** Choice (A) has different eyes and nose; (B) has a different chin; (C) has a different nose. The dark glasses and beard leave few features with which to judge (D), but nose, mouth and ears match exactly and all other choices have been eliminated.

149. **(B)** Choice (C) is clearly not the answer because she has very different ears and lips; (D) has a different nose. The decision between (A) and (B) is more difficult, but (B) is the answer because (A) has eyes that are quite a bit farther apart. As you practice at home, you can check this with a ruler. If faced with this type of need for measurement at the exam, mark distances off at the edge of a piece of paper, perhaps your answer sheet.

150. **(C)** Both (A) and (B) have noses that rule them out. Choice (D) has eyes that are set more deeply than those of the comparison face. This is not an easy determination. The eyes on (C) look larger, but you must remember that makeup can create illusions. If you find yourself having difficulty choosing a face, do give consideration to the effectiveness of various disguises. The sophisticated hairdo of (C) makes for a greater contrast from the original than the hairdo on (D), which, while shorter, still frames the face.

ANSWER SHEET FOR PRACTICE EXAMINATION 3

TEAR HERE

1. Ⓐ Ⓑ Ⓒ Ⓓ   21. Ⓐ Ⓑ Ⓒ Ⓓ   41. Ⓐ Ⓑ Ⓒ Ⓓ   61. Ⓐ Ⓑ Ⓒ Ⓓ   81. Ⓐ Ⓑ Ⓒ Ⓓ
2. Ⓐ Ⓑ Ⓒ Ⓓ   22. Ⓐ Ⓑ Ⓒ Ⓓ   42. Ⓐ Ⓑ Ⓒ Ⓓ   62. Ⓐ Ⓑ Ⓒ Ⓓ   82. Ⓐ Ⓑ Ⓒ Ⓓ
3. Ⓐ Ⓑ Ⓒ Ⓓ   23. Ⓐ Ⓑ Ⓒ Ⓓ   43. Ⓐ Ⓑ Ⓒ Ⓓ   63. Ⓐ Ⓑ Ⓒ Ⓓ   83. Ⓐ Ⓑ Ⓒ Ⓓ
4. Ⓐ Ⓑ Ⓒ Ⓓ   24. Ⓐ Ⓑ Ⓒ Ⓓ   44. Ⓐ Ⓑ Ⓒ Ⓓ   64. Ⓐ Ⓑ Ⓒ Ⓓ   84. Ⓐ Ⓑ Ⓒ Ⓓ
5. Ⓐ Ⓑ Ⓒ Ⓓ   25. Ⓐ Ⓑ Ⓒ Ⓓ   45. Ⓐ Ⓑ Ⓒ Ⓓ   65. Ⓐ Ⓑ Ⓒ Ⓓ   85. Ⓐ Ⓑ Ⓒ Ⓓ
6. Ⓐ Ⓑ Ⓒ Ⓓ   26. Ⓐ Ⓑ Ⓒ Ⓓ   46. Ⓐ Ⓑ Ⓒ Ⓓ   66. Ⓐ Ⓑ Ⓒ Ⓓ   86. Ⓐ Ⓑ Ⓒ Ⓓ
7. Ⓐ Ⓑ Ⓒ Ⓓ   27. Ⓐ Ⓑ Ⓒ Ⓓ   47. Ⓐ Ⓑ Ⓒ Ⓓ   67. Ⓐ Ⓑ Ⓒ Ⓓ   87. Ⓐ Ⓑ Ⓒ Ⓓ
8. Ⓐ Ⓑ Ⓒ Ⓓ   28. Ⓐ Ⓑ Ⓒ Ⓓ   48. Ⓐ Ⓑ Ⓒ Ⓓ   68. Ⓐ Ⓑ Ⓒ Ⓓ   88. Ⓐ Ⓑ Ⓒ Ⓓ
9. Ⓐ Ⓑ Ⓒ Ⓓ   29. Ⓐ Ⓑ Ⓒ Ⓓ   49. Ⓐ Ⓑ Ⓒ Ⓓ   69. Ⓐ Ⓑ Ⓒ Ⓓ   89. Ⓐ Ⓑ Ⓒ Ⓓ
10. Ⓐ Ⓑ Ⓒ Ⓓ   30. Ⓐ Ⓑ Ⓒ Ⓓ   50. Ⓐ Ⓑ Ⓒ Ⓓ   70. Ⓐ Ⓑ Ⓒ Ⓓ   90. Ⓐ Ⓑ Ⓒ Ⓓ
11. Ⓐ Ⓑ Ⓒ Ⓓ   31. Ⓐ Ⓑ Ⓒ Ⓓ   51. Ⓐ Ⓑ Ⓒ Ⓓ   71. Ⓐ Ⓑ Ⓒ Ⓓ   91. Ⓐ Ⓑ Ⓒ Ⓓ
12. Ⓐ Ⓑ Ⓒ Ⓓ   32. Ⓐ Ⓑ Ⓒ Ⓓ   52. Ⓐ Ⓑ Ⓒ Ⓓ   72. Ⓐ Ⓑ Ⓒ Ⓓ   92. Ⓐ Ⓑ Ⓒ Ⓓ
13. Ⓐ Ⓑ Ⓒ Ⓓ   33. Ⓐ Ⓑ Ⓒ Ⓓ   53. Ⓐ Ⓑ Ⓒ Ⓓ   73. Ⓐ Ⓑ Ⓒ Ⓓ   93. Ⓐ Ⓑ Ⓒ Ⓓ
14. Ⓐ Ⓑ Ⓒ Ⓓ   34. Ⓐ Ⓑ Ⓒ Ⓓ   54. Ⓐ Ⓑ Ⓒ Ⓓ   74. Ⓐ Ⓑ Ⓒ Ⓓ   94. Ⓐ Ⓑ Ⓒ Ⓓ
15. Ⓐ Ⓑ Ⓒ Ⓓ   35. Ⓐ Ⓑ Ⓒ Ⓓ   55. Ⓐ Ⓑ Ⓒ Ⓓ   75. Ⓐ Ⓑ Ⓒ Ⓓ   95. Ⓐ Ⓑ Ⓒ Ⓓ
16. Ⓐ Ⓑ Ⓒ Ⓓ   36. Ⓐ Ⓑ Ⓒ Ⓓ   56. Ⓐ Ⓑ Ⓒ Ⓓ   76. Ⓐ Ⓑ Ⓒ Ⓓ   96. Ⓐ Ⓑ Ⓒ Ⓓ
17. Ⓐ Ⓑ Ⓒ Ⓓ   37. Ⓐ Ⓑ Ⓒ Ⓓ   57. Ⓐ Ⓑ Ⓒ Ⓓ   77. Ⓐ Ⓑ Ⓒ Ⓓ   97. Ⓐ Ⓑ Ⓒ Ⓓ
18. Ⓐ Ⓑ Ⓒ Ⓓ   38. Ⓐ Ⓑ Ⓒ Ⓓ   58. Ⓐ Ⓑ Ⓒ Ⓓ   78. Ⓐ Ⓑ Ⓒ Ⓓ   98. Ⓐ Ⓑ Ⓒ Ⓓ
19. Ⓐ Ⓑ Ⓒ Ⓓ   39. Ⓐ Ⓑ Ⓒ Ⓓ   59. Ⓐ Ⓑ Ⓒ Ⓓ   79. Ⓐ Ⓑ Ⓒ Ⓓ   99. Ⓐ Ⓑ Ⓒ Ⓓ
20. Ⓐ Ⓑ Ⓒ Ⓓ   40. Ⓐ Ⓑ Ⓒ Ⓓ   60. Ⓐ Ⓑ Ⓒ Ⓓ   80. Ⓐ Ⓑ Ⓒ Ⓓ   100. Ⓐ Ⓑ Ⓒ Ⓓ

PRACTICE EXAMINATION 3

The time allowed for the entire examination is 3½ hours.

Directions: For each question, read all the choices carefully. Select the choice that you consider the most correct or best of all the choices. Then mark your answer on the answer sheet.

Questions 1 through 15 are based on the photographs on pages 286 and 287. You will have five minutes to memorize as many as possible of the details in these photos. The photos include mug shots and a street scene. You may not write or make any notes while studying the photos. When the time is up, answer questions 1 through 15 without referring back to the photos

285

Faces

The twelve photographs, shown below, were taken from FBI files. Study these faces carefully. Your ability to remember these faces will be tested in this examination.

Street Scene

While on foot patrol, you receive a call on your portable police radio that a robbery may be in progress at a watch repair shop. It so happens that the shop is across the street from where you are standing. What you see at this moment will help you decide what to do, and remembering what you see may be very important later on. Study this scene carefully. You will be asked questions about it in this examination.

Bonnie Freer/Photo Researchers, Inc.

Section I: Recall of Details

Directions: Questions 1 through 5 test your ability to remember the details of the street scene that you just studied. Each question is followed by four choices. Choose the one best answer (A,B,C, or D) and blacken the corresponding space on your answer sheet.

1. The boy by the dark-colored car
   (A) was opening the fill-tank cap
   (B) was carrying a large box
   (C) was passing between cars
   (D) wore a short-sleeved shirt

2. The group of men on the sidewalk were
   (A) facing one another
   (B) looking at the watch repair shop
   (C) kneeling in a circle
   (D) waiting at the bus stop

3. Nearest to the watch repair shop was a
   (A) boy standing by a dark-colored car
   (B) woman in a doorway

   (C) group of men on the sidewalk
   (D) man next to a light-colored car.

4. The dark-colored car
   (A) was a four-door sedan
   (B) carried New York State plates
   (C) was headed uptown
   (D) had a man in the driver's seat.

5. A woman on the sidewalk appeared to be
   (A) looking at the apartment windows directly above her
   (B) looking toward the watch repair shop
   (C) watching the boy by the dark-colored car
   (D) coming out of a store.

Section II: Recognition of Faces

Directions: Questions 6 through 15 test your ability to recognize faces that you have seen before. Each question comprises three faces. If one of the three faces was among the photographs that you studied, blacken the space on your answer sheet corresponding to the correctly matched face. If none of the three faces was among the FBI photographs, blacken space (D) on your answer sheet.

6. (A) (B) (C) (D) none of the three faces at the left

Section III: Judgment in Police Situations

Directions: Questions 16 through 55 are designed to test your judgment. The questions describe situations similar to those encountered by police officers on duty. Each question is followed by four choices. Choose the one best answer (A,B,C, or D) and blacken the corresponding space on your answer sheet.

16. A man comes out of a store and complains to a police officer that he has been overcharged $50 by the store owner. He wants the store owner arrested. The police officer should *first*

    (A) advise the man to hire a lawyer
    (B) go inside and ask the store owner to give the money back
    (C) go inside the store and find out what happened
    (D) tell the man that there is nothing the police can do.

17. A teenage boy stops a passing patrol car. He tells the police officers that a pipe has broken in the basement of a nearby apartment house and "everything is getting flooded." The officers should

    (A) tell the boy to find a plumber
    (B) look for some tools to fix the leak
    (C) radio the station house for assistance
    (D) investigate the matter and then decide what to do.

18. A very old man walks slowly from a bus stop to a patrol car that happens to be parked nearby. He tells the police officers that he has been visiting a friend and wants to go home now. But he says that he cannot remember his home address or how to get there. The *first* thing the officers should do is

    (A) find out if he is carrying any identification
    (B) find out if he is listed as a missing person
    (C) tell him to go back to his friend's house
    (D) take him to a hospital.

19. In general, a police officer dealing with teenagers should

    (A) establish two-way communication with them
    (B) show them that he or she can solve their problems
    (C) force them to respect the law
    (D) avoid face-to-face contact.

20. Occasionally, a police officer may be required to deal with a mentally disturbed person. In such a situation, the officer should, as a rule,

    (A) try not to frighten or excite the person
    (B) take no action unless a doctor is present
    (C) avoid speaking to the person
    (D) consider the person harmless.

21. While a man is being booked at a police station for attempted robbery, his wife enters the station. She screams and curses at the police officers there and threatens to tear up the police forms that are being filled out. The officer on duty should

    (A) give her a cup of coffee
    (B) tell her they will lock her up too
    (C) ignore the woman and continue with what they were doing
    (D) take the woman into another room and try to calm her down.

22. A patrol car is stopped on the street by a man who wants help for his sick son. The man tells the officers that he thinks his son may be ill from an overdose of drugs. On reaching the family's apartment, the police find the son unconscious. The first thing they should do is

    (A) place the son under arrest
    (B) question the father about his son's use of drugs
    (C) call for an ambulance
    (D) search for drugs.

23. In response to a call one night, a patrol car is sent to a private house. On arriving, the officers find that the house is dark and the owner is waiting for them at the front door. She explains that all of the lights suddenly went out and she does not know how to get them back on. The officers should

    (A) replace the light bulbs
    (B) tell the woman that the police do not have the time to fix lights
    (C) tell the woman to call the electric company
    (D) check the fuse box as a possible source of trouble.

24. A police officer is asked to talk to a neighborhood group about the use of force in making arrests. One person in the meeting says, "The trouble with you pigs is that you always want to beat a man's brains out." The police officer should say,

 (A) "With most criminals you must use force."
 (B) "Some people may think that, but that's not the way it is."
 (C) "Only idiots call us pigs."
 (D) "I won't talk with people who hate the police."

25. A police officer is on foot patrol near a supermarket when a young mother pushing a baby carriage stops him. She asks him to watch her child for a few minutes while she goes in to buy a couple of things. The officer should

 (A) tell her she could be arrested for interfering with a police officer's duties
 (B) agree to the request, since the delay will probably not amount to more than five or ten minutes.
 (C) agree to the request to avoid an argument, then continue to patrol after the woman has entered the store
 (D) refuse the request, since the officer should continue with his patrol.

26. In the course of a barroom argument one Saturday night, Pete Smith seriously injures three police officers. He then agrees to go quietly to the police station. This is not the first time that the local police have been injured by Smith. On the way to the station, the arresting officers should

 (A) offer to let Smith go if he will promise to give up fighting
 (B) give Smith a bruise or two so that he will think twice about striking police officers
 (C) use only as much physical force as needed to bring Smith in
 (D) try to talk Smith into giving up drinking.

27. Police officers are assigned to duty at a school where parents are picketing to get the principal removed. When the police accompany the principal as he leaves the building, some of the parents scream insults at the police and yell, "We'll get him tomorrow." The *best* course of action for the police to take is to

 (A) give summonses to the leaders of the pickets for threatening the principal
 (B) warn them that picketing will be forbidden if the insults continue
 (C) ignore the insults but watch out for any violent actions
 (D) arrest the leader of the pickets as an example.

28. Two police officers respond to a complaint of an argument between a man and his wife in their apartment. The door is opened by one of their children, and the police officers find the man and wife in the kitchen of their three-room apartment loudly threatening one another. The *first* course of action for the officers to follow is to

 (A) handcuff the man before he has a chance to strike the woman
 (B) get the husband and wife into separate rooms for a while
 (C) ask the man and wife to explain why they are upset
 (D) arrest the angrier of the two.

29. A police officer, on patrol one night, sees a woman standing alone in a vacant lot. He should

 (A) ignore the woman since she can do no harm there
 (B) ask the woman whether she needs assistance
 (C) order her to leave the lot since she has no business being there
 (D) greet her courteously and continue on patrol.

30. An officer on foot patrol hears a siren and looks up to see a car speeding in his direction. Several blocks behind is a patrol car, apparently giving chase. As the speeding car goes by, the officer should

 (A) fire his gun at the tires
 (B) attempt to flag it down
 (C) fire his gun at the driver
 (D) get as good a description of the car as he can.

31. One Sunday, the police receive a complaint that a small appliance store is open in violation of the Sunday closing law. In line with routine police procedure, an officer is sent to close the store and issue a summons to the owner. When the officer arrives at the store, the owner says that the shop is open because he badly needs the money. The officer should

    (A) issue a summons but allow the owner to remain open for a little while
    (B) close the store and forget about the summons
    (C) issue a summons and close the store
    (D) close the store and warn the owner that next time a summons will be issued.

32. The police receive a report one night that a ground-floor apartment is being burglarized. One of the two officers responding to the call enters the front door of the apartment house. The other officer, with gun in hand, goes into an alley in back of the apartment building. A few yards ahead of him, he sees someone crouching in the shadows. The officer orders the person to come out slowly. Whoever is there jumps up and dashes down the alley. The officer should

    (A) fire his gun at the fleeing person
    (B) ignore the person since there is no proof that he has done anything wrong
    (C) chase after the person and try to catch him
    (D) let the person go, but notify other police units to be on the lookout for him.

33. When a police officer responds to a call, a woman tells him that she is afraid her teenage daughter will run away while she (the mother) is in the hospital. She asks the police officer to help. The officer should

    (A) take the daughter into protective custody
    (B) tell the woman that she should not waste a police officer's time on such things
    (C) explain to the woman that this is not a police matter and tell her where she may be able to get help
    (D) give the daughter a lecture and threaten to arrest her if she runs away.

34. One evening, paint is sprayed on the window of a ground-floor apartment. The next morning the tenant of the apartment stops a passing police officer and shows her the painted window. The tenant believes that the spraying was done by a boy who lives in the apartment building, and asks the police officer to make the boy remove the paint. The officer should

    (A) tell the tenant that a police officer can act only on the basis of positive evidence
    (B) tell the boy's parents that they are responsible for having the paint removed
    (C) tell the boy's parents to punish their son
    (D) tell the tenant to forget it since "boys will be boys"

35. Late one night, an officer on foot patrol observes a middle-aged man standing outside a bar counting a large roll of bills. He knows the man as someone who lives a block away. As the officer gets closer, he realizes that the man is very drunk. The officer would be most helpful if he said,

    (A) "Get that money out of sight and learn to hold your liquor."
    (B) "If you have to count your money, do it inside the bar."
    (C) "You'd better tell me where all that money came from."
    (D) "Better put the money away and let me walk you home."

36. A police officer chases a suspected burglar down a street that is crowded with people and cars. Suddenly, the suspect turns and fires a gun, narrowly missing the officer. The officer should

    (A) continue the chase with caution
    (B) stop the chase before someone gets hurt
    (C) shoot back before the suspect gets away
    (D) fire a warning shot over the suspect's head.

37. Officer Thompson, who is stationed in a Manhattan precinct, has recently moved his family to a home in a different borough. Several of his new neighbors tell Thompson that for many years an illegal betting parlor has been operating in the rear of a nearby stationery store. According to his neighbors, the police are aware of the betting parlor, but do not interfere with its operation. Thompson has been regularly buying newspapers and magazines at the store. On the basis of what he has learned, he should

    (A) stay away from the store, and report what he has been told to the local police station
    (B) stay away from the store, but take no other action
    (C) continue to visit the store and personally investigate the truth of the information
    (D) stay away from the store and report what he has been told to his own surperiors.

38. A police officer sees a young man throw a brick through the front window of a jewelry store and disappear into a crowd at the end of the block. The *best* course of action for the officer to take is to

    (A) get into the crowd as quickly as possible in search of the young man
    (B) try to find persons who can identify the young man
    (C) request help by radio and remain near the broken window to prevent burglary
    (D) yell to nearby pedestrians to get after the escaping man.

39. A police officer on foot patrol on a Sunday night observes two men he does not recognize carrying supplies from an unfinished building to a parked car. He should

    (A) stop the two men and ask for an explanation
    (B) stay out of sight so that he can observe them unnoticed
    (C) arrest the two men and give them a chance to explain in the station house
    (D) call the police station for instructions.

40. A hysterical woman rushes up to a police officer and says she is afraid her baby has been kidnapped. She had left her baby outside a supermarket while she shopped, and the baby was gone when she came out. The *first* thing the police officer should do is

    (A) tell the woman to call her husband

    (B) hail a passing car to search the neighborhood
    (C) call the police station for assistance
    (D) make sure the baby is not in the supermarket.

41. In general, police officers should make a point of getting personally acquainted with the storekeepers, businesspeople, and residents in the area they patrol. In making themselves known, police officers should

    (A) warn that they will not allow any complaints in their area
    (B) make it plain that the police officer's job is to serve the community
    (C) make it clear that they will help the community only if the community will help them
    (D) mention that inside information is always worth money to the police.

42. While on patrol in midtown, two police officers see a well-dressed woman standing by a late-model car. She calls to them as they drive by. When they stop, the woman explains that in the course of a day of shopping she has lost her car keys. She gives her name and an address in Paterson, New Jersey. The car is locked, and she asks the officers if they can open the car and start it for her without a key. The *first* thing the officers should do is

    (A) verify ownership of the car
    (B) start the car by jumping the ignition wires
    (C) pry open a window and release the door lock
    (D) accompany the woman to the stores where she may have lost the keys.

43. A child calls the police emergency number and screams that her father is beating her mother to death. On responding to the call for help, two police officers find that the fight is over. The woman is unharmed and unwilling to press charges against her husband, who is present. The officers should

    (A) take no action, but make it clear to the woman that they are angry with her for refusing to press charges against her husband
    (B) offer their assistance and, if it is not accepted, leave
    (C) arrest the husband and take the wife to the precinct house to sign a complaint against her husband
    (D) apologize for bothering them unnecessarily and leave.

44. While off duty in a neighborhood bar, a police officer overhears a man who has had too much to drink. The man threatens to break a chair over another person's head. If the man who is drunk picks up the chair, the police officer should

    (A) avoid interfering in the matter since it is none of his business
    (B) draw his gun and force the man to drop the chair
    (C) call the nearest precinct house and request the police assistance
    (D) identify himself as a police officer and tell the man to leave the bar and go home.

45. Two police officers on patrol come upon a large and disorderly mob of men, women, and children. The crowd is throwing bricks and bottles, and several store windows have been broken. The officers should

    (A) fire one or two warning shots over the heads of the crowd
    (B) radio the precinct house and ask for assistance
    (C) mingle with the crowd in order to find out what is going on
    (D) identify and arrest the leaders of the mob.

46. A police station receives a report that a man plans to shoot himself. Two police officers are sent to the address given, which is in a neighborhood where most of the people speak Spanish. The officers find the man's wife frightened and in tears. A neighbor who does not speak Spanish tells them that the man has locked himself in the bathroom and that neither the man nor his wife speak English. The officers are not able to speak more than a few words of Spanish. The *first* thing they should do is

    (A) send for tear gas, which can be used to drive the man from the bathroom
    (B) find someone who speaks both English and Spanish so they can talk with the man and his wife
    (C) force their way into the bathroom and quickly disarm the man
    (D) get everyone out of the apartment and allow the man an hour or two to calm down.

47. Two police officers stop for lunch at a diner that has just opened under new management. After the officers have been served, the manager of the diner walks over to their table and introduces himself. He hopes they will eat often at his diner and tells them that this first lunch is "on the house." The officers should

    (A) thank him for his offer, but insist on paying for their lunch
    (B) accept his offer, but make it clear that they will pay for their lunch in the future
    (C) warn the manager about offering bribes to police officers
    (D) accept his offer and thank him for being friendly to the local police.

48. After breaking up a fight at a party, two police officers find it necessary to arrest a man. While taking him to their patrol car, they find that a small crowd has gathered on the street. The people in the crowd are friends and neighbors of the man and they angrily demand that he be set free. The *first* action that the officers should take is to

    (A) draw their guns to prevent the crowd from getting out of hand
    (B) offer to go back inside and discuss the matter with the leaders of the crowd
    (C) threaten the crowd with arrest if anyone tries to get in their way
    (D) tell them the man is under arrest and let them know where he is being taken.

49. A man runs out of a movie theater and calls to a police officer. He tells the officer that there may be a bomb in a telephone booth inside the theater. The officer hurries to the theater and finds a length of pipe wedged under a phone booth seat. Visible at one end are some electrical tape and wires. The *first* thing the officer should do is

    (A) tell the people in the theater that there is a bomb and that they should leave at once
    (B) try to remove the pipe to get a better look at it
    (C) tell the manager to have the theater emptied quickly and quietly
    (D) call the police bomb squad.

50. A small store has been broken into and money has been stolen from the cash register. The owner of the store tells one of the investigating police officers that an employee forgot to turn on the burglar alarm system the night the crime occurred. The officer should

   (A) suggest ways of preventing future burglaries
   (B) urge that the forgetful employee be fired
   (C) point out that the store is responsible for the crime
   (D) arrest the employee on suspicion of being involved in the crime.

51. A patrol car stops a truck that is being driven at night without lights. The driver of the truck is a large, powerfully built man who is slightly drunk. He climbs down from the truck cab and waits as the two police officers approach him. Suddenly, he swings at one of the officers but misses. He then turns and lunges at the second officer. The officers should

   (A) keep out of the truck driver's reach until he cools off
   (B) use physical force to stop the truck driver's attack
   (C) fire a warning shot over the driver's head to stop him
   (D) calls for police assistance on the patrol car radio.

52. The Saints, a neighborhood street gang, has been in trouble from time to time with the police. The police think that the gang may have been responsible for the recent burglary of a pawn shop, and they have questioned the gang members about that crime. Shortly after 9 P.M. one night, two officers driving on patrol see three members of the Saints standing by themselves on a corner. The officers should

   (A) drive slowly by the gang members in order to let them know that the police are watching them
   (B) take the gang members to the police station for further questioning
   (C) park the patrol car and prepare to follow the gang members on foot
   (D) search the gang members for possession of stolen goods.

53. The police receive a call from the owner of a delicatessen who reports that a man is hanging around outside his store. Two police officers promptly respond to the call and find a young man standing outside the delicatessen. From inside the store the owner points to the man, indicating that he is the person under suspicion. The officers should

   (A) remain in their car and watch the man until he leaves
   (B) tell the man to move along or they will arrest him
   (C) ask the man his name and what he is doing there
   (D) ignore the man and tell the owner he should not be so nervous.

54. Police Officer Helen Murphy is directing traffic at a busy intersection when she sees two men fighting on the sidewalk about half a block away. A crowd is already beginning to gather. She hurries to the scene of the fight and finds one of the men lying unconscious with blood on his face. The second man, who is about 6 feet tall, brushes off his jacket and turns to leave. Officer Murphy, who is 5′3″, tells the man to stay where he is. The man stops, stares at her, and says, "No lady cop can tell me what to do." The *first* thing Officer Murphy should do is

   (A) tend to the injured person and allow the second man to leave if he wants to
   (B) place the second man under arrest
   (C) draw her gun and tell the second man she will shoot if he refuses to obey her
   (D) ask some of the bystanders to grab the second man and stop him from leaving.

55. Late one night, the police receive a telephone call from a man who complains that a loud party in his apartment building is disturbing the peace. The man will not give his name. When two officers arrive at the address given, the street is quiet except for the faint sound of drums coming from someone's apartment. The officers should

   (A) locate the source of the drums and arrest the tenant for disturbing the peace
   (B) knock on several doors and ask whether the drums are bothering anyone in the apartment building
   (C) continue on patrol without taking any action regarding the drums
   (D) locate the source of the drums and ask the tenant to lower the volume of the music.

Section IV: Basic Arithmetic

Directions: Questions 56 through 65 test your ability to perform basic arithmetical operations. Each question is followed by four choices. Choose the one best answer (A, B, C, or D) and blacken the corresponding space and your answer sheet. You may use the margins for work space in solving the problems.

Answer questions 56 and 57 on the basis of the calendar shown below.

56. The first day of a special duty assignment was the third Monday of August. The assignment lasted two weeks and one day. The final day of the assignment was

(A) September 4
(B) September 3
(C) September 11
(D) September 10

57. A man works for five days each week, Tuesday through Saturday. How many days did he work in August?

(A) 22
(B) 23
(C) 24
(D) 25

58. The diagram at the bottom of column 1 shows an automobile fuel gauge. The arrow on the gauge indicates that the gas tank is

(A) ⅓ full
(B) ⅜ full
(C) ¼ full
(D) ⅝ full

59. If the time shown on the clock above represents the present time, the time in 25 minutes will be

(A) 2:55
(B) 4:55
(C) 3:50
(D) 3:25

60. Five pounds of uncut heroin are found by police in the trunk of a car. One ounce of uncut heroin is enough to make approximately 500 bags which sell for five dollars each on the street. How many five-dollar bags could have been made from the five pounds of heroin found?

(A) 50,000
(B) 40,000
(C) 25,000
(D) 2500

Answer questions 61 through 63 on the basis of the following passage.

In the police department, the time of day is given by a four-digit number between 0000 and 2400. The first two digits represent the hours from 00 to 24. The last two digits express minutes from 00 to 59. For example, 0326 hours is 3:26 A.M.; 1200 hours is noon; 1443 is 2:43 P.M.; and 2400 hours is midnight.

61. If a patrol car passed a store at 0100 and returned every 2 hours and 10 minutes after that, it would also pass the store at

(A) 0710
(B) 0330
(C) 0930
(D) 0520.

62. The time is now 2027 hours. How many hours and minutes is it before midnight?

(A) 3 hours 33 minutes
(B) 3 hours 3 minutes
(C) 4 hours 13 minutes
(D) 4 hours 3 minutes.

63. The time at which a crime occurred was 0142 hours. The police were notified of the crime a half hour later. They arrived at the scene a quarter of an hour after that. They stayed there for one hour. What time did the police leave the scene of the crime?

(A) 0732 hours
(B) 0723 hours
(C) 0327 hours
(D) 0237 hours.

Answer questions 64 and 65 on the basis of the following table.

Borough	Population 1970	1960
Bronx	1,471,701	1,424,815
Brooklyn	2,602,012	2,627,319
Manhattan	1,539,233	1,698,281
Queens	1,987,174	1,809,578
Staten Island	295,443	221,991
Total	7,895,563	7,781,984

64. For which borough was the change in number of residents greatest between 1960 and 1970?

(A) Manhattan
(B) Bronx
(C) Staten Island
(D) Queens.

65. In 1970, the population of Queens was approximately what fraction of the total population of New York City?

(A) One-half
(B) One-eighth
(C) One-third
(D) One-fourth.

Section V: Word Meaning

Directions: Questions 66 through 70 test your understanding of some words commonly found in newspapers and magazines, and often used in police work. Each question is followed by four choices. Choose the one best answer (A, B, C, or D) and blacken the corresponding space on your answer sheet.

66. A car and a truck were in an accident. The inspector who tested the truck's brakes reported that they were *defective*. By this, he meant that the brakes

    (A) were not working properly
    (B) were in good shape
    (C) had been relined
    (D) had nothing to do with the accident.

67. When taken to the station house, the woman said that she had been *previously* arrested. She meant that she had

    (A) never been arrested
    (B) been arrested illegally
    (C) been arrested by mistake
    (D) been arrested before.

68. The prisoner claimed that the wallet found in his pocket when he was arrested belonged to his wife. His story was *verified* when

    (A) the wallet was found to be empty
    (B) his wife could not be found
    (C) his wife's name was found in the wallet
    (D) his wife said she had her wallet.

69. A police officer watched a young woman cross from one side of the avenue to the other and was sure that she *disregarded* the traffic light. The officer believed that the woman

    (A) looked at the light
    (B) crossed with the light
    (C) paid no attention to the light
    (D) responded to the light.

70. During a heavy rainstorm one night, a car went off the road and hit a pole. The police officer who investigated wrote in her report that the weather *contributed* to the accident. The officer meant that the weather

    (A) caused the accident
    (B) was partly responsible for the accident
    (C) was the only explanation for the accident
    (D) had nothing to do with the accident.

Section VI: Reading Comprehension

Directions: Questions 71 through 86 test your ability to read and understand written materials. Seven reading passages are presented. Read each passage carefully and answer the questions based on each one. For each question, choose the one best answer (A, B, C, or D) and blacken the corresponding space on your answer sheet. Your answers must be based solely on the information presented in the passages.

Answer questions 71 and 72 on the basis of the following passage.

From time to time, a police officer may have to appear in court as a witness in a criminal case. The content of his or her statement is very important. The way testimony is given may create a favorable or an unfavorable impression in court. The officer should be able to talk about the kind of evidence he or she has and where the evidence came from; otherwise, cross-examination may confuse him or her and may reduce the value of what he or she has to say. If facts are reviewed before testifying, the officer will be better prepared to carry out the assignment, which is to provide accurate information in such a way that its meaning will be understood by the court.

71. Which one of the following statements regarding testimony by a police officer may be inferred from the passage?

(A) The content of the officer's testimony should make the case stronger.

(B) Not only what the officer says in court is important, but also how he or she says it.

(C) The officer should memorize all of the facts that he or she may be asked to give.

(D) How the testimony is given is more important than what is said.

72. When testifying in court, the chief responsibility of a police officer is to

(A) prepare the case ahead of time

(B) make a favorable impression

(C) avoid becoming confused during cross-examination

(D) present factual evidence in a clear manner.

Answer questions 73 and 74 on the basis of the following passage.

According to a report on police corruption, some police officers collected "pad" payments on a regular basis. These were bribes from people whose businesses would have suffered if they or their customers had received parking tickets. For example, some bar owners paid the police to allow their customers to double- or triple-park without being ticketed. Payoffs were made by construction companies and businesses that made pickups and deliveries in crowded areas. Some small companies used unlicensed drivers during rush seasons and wanted to make sure that the police did not bother them. Police corruption also took the form of "scores." These were one-time payments to police officers to overlook moving traffic violations. Taxi drivers, truck drivers, and other motorists whose livelihoods depended on having a driver's license were often willing to make such payments.

73. On the basis of the information given in the passage, which of the following statements is correct?

(A) Police corruption was supported by law-breaking citizens.
(B) In general, "pad" payments involved less money than "scores."
(C) The police should have overlooked minor violations.
(D) Taxi drivers were more likely to bribe police officers than were business people.

74. According to the passage, "pad" payments and "scores" both involved

(A) unlicensed drivers
(B) payoffs made on a regular basis
(C) police officers who were willing to be bribed
(D) seasonal city traffic conditions.

Answer questions 75 through 77 on the basis of the following passage.

As a rule, police officers arriving at the scene of an automobile accident should first care for victims who need immediate medical treatment. If necessary, the officers should ask bystanders to help warn approaching cars and keep traffic moving. People should be kept out of traffic lanes and at a safe distance from the damaged cars. This will help to avoid additional accidents at the scene and will allow for faster movement of emergency vehicles. Such action will also protect any evidence that might be important later.

75. Among the following actions that police officers might take at the scene of an accident, which one should be taken *first*?

(A) Warn approaching cars of the accident.
(B) Keep the bystanders moving.
(C) Find out which driver was responsible for the accident.
(D) Get the license plate numbers of the cars involved.

76. The *first* thing that police officers should do when they get to the scene of an accident is to

(A) take care of the injured who need immediate help

(B) ask for the help of bystanders
(C) warn oncoming cars and keep traffic moving
(D) protect evidence showing how the accident happened.

77. An important reason for keeping people out of the traffic lanes is to

(A) allow ambulances to get through
(B) allow photographers to get pictures of the accident
(C) keep crowds from forming
(D) keep souvenir hunters away from the scene.

Answer questions 78 and 79 on the basis of the following passage.

Many factors must be considered when a police officer is deciding whether or not to make an arrest. If an arrest is not considered legal, it could mean that some evidence will not be allowed in court. At other times, an arrest may tip off a suspect before evidence can be found. In all cases, an arrest takes away from a person the very important right to liberty. It is also very upsetting to a person, causing worry and possibly loss of money. On the other hand, an officer must also realize that if an arrest is delayed too long, the suspect may run away or the evidence may be destroyed.

78. In deciding whether to make an arrest, a police officer should

(A) consider whether the suspect is a known criminal
(B) realize that an innocent person could be very upset by being arrested
(C) not delay since evidence can be found later
(D) not worry about the innocent person because the courts will free the innocent.

79. A judge may refuse to accept evidence of a crime if

(A) it interfered with the suspect's right to liberty
(B) it was found after the suspect was tipped off
(C) the suspect was able to get away
(D) it was collected during an illegal arrest.

Answer questions 80 and 81 on the basis of the following passage.

The sergeant in command of a team of police officers on special assignment gave extra instructions only to the inexperienced officers in the group. Each of the experienced officers was to guard one of the four exits from a building while the sergeant led the remaining three officers through the front door.

80. The plan to be followed

(A) required the participation of all members of the team
(B) is standard operating procedure
(C) was known only to the experienced police officers
(D) did not require the sergeant to take part.

81. The total number of inexperienced officers in the group was

(A) eight
(B) seven
(C) four
(D) three.

Answer questions 82 and 83 on the basis of the following passage.

A factory hires an armed guard for its front gate. The guard is given the following instructions:

Do not let anyone enter the factory after 6 P.M. without a company identification card with a photograph on it. If a person does not have such identification, check with the Security Office for instructions. If an alarm goes off in the factory at any time, no one is allowed to leave through the front gate. Stay at your post unless the Security Office orders you to leave it.

82. At 5:15 P.M. an alarm is sounded in the factory. Shortly afterwards, a man whom the guard recognizes as a company vice president runs up and tells him to find out what the trouble is. The vice president offers to watch the gate while the guard is in the factory. The guard should

   (A) remain at the front gate and prevent anyone from leaving
   (B) follow the instructions of the vice president
   (C) enter the factory with the vice president to investigate the alarm
   (D) assume that the alarm went off by accident since it is before 6 P.M.

83. A visitor arrives at 6:15 P.M. in a chauffeur-driven car. The visitor explains that he had an appointment at 5:45 P.M. with a company official but was delayed in traffic. The guard should

   (A) allow the man to enter since his appointment was for 5:45
   (B) ask him to wait while he checks with the Security Office
   (C) ask the man to please make another appointment
   (D) permit the man to go in since he is clearly an important person.

Answer questions 84 through 86 on the basis of the following passage.

A recent newspaper story reported that, in New York City, four of the seven major types of crime increased during the first half of this year, with the rate of increase greater than 10 percent for rapes, assaults, and homicides. However, larcenies, robberies, and burglaries decreased, and the overall rate for the seven major crimes went down. Auto thefts are the seventh type of major crime. The police commissioner noted that the rise in homicides was related to the illegal weapons that were available. He estimated that about 80 percent of 8000 confiscated weapons were pistols that could easily be concealed.

84. It appears that the number of concealable pistols that were confiscated during the first six months of the year was about

   (A) 800
   (B) 1600
   (C) 6400
   (D) 8000.

85. The rate of auto thefts

   (A) increased less than 10 percent
   (B) decreased more than 10 percent
   (C) increased more than 10 percent
   (D) decreased less than 10 percent.

86. According to the paragraph, the rate of killings in New York City

   (A) was not included in the report
   (B) decreased the same as the rate for burglaries
   (C) did not change for the half year
   (D) increased during the first half of the year

Section VII: Completion of Forms

Directions: Questions 87 through 96 test your ability to fill out forms correctly. Two incidents are described, each requiring that a police form be filled out. Read the questions applying to each form. For each question, choose the one best answer (A, B, C, or D) and blacken the corresponding space on your answer sheet.

Answer questions 87 through 91 on the basis of the following passage and the Report of Aid Given form shown beneath the passage.

Police Officers Margaret Firestone and Harry Davis are partners on patrol. They see a man lying on his back on the southwest corner of Second Avenue and Sixth Street. Officer Firestone leaves the patrol car to look at him more closely. The man is dressed in clean clothes and seems to have stopped breathing. Officer Firestone bends over him, makes a quick inspection, and tells Officer Davis to send for an ambulance. She begins to administer mouth-to-mouth resuscitation. At this point, the man becomes fully conscious and states that this has happened before. He insists that all he needs is a glass of water. He does not want to go to the hospital, nor does he want to be driven home. Officer Davis gets a glass of water for the man from a nearby restaurant. The man refuses to give his name and will not wait for the ambulance. He drinks the water, thanks the officers for their help, and walks north on Second Avenue where he disappears from view. Officer Firestone then fills out a Report of Aid Given form like the one shown here.

REPORT OF AID GIVEN

Identification

Date _____

Time _____

Place _____

Name of Person Aided_____ ☐ Unknown

Nature of Problem

☐ Abandoned   ☐ Destitute   ☐ Sick
☐ Neglected   ☐ Lost   ☐ Injured

Nature of Sickness or Injury

☐ Mental   ☐ Physical   ☐ Unknown

Aid Given

☐ Artificial Respiration   ☐ Food or Water
☐ Control of Bleeding   ☐ Clothing or Blankets
☐ Temporary Splint   ☐ Other

Disposition of Case

☐ Taken Home   ☐ Left in Custody of Friend or Relative
☐ Removed to Hospital   ☐ Taken to Morgue.
☐ Left at Place of Occurrence   ☐ Other

Name of Officer Reporting_____

87. Under Identification, the correct entry for Place is
    (A) Second Avenue, Sixth Street, SW corner
    (B) Second and Seventh
    (C) corner of Sixth Avenue and Second Street
    (D) Second Avenue North, East Sixth Street.

88. Since the man refused to give his name, Officer Firestone should check the box for
    (A) Other, under Aid Given
    (B) Unknown, under Identification
    (C) Other, under Disposition of Case
    (D) Unknown, under Nature of Sickness or Injury.

89. Under Nature of Problem, the correct box to check is
    (A) Injured
    (B) Sick
    (C) Neglected
    (D) Destitute

90. The correct boxes to check under Aid Given are
    (A) Food or Water and Other
    (B) Food or Water and Clothing or Blankets
    (C) Artificial Respiration and Food or Water
    (D) Artificial Respiration and Other.

91. Under Disposition of Case, Officer Firestone should check the box of
    (A) Removed to Hospital
    (B) Left in Custody of Friend or Relative
    (C) Other
    (D) Left at Place of Occurrence.

Answer questions 92 through 96 on the basis of the following passage and the Accident Report form shown below.

At approximately 5:00 P.M. on a foggy, rainy afternoon, Police Officer Ressa arrived at the scene of an accident a few minutes after it occurred. On the basis of his own observations and from the statements of the persons involved in the accident, he decided that the accident happened this way: Mr. Goldsmith was driving his car east on Tenth Street. Tenth is a straight, one-way street that runs downhill as one goes from west to east. At the intersection of Tenth Street and Pacific Avenue, Mr. Goldsmith came to a full stop for a red light. When the light turned green, he started downhill and immediately struck Mr. Bates, a 43-year-old high school teacher who was jogging north on Pacific Avenue. Mr. Bates was not seriously injured. He admitted that he had been careless in crossing the intersection. Police Officer Ressa filled out an Accident Report form, a portion of which is shown below.

ACCIDENT REPORT

Date _____ Time _____ Location of Accident _____

Vehicle in Collison With

- ☐ Pedestrian
- ☐ Other Vehicle
- ☐ Train
- ☐ Animal
- ☐ Motorcycle
- ☐ Fixed Object
- ☐ Bicycle
- ☐ Other

Type of Traffic Control

- ☐ Police Officer
- ☐ Signal Light in Operation
- ☐ Signal Light Not in Operation
- ☐ Flashing Light
- ☐ Stop Sign
- ☐ Yield Sign
- ☐ Other
- ☐ None

Character of Road

- ☐ Straight and Level
- ☐ Straight on Hill
- ☐ Straight Approaching Hilltop
- ☐ Curve and Level
- ☐ Curve on Hill
- ☐ Curve Approaching Hilltop

Action of Pedestrian at Intersection

- ☐ Crossing With Signal
- ☐ Crossing Against Signal
- ☐ Crossing Diagonally
- ☐ Crossing, No Signal

Action of Vehicle at Time of Accident

- ☐ Going Straight Ahead
- ☐ Overtaking
- ☐ Making Right Turn
- ☐ Making Left Turn
- ☐ Making U-Turn
- ☐ Backing Up
- ☐ Starting from Parking
- ☐ Slowing or Stopping
- ☐ Parked

92. Under the section, Vehicle in Collision With, Officer Ressa should have checked the box for
    (A) Pedestrian
    (B) Other Vehicle
    (C) Fixed Object
    (D) Other.

93. The box Officer Ressa should have checked under Type of Traffic Control is
    (A) Flashing Light
    (B) Other
    (C) Signal Light in Operation
    (D) Stop Sign.

94. Under Character of Road, Officer Ressa should have checked the box for
    (A) Curve Approaching Hilltop
    (B) Straight Approaching Hilltop
    (C) Straight on Hill
    (D) Curve on Hill.

95. The box Officer Ressa should have checked under Action of Pedestrian at Intersection is
    (A) Crossing Against Signal
    (B) Crossing, No Signal
    (C) Crossing With Signal
    (D) Crossing Diagonally.

96. Officer Ressa should have checked which box under Action of Vehicle at Time of Accident?
    (A) Starting from Parking
    (B) Slowing or Stopping
    (C) Going Straight Ahead
    (D) Overtaking.

Section VII: Diagrams

Directions: Questions 97 through 100 test your ability to understand and use information presented in diagrams. Each question is followed by four choices. Choose the one best answer (A, B, C, or D) and blacken the corresponding space on your answer sheet. (You may draw on the diagrams in the test booklet if you wish.)

Answer question 97 on the basis of the street map shown below.

The city street map shown above is divided into four police patrol sectors as follows:

—Sector Adam: Bounded by Tudor Street, Newton Street, Hub Street, Athens Street, and Canal Street.

—Sector Boy: Bounded by Tudor Street, F Street, West 4th Street, Hub Street, and Newton Street.

—Sector Charles: Bounded by West 4th Street, F Street, West 2nd Street, C Street, and Hub Street.

—Sector David: Bounded by Athens Street, C Street, West 2nd Street, and Canal Street.

97. A bank is held up in the block bounded by West 4th Street, Summer Street, and Hub Street. The crime occurred in Sector

(A) David
(B) Charles

(C) Boy
(D) Adam

Answer question 98 on the basis of the passage and diagram below.

As indicated by arrows on the street map shown below, Adams and River Streets are one-way going north. Main is one-way going south, and Market is one-way going northwest. Oak and Ash are one-way streets going east, and Elm is one-way going west.

98. A patrol car heading north on River Street between Ash and Elm Streets receives a call to proceed to the intersection of Adams and Oak. In order to travel the shortest distance and not break any traffic regulations, the patrol car should turn

(A) left on Elm and right on Market
(B) left on Market and proceed directly to Oak
(C) left on Elm and right on Adams
(D) left on Oak and proceed directly to Adams

In the diagrams for questions 99 and 100, symbols are used to represent vehicles and pedestrians and their movements.

—Vehicles are shown by this symbol: front   ⬭   rear

—Pedestrians are represented by a circle: ○

—Solid lines shown the path and direction of a vehicle or person *before* an accident happened: ⟶

—Dotted lines show the path and direction of a vehicle or person *after* an accident happened: ----→

99. Mrs. Wagner was walking across the intersection of Elm Street and Willow Avenue when she was struck by a car approaching from her right. After hitting Mrs. Wagner, the car swerved left and ran into a tree. Which of the four diagrams below best represents the accident described?

100. An automobile accident occurred at the intersection of Mill Road and Grove Street. Cars 1 and 3 were proceeding south on Mill Road and Car 2 was proceeding west on Grove Street. When Car 1 stopped quickly to avoid hitting Car 2, it was immediately stuck from behind by Car 3. Car 2 continued west on Grove Street without stopping. Which of the following four diagrams best represents the accident described?

ANSWER KEY FOR PRACTICE EXAMINATION 3

1. C	21. D	41. B	61. D	81. D
2. A	22. C	42. A	62. A	82. B
3. D	23. D	43. B	63. C	83. A
4. A	24. B	44. D	64. D	84. C
5. B	25. D	45. B	65. D	85. A
6. B	26. C	46. B	66. A	86. D
7. D	27. C	47. A	67. D	87. A
8. D	28. B	48. D	68. C	88. B
9. B	29. B	49. C	69. C	89. B
10. C	30. D	50. A	70. B	90. C
11. B	31. C	51. B	71. B	91. C
12. B	32. C	52. A	72. D	92. A
13. A	33. C	53. C	73. A	93. C
14. C	34. A	54. B	74. C	94. C
15. B	35. D	55. D	75. A	95. A
16. C	36. A	56. B	76. A	96. C
17. D	37. D	57. B	77. A	97. D
18. A	38. C	58. B	78. B	98. A
19. A	39. A	59. C	79. D	99. B
20. A	40. D	60. B	80. A	100. D

EXPLANATORY ANSWERS FOR PRACTICE EXAMINATION 3

1. **(C)** In the left foreground, a boy wearing a long-sleeved shirt with the sleeves pushed up is passing between a light-colored parked car and a dark-colored double-parked car. His hands are not visible, so the answer cannot refer to anything he is carrying.

2. **(A)** The men across the street are standing in a group in front of the barber shop. Since they are facing one another, they cannot all be looking at the watch repair shop. The cars are parked at meters, so they are not at the bus stop.

3. **(D)** The man next to the light-colored car is closest to the watch repair shop.

4. **(A)** The dark-colored car is a four-door model and is unoccupied. There is no indication of direction nor can you see the license plates, so neither (B) nor (C) could be the answer.

5. **(B)** By the direction of her legs, body, and head, you can see that the woman is entering the store and is looking towards her right in the direction of the watch repair shop.

For questions 6 through 15, if you had any incorrect answers, refer back to the photographs of the faces at the beginning of this examination. You will then be able to compare the faces in the questions with those given in the face section.

16. **(C)** Before a police officer decides on the action to be taken, the officer should collect as much information as possible concerning the matter. The man may not be telling the truth.

17. **(D)** In this case also, the police officer should gather as much information as possible before he or she decides what action should be taken.

18. **(A)** If the man has any identification with him on which his address is noted, the officer may be able to take him to his residence or notify a family member of the man's whereabouts so that arrangements can be made for him to be picked up. This action would avoid any unnecessary detention, hospitalization, or investigation by the missing persons unit.

19. **(A)** Two-way communication should be established to show that the officer is not only there to enforce the laws but also to help people. The officer may not be able to solve citizen's problems, but the officer should be able to refer them to sources where they may be able to receive help. Two-way communication is the most effective means of dealing with all persons.

20. **(A)** A police officer, when dealing with an apparently mentally disturbed person, should try to keep the situation calm and not do anything to excite the individual. Since the person may not be in full control of his or her faculties, the officer should never consider the person harmless.

21. **(D)** The police officer should remember that the woman is overly upset because her husband is being arrested. The officer's best recourse in this situation is to try to calm the woman down.

22. **(C)** The officers' first concern should be getting medical attention for the son.

23. **(D)** If the police officer can help correct a situation quickly, the officer should take that appropriate action. In this case, checking the fuse box may solve the problem immediately.

24. **(B)** The officer should avoid any argument or heated debate with this individual. The officer should use statistics to back up his point.

25. **(D)** The officer is not a babysitter. His job is to patrol a post in order to prevent crime.

26. **(C)** Regardless of Smith's past history, he should be treated like anyone else. Only the force necessary to control Smith should be used.

27. **(C)** The police officers should remember that pickets stir up the emotions of the people involved. Since these people are upset, their insults should be taken as an expression of these emotions; however, the officers should remain alert for the possibility of violent action.

28. **(B)** It is apparent that the argument is a heated one. The parties should be separated so that the officers may find out each person's side of the story as well as decrease the potential for violence.

29. **(B)** A woman is not usually seen standing alone in a vacant lot. The officer should investigate to see if the woman needs any assistance.

30. **(D)** The car is apparently trying to escape from the police. If the officer steps into the path of the car to flag it down, there is a good chance that the officer will be injured or killed. If he shoots the driver or the tires of the car, the car will go out of control and may injure innocent people. Also, the officer has insufficient information to determine whether a firearm should be used in this case. At this point, the best thing the officer can do is get a good description of the car as it speeds by.

31. **(C)** This is a clear violation of the law, and the officer must comply with police procedures.

32. **(C)** The officer doesn't have sufficient information to justify the use of a firearm. There is the likelihood, however, that this person was involved in the burglary so the officer should give chase and try to apprehend the individual.

33. **(C)** This is not a police matter as there is no violation of the law involved. The only thing the officer can do is to refer the mother to an agency that may be able to help her.

34. **(A)** The tenant only *believes* that the boy sprayed the paint; there is no evidence that he *did* spray it. Therefore, no police action should be taken at this time.

35. **(D)** A drunken man displaying a large amount of money would be easy prey for a mugger. The officer knows where the man lives, and since it is only a short distance away, it would be proper for the officer to walk the man home. This would prevent the man from injuring himself because of his drunken state as well as prevent the possibility of his becoming a mugger's victim.

36. **(A)** The officer has the responsibility to try to apprehend the suspect. Since the street is crowded with people and cars, the officer should avoid returning fire. He should seek cover and proceed with caution. The officer should use whatever tactics are necessary to avoid injury to innocent persons.

37. **(D)** Because there is the possibility of illegal activity taking place in the stationery store, Officer Thompson should avoid giving the store his business. The officer has the obligation to report what he has learned to his superiors. Since local police may be involved, a report to his own superiors may be more effective than a report to the local precinct.

38. **(C)** The officer should radio a description of the young man to officers in the area and then stay near the broken window to prevent people from looting the store.

39. **(A)** Because of the day and the time, the officer should suspect that a crime may be in progress. Therefore, the officer should approach the men cautiously and ask them to identify themselves and give an explanation of their conduct.

40. **(D)** It is possible that someone could have taken the baby into the store, either to the store manager to seek assistance or to a phone to call the police. The supermarket should be checked *first* before leaving the premises where the baby was last seen.

41. **(B)** A police officer's job is to render aid and service to the community.

42. **(A)** She wants the officers to help her start the car without a key. The officers have no proof that she owns the car. Therefore, the officers should request proof that she owns the car before giving the woman any aid.

43. **(B)** Since there is no sign of injury and the woman doesn't want to press charges, the police officers can only offer their assistance. If the woman doesn't want any help, there is no reason to stay in the home.

44. **(D)** If it appears that this man is going to injure another, the officer has an obligation to get involved. If the drunken man starts to pick up the chair, the officer should identify himself and tell the man to go home. No crime has been committed so he cannot bring the man up on any charge.

45. **(B)** A large disorderly group of people throwing bricks and bottles cannot be handled by two officers alone. Shots should not be fired since someone could be easily hurt.

46. **(B)** The officers must try to open some line of communication with the man to ascertain just what is going on. They need to find someone who speaks both English and Spanish to act as a interpreter.

47. **(A)** It is not permissible for police officers to accept a meal "on the house" or to receive any other such favors or gifts. They must pay for their meal just like everyone else.

48. **(D)** Very often this type of crowd will begin to disperse after an arresting police officer informs the crowd where the violator is being taken. If this action does not have positive results, other police action may be taken. This, however, should be the *first* action.

49. **(C)** It is possible that the article in the phone booth *is* a bomb. The theater should be emptied quickly and quietly so as to avoid panic and chaos.

50. **(A)** If there is no other evidence that the employee was involved in the crime, no arrest is warranted. A police officer should not suggest that an employee be fired, but he or she can suggest ways of preventing crime from occurring.

51. **(B)** In this particular case, the officers would be justified in using physical force to subdue the individual. Such force would be considered self-defense. Two officers should be able to deal with one truck driver without backup assistance.

52. **(A)** Just the fact that three gang members are standing on a street corner shortly after 9 P.M. is not reason enough for the officers to search them, take them to the station house, or follow them. However, the officers can let the gang members know that they are being watched by driving by slowly. Visible police presence often serves as a deterrent.

53. **(C)** Since the man appears to be loitering, this would justify the police asking for identification and an explanation of conduct.

54. **(B)** A crime has been committed, and the person who committed it is present. Officer Murphy has an obligation to make an arrest.

55. **(D)** The officers can hear the sound of drums. The officers should try to ascertain which apartment the music is coming from and then inform the tenant that loud music is annoying others in the building and must be turned down.

56. **(B)** Two weeks plus one day is 15 days. Fifteen days from August 20 is September 3.

57. **(B)** The man works August 1, 2, 3, 4, 7, 8, 9, 10, 11, 14, 15, 16, 17, 18, 21, 22, 23, 24, 25, 28, 29, 30, 31—a total of 23 days.

58. **(B)** The indicator points to the third of eight markers, therefore, the gas tank is 3/8 full.

59. **(C)** The clock in the diagram shows the time to be 3:25. In 25 minutes, it will be 3:50.

60. **(B)** 1 pound = 16 ounces
16 x 5 = 80 ounces, which is 5 pounds
1 ounce yields 500 bags
500 x 80 = 40,000 bags

61. **(D)** 0100 first pass
0310 second pass
0520 third pass

62. **(A)** Convert 2400 to 2360. Then subtract 2027.
2360
−2027
0333 = 3 hours 33 minutes

63. **(C)** 0142 crime occurred
0212 police notified
0227 police arrive
0327 police leave

64. **(D)** From 1960 to 1970, the population table shows the following changes in the following directions:

Bronx (+) 46,886
Brooklyn (−) 25,307
Manhattan (−) 159,048
Queens (+) 177,596
Staten Island (+) 73,452

Therefore, Queens showed the greatest change.

65. **(D)** Divide 1,987,174 by 7,895,563 and your answer will be just over .25, or 25%.

66. **(A)** *Defective* means *imperfect* or *faulty*. The accident occurred because the truck's brakes failed.

67. **(D)** *Previously* means *at an earlier time*. This was not the woman's first arrest.

68. **(C)** To *verify* is to *prove to be true*. The wife's name in the wallet indicated that it was indeed her wallet and verified his story.

69. **(C)** To *disregard* is to *pay no attention to*. The officer watched the woman cross without looking.

70. **(B)** To *contribute to* is to *have a share in bringing about a result*. The officer noted that the rain was at least partly responsible for the accident, but did not rule out other contributing causes such as the condition of the tires or faulty driving.

71. **(B)** The second sentence says that the content of the testimony is very important. The third sentence says that the way in which the testimony is given is also important. The passage does not say that one is more important than the other.

72. **(D)** The last sentence states that the assignment is to provide accurate information in such a way that its meaning will be understood.

73. **(A)** The passage refers to people making payoffs to police for overlooking breaking of the law.

74. **(C)** Both "pad" payments and "scores" are bribes to police officers to overlook definite violations of the law. The difference between the two types of bribes is that "pad" payments are made on a regular basis for an ongoing offense, while "scores" are one-time payments.

75. **(A)** The passage states that the first action of the police should be to care for the injured. This action is not offered as an answer choice. The passage goes on to next suggest that traffic must be diverted from the scene of the accident. Bystanders may be asked to assist in directing traffic if the police officers are busy tending to the injured.

76. **(A)** This question takes you to the first sentence and the first action.

77. **(A)** The passage suggests that keeping people out of traffic lanes allows for faster movement of emergency vehicles (ambulances).

78. **(B)** The next-to-last sentence states that arrest may be upsetting.

79. **(D)** The second sentence means that illegally collected evidence may not be accepted.

80. **(A)** All of the officers, including the sergeant, had assignments. The experienced officers were to guard the doors while the inexperienced officers entered the building with the sergeant.

81. **(D)** The sergeant gave an assignment to each of the experienced officers. He then led the remaining three, inexperienced officers through the front door.

82. **(A)** The guard's instructions are that in the event of an alarm he or she must remain at the front gate and prohibit all exits until otherwise instructed by the Security Office.

83. **(B)** The instructions clearly state that the guard is not to allow admittance after 6 P.M. to anyone without an identification card. A visitor fits into the category of person without company identification. The instruction is to check with the Security Office for instructions in such instances.

84. **(C)** See the last sentence. 80% of 8000 is 6400.

85. **(A)** There are seven major types of crime: rape, assault, homicide, larceny, robbery, burglary, and auto theft. Of these, larceny, robbery, and burglary decreased. Of those crimes that increased, rape, assault, and homicide increased by more than 10%. The remaining crime, auto theft, increased by a rate of less than 10%.

86. **(D)** Refer to the first sentence of the passage. You should realize that in this question, "killings" is used as a synonym for "homicides."

87. **(A)** Refer to the second sentence of the passage.

88. **(B)** The name of the person aided is to be entered in the Identification section of the form. Since the man did not give Officer Firestone his name, she must check the box for Unknown in the Identification section.

89. **(B)** There was no mention of an injury nor of the man being neglected, so the nature of the problem must be considered an illness.

90. **(C)** The officer gave the man mouth-to-mouth resuscitation and gave him a glass of water.

91. **(C)** The man walked away from the scene after aid had been administered.

92. **(A)** Mr. Bates was jogging, therefore, he is considered a pedestrian.

93. **(C)** Mr. Goldsmith stopped for a red light. When the light turned green, he proceeded down the hill. The traffic signal was operating at the time of the accident.

94. **(C)** Refer to the third sentence of the passage.

95. **(A)** The car was proceeding east with a green light while the jogger was going north against the light.

The Correctly Filled Form

REPORT OF AID GIVEN

Identification

Date _____

Time _____

Place *Second Ave. and Sixth Street, SW corner*

Name of Person Aided_____ ☒ Unknown

Nature of Problem

☐ Abandoned   ☐ Destitute   ☒ Sick
☐ Neglected   ☐ Lost   ☐ Injured

Nature of Sickness or Injury

☐ Mental   ☒ Physical   ☐ Unknown

Aid Given

☒ Artificial Respiration   ☒ Food or Water
☐ Control of Bleeding   ☐ Clothing or Blankets
☐ Temporary Splint   ☐ Other

Disposition of Case

☐ Taken Home   ☐ Left in Custody of Friend
                                  or Relative
☐ Removed to Hospital   ☐ Taken to Morgue
☐ Left at Place of   ☒ Other
   Occurrence

Name of Officer Reporting *Margaret Firestone*

96. **(C)** Refer to the description of the accident.

The Correctly Filled Report

ACCIDENT REPORT

Date _____ Time *5:00 PM* Location of Accident *Tenth St. + Pacific Ave.*

Vehicle in Collison With

☒ Pedestrian   ☐ Motorcycle
☐ Other Vehicle   ☐ Fixed Object
☐ Train   ☐ Bicycle
☐ Animal   ☐ Other

Type of Traffic Control

☐ Police Officer   ☐ Stop Sign
☒ Signal Light in Operation   ☐ Yield Sign
☐ Signal Light Not in   ☐ Other
    Operation
☐ Flashing Light   ☐ None

Character of Road

☐ Straight and Level   ☐ Curve and Level
☒ Straight on Hill   ☐ Curve on Hill
☐ Straight Approaching   ☐ Curve Approaching
    Hilltop   Hilltop

Action of Pedestrian at Intersection

☐ Crossing With Signal   ☐ Crossing Diagonally
☒ Crossing Against Signal   ☐ Crossing, No Signal

Action of Vehicle at Time of Accident

☒ Going Straight Ahead   ☐ Making U-Turn
☐ Overtaking   ☐ Backing Up
☐ Making Right Turn   ☐ Starting from Parking
☐ Making Left Turn   ☐ Slowing or Stopping
     ☐ Parked

97. **(D)** Sector Adam is bounded by heavy black lines. The block in which the holdup occurred is marked with an X.

98. **(A)** The route is marked on the diagram. Choice (C) would be slightly longer. (B) and (D) are impossible from the given starting point.

99. **(B)** This is the only diagram that shows a vehicle approaching from the right.

100. **(D)** This is the only diagram that shows Car 2 continuing west on Grove Street. In diagram A, Car 2 is going east.

ANSWER SHEET FOR PRACTICE EXAMINATION 4

TEAR HERE

1. Ⓐ Ⓑ Ⓒ Ⓓ   21. Ⓐ Ⓑ Ⓒ Ⓓ   41. Ⓐ Ⓑ Ⓒ Ⓓ   61. Ⓐ Ⓑ Ⓒ Ⓓ   81. Ⓐ Ⓑ Ⓒ Ⓓ

2. Ⓐ Ⓑ Ⓒ Ⓓ   22. Ⓐ Ⓑ Ⓒ Ⓓ   42. Ⓐ Ⓑ Ⓒ Ⓓ   62. Ⓐ Ⓑ Ⓒ Ⓓ   82. Ⓐ Ⓑ Ⓒ Ⓓ

3. Ⓐ Ⓑ Ⓒ Ⓓ   23. Ⓐ Ⓑ Ⓒ Ⓓ   43. Ⓐ Ⓑ Ⓒ Ⓓ   63. Ⓐ Ⓑ Ⓒ Ⓓ   83. Ⓐ Ⓑ Ⓒ Ⓓ

4. Ⓐ Ⓑ Ⓒ Ⓓ   24. Ⓐ Ⓑ Ⓒ Ⓓ   44. Ⓐ Ⓑ Ⓒ Ⓓ   64. Ⓐ Ⓑ Ⓒ Ⓓ   84. Ⓐ Ⓑ Ⓒ Ⓓ

5. Ⓐ Ⓑ Ⓒ Ⓓ   25. Ⓐ Ⓑ Ⓒ Ⓓ   45. Ⓐ Ⓑ Ⓒ Ⓓ   65. Ⓐ Ⓑ Ⓒ Ⓓ   85. Ⓐ Ⓑ Ⓒ Ⓓ

6. Ⓐ Ⓑ Ⓒ Ⓓ   26. Ⓐ Ⓑ Ⓒ Ⓓ   46. Ⓐ Ⓑ Ⓒ Ⓓ   66. Ⓐ Ⓑ Ⓒ Ⓓ   86. Ⓐ Ⓑ Ⓒ Ⓓ

7. Ⓐ Ⓑ Ⓒ Ⓓ   27. Ⓐ Ⓑ Ⓒ Ⓓ   47. Ⓐ Ⓑ Ⓒ Ⓓ   67. Ⓐ Ⓑ Ⓒ Ⓓ   87. Ⓐ Ⓑ Ⓒ Ⓓ

8. Ⓐ Ⓑ Ⓒ Ⓓ   28. Ⓐ Ⓑ Ⓒ Ⓓ   48. Ⓐ Ⓑ Ⓒ Ⓓ   68. Ⓐ Ⓑ Ⓒ Ⓓ   88. Ⓐ Ⓑ Ⓒ Ⓓ

9. Ⓐ Ⓑ Ⓒ Ⓓ   29. Ⓐ Ⓑ Ⓒ Ⓓ   49. Ⓐ Ⓑ Ⓒ Ⓓ   69. Ⓐ Ⓑ Ⓒ Ⓓ   89. Ⓐ Ⓑ Ⓒ Ⓓ

10. Ⓐ Ⓑ Ⓒ Ⓓ   30. Ⓐ Ⓑ Ⓒ Ⓓ   50. Ⓐ Ⓑ Ⓒ Ⓓ   70. Ⓐ Ⓑ Ⓒ Ⓓ   90. Ⓐ Ⓑ Ⓒ Ⓓ

11. Ⓐ Ⓑ Ⓒ Ⓓ   31. Ⓐ Ⓑ Ⓒ Ⓓ   51. Ⓐ Ⓑ Ⓒ Ⓓ   71. Ⓐ Ⓑ Ⓒ Ⓓ   91. Ⓐ Ⓑ Ⓒ Ⓓ

12. Ⓐ Ⓑ Ⓒ Ⓓ   32. Ⓐ Ⓑ Ⓒ Ⓓ   52. Ⓐ Ⓑ Ⓒ Ⓓ   72. Ⓐ Ⓑ Ⓒ Ⓓ   92. Ⓐ Ⓑ Ⓒ Ⓓ

13. Ⓐ Ⓑ Ⓒ Ⓓ   33. Ⓐ Ⓑ Ⓒ Ⓓ   53. Ⓐ Ⓑ Ⓒ Ⓓ   73. Ⓐ Ⓑ Ⓒ Ⓓ   93. Ⓐ Ⓑ Ⓒ Ⓓ

14. Ⓐ Ⓑ Ⓒ Ⓓ   34. Ⓐ Ⓑ Ⓒ Ⓓ   54. Ⓐ Ⓑ Ⓒ Ⓓ   74. Ⓐ Ⓑ Ⓒ Ⓓ   94. Ⓐ Ⓑ Ⓒ Ⓓ

15. Ⓐ Ⓑ Ⓒ Ⓓ   35. Ⓐ Ⓑ Ⓒ Ⓓ   55. Ⓐ Ⓑ Ⓒ Ⓓ   75. Ⓐ Ⓑ Ⓒ Ⓓ   95. Ⓐ Ⓑ Ⓒ Ⓓ

16. Ⓐ Ⓑ Ⓒ Ⓓ   36. Ⓐ Ⓑ Ⓒ Ⓓ   56. Ⓐ Ⓑ Ⓒ Ⓓ   76. Ⓐ Ⓑ Ⓒ Ⓓ   96. Ⓐ Ⓑ Ⓒ Ⓓ

17. Ⓐ Ⓑ Ⓒ Ⓓ   37. Ⓐ Ⓑ Ⓒ Ⓓ   57. Ⓐ Ⓑ Ⓒ Ⓓ   77. Ⓐ Ⓑ Ⓒ Ⓓ   97. Ⓐ Ⓑ Ⓒ Ⓓ

18. Ⓐ Ⓑ Ⓒ Ⓓ   38. Ⓐ Ⓑ Ⓒ Ⓓ   58. Ⓐ Ⓑ Ⓒ Ⓓ   78. Ⓐ Ⓑ Ⓒ Ⓓ   98. Ⓐ Ⓑ Ⓒ Ⓓ

19. Ⓐ Ⓑ Ⓒ Ⓓ   39. Ⓐ Ⓑ Ⓒ Ⓓ   59. Ⓐ Ⓑ Ⓒ Ⓓ   79. Ⓐ Ⓑ Ⓒ Ⓓ   99. Ⓐ Ⓑ Ⓒ Ⓓ

20. Ⓐ Ⓑ Ⓒ Ⓓ   40. Ⓐ Ⓑ Ⓒ Ⓓ   60. Ⓐ Ⓑ Ⓒ Ⓓ   80. Ⓐ Ⓑ Ⓒ Ⓓ   100. Ⓐ Ⓑ Ⓒ Ⓓ

PRACTICE EXAMINATION 4

The time allowed for the entire examination is 3½ hours.

Directions: For each question, read all the choices carefully. Select that choice which you consider the most correct or the best of all choices. Then mark your answer on the answer sheet.

Questions 1 through 15 are to be answered on the basis of the police action described in the following passage. You will have ten minutes to read and study the description of the incident. Then you will have to answer 15 questions about the incident without referring back to the description of the incident.

Police Officers Brown and Reid are on patrol in a radio car on a Saturday afternoon in the fall. They receive a radio message that a burglary is in progress on the fifth floor of a seven-floor building on the corner of 7th Street and Main. They immediately proceed to that location to investigate and take appropriate action.

The police officers are familiar with the location and they know that the Fine Jewelry Company occupies the entire fifth floor of the building. They are also aware that the owner, who is not in the office on weekends, often leaves large amounts of gold in his office safe. The officers, upon arrival at the scene, lock their radio car and proceed to look for the building superintendent in order to get into the building. The superintendent states that he has not seen or heard anything unusual, although he admits that he did leave the premises for approximately one hour to have lunch. The officers start for the fifth floor, using the main elevator. As they reach that floor and open the door, they hear noises followed by the sound of the freight elevator door in the rear of the building closing and the elevator descending. They quickly run through the open door of the Fine Jewelry Company and observe that the office safe is open and empty. The officers then proceed to the rear of the building and use the rear staircase to reach the ground floor. They open the rear door and go out onto the street where they observe four individuals running up the street, crossing at the corner. At that point, the police officers get a clear view of the suspects. There are three males and one female. One of the males appears to be white, one is obviously Hispanic, and the other male is black. The female is white.

The white male is bearded. He is dressed in blue jeans, white sneakers, and a red and blue jacket. He is carrying a white duffel bag on his shoulder. The Hispanic male limps slightly and has a large dark moustache. He is wearing brown pants, a green shirt, and brown shoes. He is carrying a blue duffel bag on his shoulder. The black male is clean-shaven, wearing black pants, a white shirt, a green cap, and black shoes. He is carrying what appears to be a tool box. The white female is carrying a sawed-off shotgun, has long brown hair, and is wearing white jeans, a blue blouse, and blue sneakers. She has a red kerchief around her neck.

The officers chase the suspects for two blocks without being able to catch them. At that point, the suspects separate. The white and black males quickly get into a black 1983 Chevrolet station wagon with Connecticut license plates with the letters AWK on them and drive away. The Hispanic male and the white female get away in an old light blue Dodge van. The van has a prominent CB antenna on top and large yellow streaks running along the doors on both sides. There is a large dent on the right rear fender and the van bears New Jersey license plates which the officers are unable to read.

The station wagon turns left and enters the expressway headed towards Connecticut. The van makes a right turn and proceeds in the direction of the tunnel headed for New Jersey.

The officers quickly return to their radio car to report what has happened.

Do not refer back to the passage while answering questions 1 through 15.

1. The officers were able to read the following letters from the license plates on the station wagon:
   - (A) WAX
   - (B) EWK
   - (C) AUK
   - (D) AWK.

2. The van used by the suspects had a dented
   - (A) left front fender
   - (B) right front fender
   - (C) right rear fender
   - (D) left rear fender.

3. The officers observed that the van was headed in the direction of
   - (A) Long Island
   - (B) Pennsylvania
   - (C) New Jersey
   - (D) Connecticut.

4. The best description of the female suspect's hair is
   - (A) short and light in color
   - (B) long and light in color
   - (C) short and dark in color
   - (D) long and dark in color.

5. The suspect who was wearing a white shirt is the
   - (A) white male
   - (B) Hispanic male
   - (C) black male
   - (D) white female.

6. The suspect who wore white jeans is the
   - (A) white male
   - (B) Hispanic male
   - (C) black male
   - (D) white female.

7. The Hispanic male suspect carried a duffel bag of what color?
   - (A) Yellow
   - (B) Red
   - (C) Blue
   - (D) Brown.

8. Of the following, the best description of the shoes worn by the Hispanic suspect is
   - (A) white sneakers
   - (B) black shoes
   - (C) black boots
   - (D) brown shoes.

9. The suspect who was carrying the white duffel bag was the
   - (A) white female
   - (B) black male
   - (C) Hispanic male
   - (D) white male.

10. The suspect who was carrying the shotgun was the
    - (A) white female
    - (B) black male
    - (C) Hispanic male
    - (D) white male.

11. The green cap was worn by the
    - (A) white female
    - (B) black male
    - (C) Hispanic male
    - (D) white male.

12. The suspect who limped when he or she ran was the
    - (A) white female
    - (B) black male
    - (C) Hispanic male
    - (D) white male.

13. Of the following, the best description of the station wagon used by the suspects is
    - (A) 1983 black Chevrolet station wagon
    - (B) 1981 blue Ford
    - (C) 1981 green Dodge
    - (D) 1986 red Ford.

14. The best description of the suspects who used the station wagon to depart is
    - (A) a black male and a white female
    - (B) a black male and a white male
    - (C) a white female and a Hispanic male
    - (D) a black male and a Hispanic male.

15. The van's license plates were from which of the following states?
    - (A) New York
    - (B) Delaware
    - (C) New Jersey
    - (D) Connecticut.

16. Police officers are often assigned to the scene of a fire to control traffic and at times to close off a street to all traffic except emergency vehicles. Two officers assigned to this duty arrive in a radio car which they park across one end of a street, blocking traffic. After locking their radio car, they then proceed to the other end of the street on foot to block off traffic at that end. Their action may be considered.

   (A) improper, because they should have remained in their car in order to be able to move quickly if they were needed
   (B) proper, since a person who may have started the fire would be effectively trapped
   (C) improper, because their car was left unattended and therefore could not be moved to permit emergency vehicles to enter
   (D) proper, because the street is now closed to all but emergency vehicles.

17. The characteristics that should be emphasized in a wanted person report are those which most easily set an individual apart from the general public. Which one of the following descriptions would be of greatest help to a police officer trying to locate a wanted person in a large crowd of people on a cold winter day?

   (A) The person is wearing a blue coat and has short cropped hair.
   (B) The person has a patch on his right eye and a long thin scar on his left cheek.
   (C) The person talks with a lisp and has two upper front teeth missing.
   (D) The person has a scar on his right knee and has blue eyes.

18. There are persons living or working in the city who have the privilege of "diplomatic immunity." Police officers who come into contact with such persons are instructed not to issue them summonses, arrest them, or detain them. While on duty, an officer encounters two men having an argument over an automobile accident. In the presence of the officer, one man, Mr. Mont, punches the other man, Mr. Paul. The officer separates the two men and asks to see their driver's licenses and their registrations. Mr. Paul produces his license, but Mr. Mont does not produce his. However, Mr. Mont produces a card issued by the United States Department of State showing that he is a foreign diplomat entitled to diplomatic immunity. Based on the foregoing, the police officer should

   (A) escort both men to the police station to settle their dispute
   (B) arrest Mr. Mont for hitting Mr. Paul
   (C) issue a summons to Mr. Mont for not having his license or registration with him
   (D) allow Mr. Mont to leave the scene.

19. Police officers are instructed to act in the following manner when dealing with a case of child rape: first, call for medical assistance; second, calm the parents because a hysterical reaction on their part may further upset the child; and third, using patience and understanding, question the child carefully. A police officer on foot patrol is stopped by a man who shouts that a neighbor's child has just been raped. The officer goes to the scene of the alleged crime where he is told by a hysterical mother that her daughter was raped in the apartment while she was out shopping. The mother screams that she believes the man is on the roof. The police officer would be acting properly if he *first*

   (A) called for medical assistance
   (B) attempted to calm the hysterical parent
   (C) went up to the roof to apprehend the accused man
   (D) questioned the child as to what actually took place.

Questions 20 and 21 are to be answered solely on the basis of the following passage and sign.

Police officers are required to enforce parking regulations. "Parking" is defined as stopping a vehicle at a curb and leaving the vehicle. "Standing" is defined as stopping a vehicle at a curb with the driver remaining in or next to the vehicle. Regulations state that when standing is forbidden, parking is also forbidden. However, standing is always permitted unless a sign clearly indicates, "No Standing." The following traffic sign is posted on Main Street.

```
┌─────────────────────────┐
│                         │
│      NO PARKING         │
│    10 A.M. to 1 P.M.    │
│    Mon., Wed., Fri.     │
│                         │
│   ───────────────────   │
│                         │
│      NO STANDING        │
│    8 A.M. to 6 P.M.     │
│    Tues., Thurs., Sat.  │
│                         │
└─────────────────────────┘
```

20. The preceding information and sign would indicate that parking is permitted on Main Street at

(A) 9 A.M. Tuesday
(B) 12 noon Wednesday
(C) 3 P.M. Saturday
(D) 4 P.M. Friday

21. The information and sign would indicate that standing is permitted on Main Street at

(A) 11 A.M. Tuesday
(B) 12 noon Wednesday
(C) 5 P.M. Saturday
(D) 5 P.M. Thursday

Questions 22 through 30 are to be answered solely on the basis of the following passage. The arrest form to be used contains 34 numbered boxes. Read the passage thoroughly and review the Report of Arrest form before attempting to answer the questions.

Police Office James Wilson, on foot patrol, passes a delicatessen late one night and hears a male voice shouting for help. The cries seem to be coming from inside the delicatessen. Officer Wilson enters the store through the front door where he is met by the owner, Robert Connors, who tells the officer he has just been robbed by a tall, slim, young, white man who can still be seen running down the street. The officer chases after the youth who climbs into a light blue two-door 1973 Oldsmobile, bearing the license plate 452-XCP. The car fails to start after several attempts and Officer Wilson catches up to it and arrests its occupant in front of 1139 Avenue of the Americas. The arrest has taken place approximately three minutes after the crime had been committed. The officer then takes the prisoner to the Midtown Precinct North, 305 West 54th St., where it is determined that the prisoner's legal name is John Wright, that he lives alone in apartment 3B at 457 Willis Avenue, Bronx, and his telephone number is 752-8116. Wright's nickname is "Slim" and he is single. He was born in New York City on February 14, 1957, and his Social Security number is 073-16-9812. Wright is employed by the Wellmade Blouse Company, 262 West 37th St., NYC. An arrest record is completed and assigned the number 18431.

Connors arrives at the precinct and is able to describe the incident in detail. He states that at approximately 10:30 P.M. on August 14, 1979, a young, slim, white man entered his store. He approximated the weight of the man to be 145 lbs. and his height to be 5'11". The man had brown hair and eyes. Connors said he went to wait on the man, who suddenly pointed a knife at Connors and said, "Give me all your money or else." Connors noticed that the man had a red and blue tattoo of the head of an Indian chief on his right forearm. Connors picked up an empty soda bottle from the counter and threw it at the man, hitting him in the chest. The man turned and ran out of the store, heading south on the Avenue of the Americas. Connors then headed for the door, yelling for help.

Connors was born on June 17, 1925 and he lives with his wife at 1143 57th St., Brooklyn, NY. His business address is 1151 Avenue of the Americas, NYC. His home telephone number is 852-8817 and his business phone number is 575-7623.

REPORT OF ARREST

ARREST INFORMATION	(1) Date of arrest	(2) Time of arrest	(3) Place of arrest	(4) Precinct	(5) Arrest number

DESCRIPTION OF INCIDENT

(6) Prisoner's weapon (description)	(7) Date and time
(8) Prisoner's auto (color, year, make, model, license plate number, state)	

(9) Type of business	(10) Location of incident (be specific)

DESCRIPTION OF PRISONER

(11) Last name First name Middle initial	(12) Date of birth

(13) Sex	(14) Race	(15) Eyes	(16) Hair	(17) Weight	(18) Height	(19) Age

(20) Address City State	(21) Apt. no.	(22) Home phone number

(23) Citizenship Citizen ☐ Non-Citizen ☐	(24) Place of birth	(25) Marital status

(26) Social Security number	(27) Where employed (company and address)

(28) Nickname	(29) Scars, tattoos (describe fully and give location)

DESCRIPTION OF COMPLAINANT

(30) Last name First name Middle initial	(31) Date of birth

Telephone Numbers		(34) Address City State
(32) Business	(33) Home	

22. Which one of the following dates should be entered in the box numbered (1)?

(A) August 15, 1979
(B) August 14, 1979
(C) August 22, 1979
(D) August 23, 1979.

23. Which one of the following times should be placed in the box numbered(2)?

(A) 10:33 P.M.
(B) 11:15 P.M.
(C) 11:13 P.M.
(D) 10:48 P.M.

24. Which one of the following should be placed in the box numbered (7)?

(A) 8/15/79, 10:30 A.M.
(B) 8/15/79, 10:30 P.M.
(C) 8/14/79, 10:30 A.M.
(D) 8/14/79, 10:30 P.M.

25. Which of the following should be entered in the box numbered (6)?

(A) Gun
(B) Ax
(C) Knife
(D) Bottle.

26. Of the following, which one should be entered in the box numbered (8)?

(A) Light blue, 1973 Oldsmobile, two-door, 452-XCP, New York
(B) Light blue, 1973 Oldsmobile, four-door, 452-XCP, New York
(C) Light blue, 1972 Oldsmobile, two-door, 452-CXP, New York
(D) Light blue, 1973 Oldsmobile, four-door, 542-XCP, New York.

27. Which of the following should be entered in the box numbered (12)?

(A) 6/17/25
(B) 4/14/57
(C) 2/14/57
(D) 2/17/57.

28. Of the following, which should be entered in the box numbered (27)?

(A) Wellmaid Blouse Company, 252 West 37th St., NYC
(B) Wellmade Blouse Company, 262 West 37th St., NYC
(C) Wellmade Blouse Company, 226 West 37th St., NYC
(D) Wellmaid Blouse Company, 262 West 37th St., NYC.

29. Of the following, which one should be entered in the box numbered (34)?

(A) 1143 57th St., Brooklyn, New York
(B) 262 West 37th St., New York City
(C) 457 Willis Avenue, Bronx, New York
(D) 305 West 54th St., New York City.

30. Of the following, which one should be entered in the box numbered (32)?

(A) 852-8817
(B) 122-4552
(C) 752-8818
(D) 575-7623.

Study the following definitions. You will be asked questions about them.

Definitions of Crimes Listed Alphabetically

Arson is committed when an individual intentionally starts a fire that causes damage to a building or that ignites an explosion.

Assault is committed when a person intentionally causes physical injury to another person; or when a person acting recklessly causes physical injury to another person.

Burglary is committed when an individual, without authorization, enters or remains in a building with the intent of committing a crime.

Criminal Mischief is committed when a person intentionally damages the property of another person, having no right to do so, nor any reasonable ground to believe that he has the right to do so.

Criminal Trespass is committed when a person enters or remains in a building he has no right to be in and, while there, possesses, or has knowledge of another person accompanying him possessing, a weapon.

Criminally Negligent Homicide is committed when the behavior of an individual creates a substantial risk for others and results in the unintentional death of a person.

Felony Murder is committed when a person, acting alone or with others, commits or attempts to commit the crimes of robbery, burglary, kidnapping, arson, or rape, and in the course and furtherance of such crime, or immediate flight therefrom, he, or another participant, if there be any, causes the death of a person other than one of the participants.

Harassment is committed when an individual, with intent to annoy or frighten another individual, does strike, shove, kick, or subject that individual to physical contact, or attempts or threatens to do the same, or uses abusive or obscene language, or makes an obscene gesture in a public place, or follows a person in a public place, or repeatedly engages in conduct which serves no legitimate purpose, but which results in alarming or seriously annoying another person.

Jostling is committed when a person, with intent, unnecessarily places his hand near a person's pocket or handbag, or pushes or crowds another person at the same time that another participant's hand is in the proximity of such person's pocket or handbag.

Larceny is committed when a person intentionally deprives another of property or wrongfully takes, obtains, or withholds property from the owner of that property without the use of force, violence, or threat of injury. Larceny is committed, for example, when property is obtained under false pretenses, finding and not returning lost property, or the intentional issuance of a bad check.

Manslaughter is committed when one person recklessly causes the death of another person; when a person causes the death of another person while in the act of intentionally causing serious physical harm to that person; when a person, intending to cause the death of another person, causes that death while acting under the influence of an extreme emotional disturbance.

Menace is committed when a person, by physical threat, intentionally places, or attempts to place, another person in a state of fear of imminent and serious physical injury.

Murder is committed when a person, following a period of lengthy planning, intentionally causes the death of another person.

Reckless Endangerment is committed when a person, failing to exercise caution, engages in conduct which creates a substantial risk of serious injury to another person.

Reckless Endangerment of Property is committed when a person, in the act of failing to exercise proper caution, engages in conduct which creates a risk of damage to the property of another person.

Robbery is committed when a person, against another person's will, takes property from that person.

Questions 31 through 42 are to be answered on the basis of the preceding legal definitions of crimes. Although these definitions may vary slightly from state to state, you are to answer the questions solely on the basis of the definitions stated here.

31. Jane Wills finds a diamond ring on the sidewalk of a busy street. She keeps it. According to the definitions, Wills committed

    (A) the crime of larceny
    (B) the crime of burglary
    (C) the crime of robbery
    (D) none of the listed crimes.

32. Ephriam Towne is waiting at a bus station to hand over a package of expensive jewelry to a representative of the XYZ Transfer Company. Phil Shute learns of the shipment and decides to steal the package. He goes to the bus station, presents himself to Towne, and says he is from XYZ. Towne gives Shute the package believing he is from XYZ. Shute is not armed. The definitions indicate that Shute committed the crime of

    (A) robbery
    (B) burglary
    (C) criminal mischief
    (D) larceny.

33. Leo Charles tries out his new sports car. He drives 70 miles an hour on a school street during school hours and accidentally hits and kills a child. According to the legal definitions, Charles has committed the crime of

    (A) criminally negligent homicide
    (B) menacing
    (C) felony murder
    (D) murder.

34. Conrad Hill and Leonard Burke are walking when they pass a museum. It is late at night, long after the museum ordinarily closes to the public. Hill notices that the front door is open and he suggests that they go in and have a private visit to the museum as a prank. Hill happens to have a flashlight with him. Unknown to Hill, Burke has a concealed gun on his person that is an illegal weapon. Ten minutes after they have entered the museum the two men hear footsteps approaching. They dash out of the museum the same way they had entered it. According to the definitions given,

    (A) both Hill and Burke committed the crime of criminal trespass
    (B) neither Hill nor Burke committed the crime of criminal trespass
    (C) Burke committed the crime of criminal trespass, Hill did not
    (D) Hill committed the crime of criminal trespasss, Burke did not.

35. Which one of the following is the best example of a burglary based upon the definitions given?

    (A) Mr. Samuel's car breaks down in the middle of the night while he is driving on a lonely road. He locates a nearby house which is unoccupied in order to find shelter from the rain.
    (B) During working hours, Wilson, a mechanic, enters the locker room of the factory where he is employed and steals tools from another mechanic's locker.
    (C) Burns, a teenager, passes the open door of a warehouse. He does not see anybody inside the warehouse, but he notices a portable radio on a desk. He enters the warehouse with the intention of stealing the radio, but before he can do so, he hears approaching footsteps and leaves without taking anything.
    (D) Mr. Jurow enters a drug store with the intention of purchasing some toothpaste. The clerk is busy at the back of the store. Jurow, spotting the toothpaste he wants, removes it from the shelf, puts it in his pocket, and leaves.

36. As a result of a dispute over a parking space, Anne Blount and Bea Wallace engage in an argument during which Blount pushes Wallace in an attempt to scare her. Wallace is not hurt, but she makes an obscene gesture in the direction of Blount. Referring to the definitions given, which one of the following best describes the incident?

    (A) Blount committed assault and Wallace committed harassment.
    (B) Blount and Wallace both committed harassment.
    (C) Neither Blount nor Wallace committed harassment.
    (D) Wallace committed assault and Blount committed harassment.

37. William Hammer, fully intending to scare James Bates, drives his car at high speed in the direction of Bates who quickly jumps out of the path of the vehicle. In turning in the direction of Bates, Hammer narrowly misses Fred Collins, a bystander. Neither Bates nor Collins is injured. According to the definitions, Hammer

    (A) did not commit an assault against Bates or Collins
    (B) did not commit a crime
    (C) committed an assault against Bates and Collins
    (D) committed an assault against Collins only.

38. Jon Ochtes picks the pocket of Will Ronge and takes his wallet. Ronge is unaware that his wallet has been taken. According to the definitions, Ochtes committed the crime of

    (A) robbery
    (B) burglary
    (C) larceny
    (D) criminal trespass.

39. James Calvin is driving his car and has as his passenger his four-year-old daughter, Pamela. Calvin's car is suddenly struck by another car and as a result of the accident Pamela is instantly killed. Calvin, upon learning of his daughter's death, approaches the driver of the other vehicle, takes out a gun and shoots him dead. The definitions indicate that Calvin had committed the crime of

    (A) felony murder
    (B) criminally negligent homicide
    (C) murder
    (D) manslaughter.

40. James Floyd has an argument with John Rudd. Floyd then sets fire to Rudd's car, totally destroying it. According to the definitions given, James Floyd has committed the crime of

    (A) arson
    (B) criminal mischief
    (C) reckless endangerment of property
    (D) harassment.

41. Roger Brown enjoys, and engages in, the practice of making obscene gestures towards passengers on subway trains. According to the definitions given, when Brown is in the act of making obscene gestures, he is committing the crime of

    (A) menace
    (B) jostling
    (C) reckless endangerment
    (D) harassment.

42. Robert Huron, after riding his bike through the park, decides to lie down and take a nap. He leaves his bicycle next to him and dozes off. Thomas Hunt, observing that Huron is asleep, decides to steal the bicycle. Huron awakens before Hunt removes the bicycle and he starts after Hunt who pulls out a gun, points it at Huron, threatens to kill him, and takes Huron's bicycle. According to the definitions given, Hunt committed the crime of

    (A) robbery
    (B) burglary
    (C) larceny
    (D) criminal mischief.

Questions 43 and 44 are to be answered solely on the basis of the following passage.

Police officers assigned to search an office building in order to apprehend a criminal should search every office, rest room, and storage area. They should ask all individuals in the building if they have seen the criminal.

43. Two male police officers are assigned to search an office building for a male prowler who was seen in the building. They search the men's rest rooms but not the women's rest rooms. Their actions can be described as

(A) proper; the prowler was male so he could not be hiding in a women's rest room
(B) improper; all rest rooms should have been searched
(C) proper; if the male had entered a women's rest room, females would have screamed
(D) improper; an open window in a women's rest room would have indicated the means of escape.

44. Two officers, assigned to search an office building in search of a prowler, ask everyone on each of the floors if he or she has seen the prowler. On one floor, they encounter a seven-year-old girl who is visiting her mother. They ask the girl if she has seen the prowler. Their action in this matter is to be considered

(A) proper; otherwise the child would feel neglected
(B) improper; their questioning of the girl would upset her
(C) proper; the girl may have seen the prowler
(D) improper; children should be kept out of such matters.

Questions 45 and 46 are to be answered solely on the basis of the following passage.

Police officers assigned to patrol in a radio car are instructed to adhere to the following rules concerning the use of the police radios in patrol cars.

1. The use of the radio is to be restricted to performance of duty only.
2. All conversations should be to the point and as short as possible.
3. Names of people are not to be used.
4. All conversations should begin by identifying the vehicle by number.
5. A message received is to be acknowledged by "ten-four."

45. Police Officers Abel and Flynn apprehend two men in the act of robbing a jewelry store. They place the men in Patrol Car 14 and radio in a report of the activity. Which one of the following messages would be in conformance with the procedure given?

(A) "Officers Abel and Flynn, car one four, proceeding to station house with two prisoners."
(B) "Car one four, proceeding to station house with two prisoners."
(C) "Car one four, Officers Abel and Flynn, proceeding to station house with two prisoners."
(D) "Car one four, proceeding to station house with prisoners Bossey and Warren."

46. Officer Ahearn has an appointment for dinner with Officer Tomkins. During the afternoon, Officer Ahearn suddenly realizes that he cannot meet Officer Tomkins. He is on patrol in a radio car and he knows that Tomkins is in another radio car on patrol. It is snowing heavily and Ahearn advises Tomkins over the car radio that he will not be able to have dinner with him. The action of Officer Ahearn is

(A) proper, because he effectively used the radio to cancel an appointment he could not keep
(B) improper, because he violated the procedure for the use of car radios
(C) proper, because he was able to cancel the appointment in time
(D) improper, because he should not have cancelled the appointment.

Questions 47 through 49 are to be answered solely on the basis of the following passage.

Bomb threats must be handled carefully. When responding to a bomb threat in a building, police officers should adhere to the following instructions.

1. Proceed immediately to the scene of the reported bomb.
2. Advise the person in charge of the building as to whether or not the building should be evacuated.
3. Advise the people in the building not to turn the lights on or off because this may set off the bomb.
4. Avoid using portable radios because this, too, may set off the bomb.
5. Open doors and windows because this action may limit the effectiveness of the bomb if it goes off.
6. Search the building thoroughly.
7. Avoid contact with out-of-place objects.
8. Advise the person in charge of the building that it is not necessarily safe even if no bomb is found.

47. Police Officers Lane and Gold respond to a report of a bomb in a large office building. They report to the person in charge of the building and suggest evacuating the building. The officers commence to search the building carefully. In a second floor rest room, they find a small black suitcase hidden behind a radiator. The officers immediately call for help on their portable radio. The officers acted

(A) improperly; the officers should not have used their portable radio to call for help
(B) properly; they called for help as soon as they found what appeared to be the bomb
(C) improperly; they should have evacuated the building before beginning their search
(D) properly; they informed the building manager that they had found the bomb.

48. Officer Groom, responding to a report of a bomb in a building, informs Mr. Goff, who is in charge of the building, of the reported bomb and the building is evacuated. Officer Groom tells Mr. Goff that the people, before leaving the building, should be told not to touch any unfamiliar object and to turn off all lights. The officer's instructions to Mr. Goff were

(A) improper; the decision to evacuate the building was wrong
(B) proper; the people in the building were protected from injury

(C) improper; the lights should not have been turned off
(D) proper; Officer Groom's instructions limited possible damage to the building.

49. While responding to a report of a bomb in a large office building, Officer Samuels, during his search of the building, notices an expensive-looking suitcase underneath a workbench in the boiler room. The area is dusty but the suitcase is clean of any dust. Officer Samuels hears a ticking sound coming from the suitcase and he proceeds to carefully open it, finding a pair of pajamas, a bathrobe, and an alarm clock as its contents. According to the procedure covering reports of bombs, Officer Samuels' actions were

(A) improper; he should not have touched the property of another person
(B) proper; his actions made the evacuation of the building unnecessary
(C) improper; he should not have touched the suitcase
(D) proper; he did determine that there was no bomb.

336 / *Police Officer*

Questions 50 and 51 are to be answered on the basis of the procedure described in the following passage.

Quite often a police officer is required to give assistance to an injured person. Upon responding to a call to assist an injured person, a police officer should be guided by the following procedure:

1. Administer first aid.
2. Call for medical assistance.
3. Call again if the ambulance does not respond within 20 minutes.
4. Accompany the injured person to the hospital if he or she is unconscious or unidentified.
5. Witness the search of an unconscious or unidentified person.
6. Attempt to identify the person who is unconscious or unidentified by a search of his or her property.

50. Officer Hawthorne, on patrol on a cold winter night, observes an old man falling down the icy steps of his apartment house. When he reaches the man, he finds him bleeding profusely from a head wound. Officer Hawthorne is able to control the bleeding; however, the man lapses into unconsciousness. The officer calls for an ambulance, which arrives in 15 minutes, and Officer Hawthorne accompanies the man to the hospital. The officer remains present while the man is searched by the hospital staff. The officer examines the man's property and discovers it consists of an empty wallet, keys, and a comb. The actions taken by Officer Hawthorne were

(A) improper; the first aid given by the officer was not proper because the man lapsed into unconsciousness
(B) proper; the officer followed the procedure
(C) improper; no attempt was made to establish the man's identity before the ambulance was summoned
(D) proper; the actions of the officer enabled the victim to be identified.

51. Officer Alcorn, while on patrol, observes a man lying in the front yard of a two-family house. Upon questioning, the man reveals that he fell while repairing the roof of his house. He says he is in a great deal of pain and unable to move. Officer Alcorn summons an ambulance and gives the man first aid. He then requests that the man give him his name but the man refuses. The ambulance arrives in 15 minutes, and Officer Alcorn resumes patrol. Officer Alcorn failed to fulfill his obligations in this incident because he

(A) did not make a second call for the ambulance when the man was in great pain
(B) failed to accompany the man to the hospital
(C) did not attempt to locate a physician while waiting for the ambulance
(D) failed to relieve the injured man's pain through the administration of proper first aid.

Questions 52 through 54 are to be answered solely on the basis of the following procedure.

1. When a prisoner requests medical attention or is in apparent need of it, the police officer should arrange for the prisoner to be promptly examined by a doctor.
2. In the event that a prisoner is in need of medical treatment, the police officer should notify a supervisor immediately so that an ambulance can be summoned. Prisoners who are drug addicts and who are in need of treatment for their addiction should be taken to a hospital by a radio car.
3. Under no circumstances should a police officer prescribe any medication for a prisoner.
4. A police officer should not attempt to diagnose a prisoner's illness or injury and should not attempt to treat the prisoner except in a situation where first aid is required. First aid should be administered promptly.
5. A doctor is the only one authorized to administer medicine to a prisoner. When a doctor is not available, the police officer in charge of the prisoner should then give him or her the medicine and watch him or her take it.

52. Alan Fox, a prisoner well known to police because of his long record, is in custody when he claims that he has a severe headache as a result of being badly beaten. There are no apparent signs of a physical injury, but the prisoner demands medical attention. The police officer in charge of Alan Fox should

(A) consider the prisoner's long record before deciding to call a doctor
(B) give the prisoner aspirin tablets
(C) ignore the prisoner's request for medical attention since there are no apparent physical injuries
(D) see that Alan Fox is promptly examined by a doctor.

53. It is a hot summer day and Officer David Stone has in his custody a prisoner who is a drug addict. The prisoner opens his shirt to reveal a large unhealed wound which is obviously infected. Officer Stone suggests to the prisoner that he call a doctor in to examine him, but the prisoner refuses, saying the wound is of no consequence. In this instance, Officer Stone should

(A) request that his supervisor call an ambulance

(B) closely examine the wound in order to evaluate its severity
(C) adhere to the prisoner's wishes and do nothing about the matter
(D) take the prisoner at once to a hospital in a radio car.

54. Melanie Feeney, a prisoner, is in court waiting to make an appearance. She informs Officer Dorkin, who is guarding her, that she is terrified and about to faint. She states that a tranquilizer would relieve her anxiety. Police Officer Dorkin takes tranquilizers on occasion and happens to have some with him. These tranquilizers are prescribed by Officer Dorkin's physician. Officer Dorkin offers Feeney a tranquilizer and she takes it. Police Officer Dorkin acted

(A) properly; his action relieved the situation
(B) improperly; all medicines given to a prisoner must be prescribed by a doctor
(C) properly; he watched her take the medicine
(D) improperly; he should have summoned an ambulance.

Questions 55 and 56 are to be answered solely on the basis of the following procedure.

A police officer responding to complaints of noise should

1. Interview the person who lodged the complaint.
2. Go to the location of the noise.
3. Ascertain the source of the noise and interview those people responsible for it.
4. Correct the situation, if possible, by the giving of advice or a warning.

55. Responding to a complaint of noise, Police Officer Levin enters a small apartment building and is approached by an elderly man who says he called in the complaint. He states that a party has been going on all night in apartment 2B, up the hall. As Officer Levin approaches the apartment, he is met by two people who are leaving it. He asks them how long the party will continue and they answer that it should be over in a few minutes. Levin then tells the complainant that the party will be over very shortly. Officer Levin in this instance acted

(A) correctly; he found out for the complainant when the party would end
(B) incorrectly; he should have directed that all the guests leave the party immediately
(C) correctly; he spoke to both the complainant and the party guests
(D) incorrectly; he should have spoken to the people who lived in the apartment.

56. Police Officer Smythe responds to a complaint of excessive noise from residents in an apartment house. When he arrives, a couple tells him that a baby has been crying loudly all night in an apartment directly over them. Officer Smythe can hear the crying clearly. However, he tells them that he can do nothing about a crying baby. He then returns to his car and resumes patrol. His action in this matter was

(A) improper; he should have investigated the matter fully before leaving
(B) proper; he had determined that the baby's crying resulted from being ill
(C) improper; he should have advised the couple that a baby cannot continue crying forever
(D) proper; the matter was not serious enough to justify a complaint.

Questions 57 through 60 should be answered solely on the basis of the following passage.

When a police officer arrives at the scene of an attempted murder, he or she should follow the procedure indicated below:

1. Determine if the victim is alive by checking breathing, pulse, and reflexes.
2. Administer necessary first aid if the victim is alive.
3. Request the victim's identity and the identity of the attacker if the victim is conscious.
4. Move bystanders back from the immediate area but ask them to remain in the general area.
5. Request identification from witnesses to the attack.
6. Question each of the witnesses out of earshot of the other witnesses.

Officer Mayfield, on patrol in a police car, responds to a report of an attempted murder. The officer enters an apartment house and finds a woman lying unconscious on the lobby floor. She is surrounded by a number of people. Officer Mayfield checks her pulse, which he finds to be weak, but she is still alive. At this point, he orders everyone from the area. One resident, Gerald Bowen, runs into the lobby and says, "I saw just what happened, and the man who did it is escaping through the rear door. He is wearing a navy blue jacket. Get him." Officer Mayfield tells Bowen to stay with the victim until he gets back. The officer then proceeds out the rear door.

A few minutes later the officer returns and says that he saw the alleged attacker jump into a car and get away. The officer observes the victim and determines that her condition has not appreciably changed. Some of the people who had been there earlier have returned together with several new people. An ambulance arrives to take the woman to the hospital. Officer Mayfield takes Bowen aside to question him further.

57. Officer Mayfield's direction to the people near the victim to leave the building was
   (A) improper; he should have requested that the people remain nearby
   (B) proper; a victim to a crime should not remain on public view
   (C) improper; he should have told the people to leave and not return
   (D) proper; bystanders interfere with police investigations.

58. Police Officer Mayfield's checking for signs of life on the victim was
   (A) proper; this information was needed before the attacker could be charged
   (B) improper; the officer should have first given his attention to the attacker
   (C) proper; checking the victim's condition is the officer's first responsibility
   (D) improper; only a doctor can determine if a person is dead or alive.

59. Officer Mayfield's action in letting Bowen watch the victim while he went after the at-

tacker is considered.
   (A) proper; it enabled him to go after the attacker
   (B) improper; Bowen had not identified himself at that point
   (C) proper; Bowen did not permit any of the bystanders to disturb the woman
   (D) improper; the officer should have directed his immediate attention to giving possible first aid to the victim.

60. Police Officer Mayfield's action in removing Bowen from the group of bystanders is considered.
   (A) proper; witnesses should not be questioned in the vicinity of the crime.
   (B) improper; Bowen's story could have been corrected or added to if the rest of the bystanders could have heard the questioning
   (C) proper; witnesses should be questioned away from other witnesses
   (D) improper; it would have saved time if the entire group was asked at one time what they had seen.

Questions 61 through 65 are to be answered solely on the basis of the following passage.

Police officers responding to complaints of loud or violent disagreements between members of a family are directed to follow the procedure below.

1. When knocking on the door of the apartment in which the dispute is taking place, do not stand directly in front of it.
2. Separate the people taking part in the dispute by taking them into different rooms.
3. Attempt to calm the people involved while interviewing them.
4. Stay out of the dispute; do not take sides.
5. If an insult is directed at you, ignore it.
6. Advise the parties in the argument where they may go for counseling.
7. Do not say anything which will direct the people's anger at you.
8. Make no arrests unless one of the participants is hurt.

61. Two officers, arriving at the scene of a family dispute, separate a screaming couple into different rooms. The wife shouts that her husband is having an affair with his secretary and that she is going to file for divorce. The wife picks up the ringing telephone, listens briefly, and then slams it down. She shouts to her husband, "Your secretary just called, but she didn't leave a message." At this point it would be proper for the police officer to advise that the

(A) husband end this affair at once
(B) wife go ahead with her divorce plans
(C) wife trust her husband
(D) couple seek the help of local marriage counselors.

62. Two officers respond to a complaint of gunshots and loud arguing taking place in an apartment. They approach the apartment and hear a television set playing. They stand in front of the door, knock on it, and are told to enter. A man and a woman are sitting on a couch watching a murder mystery on television. The couple states that they have been watching the program for almost two hours. The officers evaluate the situation and decide that a mistake has been made. They apologize and leave. One of the actions taken by the officers does not conform to the procedure for dealing with this type of situation. This occurred when they

(A) determined that a mistake had been made and they apologized and left the premises

(B) interviewed the people involved in the complaint
(C) investigated the complaint even though they could hear no argument
(D) stood in front of the door while knocking on it.

63. Two police officers are assigned to respond to a family dispute taking place in an apartment. The officers approach the door leading to the apartment and hear loud arguing. They knock and the husband opens the door. He tells the officer that an argument is taking place because of his wife's excessive drinking habits. The wife is sitting on the couch with what appears to be a glass of whiskey in her hand. The officers advise the husband that if the problem should occur again, he should call the police. The actions of the officers in this situation were

(A) improper; the officers should have interviewed both parties, the husband and the wife
(B) proper; no one was hurt, so the officers left
(C) improper; the officers should have ordered the wife to stop drinking
(D) proper; the officers advised the husband to call the police if they were needed.

64. Officers Cohn and Blue respond to a family dispute that involves a young couple and the mother of the wife. They enter the apartment and notice that it is very dusty and untidy. The couple is dressed in soiled clothing and the husband has not shaved in days. The wife's mother tells the officers that the couple are a pair of "good-for-nothings" and that she is always arguing with her daughter. Officer Blue then tells the couple to clean themselves and the apartment. In response to this remark, the couple angrily states that they can live in whatever manner they please. Of the following, Officer Blue's statement to the couple can be evaluated as

(A) inappropriate; he should have told the mother not to interfere
(B) appropriate; he did give good advice to the couple
(C) inappropriate; he should not have angered the couple
(D) appropriate; people should not be permitted to live in a dirty apartment.

65. Two officers are responding to a complaint of a family dispute taking place in an apartment. As they approach the door to the apartment, they are able to hear loud arguing and the sound of things being thrown about. After knocking on the door, they are admitted by the wife who tells them that her husband has been throwing dishes at the wall and she wants him locked up. The husband states that the wife is constantly nagging him to make more money and that he is being driven out of his mind. At this point, both parties resume shouting. The officers arrest the husband and take him to the police station. The procedure followed by the officers was

(A) improper; they should not have arrested the husband
(B) proper; they prevented the husband from hurting his wife
(C) improper; both husband and wife should have been arrested
(D) proper; the husband in all probability started the fight.

Questions 66 through 68 should be answered solely on the basis of the information given in the following passage.

Preparations to deal with community demonstrations should take place before they actually occur. A police officer should try to accomplish all of the following:

1. Determine possible problems in the community through discussions with community members.
2. Determine the locations of demonstrations that are being planned in the community.
3. Determine from its leaders what plans have been made before the demonstration is to take place.
4. Speak to the owners of businesses in the community to determine if they have any information concerning possible demonstrations.

66. Police Officer Wynne, while on foot patrol, observes a small group of angry residents leaving the house of a community leader. Members of the group are shouting that it is time to hold a public demonstration. Officer Wynne approaches the group and inquires about the nature of their problem. They walk away from him. He then approaches the community leader who is standing in front of his house and asks him why the citizens are so angry. The community leader tells Officer Wynne to mind his own business and to stick to doing police work. In this instance, Officer Wynne acted

(A) correctly, mainly because the officer was trying to prevent a demonstration from taking place
(B) incorrectly, mainly because the residents made it clear that they did not want his help
(C) correctly, mainly because he attempted to determine the nature of the problem
(D) incorrectly, mainly because the actions of the officer made the community leader angry.

67. Police Officer Stanley observes a woman in a park addressing a large group of women. A man approaches the officer and informs him that the woman is organizing a protest against the lack of high-paying jobs for wo-

men. At this point, the speaker advises the group to prepare for the demonstration and calls the rally to an end. Officer Stanley should

(A) order the woman to accompany him to the station house
(B) attempt to determine from the woman what her plans are for the demonstration
(C) tell the woman that she may not hold any more meetings concerning this issue in public
(D) attempt to determine from the woman why she is involving others in her problem.

68. A police officer on foot patrol is approached by the owner of a restaurant who informs him that a meeting of 15 community residents has just taken place in his establishment where they discussed demonstrating against the proposed opening of a drug addiction center in the neighborhood. They had asked the restaurant owner if he wished to take part in the demonstration. In this situation, the police officer would be acting properly if he requested that the restaurant owner

(A) not become involved
(B) find out where the group plans to meet in the future
(C) explain why he refused to become involved in the demonstration
(D) have the leaders call the station house.

Questions 69 through 74 are to be answered solely on the basis of the procedure described in the following passage.

A police officer responding to a situation that involves a person or persons who seem to be dead should take the following steps:

1. The officer should assume that the person is alive unless the officer is absolutely sure that he or she is dead.
2. If the officer is absolutely sure that the person is dead, and if the body is in public view, the body should be covered with a waterproof covering.
3. The officer should summon a sergeant to the scene.
4. The officer should immediately call the homicide detectives if the death is suspicious.
5. The body should be searched for identification if the death took place in a public area. In the event that the death took place in the apartment or home of a person who lived alone, both the body and the apartment or home are to be searched. All searches must be witnessed by a sergeant.
6. Property of a dead person may be released only to a relative who lived with the deceased.
7. A police officer, when informing the relatives of a death, should be considerate and tactful. If possible, the officer should inform the family of the death in the presence of friends and neighbors. The officer should be sure not to make statements that would further upset the family, such as, "This death probably could have been avoided if you had taken him to a doctor."
8. Do not notify relatives or family of a death over the telephone. However, if you receive a call from a relative concerning the person's condition, you may inform the relative of the death.

69. A police officer is summoned to the scene of an accident. The victim, a young woman, is lying on the street, apparently dead. She is surrounded by bystanders. In this situation, the officer should first
   (A) cover the body with a waterproof covering
   (B) notify the homicide detectives
   (C) search the body to determine its identity
   (D) check to see if the woman is alive.

70. A police officer is sent to an apartment in which a man has died. The man had been living alone in the apartment. The officer has reason to believe that there is a suspicious aspect to the man's death. At this point, the officer should call
   (A) a doctor
   (B) the man's relatives
   (C) an ambulance
   (D) homicide detectives.

71. A police officer is sent to the apartment of an elderly man who apparently has been dead for a few days. The officer closes the door to the apartment and is now alone with the body. His first act should be to
   (A) summon a sergeant
   (B) search the apartment
   (C) search the body
   (D) cover the body

72. A police officer, while searching the apartment of a dead man who had lived alone, is approached by the man's sister who requests permission to remove a few family albums from the apartment. The officer, in this instance, should
   (A) give her the albums since she is the dead man's sister
   (B) not give her the albums since she did not live with the dead man
   (C) give her the albums since they contain family pictures
   (D) not give her the albums until she proves she is the deceased's sister.

73. A police officer has been assigned to notify a woman's family that she has died. Before the officer can notify the family, a member of the family calls concerning the woman's condition. The officer should respond to the call by

(A) informing the caller of the woman's death

(B) stating that the woman's condition cannot be given over the telephone

(C) stating that he is on his way over to inform the family personally

(D) stating that he can only reveal the condition of the woman in the presence of friends or neighbors.

74. A police officer is informing the family of a deceased man that the man died following a heart attack. The officer suspects that the man could have been saved if the family had been with him at the time of his attack. The officer decides to keep this opinion to himself. The officer's decision is

(A) proper; the officer did not know for certain that the man could have been saved

(B) improper; this information may have helped to prevent future similar deaths to other members of the family

(C) proper; he spared the family from additional upset

(D) improper; he withheld information that the family was entitled to have.

75. Quite often police officers are required to testify in court concerning arrests made several months earlier. Officers should testify honestly, offering only factual information. A police officer is testifying concerning an arrest he had made five months previously. He is requested to give the weather conditions on the day of the arrest. The officer had not recorded this information at the time of the arrest and he cannot recall what the conditions were. He answers, "I do not recall." The officer's answer is

(A) proper; the officer does not know the answer to the question

(B) improper; the officer should have guessed

(C) proper; the officer needs more time to form his answer

(D) improper; this type of answer will discredit the balance of his testimony.

76. A police officer attempting to extract information from a witness should not ask questions that can be answered by a "yes" or "no." A police officer is interviewing a witness to a car accident that resulted in serious injury to two people. The officer has reason to believe that the car involved went through an intersection against the light. Of the following, the proper question for the officer to ask the witness would be

(A) "Did you see the car go through a red light?"

(B) "Can you recall if the light turned red before the car went through the intersection?"

(C) "What color was the light at the time the car went through the intersection?"

(D) "Was the light red when the car went through the intersection?"

77. A police officer should not ask leading questions, that is, questions which suggest the answer that the officer desires. A police officer is called to the scene of an accident that involved a red and a green car. It would be proper for the officer to ask a witness to the accident,

(A) "You observed the red car hit the green car, didn't you?"

(B) "You did see the green car hit the red car?"

(C) "The red car caused the accident, didn't it?"

(D) "Just what caused the accident between the red car and the green car?"

Answer questions 78 and 79 solely on the basis of the following information.

When engaging in conversations with the public, police officers should be guided by the following:

1. If angry, calm yourself down before engaging in conversation with the public.
2. Be courteous to citizens at all times.
3. When you are insulted by the public, you should overlook it.
4. Do not express your personal views on controversial topics when on duty.
5. Be understanding of the citizen's point of view.
6. Never raise your voice during a conversation with a citizen.

78. A police officer very strongly believes that there is no gasoline shortage of any consequence and that the high price of gasoline is the responsibility of the gas station owners. While he is walking patrol, he encounters a gasoline station owner who complains that everyone is holding the owners responsible for the high price of gasoline while the blame should be placed on the large oil companies. An appropriate reply on the part of the police officer would be to tell the owner that

(A) the gas station owners are responsible for the high price of gasoline
(B) many people may agree with the owner
(C) he is making a lot of money and should not complain
(D) the large oil companies and their practices are responsible for the high price of gasoline.

79. A police officer, driving a radio car down a narrow one-way street, observes a van approaching him in the wrong direction. The driver of the van mounts the sidewalk and stops, narrowly missing the radio car. Laughter is coming from the back of the van. The officer is upset and angry. The driver of the van laughingly shouts to the police officer, "Man, what's happening?" In this instance, it would be most appropriate for the officer to

(A) shout, "You almost killed me!"
(B) calm down and say to the driver, "You were going the wrong way on a one-way street."
(C) shout at the driver, "I'll get you good now!"
(D) calm down and say, "Hey you, how many drinks have you had?"

Answer questions 80 and 81 based solely on the following procedure.

When speaking to a traffic violator, a police officer should adhere to the following procedure:

1. Use the words "Sir" or "Ma'am" until the officer gets to know the name of the violator; then the use of Mr. Jones or Ms. Smith is proper.
2. Advise the driver of the violation he or she has committed.
3. Do not argue with the motorist.
4. Be impersonal in your conversation; do not mention yourself.
5. Do not be critical of the motorist.

80. Officer Thomas stops a motorist for speeding. The officer approaches the car, and the driver, a man whom the officer never met before, says, "I haven't done anything wrong. Why did you stop me?" An appropriate reply from Officer Thomas would be

(A) "I stopped you for speeding."
(B) "You were speeding."
(C) "Sir, you were exceeding the speed limit."
(D) "Sir, I know exactly how fast you were going. You were speeding."

81. Officer James Lane stops a motorist because of erratic driving on a busy highway. The motorist had come close to hitting several cars. As the officer approaches the motorist's car, he notices that there are three additional occupants in the car. The motorist extends his license to the officer who notes his name as being William Doran. The motorist asks the officer why he was stopped, declaring that he was not driving too fast. Officer Lane, in attempting to get the motorist to realize the seriousness of his violation, calmly says, "Mr. Doran, you are a lousy driver." Officer Lane's statement to the motorist was

(A) improper; the officer should have asked the motorist how much he had had to drink
(B) proper; the officer was truthful to the motorist
(C) improper; the officer had criticized the motorist
(D) proper; the officer had notified the driver of the violation he had committed.

Questions 82 through 85 are to be answered solely on the basis of the following information.

In order to further public relations between the police department and members of the community, a police officer should:

1. Refrain from showing anger to another person, even if being subjected to unpleasant behavior by that person.
2. At all times be fair and impartial.
3. Display interest in the problems of people
4. Encourage people to cooperate with police.
5. Always give the reason for his or her actions while complying with a request or taking police action.

82. A police officer is walking past a kindergarten while on foot patrol and encounters a group of parents who complain that the nearby streets are unsafe for children to cross because there are no traffic lights. One parent yells that her child was almost hit by a car a week ago. Another parent shouts that the police do not care. The police officer has two small children of his own and thinks that the parents are being unfair. He says loudly that the police do care and that he has children of his own. The police officer acted

(A) incorrectly; he should not have responded to the complaints of the parents
(B) correctly; he did point out that police officers are also members of the community
(C) incorrectly; he did not respond properly to the parents
(D) correctly; he stated that the police do care about the safety of the children.

83. A police officer is slowly driving his patrol car past a large park. The officer notices a group of teenagers running through the park and jumping over the benches. Loud rock music is blaring from several radios they are carrying. An elderly woman beckons to the officer and complains that the older people also use the park and are being disturbed by the teenagers. She continues her complaint, which is interrupted by the officer informing her that young people have a right to use the park also. In this instance, the officer acted

(A) incorrectly; he did not show proper interest in the elderly woman's problem
(B) correctly; he was fair and impartial
(C) incorrectly; he should have removed himself from the problem because it is controversial

(D) correctly; he did defend the rights of the teenagers.

84. A police officer on foot patrol observes two people in a heated argument. One is a well-dressed woman and the other is a shabbily dressed pretzel vendor. The woman claims that she gave the vendor a five-dollar bill and that he gave her change for only a dollar. The police officer directs the pretzel vendor to give the woman four dollars more. The action of the police officer in this situation can be evaluated as

(A) improper; it was apparent that the woman was trying to cheat the vendor
(B) proper; street vendors continually engage in this type of practice
(C) improper; he should have permitted the vendor to give his side of the dispute
(D) proper; he forced the vendor to pay the money he owed the woman.

85. A police officer on foot patrol on a hot, humid summer day observes a group of teenagers turning on a fire hydrant which does not have a sprinkler cap. Knowing that this will result in a waste of water and reduced water pressure, the officer closes off the hydrant and orders the teenagers not to turn it on again. The police officer acted

(A) incorrectly; he did not tell the teenagers the reason for his actions
(B) correctly; the teenagers should go to a pool in order to cool off
(C) incorrectly; he should have permitted the hydrant to stay on while the teenagers obtained a sprinkler cap
(D) correctly; the officer will now be respected by the teenagers.

Questions 86 through 88 are to be answered solely on the basis of the following information.

Police officers, while questioning witnesses or potential witnesses, should attempt to collect as much information as possible. In order to accomplish this, police officers should follow the guidelines listed below:

1. Conversation should be kept informal.
2. Every effort should be made to avoid unpleasant expressions or gestures.
3. The person questioned should be encouraged to speak and never hurried or pressured.
4. Never ask questions that imply the person may have done something wrong.
5. Display an interest in the individual's problems.

86. A police officer is interviewing a woman who lives next to an apartment that has been robbed. The officer's tour of duty is scheduled to end shortly. The officer asks if the woman had heard or seen anything unusual. The woman starts answering, but she stutters severely and the police officer realizes that it will take a considerable amount of time to complete the interview. He tells her, therefore, to try to speed it up because he is going off duty soon. His action in this matter was

(A) improper; he should not have told the woman why he is in a hurry
(B) proper; he attempted to finish the interview before his tour of duty was completed
(C) improper; he should not have hurried the woman
(D) proper; in this manner he will be able to get needed information more quickly.

87. A police officer is interviewing a witness to a crime. The witness has indicated that she wishes to be cooperative, but in response to a question concerning an important issue, the witness states that she does not know the answer. The police officer then says, "Give some thought to the matter; the answer may come to you later. Call me if it does." The officer's statement can be evaluated as being

(A) improper; a more forceful approach would have provided the information sought

(B) proper; this type of response would entice an uncooperative witness to supply the need information
(C) improper; the information was needed at once
(D) proper; this type of statement may lead to obtaining the wanted information.

88. Police Officer Mary Burns is interviewing a witness to a serious car accident. The accident resulted in the death of the witness' brother who had been the driver of one of the vehicles involved. Officer Burns asks the witness if his brother had been drinking before the accident. The witness replies angrily that his brother was sober, cursing the officer for implying otherwise. At this point it would be most appropriate for Officer Burns to

(A) indicate that she was offended by the witness' language
(B) tell the witness that she understands that being interviewed so shortly after the accident must be quite a difficult ordeal for him
(C) indicate her anger at being cursed at by the witness by repeating the curse words
(D) tell the witness that his apparent failure to cooperate is an indication that he is withholding vital information.

Questions 89 through 91 are to be answered solely on the basis of the following information.

It is essential that police officers, while questioning people taken into custody, give them as much information as possible concerning the crime for which they have been arrested. In order to accomplish this, and at the same time gain the cooperation of the people they take into custody, the procedure below should be followed:

1. Be sympathetic.
2. Lighten the person's fear of the punishment he or she faces.
3. Convince the person that his or her family will understand if he or she confesses to the crime.
4. Attempt to convince the person that if he or she wishes to confess, he or she is not squealing on partners in the crime, that if they were caught, they would squeal.
5. If the person in custody seems reluctant to admit guilt, point out the fact that the police possess enough evidence for a conviction without a confession.

89. Two police officers, responding to a call that a liquor store is being robbed, are able to capture and arrest a suspect. Two other men who participated in the robbery get away. The arrested man indicates that he would be willing to give the officers the names of the other two men, but if he did, he would be considered an informer. It would be appropriate at this point for the officers to tell the man they have in custody that

(A) his partners would have told on him if they had been caught
(B) the facts point to the guilt of his partners
(C) he will receive a longer jail term if he does not tell them the names of his partners
(D) his partners will not hold it against him if he reveals their names.

90. Police Officer Jane Paxton has just taken a man into custody for the commission of a minor crime. During questioning, the man remains silent, finally telling Officer Paxton that he is very much ashamed and he fears what his family will think when they discover his predicament. He states that if he confesses to the crime his family will never forgive him. Officer Paxton should tell the man that

(A) he should immediately confess before everyone finds out how stupid he is for committing the crime

(B) his family is likely to forgive him if he confesses to the crime
(C) since his family will not forgive him anyway, he should confess to the crime
(D) if he does not confess at once, she will personally tell his family.

91. A police officer on foot patrol observes a woman run out of a department store with a small television set in her arms. She is followed by a security guard who shouts, "Stop that woman! She has just stolen a television set!" The police officer chases the woman, who runs to a station wagon and places the set in the back of it. The driver of the station wagon, seeing the approaching officer, drives away before the woman can get into the car. At this point, the officer arrests the woman. She claims that she has not committed any crime and that she is willing to fully cooperate with the police. It would be most appropriate for the police officer to tell the woman that

(A) she is a thief and she should admit to it
(B) she will have her day in court
(C) she is only hurting herself by not admitting to her guilt
(D) he and the security guard can both testify against her since they both saw her running from the store with the television set in her arms.

Questions 92 through 98 are to be answered solely on the basis of the following instructions.

Officers should adhere to the following procedure for dealing with persons who display indications of mental illness:

1. Attempt to determine the cause of the person's being upset.
2. Calm the individual and reassure him or her that you are there to help.
3. Under no circumstances laugh at or make fun of the individual.
4. Do not threaten or bully the individual.
5. Do not show anger if subjected to insulting remarks.
6. Try to reason with the individual unless there is imminent danger.
7. Do not dare an individual to carry out a threat he or she has made against self or others.

Very often mentally ill individuals do not appear to be mentally ill. Others indicate that they suffer from mental illness by their dress or by acts of violence to themselves or to others. When police officers encounter a person who appears to be mentally ill, they must closely follow the procedure described above.

Questions 92 through 94 are to be answered on the basis of the aforementioned procedure and the following incident.

92. A police officer on foot patrol is approached by a citizen and told that a man is threatening to jump from the top floor of a nearby building. As the officer approaches the building, he sees the man standing on a narrow ledge threatening to jump. The police officer takes the elevator to the top of the building and is told by the elevator operator that the man is upset because his wife recently left him. The elevator operator also says that the man had been released from a mental institution only a short time ago. As the officer approaches, the man on the ledge threatens to jump. At this point it would be appropriate for the police officer to say,

(A) "Get off that ledge. Everybody has troubles."
(B) "Your wife has just arrived. Come on in and talk to her."
(C) "If I dare you to jump, you won't do it."
(D) "Come off that ledge, Romeo."

93. The police officer pulls the man to safety. The man then calls the officer a "racist pig." In response to the insult, the officer answers, "I just saved your life, you fool." The officer's remark was

(A) inappropriate; the officer should have said, "Your wife was right all the time."
(B) appropriate; police officers should not be insulted
(C) inappropriate; the officer should not have displayed his anger
(D) appropriate; he put the man in his place.

94. The man starts to curse the officer. The officer replies to these insults by saying, "You are going to be put away forever." This statement by the police officer was

(A) inappropriate; the police officer threatened the man with something he could not carry out
(B) appropriate; the man would probably be happy in a mental institution
(C) inappropriate; he should not have threatened the man
(D) appropriate; he advised the man correctly concerning his future.

Questions 95 through 98 are also to be answered on the basis of the procedure for dealing with persons who display indications of mental illness and are based on the incident described below.

Officer Cummings, on foot patrol several blocks away from the United Nations, encounters a crowd of people in front of a building. The officer forces his way through the crowd to find a man dressed as Mickey Mouse. Officer Cummings asks the man, "What seems to be the matter?" The man answers, "I have been appointed Disneyland's representative to the United Nations, and I am here to take my seat." Cummings laughs, and in a loud voice heard by the crowd says, "Donald Duck is Disneyland's official representative. Go see him." Officer Cummings then quietly says to the man, "Disneyland is not a real country. Therefore, it is not entitled to be represented at the United Nations."

95. Officer Cummings' question to the man was

(A) inappropriate; Cummings should have ordered the man to leave

(B) appropriate; Cummings in this way assured the man that he would get the help he needed

(C) inappropriate; Cummings should have first calmed the man down

(D) appropriate; the question led to the source of the trouble.

96. Officer Cummings reacted to the man's answer

(A) properly; the man's reply was funny

(B) improperly; the man's reply was not funny

(C) properly; the officer had indicated to the man how silly his story was by laughing

(D) improperly; the officer should not have laughed at the man.

97. Officer Cummings' remarks that were heard by the crowd were

(A) inappropriate; he should not have made fun of the man

(B) appropriate; they indicated to the crowd that Officer Cummings knew how to handle the situation

(C) inappropriate; the crowd gained the impression that the officer believed the man

(D) appropriate; they tended to reduce the tension.

98. Officer Cummings' remark, "Donald Duck is Disneyland's official representative. Go see him" was

(A) appropriate; it indicated to the man that the officer was there to help him

(B) inappropriate; the officer at that point should not have disagreed with the man's story

(C) appropriate; the man would be receptive to the explanation

(D) inappropriate; the officer should have been truthful to the man

ANSWER KEY FOR PRACTICE EXAMINATION 4

1. D	21. B	41. D	61. D	81. C
2. C	22. B	42. A	62. D	82. C
3. C	23. A	43. B	63. A	83. A
4. D	24. D	44. C	64. C	84. C
5. C	25. C	45. B	65. A	85. A
6. D	26. A	46. B	66. C	86. C
7. C	27. C	47. A	67. B	87. D
8. D	28. B	48. C	68. B	88. B
9. D	29. A	49. C	69. D	89. A
10. A	30. D	50. B	70. D	90. B
11. B	31. A	51. B	71. A	91. D
12. C	32. D	52. D	72. B	92. B
13. A	33. A	53. A	73. A	93. C
14. B	34. C	54. B	74. C	94. C
15. C	35. C	55. D	75. A	95. D
16. C	36. B	56. A	76. C	96. D
17. B	37. A	57. A	77. D	97. A
18. D	38. C	58. C	78. B	98. B
19. A	39. D	59. D	79. B	
20. D	40. B	60. C	80. C	

EXPLANATORY ANSWERS FOR PRACTICE EXAMINATION 4

1. **(D)** Refer to the third sentence of the fourth paragraph.

2. **(C)** Refer to the last sentence of the fourth paragraph.

3. **(C)** Refer to the second sentence of the fifth paragraph.

4. **(D)** Refer to the next-to-last sentence of the third paragraph.

5. **(C)** Refer to the seventh sentence of the third paragraph.

6. **(D)** Refer to the next-to-last sentence of the third paragraph.

7. **(C)** Refer to the sixth sentence of the third paragraph.

8. **(D)** Refer to the fifth sentence of the third paragraph.

9. **(D)** Refer to the third sentence of the third paragraph.

10. **(A)** Refer to the next-to-last sentence of the third paragraph.

11. **(B)** Refer to the seventh sentence of the third paragraph.

12. **(C)** Refer to the fourth sentence of the third paragraph.

13. **(A)** Refer to the third sentence of the fourth paragraph.

14. **(B)** Refer to the third sentence of the fourth paragraph.

15. **(C)** Refer to the third sentence of the fourth paragraph.

16. **(C)** The course of action as stated should first be evaluated as improper. The parked unattended police car could not be easily moved to permit arriving emergency vehicles to enter the street.

17. **(B)** The long thin scar on the cheek would be highly visible. The eye patch also makes for good identification because very few people wear them. Points of identification must be distinctive or unusual, visible, and not easily subject to change.

18. **(D)** The police officer has no other choice than to respect Mr. Mont's right to diplomatic immunity.

19. **(A)** Procedures, rules, and regulations are implemented so that certain situations will be handled in the best possible manner. The police officer has no choice but to follow them. As stated, medical assistance for the rape victim should be summoned *first*.

20. **(D)** This is a restrictive sign. It indicates only when parking or standing is not permitted. According to the sign, parking is permitted at 4 P.M. Friday. There is no regulation concerning standing at this time.

21. **(B)** There is no restriction against standing on Wednesdays according to the sign and the accompanying instructions.

22. **(B)** Refer to the second sentence of the second paragraph.

23. **(A)** In the first paragraph, it is stated that the arrest took place approximately three minutes after the crime was committed. In the second sentence of the second paragraph, the owner of the store stated that the crime was committed at 10:30 P.M.

24. **(D)** Refer to the second sentence of the second paragraph for the date and time of the incident.

25. **(C)** Refer to the fifth sentence of the second paragraph.

Correctly Filled Arrest Report

REPORT OF ARREST

ARREST INFORMATION	(1) Date of arrest 8/14/79	(2) Time of arrest 10:33 P.M.	(3) Place of arrest 1139 Ave of Americas	(4) Precinct Midtown North	(5) Arrest number 18431

DESCRIPTION OF INCIDENT

(6) Prisoner's weapon (description)
Knife

(7) Date and time
8/14/79
10:30 P.M.

(8) Prisoner's auto (color, year, make, model, license plate number, state)
Light Blue, 1973 Oldsmobile, 2-door, N.Y. 452-XCP

(9) Type of business
Delicatessen

(10) Location of incident (be specific)
1151 Ave of Americas N.Y.C.

DESCRIPTION OF PRISONER

(11) Last name First name Middle initial
Wright, John

(12) Date of birth
2/14/57

(13) Sex M	(14) Race W	(15) Eyes Brown	(16) Hair Brown	(17) Weight 145	(18) Height 5'11"	(19) Age 22

(20) Address City State
457 Willis Ave, Bronx, N.Y.

(21) Apt. no.
3B

(22) Home phone number
(212)
752-8116

(23) Citizenship Citizen ☒ Non-Citizen ☐

(24) Place of birth
N.Y.C.

(25) Marital status
Single

(26) Social Security number
073-16-9812

(27) Where employed (company and address)
Wellmade Blouse Company
262 W. 37 St., N.Y.C.

(28) Nickname
Slim

(29) Scars, tattoos (describe fully and give location)
red and blue tattoo of head of Indian Chief on right forearm

DESCRIPTION OF COMPLAINANT

(30) Last name First name Middle initial
Connors, Robert

(31) Date of birth
6/17/25

Telephone Numbers

(32) Business 515-7623	(33) Home 852-8817	(34) Address City State 1143 57 St., Brooklyn, N.Y.

26. **(A)** Refer to the fourth sentence of the first paragraph.

27. **(C)** Refer to the end of the first paragraph.

28. **(B)** Refer to the next to last sentence of the first paragraph. Watch the spelling.

29. **(A)** Refer to the first sentence of the third paragraph.

30. **(D)** Refer to the last sentence of the third paragraph.

31. **(A)** According to the definition of larceny, one may be considered guilty of this crime if found property is not returned to its owner.

32. **(D)** Larceny also involves obtaining property under false pretenses, which is the situation here.

33. **(A)** Leo Charles' behavior created substantial risk to schoolchildren in the area, and his criminally negligent behavior resulted in the death of a child. Charles did not intend to kill the child.

34. **(C)** Burke committed the crime of criminal trespass because he possessed a weapon. Hill is not guilty of criminal trespass because he did not know that Burke was carrying a concealed weapon.

35. **(C)** The difference between choices (B), (C), and (D) is the *intent* to enter into the building for the purpose of committing a crime. Wilson did not have previous intent to steal the tools; Mr. Johnson did not plan to steal the tooth paste.

36. **(B)** Blount and Wallace both committed harassment: Blount because she pushed Wallace in an attempt to scare her and Wallace because she made an obscene gesture at Blount.

37. **(A)** William Hammer did not injure either Bates or Collins so he is not guilty of assault. He was, however, intentionally reckless.

38. **(C)** Larceny is the wrongful taking of property from the owner without use of force, violence, or threat of injury.

39. **(D)** Since Calvin may be considered "under the influence of an extreme emotional disturbance" over the death of his daughter, the crime Calvin committed was manslaughter.

40. **(B)** The definition of the crime of criminal mischief involves the intentional destruction of another's property. This was not arson because a car is not a building and there was no explosion.

41. **(D)** Making obscene gestures in public places is considered harassment.

42. **(A)** Thomas Hunt took the bicycle from Robert Huron against Huron's will.

43. **(B)** Police rules and regulations must be followed exactly. Although the officers are male, they should have checked the women's rest room because the prowler may have been hiding there.

44. **(C)** The action of the officers must be evaluated as proper. The seven-year-old girl could have supplied the information necessary to apprehend the prowler. There is no harm in asking the girl.

45. **(B)** Rule 3 prohibits the use of names, therefore, choices (A), (C), and (D) are incorrect. Choice (B) avoids the use of names and adheres to the rest of the rules.

46. **(B)** Officer Ahern's actions must be evaluated as improper. In choosing between (B) and (D), whether Ahern should have cancelled the appointment is immaterial to the situation in question, therefore, (B) must be chosen as the correct answer.

47. **(A)** The action of the officers was improper. Rule 4 prohibits the use of portable radios since they may in some way trigger the bomb.

48. **(C)** Rule 3 states that lights should not be turned off or on because of the possibility of setting of the bomb.

49. **(C)** Officer Samuel's action should be evaluated as improper because the handling of the suspicious suitcase should have been left to a specialist in bomb control. Officer Samuel was very fortunate that the suitcase did not contain the bomb since he could have set it off by opening the suitcase.

50. **(B)** According to the procedure, Officer Hawthorne acted properly. In choosing between (B) and (D), recall that the victim could not be identified, therefore, (B) should be selected as the correct answer. Profuse, uncontrolled bleeding is the greatest danger to life.

Officer Hawthorne acted correctly in trying to stop the man's bleeding first.

51. **(B)** Rule 4 of the procedure indicates that Officer Alcorn should have accompanied the man to the hospital since the man refused to identify himself.

52. **(D)** Refer to Rule 1. An officer should never assume the responsibility of deciding whether or not a prisoner requires the services of a doctor.

53. **(A)** Refer to Rule 2. It is apparent that the prisoner requires medical attention even though there is no emergency. Medical attention is required for the prisoner's wound, not his drug addiction, therefore, an ambulance should be called.

54. **(B)** Officer Dorkin acted improperly. Rule 3 states that *under no circumstances* should a police officer prescribe medication for a prisoner. Medicine prescribed for Officer Dorkin might have been harmful to the prisoner.

55. **(D)** Police Officer Levin acted incorrectly since he spoke only with people leaving the party and not with the people who lived in the apartment (the source of the complaint). Choice (D) is better than choice (B), because if Officer Levin had ordered all the guests to leave the party, he would have been exceeding his authority.

56. **(A)** Police Officer Smythe's actions were decidedly improper. He made no investigation. Choosing between (A) and (C), (A) is a far better choice than (C). The couple with the baby might have needed the assistance of the officer.

57. **(A)** Officer Mayfield acted improperly in that by ordering all bystanders away from the area, he could have lost track of important witnesses to the crime. He violated Rule 4 of the procedure.

58. **(C)** Checking the victim for signs of life is the first step the officer should take. Immediate medical attention may be needed to save a victim in a life or death situation.

59. **(D)** Officer Mayfield's action in this instance was improper. Choosing between (B) and (D), remember that the officer's *first* responsibility is to see to the medical necessities of the victim of the crime.

60. **(C)** Officer Mayfield acted properly according to Rule 6 of the procedure. A witness should be questioned out of earshot of other witnesses so that his or her testimony does not influence other witnesses to the crime.

61. **(D)** Refer to Rule 6 of the procedure and select choice (D).

62. **(D)** Refer to Rule 1 of the procedure and select choice (D). The reason for not standing in front of the door is that if the inhabitants of the apartment had a gun, the officer would be vulnerable if the weapon were fired at the door.

63. **(A)** The actions of the officers should be evaluated as improper. They should have interviewed both the husband and wife to get both sides of the story.

64. **(C)** Officer Blue's statement was inappropriate. Refer to Rules 4 and 7 and then select (C) as the correct answer. A police officer does not have the authority to direct an individual to change his or her mode of living if it is not unlawful.

65. **(A)** The officers acted improperly. No arrest should have been made since no one was hurt (see Rule 8).

66. **(C)** Officer Wynne acted properly although he did not find out any information. Choice (A) is incorrect because there was definite indication that a demonstration was going to take place.

67. **(B)** Officer Stanley does not have the authority to take the courses of action outlined in choices (A) and (C). If the officer could learn more of the woman's plans for the demonstration, it would be helpful to the police in dealing with demonstrators.

68. **(B)** This information could possibly help police deal with the situation.

69. **(D)** Refer to Rule 1 of the procedure. The first thing the officer should do is ascertain that the woman is indeed dead.

70. **(D)** Refer to Rule 4 of the procedure.

71. **(A)** Refer to Rule 3 of the procedure. The police officer should summon a sergeant to the scene before doing anything else.

72. **(B)** Refer to Rule 6. The sister did not live with the dead man, therefore, the albums may not be released to her.

73. **(A)** Permission to inform the caller of the death of a relative is given in Rule 8 of the procedure.

74. **(C)** The officer's action is proper. According to Rule 7, a statement that would further upset the family of the deceased should not be made.

75. **(A)** The officer is required to testify honestly. If he does not remember the exact situation, he must say so. If he does not know the answer to the question now, more time will not be of any help to him.

76. **(C)** Of the choices given, (C) is the only question which will not elicit "yes" or "no" as an answer.

77. **(D)** Choices (A), (B), and (C) are all leading questions. Choice (D) is objective, and, therefore, a good question to ask.

78. **(B)** A police officer on duty should not offer an opinion in a controversial matter according to Rule 4. The response in choice (B) is noncommittal.

79. **(B)** The officer, in this instance, should keep calm and address the point at issue. Extraneous comments or outrage are only likely to aggravate the situation.

80. **(C)** Refer to Rules 1 and 2 of the procedure.

81. **(C)** The officer acted improperly according to the procedure because he criticized the driver's ability (see Rule 5) and did not advise him of his violation (Rule 2). There is no mention in the question that the driver had been drinking.

82. **(C)** The police officer acted improperly. The officer's response should have been specific in pointing out exactly what the police do to protect the children in the area.

83. **(A)** The police officer acted incorrectly. The officer was responding to a complaint on the part of the woman, but he has done nothing to ensure that her rights will not be violated.

84. **(C)** The action of the officer was improper. The vendor should have been afforded the opportunity to give his side of the story.

85. **(A)** The action of the officer is incorrect since no explanations were made to the teenagers. Such actions will only cause the teenagers to resent authority figures such as the police.

86. **(C)** The officer's actions must be considered improper. The officer should not have hurried the woman. She may have important information regarding the robbery.

87. **(D)** The officer's action was proper since it may lead to obtaining wanted information. Choice (B) is incorrect since the question states that the witness is cooperative.

88. **(B)** The witness' response, considering the circumstances, could be considered normal. The other choices contain courses of action that would only make matters worse.

89. **(A)** The objective of the officers is to get the prisoner to supply the names of the other parties involved. Refer to Rule 4 of the procedure.

90. **(B)** Refer to Rule 3 of the procedure. If the officer is sufficiently convincing, the man is likely to confess.

91. **(D)** This approach is most direct, and it will probably convince the woman to cooperate with the police in the upcoming proceedings.

92. **(B)** The objective of the officer is to distract the man and gain his attention. Telling him that his wife is there may get him to move off the ledge and come back into the building.

93. **(C)** The officer's response was inappropriate. A police officer must contain any personal anger against an individual he or she may come in contact with during the performance of duties.

94. **(C)** The remark made by the officer is inappropriate because, under these circumstances, no threat should be made. See Rule 4 of the procedure.

95. **(D)** Officer Cummings' question was appropriate in that it opened up a line of communication with the man. A choice has to be made between (B) and (D). Choice (B) is incorrect because Cummings did not assure the man that he would get help.

96. **(D)** According to the procedure, Officer Cummings acted improperly (refer specifically to Rule 3). His laughter could have become infectious, especially since he represented authority to the crowd. Laughter was indeed not called for and could have been emotionally harmful to the man.

97. **(A)** Officer Cummings' remarks were inappropriate. Again refer to Rule 3. An officer of the law should never make fun of a person who appears to be mentally ill.

98. **(B)** Again, Officer Cummings' remark was inappropriate for the same reason as given in question 97.

ANSWER SHEET FOR PRACTICE EXAMINATION 5

1. Ⓐ Ⓑ Ⓒ Ⓓ
2. Ⓐ Ⓑ Ⓒ Ⓓ
3. Ⓐ Ⓑ Ⓒ Ⓓ
4. Ⓐ Ⓑ Ⓒ Ⓓ
5. Ⓐ Ⓑ Ⓒ Ⓓ
6. Ⓐ Ⓑ Ⓒ Ⓓ
7. Ⓐ Ⓑ Ⓒ Ⓓ
8. Ⓐ Ⓑ Ⓒ Ⓓ
9. Ⓐ Ⓑ Ⓒ Ⓓ
10. Ⓐ Ⓑ Ⓒ Ⓓ
11. Ⓐ Ⓑ Ⓒ Ⓓ
12. Ⓐ Ⓑ Ⓒ Ⓓ
13. Ⓐ Ⓑ Ⓒ Ⓓ
14. Ⓐ Ⓑ Ⓒ Ⓓ
15. Ⓐ Ⓑ Ⓒ Ⓓ
16. Ⓐ Ⓑ Ⓒ Ⓓ
17. Ⓐ Ⓑ Ⓒ Ⓓ
18. Ⓐ Ⓑ Ⓒ Ⓓ
19. Ⓐ Ⓑ Ⓒ Ⓓ
20. Ⓐ Ⓑ Ⓒ Ⓓ

21. Ⓐ Ⓑ Ⓒ Ⓓ
22. Ⓐ Ⓑ Ⓒ Ⓓ
23. Ⓐ Ⓑ Ⓒ Ⓓ
24. Ⓐ Ⓑ Ⓒ Ⓓ
25. Ⓐ Ⓑ Ⓒ Ⓓ
26. Ⓐ Ⓑ Ⓒ Ⓓ
27. Ⓐ Ⓑ Ⓒ Ⓓ
28. Ⓐ Ⓑ Ⓒ Ⓓ
29. Ⓐ Ⓑ Ⓒ Ⓓ
30. Ⓐ Ⓑ Ⓒ Ⓓ
31. Ⓐ Ⓑ Ⓒ Ⓓ
32. Ⓐ Ⓑ Ⓒ Ⓓ
33. Ⓐ Ⓑ Ⓒ Ⓓ
34. Ⓐ Ⓑ Ⓒ Ⓓ
35. Ⓐ Ⓑ Ⓒ Ⓓ
36. Ⓐ Ⓑ Ⓒ Ⓓ
37. Ⓐ Ⓑ Ⓒ Ⓓ
38. Ⓐ Ⓑ Ⓒ Ⓓ
39. Ⓐ Ⓑ Ⓒ Ⓓ
40. Ⓐ Ⓑ Ⓒ Ⓓ

41. Ⓐ Ⓑ Ⓒ Ⓓ
42. Ⓐ Ⓑ Ⓒ Ⓓ
43. Ⓐ Ⓑ Ⓒ Ⓓ
44. Ⓐ Ⓑ Ⓒ Ⓓ
45. Ⓐ Ⓑ Ⓒ Ⓓ
46. Ⓐ Ⓑ Ⓒ Ⓓ
47. Ⓐ Ⓑ Ⓒ Ⓓ
48. Ⓐ Ⓑ Ⓒ Ⓓ
49. Ⓐ Ⓑ Ⓒ Ⓓ
50. Ⓐ Ⓑ Ⓒ Ⓓ
51. Ⓐ Ⓑ Ⓒ Ⓓ
52. Ⓐ Ⓑ Ⓒ Ⓓ
53. Ⓐ Ⓑ Ⓒ Ⓓ
54. Ⓐ Ⓑ Ⓒ Ⓓ
55. Ⓐ Ⓑ Ⓒ Ⓓ
56. Ⓐ Ⓑ Ⓒ Ⓓ
57. Ⓐ Ⓑ Ⓒ Ⓓ
58. Ⓐ Ⓑ Ⓒ Ⓓ
59. Ⓐ Ⓑ Ⓒ Ⓓ
60. Ⓐ Ⓑ Ⓒ Ⓓ

61. Ⓐ Ⓑ Ⓒ Ⓓ
62. Ⓐ Ⓑ Ⓒ Ⓓ
63. Ⓐ Ⓑ Ⓒ Ⓓ
64. Ⓐ Ⓑ Ⓒ Ⓓ
65. Ⓐ Ⓑ Ⓒ Ⓓ
66. Ⓐ Ⓑ Ⓒ Ⓓ
67. Ⓐ Ⓑ Ⓒ Ⓓ
68. Ⓐ Ⓑ Ⓒ Ⓓ
69. Ⓐ Ⓑ Ⓒ Ⓓ
70. Ⓐ Ⓑ Ⓒ Ⓓ
71. Ⓐ Ⓑ Ⓒ Ⓓ
72. Ⓐ Ⓑ Ⓒ Ⓓ
73. Ⓐ Ⓑ Ⓒ Ⓓ
74. Ⓐ Ⓑ Ⓒ Ⓓ
75. Ⓐ Ⓑ Ⓒ Ⓓ
76. Ⓐ Ⓑ Ⓒ Ⓓ
77. Ⓐ Ⓑ Ⓒ Ⓓ
78. Ⓐ Ⓑ Ⓒ Ⓓ
79. Ⓐ Ⓑ Ⓒ Ⓓ
80. Ⓐ Ⓑ Ⓒ Ⓓ

81. Ⓐ Ⓑ Ⓒ Ⓓ
82. Ⓐ Ⓑ Ⓒ Ⓓ
83. Ⓐ Ⓑ Ⓒ Ⓓ
84. Ⓐ Ⓑ Ⓒ Ⓓ
85. Ⓐ Ⓑ Ⓒ Ⓓ
86. Ⓐ Ⓑ Ⓒ Ⓓ
87. Ⓐ Ⓑ Ⓒ Ⓓ
88. Ⓐ Ⓑ Ⓒ Ⓓ
89. Ⓐ Ⓑ Ⓒ Ⓓ
90. Ⓐ Ⓑ Ⓒ Ⓓ
91. Ⓐ Ⓑ Ⓒ Ⓓ
92. Ⓐ Ⓑ Ⓒ Ⓓ
93. Ⓐ Ⓑ Ⓒ Ⓓ
94. Ⓐ Ⓑ Ⓒ Ⓓ
95. Ⓐ Ⓑ Ⓒ Ⓓ
96. Ⓐ Ⓑ Ⓒ Ⓓ
97. Ⓐ Ⓑ Ⓒ Ⓓ
98. Ⓐ Ⓑ Ⓒ Ⓓ
99. Ⓐ Ⓑ Ⓒ Ⓓ
100. Ⓐ Ⓑ Ⓒ Ⓓ

PRACTICE EXAMINATION 5

The time allowed for the entire examination is 3½ hours.

Directions: Each question has four suggested answers, lettered (A), (B), (C), and (D). Decide which one is the best answer, and on the sample answer sheet, locate the question number and darken the area corresponding to your answer choice with a soft pencil.

Questions 1 through 15 are to be answered on the basis of the description of the police action which follows. You will have ten minutes to read and study the description. Then you will have to answer the 15 questions about the incident without referring back to the description of the incident.

Police Officers Smith and Jones were working a midnight to 8 A.M. tour of duty. It was a Saturday morning in the month of July and the weather was clear. At about 4:30 A.M., Officers Smith and Jones received a radio call reporting a burglary in progress at 777 Seventeenth Street, the address of an appliance store.

Upon their arrival at the scene, the officers could not find evidence of a break-in. However, as the officers continued their investigation, they heard noises coming from the rear of the building. As the officers raced to the rear of the building, they saw four people alighting from the roof, by way of a ladder, and climbing over a fence that leads to the rear of a warehouse. As the officers climbed over the fence, they observed two of the people running into an alleyway on the west side of the warehouse and the other two people running into a parking lot on the east side of the warehouse.

Officer Smith, using a walkie-talkie, called for assistance and proceeded to give chase after the two persons who entered the alley. The description of the two individuals was as follows: One was a male white, wearing light pants, a blue shirt, and white sneakers, with long blond hair, and carrying what appeared to be a portable T.V. set. The other was also a male white, wearing dungarees, a white T-shirt, and cowboy boots, with short dark hair, and carrying what appeared to be a portable cassette-stereo-radio.

Officer Jones continued to give chase to the two individuals who had entered the parking lot. The description of these two individuals was as follows: One was a male Hispanic, wearing dark pants, a yellow shirt, and dark shoes, with long dark hair, and carrying what appeared to be a video recorder. The other was a male black, wearing dungarees, a white T-shirt, and white sneakers, with a bald head, and carrying what appeared to be a baseball bat and portable T.V. set.

As Officer Smith emerged from the alley onto the sidewalk, he again observed the two individuals he had been chasing. They were entering a dark blue Chevrolet with New York license plates, beginning with the letters AKG. The vehicle drove west on Seventh Street. The male with the long blond hair appeared to be driving.

As Officer Jones reached the parking lot, he observed the two individuals he was pursuing speed off in a white station wagon, heading west on Seventh Street. The license plates could not be discerned. Officer Jones found a broken portable T.V. set in the parking lot.

Officer Smith broadcast this additional information, and both officers then quickly returned to their radio car to conduct a search of the area.

Do not refer back to the description while answering questions 1 through 15.

1. Officers Smith and Jones responded to a "burglary in progress" call at approximately

   (A) midnight
   (B) 8:00 A.M.
   (C) 4:30 P.M.
   (D) 4:30 A.M.

2. This suspects in the burglary gained entrance to the store by

   (A) breaking a front window
   (B) breaking a rear window
   (C) breaking in from an adjoining warehouse
   (D) using a ladder to get to the roof.

3. The suspects, when fleeing from the burglary,

   (A) all ran into an alleyway
   (B) all ran into a parking lot
   (C) all ran into a warehouse
   (D) went in different directions.

4. The male white with the long blond hair was carrying what appeared to be a

   (A) portable T.V. set
   (B) portable cassette-stereo-radio
   (C) video recorder
   (D) portable cassette player.

5. The male Hispanic was carrying what appeared to be a

   (A) video recorder
   (B) portable cassette-stereo-radio
   (C) portable T.V. set
   (D) portable cassette player.

6. The male white with the short hair was carrying what appeared to be a

   (A) portable T.V. set
   (B) portable cassette-stereo-radio
   (C) video recorder
   (D) portable cassette player

7. The suspect wearing cowboy boots was the

   (A) male white with long blond hair
   (B) male black
   (C) male Hispanic
   (D) male white with short hair.

8. The suspect wearing light pants and blue shirt was the

   (A) male black
   (B) male white with long blond hair
   (C) male Hispanic
   (D) male white with short hair.

9. The suspect wearing dark pants and a yellow shirt was the

   (A) male white with long blond hair
   (B) male black
   (C) male white with short hair
   (D) male Hispanic.

10. When the suspects were fleeing, the two male whites entered a

    (A) blue station wagon with unknown license plates
    (B) white station wagon with New York license plates beginning with the letters AKG
    (C) blue Chevrolet with New York license plates beginning with the letters AKG
    (D) white Chevrolet with unknown license plates.

11. From reading the description of the incident, one could assume

    (A) that Seventh Street is one way westbound
    (B) that Seventh Steet is a two-way street
    (C) that Seventh Street is one way eastbound
    (D) none of the above.

12. Upon entering the parking lot, Officer Jones found a broken portable T.V. set that has apparently been dropped by the

    (A) male white with blond hair
    (B) male white with dark hair
    (C) male black
    (D) male Hispanic.

13. The male black was

    (A) bald, and wearing dark pants, a yellow shirt, and dark shoes
    (B) bald, wearing dungarees, a white T-shirt, and white sneakers
    (C) wearing dungarees, a white T-shirt, and cowboy boots, and had dark hair
    (D) bald, and wearing light pants and a blue shirt.

14. The suspect who was carrying the baseball bat was also carrying what appeared to be a

    (A) portable T.V. set
    (B) video recorder
    (C) portable cassette-stereo-radio
    (D) portable cassette player.

15. A description of the suspects was broadcast to other police units so that they could assist in searching the area. This was done by
    (A) both Officers Jones and Smith as they both had walkie-talkies
    (B) Officer Jones as he had a walkie-talkie
    (C) Officer Smith as he had a walki-talkie
    (D) both officers upon returning to their radio car.

16. In the investigation of a homicide case, it is desirable to have photographs taken of the body in its original condition and position. Of the following, the best reason for this practice is that the photographs
    (A) show the motive for the hoimicide and thus indicate likely suspects
    (B) indicate if the corpse has been moved in any way
    (C) form a permanent record of the body and the scene of the crime
    (D) reveal the specific method used in committing the homicide.

17. A police officer hears two shots fired and proceeds in the direction of the shots. He comes upon an intoxicated man who is angrily screaming at a woman. The officer notices that the handle of a pistol is protruding from the man's pocket and orders him to surrender the pistol. The man apparently ignores the order and continues screaming at the woman. For the officer now to fire a warning shot over the man's head would be
    (A) bad; it is quite possible that the man is so intoxicated that he did not clearly hear or understand the officer's order
    (B) bad; the officer should realize that an intoxicated person is not entirely responsible for his actions
    (C) good, the warning shot will impress the man with the seriousness of the situation
    (D) good; since the man had already fired twice, the officer should take no further chances.

18. The practice of writing down confessions while a suspect is being questioned is
    (A) bad, chiefly because the time taken to put a confession into written form may prove to be a waste of time since it may later be declared to be inadmissible as evidence in court
    (B) bad, chiefly because this may cause the suspect to withhold information when he or she knows that the confession is being recorded
    (C) good, chiefly because the suspect cannot claim at a later date that the information was obtained by force
    (D) good, chiefly because the suspect is thereby given more time to gather his or her thoughts and give the information wanted by the police.

19. It is important for a police officer to be thoroughly familiar with the street locations, house numbers, and alleys on his or her post. In the event that the police officer is searching for a prowler reported to be on his or her post, this familiarity will be of greatest value in that it will enable the police officer to
    (A) capture the prowler more quickly by going directly to the usual haunts of those previously arrested for the same violation
    (B) anticipate possible avenues of flight which the prowler might take from the location where he was reported seen.
    (C) conduct a systematic search of the surrounding area
    (D) know which buildings are unoccupied and search for the prowler there first.

20. An escaped prisoner has been wounded and is lying flat on his stomach with his head turned to one side. The one of the following directions from which a police officer should approach the prisoner in order to make it most difficult for the prisoner to fire quickly and accurately at the police officer is from the side
    (A) directly behind the prisoner's head
    (B) facing the top of the prisoner's head
    (C) facing the prisoner's face
    (D) facing the prisoner's heels.

21. A gas main explosion has caused some property damage. Examination by an emergency repair crew clearly indicates that no further explosions will occur. Nevertheless, rumors are circulating that more explosions and greater damage are going to occur. This situation has resulted in a high degree of fear among local residents. The best of the following actions for a police officer on duty at the scene to take *first* would be to

   (A) ignore the rumors since they are false and no real danger exists
   (B) inform the people of the true circumstances of the emergency
   (C) question several people at the scene in an attempt to determine the source of the rumors
   (D) order everyone to leave the area quickly and in an orderly fashion.

22. A police officer finds a young child wandering about a residential neighborhood. After unsuccessfully questioning the child as to the location of his home, the officer phones police headquarters and is informed that no child meeting the description given by the officer has been reported as lost. The officer decides to make inquiries about the child in the immediate area before taking any other action. This action is advisable chiefly because

   (A) the child's parents probably know of his whereabouts since no report of the missing child has been received at headquarters
   (B) the child has probably been away from home only a short time since no report of the missing child has been received at headquarters
   (C) the child is less likely to become emotionally disturbed if he remains in his own neighborhood
   (D) young children, when lost, never wander more than a short distance from home.

23. While a police officer in plain clothes is following and watching a suspect in a homicide case, the officer becomes convinced that the suspect realizes he is being watched. The suspect's identity is known to the police, but he is also known to have changed his place of residence frequently during the past few months. The officer does not have sufficient evidence to arrest the suspect at this time. Of the following, the best action for the officer to take is to

   (A) approach the suspect, inform him that he is being followed, and demand an explanation of his suspicious past conduct
   (B) continue to follow the suspect until an opportunity is presented for the officer to telephone for a replacement
   (C) continue to follow the suspect since he will probably commit an illegal act eventually
   (D) discontinue following the suspect and attempt to gain evidence by other means.

24. While issuing a summons to the manager of a movie theater for allowing a child under 16 to remain in the theater without a parent or guardian at an R-rated movie, a police officer requests identification from the manager. The manager hands his wallet to the officer and says that his operator's license is in the wallet. The officer should not accept the wallet mainly

   (A) because the sorting of papers and cards contained in the wallet would be too time consuming for the officer
   (B) to discourage the manager from any possible bribery offer
   (C) to lessen the possibility that the manager will later claim that money or papers were taken from the wallet
   (D) to minimize the temptation for the officer to look at papers or cards of a personal nature.

25. Probationary Police Officers A and B are given a special assignment by the sergeant. Officer B does not fully understand some of the instructions given by the sergeant concerning the carrying out of the assignment. Of the following, it would be best for Officer B to

   (A) proceed with those parts of the assignment he understands and ask for an explanation from the sergeant when he can go no further
   (B) observe Officer A's work carefully in order to determine how the assignment is to be carried out
   (C) ask the sergeant to explain that portion of the instructions which he does not fully understand before starting the assignment
   (D) suggest to Officer A that he supervise the operation since he probably understands the sergeant's instructions better.

26. A police officer responds at night to a telephone complaint that a prowler has been observed at a particular location. The officer arrives at the location and notices someone who appears to fit the description of the prowler previously given by the complainant. In approaching this individual, it would be best for the police officer to

   (A) consider this individual to be a potentially dangerous criminal
   (B) avoid taking any precautionary measures since there is no way of knowing whether any offense has been committed
   (C) consider that this individual is probably harmless and is only a "Peeping Tom"
   (D) fire a warning shot over the man's head.

27. A police officer has been asked by a merchant on his post to recommend the best make of burglar alarm for his store. The chief reason why the police officer should not make any specific recommendation is that

   (A) he does not have enough technical knowledge of the operation of burglar alarms
   (B) the merchant may interpret the officer's recommendation as an official police department endorsement
   (C) such a recommendation would imply that the police are incapable of protecting the merchant's property
   (D) he is not likely to know the prices of the various makes and models available.

28. Two police officers in a radio patrol car stop a car which they recognize as having been reported stolen. The police officers immediately separate the two occupants of the car and proceed to question them apart from each other. Of the following, the most important reason for questioning them separately is to

   (A) give each suspect an opportunity to admit guilt out of the presence of the other suspect
   (B) prevent the suspects from agreeing on an explanation of their presence in the car
   (C) prevent the errors which may arise when attempting to record in a notebook two separate statements being made at the same time
   (D) determine which of the two suspects actually planned the theft of the car.

29. While on patrol, you are informed by the manager of a supermarket that an object which appears to be a homemade bomb has been discovered in his market. Your first reaction should be to

   (A) go to the market amd make sure that everyone leaves it immediately
   (B) go to the market, examine the bomb, and then decide what action should be taken
   (C) question the manager in detail in an effort to determine whether this really is a bomb
   (D) telephone the bomb squad for instructions as to how the bomb should be rendered harmless.

30. A police officer on post would be most likely to make a regular hourly signal-box call to the precinct, rather than an immediate call, when he or she

   (A) discovers that a traffic signal light is not functioning properly
   (B) discovers what appears to be an abandoned car on the post
   (C) notices a street name sign which has been damaged
   (D) overhears a conversation relating to a possible disturbance between two groups of teenagers.

31. The most reasonable advice that a police officer can give to a merchant who asks what he should do if he receives a telephone call from a person he doesn't recognize regarding an alleged emergency at his store after ordinary business hours is that the merchant should go to the store and, if police officers are not at the scene, he should

    (A) continue past the store and call the police for assistance
    (B) continue past the store, and return and enter it if there doesn't appear to be an emergency
    (C) enter the store and ascertain whether the alleged emergency exists
    (D) enter the store only if there is no one apparently loitering in the vicinity.

32. A police officer is asked by a citizen for directions to a candy store which the officer knows is under observation for suspected bookmaking activity. In such a situation, the police officer should

    (A) give the proper directions to the citizen
    (B) give the proper directions to the citizen but explain that the store is under observation
    (C) pretend not to know the location of the store
    (D) tell the citizen that he may be arrested if the store is raided.

33. Whenever a crime has been committed, the criminal has disturbed the surroundings in one way or another by his or her presence. The *least* valid deduction for the police to make from this statement is that

    (A) clues are thus present at all crime scenes
    (B) even the slightest search at crime scenes will turn up conclusive evidence
    (C) the greater the number of criminals involved in a crime, the greater the number of clues likely to be available
    (D) the completely clueless crime is rarely encountered in police work

34. It is suggested that a suspect should not be permitted to walk in or about the scene of a crime where fingerprints may be present until a thorough search has been made for such evidence. This suggested procedure is

    (A) good; the suspect would, if permitted to walk about the scene, smear all fingerprints that might be found by police investigators
    (B) bad; the return of a suspect to the scene of a crime provides an opportunity to obtain additional fingerprints from the suspect
    (C) good; if the suspect handled any objects at the scene, the value of any original fingerprints, as evidence, might be seriously impaired
    (D) bad; the return of a suspect to the scene of a crime provides an opportunity to identify objects that had been handled during the commission of the crime.

35. A police officer is the first one to arrive at the scene of a murder. The suspect offers to make a statement concerning the crime. The police officer refuses to accept the statement. The officer's action was

    (A) good; interrogation of suspects should be performed by experienced detectives
    (B) poor; the suspect may later change his mind and refuse to make any statement
    (C) good; the officer will be too busy maintaining order at the scene to be able to accept the statement
    (D) poor; a statement made by the suspect would quickly solve the crime.

Answer questions 36 through 45 on the basis of the following legal definitions.

Burglary is committed when a person enters a building to commit a crime therein.

Larceny is committed when a person wrongfully takes, obtains, or withholds the property of another.

Robbery is the forcible stealing of property. If a person, while committing a larceny, uses or threatens the *immediate* use of force, the crime changes from larceny to robbery.

Sexual Abuse is committed when a person subjects another person to sexual contact without the second person's consent or when a person has sexual contact with another person less than 17 years of age. (A person less than 17 years of age cannot legally consent to any sexual conduct.) "Sexual contact" may be defined as touching the sexual or other intimate parts of a person to achieve sexual gratification.

Sexual Misconduct is committed when a male has sexual intercourse with a consenting female who is at least 13 years of age but less than 17 years of age.

Harrassment is committed when a person intends to harass, annoy, or alarm another person and does so by striking, shoving, kicking, or otherwise subjecting the other person to physical contact.

Assault is committed when a person unlawfully causes a physical injury to another person.

36. James Kelly enters the home of Mary Smith with the intention of taking Mary's portable T.V. set. While Kelly is in the apartment, Mary wakes up and attempts to retrieve her T.V. set from Kelly. Kelly punches Mary in the face and flees with the T.V. set. Kelly can be charged with

(A) burglary and larceny
(B) burglary only
(C) robbery and larceny
(D) burglary and robbery.

37. John Brown enters a department store with the intention of doing some shopping. Brown has a .38 caliber revolver in his coat pocket and also has a criminal conviction for armed robbery. As he passes the jewelry counter, he notices an expensive watch lying on the showcase. He checks to see if anyone is watching him, and, when he feels that he is not being observed, he slips the watch into his pocket and leaves the store. Brown could be charged with

(A) larceny
(B) burglary and larceny
(C) burglary and robbery
(D) robbery.

38. Tom Murphy enters a crowded subway car. He positions himself behind a woman and starts to touch her buttocks with his hand. The woman becomes very annoyed and starts to move away. As she does so, Murphy reaches into her pocketbook and removes $10. He then exits the train at the next station. Murphy could be charged with

(A) robbery, larceny, and sexual misconduct
(B) burglary, robbery, and sexual abuse
(C) burglary, larceny, and sexual misconduct
(D) larceny and sexual abuse.

39. Ed Saunders entered the apartment of Jane Robers with the intent to sexually abuse her. However, Robers was not at home and Saunders left the apartment. Saunders could be charged with

(A) sexual abuse
(B) sexual misconduct
(C) burglary
(D) none of the above as a crime did not take place because Robers was not at home.

40. Frank Taylor entered the apartment of his 16-year-old girlfriend, Doris, to have sexual intercourse with her. Doris consented to this sexual conduct and they engaged in intercourse. Taylor could be charged with

    (A) burglary
    (B) sexual misconduct
    (C) both burglary and sexual misconduct
    (D) no crime as Doris consented to the activity.

41. Brian Jones asks his 17-year-old girlfriend, Mary, if she would like to go to a motel and have sexual intercourse. She agrees and they go to the motel. Jones could be charged with

    (A) burglary
    (B) sexual misconduct
    (C) both burglary and sexual misconduct
    (D) no crime as she consented to the activity.

42. Bill is at a party at Joan's house. An argument ensues among several of the guests. Bill overhears Helen make a derogatory comment about him. He walks up to Helen and demands she "apologize or else." Helen refuses to apologize; Bill slaps her in the face and then rushes from the apartment. Bill could be charged with

    (A) assault
    (B) burglary and assault
    (C) harassment
    (D) burglary and harassment.

43. Joe is on his way to work. He is in a very bad mood. As he enters the warehouse where he works, he slips and falls to the floor. This only escalates his foul mood. As he is getting up, he sees a fellow worker who had made some unkind remarks to him two days before. Joe picks up a piece of board that is lying on the floor, walks up to the other worker, and hits him across the arm. This causes the other worker to suffer a broken arm. Joe could be charged with

    (A) assault
    (B) burglary and assault
    (C) harassment
    (D) none of the above as Joe was emotionally upset.

44. Jim enters a school through a rear window at 2:00 A.M. He wants to take a movie projector that he knows is kept in a specific room. He enters the room, takes the projector, and starts to leave when he is confronted by a security guard. The guard attempts to grab Jim; however, Jim slips away. As the guard again attempts to apprehend him, Jim swings the projector, striking the guard in the face. The guard falls to the floor unconscious and suffers a broken nose. Jim could be charged with

    (A) burglary, larceny, and robbery
    (B) robbery, larceny, and assault
    (C) burglary, larceny, and assault
    (D) burglary, robbery, and assault.

45. Sue invites Tom to her apartment for dinner. After dinner, Tom decides that he would like to have a sexual encounter with Sue. She attempts to discourage his advances. Tom then proceeds to hold her down on the couch and to fondle her breasts and touch her private parts. When Sue starts to scream, Tom rushes from the apartment. Tom could be charged with

    (A) burglary and sexual abuse
    (B) burglary and sexual misconduct
    (C) sexual abuse
    (D) no crime as Sue invited him to her apartment.

46. It is important that the police give proper attention to the investigation of apparently minor, as well as major, complaints made by citizens. Of the following, the one which is the *most* valid reason for doing so is that

    (A) minor complaints may be of great importance in the mind of the complainant
    (B) minor complaints are more readily disposed of
    (C) minor complaints may be an indication of a serious police problem
    (D) police efficiency is determined by the attitude shown towards citizens complaints.

47. Hearsay evidence may be defined as testimony by one person that another person told him or her about a criminal act which that other person had witnessed. Hearsay evidence is usually *not* admissible in a criminal trial mainly because

    (A) hearsay evidence is consistently biased and deliberately distorted
    (B) hearsay evidence is usually not relevant to the issues of the case
    (C) such evidence is usually distorted by both the original witness and the person to whom the observations were stated
    (D) the actual witness to the criminal act is not being examined under oath.

48. "Arrests should not be given too much weight in the appraisal of a police officer's performance since a large number of arrests does not necessarily indicate that a good police job is being done." This statement is

(A) true, factors other than the number of arrests made must also be considered in judging police effectiveness

(B) false; the basic job of the police is to suppress crime and the surest measure of this is the number of arrests made

(C) true; arrest figures are not indicative in any way of a police officer's efficiency

(D) false; although some police officers are in a better position to make arrests than others, the law of averages should operate to even this out.

49. "Arson is a particularly troublesome crime for the police." Of the following statements, the one which is the *most* important reason why this is so is that

(A) arsonists usually seek the protection of darkness for their crimes

(B) arson occurs so infrequently that the police lack a definite approach for combatting it

(C) important evidence is frequently destroyed by the fire itself.

(D) witnesses find it difficult to distinguish arsonists from other criminals.

50. "Undoubtedly, the police have an important contribution to make to the welfare of youth." Of the following, the principal reason for this is that

(A) effectiveness is a result of experience and the police have had the longest experience in youth work

(B) no other agency can make use of the criminal aspects of the law as effectively as the police

(C) the police are in a strategic position to observe children actually or potentially deliquent and the conditions contributing thereto

(D) welfare agencies lack an understanding of the problems of youth.

51. An apparently senile man informs a police officer that he is returning from a visit to his daughter and that he is unable to find his way back home because he has forgotten his address. Of the following courses of action, the *first* one that should be taken by the officer is to

(A) question the man in an effort to establish his identity

(B) request the police missing persons section to describe to you any person recently reported as missing

(C) suggest that the man return to his daughter for travel directions to his home

(D) telephone a description of the man to the precinct station house.

52. Of the following facts about a criminal, the one which would be of most value in apprehending and identifying the criminal would be that he

(A) drives a black 1980 Chevrolet sedan with chrome license-plate holders

(B) invariably uses a .38 caliber Colt blue steel revolver with walnut stock and regulation front sight

(C) talks with a French accent and has a severe stutter

(D) usually wears three-button single-breasted "Ivy League" suits with white oxford cloth button-down-collar shirts

53. A pawnshop dealer has submitted to the police an accurate and complete description of a wristwatch which he recently purchased from a customer. The one of the following factors that would be most important in determining whether this wristwatch was stolen is the

(A) degree of investigative perservance demonstrated by the police

(B) exactness of police records describing stolen property

(C) honesty and neighborhood reputation of the pawnbroker

(D) time interval between the purchase of the wristwatch by the pawnbroker and the report made to the police.

54. A police officer at the scene of a serious vehicular accident requests two witnesses to the accident not to speak to each other until each one has given a statement to the officer concerning the accident. The most likely reason for this request by the police officer is that if the witnesses were allowed to speak to each other at this time they might

(A) become involved in a violent quarrel over what actually occurred

(B) change their opinion so that identical statements to the police would result

(C) discuss the possibility of a bribe offer to either of them by one of the operators involved in the accident

(D) have their original views of the accident somewhat altered by hearing each other's view of the accident.

55. "Tests have shown that sound waves set up by a siren have a greater intensity ahead than at either side or at the rear of a police car." On the basis of this quotation, it would be most reasonable for the operator of a police car, when responding to the scene of an emergency and using the siren, to expect that a motorist approaching an intersection from

(A) a side street may not stop his vehicle as soon as a more distant motorist directly ahead of the police car

(B) directly ahead may not stop his vehicle as soon as a more distant motorist approaching from the rear of the police car

(C) directly ahead may not stop his vehicle as soon as a more distant motorist approaching from the side of the police car

(D) the rear of the police car may stop his vehicle before the less distant motorist approaching from a side street.

56. A police officer is guarding the entrance of an apartment in which a homicide occurred. While awaiting the arrival of the detectives assigned to the case, the officer is approached by a newspaper reporter who asks to be admitted. The police officer refuses to admit the reporter. The officer's action was

(A) wrong; the police should cooperate with the press

(B) right; the reporter might unintentionally destroy evidence if admitted

(C) wrong; experienced newspaper reporters can be trusted to act intelligently in situations such as this.

(D) right; this reporter should not be given an advantage over other reporters.

57. A phone call is received at police headquarters indicating that a burglary is now taking place in a large loft building. Several radio motor patrol teams are dispatched to the scene. In order to prevent the escape of the burglars, the two police officers arriving first at the building, knowing that there is at least one entrance on each of the four sides of the building, should first

(A) station themselves at diagonally opposite corners outside of the building

(B) enter the building and proceed to search for the criminals

(C) station themselves at the most likely exit from the building

(D) enter the building and remain on the ground floor attempting to keep all stairways under observation.

58. Soon after being appointed a police officer, you decide that some of the rules and regulations of the police department are unwise. It would be best for you to

(A) carry out these rules and regulations regardless of your opinion

(B) make any changes that you decide are necessary

(C) not do your job until some changes are made

(D) disregard these rules and regulations and use your own good judgment.

59. In most cases, a written report about a serious accident is better than an oral report, mainly because a written report

(A) includes more of the facts

(B) can be referred to later

(C) takes less time to prepare

(D) is more accurate.

60. Officers assigned to regular posts for an extended period of time should try to establish friendly relations with the people in the area. For officers to follow this procedure is generally

(A) advisable, mainly because the officers will be more likely to get the cooperation of the residents when needed
(B) inadvisable, mainly because it will take the officer's attention away from their regular duties
(C) advisable, mainly because it will help officers to impress their superior officers
(D) inadvisable, mainly because the people may be encouraged to take advantage of this friendliness to commit minor violations.

Assume that a police officer at a certain location is equipped with a two-way radio to keep him in constant touch with his security headquarters. Radio messages and replies are given in code form, as follows:

Radio Code for Situation	J P M F B
Radio Code for Action to be Taken	o r a z q
Radio Response for Action Taken	1 2 3 4 5

Assume that each of the above capital letters is the radio code for a particular type of situation, that the small letter below each capital letter is the radio code for the action a police officer is directed to take, and that the number directly below each small letter is the radio response the police officer should make to indicate what action was actually taken.

In each of the following questions, 61 through 66, the code letter for the action directed (Column 2) and the code number for the action taken (Column 3) should correspond to the capital letters in Column 1.

- If only Column 2 is different from Column 1, mark your answer (A).
- If only Column 3 is different from Column 1, mark your answer (B).
- If both Column 2 and Column 3 are different from Column 1, mark your answer (C).
- If both Columns 2 and 3 are the same as Column 1, mark your answer (D).

SAMPLE QUESTION

Column 1	Column 2	Column 3
JPFMB	orzaq	12453

The code letters in Column 2 are correct, but the numbers "53" in Column 3 should be "35." Therefore, the correct answer is (B).

	Column 1	Column 2	Column 3
61.	PBFJM	rqzoa	25413
62.	MPFBJ	zrqoa	32541
63.	JBFPM	oqzra	15432
64.	BJPMF	qaroz	51234
65.	PJFMB	rozaq	21435
66.	FJBMP	zoqra	41532

Answer questions 67 through 76 solely on the basis of the following narrative and Assistance Report. The report contains 20 numbered boxes. First read the narrative and the information given concerning the form, and then study the form thoroughly before answering the questions.

It was 9:30 A.M., Sunday, June 14, 1989. Officers Whelan and Murphy of the 2nd Precinct, riding in patrol car 1294, received a radio call of an injury at the N.W. corner of Seventh Avenue and 83rd Street. The location of the injury was within the confines of the 3rd Precinct; however, the 3rd Precinct did not have any cars available to respond.

Upon arriving at the scene, Officers Whelan and Murphy found a male white, approximately 28 years of age, lying on the sidewalk. The man was bleeding moderately from a cut on the forehead. When questioned by the officers, the man identified himself as John Mandello, and he stated that someone ran up behind him and pushed him to the ground, causing him to strike his head on the sidewalk. The person who pushed him to the ground also took a wallet containing $100 from his rear left pocket. Officer Whelan informed Mr. Mandello that an ambulance was on the way. Mr. Mandello stated that he would take care of the injury himself and did not want any medical assistance.

Officer Whelan cancelled the ambulance and proceeded to take the information to be included in the report. As he was doing so, Officer Whelan noticed that the corner street light was not working.

Just as Officer Whelan was finishing getting the information, he and Officer Murphy heard what sounded like brakes screeching and cars colliding. The two officers ran around the corner and saw a car on the southeast corner sidewalk of 82nd Street and Seventh Avenue. They also observed a van, lying on its side, in the intersection of 82nd Street and Seventh Avenue. Officer Murphy ran back to his patrol and car and put in a call for an additional 2nd Precinct patrol car to handle traffic conditions. The accident had occurred within the confines of the 2nd Precinct.

Officer Whelan checked the car that was on the sidewalk. The car, after colliding with the van, apparently mounted the sidewalk and went through the front window of a men's clothing store, setting off the burglar alarm. The driver was lying on the front seat with moderate bleeding from a cut on his head and had what appeared to be a broken arm. The driver of the car was identified as Joe Serrano, a male white, 29 years of age, residing at 384 Lincoln Place, Apt. 4E, Brooklyn, NY.

Officer Murphy went to the van and, with the help of several passersby, pulled the driver out. The driver was unconscious. A search of the unconscious van driver's wallet identified him as Juan Rodriguez, a male Hispanic, 24 years of age, residing at 98 Fourth Avenue, Apt. 1, Newark, NJ.

An ambulance from Washington Hospital arrived at the scene. The ambulance attendant, John Francis, administered first aid to both drivers who were then removed to Washington Hospital.

Further investigation produced two witnesses to the accident. The first witness was Mary Randolph of 876 First Avenue, Apt. 2S, NYC; the second was Helen Sweeney of 684 Broadway, Apt. A, NYC. The witnesses stated to Police Officer Whelan that the traffic light at the intersection of 82nd Street and Seventh Avenue was not working.

Mr. Thomas Serrano of 384 Lincoln Place, Apt. 4E, phone 287-8777 was notified that his brother, Joe, was admitted to Washington Hospital. The admission number for Joe Serrano was 18764.

No friends or relatives of Juan Rodriguez could be notified that he was admitted to Washington Hospital. His admission number was 18763.

ASSISTANCE REPORT

1. Date	2. Last name First name M.I.	3. Age	4. Sex	5. Color

6. Time	7. Residence (including county, apt. # & Zip Code)

8. Location of occurrence (including county, apt. # & Zip code)

9. Illness or injury	10. Precinct and report number

11. Check: ☐ sick ☐ mentally ill ☐ injured ☐ dead	12. Taken to: Name of ☐ hospital ( ) ☐ morgue ( )

13. Admission number	14. Name of Doctor or ambulance attendant

15. Person notified	Relationship

16. Witnesses

17. Remarks

18. Additional required reports (Check appropriate boxes, if any)

        ☐ Crime report   ☐ Morgue report

        ☐ Vehicle accident report   ☐ Street injury report

19. Other agency notifications

20. Reporting Officer

    Rank   Name   Number   Precinct

A police officer is required to prepare an Assistance Report whenever an occurrence which requires that a person receive medical aid or assistance comes to the officer's attention. However, if a person is sick at his or her own residence, an Assistance Report is not required. The officer then need only make a log book entry.

Box #1 will indicate the date that the report is being prepared. If the occurrence happened on a date that is different from the date of the report, the date of occurrence will be listed under Remarks, box #17. The reason for the delay in reporting the incident will also be noted under Remarks, box #17.

Box #8 will give the specific location of the occurrence, i.e., 374 First Street, Apt. 1D; Front of 374 First Street on sidewalk; N.W. corner of 86th Street and First Avenue.

Box #9 will indicate, to the best of your knowledge, the illness or injury sustained, i.e., cut on forehead, dizziness, etc. The official doctor's or hospital's diagnosis, if available, will be listed under Remarks, box #17.

Box #10 will list the precinct of the site of the incident and the precinct report number.

Check the appropriate circumstance in box #11.

Check the appropriate disposition in box #12. If a person is treated at his or her home and is not removed to another location, no report is required. If a person is removed to a hospital or morgue, check the appropriate box and list the name of the hospital or morgue. If a person refuses medical assistance, write "refused assistance" in box #12. If a person is treated at another location other than his or her home and is not removed to a hospital or morgue, state such facts under Remarks, box #17.

The hospital admission number is listed in box #13 only if a relative or a friend cannot be notified that the person is being admitted to the hospital.

Box #14 will indicate the name of the doctor or ambulance attendant who treated the individual.

Box #15 will list the name and address of the friend or relative who was notified of the person's admission to the hospital. The relationship of the person notified to the person admitted will also be listed, i.e., friend, wife, brother, etc.

Box #16 will indicate the names and addresses of any witnesses.

Box #17 will contain a short description of the incident.

Box #18, check the appropriate box for any additional forms that may be needed. Check *crime report* if medical assistance was made necessary as the result of a criminal act. Check *vehicle accident report* if the incident involved a motor vehicle accident. Check *morgue report* if the individual involved dies. Check *street injury report* if the person was injured as a result of a defect in a street or sidewalk.

Box #19 will list the names of any other city agencies that may have to be notified, i.e., damaged or broken traffic or street lights—Traffic Department; potholes in the street or broken sidewalks—Department of Highways; broken or damaged fire hydrants or water mains—Department of Water Supply, etc.

Box #20 will contain the rank, name, and command of the police officer making the report.

All other boxes not specifically mentioned are self-explanatory.

Questions 67 through 70 are to be answered solely on the basis of the information relating to the case of John Mandello.

67. An assistance report

    (A) would not be required because Mr. Mandello refused medical assistance

    (B) would not be required; only a police officer's log entry would be necessary

    (C) would be required, and the precinct that would be listed in box #10 would be the 2nd Precinct

    (D) would be required, and the precinct number that would be listed in box #20 would be the 2nd Precinct.

68. In box #9, the officer would

    (A) enter the official hospital diagnosis when it became available

    (B) enter the description of the illness or injury in his own words

    (C) make a reference to see box #17, Remarks, for the official diagnosis

    (D) enter "refused medical assistance."

69. In box #18, the officer would check the box(es) for

    (A) street injury report, because Mr. Mandello was injured when his head struck the sidewalk

    (B) street injury report, because the injury was incurred when Mr. Mandello's head struck the sidewalk, and crime report, because he was apparently the victim of a robbery

    (C) crime report only

    (D) No additional report would be required because Mr. Mandello refused medical assistance.

70. In box #19, the officer would

    (A) enter Traffic Department

    (B) enter Department of Highways

    (C) enter both Traffic Department and Department of Highways

    (D) make no entry as no additional agency would have to be notified.

Answer questions 71 through 76 based on the information given regarding Joe Serrano and Juan Rodriguez.

71. Box #13 would be

    (A) filled in only in the case of Mr. Serrano

    (B) filled in only in the case of Mr. Rodriguez

    (C) filled in the cases of both Mr. Serrano and Mr. Rodriguez

    (D) left blank in both cases.

72. The official hospital diagnoses of Mr. Serrano's injuries were a laceration of the forehead and a fracture of the right arm. This information would

    (A) be listed in box #17, Remarks

    (B) be listed in box #9, Illness or injury

    (C) be listed in box #14 next to the doctor's name

    (D) not be listed in the report.

73. In regard to the proper preparation of the Assistance Report, select the correct answer from the choices given below.

    (A) In box #10, the number of the precinct that would be entered would be the 2nd Precinct.

    (B) In box #20, the number of the precinct that would be entered would be the 3rd Precinct.

    (C) In box #10, the number of the precinct that would be entered would be the 3rd Precinct.

    (D) The admission number for Mr. Serrano, 18763, would be entered in box #13.

74. In box #18, the additional report(s) that would be required is (are)

    (A) a crime report

    (B) a street injury report

    (C) a vehicle accident report

    (D) a vehicle accident report and a crime report.

75. Based on the information given by the witnesses, box #19 would contain the name(s) of which other agency or agencies?

(A) Traffic Department
(B) Traffic Department and Highway Department
(C) Highway Department
(D) Building Department.

76. In preparing the Assistance Report,

(A) the caption "Sick" would be checked in box #11
(B) the relationship of the person notified in the case of Mr. Serrano would be "father" and would be entered in box #15
(C) the location of the occurrence would be the intersection of 83rd Street and Seventh Avenue and would be entered in box #8
(D) the name John Francis would be entered in box #14.

Answer questions 77 through 80 on the basis of the information given in the following passage.

The public often believes that the main job of a uniformed officer is to enforce laws simply by arresting people. In reality, however, many of the situations that an officer deals with do not call for the use of the power of arrest. In the first place, an officer spends much of his or her time *preventing* crimes from happening, by spotting potential violations or suspicious behavior and taking action to prevent illegal acts. In the second place, many of the situations in which officers are called on for assistance involve elements like personal arguments, husband-wife quarrels, noisy juveniles, or emotionally disturbed persons. The majority of these problems do not result in arrests and convictions, and often they do not even involve illegal behavior. In the third place, even in situations where there seems to be good reason to make an arrest, an officer may have to exercise very good judgement. There are times when making an arrest too soon could touch off a riot, or could result in the detention of a minor offender while major offenders escaped, or could cut short the gathering of necessary on-the-scene evidence.

77. The passage implies that most citizens

(A) will start to riot if they see an arrest being made
(B) appreciate the work that law enforcement officers do
(C) do not realize that making arrests is only a small part of law enforcement
(D) never call for assistance unless they are involved in a personal argument or a husband-wife quarrel.

78. According to the passage, one way in which law enforcement officers can prevent crimes from happening is by

(A) arresting suspicious characters
(B) letting minor offenders go free
(C) taking action on potential violations
(D) refusing to get involved in husband-wife fights.

79. According to the passage, which of the following statements is *not* true of situations involving emotionally disturbed persons?

(A) It is a waste of time to call on law enforcement officers for assistance in such situations.
(B) Such situations may not involve illegal behavior.
(C) Such situations often do not result in arrests.
(D) Citizens often turn to law enforcement officers for help in such situations.

80. The last sentence in the passage mentions "detention of minor offenders." Of the following, which best explains the meaning of the word "detention" as used here?

(A) Sentencing someone
(B) Indicting someone
(C) Calling someone before a grand jury
(D) Arresting someone.

Answer questions 81 through 84 on the basis of the information given in the following passage.

Automobile tire tracks found at the scene of a crime constitute an important link in the chain of physical evidence. In many cases, these are the only clues available. In some areas, unpaved ground adjoins the highway or paved streets. A suspect will often park his or her car off the paved portion of the street when committing a crime, sometimes leaving exellent tire tracks. Comparison of the tire track impressions with the tires is possible only when the vehicle has been found. However, the initial problem facing the police is the task of determining what kind of car probably made the impressions found at the scene of the crime. If the make, model, and year of the car which made the impressions can be determined, it is obvious that the task of elimination is greatly lessened.

81. The one of the following that is the most appropriate title for this passage is

(A) The Use of Automobiles in the Commission of Crimes
(B) The Use of Tire Tracks in Police Work
(C) The Capture of Criminals by Scientific Police Work
(D) The Positive Identification of Criminals Through Their Cars.

82. When searching for clear signs left by the car used in the commission of a crime, the most likely place for the police to look would be on the

(A) highway adjoining unpaved streets
(B) highway adjacent to paved streets
(C) paved streets adjacent to a highway
(D) unpaved ground adjacent to a highway.

83. Automobile tire tracks found at the scene of a crime are of value as evidence in that they are

(A) generally sufficient to trap and convict a suspect

(B) the most important link in the chain of physical evidence
(C) often the only evidence at hand
(D) circumstantial rather than direct.

84. The primary reason that the police try to determine the make, model, and year of the car involved in the commission of a crime is to

(A) compare the tire tracks left at the scene of the crime with the type of tires used on cars of that make
(B) determine if the mud on the tires of the suspected car matches the mud in the unpaved road near the scene of the crime
(C) reduce, to a large extent, the amount of work involved in determining the particular car used in the commission of a crime
(D) alert the police forces to question the occupants of all automobiles of this type.

Answer questions 85 through 88 on the basis of the information given in the following passage.

When stopping vehicles on highways to check for suspects or fugitives, the police use an automobile roadblock whenever possible. This consists of three cars placed in prearranged positions. Car number one is parked across the left lane of the roadway with the front diagonally facing toward the center line. Car number two is parked across the right lane, with the front of the vehicle also toward the center line, in a position perpendicular to car number one and approximately 20 feet to the rear. Continuing another 20 feet to the rear along the highway, car number three is parked in an identical manner to car number one. The width of the highway determines the angle or position in which the autos should be placed. In addition to the regular roadblock signs, and the use of flares at night only, there is an officer located at both the entrance and exit to direct and control traffic from both directions. This type of roadblock forces all approaching autos to reduce speed and zigzag around the police cars. Officers standing behind the parked cars can most safely and carefully view all passing motorists. Once a suspect is inside the block, it becomes extremely difficult to crash out.

85. Of the following, the most appropriate title for this passage is
   (A) The Construction of an Escape-Proof Roadblock
   (B) Regulation of Automobile Traffic Through a Police Roadblock.
   (C) Safety Precautions Necessary in Making an Automobile Roadblock.
   (D) Structure of a Roadblock to Detain Suspects or Fugitives.

86. When setting up a three-car roadblock, the relative positions of the cars should be such that
   (A) the front of car number one is placed diagonally to the center line and faces car number three
   (B) car number three is placed parallel to the center line and its front faces the right side of the road
   (C) car number two is placed about 20 feet from car number one and its front faces the left side of the road
   (D) car number three is parallel to and about 20 feet away from car number one.

87. Officers can observe occupants of all cars passing through the roadblock with greatest safety when
   (A) warning flares are lighted to illuminate the area sufficiently at night
   (B) warning signs are put up at each end of the roadblock
   (C) they are stationed at both the exit and the entrance of the roadblock
   (D) they take up positions behind cars in the roadblock.

88. The type of automobile roadblock described in the passage is of value in police work because
   (A) a suspect is unable to escape its confines by using force
   (B) it is frequently used to capture suspects with no danger to police officers
   (C) it requires only two officers to set up and operate
   (D) vehicular traffic within its confines is controlled as to speed and direction.

Answer questions 89 through 91 on the basis of the information given in the following passage.

When police officers search for a stolen car, they first check for the color of the car, then for make, model, year, body damage, and finally license number. The first five checks can be made from almost any angle, while the recognition of the license number is often not immediately apparent. The serial number and motor number, though less likely to be changed than the easily substituted license number, cannot be observed in initial detection of the stolen car.

89. According to the passage, the one of the following features that is *least* readily observed in checking for a stolen car in moving traffic is the

(A) license number
(B) serial number
(C) model
(D) make.

90. The feature of a car that cannot be determined from most angles of observation is the

(A) make

(B) model
(C) year
(D) license number.

91. Of the following, the feature of a stolen car that is most likely to be altered by a car thief shortly after the car is stolen is the

(A) license number
(B) motor number
(C) color
(D) minor body damage.

Answer questions 92 and 93 on the basis of the information given in the following passage.

A survey has shown that crime prevention work is most successful if the officers are assigned on rotating shifts to provide around-the-clock coverage. An officer may work days for a time and then be switched to nights. The object of the night work is to enable the officer to spot conditions inviting burglars. Complete lack of, or faulty locations of, night lights and other conditions that may invite burglars, which might go unnoticed during daylight hours, can be located and corrected more readily through night work. Night work also enables the officer to check local hangouts of teenagers, such as bus and railway depots, certain cafes or pool halls, the local roller rink, and the building where a teenage dance is held every Friday night. Detectives also join patrol officers cruising in radio patrol cars to check on teenagers loitering late at night and to spot-check local bars for teenagers.

92. The most important purpose of assigning officers to night shifts is to make it possible for them to

(A) correct conditions that may not be readily noticed during the day
(B) discover the location of and replace missing and faulty night lights
(C) locate criminal hangouts
(D) notice things at night that cannot be noticed during the daytime.

93. The type of shifting of officers that best prevents crime is to have

(A) day-shift officers rotated to night work
(B) rotating shifts provide sufficient officers for coverage 24 hours daily
(C) an officer work around the clock on a 24-hour basis as police needs arise
(D) rotating shifts to give officers varied experience.

Answer questions 94 and 95 on the basis of the information given in the following passage.

Proper firearms training is one phase of law enforcement that cannot be ignored. No part of the training of a police officer is more important or more valuable. The officer's life, and often the lives of his or her fellow officers, depend directly upon skill with the weapon he or she is carrying. Proficiency with the revolver is not attained exclusively by the volume of ammunition used and the number of hours spent on the firing line. Supervised practice and the use of training aids and techniques help make the shooter. It is essential to have a good firing range where new officers are trained and older personnel practice in scheduled firearms sessions. The fundamental points to be stressed are grip, stance, breathing, sight alignment, and trigger squeeze. Coordination of thought, vision, and motion must be achieved before the officer gains confidence in shooting ability. Attaining this ability will make the student a better officer and enhance his or her value to the force.

94. A police officer will gain confidence in his or her shooting ability only after having

(A) spent the required number of hours on the firing line
(B) been given sufficient supervised practice
(C) learned the five fundamental points
(D) learned to coordinate revolver movement with sight and thought.

95. Proper training in the use of firearms is one aspect of law enforcement that must be given serious consideration chiefly because it is the

(A) most useful and essential single factor in the training of a police officer

(B) one phase of police officer training which stresses mental and physical coordination
(C) costliest aspect of police officer training, involving considerable expense for the ammunition used in target practice
(D) most difficult part of police officer training, involving the expenditure of many hours on the firing line.

Answer questions 96 through 98 on the basis of the information given in the following passage.

In addition to making the preliminary investigation of crimes, police patrol officers should serve as eyes, ears, and legs for the detective division. The patrol division may be used for surveillance, to serve warrants and bring in suspects and witnesses, and to perform a number of routine tasks for the detectives which will increase the time available for tasks that require their special skills and facilities. It is to the advantage of individual detectives, as well as of the detective division, to have patrol officers working in this manner. More cases are cleared by arrest, and a greater proportion of stolen property is recovered when, in addition to the detective regularly assigned, a number of patrol officers also work on the case. Detectives may stimulate the interest and participation of patrol officers by keeping then informed of the presence, identity or description, hangouts, associates, vehicles, and method of operation of each criminal known to be in the community.

96. According to this passage, a patrol officer should

(A) assist the detective in certain routine functions
(B) be considered for assignment as a detective on the basis of patrol performance
(C) leave the scene once a detective arrives
(D) perform as much of the detective's duties as time permits.

97. According to this passage, patrol officers should aid detectives by

(A) accepting assignments from detectives which give promise of recovering stolen property
(B) making arrests of witnesses for the detective's interrogation

(C) performing all special investigative work for detectives
(D) producing for questioning individuals who may aid the detective in investigation.

98. According to this passage, detectives can keep patrol officers interested by

(A) ascertaining that patrol officers are doing investigative work properly
(B) having patrol officers directly under their supervision during an investigation
(C) informing patrol officers of the value of their efforts in crime prevention
(D) supplying the patrol officers with information regarding known criminals in the community.

Answer questions 99 and 100 on the basis of the information given in the following passage.

The medical examiner may contribute valuable data to the investigator of fires that cause fatalities. By careful examination of the body of any victims, the examiner not only establishes cause of death, but may also furnish, in many instances, answers to questions relating to the identity of the victim and the source and origin of the fire. The medical examiner is of greatest value to law enforcement agencies because he or she is able to determine the exact cause of death through an examination of tissue of apparent arson victims. Thorough study of a burned body or even of parts of a burned body will frequently yield information which will help to clarify the problems confronting the arson investigator and the police.

99. According to the passage, the most important task of the medical examiner in the investigation of arson is to obtain information concerning the
    (A) identity of arsonists
    (B) cause of death
    (C) identity of victims
    (D) source and origin of fires.

100. The central thought of the passage is that the medical examiner aids in the solution of crimes of arson when
    (A) a person is burnt to death
    (B) identity of the arsonist is unknown
    (C) the cause of the fire is known
    (D) trained investigators are not available.

ANSWER KEY FOR PRACTICE EXAMINATION 5

1. D	21. B	41. D	61. D	81. B
2. D	22. B	42. C	62. C	82. D
3. D	23. B	43. A	63. B	83. C
4. A	24. C	44. D	64. A	84. C
5. A	25. C	45. C	65. D	85. D
6. B	26. A	46. C	66. A	86. C
7. D	27. B	47. D	67. D	87. D
8. B	28. B	48. A	68. B	88. D
9. D	29. A	49. C	69. C	89. B
10. C	30. C	50. C	70. A	90. D
11. D	31. A	51. A	71. B	91. A
12. C	32. A	52. C	72. A	92. A
13. B	33. B	53. B	73. A	93. B
14. A	34. C	54. D	74. C	94. D
15. C	35. B	55. A	75. A	95. A
16. C	36. D	56. B	76. D	96. A
17. A	37. A	57. A	77. C	97. D
18. B	38. D	58. A	78. C	98. D
19. B	39. C	59. B	79. A	99. B
20. A	40. C	60. A	80. D	100. A

Explanatory Answers for Practice Examination 5

1. **(D)** Refer to the third sentence of the description.

2. **(D)** The officers observed the suspects alighting from the roof by way of a ladder.

3. **(D)** The two male whites ran into an alleyway and the male black and male Hispanic ran into a parking lot.

4. **(A)** This information is included in the description of the male white with long blond hair.

5. **(A)** This information is included in the description of the male Hispanic.

6. **(B)** This information is included in the description of the male white with short hair.

7. **(D)** This information is included in the description of the male white with short hair.

8. **(B)** This information is included in the description of the male white with long blond hair.

9. **(D)** This information is included in the description of the male Hispanic.

10. **(C)** This is the description of the vehicle in which the two male whites fled.

11. **(D)** The description states only that the escape vehicles fled west on Seventh Street. There is no information as to what type of street Seventh Street is.

12. **(C)** Both the male black and male Hispanic entered the parking lot. However, it was the male black who was carrying what appeared to be a portable T.V. set.

13. **(B)** This information is included in the description of the male black.

14. **(A)** This information is included in the description of the male black.

15. **(C)** The description refers only to Officer Smith using a walkie-talkie and broadcasting information.

16. **(C)** Photographs form a permanent record of how the crime scene appeared when the police arrived. These pictures can be used at a criminal trial to show how the crime scene looked.

17. **(A)** There is no immediate danger to the officer or to the woman since the gun is in the man's pocket. Therefore, it is not necessary or proper for the officer to fire a shot. The officer should repeat his order before taking any further action.

18. **(B)** If the suspect observes that notes are being taken, he or she may freeze up or not talk as freely because he knows that what he or she is saying will become part of the permanent record.

19. **(B)** Being familiar with the post allows a police officer to anticipate the easiest avenues of escape from specific locations.

20. **(A)** The prisoner would either have to roll over or turn his head completely around to see the officer in order to shoot accurately. The time required for this type of movement would allow the officer to take cover or to fire the first shot.

21. **(B)** Ignoring the rumors or not supplying the true circumstances of the emergency as soon as they are available only increases the fear people may have and may result in a possible panic situation.

22. **(B)** If a child has been missing for an extended period of time, police headquarters usually would have received information concerning the child.

23. **(B)** If the plainclothes officer were to stop following the suspect now, he would be difficult to locate again since he is known to have changed residences frequently.

24. **(C)** The police officer should always request that only the needed identification papers be produced. If the police officer accepts the wallet and goes through it for identification papers, there is a possibility that a complaint could be made that money and other personal items were missing when the wallet was returned.

25. **(C)** If a police officer doesn't fully understand the instructions given by a supervisor, the officer should immediately ask for clarification from the person giving the instructions so that he or she can carry out the assignment properly.

26. **(A)** A police officer should always be alert and on guard until the nature of the situation in which he or she is involved is made completely clear.

27. **(B)** Police officers and police departments should never recommend a specific product or business. Endorsements tend to indicate favoritism and police officers should always be impartial.

28. **(B)** Suspects and witnesses should always be questioned separately so that the description that one person gives does not influence the description given by any other persons at the scene.

29. **(A)** If there is the slightest chance that the object could be a bomb, all persons should be removed from the location for safety reasons.

30. **(C)** All of the other choices require immediate police action; a damaged street name sign does not.

31. **(A)** The call could be a set-up for robbing both the owner and his store. If there were a real emergency, the police would most likely be on the scene.

32. **(A)** The citizen may have a legitimate reason for going to the store. Information regarding a criminal investigation should not be divulged to the public.

33. **(B)** In most cases it takes a thorough search of the crime scene to uncover the clues left by the criminal. Most clues in and of themselves are not conclusive. However, when used collectively, they form the foundation for proving the guilt or innocence of the suspect.

34. **(C)** In a criminal prosecution, it would have to be shown that the fingerprints were found prior to the suspect's walking around or entering the scene.

35. **(B)** A statement should be taken as soon as the suspect offers to make one. The suspect may feel an immediate need to tell someone what happened. A delay in taking the statement may cause the suspect to remain silent about the matter.

36. **(D)** The situation fits both the definition of burglary (to enter a building to commit a crime) and of robbery (stealing by force—in this case, the punch in the face).

37. **(A)** John Brown can be charged with larceny only as there was no intent to commit a crime when he entered the store, and there was no force used.

38. **(D)** The charges are sexual abuse (touching of the buttocks) and larceny (taking $10 from the pocketbook). No force was used to remove the money, thus eliminating the charge of robbery.

39. **(C)** To charge a person with burglary, it only must be shown that the building was entered with the intention of committing a crime therein. (In this case, the crime was sexual abuse.) Despite the fact that Saunders was not successful in committing the crime he intended, the intention was there.

40. **(C)** Taylor's intention for entering the apartment was to have sexual intercourse with his 16-year-old girlfriend, a crime because she is less than 17 years of age. He could be charged with burglary (intent to commit a crime) and sexual misconduct (sexual intercourse with a female less than 17 years of age).

41. **(D)** Mary is 17 years old and gave her consent.

42. **(C)** There was neither any intention to commit a crime when Bill entered the building nor was there any injury incurred. For the charge to be assault, there must be some kind of injury.

43. **(A)** Joe had no intent to commit a crime before he entered the warehouse. He caused an injury to a fellow worker, a broken arm, by his actions; therefore, the charge of assault could be preferred. Emotional disturbance is not a valid excuse for such actions.

44. **(D)** The charges are burglary (entering the school with the intention of taking a movie projector), robbery (using force on the security guard to take the projector), and assault (causing an injury, the broken nose, to the security guard).

45. **(C)** Because Tom used force to touch Sue's private parts, he could be charged with sexual abuse. Since there was no intention to commit the crime prior to his entering her apartment, the possibility of a burglary charge is eliminated.

46. **(C)** Minor complaints, when properly investigated, can show a pattern of conduct that could lead to a major problem for the police.

47. **(D)** With the exception of a few narrowly defined situations, the courts demand that actual witnesses be examined under oath.

48. **(A)** A police officer does a multitude of things other than arrest people. The officer responds to sick, injured, and emotionally disturbed people calling for help. He or she handles vehicle accidents, family disputes, lost children, traffic problems, and so on. The officer's effectiveness should be based on how the officer handles the entire spectrum of his or her duties rather than on the number of arrests he or she makes in a given period of time. (C) is not the best answer because of the exclusionary word *any*. Arrest figures are some indication of a police officer's efficiency.

49. **(C)** Fire destroys valuable clues that are usually found at a crime scene. Investigation is made considerably more difficult as a result.

50. **(C)** When the police observe potential delinquent-producing conditions, they can take immediate action to correct them.

51. **(A)** By questioning the man first, the officer may be able to ascertain who he is and where he lives, and thereby return him to his home without any further delay.

52. **(C)** The suspect's accent and stuttering are more or less permanent conditions. The other habits mentioned could be readily changed as needed.

53. **(B)** Police descriptions must be accurate in order to match the article to the complainant. For example, just listing the watch as a yellow metal man's wristwatch would fit thousands of complaints of lost or stolen watches.

54. **(D)** Witnesses and suspects should always be separated when being questioned or giving statements so that the statement one makes does not influence what the others might say.

55. **(A)** This information is stated clearly in the quotation itself.

56. **(B)** Until a crime scene is properly searched and investigated, no one other than those assigned directly to the case should be allowed to enter the area because of the possibility that valuable evidence will be destroyed.

57. **(A)** By stationing themselves in this manner, the two officers would be able to observe all four sides of the building.

58. **(A)** In order to function effectively, police departments have specific rules and regulations that must be followed. Individual police officers must follow the rules; they cannot change or disregard these rules because they think they are unwise or unnecessary. All changes will be made by the chiefs of the respective departments.

59. **(B)** With the passage of time, accurate mental recall of an incident decreases. Written reports should always be prepared for future reference, especially if the case may go to court.

60. **(A)** Once the people in the neighborhood get to know the police officer who is regularly assigned, they are more likely to cooperate. People don't generally cooperate with strangers, even if the stranger is a police officer.

61. **(D)** All the letters in Column 2 and all the numbers in Column 3 are in sequence with the capital letters in Column 1.

62. **(C)** When compared to Column 1, the letters (Column 2) z, q, o, and a and the numbers (Column 3) 5 and 4 are out of sequence.

63. **(B)** When compared to Column 1, all the letters in Column 2 are in their proper sequence, however, the numbers 2 and 3 in Column 3 are out of sequence.

Assistance Report on John Mandello Completed with Information Supplied

ASSISTANCE REPORT				
1. Date 6/14/89	**2. Last name First name M.I.** Mandello, John	**3. Age** Approx. 28	**4. Sex** M	**5. Color** W
6. Time 9:30 A.M.	**7. Residence (including county, apt. # & Zip Code)**			

8. Location of occurrence (including county, apt. # & Zip code)
N.W. Corner, Seventh Avenue and 83rd Street, New York

9. Illness or injury Cut on forehead	**10. Precinct and report number** 3

11. Check: ☐ sick ☐ mentally ill ☒ injured ☐ dead	**12. Taken to:** Refused assitance ☐ hospital ( ) ☐ morgue ( )	**Name of**

13. Admission number	**14. Name of Doctor or ambulance attendant**

15. Person notified	**Relationship**

16. Witnesses

17. Remarks
Victim was pushed from behind; fell to sidewalk and struck forehead; wallet containing $100.00 was removed from pocket.

18. Additional required reports (Check appropriate boxes, if any)
☒ Crime report   ☐ Morgue report
☐ Vehicle accident report   ☐ Street injury report

19. Other agency notifications
Traffic Department

20. Reporting Officer

Rank   Name Whelan   Number   Precinct 2

Assistance Report on Juan Rodriquez Completed with Information Supplied

ASSISTANCE REPORT

1. Date 6/14/89	2. Last name First name M.I. Rodriguez, Juan	3. Age 24	4. Sex M	5. Color Hispanic

6. Time Shortly after 9:30 A.M.	7. Residence (including county, apt. # & Zip Code) 98 Fourth Ave., Apt. 1, Newark, N.J.

8. Location of occurrence (including county, apt. # & Zip code)

82 Street and Seventh Ave, New York, N.Y.

9. Illness or injury Unconscious	10. Precinct and report number 2nd

11. Check: ☐ sick ☐ mentally ill ☒ injured ☐ dead	12. Taken to: ☒ hospital (Washington) ☐ morgue ( ) Name of

13. Admission number 18763	14. Name of Doctor or ambulance attendant John Francis, ambulance attendant

15. Person notified	Relationship

16. Witnesses

Mary Randolph, 876 First Ave., Apt. 2S, N.Y.C.
Helen Sweeney, 684 Broadway, Apt. A, N.Y.C.

17. Remarks

Collision of car and van at intersection of inoperative signal. Car mounted sidewalk and entered window of men's clothing store, setting off burglar alarm. Both drivers injured. No other injuries.

18. Additional required reports (Check appropriate boxes, if any)
    ☐ Crime report   ☐ Morgue report
    ☒ Vehicle accident report   ☐ Street injury report

19. Other agency notifications
    Traffic

20. Reporting Officer

Rank	Name	Number	Precinct 2

Assistance Report on Joe Serrano Completed with Information Supplied

ASSISTANCE REPORT

1. Date	2. Last name First name M.I.	3. Age	4. Sex	5. Color
6/14/89	Serrano, Joe	29	M	W

6. Time	7. Residence (including county, apt. # & Zip Code)
Shortly after 9:30 A.M.	384 Lincoln Place, Apt. 4E, Brooklyn, N.Y. (Kings)

8. Location of occurrence (including county, apt. # & Zip code)

82nd St. and Seventh Ave., N.Y.C.

9. Illness or injury	10. Precinct and report number
bleeding from cut on head; possible broken arm	2nd

11. Check:	12. Taken to:	Name of
☐ sick ☐ mentally ill ☒ injured ☐ dead	☒ hospital (Washington) ☐ morgue ( )	

13. Admission number	14. Name of Doctor or ambulance attendant
	John Francis, ambulance attendant

15. Person notified		Relationship
Thomas Serrano 384 Linclon Place, Apt. 4E Brooklyn, N.Y. 287-8777		brother

16. Witnesses

Mary Randolph, 876 First Ave, Apt. 2S, N.Y.C.
Helen Sweeney, 684 Broadway, Apt. A, N.Y.C.

17. Remarks

Collision of car and van at intersection of inoperative signal. Car mounted sidewalk and entered window of men's clothing store setting off burglar alarm. Hospital diagonsis of forehead laceration and right arm fracture. Other driver injured.

18. Additional required reports (Check appropriate boxes, if any)

☐ Crime report   ☐ Morgue report
☒ Vehicle accident report   ☐ Street injury report

19. Other agency notifications

Traffic

20. Reporting Officer

Rank   Name   Number   Precinct 2

64. **(A)** When compared to Column 1, all the numbers in Column 3 are in their proper sequence, however, the letters a and o in Column 2 are out of sequence.

65. **(D)** When compared to Column 1, all the letters in Column 2 and all the numbers in Column 3 are in proper sequence.

66. **(A)** When compared to Column 1, all the numbers in Column 3 are in proper sequence, however, the letters r and a in Column 2 are out of sequence.

67. **(D)** The person is treated at a location other than his home. If he were treated at home, a report would not be required. The reporting officer is from the 2nd Precinct. The incident occurred in the 3rd Precinct.

68. **(B)** The directions for box #9 state that the officer will enter the nature of the illness or injury to the best of his or her knowledge.

69. **(C)** Mr. Mandello was the victim of a robbery; therefore, a crime report is required. A street injury report is not required because he was not injured as a result of a defect in the sidewalk.

70. **(A)** As he was taking the information for the Assistance Report, Officer Whelan noticed that the corner streetlight was not working.

71. **(B)** An admission number is required only when a relative or friend can't be notified that a person was admitted to a hospital. This is true only in the case of Mr. Rodriguez.

72. **(A)** The directions for preparing the report state that the official diagnosis will be listed in box #17, Remarks.

73. **(A)** The incident involving Mr. Serrano and Mr. Rodriguez occurred in the 2nd Precinct. Mr. Serrano's admission number is not recorded because his brother was notified that he was taken to the hospital. In addition, the number listed for Mr. Serrano in choice (D) is incorrect.

74. **(C)** Only a vehicle accident report is required. There was no crime involved and the accident was not caused by a defect in the roadway, thus eliminating a street injury report.

75. **(A)** The witnesses state that the traffic light was not working, therefore the Traffic Department should be notified.

76. **(D)** John Francis was the ambulance attendant who responded. The victims were not sick; they were injured. Mr. Serrano's brother, not his father, was notified as to his injury in an accident which occurred on Seventh Avenue and 82nd Street.

77. **(C)** Refer to the first sentence of the passage.

78. **(C)** Refer to the third sentence of the passage.

79. **(A)** It is stated in the fourth sentence that many of the situations in which police assistance is required involve emotionally disturbed persons.

80. **(D)** A police officer arrests; the courts sentence, indict, or call people before a grand jury. Detention is holding in custody.

81. **(B)** The passage talks exclusively about tire tracks. No mention is made of autos being used in the commission of crimes, of scientific police work, or of positive identification through cars.

82. **(D)** Refer to sentences 3 and 4 of the passage.

83. **(C)** Refer to the second sentence of the passage.

84. **(C)** Refer to the last sentence of the passage.

85. **(D)** The paragraph doesn't state that the type of roadblock mentioned is escape-proof, but it does state that the roadblock described will force all approaching vehicles to reduce speed and make it extremely difficult for vehicles to crash out of the roadblock.

86. **(C)** Refer to the fourth sentence of the passage. If the car is parked in the right lane with its front facing the center line, the front is necessarily facing the left side of the road. Car #3 is 40 feet from car #1.

87. **(D)** Refer to the next-to-last sentence of the passage.

88. **(D)** Refer to the third from the last sentence of the passage.

89. **(B)** Refer to the last sentence of the passage.

90. **(D)** Refer to the second sentence of the passage.

91. **(A)** Refer to the last sentence of the passage. The changing of color or the repairing of body damage could not be accomplished in a short period of time.

92. **(A)** Refer to the fourth sentence of the passage. The key word here is "correct." Choice (A) uses the word "correct" which is used in the fourth sentence; choice (D) uses the word "notice." Correction is *most* important.

93. **(B)** Refer to the first sentence of the passage.

94. **(D)** Refer to the next-to-last sentence of the passage.

95. **(A)** Refer to the second sentence of the passage.

96. **(A)** The first sentence of the passage states that the patrol officer "should serve as eyes, ears, and legs for the detective division." No statement in the passage makes any mention of police officers being considered for assignment to the detective division, leaving the scene when detectives arrive, or performing detectives' duties.

97. **(D)** Refer to the second sentence of the passage.

98. **(D)** Refer to the last sentence of the passage.

99. **(B)** Refer to the third sentence of the passage.

100. **(A)** Refer to the first sentence of the paragraph. The medical examiner deals with dead human bodies, not with trying to identify arson suspects or with determining the causes of a fire.

THE POLICE ACADEMY

The First Step in Your Law Enforcement Career

BY STEVE ALBRECHT

ABOUT THE AUTHOR

Steve Albrecht is nationally known for his written work on police officer safety and tactics. He has been with the San Diego Police Department since 1984, first as a regular officer and now as a reserve. He is a member of the American Society of Law Enforcement Trainers and contributes articles to police publications across the country. He is the author of *STREETWORK: The Way To Police Officer Safety & Survival* (Paladin) and is co-author, with John Morrison, of *CONTACT & COVER: Two-Officer Suspect Control* (Charles C. Thomas).

THE POLICE ACADEMY

Police work is one of the few professions—besides baseball umpiring—where you have to start out perfect and get better each day. It's also a profession that puts a tremendous emphasis upon training. You'll start the first day of your law enforcement career in a training mode and continue with it every day after that. As long as you wear the badge of a police officer, you will spend a large part of your time learning on the job.

This job requires you to carry an extraordinarily broad range of knowledge. During an average patrol shift, you'll be called upon to solve a variety of problems, mediate disputes, investigate criminal cases, and respond to any number of different service requests ranging from the life-threatening to the mundane.

New police officers like to think of themselves as true "crime fighters." Equipped with a badge, gun, and uniform, many new cops envision themselves chasing "bad guys," making dozens of felony arrests, and solving major crimes on a constant basis. Unfortunately, this is not really how the job goes. Studies of law enforcement tell us you'll probably spend only 20 percent of your patrol time actually in an enforcement position. The rest of the time you'll answer citizen complaints, questions, and requests, write reports, participate in administrative or training tasks, or just randomly patrol your area waiting for calls.

The 20-percent figure that relates to enforcement—issuing citations, making arrests, and protecting life and property—is certainly an important part of your job as a police officer, but it's really only one of your many functions.

Our society is a diverse and ever-changing place, filled with people who have different cultural backgrounds, ethical values, and moral standards. The residents of a city interact with the police in a variety of matters, not just during enforcement situations. Since enforcement is such a small part of your job, you have to bring other "people" skills to bear. The citizens of this country look to the police for protection and service, and by its nature, police work is a reactive, service "business."

If you have been hired as a police officer, you have already met a number of high standards. You've passed a series of rigorous mental, physical, medical, and psychological tests. And you have convinced key city and police department personnel that you have the high morals, positive ethical values, and stable personality traits needed to do the job in a humane and intelligent manner.

But surviving the hiring process is only the start of your exposure to the world of police service. The next phase of your development as an officer—your introduction to law enforcement—begins in the Police Academy.

It's here that you will spend the next four to six months of your life, learning what it means to be a police officer. In the sections that follow, you'll get a complete overview of a typical police academy facility, including the information you'll need to have before you begin your training. Some information may not exactly match what you already know or what you've been told about the police academy in your area, but most of it pertains to the overall police training experience.

Different agencies require different things from their police officer trainees. Some police departments—like the LAPD—stress extensive physical training sessions and spend a significant amount of time teaching recruits to speak Spanish. This emphasis on second-language skills reflects the cultural necessities of the area.

Other agencies—like the San Diego Police Department—have established a "phase training" program where police officer trainees rotate back and forth between academy classes and actual participation in street patrol with senior Field Training Officers. This hands-on experience helps to prepare new officers for the stress of police work by introducing them to it in carefully controlled stages.

Some police academies require the recruits to live at the facility—much like the military. Federal and state law enforcement agencies usually require their trainees to live on-site, while city and county academies allow their cadets to commute from home.

Other police training centers operate in conjunction with state universities or with local community college facilities. But no matter how or where the academy for your agency functions, the values you learn are the same.

On the west coast or east, from a small midwestern training center or from a large southern regional facility that covers an entire state, you'll come away from your academy experience with the following traits and abilities:

• **Discipline.** You will know how to take orders and give them, especially during moments of extreme stress.
• **Teamwork.** You will recognize the need to work together as a unit, either with a partner or even with several dozen other officers.
• **Camaraderie.** You will establish personal friendships that last for your entire career and beyond.
• **Esprit-de-corps.** You will forge an intense commitment to your "brothers and sisters in arms" that permeates your working relationships and even your entire way of life.
• **Courtesy, tact, and control.** You will use these traits to handle any situation, politely, safely, humanely, and above all, professionally.
• **Tactical survival skills.** You will receive the best officer safety material available and learn the latest patrol theories designed to save your life.
• **Professionalism.** You will become a total law enforcement professional, taught to protect and serve with skill and a strong sense of commitment that the career you have chosen is both right and necessary in our society today.

Pre-Academy Preparations

Your entrance into the police academy really begins long before you get there. An old police maxim fits here: Forewarned is forearmed. The more you can prepare yourself—both mentally and physically—for the rigors of academy training, the better you'll do. This may sound simplistic and obvious, but the reasoning is clear. A little preparation before you start can save you from an enormous amount of hardship later.

Police academy training instructors can all remember police officer candidates who had all the "on paper" qualifications to make it to the academy. Typically, these people seemed to have it all. They scored well on written tests, showed impressive skills during the many interviews, and even had the strength and health to pass the physical and medical tests. But once they arrived at the academy—with its built-in stressors and physical requirements—they folded under the pressure.

In some instances, people who reach the academy stage find themselves quite disillusioned by the pressure, the workload, and the physical side of police work. This disillusionment often leads to their dismissal because of low test scores and poor physical performance. More frequently, they quit on their own.

To get through a typical police academy, you need more than just high test scores and physical strength; you need mental toughness as well. The biggest, "baddest," or smartest people don't always make it because the police academy calls for so many other characteristics from its students. Humility, internal courage, and enthusiasm count for just as much as physical virtues.

Another common mistake comes when new enrollees underestimate the amount of classroom study required. Most academy programs are designed around a college curriculum, offering from 12 to 18 units to officer-graduates. To learn and retain this much material, academy students have to spend much of their off-time studying their notes and reading their textbooks. With today's academy programs, it's just not possible to "wing it" and get by without extensive study. The classroom work is demanding and calls for mental discipline. Scanning your criminal law book and reading a few cryptic notes will not suffice. If you don't devote a substantial portion of your off-hours to studying this large amount of material, you won't make it to graduation day.

The skills you bring to the academic portion of the academy are largely in place when you get there. You may want to review some books on how to study efficiently, take good notes, and manage your time effectively. You will learn and succeed in the police academy by maximizing your in-class time, working at home at a specific pace, and following a planned study schedule.

But except for reviewing some helpful techniques, there is very little you can do to improve upon the common sense you already carry. Reading legal textbooks and police training manuals may give you an idea of what to expect, but for the most part, your instructors will teach you everything you'll need to know to function in the field.

Since you can't really prepare for the academic rigors, you can focus your attention on one key area you can improve: your level of physical fitness.

Most academy physical fitness programs stress the same three elements: upper body strength, cardiovascular endurance, and joint and muscle flexibility. The key to your success in these demanding areas starts with your pre-academy fitness level. It's just not possible to "work" yourself into shape once you get there. You've probably seen or heard stories about professional athletes who come to training camp for their sport grossly overweight or out of shape. They quickly fall behind their teammates and spend most of their time in a catch-up position.

Being out of shape is just as demanding mentally as it is physically. Since your body is under tremendous stress during hard exercise, your mind cannot "relax" either. If you couple this exercise-induced stress with the additional pressures from the academy training officers and competition from your classmates, you can find yourself far behind in a short period of time.

If you train correctly and work hard before your academy classes begin, you'll find the exercise programs much easier than if you don't. You don't want to start off with the handicap of being out of shape. Come to the academy in the best shape of your life, and try to improve upon that once the physical training sessions begin.

In some academy programs, you'll be given a list of equipment to purchase before you arrive. In some cases, your department will give you various items; in others, you'll have to buy them. Usually, you're required to buy your uniforms, dress jacket, cold and rainy weather clothes, footwear, and leather gear.

Most departments will give you a duty weapon, a baton, a helmet, a whistle, Mace, and other similar department-issue items. These items belong to the agency, even though you will use them for your entire career. Should you decide to leave the department, you'll need to return any equipment issued to you.

A few police agencies issue a badge and a photo identification card to trainees just before the academy formally begins. If your agency does this, you'll get instructions on how and when to wear your badge, including some careful admonishments about off-duty considerations and the potential for misuse and abuse of your new authority.

Most agencies see the badge and police officer ID card as something to be earned through hard work and dedication and issue it only after you complete the academy, usually at the graduation ceremony.

In most programs, you'll be given the textbooks, paperwork, report forms, and other written materials needed to complete the academic portions of the academy.

If your agency requires you to buy uniforms and leather gear, do yourself a favor and buy the best you can afford. Shopping at cut-rate uniform or police equipment shops can lead to problems later. With uniforms, your appearance is critical to your professionalism, inside the academy and later, out in the field. Don't skimp here. Buy quality uniforms and have them tailored to fit your body.

Nowhere is this sense of quality more important than with your leather gear and police equipment. The quality and durability of your holster, handcuff case, and baton ring could affect your safety. Respected, namebrand equipment may save you from injuries or death; poor-quality "knockoffs" could threaten your survival if they fail. Buy the best leather gear and equipment you can afford and then take care of it as if your life depended on it, because it just might.

With an understanding of the nature of police work, the goals of police academy training, and the mental and physical preparations you'll need, you're ready to look at academy life—one of the most exciting and demanding parts of your law enforcement career.

Dealing with the "Boot Camp" Environment

It's no secret that the police academy is much like military basic training. As in the military, you'll be required to respond to orders quickly, march in a structured fashion to and from various locations, salute when necessary, answer your training officers with a stout "Yes Sir!" or "Yes Ma'am!" when called upon, and generally assume a role of the classic "cadet," "recruit," or "trainee." It seems as if the academy training officers are always yelling and mostly at you. There are good reasons for this: discipline, obedience, and unity are the orders of the day.

On the first day of the academy, the training officers in charge of your class will carefully point out the rules and regulations of the facility. They'll also teach you how to walk, how to talk, how to act, and how to move on command. Any attempt at horseplay, showing off, or other childish moves that jeopardize the safety and success of your classmates will be met with swift and decisive punishment.

As one veteran instructor puts it, "Unless you want to spend all of your time doing pushups or writing 500-word essays on the importance of discipline, you had better 'toe the mark' and do what we tell you."

There are many reasons most police training academies follow this military model. Some are based upon safety concerns (especially when dealing with firearms, defensive tactics, pursuit-driving and other potentially dangerous training programs), others relate to the need to unite, train, and control a large group of people in a minimum amount of time, and still others are linked to the histories and traditions of that particular agency.

Police work is similar to the military in more than just its use of titles—Officer, Sergeant, Lieutenant, Captain, Commander, Chief, etc. Both organizations deal with life-and-death situations in many hostile environments. Each requires its people to respond to specific orders during periods of great personal danger and stress. With these similarities in mind, it's not surprising the police department trains just like the military. In many foreign countries, the police and the military work in conjunction with each other, even to the point of near interchangeability.

Some new recruits are quite comfortable with this enormous emphasis on the paramilitary. Other trainees find it terrifying and have a hard time concentrating on the tasks at hand. The people who seem to react the best are those who have had actual prior military experience. They still remember how to march and how to speak to superiors, so they have a significant edge over their classmates. The academy training officers usually recognize or identify these people and assign them "squad leader" roles to help the others. Learning from your peers is easier than learning from a large man in a khaki uniform who seems to take great delight in yelling at you.

Most officers who have gone through the academy experience will say that after a short period, it becomes easier to respond in this military fashion. What seems foreign and difficult at first will get easier, especially if you concentrate and work hard to conform. Still, you'll do much better if you can develop a thick skin before you begin the academy program. The trick is to follow the orders, complete the tasks you're given, and show effort and enthusiasm at all times. Don't take any verbal abuse from your training officers or instructors as a personal attack.

Rest assured that these people have your best interests in mind. They want you to make it to graduation day, and they will never hit you, curse you, or allow you to do anything unsafe or dangerous. Keep in mind that they aren't picking on you. They're merely exercising their lungs and reinforcing the level of discipline that must pervade the academy setting. It's all for your own good, although it's often difficult to keep this in mind as you complete your fiftieth pushup on a hot summer day.

One key tenet of police work is the strong sense of camaraderie and unity. Large academy classes are often broken into two separate squads and each competes against the other for the top class honors. Some academy classes, like those of the LAPD, use full-size military flags with their class colors, emblem, and slogan printed on them. Many academy classes have a "fight" slogan which they yell out at the beginning and end of each day, before each break, and during rigorous physical training sessions. These class mottos serve to reinforce the concepts of teamwork, unity of command, tradition, pride, and aggressiveness—all good qualities for today's police officers.

The concept of the "Thin Blue Line" —that the police are the first and only defense against the criminals and other bad people in our society—continually permeates the academy training process. The training officers want you to think and act as individuals, but never at the expense of the group. They will teach you how to help each other survive not only the academy process but life on the streets as well.

This concept runs throughout the academy experience, probably because most times law enforcement is a lonely profession. Few people would go out of their way to help a police officer in dire need, either because they dislike the police or, more likely, because they don't want to "get involved."

As a solo patrol officer making a traffic stop at 2:00 a.m., you can feel that help is a world away. But when the chips are down, your brothers and sisters in arms will drop whatever they're doing and race to your side—no questions asked.

How many other professions offer this kind of support? Where else can you find someone willing to risk his or her life for you when necessary? Above all else, law enforcement is a team effort, and the academy teaches this to you each day.

The rewards and punishments doled out by your training officers have a "one size fits all" flavor. You'll usually be rewarded as a group, and punished as one too. Class unity is a constant goal, so if one trainee violates the rules, his or her associates may share the blame. This isn't to say that individual punishments don't exist, but rather that the instructors use their knowledge of group dynamics to teach discipline and order by involving everyone.

The best way to deal with the discipline and paramilitary structure of academy training is to accept it as a part of your law enforcement training process. Don't take anything too personally—it won't last forever. Monitor your stress level the best you can, and realize that your training officers want you to succeed.

Classroom Conduct

The time you spend in the academy classroom environment represents about 60 percent of your total training time. You'll spend another 20 percent of time involved with physical training and defensive tactics activities, and you'll spend the last 20 percent outside the classroom, with driving and firearms training, role plays, and trips to off-site agencies. Since you'll spend the majority of your training time in class, it helps to know what to expect, what to ask, and how to respond to questions, orders, and requests.

Your day will usually begin outside the classroom—in uniform and in orderly rows, ready for a careful inspection. Under the direction of your training officers, you and your classmates will practice marching short distances. Then you'll line up for a uniform and equipment inspection, listen to some announcements about the activities of the day, and then "fall out" for the classroom lectures.

Most police academy courses are taught by experienced, highly qualified veteran officers. The positions of academy training officer and academy course instructor are highly coveted jobs, so the competition among officers is fierce. This competition almost guarantees that you will get some of the finest teachers available. These people know their subjects and can spice the classroom lectures with some carefully chosen "war stories" that illustrate the need to do things correctly in the field.

The course material itself is specifically written and created to stress the most important parts of each subject. There is very little "fat" in a standard police academy curriculum. The organizers know they have only a limited amount of time to teach you and your classmates a wide variety of necessary information. As such, nearly everything your instructors discuss relates to material you must know to pass an exam.

The instructors who teach the various academy subjects are responsible for explaining certain core material mandated by the state. Each state has its own learning requirements for its police officers, and the instructors are expected to teach to these criteria. This isn't to say that you won't hear an abundance of stories, bad jokes, or inside police gossip, just that you can expect the bulk of the classroom material to relate to specific, testable material you'll need to remember later in the academy and later in your career.

Academy classroom etiquette is similar to that of most college-type classrooms, with a few important exceptions. In a college class, the room level is fairly informal, and the discussions usually bounce back and forth between students and the teacher. In the academy, discipline in the classroom is much more important. To ask a question, you'll usually need to raise your hand, wait to be called on, and stand and address the instructor formally, "Sir, Trainee Jones. I wanted to ask about . . . . "

While this kind of formality is popular with your training officers, it's usually less important to the instructors, who will tell you how to address them once their class begins. This formal style serves a few purposes. It shows respect to the instructors; it helps build a foundation of discipline in the classroom; and it allows each student to speak without interruption.

Most academy subjects are taught in blocks of instruction, ranging from two-hour overviews to 80-hour, in- depth looks. Lectures for these blocks, however, usually last for 50 minutes at a time to allow for frequent breaks. At many academies the break procedure is the same: get dismissed by the instructor, "fall in" to ranks outside the classroom, wait to be marched to the break area by a training officer or chosen student, and then get dismissed for a break. Returning to the classroom is usually less structured, as long as you come back on time for the next lecture session.

Lectures

It's hard to overstress the importance of good study habits. Academy courses are dense and force you to cover a lot of material in a short period. Your success in the classroom lies in your ability to take good notes, ask appropriate questions when you need further clarification, study efficiently, and score well on the exams.

In most academy classes, you must score at least a 70 to pass the exams. If you fail an exam, you'll usually be given one opportunity to "remediate" or retake that exam. If you fail the exam the second time you could fail out of the academy program—"wash out," to put it bluntly. While this sounds harsh, it does illustrate the need for good study habits and hard work.

Effective studying starts with good notetaking. One of the easiest ways to take notes efficiently is to use a technique called "mind-mapping." To use this method, start with a clean sheet of paper and write the title or the subject of the lecture right in the center of the page. From there, draw lines that radiate from the center, attaching a word, phrase, or key piece of information to each line. Each time you hear a new piece of information, start a new line or add it to an existing line. Some people call these "spider diagrams" because they look like webs. They are also called "mind-maps" because the ideas look like cities and the lines look like roads.

Anytime you take notes in an academy lecture, be sure to listen carefully to the instructor. He or she will usually tell you what material you'll "see again," meaning that it relates to test questions. Make extra notes about these items and study them in particular later.

Since most academy courses are taught in core modules, that's how you'll take the exams as well—in sections. Instead of one huge 500-question test that covers all your knowledge, you'll usually take a series of 10- to- 50-question multiple-choice tests on each subject. Most academies use multiple-choice exams because they're easier to create and grade, and aren't completely subjective in the grading, as are essay tests.

In most cases, the test will follow the conclusion of the last block of instruction for that subject. That means you'll have a test about every two weeks. You'll know from your master schedule when each subject concludes and when the exam blocks will arrive. This gives you ample time to plan your study sessions accordingly.

In the interest of speed and accuracy, many academies use electronic scoring machines to grade exams. Since many of the tests are reused with future classes, you'll mark your answers on a special tally sheet rather than on the test itself. This method has many benefits, besides making life easier for your training officers who have to grade each test. Because the machine can score several hundred exams in a short period, you can get the results back immediately. This can do wonders for your morale, because you won't have to worry about your scores overnight or, worse, over a weekend. You get immediate feedback; 70 percent and above is a passing grade, and anything below that means you have to retake the test.

Some academy programs allow you to retake a failed exam the next day. Others will let you take it at the end of the same day, allowing you ample study time to prepare again. It's important that you pass the first time. A failed exam can put you behind your fellow classmates and add to your mental burdens. The academy program is stressful enough without having to retake exams. Further, you run the risk of expulsion if you don't pass the make-up exams.

After you've received your test papers back, your training officers will go over each test question and each answer with the entire class. Here, you can learn from your mistakes and reinforce the material you've learned. Remember again that the academy program continues to build upon your knowledge. The more you can retain and recall, the better you'll do on future exams.

This question-and-answer exam review serves an even more important purpose: it gives you the right to have certain test questions thrown out if a majority of your fellow classmates got the wrong answer as well. Say, for example, you took an extensive exam on first aid procedures. If your instructor gave you one answer and the test asks for something completely different, you can ask to have that question deleted. This protects your grade and tells the training officers and instructors what parts of the lectures they might need to improve.

If you're a bit apprehensive about the amount of study involved in the academy, consider getting some help from your fellow classmates. One of the best ways to study is in groups. Informal study sessions are usually held at a student's home or some other convenient meeting place. Besides the obvious benefits of review and reinforcement, these study sessions also offer a good way to get to know your fellow officers.

However you study—alone or in groups—make sure you stay on track and current with the material. As with most college-type classes, academy courses usually require some cumulative knowledge, meaning that things you learned in the first week will apply to courses that come later.

404 / Police Officer

Since you now know the academy classroom format, you'll want to know more about the specific subjects of study. What follows is an annotated list of topics covered during a typical academy program. While a few of these topics may not pertain to your individual agency, the list helps you know what to expect. Don't think that you'll have to know anything about these subjects before you get to the academy. Your instructors will make sure you know each one thoroughly before you leave.

Academy Subjects

Here's an overview of the criminal law classes, patrol theory, first aid, and evidence courses required to graduate. The subjects may differ in scope and content, since different academies stress different subjects. For the most part, this list represents the core of a typical police academy program.

ALCOHOLIC BEVERAGE CONTROL LAWS. This subject deals with the rules and regulations surrounding alcoholic beverage sales and distribution, including types of liquor store, bar, and restaurant licenses; underage minors violations; and the enforcement of similar vice laws. Patrol officers and detectives spend a good deal of their time dealing with alcohol-related problems in bars, taverns, and liquor stores. This class gives information crucial to the law enforcement aspects of these problems.

CHEMICAL WEAPONS TRAINING. Although most of the chemical weapons training calls for outdoor activities (and exposures), there is a significant amount of class time involved too. You'll learn the dynamics of chemical weapon assaults; chemical weapon types and ingredients; effective usage as a defensive weapon; first aid; and proper suspect handling techniques after exposure.

CITATIONS. The training involves how and when to write citations for traffic, misdemeanor, drug, and alcohol violations. This section uses sample citation forms to illustrate the written formats. Since "cite" writing makes up a large part of the police patrol function, the lectures include specific officer safety techniques. You'll be given several "street scenarios" and will be asked to write a variety of sample citations for each.

COMMUNITY RELATIONS. Since our cities are represented by a growing and diverse number of ethnic groups, this section explains the customs of many races and how to build better cultural relations; meet community needs; follow noncultural, unbiased standards for law enforcement; conduct community meetings; form citizen awareness groups; make citizen contacts; suggest referrals and recommend social service agencies; and create crime and drug prevention programs for neighborhoods, businesses, and schools.

CONSTITUTIONAL LAW. Here you'll learn more about the Constitution, the Bill of Rights, and the amendments that relate specifically to the judicial system and to police work. This information is especially useful when coupled with patrol practices involving search and seizure, laws of arrest, interrogation, report writing, and court testimony.

CORRECTIONS. This module follows the booking procedures for arrested suspects, including bail; in-custody care; probation and parole; city and county jail procedures; the roles and functions of the Sheriff's Department; and an overview of the state prison system.

THE COURT SYSTEM. This overview covers the entire judicial process, including trials, hearings, and arraignments; pleas and plea bargains; complaints; indictments; appeals; felony and misdemeanor cases; district and city attorneys; subpoenas; traffic court; family court; and juvenile court. You'll learn more about the arrest "cycle," from the initial arraignment and the preliminary hearing to the jury selection, the court case, the verdict, and the sentencing hearing.

COURTROOM TESTIMONY. Focusing on courtroom etiquette and preparedness, this section explains court procedures, testimony techniques, and the use of reports as a prosecution and defense tool. You'll probably see a mock trial, with careful explanations of your role in the court proceedings.

CRIMINAL LAWS. This section is one of the most comprehensive parts of academy training. It covers all phases of the law as it pertains to police work, such as the laws of arrest; search and seizure rules; stop and frisk requirements; detentions; the definitions of "reasonable suspicion" and "probable cause"; "Miranda" warnings; laws relating to property crimes, personal crimes, the Penal Code, Health & Safety codes, juvenile crimes, Welfare & Institution codes, and the Vehicle Code; citizens' arrests; and powers of arrest and release. This section is often taught by ranking district attorneys, city attorneys, or, in some cases, former police officers who have themselves become prosecuting attorneys.

DEADLY FORCE ISSUES. Another of the important core elements in any academy training program, this section will utilize highly focused and detailed discussions, role playing, and video training simulations. The issues themselves include use of firearms; warning shots; "fleeing felon" decisions; the use of shotguns; the use-of-force continuum; deadly force decision-making techniques; stress control; and the potential for civil or criminal liability actions against officers who misuse deadly force.

DEATH CASES. This topic includes death case procedures, crime scene and evidence protection, report writing, and an overview of the Coroner's Office.

DEFENSIVE TACTICS. Another important core element in your academy training, the defensive tactics module emphasizes the defensive rather than offensive side of effective suspect control. It includes classroom lectures; gymnasium training; armed and unarmed handcuffing procedures; armed and unarmed self-defense; baton training; the carotid neck restraint; search procedures; the use of chemical weapons; high-risk arrest tactics; crowd and riot control; and the potential for civil liability of officers who misuse defensive tactics, arrest and control procedures, or police weaponry.

DISTURBANCE CALLS. Since many officers are killed or injured while handling disturbance calls, this section explains the dynamics of disturbance calls; one- and two-officer safety issues; conflict management; cultural issues; family fights; child custody cases; emotionally disturbed persons; domestic violence; social services and referrals; report procedures; and arrest criteria.

DRIVER'S LICENSES. Taught by State Motor Vehicle investigators, this class explains the issuance and use of driver's licenses, ID cards, vehicle license plates, and VIN numbers. You'll see examples of fraudulent documents to help you recognize them in the field.

DUI ARRESTS. Because drunk driving arrests are growing in response to public awareness, this section shows how to identify, stop, arrest, and book the suspected driver. It includes discussions and examples of the Field Coordination Test; officer safety factors; accident scenes involving the drinking driver; public safety issues; awareness campaigns; arrest, impound, and booking procedures; reports; State Motor Vehicle requirements; and potential civil liability problems.

EVIDENCE. Patrol officers are often called on to collect and recover evidence from crime scenes. This course explains collection techniques; impounding procedures; chain of custody; how to take photos and make crime scene diagrams; fruits of the crime; instrumentalities of the crime; and practical exercises to help recover trace amounts of evidence, such as fingerprints, hairs, fibers, and soil.

FIREARMS TRAINING. This is another significant core module, involving classroom lectures; gun safety rules; range practice; two-hand, one hand, barricade, prone, and stress shooting; reloading; cleaning the weapon; shotgun training; and weapons identification.

FIRST AID TRAINING. While this course probably won't make you a paramedic, it does provide enough information to allow you to stabilize most injury cases, from minor problems to life-threatening wounds. The subjects include first aid application and theory; CPR certification; field problems and role play; and first aid testing and certification.

INTERVIEWS AND INTERROGATIONS. Since most crimes come to police attention "after the fact," a police investigation is only as good as the officer asking the questions. This course teaches techniques for interviewing victims and witnesses; techniques for interrogating suspects; and the dynamics of human communication, including "active listening," body language, and lie detection.

OFFICER SAFETY AND SURVIVAL. Police work is a dangerous profession and is getting more so each day. This class is probably one of the most demanding and powerful sections of the academy. This no-nonsense module looks at mental and physical awareness; patrol theory; radio call response; low- and high-risk arrest tactics; assaults involving knives, guns, and other weapons; disarmings; gun retention; role plays; the use of force; uses of gun, baton, and defensive tactics; stress control; and the "survival" mindset.

PATROL THEORY. This section teaches trainees how to patrol the streets, either on a foot beat or from the seat of a police car. It explains the proper response to radio calls, self-initiated activity, citations, field interviews, and referrals. It covers crimes in progress; building searches; using the police radio; car stops; pedestrian stops; observation techniques; officer safety; officer survival; and modern patrol practices.

PENAL CODE. Coupled with detailed explanations in the law section, the discussion of the Penal Code shows officers how to use this law book and explains the crime elements, violations, and enforcement sections.

PHYSICAL TRAINING LECTURES. More than a few police officers in this country die of heart attacks. Some of these attacks are brought on by poor dietary habits, lack of exercise, and far too much stress. Other officers are forced into early retirement because of chronic back and knee ailments. The PT classroom module discusses health issues that relate to police officers, including diet and exercise plans, injury prevention, and stress control.

POLICE HISTORY AND ETHICAL PRINCIPLES. A course module will offer an overview of the history and principles of law enforcement in the U.S.; ethics and conduct; on- and off-duty habits; individual department policies and procedures; the police chain of command; and the administration of justice in the community.

REPORT WRITING. You'll spend most of your career writing reports of some type. This important module explains the nature and scope of police reports; terminology, procedures, and forms; narratives; interviews and interrogations; crime cases; arrest reports; impounds; narcotics arrests; drunk driver arrest reports; auto theft reports and recoveries; crime descriptions; courtroom procedures; and civil liability precautions.

TRAFFIC ACCIDENT INVESTIGATION. This section explains the proper procedures to be used to respond to vehicle accidents, including safe response; flare patterns; injuries; evidence; vehicle impounds; collision reports; victim, driver, and witness statements; traffic direction; scene protection; measurements; and collision investigation techniques.

VEHICLE CODE. This course offers detailed explanations of state traffic laws. The discussion of the Vehicle Code shows officers how to use this law book in the field, including the administrative and enforcement sections, and specific traffic violations to remember.

VEHICLE OPERATIONS. A typical police patrol officer will spend more time behind the wheel of a police car than at nearly any other on-duty activity. This important section includes classroom study; emergency vehicle traffic laws; emergency vehicle operations; pursuit driving techniques; pursuit policies; accident prevention; and civil liability issues.

Physical Training

While the classroom portion of your academy training takes up the bulk of your time, you will spend a significant part of your days and weeks doing some kind of physical training (PT). How well you do during these PT sessions will depend upon two things: your level of fitness before the academy begins and your ability to work hard and ignore the pain and discomfort that come with difficult physical exercise. The good news is that you can control each of these factors. The bad news is that if you don't, you may fail the academy program.

Like classroom work, police academy physical training can be extremely difficult. If you aren't prepared for it in advance, you'll fall behind your classmates, add to your existing stress level, risk the wrath of your training officers, and possibly even get dismissed from the academy.

Police work is a physically and mentally demanding occupation. It takes place in all kinds of weather, in some of the worst neighborhoods imaginable, and under the most difficult stressors a human being can face. Police work can be painful, involving severe bodily injury and even death to the officer. It requires upper and lower body strength, flexibility, cardiovascular stamina, and lastly, plain old-fashioned guts. If you lack some of these physical requirements, fear not, because academy PT sessions will teach you to overcome physical pain and carry on.

The best way to succeed in PT is to be in shape before it begins. Some hard work on your part before the academy starts will save you much grief later. It's just not possible to get in shape when you get there. You don't have the luxury of time (or a stress-free training environment) to help you ease your way into it.

If you have any preconceived notions about police officers being the largest people around, get rid of them. The old days of the burly, door-filling cops on the beat are over. Today's officers are leaner, more health conscious, and more fit than ever before. More officers are exercising, eating correctly, quitting smoking, and actually working to reduce their on- and off-duty stresses.

Your personal PT program should begin at least four months before the actual academy starts. This will give you plenty of time to get physically and mentally ready for the classroom courses and PT sessions. Consider these four steps as a part of your pre-academy training plan.

QUIT SMOKING

If you don't smoke, don't start. As stressful as police work can be, a cigarette won't help any. Taking up the habit to kill time or calm your nerves is just a bad idea. Health studies tell us that heavy smokers face more sick days, higher health-care bills, and more respiratory problems than nonsmokers.

If you do smoke, it's time to quit. The police academy theory of PT is based on one idea: constant movement. If you aren't running somewhere at double-time speed, you'll be marching or walking quickly. If you're a medium-to-heavy smoker, you will pay the price during these training and marching sessions. Quit now and give your lungs a break. You'll need the oxygen later on those long training runs, and you'll certainly see a definite improvement in your fitness level.

Many progressive police academies actively discourage smoking. They know how harmful it is to the health and safety of their new officers, so they create barriers that make it hard for you to continue smoking, such as no "smoke breaks," restricted smoking areas, and added peer pressure from training officers and fellow classmates to give up the habit.

LOSE WEIGHT

If you can lose any extra weight before the academy, you'll find it very easy to keep it off once the PT sessions start. In fact, you may even find you have to eat more food, more frequently, just to maintain your current weight. If you go through your academy program during hot summer or cold winter months, you'll probably need to increase your intake of calories and fluids to keep up. The PT sessions can take a lot out of you.

Proper weight control also makes it easier for you to run long distances. Since it's no longer necessary to be built like a pro football player to work as a police officer, you should focus your pre-academy training efforts toward slimming down to a leaner body weight. Many new recruits who spent hours in the health spa "pumping iron" have found the extra muscle bulk actually hindered their performance. Carrying extra weight, even if it's mostly muscle, can slow you down.

The trick is to be strong and muscular, without any unnecessary muscle mass or fat to carry around. Unless you're an experienced athlete with years of work behind you, don't try to bring any extra muscle weight to the academy. If you're too heavy, you're probably too slow as well. Lean and mean is the idea here. You can certainly lift weights before and during the academy, but keep the weights light and the number of repetitions high to "tone up" rather than "bulk up."

Start a sensible diet program when you begin your pre-academy conditioning program. Lose the extra weight slowly and safely by drinking plenty of water, taking vitamins, and eating a balanced and reduced-calorie diet as you train. Just remember you'll have to carry any extra pounds with you on those long academy training runs.

WALK / RUN / SPRINT

If you're more than a weekend athlete, you're probably already used to running or jogging at least three or four times per week. If so, continue your present training pace and add some long runs, some sprints and speed work, and plenty of pre- and post-run stretching to your workouts. If you don't run regularly, do yourself a favor and start your training by walking first. Many overeager police cadets have set themselves back with serious injuries by overtraining. Go to the bookstore and get a good book on walking. Follow the advice concerning the choice of shoes, walking courses, and training times. Start slowly, work hard during every session, and focus on strengthening your leg and back muscles as you walk. Some carefully planned walking workouts will prepare your body safely and efficiently for the runs to follow.

Once you've worked up to a brisk walking pace, you can start your pre-academy running program. The secret here again is not to overdo it and risk an injury that could set you back for months. Run at a "talking pace"—a speed where you can hold a conversation without gasping—for the first few weeks. Make sure you have a good pair of running shoes—not tennis or basketball sneakers—that support your ankles and protect your legs from the inevitable pounding from hard running surfaces.

While some experts say you can run on a near-daily basis, as long as you alternate one "hard" day with one "easy" day, other sports trainers aren't so sure. A good rule of thumb is to run every other day and rest your legs, lungs, and heart on your off days. Many people like to run on Mondays, Wednesdays, and Fridays, with a longer distance run on Sunday. Then they rest Monday and start up again Tuesday with the every-other-day pace. Pick a schedule that works for you and stick with it. If you want to increase your mileage, go up about 10 percent every other week. For example, if you can run 10 total miles per week with little difficulty, go up to 11, and so on.

Too much running can cause you a host of problems, from blisters to shin splints, and even stress fractures and broken bones. Be sensible, run "softly" on well-cushioned surfaces, and concentrate on quality training sessions rather than quantity. Run in a way that causes you to roll along heel to toe, rather than on the balls of your feet. Run straight upright, so that your body doesn't bounce. If the horizon in front of you shakes about, you're probably moving your upper body too much.

To give you some variety during your running workouts, you may want to try some "wind sprints." Go to a local high school football field and pace off 40 yards. Try running a few warmup sprints at half-speed and then "kick it into gear." Run six to ten full-speed sprints to get your heart rate up and increase your leg-muscle flexibility. Sprint workouts offer a good change of pace and can prepare you for a variety of academy running assignments. Remember to stretch before and after every running workout, especially if you plan to do any sprinting.

USE YOUR BODY WEIGHT

If you were to get a dime for every push-up you'll do in the police academy, you could retire at an early age. The standard gym-class pushup is a mainstay of most academy PT sessions. You'll do them as punishment in a group; you'll do them as punishment for an individual mistake; and you'll do them by the carload in your formal PT sessions.

As you're doing these pushups with your classmates, you'll all collectively wonder when your training officers will get tired and ask you to stop. Unfortunately, they have several secret weapons at their disposal. First, if they get tired, they simply stand up and continue counting. So while they've stopped at 37, you have to go on until 50. Secondly, if they get tired at 50, they just ask another instructor to take over until you reach 100. Lastly, if you don't yell loudly during the count portion, these fine instructors will pretend they lost track, and you'll have to start again from pushup number one!

Seriously, since the pushup exercise is so much a part of academy PT, you'll want to do many hundreds of them as part of your pre-academy training program. As with most body-weight resistance exercises, pushups get easier the more you do them.

As with running, if you haven't done this type of exercise in some time, you'll need to start slowly. Give yourself small goals and try to meet them each day. Start with 10 pushups per session, go to 25, and then go to 50. Increase the number of times you practice pushups from once or twice per day on up to 10 times per day. Use good form, breathe correctly (inhale going down, exhale coming up), and stick with them. The more you do now, the easier they are to do later, especially when a large, uniformed man is yelling in your ear.

Like pushups, situps are another standard-issue academy exercise. And while pushups build your arms, shoulders, and chest, situps strengthen your abdominal muscles and, to a lesser extent, your lower back and hip joint area. Many police officers have had to retire early with long-term medical disabilities because of weak backs. Many of these problems stem from the constant wear and tear on your stomach muscles. Police gun belts, bullet-proof vests, heavy shoes, and other equipment can add up to 30 pounds to an officer's body weight. This can cause stomach muscles to sag and become more prone to injuries like hernias, ruptures, and lateral low-back ailments.

Do your back and stomach a favor. Start a situp program with your pushup regimen. Choose a target number and meet it every day. Use good form; don't pull on the back of your neck with your hands; and protect your seat with a towel or pad.

Lastly, many training academies ask their officers to do pullups as a part of PT. The typical pullup movement requires an above-average amount of upper-body strength and it offers a good way to show improvements in overall fitness levels. As with your pre-academy conditioning exercises, start slowly and build yourself up to multiple pullup sets. If you can't do one pullup, make that your goal and work hard to achieve it. Use your determination and concentrate on good form. Try to do one, five, or ten more of everything than you did in the previous day.

The paramilitary model that covers the classroom discipline in the academy also reaches the PT sessions. Those trainees with prior military experience will be fairly comfortable with the group exercise process. If you don't have a military background, you'll have to make a few adjustments.

Most academy PT classes run for one hour to one hour and fifteen minutes. Some sessions will take place early in the morning, before classes begin; others will start just before lunch, and still others will cover the last hour of the work day. Nearly every session will include a running program followed by a vigorous session of mat work, which includes the usual pushups, situps, leg lifts, abdominal crunches, pullups, and even bar dips.

You'll begin with a set of warm-ups and calisthenics, which you'll do as a group, counting loudly enough to impress your training officers. From there, you'll form two single-file lines and begin the run of the day.

Running in formation like this takes a careful step. Too close and you'll stomp on the person in front of you; too far away and you'll risk falling behind. Since most training runs are held on the roads around the academy facility, you'll need to pay strict attention to the terrain and the potential hazards in the street, such as curbs, fire hydrants, and mail boxes.

A few academy classes like to run in the traditional Army style, with everyone staying together and running at a comfortable pace so the slowest runner can keep up. Most PT instructors, however, prefer to start the class together and then let the faster runners set the pace. This tends to spread the group out in a long line, but it allows everyone to work at a rate that is personally best. To keep the "gazelles" under control, a training officer will often set a fast pace and keep everyone else behind. Another training officer will anchor the end of the line to encourage the stragglers with a few well-chosen words and to push them along.

If you're out of shape, this spread-out method can be unbearable. Just when you catch up to the leaders of the pack—who jog in place until you arrive—they start up again, giving you no break whatsoever. This should tell you how important pre-academy fitness is to your mental and physical health. Unless you want your eardrums to ring with the howls of your training officers, get in shape and be ready to run at a brisk pace when necessary.

The only thing that makes this kind of running enjoyable—besides knowing that it can't last forever—is the cadence calling. Just like the military, many academies use marching songs and rhymes to encourage the recruits and take their minds off their labored breathing. These songs, limericks, and marching poems are always inspirational, usually motivational, and occasionally humorous. They also encourage group unity, promote discipline, and help to pass the time a bit.

After a stimulating run, it's off to the gym room or exercise area for some more calisthenics. You will usually line up in rows and begin a whole series of pushups and situps. These exercises aren't particularly difficult, but coupled with the running program, they can really tire you out.

As with all PT exercises, the more you can do before the academy begins, the easier it will be for you to complete each exercise session. During all sessions, try to stay up with the training officers and match them exercise for exercise. You'll improve your conditioning, and this makes for a better impression among your peers and trainers.

If your PT program takes place before class begins, you'll probably have just enough time to shower and dress for the start of the day. If the session ends at lunch or at the close of the day, take some extra time to eat properly and drink plenty of fluids, especially water. If you eat sensibly, minimizing the junk food, sodas, and fast-food items, you'll help your physical performance and feel better as well.

Besides the obvious cardiovascular and upper-body strength benefits, most academy

PT sessions are designed to build the muscles of the abdomen, lower back, and back and knee joints. Since so many officers suffer career-threatening health problems in these vital areas, injury prevention is a critical part of your overall fitness plan while you attend the academy. Tell your instructors anytime you feel any unusual pains or anything other than normal muscle soreness.

Work hard to keep your knee joints strong and flexible. Concentrate on your stomach muscles to prevent back and stomach injuries. Run carefully and efficiently to avoid any foot or leg problems. Think of your academy PT sessions as the gateway to a career of lifelong fitness and injury prevention.

Arrest and Control Classes

Many academies have a "mat room" especially designed for police defensive training. This area is covered with thick wrestling-style mats, and there are usually heavy boxing-type "body punching" bags in various locations around the room. The mats help protect you during defensive tactics training, and the bags are for baton strikes and punching practice.

You'll spend most of your time in the mat room doing PT work—pushups, situps, etc. Except for the classroom courses, you'll go through most of your arrest and control classes and defensive tactics work here, too.

Notice the key word "defensive." By its nature, police work is filled with opportunities for officers to prevent physical confrontations. We use defensive rather than offensive movements for a variety of reasons, besides just to protect ourselves. The defensive mode promotes better officer safety tactics; it's more effective as a suspect control technique; and it prevents undue civil liability suits against officers and their departments.

The days of the baton-swinging, head-beating officer are long over. With the potential for unlawful injuries to suspects and the tremendous risk of civil liability for excessive force, police academies have turned their attention towards defensive tactics that protect officers and suspects alike.

Some trainers like to teach judo "safe-falling" techniques, tumbling movements, ground and foot fighting movements, boxing and wrestling techniques, and other "street" fighting maneuvers.

For these defensive tactics drills, you'll partner up with a fellow classmate. Most of these activities call for one officer to be "the cop" and one to be "the crook." You'll switch back and forth as you practice the hands-on techniques over the one- to two-hour class sessions.

Whether you're learning to use the police baton, a handcuffing technique, or an empty-hand control technique, the key to your success in defensive tactics training lies in correct practice and repetition. You must exercise the proper control to protect yourself and your partner from injuries. Some officers have been badly injured during these sessions because of an overzealous partner or because they failed to practice safely and carefully. On the other hand, the only way you'll learn to perform these techniques correctly (and safely) is to practice them over and over again.

The human body, in terms of police training, thrives on repetition. Constant, unrelenting practice involving several hundred or even several thousand repetitions will build a sense of "muscle memory" into your brain and muscles. With sufficient practice, each of these moves can become almost instinctive, requiring no thought, just action.

Your defensive tactics training instructors know this, so you'll spend most of your time learning new techniques and drilling with them over and over again. The more you can practice in the gym, the better you will follow the techniques in the field, where it really counts.

Many hands-on techniques for police work are based on the martial art aikido, which focuses on wrist, elbow, and shoulder-joint pressures and throwing techniques. You won't need any previous martial arts experience to learn these movements, but you may want to review some aikido or other martial arts books at the bookstore or library. Sometimes it helps to see these grappling techniques as they are broken down in step-by-step photographs.

Police baton training in the academy depends upon the equipment used by your local agency. Some police departments use the straight baton and others use an expandable straight baton. Some agencies train officers to use the PR-24 side-handle baton and others prefer the Orcutt Police Nunchakus. Whatever equipment you use, keep these rules in mind: train safely—these are potentially deadly weapons—and train consistently, using many drills and repetitions to hone your skills.

Dress Codes

Most academies require their trainees to maintain three different types of uniform: the dress uniform, the arrest and control uniform, and the PT uniform. Each serves its own purpose. Since the word "uniform" is defined as "official clothing; one that does not vary," you can imagine that police academy clothing is all the same. You will dress exactly the same as your classmates, even down to the color of your socks. You'll also have the same haircut, the same color dress shoes, and, hopefully, the same enthusiastic attitude. Only your training officers and instructors will dress differently from you, and they do not particularly encourage your individuality.

The dress uniform is usually the uniform of the agency that hired you. Some academies have trainees wear the actual uniform of the police agency, while others use a training uniform of blue or khaki brown. In the latter example, you would begin wearing the traditional uniform of your agency at your graduation. In any case, the dress uniform is usually worn during the classroom sessions.

The arrest and control uniform also varies. Most cadets wear "nametag" T-shirts with their last names printed on the front and back for ease in identification (and yelling at). Some academies have trainees wear T-shirts, standard blue jeans, and running shoes for defensive tactics classes, while other classes use T-shirts, sweatpants, and running shoes. In either case, the purpose of the uniform is comfort, durability, freedom of movement, easy identification, and safety. Few academies want their people to wrestle and fight in dress uniforms, since it's expensive to fix torn clothes.

The PT uniform consists of the "nametag" T-shirt, running shorts, white socks, and running shoes. This uniform is used strictly for PT sessions because it's cool and comfortable and allows free movement.

For nearly every defensive tactics session, you'll use the arrest and control uniform. You'll also wear your gunbelt, baton, and unloaded handgun. Since safety is a constant issue, every arrest and control session starts with a handgun inspection to make certain no live ammunition is anywhere near your gun. Then after a quick warm-up session involving some stretching and pushups, you'll begin the course of instruction for the day.

Role Plays

A weary patrol officer once said that all of police work is just "street theater." This refers to a cop's ability to portray certain characters while out in the field. In some cases, you'll have to be the concerned and empathetic helper when talking to an emotionally disturbed or suicidal person. In others, you'll have to play the "heavy," the strict authoritarian figure, especially in the face of certain violence. And in others, you may have to act as if you aren't the slightest bit afraid, even though, inside, you may be shaking like a leaf. Police patrol work requires much of its officers, and playing different roles is just part of the job. You learn to play these parts in the police academy.

As the academy training begins to wind down, your training officers and instructors will begin to give you more autonomy, more leeway in your decision-making activities. You'll still have the discipline that is a part of academy life, but you'll be placed in certain situations and be asked to respond like a professional law enforcement officer. These situations are called "role plays," and they resemble small theater skits in that they call for you to act out a part and respond to other people doing the same.

In a typical role-play scenario, you and your partner will be asked to answer a radio call regarding some in-progress or after-the-fact crime. You'll go to the scene, meet the participants, and take the appropriate police action. During this role-play scenario, your training officers and instructors will supervise your actions and grade your performance. Here, under the controlled conditions of the academy, you can make mistakes and learn from them. You don't always have that luxury in the field, where your mistakes could cost your life.

These role plays could involve something simple, like a burglary report, or something life-threatening, like a liquor store robbery or a high-risk vehicle stop. In each example, you'll be expected to respond just as you would if it were a live, real-life field problem. Now is the time to put your skills and training to use. Your success in these role plays in the academy can mean continued success on the streets later.

Weapons Training

Besides the role-playing work, you will spend a significant portion of your academy time at the police range, practicing with your duty firearm. Coupled with your classroom training on deadly force issues, the firearms module is critical to your development as a professional police officer.

Anytime you are not at a police range or in some other training capacity, you are responsible for every bullet that leaves your gun. These days, it just doesn't matter that an officer says he or she "meant to do the right thing." Civil liability and deadly force go hand in hand. You must know when to draw your weapon and how to operate it safely. The instructors at the police range will teach you how to do both.

As with the movements you make in the defensive tactics and arrest and control classes, safety and repetition are the keys to your success on the firing line. You must always realize that you are holding a loaded handgun, capable of delivering deadly force in a split-second. Discipline and attention to the details of safety are the rules of the police range. Rest assured that your instructors will make sure you pay attention and follow their explicit directions.

Some police agencies favor the standard .38-caliber police handgun while others are going with the 9mm semi-automatic pistol. There are arguments pro and con for each, but whatever gun you're given, treat it as if it were a member of your family. Barring damage or malfunction, you will carry that gun for the rest of your police career. You may have to call upon it to save your life or the life of someone else.

Your instructors will show you how to shoot your weapon from a variety of hand and body positions. You'll learn how to clean it, disassemble and reassemble it, and carry and draw it in a stressful situation. You'll probably shoot over one thousand rounds before your academy training ends—sometimes at night, sometimes in bright sunlight. You'll shoot lefthanded and right, from your knees, from your stomach, and from behind barricades of all shapes and sizes. You'll shoot at close range and over long distances, under timed conditions, with a partner, and on your own.

Since most law enforcement agencies use the standard police shotgun, you'll learn just as much about that weapon as you will about your handgun. By the end of your training, you'll know how to break the shotgun down into pieces and rebuild it. You'll shoot it in a variety of positions, settings, and lighting conditions, using different ammunition loads. Other agencies use police rifles, involving similar training and repetition as with the police shotgun.

As in the role plays, at the range you'll be under the watchful eyes of your training officers and firearms instructors. And like the role-play exercises, the police range is the place to make mistakes and learn from them. Any mistake involving a firearm that you make in the street could end in a tragedy.

Emergency Vehicle Driving

Other outdoor academy work will take place on the driving course. Since you'll spend the majority of your random patrol time behind the wheel of a car, you'll need some extensive training in emergency vehicle driving. Some large-city law enforcement agencies average over one police equipment accident per day. Not only is it expensive to repair these cars, but an accident often results in injuries to officers and civilians and the distinct possibility of a court case against the officer and the department.

Because your instructors assume you already have some average or better-than-average behind-the-wheel skills, the driving portion of your academy training usually focuses on emergency techniques to help you during high-risk pursuit-type operations. This includes "speed" braking, driving in reverse, "slalom" turn driving, high-speed turning, and skid control. Because you spend so much time behind the wheel—and a moving car can be just as much of a deadly weapon as a gun—it's essential that you appreciate your degree of responsibility every time you operate a police vehicle in a normal or emergency situation.

Field Trips

Some academies send their trainees out to various criminal justice facilities for some familiarization training. Most recruits enjoy these short "field trips" because a trip offers a change of pace and gets the recruits away from the day-to-day grind of the academy. Usually, the instructor for that particular subject will lead a tour or arrange to have a representative take the recruits around the facility.

Because officers will interact with other public service agencies, it helps to know where these places are located and how they operate. Your academy may schedule tours and short trips to the facilities listed below.

CITY AND COUNTY JAIL TOUR. Since many city law enforcement agencies contract their custodial inmate services with the county sheriff, deputies rather than police officers will work in these facilities. A jail tour helps new officers understand the booking and detention procedures as well as the duties and responsibilities of the sheriff's department for inmate housing, transportation, and care inside the jail. Some academy classes will tour both the men's and the women's detention facilities on separate days.

JUVENILE HOLDING CENTERS. Because juvenile inmates are held in locations separate from those for adults, officers will tour the youth facilities. The laws and restrictions surrounding the housing of juvenile inmates are quite strict, so trainees will have to learn how arrest and booking procedures differ from those of adult suspects.

FAMILY AND CHILD PROTECTIVE SERVICES. Many cities have social service facilities to care for abandoned, abused, or injured children. These places also care for foster children, wards of the court, and other children involved in noncriminal matters that come to the attention of the police.

COURTHOUSE TOUR. This tour covers the city or county courthouses and explains to new officers how and where the trials take place. Coupled with the classroom lectures that cover courtroom procedures, this trip takes recruits through the criminal justice cycle that begins after an arrest is made.

CORONER'S OFFICE TOUR. Usually an exciting and fascinating trip, the Coroner's Office tour supplements the classroom lectures for death cases and crime scene investigations. In some cities, police recruits will watch an actual autopsy. Members of the Coroner's Office will explain when an autopsy is necessary in a death case and how the evidence is collected, analyzed, and processed. Many trainees find this tour quite informative—once they get over the initial shock of being around so many dead bodies.

These field trips give recruit officers a different perspective about the criminal justice process and the social service organizations in their area. The trips also expose recruits to other available sources of help and information once they get into the field. These trips, combined with the classroom lectures, exercises, and tests, help put some reality into the academy training.

Graduation and Beyond

The only event more important than starting the academy is finishing it. And the only day more exciting than the first one is graduation day. Here you'll see the payoff, the culmination of your hard work, the sweat, the exams, and the extra effort.

Graduation Day is an exciting time for all new officers. The drudgery of the academy is finally over. No more marching, saluting, or those heavy doses of discipline. You can now dispense with the constant stream of "yes sirs" and "yes ma'ams" that have been a part of your vocabulary for the past months. It's time to celebrate your efforts with a graduation ceremony steeped in the tradition and history of your agency. You'll get your badge—a centuries-old symbol of the public trust. You'll also get to meet your police chief and the command staff. It's a proud moment for your relatives and loved ones, and it's an even prouder moment for you. Celebrate your accomplishments and salute your fellow classmates.

The Field Officer Training Phase

There's an old saying in law enforcement that goes, "The academy teaches you to be a police officer and the streets teach you to be a cop." The distinction is an important one.

The material you learned in the academy is a valuable and necessary part of your development as a police officer, but the only way you can earn the title of "street cop" is to hit the streets and prevent crime. Rest assured that you won't be asked to do this by yourself. For the first few months of your patrol career, you'll be under the wing of an experienced Field Training Officer (FTO).

Some new officers say the Field Training phase is even more stressful and difficult than the academy. This may be because the academy is a relatively safe environment. Nobody can assault or injure you there, and except for all the yelling and screaming done by the training officers, it's a fairly calm place. The streets, on the other hand, are rarely calm and hardly offer much safety, especially in some of the more vehemently anti-police neighborhoods.

For all its stresses, the academy is still a structured, orderly place well-suited for learning. Street patrol, with its hours of boredom interspaced with minutes of high excitement, offers a much more difficult learning environment. It's indeed possible to magnify the consequences of your mistakes, especially when it comes to your safety, the safety of your partner, and that of the people you're supposed to protect. The ever-present news media hardly help the situation; your mistakes can now be captured for eternity on videotape. You're now in the "fishbowl," under constant public scrutiny, with many eyes upon you.

To minimize the mistake process and make sure you learn to be a good, safe street cop, most police agencies have developed an entire program based on the training needs of new officers. Your initial meeting with your partner, the Field Training Officer, will include your introduction to the "bible" of street policing, the Critical Task book. Other agencies may refer to it differently, perhaps as the Patrol Guide, but however it's called, the book is basically a checklist of your duties and responsibilities as a patrol officer.

Just as it's titled, the Critical Task book is a book filled with various critical and essential police tasks that you must identify and complete with the approval of your FTO. Your FTO will explain each of the tasks, ranging from checking the equipment in your police car before the beginning of a shift, to proper radio procedures, to handling domestic disturbance calls, to high-risk arrests, to issuing parking citations, to working with the computer records back at the station, to writing complete and effective reports. If you do something as a police officer, you'll find it in this Critical Task book.

You may even be asked to complete "homework" assignments, ranging from map book location problems to sample arrest and crime case reports. You'll complete these assignments on your own and turn them in on time.

Besides teaching you how to do this demanding job safely and effectively, your FTO will document your daily activities on paper. The FTO's report includes an evaluation of your work habits, strengths, weaknesses, mistakes, and good points. Depending upon the length of time you spend with your FTO, he or she will write biweekly evaluation reports to show that you are "on schedule" and progressing in a timely manner.

These biweekly reports are reviewed by the training division personnel who also monitor your progress and by a number of other supervisors up the line. Rest assured that your agency wants you to make it through this street patrol training phase and to become a full-fledged member of the department. Officers who can work alone or without constant supervision offer the best service to their department. The Field Training Phase teaches you how to work alone and with a partner.

The length of the Field Training Phase varies from agency to agency. Some departments put new academy graduates through a four-month program, rotating their partners, shift hours, and duty areas each month. Others will cycle new officers back and forth each month between the academy classroom and the field until they graduate. Other departments will send a new officer to his or her permanent duty assignment immediately upon graduation, with no area or shift rotation at all. Still other agencies will assign new graduates to one station for their entire one-year (or 18-month) probationary period. After they clear probation, they can request a transfer to another station.

During this critical probationary period, the officer must work hard and meet all of the required job performance objectives. Probationary officers have very few civil service rights and can be quickly terminated for crucial mistakes, judgment errors, or hazardous off-duty incidents. Where the veteran officer may have some protection from discharge by the civil service board, the probationary officer does not. The probationary period forces new officers to demonstrate their skills and knowledge to the police agency that hired them.

Getting through the field training phase is quite similar to succeeding in the academy: listen, do as you're told, ask questions when necessary, and practice doing the right things over and over again. Your FTO will suggest ways to do the job more effectively. Take what you learn from each training officer you encounter in the field. Just like the academy training officers and course instructors, the Field Training Officers in your department are chosen for their police skills and their ability and desire to train new officers to function in the field. They're usually the finest officers in the department.

Listen to their suggestions, take their criticisms in stride, and learn from your mistakes. Don't rationalize your behavior with statements like, "What I really meant to do was . . . ." or "I meant to do that but didn't because . . . ." Your FTO partners will try to give you the benefit of their experience. Watch how they work, observe their safety habits, and make these part of your own operating plan. Learn from them and continually tell yourself you can do this job safely and successfully.

Recruiting studies show that for every one person a police agency hires and puts through an academy, it turns away nearly 90 applicants, for one reason or another. Police work truly is a profession for an elite and qualified few. Consider yourself part of a proud and honorable calling.

Many people in this country admire law enforcement and have the utmost respect and admiration for police officers. Plenty of people will tell you, "You know, I always thought I could be a cop." The difference between them and you is that you put forth the effort and did what was asked. You have become a law enforcement officer.

ARCO BOOKS

FOR LAW ENFORCEMENT POSITIONS

ACWA: Administrative Careers With America
Border Patrol Agent
CIA Entrance Examinations
Civil Service Psychological and Psychiatric Tests
Correction Officer
Correction Officer Promotion Tests
Court Officer / Senior Court Officer / Court Clerk
Drug Enforcement Agent
Emergency Dispatcher / 911 Operator
Federal Law Enforcement Jobs
FBI Entrance Examination
Police Officer
Police Sergeant / Lieutenant / Captain
Probation Officer / Parole Officer
SF 171: The Federal Employment Application Form
Special Agent / Treasury Enforcement Agent
State Trooper / Highway Patrol Officer / State Traffic Officer
Traffic Enforcement Agent
You as a Law Enforcement Officer

AVAILABLE AT BOOKSTORES EVERYWHERE

PRENTICE HALL

CIVIL SERVICE BOOKS

TEST PREPARATION

Accountant / Auditor
Air Traffic Controller Qualifying Test
Air Traffic Controller Training Program
American Foreign Service Officer
Assistant Accountant
Auto Mechanic / Automotive Serviceman
Beginning Clerical Worker
Bookkeeper / Account Clerk
Building Custodian / Building Superintendent / Custodian Engineer
Bus Operator / Conductor
Case Worker
Computer Specialist GS 5-9
The Corey Guide to Postal Exams
Distribution Clerk, Machine
Electrician / Electrician's Helper
Federal Clerk / Steno / Typist
File Clerk / General Clerk
Fire Department Lieutenant / Captain / Battalion Chief
Firefighter
Gardener / Grounds Maintenance Worker
Investigator / Claim Examiner
Librarian
Machinist / Machinist's Helper
Mail Handler / Mail Processor
Maintenance Mechanic
Maintenance Worker / Mechanical Maintainer
Mark-up Clerk / Clerk Typist / Clerk Stenographer—U.S. Postal Service
Office Aide
Office Associate
Plumber / Steam Fitter
Police Administrative Aide
Postal Exams Handbook
Post Office Clerk / Carrier
Preparación para el Examen de Cartero
Principal Administrative Associate / Administrative Assistant
Principal Clerk / Principal Stenographer
Rural Carrier
Sanitation Worker
School Secretary
Senior Clerical Series
Special Officer / Senior Special Officer / Bridge and Tunnel Officer
Staff Analyst / Associate Staff Analyst
Track Worker
Train Operator / Tower Operator / Assistant Train Dispatcher
Transit Electrical Helper

CAREERS / STUDY GUIDES